A COMMUNITARIAN THEORY OF WTO LAW

Since 1995 there has been intense debate about whether the World Trade Organization (WTO) Agreement is just. Many observers point to the association of the treaty with intensive interdependence and the disruptive effects of globalization to assert that it is unjust, particularly when viewed from the perspective of human rights.

Nevertheless, justice in sovereign terms is different from justice in human terms. This book puts forward a theory of WTO law to explain the difference. The theory explains how economic interdependence gives rise to an interactive view of the relationship between different forms of justice and generates interdependent obligations under WTO law.

In an era of fresh concern about interdependence, however, the international trading system appears to be uncoupling. The theory's emphasis on interdependence accounts for the way in which this development is happening and how in response the WTO Agreement appears to be evolving away from a constitutive framework towards something more contractual. In the meantime, the theory also suggests how WTO dispute settlement might have continuing relevance as a locus for transformative solutions to international economic problems.

Taken together, the theory's insights may assist in outlining a general theory of law.

CHIOS CARMODY is Associate Professor at the University of Western Ontario Faculty of Law in London, Ontario, Canada. He currently teaches courses in International Trade Law, Public International Law and Contracts. He has been Canadian National Director of the Canada–United States Law Institute since 2002.

CAMBRIDGE STUDIES IN INTERNATIONAL AND COMPARATIVE LAW: 181

Established in 1946, this series produces high quality, reflective and innovative scholarship in the field of public international law. It publishes works on international law that are of a theoretical, historical, cross-disciplinary or doctrinal nature. The series also welcomes books providing insights from private international law, comparative law and transnational studies which inform international legal thought and practice more generally.

The series seeks to publish views from diverse legal traditions and perspectives, and of any geographical origin. In this respect it invites studies offering regional perspectives on core *problématiques* of international law, and in the same vein, it appreciates contrasts and debates between diverging approaches. Accordingly, books offering new or less orthodox perspectives are very much welcome. Works of a generalist character are greatly valued and the series is also open to studies on specific areas, institutions or problems. Translations of the most outstanding works published in other languages are also considered.

After seventy years, Cambridge Studies in International and Comparative Law sets the standard for international legal scholarship and will continue to define the discipline as it evolves in the years to come.

A list of books in the series can be found at the end of this volume.

A COMMUNITARIAN THEORY OF WTO LAW

CHIOS CARMODY
University of Western Ontario

CAMBRIDGE
UNIVERSITY PRESS

CAMBRIDGE
UNIVERSITY PRESS

Shaftesbury Road, Cambridge CB2 8EA, United Kingdom

One Liberty Plaza, 20th Floor, New York, NY 10006, USA

477 Williamstown Road, Port Melbourne, VIC 3207, Australia

314–321, 3rd Floor, Plot 3, Splendor Forum, Jasola District Centre, New Delhi – 110025, India

103 Penang Road, #05–06/07, Visioncrest Commercial, Singapore 238467

Cambridge University Press is part of Cambridge University Press & Assessment, a department of the University of Cambridge.

We share the University's mission to contribute to society through the pursuit of education, learning and research at the highest international levels of excellence.

www.cambridge.org
Information on this title: www.cambridge.org/9780521879002

DOI: 10.1017/9780511843280

First published 2024

A catalogue record for this publication is available from the British Library.

Library of Congress Cataloging-in-Publication Data
Names: Carmody, Chios, author.
Title: A communitarian theory of WTO law / by Chios Carmody.
Other titles: Communitarian theory of World Trade Organization law
Description: Cambridge, United Kingdom ; New York, NY : Cambridge University Press, 2023. | Series: Cambridge studies in international and comparative law | Includes bibliographical references and index.
Identifiers: LCCN 2022056921 | ISBN 9780521879002 (hardback)
Subjects: LCSH: World Trade Organization. | World Trade Organization. | Foreign trade regulation.
Classification: LCC K4610 .C365 2023 | DDC 382/.92–dc23/eng/20230403
LC record available at https://lccn.loc.gov/2022056921

ISBN 978-0-521-87900-2 Hardback

For my parents

Zoë Chios Carmody (1939–) and George Richard Carmody (1938–2011),

who sought a better world

We are people because of other people.

Tswana proverb

CONTENTS

FIGURES

PREFACE

> Can you see anything? . . .
> Yes, wonderful things.[1]

This book puts forward a theory of the law of the World Trade Organization (WTO). It began with my doctoral dissertation on remedies in WTO law at Georgetown University Law Center in 1997–2001, which was a short, hurried piece of work I was dissatisfied with.

A remedy is traditionally given by a court or tribunal to correct an injury. However, the remedial formula set out in Art. 19.1 of the WTO Dispute Settlement Understanding (DSU) simply recommends that a WTO member country found to be non-compliant with the WTO Agreement bring its laws "into conformity" with its commitments under the treaty. Such a formula seemed too cryptic and open-ended to be completely corrective.

At the time there was a lot of interest in DSU provisions, which provide for the possibility of countermeasures should a defendant country be unable to bring itself into immediate compliance with the WTO Agreement. In WTO dispute settlement a successful complainant country is given the option of negotiating temporary compensation if immediate withdrawal of the impugned measure is impracticable. If compensation cannot be agreed, then as a "last resort" the complainant is permitted to selectively close its market to the defendant by temporarily suspending concessions or other obligations.

Commentators were intrigued by the possibility of countermeasures since they seemed to fulfill a long-held desire to make international law more afflictive, and, to that extent, presumably more effective. There was

[1] Remarks between the archeologist Howard Carter and his patron, George Herbert, Earl of Carnavon, on Carter's initial glimpse into the tomb of Tutankhamun, Pharaoh of Egypt (reigned 1334–1325 BCE) in the Valley of the Kings, December 1922. Howard Carter & A. C. Mace, *The Tomb of Tutankhamen*. 35 (Barrie & Jenkins, London; 1972).

a lot written about countermeasures under the DSU and some early WTO litigation involving them in cases such as *EC – Bananas III* and *EC – Hormones*.

Still, the enormous attention devoted to countermeasures seemed to me to obscure the deeper pattern of what was happening in WTO law. As time passed it became apparent that rather than retaliating against each other, WTO member countries were using individual disputes or groups of disputes to work out accommodative solutions. These solutions were often arrived at obliquely and elicited only intermittent attention in commentary but in my thinking they were evidence of a creative, flexible legal system at work.

I struggled for several years to find some way of rationalizing this facilitative role as the ultimate purpose of remedies under the WTO Agreement. There seemed to be no easy way to explain it.

This, then, was the genesis for the theory set out in this book. It began in an effort to explain the peculiar shape of remedies in WTO dispute settlement.

At the same time, there were a number of other themes that attracted my interest. One was interdependence. Interdependence has always been important in human and international affairs. At the end of the Cold War, however, the inclination to depend on others for economic benefit appeared to go into overdrive. Immense, highly sophisticated supply and value chains emerged that spanned the globe and wove together producers and consumers. I wondered how this intensive reliance might condition the legal engagements entered into under the WTO Agreement and influence its remedies.

I was also interested in the shape of WTO obligations. In an exchange with Joost Pauwelyn in the *European Journal of International Law* in 2003–2006, Pauwelyn suggested that WTO obligations are fundamentally bilateral and "private" since they are about "trade" between pairs of countries.[2] He made reference to the bilateral way in which trade concessions are negotiated, to the bilateral form of much WTO dispute settlement and to the apparent consistency of certain WTO rules with leading restatements of international law concerning bilateral obligations.

In response I made the opposite case.[3] I referred to the way in which a key feature of the WTO Agreement – arguably its most important innovation – is nondiscrimination obligations that make one WTO

[2] Joost Pauwelyn, "A Typology of Multilateral Treaty Obligations" 14:5 *E.J.I.L.* 907 (2003).

[3] Chios Carmody, "WTO Obligations as Collective" 17:2 *E.J.I.L.* 419 (2006).

member country extend trade concessions and commitments "immediately and unconditionally" to the entire WTO membership. These effectively create a "public" good in the special and limited sense of the WTO membership as a relevant "public." I backed up my position by referring to the way in which certain features of WTO law are more consistent with classic descriptions of multilateral obligations in international law.

Nevertheless, on that occasion my ultimate conclusion was that WTO obligations are not purely bilateral *or* multilateral. Instead, they can be identified as "interdependent," an intermediate category of obligation wherein the relationship is not one-to-one as in bilateral obligations, nor one-to-all as in multilateral obligations, but one-to-some.

The interdependent label seemed to be consistent both with the way that the obligations arose (i.e. through the interdependence of states and economic operators) and the way that WTO member behavior is in fact carefully calibrated to the behavior of other WTO members, particularly major ones. Over time this identification seemed to offer a particularly accurate description of what was happening under the WTO Agreement as intensive interdependence exposed certain vulnerabilities and the possibility of its "weaponization," and how in response, certain member states appeared to be "dialing back" their WTO obligations.

Finally, I was interested in whether or not any link or connection could be drawn between my observations about WTO law and those pertaining to classic Aristotelian ideas of corrective and distributive justice.

Eventually, I came to the conclusion that WTO remedies are broad and open-ended because the law is chiefly distributive and obligation-oriented. Its aim is to ensure the equal distribution of expectations of market access *ex ante* rather than the fair correction of trade injury *ex post*. This is for the greater purpose of facilitating interdependence. In the intervening years, however, experience has exposed what amounts to a crisis of faith in the value of interdependence, with the result that the community of the WTO Agreement now appears to be decoupling.

Again, I searched for a plausible way to fit these features of the law together. The most appropriate way to do so appeared to be to devise a theory. The result is what is outlined in succeeding chapters.

ACKNOWLEDGMENTS

To see is itself a creative operation, requiring an effort.[1]

Henri Matisse's words above convey something of the effort it has been to "see" both the theory and its operation in WTO law and write this book.

The book would not have been completed without the insight and encouragement of many people. Several deserve special mention.

I am grateful to the late John Jackson (1932–2015), who taught for many years at the University of Michigan Law School before moving to Georgetown University Law Center in 1998. John was my doctoral supervisor at Georgetown and originally directed me toward the subject of remedies in WTO law as a thesis topic. I am thankful for his direction and insight.

Frieder Roessler, formerly Legal Advisor to the General Agreement on Tariffs and Trade (GATT) and subsequently Executive Director of the Advisory Centre for WTO Law (ACWL), was also an inspiration. Frieder gave a course on WTO law that I attended at Georgetown Law in the fall of 1997. His approach was very clear and systematic, and as a result, I began to wonder if it might be possible to outline a system of ideas in the form of a theory to describe WTO law as a whole.

Another person to whom I owe great thanks is Peter Gerhart at Case Western Reserve University School of Law. Peter is a wonderfully rigorous thinker, who has written several books on legal theory himself.[2] In an exchange in 2000 he was the first person to suggest that rather than characterize WTO obligations as "either/or" – that is, as *either* bilateral *or* multilateral – they might have a dual nature.

[1] Henri Matisse in Hilary Spurling, *The Unknown Matisse*, xx (Knopf, New York; 1998)

[2] See Peter Gerhart, *Tort Law and Social Morality* (2010); Peter Gerhart, *Property Law and Social Morality* (2013); Peter Gerhart, *Contract Law and Social Morality* (2022).

I would also like to make special mention of my father, George Carmody (1938–2011), a geneticist who taught for several decades at Carleton University. In a discussion with him in March 2005 I related Gerhart's observation about the dual nature of WTO obligations. My father suggested to me that what arises in the treaty isn't a dualism so much as a hybrid. He insisted that I would have to derive a series of "third" values arising from the interaction and interdependence of the various elements of the hybrid. I proceeded to follow his suggestion, which provided the framework outlined in Fig. 1.6 and the essential structure of this monograph.

In addition, there are a number of other people to acknowledge.

I am very grateful to Cherise Valles of the ACWL, who organized a mini-symposium on an early version of the ideas outlined in my response to Pauwelyn in 2005. The symposium was an opportunity to obtain valuable feedback and convinced me that a more complete exposition of the ideas involved was feasible.

Over the years I have also had the opportunity to present portions of my thinking on a number of occasions. I must thank the late Karen Knop, Valerie Hughes, Samuli Seppänen, Martin Björklund, Susan Karamanian, Jeff Dunoff, Sungjoon Cho, Changfa Lo, Shin-yi Peng, Christopher Parlin, Arman Savarian, Filippo Fontanelli, Antonio Segura Serrano, Lisa Toohey, Gillian Moon, Joanna Gomula, Stephan Wittich, Debra Steger and Don McRae. I must also thank Emilia Porges and Tomer Broude for inviting me to present a synopsis of this work at the American Society of International Law (ASIL) International Economic Law Research Colloquium in 2009. Later that same year I was also able to meet with Sanne Taekema to discuss the role of ideals in law. Sanne's book *The Concept of Ideals in Legal Theory* (2003) was formative in developing my thinking concerning the role of equality and fairness as "master ideals" of justice. I am also grateful to Francine MacKenzie of Western University's History Department, who provided a useful historical overview of GATT and the WTO Agreement, and to Todd Weiler and Paul Moën for their insights and occasional humor. Americo Beviglia Zampetti kindly provided me with an advance copy of his book, *Fairness in the World Economy* (2006), as did Ronnie R.F. Yearwood of *The Interaction between World Trade Organization (WTO) and External International Law* (2011). I deeply appreciate their unconditional willingness to share their work.

Drafts of the first chapter were written while I was on sabbatical at the Jean Monnet Center, New York University (NYU), in 2005–2006. I am very grateful to the Center's Director, Joseph Weiler, for making my stay there possible and for offering me the opportunity to present some of my ideas in the context of the Center's seminar series. On that occasion Eyal Benvenisti and Armin von Bogdandy provided insightful feedback. Rebecca Laforgia also visited me at NYU one sunny day in April 2006 and buoyed me with her insight and enthusiasm for this project.

I am also grateful for a second sabbatical leave spent at the University of Toronto Faculty of Law in 2012–2013, where the middle chapters of this book began to take shape. During that time Associate Dean Ian Lee and his successor in post, Jim Phillips, as well as Jutta Brunnée, graciously extended the Faculty's resources to me.

At the Canada–United States Law Institute, the late Richard Cunningham (1942–2021) and Lawrence Herman – as well as my fellow Institute directors Steve Petras, Ted Parran and Michael Scharf – have been tremendous colleagues and steadfast in their support for this work.

I am most thankful to Maureen Irish and Stephen Pitel, who read the entire manuscript and offered comments, and to a number of others who offered to read chapters and did the same, including Joanna Langille, Petros Mavroidis, Graham Cook, Gabrielle Marceau, Asif Qureshi, Shai Dothan and Joanna Gomula. They have been excellent debaters and friends, as has been the late Armand de Mestral. Michael Byers kindly put me in touch with Philip Allott, who was very hospitable, welcoming me to Cambridge for a day in June 2010 to discuss legal theory and some of the ideas contained in the developing manuscript.

At Cambridge University Press I am thankful to John Berger, Jackie Grant, Tom Randall and Gemma Smith, who were very patient with me during the long years of writing and who shepherded the manuscript through the editorial process with dispatch once it was received. Annerufina Raymond and Marijasintha Jacob Srinivasan at Straive were exemplars of patience and useful advice. I also benefitted greatly from comments supplied by two unidentified reviewers at the review stage.

At the University of Western Ontario Faculty of Law I am particularly grateful to several people. Dean Ian Holloway, QC, and his two successors, Iain Scott and Erika Chamberlain, gave me the valuable opportunity to teach and conduct research in international law, something that enabled me to develop the focus necessary for a book of this type. Their generosity and that of the University's research arm, Research Western, afforded me a number of opportunities to travel in order to present ideas and test out my thinking. I am also very grateful for funding from the Law Foundation of Ontario over several summers to hire student research assistants, including Peter Kucherepa, Janice Ho, Ryan Brown, Michelle Dekens, Michael Kelly and Alexander Will. They helped considerably in several phases of this work.

More generally, I would like to thank Western Law colleagues, who have provided support and encouragement in countless ways as the manuscript moved forward: Stephen Pitel, Dale Ives, Jason Neyers, Rande Kostal, Valerie Oosterveld, Sara Seck, Margaret Martin, the late Tim Edgar, Randal Graham, Michael Coyle, Zoë Sinel, Melanie Randall, Joanna Langille and Ryan Liss. I am proud to work with such fine colleagues. They inspire me daily with their commitment to excellence in legal education and research.

I must add that a strong, well-financed system of public education is a tremendous asset, one vital to the creation of community. I must therefore thank the people and government of Ontario for their continuing support of my institution and others like it.

I would be remiss if I implied that anyone above is responsible for any errors found in this book. Those are wholly my own.

Chios Carmody
London, Ontario
1 August 2023

1

A Theory of WTO Law

theory, as of a system of knowledge.[1]

1.1 Why a Theory?

This book puts forward a theory of the law of the World Trade Organization (WTO). A "theory" is a "system of ideas," with the emphasis being on the "system," or set of relationships, regularly exhibited between those ideas.[2]

In this book I make the principal point that WTO law is about interdependence as reflected in varying conceptions of the good. The theory emphasizes how WTO law reflects regular relationships between classic forms of justice that work to sustain the good.

Before going into detail on this point, however, I think it is important to address some potential objections to a theory, both as a way of providing some background to the subject and underlining the importance of what is advanced here.

One potential objection is the fact that WTO disputes are difficult to assimilate with justice, at least if justice is thought about in corrective terms. Most WTO disputes are initiated by a single complainant country and defended by a single respondent country. If the complaint is made out, the proceedings normally end in a cryptic direction to the wrongdoing country to bring its laws and regulations "into conformity" with the organization's basic treaty, WTO Agreement. No compensation is automatically payable.

[1] S.v. "Basis," in *Webster's New World Dictionary*, 1564 (Simon & Schuster, New York; 1976), quoted in *EC – Sardines*, WT/DS231/R, para. 7.110 (29 May 2002).

[2] S.v. "Theory," *Shorter Oxford English Dictionary* (5th ed.) 3236 (Oxford University Press, Oxford; 2002).

Another potential objection is the lack of any direct reference to "justice" in WTO texts. When the WTO Agreement was concluded in 1994 member governments spoke chiefly of the new treaty as contributing to the rule of law, not justice, and since that time criticism of the treaty by human rights advocates, environmental activists and others has left the impression of it in many quarters as unjust.[3]

A further potential objection is encapsulated in the question, why is such a theory necessary? After all, until recently WTO dispute settlement has functioned reasonably well without a theory, and so it might be queried whether one is required or useful.

Over time, however, eminent commentators have implied that a theory *is* useful, either by alluding to one or trying to define its contents in some preliminary way. For instance, as long ago as 1983 Ernst-Ulrich Petersmann observed with respect to the WTO Agreement's forerunner, the General Agreement on Tariffs and Trade (GATT 1947), that "a comprehensive economic theory of [the international economic system] is not to be found in the (neo) classical treatises on political economy." Petersmann went on to note that:

> an order should be characterized by a coherent system of starting points, objectives, principles, and institutional and instrumental means that can achieve the formulated objectives in an orderly fashion.[4]

More recently in 2005, Thomas Cottier, Matthias Oesch and Thomas Fisher observed that "the absence of a long-standing legal theory or

[3] For criticisms of the WTO, see OXFAM International, *Rigged Rules and Double Standards* (2002), observing:

> The problem is not that international trade is inherently opposed to the needs and interests of the poor, but that the rules that govern it are rigged in favour of the rich . . . Many of the rules of the World Trade Organization . . . on intellectual property, investment, and services protect the interests of . . . countries and powerful TNCs, while imposing huge costs on developing countries. This bias raises fundamental questions about the legitimacy of the WTO.

See also Sarah Joseph, *Blame It on the WTO* (Oxford University Press, Oxford; 2011) (offering a critique of the organization and its legal system from a human rights perspective).

[4] Ernst-Ulrich Petersmann, "International Economic Theory and International Economic Law: On the Tasks of a Legal Theory of International Economic Order" in R. St. J. Macdonald & D. M. Johnston (eds), *The Structure and Process of International Law* 234–235 (Martinus Nijhoff, Boston; 1983).

tradition of international trade regulation explains why even basic questions of international trade law are still in the open."[5]

The statements of Petersmann, Cottier and others infer that whatever the current state of thinking about WTO law, a theory is desirable because it conforms with the general intuition that a theory is rational.

There will be limits to this rationality of course. That is because any theory is a distillation. Anne Peters has pointed out how all theories involve simplification. The benefit of simplification is explanatory. "The simpler the theory, the better you understand [it]."[6]

At the same time, the simplicity of a theory can generate uncertainty about its explanatory power and elicit criticism.[7] No theory will explain everything and as I intend to show, that is certainly true of the theory put forward in this book.

Instead, what is highlighted by the theory is tendencies as opposed to certainties. As such, some phenomena of WTO law will be explained relatively well by the theory whereas others will not. The theory aims to strike a balance between simplification and explanation. Its shortcomings will spur the quest for other, more accurate theories.

A theory like this one is likely to be useful in a number of ways. First, it will provide an overview, or "map," of the WTO legal system. With it we will no longer be left to "wander around among the differences"[8] of WTO provisions and cases. Rather, there will be something more schematic to guide legal thinking.

Second, reasoning about WTO law often takes place from within the law – its existing texts and jurisprudence – whereas the theory outlined here analyzes the body of law by means of concepts beyond it, notably community and justice. This approach is particularly promising because there continues to be much debate about the future of the WTO as a

[5] Thomas Cottier et al., *International Trade Regulation* 47 (Cameron May, London; 2005).

[6] Anne Peters, "Realizing Utopia as a Scholarly Endeavour" 24:2 *Eur. J. Int'l L.* 533 at 536 (2013), quoting Gregory Chaitin, "The Limits of Reason" 294:3 *Scientific American* 74 (2006).

[7] "[T]here must come a point where gaps between the *explanadum* and the *explanans* cast doubt on the value of the explanation." Peter Cane, "The Anatomy of Private Law Theory" 25:2 *Ox. J. L. S.* 203 at 207 (2003).

[8] H. Patrick Glenn, *Legal Traditions of the World* (5th ed.) at 153 (Oxford University Press, Oxford; 2014).

community and about the ultimate justice of WTO law, issues which, as of the time of this writing, have provoked a variety of reactions, including an impasse over the role of the WTO dispute settlement system's court of appeal, the Appellate Body, which in late 2019 suspended operation. To that extent, the theory may offer a diagnosis for what currently ails the WTO.

Third, a theory is useful because it is predictive. It will provide some indication of how WTO law is likely to evolve in future.

In response then to the question posed at the outset of this chapter, why a theory?, there are several answers. A theory is useful because it is rational as well as analytic, diagnostic and predictive.

There is something else too. This is the possibility of using the theory to outline a theory of law in general. At a time of some pessimism about the likelihood of ever successfully identifying a general theory of law, I will suggest that what is observed in WTO law is in some degree an illustration of how law does justice in *any* community.[9] Such an assertion might appear grandiose – even foolish – but in my view it is nothing more than recognition of the fact that what has happened in the course of WTO law's short history is the emergence of regular relationships expressive of the need for justice in a community.

1.2 The Outline of a Theory

The word "theory" is often associated with abstraction and complexity. It is therefore worthwhile providing a synopsis of what is put forward here in order to summarize the theory's contents and help direct subsequent discussion.

The theory outlined in this book is a three-fold theory. It is, first and foremost, a *theory of community*, a theory about how individual actors come together and depend upon each other to produce certain things they hold together and value that I will refer to as "goods."

Second, the theory is a *theory of justice*, or in other words, a theory about how members of a community regularly conceive of what is right or correct in relation to goods.

[9] Joseph Raz, *Between Authority and Interpretation* 17 (Oxford University Press, Oxford; 2009). In chapter 2, Raz asks the question "can there be a theory of law?" but concludes that he is less than completely confident a workable theory can be identified.

A Theory of Community

|

A Theory of Justice

|

A Theory of Law

Figure 1.1 A communitarian theory outline

Third, the theory is a *theory of law*, a theory about how legal elements relate to each other in an effort to do justice as it relates to goods.

A preliminary outline of the theory's structure can be summarized as shown in Figure 1.1.

In sum, the theory posits that the law does justice in order to sustain the good of the community.[10] Again, it is helpful for the purposes of subsequent discussion to briefly outline these ideas a little further.

1.2.1 A Theory of Community

The foundation of a theory of law lies in interdependence, a phenomenon rooted in biology. Humans are members of a uniquely interdependent species.[11] We create and rely upon many goods that could not be produced by one individual in a single human lifetime. These include vaccines, jet travel and the internet.

[10] The theory's three-fold structure prioritizing community is dictated by the fact that "[w]e treat community as prior to justice and fairness in the sense that questions of justice and fairness are regarded as questions of what would be fair or just within a particular community." Ronald Dworkin, *Law's Empire* 208 (Belknap Press, Cambridge, MA; 1986).

[11] Paul Seabright has written:

> *Homo sapiens sapiens* is the only animal that engages in elaborate task-sharing – the division of labour as it is sometimes known – between genetically unrelated members of the same species. It is a phenomenon as remarkable and uniquely human as language itself. Most human beings now obtain a large share of the provision of their daily lives from others to whom they are not related by blood or marriage.
>
> (Paul Seabright, *The Company of Strangers* 1 (Princeton University Press, Princeton, NJ; 2004)).

In the latest phase of interdependence from 1990 on the "blend of Western industrial know-how and Asian manufacturing muscle" has fueled a "hyper-globalisation of supply chains" that has left an impression of the world as "flat."[12] Although there are some indications that this hyper-globalizing trend has moderated, interdependence in the form of global supply and value chains remains enormously important.[13]

Some idea of its importance was given in *US – Aircraft*, a WTO dispute concerning subsidies granted to the US aircraft industry. There, a WTO dispute settlement panel detailed the multinational list of suppliers involved in assembling the Boeing 787:

> Completion of sub-assemblies and integration of systems takes place in Everett, Washington, with many components being pre-installed before delivery to Everett. The 787 composite wings are being manufactured by Mitsubishi Heavy Industries. The horizontal stabilizers are being manufactured by Alenia Aeronautica in Italy, and various parts of the fuselage sections are being built by Alenia in Italy, Vought in Charleston, South Carolina, Kawasaki Heavy Industries and Fuji Heavy Industries in Japan, Alenia in Italy and Spirit Aerosystems in Wichita, Kansas. The main landing gear and nose landing gear are being supplied by the French company Messier-Dowty, while passenger doors are being made by

[12] "Flatness" is Thomas Friedman's metaphor for viewing the world today as a level-playing field in terms of commerce wherein all competitors have an equal opportunity. Thomas L. Friedman, *The World Is Flat* (Farrar, Straus & Giroux, New York; 2005). See also Vijay Vaitheeswaran, "A Slow Unravelling" 432:9151 *The Economist* 3 (13 July 2019).

[13] David Brooks, "Globalization Is Over. The Global Culture Wars Have Begun" *The New York Times* (8 Apr. 2022) Brooks notes how in the immediate aftermath of the Cold War:

> [i]t seemed as if there would be a global convergence around a set of universal values – freedom, equality, personal dignity, pluralism, human rights. . . . The world is not converging anymore; it's diverging. The process of globalization has slowed and, in some cases, even kicked into reverse . . . Sure, globalization as flows of trade will continue. But globalization as the driving logic of world affairs – that seems to be over.

For a more equivocal account, see Jeanna Smialek & Ana Swanson, "The Era of Cheap and Plenty May Be Ending" *The New York Times* (3 May 2022) (noting how if supply chain turmoil and geopolitical conflicts result in a reversal or reconfiguration of global production a decades-long decline in the prices of many goods could come to an end).

> Latécoère in France, and the cargo, access and crew escape doors by Saab in Sweden.[14]

The panel noted that as a result of globalized manufacturing, Boeing has "shifted responsibility for detailed component design to suppliers, and focuses on systems integration, managing overall requirements, as well as the assembly process. The 787 is essentially assembled from large sub-structures designed and produced by suppliers."[15]

The panel's description of the Boeing 787's assembly process is emblematic of the way that what has arisen through interdependence is an elaborate network of relationships. Much modern production and consumption is characterized by them. They value coordination and integration so that delivery of the final product becomes a unity.

Unity places demands on supply and value chain participants. They need to consider matters differently than they would if acting independently. Regular reliance means that actors have to pay at least as much attention to what they are required to do as to what they want to do.

The experience of Boeing and other actors demonstrates the way that interdependence modifies thinking. Similarly in this book, I maintain that the modification generated by WTO law is primarily mind-driven. The "security and predictability"[16] that are repeatedly identified as

[14] *United States – Civil Aircraft (Second Complaint)*, WT/DS353/R, appendix VII.F.1, para. 25 (31 Mar. 2011). For similar observations of the Boeing 787 as emblematic of interdependence, see Michele Ruta & Mika Saito, "Chained Value" *Finance & Development* 52 (Mar. 2014).

[15] *United States – Civil Aircraft (Second Complaint)*, WT/DS353/R, appendix VII.F.1, para. 24 (31 Mar. 2011). WTO Director-General Pascal Lamy has described a similar phenomenon in the global textiles value chain. See "What Cannot Be Counted Does Not Count" (speech by WTO Director-General Pascal Lamy to the Economic Development Foundation (IKV) and the Economic Policy Research Foundation of Turkey (TEPAV), Istanbul, 14 Mar. 2013).

[16] In *EC – Computer Equipment*, WT/DS62/AB/R, para. 82 (5 June 1998) the Appellate Body observed that "the security and predictability of 'the reciprocal and mutually advantageous arrangements directed to the substantial reduction of tariffs and other barriers to trade' is an object and purpose of the WTO Agreement, generally, as well as of the GATT 1994." This reference has been cited in numerous other decisions: see *EC – Chicken Cuts*, WT/DS269/AB/R, para. 243 (12 Sept. 2005); *EC – Bananas III*, WT/DS27AB/RW2/ECU, para. 433 (26 Nov. 2008). In *China – Automobile Parts* the panel referred to it as the "*main* purpose" of the WTO Agreement: see *China – Automobile Parts*, WT/DS339, 340, 342/R para. 7.460 (18 July 2008) [emphasis added].

Figure 1.2 A theory of community

constituting the core of WTO disciplines are closely linked to interdependence in that they afford officials, producers and consumers in member countries an extended horizon on which to plan. The ultimate purpose of this coordination is to produce goods.[17]

In light of these ideas, it is possible to begin outlining a theory of community as shown in Figure 1.2.

In economics goods are characterized by different degrees of exclusivity and rivalry.[18] Exclusivity refers to the way in which a good's use may be limited or restricted to some individual or group. Rivalry refers to the way a good's use may diminish its benefits for others.

The combination of exclusivity and rivalry results in four different categories of goods. First, there are exclusive, rivalrous private goods such as real estate. Second, there are exclusive, nonrivalrous "club" goods such as toll roads or the internet. Third, there are nonexclusive, rivalrous common goods such as natural resources. Fourth, there are nonexclusive, nonrival "public" goods such as public health.[19]

As I will explain, the arrangements establishing the WTO Agreement create a "club" good. This is in the sense that the concessions and commitments made by member countries under it are reserved to the WTO membership, and that at least in theory, one member's access does not diminish the treaty's benefits for others.

At the time of the WTO Agreement's inauguration in 1995, there was broad consensus about the advantages of this good. Over time, however, the sense of benefit and mutual advantage from it has decreased due to misgivings about unconditional interdependence. As a result, the club good of the WTO Agreement now appears to be splintering into a

[17] Aristotle posited that all human actions can be traced to some good. "Every art and every inquiry, and similarly every action and pursuit, is thought to aim at some good; and for this reason the good has rightly been declared to be that at which all things aim." Aristotle, *Nicomachean Ethics* (2nd ed.) 1094a1 (Terence Irwin, trans., 1999).

[18] Moya Chin, "What Are Global Public Goods?" 58:4 *Finance & Development* 62 (Dec. 2021).

[19] Ibid.

series of bilateral relationships more appropriately likened to private goods. This evolution is emblematic of the way in which the conception of the good can change and how it reflects the changing nature of the community.

1.2.2 A Theory of Justice

Notwithstanding these ideas, actors are unlikely to come together to produce goods without some assurance that they are better off by doing so. This gives rise to a preoccupation in a community with justice.

In this book I take the view that the idea of justice can be distilled into the essence proposed by Herbert Hart in 1958 when he observed that justice consists:

> of two parts: a uniform or constant feature, summarized by the precept "Treat like cases alike" and a shifting or varying criterion used in determining when, for any given purpose, cases are alike or different.[20]

A respected body of opinion championed by a number of scholars including Neil MacCormick later refined these ideas to assert that justice is fundamentally composed of values of equality plus fairness.[21] The basic relationship can be represented as follows:

$$\text{Justice} = \text{Equality} + \text{Fairness}$$

As I will show, the experience of WTO law suggests that the basic relationship above is accompanied by two provisos:

$$\text{Proviso \#1: Equality} \neq \text{Fairness}$$
$$\text{Proviso \#2: Equality} > \text{Fairness}$$

[20] Herbert L. A. Hart, *The Concept of Law* (2nd ed.) 160 (Oxford University Press, London; 2006).

[21] Sanne Taekema observes that the combination of equality and fairness at the core of the concept of justice is also forwarded by Neil MacCormick, *Legal Reasoning and Legal Theory* 73 (Clarendon Press, Oxford; 1978). Fairness as the core of justice is proposed by David Miller, *Principles of Social Justice* (Harvard University Press, Cambridge, MA; 1976). Justice as equal treatment can also be found in Gustav Radbruch, *Legal Philosophy* 278 (Quelle & Meyer, Leipzig; 1932), Herbert L. A. Hart, *The Concept of Law* 159 (Oxford University Press, Oxford; 1994), James Harris, *Property and Justice* 171 (Clarendon Press, Oxford; 1996), and Aristotle in the *Nicomachean Ethics*. See Sanne Taekema, *The Concept of Ideals in Legal Theory* 192 n. 31 (Kluwer Law International, The Hague; 2003).

Proviso #1 (i.e. Equality $\neq$ Fairness) emphasizes how the distinction ordinarily made between "equality" and "fairness" implies that the two terms do not mean the same thing.

The ascription of distinct meanings to equality and fairness dovetails with recent research in anthropology and evolutionary psychology, which indicates that fairness, in particular, is a uniquely human trait, something not observed in our closest genetic relatives.[22] As David Schmidtz has noted, what makes a result "fair [is] not that our slices are equal – they may not be – but that neither of us has grounds for complaint."[23] From this set of insights, some evolutionary psychologists hypothesize that it is a sense of fairness – a sense that all participants will be treated "appropriately," if not equally – that is key to explaining individuals' extraordinary ability to cooperate.

Still, this set of observations leaves open an important question: if fairness is so important and if it has played such a central role in human evolution, why are human communities not entirely fairness-based? Many commentators have observed that fairness cannot serve as the basis for all human relations otherwise the law risks becoming purely subjective.[24]

[22] "Patience, Fairness and the Human Condition" 385:8549 *The Economist 67* (6 Oct. 2007); Keith Jensen et al., "Chimpanzees Are Rational Maximizers in an Ultimatum Game" 318 *Science* 107 (2007).

[23] David Schmidtz, *Elements of Justice* 186 (Cambridge University Press, Cambridge; 2006).

[24] Thus, Ronald Dworkin has observed:

> Some philosophers deny the possibility of any fundamental conflict between justice and fairness because they believe that one of these virtues in the end derives from the other. Some say that justice has no meaning apart from fairness, that in politics, as in roulette, whatever happens through fair procedures is just. That is the extreme of the idea called justice as fairness. Others think that the only test of fairness in politics is the test of result, that no procedure is fair unless it is likely to produce political decisions that meet some independent test of justice. That is the opposite extreme, of fairness as justice. Most political philosophers – and I think most people – take the intermediate view that fairness and justice are to some degree independent of each other, so that fair institutions sometimes produce unjust decisions and unfair institutions just ones.
>
> (Dworkin, *Law's Empire* (177)

Herbert Hart observed:

> The distinctive features of justice and their special connection with law begin to emerge if it is observed that most of the criticisms made in terms of just and unjust could almost equally well be conveyed by the words "fair" and "unfair." Fairness is plainly not coextensive with morality in general;

The natural limits to fairness infer that in an impersonal community another value becomes important.[25] This is equality.

For a long time equality has been the preeminent ideal of a political community, at least in Western thinking.[26] In contemporary life it assumes added importance because increased specialization forces actors to engage in many transactions to meet their daily needs. These transactions do not guarantee that actors will be relatively better off than their peers, only that they will have no "grounds for complaint."

This paradox leads to Proviso #2 (i.e. Equality > Fairness). The proviso introduces a priority in the relationship between equality and fairness. It holds that equality is the primary ideal whereas fairness is the secondary ideal. One way of understanding the priority is to recognize that actors and institutions do fairness in order to attain equality. They participate in all kinds of inequalities for the purpose of realizing whatever equality is deemed to be.

A theory of justice can then be outlined and linked to the theory of community put forward earlier as shown in Figure 1.3.

> references to it are mainly relevant in two situations in social life. One is when we are concerned not with a single individual's conduct but with the way in which classes of individuals are treated, when some burden or benefit falls to be distributed among them. Hence what is typically fair or unfair is a "share." The second situation is when some injury has been done and compensation or redress is claimed.
>
> (Herbert Hart, *The Concept of Law* 158 (1994))

[25] Anthropologists suggest cognitive limits to the number of individuals that it is possible to maintain stable social relationships with. One of these measures, "Dunbar's Number," proposes that the number lies in the vicinity of 150. Numbers larger than this generally require more restrictive rules, laws, and enforced norms to maintain a stable, cohesive group. See David Schiefer & Jolanda van der Noll, "The Essentials of Social Cohesion: A Literature Review" 132 *Soc. Indic. Res.* 579 (2017) (positing that "(in)equality, quality of life, and shared values represent antecedents and consequences of social cohesion, instead of constitutive elements" and that "a cohesive society is characterized by close social relations, pronounced emotional connectedness to the social entity, and a strong orientation toward the common good." In particular, orientation toward the common good is defined as "feelings of responsibility for the common good . . . [and] acceptance of and compliance to the social order and social rules versus anomy.").

[26] Amartya Sen has observed that "every normative theory of social arrangement that has [at all] stood the test of time seems to demand equality of something – something that is regarded as particularly important in that theory." Amartya Sen, *Inequality Reexamined* 13 (Harvard University Press, Cambridge, MA; 1995).

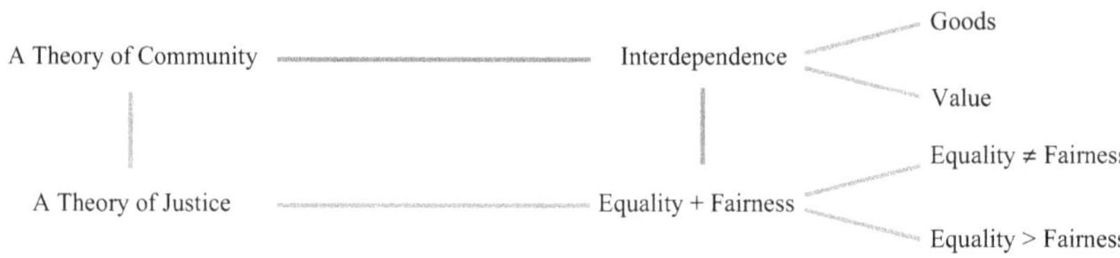

Figure 1.3 A theory of community and justice

This combination suggests that actors come together and cooperate in communities to produce goods according to ideals of equality and fairness. These ideals are communally determined and unequal although not for that reason alone unjust. What matters, as mentioned, is that actors have no "grounds for complaint."

The theory of justice put forward in this book is therefore communitarian. In that respect it differs from other theories and accounts of justice based on liberalism, or the school of thought that has traditionally emphasized the importance of the individual and the gradual reform of institutions.[27]

Communitarian thinking took shape in the 1970s largely in response to the work of John Rawls. In *A Theory of Justice* (1969), Rawls put forward the now-famous liberal view that individuals coming together in a prototypical community would agree to two key principles of justice:

1. that each person should have an equal right to basic liberties (the "liberty principle")
2. that social and economic inequalities would be arranged to be of the greatest benefit to the least-advantaged members of the community (the "difference principle").[28]

Communitarian thinkers took issue with these principles in several respects. Their most persistent criticism of Rawls's work has been that it is inaccurate to maintain, as Rawls initially appeared to do, that a Rawlsian theory of justice is universally true.[29]

[27] "By definition," Maurice Cranston says, "a liberal is a man who believes in liberty." Maurice Cranston, "Liberalism" in *The Encyclopedia of Philosophy*, Paul Edwards (ed.), 458–461 (1967). See also Shane Courtland & David Schmidtz, s.v. "Liberalism" in *Stanford Encyclopedia of Philosophy* (22 Feb. 2022).

[28] John Rawls, *A Theory of Justice* (rev'd. ed.) 53 (Belknap Press, Cambridge, MA; 1999).

[29] Instead, communitarians argue that justice in the real world is far from consistent with either principle but rather depends on a range of factors. "Standards of justice must be

Despite the persistence of a communitarian critique of Rawlsian ideas, however, leading communitarian critics of Rawls have never offered "a grand communitarian theory as a systematic alternative to liberalism."[30] Communitarian emphasis on the particularity of communities and the uniqueness of justice in each community make it difficult to say much that is definitive about communitarian thinking. To this day there remains no standard account of what a communitarian vision of justice would look like.[31]

In this book I undertake the task of outlining a communitarian theory of justice with the help of illustrative examples drawn in the first instance from WTO law. I agree with the basic communitarian thesis that justice is a product of community. At the same time, I posit that although the justice done in a community is community-specific, it will display some combination of the two ideals of justice mentioned above: equality and fairness. A community's particular expression or "identity"[32] of these will therefore be distinct.

This position may appear superficially similar to that of Rawls but in the first instance draws more heavily on the work of Aristotle.

Aristotle was interested in many things including the nature of community, or as he put it, what "holds people together."[33] He concluded that what holds people together is justice. This conclusion suggests that the ideas of equality and fairness highlighted above need to be operationalized in standard forms of justice.

In the *Nicomachean Ethics* Aristotle posited that a community will exhibit justice in two forms: *corrective* and *distributive*. Corrective justice applies to private goods and plays a rectificatory role in transactions.

found in forms of life and traditions of particular societies and hence can vary from context to context." "Communitarianism" in *The Stanford Encyclopedia of Philosophy* (first published Thursday 4 Oct. 2001; substantive revision Friday 15 May 2020).

30 Ibid.

31 Ibid.

32 I thank Fiona Smith for suggesting use of this term in relation to the expression of justice within a particular community.

33 "In reality, this measure is need, which holds everything together; for if people needed nothing, or needed things to different extents, there would be either no exchange or not the same exchange." Aristotle, *Nicomachean Ethics* 1133a28–30; also "Now clearly need holds [a community] together as a single unit, since people with no need of each other, both of them and either one, do not exchange, as they exchange whenever another requires what one has oneself, such as wine, when they allow the export of corn. This, then, must be equalized." Ibid.1133b7–11.

It is the justice most familiar in daily life. Thus, when people are wrongfully deprived of their property, they are entitled to have it returned or to be compensated.

Distributive justice, by contrast, applies to public goods such as "honours or wealth or anything else that can be divided among members of a community who have a share in the political system."[34] When a breach of the public good occurs, the wrongdoer is usually deprived of community. An example is the case of a convicted criminal whose wrong – a crime – is a wrong done to the entire community and whose traditional penalty is imprisonment, in effect a deprivation of community.[35]

In this book I likewise posit that law in a community will express some combination of corrective and distributive justice. However, while accepting Aristotle's two-fold arrangement of justice, I do some with some modifications.

Aristotle's original formulation inferred that the metric of corrective justice is equality – you get back what you've lost – whereas the metric of distributive justice is fairness – you get back what you're entitled to. His position on these points has caused centuries of confusion among commentators who have plainly noted that the outcome of many corrective operations is *not* equal.[36]

[34] Ibid. at 1131a25–29.

[35] Outlawry and renegade behavior as emblematic of distinctive communities have populated the folklore of many traditions, Famous depictions of prison "communities" include Arthur Koestler's *Darkness at Noon* (The MacMillan Company, New York; 1941) and Alexander Solzhenitsyn's *One Day in the Life of Ivan Denisovitch* (Dramatic Publishing Company, Chicago; 1963).

[36] For instance, in the Anglo-American common law, recovery for breach of contract is linked to protection of an "expectation interest," which is said to give the injured party the "benefit of the bargain." *Restatement (Second) of the Law – Contracts*, s. 344. This is not, however, the only interest protected:

> The promisee may have changed his position in reliance on the contract by, for example, incurring expenses in preparing to perform, in performing, or in foregoing opportunities to make other contracts. In that case, the court may recognize a claim based on his reliance rather than on his expectation . . . The interest protected in this way is called "reliance interest." Although it may be equal to the expectation interest, it is ordinarily *smaller* because it does not include the injured party's lost profit.
>
> (Ibid. [emphasis added])

My solution to this problem is to modify Aristotelian ideas by positing the reverse.[37] In corrective operations you get what you're entitled to get whereas in distributive ones you get what everyone merits as a member of the community.

What justifies such a rearrangement? First, the metric of corrective justice is fairness or what is appropriate because there are competing communal demands in any corrective operation. Simply put, a community does not have unlimited resources with which to correct injury, and indeed, in many instances has a vested interest in minimizing the communal cost of correction. Rules on settlement and court costs in many legal systems prove this point.[38]

The Restatement goes on to note that:

> In some situations a court will recognize yet a third interest and grant relief to prevent unjust enrichment. This may be done if a party has not only changed his own position in reliance on the contract but has also conferred a benefit on the other party by, for example, making a part payment or furnishing services under the contract. The court may then require the other party to disgorge the benefit that he has received.

This third interest is referred to as the "restitution interest." The Restatement observes that "[a]lthough it may be equal to the expectation or reliance interest, it is *ordinarily smaller* because it includes neither the injured party's lost profit nor that part of his expenditures in reliance that resulted in no benefit to the other party." Ibid. [emphasis added]. The Restatement adds that "in situations in which a court grants such relief as justice requires, the relief may not correspond precisely to any of these interests."

37 This is not the first time this reconceptualization has been put forward. Izhak Englard reveals how outlines of this same reconceptualization of Aristotle's work – the core of which constitutes an inversion of values underlying the traditional distinction and their eventual reconciliation – was prefigured in a fragmentary way by a number of renaissance and humanist scholars, including the French jurist and political philosopher Jean Bodin, the German scholastic and theologian Valentin Wudrian and the Italian philosopher and historian Giambattista Vico, Their views are surveyed in Izhak Englard, *Corrective and Distributive Justice: From Aristotle to Modern Times* (Oxford University Press, Oxford; 2009). For references to Bodin see ibid., pp. 131–133, Wudrian see pp. 133–135, Vico see pp. 156–158.

38 This is evident in the shape of rules concerning court costs. Traditionally, the "English Rule" provides that the party who loses in court pays the other party's legal costs. The English Rule contrasts with the "American Rule" under which each party is generally responsible for paying its own legal fees. In either case, however, recovery is not 100 percent. See Christopher Hodges, "Settlement and its pitfalls in England and Wales" in Christopher Hodges & Astrid Stadler, *Resolving Mass Disputes* 106 (Edward Elgar, Cheltenham: 2013); Mark Anderson, "Settlement or Roll the Dice?" 28:1 *Litigation* 37 (Fall 2001).

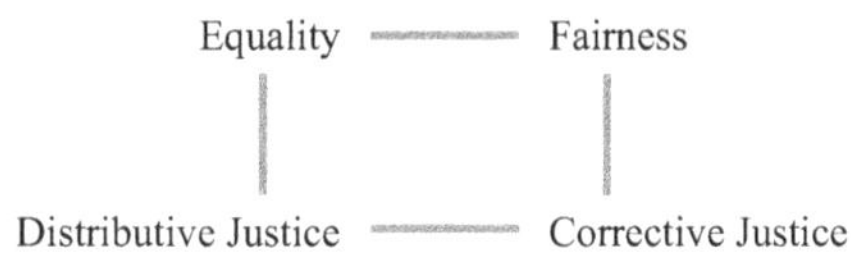

Figure 1.4 The structure of justice

Second, the metric of distributive justice is more appropriately regarded as equality or what is necessary to affirm the equality of actors in the community.[39]

This rearrangement of Aristotle's ideas can be depicted as shown in Figure 1.4.

The rearrangement infers that the basic relationship postulated in Proviso #2 above between equality and fairness (i.e. Equality > Fairness) is reproduced between distributive and corrective justice (i.e. Distributive Justice > Corrective Justice). Distributive justice is primary, whereas corrective justice is secondary.

On further reflection, however, it also becomes evident that the traditional Aristotelian categories of justice are conservative. They do not envisage any transformation of the good over time. Contemporary thinking recognizes this deficiency. It appreciates that a just legal system, as the hallmark of a sustainable community, must adapt to evolving ideas about the good.

This realization leads to the conclusion that over time there must be a point at which equality and distributive justice merge with fairness and corrective justice. Here the overarching aim of justice is transformative. What does transformative justice transform? Fundamentally it transforms legal relations with respect to the good.

The doing of transformative justice will result in what is deemed to be just – not ideal or "perfect" justice, but simply justice *eo instante*, the best that can be done in the instant moment. That justice inevitably will be perceived by some as unjust, a factor that provides a continuing impetus for reform.

[39] Hanoch Dagan, "The Distributive Foundation of Corrective Justice" 98 *Mich. L. Rev.* 138 at 140 (1999) ("the legal choice among . . . pecuniary remedies is not a matter of legal technicality, but rather requires a choice among varying conceptions of the plaintiff's entitlement. This choice, in its turn, is a normative choice that implicates the prevailing background ethos of the society at issue and is deeply influenced by the society's complex conceptions of self and of community.")

The doing of equality via distributive justice and of fairness via corrective justice then encourages "accommodative relationships between groups with competing interests."[40] The accommodation is reached in order to sustain the community. It serves as the basis for an interactive and interdependent view of the relationship between distributive and corrective justice, which I go on to develop in Chapter 3.

How exactly does this theory of justice manifest in WTO law? As will be seen, WTO law is structured chiefly as an egalitarian and distributive legal system. Its principal aim is to ensure the "security and predictability"[41] of trade concessions and commitments made by member countries that every other member country is deemed to have an equal expectation of. When injury occurs, the obligation on a wrongdoing country in WTO dispute settlement is to settle the dispute or withdraw the offending measure, action which is understood to restore the equality of competitive conditions.

A second aspect of WTO law is more evidently equitable and corrective. Correction is apparent in certain instances of permissible counteraction and authorizations of countermeasures under the WTO Agreement. As will be discussed, such action, though nominally "equivalent" to the injury sustained, is rarely in fact so and is more likely to be a matter of what is appropriate or "fair."

Finally, the interaction of distributive and corrective justice in WTO law generates transformative justice. Transformation is particularly evident in a number of settlements achieved under WTO dispute settlement. This typology of justice explains how even though WTO arrangements do not allow for equal counteraction in every instance, they might nevertheless still be considered just.

1.2.3 A Theory of Law

The theories of community and justice outlined above serve as background for a theory of WTO law. In sum, their ideas of the "good" and what is just condition the nature of the WTO legal system. To appreciate this point, some further explanation is necessary.

[40] Law Commission of Canada, "From Restorative Justice to Transformative Justice: Discussion Paper," Law Commission of Canada Catalogue No. JL2–6/1999 (1999).

[41] *EC – Computer Equipment*, WT/DS62/AB/R, para. 82 (5 June 1998).

A convenient starting point for identifying a theory of WTO law is to ask what is *legal* about the WTO Agreement. In other words, what gives the treaty its lawful, binding character? In *Maritime Delimitation and Territorial Questions (Qatar* v. *Bahrain)*[42] the International Court of Justice (ICJ) held that the essence of a legal agreement in international law is whether or not a particular agreement – in that case the minutes of a meeting – discloses an intention to be bound:

> the Minutes ... do not merely give an account of discussions and summarize points of agreement and disagreement. They enumerate the commitments to which the Parties have consented. They thus create *rights and obligations* under international law for the Parties.[43]

The Court's reference to "rights and obligations" is behind my insistence, pursued more fully in subsequent chapters, at focusing on rights and obligations as the basis of a theory of law. Their arrangement, the contrapuntal stress they create, and the way they simultaneously work to "constrain and enable"[44] actors' behavior offer insight into why WTO law is as it is.

In law the traditional relationship of rights and obligations is correlative. Each right is considered to be matched by a single offsetting obligation (i.e. Right = Obligation).[45] In WTO law, however, the jural matrix is

[42] [1994] I.C.J. Reports 112 at 121.

[43] Ibid., para. 25 [emphasis added]. Similarly, Robert Jennings and Arthur Watts have concluded "that the decisive factor is still whether the instrument is intended to create international legal *rights and obligations* between the parties" Robert Jennings & Arthur Watts, *Oppenheim's International Law* (9th ed.) 1202 (Longman, Harlow; 1996) [emphasis added].

[44] Jutta Brunnée & Stephen Toope, "International Law and Constructivism: Elements of an Interactional Theory of International Law" 39 *Colum. J. Transnat'l L.* 19 at 31 (2000).

[45] The idea of a correspondence between rights and obligations was recognized by early philosophers but developed most insightfully by Wesley Hohfeld, who postulated that there are rights and associated privileges, powers and immunities, and that there are also correspondent obligations and associated no-rights, liabilities and disabilities. When integrated, these form correlative pairs of legal relationships in the form of right-obligation, privilege-no right, power-liability and immunity-disability. See Wesley Hohfeld, *Fundamental Legal Conceptions as Applied in Judicial Reasoning* 36 (1919, rev'd. ed., Lawbook Exchange Ltd., Clark, NJ; 2010). Onora O'Neill has warned about the illusory nature of "manifesto rights," that is, rights for which there are no associated obligations:

> The most questionable effect of putting rights first is that those rights for which no allocation of obligations has been institutionalized may not be taken seriously. When obligations are unallocated it is indeed right that they should be met, but nobody can have an effective right – an

more complex. GATT's Most Favored Nation (MFN) obligation causes obligations owed by one member country to be owed simultaneously to the *entire* WTO membership. Due to this and other nondiscrimination provisions in the treaty, the general orientation of the WTO legal system is toward obligations. Hence, obligations are primary whereas rights are secondary (i.e. Obligation > Right).

That same orientation is also discernible in the WTO Agreement structurally. Many commentators have taken to describing WTO legal arrangements as either a "contract" or a "constitution." The most authoritative reference to contractualism is the WTO Appellate Body's statement in *Japan – Alcoholic Beverages* that:

> The WTO Agreement is a treaty – the international equivalent of a *contract*. It is self-evident that in an exercise of their sovereignty, and in pursuit of their own respective national interests, the Members of the WTO have made a bargain. In exchange for the benefits they expect to receive as Members of the WTO, they have agreed to exercise their sovereignty according to the commitments they have made in the WTO Agreement.[46]

The Appellate Body's statement in *Japan – Alcoholic Beverages* emphasizes the limited nature of the treaty and its legal system. The WTO Agreement is a "contract," and national sovereignty is constrained only to the extent that countries have made commitments under it. Thus, WTO law would appear to be composed of rights that countries

> enforceable, claimable or waivable right – to their being met. Such abstract rights are not effective entitlements. If the claimants of supposed "rights" to food or development cannot find where to lodge their claims, these are "empty "manifesto" rights."
>
> (Onora O'Neill, *Bounds of Justice* 126 (Cambridge University Press, Cambridge; 2000))

[46] *Japan – Taxes on Alcoholic Beverages*, WT/DS8/AB/R, p. 14 (4 Oct 1996) [emphasis added]. Jeffrey Waincymer notes that:

> [s]cholars have sought to distinguish between a contractarian versus constitutional approach to the GATT/WTO system. Contract interpretation tends to look at the intent of the parties at the time of the signing of the agreement. Constitutional lawyers vary their approach. Some would argue that a constitutional document must also be interpreted in its historical context. Others argue that it must be updated for modern times.
>
> (Jeffrey Waincymer, *WTO Litigation* 400–401 (Cameron May, London; 2002))

have limited for the purpose of enjoying the benefits extended under the treaty.[47]

A second view of the WTO Agreement is constitutive. This is in the sense that the treaty establishes the WTO as an international organization.[48] In addition, John Jackson and others have referred to the WTO Agreement as a "constitution" and Gail Evans has made the observation that "WTO law may be explained as a trade constitution having the capacity to universalize norms of substantive law."[49] Accordingly, WTO law would appear to be composed of obligations that are more constraining and limitative.[50]

[47] Generally speaking, countries have found a contractual conception of the treaty appealing and have referred to it on a number of occasions. See, for example, statement by Brazil in *EC – Poultry*, WT/DS69/AB/R, para. 15 (13 July 1998) (describing the WTO Agreement as "an international treaty laying down *contractual* obligations and not *erga omnes* obligations."); Argentina in WT/DSB/M/42, p. 14 (13 Feb. 1998) (referring to SPS obligations as "*contractual* international obligations"); China in WT/GC/M/173, para. 6.38 (26 July 2018) ("The WTO Agreement is a set of contracts achieved through negotiations. Within the scope of those contracts, Members abide by the conditions set forth in the contracts. Beyond the scope of those contracts, Members have their own policy space."). For commentators supportive of this view, see Joost Pauwelyn, "A Typology of Multilateral Treaty Obligations" 14:5 *E.J.I.L.* 907 (2003) ("Put differently, the values, aspirations and priorities of close to 150 WTO Members remain far too diverse for WTO norms to be streamlined into constitutional-type obligations" Ibid. at 938). Similarly, Petros Mavroidis has referred to the WTO Agreement as an "incomplete contract." In his view negotiators were "well aware that various [governmental] policies . . . might have an impact on trade, and that is why they decided to discipline the exercise of these policies. They did not, however, proceed to enumerate every one of them, nor did they provide specific disciplines for each." Petros Mavroidis, *The General Agreement on Tariffs and Trade: A Commentary* 127 (Oxford University Press, Oxford; 2005).

[48] "The constitution sets the pattern for the legal order of the international organization. Further rules develop from the operation of its organs. The power of these organs to take decisions stems from the constitution." Henry Schermers & Niels Blokker, *International Institutional Law* (6th ed.) 722 (Martinus Nijhoff Publishers, Leiden; 2018). See also WTO Agreement Art. 1 ("The World Trade Organization . . . is hereby established.").

[49] Gail Evans, *Lawmaking under the Trade Constitution* 44 (Kluwer Law International, The Hague; 1999). For a range of constitutional views, see John Jackson, *The World Trade Organization* (Royal Institute of International Affairs, London; 1998); Deborah Cass, *The Constitutionalization of the World Trade Organization* (Oxford University Press, Oxford; 2005). Also Peter Gerhart, "Two Constitutional Visions of the World Trade Organization" 24 *U. Pa. J. Int'l Econ. L.* 1 (2003).

[50] "The validity of each rule [of an international organization] will depend on the constitution [of the organization], the basis of the legal order." Schermers & Blokker, *International Institutional Law* 722.

The record of WTO law infers a certain priority or orientation between "contract" and "constitution." That is because WTO member countries are limited in the degree to which they can "contract out" of their WTO obligations.[51] From this requirement it is possible to conclude that the WTO legal system is more constitutive than contractual (i.e. Constitution > Contract).

The same orientation is also visible in the temporal perspective of WTO law. WTO law applies over time in a succession of moments progressing from the past to the future. This continuum demonstrates the same general orientation as the other conceptual pairs introduced above in the sense that WTO law is always open to renegotiation and change (i.e. Future > Past).[52]

Finally, the same orientation is visible in WTO law's reasoning, which is either deductive or inductive. Deduction is the logic of what "will be" based on assumptions.[53] By contrast, induction is the logic of what "is" or "was" based on proof.[54]

WTO law depends heavily on deductive reasoning and presumption. There is, for example, the well-known presumption in WTO law which provides that "[i]n cases where there is an infringement of the obligations assumed under a covered agreement, the action is considered *prima facie* to constitute a case of nullification or impairment." Case law has generally upheld the principle that while the presumption is formally rebuttable, in practice, it had "operated as an irrefutable presumption."[55] This conclusion follows from a number of GATT-era cases wherein

[51] See *Turkey – Textiles*, WT/DS34/R (31 May 1999), at para. 9.178 ("In our view, however, a bilateral agreement between two Members . . . does not alter the legal nature of the measures at issue or the applicability of the relevant GATT/WTO provisions"); *EC – Bananas III*, WT/DS27/AB/R (9 Sept. 1997), at paras. 164–170 (the Appellate Body, in examining the Lomé Convention, concluded that unless explicitly authorized by a waiver, provisions of the Convention could not alter rights and obligations of WTO members).

[52] See WTO Art. III:2 (contemplating change through future negotiation). The theme of change has also been addressed in WTO dispute settlement. Thus, in *Japan – Alcoholic Beverages* the Appellate Body observed, "WTO rules are not so rigid or so inflexible as not to leave room for reasoned judgements in confronting the endless and ever-changing ebb and flow of real facts in real cases in the real world." WT/DS8/AB/R, p. 31 (4 Oct. 1996).

[53] J. S. Covington, Jr., *The Structure of Legal Argument and Proof* 7–8 (John Marshall Pub. Co., Houston, TX; 1993).

[54] Ibid., p. 8.

[55] See *U.S. – Taxes on Petroleum*, 34th B.I.S.D. Supp. 156–157, para. 5.1.7 (17 June 1987).

nullification or impairment was found even for measures that had no demonstrable trade effect.[56]

The presumption mentioned above lies at the heart of the WTO legal system inasmuch as it conditions when state responsibility will be triggered. Much less often does WTO law depend on induction and proof. Proof can be particularly hard to supply in a system without a mechanism for discovery such as WTO dispute settlement, hence the priority of deduction versus induction (i.e. Deduction > Induction).

The regular orientation of elements suggests that the theory of law set out above can be joined to the theories of community and justice outlined earlier. In addition, the alignments observed between conceptual pairs in the theoretic framework above are not only "horizontal" (i.e. between elements of the *same* pair) but also "vertical" (i.e. between elements of *different* pairs). In other words, there is a link between ideas of obligation, constitution, an *ex ante* perspective and deduction. This link is evident inasmuch as an order of obligations is often referred to as a constitution, which is a document "for the future"[57] within which much is presumed. Likewise, a link is observed between rights, contract, an *ex post* perspective and induction since a contract is frequently described as expressing the will – or rights – of parties and breach is determined by proof of injury after-the-fact.[58]

These ideas can now be assembled and arranged together as shown in Figure 1.5.

From the foregoing arrangement, it then becomes possible to identify two distinct "idea-complexes"[59] at work in WTO law. In one idea-

[56] For instance, in *Japan – Leather*, B.I.S.D. 31st Supp. 94 (15–16 May 1984) "the panel wished to stress that the existence of a quantitative restriction should be presumed to cause nullification or impairment not only because of the effect it had on the volume of trade but also for other reasons e.g., it would lead to increased transaction costs and would create uncertainties which would affect investment plans." Ibid., paras. 55–56.

[57] "A constitution is framed for ages to come, and is designed to approach immortality as nearly as human institutions can approach it." *Cohens* v. *Virginia*, 19 U.S. (6 Wheaton) 264 at 387 (1821) (Marshall C. J.); "A constitution . . . is drafted with an eye to the future. Its function is to provide a continuing framework for the legitimate exercise of governmental power . . ." *Hunter* v. *Southam* [1984] 2 S.C.R. 145 at 155 (Dickson J.).

[58] Randy Barnett, "A Consent Theory of Contract" 86:2 *Columbia L. Rev.* 269 at 272 (1986) ("Will theories depend for their moral force upon the notion that contractual duties are binding because they are freely assumed by those who are required to discharge them.")

[59] Philip Allott, *The Health of Nations* 47 (Cambridge University Press, Cambridge; 2002) (noting how according to the nineteenth century English legal theorist John Austin "[l]aw . . . was to be seen as a species of command . . . [and] [t[he idea-complex of sovereignty, command, sanction and obedience was all the lawyer needed to know about the theory of law.").

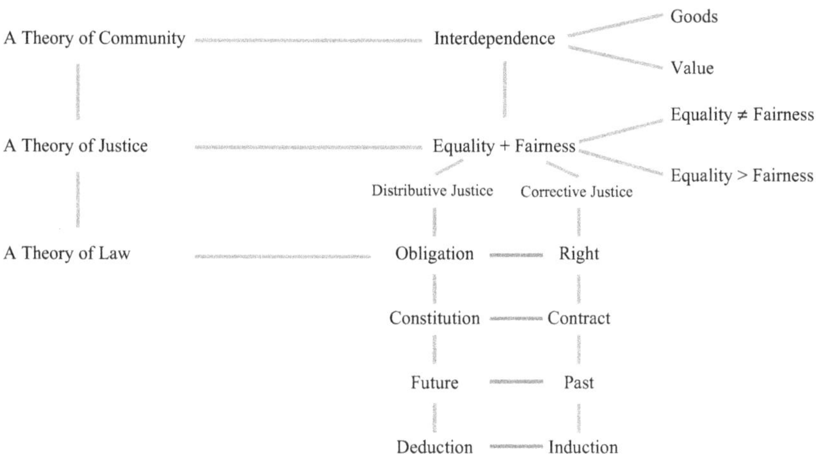

Figure 1.5 A communitarian theory of law (preliminary)

complex the law is about the attainment of equality as a matter of distributive justice. In the other it is about the attainment of fairness as a matter of corrective justice. The two complexes describe the law in a single moment.[60]

The theory's division of the law into separate idea-complexes is attractive. It streamlines the law, highlighting its contrasting tendencies.

Nevertheless, the division also involves considerable simplification and, taken literally, might be dismissed as a kind of *reductio ad absurdem*. That is because, as mentioned, the conception of the good is not static and justice is not purely a matter of equality or fairness but rather aims at transformation.

This preoccupation with transformation emerges from integration. Integration is evident in the way that the two elements of each conceptual pair outlined above over time tend to merge to create a *tertium quid* or "third thing," defined as "something novel, yet also dependent on what went on before."[61]

The impulse to transformation modifies thinking about legal relationships, notably the conception of obligations and rights in relation to

[60] On the traditional timeless perspective sought in analytic jurisprudence see Dan Priel, "Analytic Jurisprudence in Time" in Thomas Bustamante & Thiago Lopes Decat (eds), *Philosophy of Law as an Integral Part of Philosophy* 213 (Hart, Oxford; 2020).

[61] Alan Brudner & Jennifer Nadler, *The Unity of the Common Law* (2nd ed.) 2 (Oxford University Press, Oxford; 2013).

goods. As a result, obligations and rights become interdependent.[62] Working together they generate a *sui generis* legal system, which conditions the behavior of actors in distinctive ways within the system that are not observed – at least not to the same degree – outside the system.

Similarly, in the case of a legal structure, the interaction of constitutive and contractual frameworks generates what I term a "contractual constitution," a structure whose content is fluid but whose boundaries are essentially fixed.

In the case of temporal perspectives, the interaction of *ex ante* perspectives with *ex post* perspectives generates a contemporary perspective with an emphasis on law doing justice *eo instante* (i.e. in the present).

Finally, in the case of reasoning the interaction of deductive logic in the form of presumptions and inductive logic in the form of requirements for proof generates abductive logic, often called "an intelligent guess"[63] or "inference to the best explanation."[64]

The foregoing ideas can then be depicted altogether as shown in Figure 1.6.

The task of identifying a theory of law then becomes one of furnishing proof of these conceptual pairs and their associated relationships by means of examples drawn from WTO law.

1.3 Of Relationships and a System

In the previous section, I discussed how conceptual pairings in both justice and law exhibit the same relationships of correlation, subordination and integration. However, the core of a theory of law is somewhat more complex than this and needs to be more fully explained.

To review, the theoretic background suggests that the first relationship between elements is one of *correlation*. In short, where there is equality

[62] Philip Allott has described the transformation of the international community as follows: "the self-transformation of international society might represent it as a process of processes, a set of highlight charged psychic force-fields, overlapping and interacting in a multiple dialectic of change, negating and re-enforcing and surpassing each other, a revolution of declining expectations within a revolution of rising expectations." Philip Allott, *Eunomia* xxv (Oxford University Press, Oxford; 1990).

[63] Covington, *The Structure of Legal Argument and Proof* 3.

[64] Ibid., 4.

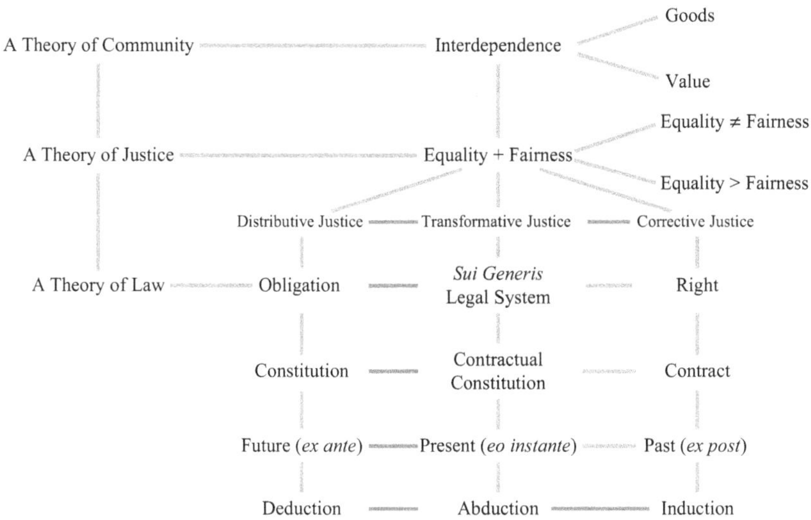

Figure 1.6 A communitarian theory of law

and distributive justice there will be a need for fairness and corrective justice. Here, the existence of obligations implies corresponding rights (i.e. Obligation/Right).

The second relationship is one of *subordination*. Equality and distributive justice tend to be primary, whereas fairness and corrective justice tend to be secondary. Here, obligations are primary whereas rights are secondary (i.e. Obligation > Right).

The third – and new – relationship is one of *transition*. Transition infers that at their outer limits, equality and distributive justice will convert or transition into their conceptual opposites of fairness and corrective justice, and vice versa (i.e. Equality/Distributive Justice = Fairness/Corrective Justice). Transition is observed in the way that equality tends to splinter into fairness positions and, likewise, that multiple instances of fairness generate contradiction and demands for egalitarian unity.[65]

Transition is similarly exhibited in the relationship between obligations and rights in WTO law. This is in the sense that WTO members

[65] Philip Allott has observed, "[t]he limits of a right amount to a peripheral duty . . . not to exceed those limits . . . [t]he limits of a duty amount to a peripheral right . . . not to be required to go beyond those limits." Allott, *Eunomia* 162.

are only bound to the extent of their obligations, beyond which they are generally free to exercise their rights (i.e. Obligation = Right). The same tendency is also exhibited between constitution and contract (i.e. Constitution = Contract), future and past (i.e. Future = Past), and deduction and induction (i.e. Deduction = Induction).[66] Transition is a reflection of the way in which each conceptual pair in the theory forms what Jack Balkin has termed a "nested opposition."[67]

Finally, the fourth relationship is one of *integration*. I have already mentioned how the interaction of equality and fairness generates justice – not "ideal justice," but justice in the present that is transformative (Distributive Justice + Corrective Justice = Transformative Justice).

Similarly, obligations and rights generate a *sui generis* legal system (i.e. Obligation + Right = *Sui Generis* Legal System), constitution and contract generate a "contractual constitution" (i.e. Constitution + Contract = Contractual Constitution), *ex ante* perspectives and *ex post* perspectives generate an *eo instante* perspective (i.e. Future + Past = Present), and deduction and induction generate abduction (i.e. Deduction + Induction = Abduction).

These four recurrent relationships at the level of both justice and law emphasize how the theory put forward in this book works in a coherent way as a "system." Consequently, the idea of system needs to be examined and explained.

[66] The same oscillation is observed in the law of international organizations generally. Jan Klabbers has noted, for instance, that "[T]his constant oscillation between the organisation and its members has given rise to a rather volatile set of legal rules and principles governing international organisations." Jan Klabbers, "The Changing Image of International Organizations" in Jean-Marc Coicaud & Veijo Heiskanen (eds), *The Legitimacy of International Organizations* 227 (United Nations University Press, Tokyo; 2001).

[67] A nested opposition "involve[s] a relation of dependence, similarity or containment between ... opposed concepts." Jack Balkin, "Nested Oppositions" 99 *Yale L.J.* 1669 at 1671 (1990). Nesting also calls upon deconstructionist ideas of "*différance*" and "*trace*." "*Différance*" was the term of art used by Jacques Derrida to describe the mutual dependence and differentiation of concepts. "*Trace*" is the retention of absent concepts that remain present in the understanding of other concepts. Balkin, ibid. at 1676. Balkin also notes that each opposition is traceable to a larger "idea complex" exhibiting its own particular concern and rationality. Balkin terms this a "countervision which is opposed to the dominant vision enforced by the law." He also notes that "it makes more sense to emphasize that the countervision one proposes is always immanent in the vision one is critiquing." Ibid. at 1688.

Systems theory suggests that a system exhibits at least five characteristics.[68] First, a system displays coherence and unity. The components of a system relate to each other more closely and regularly than those outside the system. Second, a system is exclusive. It is "closed" to external influence in some degree, and as a result, manifests its own distinctive rationality. Third, a system is ordinarily considered to be self-regulating. That regulation may take the form of correspondence as in a symmetry, or conditionality as in a sequence, or it may assume certain classic forms through its link to a common regulating factor such as a constitution. Fourth, a system displays transformed properties that are different from its constituent elements. These may take the form of independent attributes or identity. Fifth, a system aims to achieve a certain purpose. In legal systems, for instance, the principal purpose of the system is often said to be to do justice.[69]

The systematic character of WTO law is well-known. In *Brazil – Dessicated Coconut*, for instance, the Appellate Body observed that:

> The WTO Agreement is fundamentally different from the GATT *system* which preceded it. The previous *system* was made up of several agreements, understandings and legal instruments, the most significant of which were the GATT 1947 and the nine Tokyo Round Agreements, including the Tokyo Round SCM Code. Each of these major agreements

[68] For an attempt to define the criteria of a system, see Donella Meadows, *Thinking in Systems* (Chelsea Green Publishing, White River Junction, VT; 2008). Indications of these same criteria are discernible in WTO law. In *China – Electronic Payment Services*, for instance, the panel put forward the view that a "system [is] composed of several elements. Those elements could be considered, individually, as services in their own right." Ibid. at para. 7.58. The United States added that "the various elements of the system are *integrated and necessary* to facilitate a payment card transaction and, as such, constitute a single service. In our view, all elements of the system, together, are necessary for the payment card to materialize. None of the elements of the "system", individually, would be sufficient to process a payment card transaction. *Each of them must be integrated into a whole.*" Ibid. at para. 7.59:

(*China – Electronic Payment Services*, WT/DS413/R, (16 July 2012) [emphasis added]).

[69] John Maxcy Zane, *The Story of Law* (2nd ed.) 104 (Liberty Fund, Indianapolis, IN; 1927, reprint. 1998). See also *Hurtado* v. *California*, 110 U.S. 516 at 535 (1884) ("Law is something more than mere will exerted as an act of power."). Stephen Smith has observed that today there is "general agreement that a central feature, if not *the* central feature, of [law's] self-understanding is law's claim to authority – the claim or belief that law is morally justified." Stephen Smith, *Contract Theory* 15 (Oxford University Press, Oxford; 2003). Moreover, "a good theory of law ought to show that the law *is*, in fact, morally justified." Ibid., p. 17 [emphasis in original].

> was a treaty with different membership, an independent governing body and a separate dispute settlement mechanism ... Unlike the previous GATT *system*, the WTO Agreement is a single treaty instrument which is accepted by the WTO Members as a "single undertaking."[70]

The Appellate Body went on to detail how the WTO system alters behavior through the concurrent operation of obligations and rights, in that case involving disciplines on countervailing action by member countries to address trade-distorting subsidies:

> The [GATT and WTO] SCM Agreements do not merely impose additional substantive and procedural obligations on a potential user of countervailing measures. Rather, the SCM Agreements and Article VI together define, clarify and in some cases modify *the whole package of rights and obligations* of a potential user of countervailing measures.[71]

What is apparent from these excerpts is the idea that WTO obligations and rights function "concurrently and cumulatively"[72] as a system to shape states' behavior in a single moment. No one element is individually responsible for doing so. Instead, all elements work *together* systematically to transform the relationships in question. In *Brazil – Dessicated Coconut* the Appellate Body confirmed this understanding by referring to the WTO Agreement as "an integrated *system*."[73]

1.4 A Theory as Theory

The communitarian theory outlined above naturally raises the question, what kind of a theory is this? Where does it fit within the constellation of generally accepted theories of law?

Theories of law traditionally take as their starting point the "semantic" theories of natural law and positivism.[74] Natural law considers the law to

[70] *Brazil – Dessicated Coconut*, WT/DS22/AB/R, pp. 11–12 (21 Feb. 1997) [emphasis added].

[71] Ibid., p. 17, quoting *Brazil – Dessicated Coconut*, WT/DS22/R, para. 246 (17 Oct. 1996).

[72] *U.S. – Oil Country Tubular Goods Sunset Reviews*, WT/DS268/RW, para. 7.129 (30 Nov. 2006).

[73] *Brazil – Dessicated Coconut*, WT/DS22/AB/R, p. 11 (21 Feb. 1997) [emphasis added].

[74] Andrei Marmor & Alexander Sarch, "The Nature of Law" in *Stanford Encyclopedia of Philosophy* (22 Aug. 2019) ("In the course of the last few centuries, two main rival philosophical traditions have emerged about the nature of legality. The older one, dating back to late medieval Christian scholarship, is called the natural law tradition. Since the early 19th century, natural law theories have been fiercely challenged by the legal positivism tradition.")

be dictated by higher authority or reason and to be essentially coextensive with justice. Positivism, by contrast, considers the law to be "posited" by those with the authority to do so and hence to be something that may depart from justice.[75]

The two semantic theories are often thought to be separate and distinct. However, the communitarian theory put forward in this book appears to combine both. That is because in highlighting interdependence the theory emphasizes how natural law impulses in the form of obligations and positivist impulses in the form of rights are present and reconciled within a single legal system. To that extent, the theory can be thought of as a synthesis.

The foregoing observations apply primarily to the theory's character as a theory of law. However, as mentioned, the theory outlined here is a combined theory of community, justice and law. It is therefore worthwhile saying something about the theory as a theory of community and justice before returning to the matter of its characterization as a theory of law.

Earlier I said that leading communitarians have never offered a comprehensive theory as a systematic alternative to liberalism. As a result, there continues to be no standard account of what a communitarian theory of law would look like nor any definitive list of what its central tenets might be.

In this book I take the view that the essence of community arises out of what actors share, or in other words, what they have in common and value. It stands to reason that what they share and value they will seek to protect, adjust and transform.

This simple assertion might not be enough for the purposes of identifying a defensible theory of community, however. Instead, a conceptual framework appears necessary. Such a framework may be sourced in thinking about the international community.

[75] Reduced to its simplest, the distinction between [natural law and positivism] is that natural law theories argue that the status of *law* depends not simply on the fact that it has been laid down in whatever way or ways are recognised by the legal system of which it is part, but also on some additional factor or factors external to that system. Positivist theories, on the other hand, argue that the status of *law* attaches to anything which has been laid down (or *posited*) as law in whatever way or ways is or are recognised by the legal system in question.

(Ian McLeod, *Legal Theory* 18–19 (Palgrave MacMillan, Basingstoke; 2005) [emphasis in original])

In 1998 Bruno Simma and Andreas Paulus observed that "[t]here seems to be general agreement that the factual element of a community, namely, a sufficient degree of interdependence, is present in the international system."[76] Simma and Paulus went on to identify the international community's values and institutions.

They referred to three traditions of thought about the international community, each of which "is connected to a certain reception of values incorporated in the international system"[77] First, there is a Hobbesian or "realist" tradition in which "states are seen as being in a permanent situation of cold or hot war," where "[i]nternational law merely duplicates the power structure."[78] Second, there is a Kantian or universalist tradition that "sees at work in international politics a potential community of mankind" whose systemic value is justice. This tradition may justify "community intervention for the protection of individuals against their own state."[79] Third, there is a Grotian or internationalist tradition in which "international society is composed of states ... [and] cooperation between states is considered possible ... in order to realize common values and interests."[80]

Simma and Paulus went on to divide the Grotian tradition into two strands. One is "Vattelian" and international only in a narrow sense. "It emphasizes the international interest of states." Here, "[c]ooperation is the exception, not the rule." The main value "is not cooperation, but order."[81] The other strand is "truly Grotian" or "neo-Grotian" "because of its modern emphasis on institutions."[82] It "sees the international system on its way to becoming an 'organized state community' with an emphasis on common interests, the development of common values and the creation of common institutions."[83] Its paramount value is "solidarity between peoples."[84]

An examination of WTO arrangements and certain terminology emanating from WTO dispute settlement suggests that the concept of

[76] Bruno Simma & Andrea Paulus, "The 'International Community': Facing the Challenge of Globalization" 9 *E.J.I.L.* 266 at 269 (1998).
[77] Ibid.
[78] Ibid.
[79] Ibid. at 270.
[80] Ibid.
[81] Ibid.
[82] Ibid.
[83] Ibid. at 271.
[84] Ibid.

community prevailing under the WTO Agreement is primarily "neo-Grotian." As I will show, WTO dispute settlement has managed to identify a club good arising from concessions and commitments made by member countries that involves their common interest. This good emerges from interdependence.

Nevertheless, the theory also suggests that the idea of the good is not completely stable. Its character and identity can change.

As mentioned, at the time of the WTO Agreement's conclusion in 1994 there was a strong consensus about the advantages of unconditional interdependence. The Cold War had just ended and there was a desire to restructure the international economic system. In that era it was relatively easy to associate the new treaty with distributive justice and an *ex ante* perspective on its arrangements summed up in the phrase "the equality of competitive conditions."

Accompanying this consensus was a new streamlined system of dispute settlement in the WTO composed of panels and an Appellate Body, which raised hopes that countries would submit their differences to "fair, prompt and effective" resolution of trade disputes.[85] Where no settlement could be achieved or compensation negotiated, trade sanctions could follow. On this view WTO law would promote "self-enforcing trade".[86]

The idea of "self-enforcing trade" was a popular one and promoted a second, competing conception of community under the WTO Agreement as "Kantian or possibly "Vattelian". According to that conception, member countries would complain against each other for violations of the treaty, and where necessary, invoke countermeasures to promote compliance. The chief concern of the community would be achieving "justice" or instilling "order."

The difficulty with that conception is that it is at odds with the treaty's community, which remains more evidently Grotian. As I will explain, WTO law does not offer compensation for trade injury in the past and is instead primarily distributive and forward-looking. A Kantian or Vattelian conception also seems to ignore or downplay several practical issues that arise in countries' invocation of countermeasures and the point made earlier that corrective justice imposes costs on a community. Consequently, it has been little realized in practice.

85 *US – FSC*, WT/DS108/AB/R, para. 166 (24 Feb. 2000).

86 See, for example, Chad Bown, *Self-Enforcing Trade: Developing Countries and WTO Dispute Settlement* (Brookings Institution Press, Washington, DC; 2009).

Three decades on, however, both the unconditional interdependence provided for in WTO arrangements and WTO dispute settlement are viewed much more cautiously. While there remains support for the idea of comparative advantage on which WTO arrangements are based, the combined effects of trade liberalization and technical change have caused governments to rethink, and in some cases reduce, their commitment to it. This development, together with growing inequality in many countries and unease at vulnerabilities stemming from interdependence, lies at the core of current concern with the WTO Agreement.

This development is suggestive of the way that the good emanating from the WTO Agreement as a community has come to be regarded as less good, and in certain quarters, as "bad." Movement away from a view of the treaty as a relatively unified club good now appears to be taking place. Along with it, there appears to be a parallel movement away from WTO law as a matter of equal opportunity *ex ante* toward one involving debate about the fairness or unfairness of specific outcomes *ex post*.

One solution to current difficulties may lie in remaking the WTO dispute settlement system into something more evidently Kantian and corrective, but this option would appear to undercut the primarily distributive nature of the treaty and the fact that countermeasures between pairs of countries in the image of action for breach have not proven popular.

The net result suggests that justice under WTO law is far more complex than simply protecting the equality of competitive conditions or promoting correction. Ultimately, the theory put forward in this book suggests that justice is concerned with "solidarity between peoples" and transformation.

Transformation is visible in many settlements reached in WTO dispute settlement. It is also visible in current efforts to reform and repurpose the WTO as an organization.

All of the above hints at a more modest role for the WTO in terms of justice, not as a Kantian "trade enforcer" but as a setting within which common positions can be worked out, with some attention paid to law. Perhaps the best that can be hoped for at present is a "forum organization"[87] in line with Simma and Paulus's idea of a neo-Grotian community.

[87] Schermers & Blokker, *International Institutional Law* 764 (describing a forum organization as "a platform for discussion amongst members, for coordination of policies, and for exchange of views on items of common interest" as opposed to the enforcement of binding rules).

Earlier I said that a communitarian theory achieves a synthesis of natural law and positivism. It bears considering what this synthesis involves.

Most wholesale theories of law are preoccupied with identifying the ultimate source of legal obligation, or in other words, where legal obligations come from.

Efforts to answer this question in domestic law – at least in the Anglosphere – focus on "a few key figures and their central claims."[88] These include the command theory of John Austin,[89] Herbert Hart's theory of law as the union of primary and secondary rules,[90] Hans Kelsen's theory of a legal system as resting upon a fundamental norm (*grundnorm*),[91] Joseph Raz's service conception of authority and sources thesis,[92] and Ronald Dworkin's theory of interpretation.[93] These authorities have been supplemented by an array of other theories and approaches in recent decades, generally of more limited scope,

[88] Dennis Patterson (ed.), *A Companion to Philosophy of Law and Legal Theory* (2nd ed.) 2 (Wiley Blackwell, Malden, MA; 2010).

[89] John Austin was a noted English legal theorist who influenced Anglo-American law with his analytical approach to jurisprudence and his theory of legal positivism in his major work, *The Province of Jurisprudence Determined* (J. Murray, London; 1832). Austin's particular theory of law is often called the "command theory of law" because the concept of command lies at its core, resting on three-fold concepts of sovereignty, command, and sanction.

[90] Hart's book *The Concept of Law* (1994) presents his theory of legal positivism within the framework of analytic philosophy. In *The Concept of Law* Hart made a distinction between primary and secondary legal rules, where a primary rule governs conduct and a secondary rule allows the creation, alteration or extinction of primary rules.

[91] A basic norm (*grundnorm*) is a concept in Hans Kelsen's *Pure Theory of Law* (rev'd. ed.) (The Lawbook Exchange, Clark, NJ; 2005). Kelsen used this term to denote the basic norm, order or rule that forms the underlying basis for a legal system. His theory is based on a need to find a point of origin for all law, from which basic law and the constitution can gain their legitimacy.

[92] Joseph Raz maintains that legal commands are exclusionary reasons for action and for the "service conception" of authority, according to which those subject to an authority "can benefit by its decisions only if they can establish their existence and content in ways which do not depend on raising the very same issues which the authority is there to settle." This, in turn, supports Raz's argument for legal positivism, in particular "the sources thesis," or "the idea that an adequate test for the existence and content of law must be based only on social facts, and not on moral arguments." Massimo Renzo & Leslie Green, "Legal Obligation and Authority" in *The Stanford Encyclopedia of Philosophy* (30 June 2022).

[93] Dworkin's book *Law's Empire* posited the hypothetical scenario in which judges interpret the law in terms of consistent moral principles, especially justice and fairness.

attempting to theorize the law in one field, or with respect to one particular doctrine or cause of action.[94]

Theories of international law have likewise been preoccupied with identifying the ultimate source of legal obligation but have traditionally approached the job of theory from the perspective of consent.[95] Generally speaking, they appear to forward a mix of natural law and positivist explanations.[96] More recently, some theorists have also attempted to discern whether international law exhibits a "deep structure" based on alternating utopian (i.e. idealist) and apologist (i.e. realist) accounts, but have had difficulty linking these to any larger framework or explanation such as "non-will-related justice."[97]

What is apparent from these efforts is that theories of domestic and international law come at the question of the ultimate source of legal obligations by means of their own frames and rationalities. Notwithstanding the difference, what commentators in both spheres seem to conclude is that the source of obligations is found in no single category or source of law but rather in their combination.[98] The idea of obligation then may be said to arise from the totality of a legal system.

[94] Paul Rubin, "Why Is the Common Law Efficient?" 6 *J. Legal Studies* 51 (1977); George Priest, "The Common Law Process and the Selection of Efficient Rules" 6 *J. Legal Studies* 65 (1977); John Goodman, "An Economic Theory of the Evolution of the Common Law" 7 *J. Legal Studies* 393 (1978); R. Peter Terrebonne, "A Strictly Evolutionary Model of Common Law" 10 *J. Legal Studies* 397 (1981).

[95] Allen Buchanan & David Golove, "Philosophy of International Law" in Jules Coleman et al., *The Oxford Handbook of Jurisprudence and Philosophy of Law* (Oxford University Press, Oxford; Jan. 2004) (noting "the traditional view according to which state consent is both necessary and sufficient for the legitimacy of norms within the international legal system." Ibid. at 50).

[96] David Bederman, *The Spirit of International Law* 17 (University of Georgia Press, Athens, GA; 2002) ("the naturalist-positivist dualism has been regarded as the crucial dialectic of international law").

[97] Martti Koskenniemi, "International Legal Theory and Doctrine" in *Max Planck Encyclopedia of Public International Law*, para. 21 (2005).

[98] Thus, Stephen Waddams has observed that "Often a legal obligation has been derived not from a single concept but from the interaction of two or more concepts in such a way as to preclude the allocation of the legal issue to a single category." Stephen Waddams, *Dimensions of Private Law* 1 (Cambridge University Press, Cambridge; 2003). See also José Alvarez, *The Public International Law Regime Governing International Investment* 232 (Hague Academy of International Law, The Hague; 2011) (noting that "strict positivism" does not explain the shape of international investment law).

If this is true, then a communitarian theory of law can offer a more coherent and detailed understanding of the ultimate source of legal obligations because of its foundation in "system."

Still, this bare identification of "system" as the ultimate source of legal obligations may appear a little broad-brush and will not be enough for those who expect theories of law to be more precise. That is why I refer to the four relationships of correlation, subordination, transition and integration identified earlier. They impart a certain direction, or dynamic, in the system. At the same time, commentators will demand to know what the practical consequences of such an identification are.

One immediate consequence is interpretative. For instance, where the question of an obligation arises, a communitarian theory of law suggests that the legal element is likely to be interpreted in a broad and plenary way – to be constitutive, prospective and presumptive, and to involve equal application of the law. Likewise, where the question of a right arises, a communitarian theory suggests that the legal element is likely to be interpreted in a narrow and exceptional way – to be contractual, retrospective and proof-oriented, and to involve fair application of the law.

As I will show, examples of these interpretative practices are frequent in the WTO legal system. Do the same practices hold in every instance? I will suggest that they are likely to, but not invariably. This qualification is tied to a point made earlier, namely, that the theory put forward in this book emphasizes tendencies as opposed to certainties.[99] Particular fact patterns may exhibit in a contrary way (i.e. Equality < Fairness, Obligation < Right). The foregoing interpretative conventions are discernible in WTO law, but in Chapter 7 I will show how they also exhibit to a degree in international investment law. This projection supplies an example of the theory's "illuminating power."[100]

Another consequence of the relationships outlined above is to identify a gradual oscillation, or movement, between the idea-complexes that are part of a theory. In the normal course the conception of the law should move back and forth among polarities, though not necessarily in a

[99] On tendencies in law, see Catherine Valcke, "Contractual Interpretation at Common Law and Civil Law" in Jason Neyers (ed.), *Exploring Contract Law* 77 at 112 (Hart Publishing, Oxford; 2008).

[100] I would like to thank Maureen Irish for suggesting the use of this phrase.

monolithic fashion. It seems fairly clear, for instance, that current WTO arrangements are moving away from an obligation-based constitutive regime toward something more rights-based and contractual. In line with this trajectory, some commentators also forecast a further move back toward obligation-based constitutionalism at some point in the future.[101]

One theorist whose work this theory may recall is Hans Kelsen. Kelsen's "pure" theory of law posited that law should be logically self-supporting and should not depend on extralegal values such as justice. Instead, Kelsen believed that law should be traceable to some basic norm or assumption (the *Grundnorm*) accepted by a substantial proportion of the community.

Kelsen's ideas differ from the ones I put forward here in their eschewal of justice. For Kelsen justice was "an irrational ideal . . . not subject to cognition."[102] That rejection deprives his theory of the directing impulse that justice as equality instills. Instead, the relationships he foresaw were organized hierarchically, with subordinate norms being linked to higher-level ones and ultimately to the basic norm. Again, this conception differs from the view taken here wherein law is composed organically as the product of an interactive system. I submit that this systematic conception provides a more accurate description of the workings of a legal system than Kelsen's does and is more in line with

[101] See Meinhard Hilf & Tim René Salomon, "Running in Circles: Regionalism in World Trade and How It Will Lead Back to Multilateralism" in Ulrich Fastenrath et al. (eds), *From Bilateralism to Community Interest: Essays in Honour of Bruno Simma* 257 at 267 (Oxford University Press, Oxford; 2011) ("after being subject to [fragmentation] for some time, States will consequently start to look for a solution in order to somehow limit the variety of dispute settlement systems to its lowest common denominator."); Alan Wolff, "WTO 2025: Getting Back to the Negotiating Table" 22-7 Peterson Institute for International Economics Briefing Paper 10 (May 2022) ("Fragmentation of the trading system is not a sustainable long-term trend. There will be a return to multilateralism."). For broader accounts of this same oscillatory movement between multilateralism and unilateralism detected in international law, see Matthew Craven, "Unity, Diversity and the Fragmentation of International Law" XIV *Finnish Yearbook I.L.* 3 at 12 (2003) (referring to the fact that "progressive systematization [of international law] appears in tension with that of fragmentation . . . A system is a system by reason of its ability to unify a diversity of experience – it must be simultaneously homogenous and heterogenous, unified but multipolar.").

[102] Hans Kelsen, *General Theory of Law and State* 13 (Transaction Publishers, New Brunswick, NJ; 2008).

contemporary understanding of power in a community as being exercised both vertically and horizontally.[103]

Where Kelsen and my theories parallel each other, however, is in their monism. Both he and I make little or no distinction between international and domestic law and regard their structures as essentially the same.[104] Some commentators continue to assert the centrality and vitality of such differences.[105] In this book I have suggested that the idea of basic structural sameness in law is reinforced by similar structures of justice.[106] The fact that these structures might express differently in different systems is more a matter of "identity," that is, how the particular legal system is situated between polarities

[103] See Ann Marie Clark et al., "The Sovereign Limits of Global Civil Society" 51:1 *World Politics* 1 (1998) (arguing that the concept of global civil society sets a more demanding standard for the evaluation of transnational political processes than has been applied in prior accounts of transnational activity); Robert O'Brien et al., *Contesting Global Governance* (Cambridge, Cambridge University Press; 2000) (arguing that there is a transformation in the nature of global economic governance as the result of the multilateral economic institution-global society movement encounter, pluralizing governance structures).

[104] Kelsen, *General Theory of Law and State* 13.

[105] "[T]wo features of international law most commonly invoked by those who call into question its legal character are the absence of a centralized system of enforcement and the role of state consent in the formation of rules of international law." See John Tasioulas & Guglielmo Vendirame, "Philosophy of International Law" in *Stanford Encyclopedia of Philosophy* (12 May 2022). Herbert Hart maintained that:

> the absence of an international legislature, courts with compulsory jurisdiction, and centrally organized sanctions have inspired misgivings . . . the absence of these institutions means that the rules for states resemble that form of social structure, consisting of primary rules of obligation . . . [However] international law not only lacks the secondary rules of change and adjudication which provide for legislature and courts, but also a unifying rule of recognition specifying "sources" of law and providing general criteria for the identification of its rules.
>
> (Hart, *The Concept of Law* 214 (1994))

[106] Pavlos Eleftheriadis differs: "Although the distinction between distributive and corrective justice is old and well understood, it has not, for the most part, been deployed in the debates concerning international justice. It appears that when scholars refer to justice in the international context, they only have in mind distributive claims. If distributive claims cannot be justified, then justice is irrelevant." Pavlos Eleftheriadis, "Corrective Justice among States" 2 *Jus Cogens* 7 at 14 (2020). The concern with distributive justice in international affairs is often traced to the work of John Rawls, Michael Blake & Taylor Smith, "International Distributive Justice" in *Stanford Encyclopedia of Philosophy* (4 May 2020) (noting that "international justice has been a central research topic only in recent years" and that "modern dialogue about international distributive justice can be largely traced to the initial publication of Rawls's *A Theory of Justice*.").

of equality/distributive justice and fairness/corrective justice, than any presence or absence of elements that might undermine the theory's architecture.

The theory of law based on justice in this book will also draw comparison with the work of John Rawls. A communitarian theory parallels but also differs from Rawls's work in a number of ways.

Rawls's theory of justice was contractarian. By comparison, the theory I put forward in this book is communitarian. Rawls regarded the basic settlement about justice among actors within a community as occurring in a single moment, with only modest attention paid to the need for updating. The theory here exhibits greater awareness of the requirement for ongoing reform. This pivotal distinction generates a series of further differences in our respective positions.

As mentioned, Rawlsian thinking is premised on the founding of a prototypical community, a view that naturally lends itself to a focus on distributive justice.[107] For this reason Rawls addressed only minimally the problem of dealing with issues of justice correctively *ex post* such as the WTO membership now confronts.

In addition, Rawls's work left open the all-important question of how distributive and corrective justice are related. Many commentators today adhere to either a "dependent" view of the relationship[108] or, alternatively, one of distributive and corrective justice as independent and autonomous of each other.[109]

107 "Taking Rawls at his word, his principles of justice apply to the basic structure [of society]; they do not apply to transactions within that structure, which may be subject to other principles of justice." Steven Walt, "Eliminating Corrective Justice" 92:7 *Virginia. L. Rev.* 1311 at 1316 (2006).

108 Steven Heyman, "Aristotle on Political Justice" 77 *Iowa L. Rev.* 851 at 856 (1992) ("the law that governs corrective justice is not purely 'private law', a law that focuses solely on the private interests of the parties. Instead, the law of corrective justice is inherently political, in the sense that it is directed toward the good of the community"); see also Dagan, "The Distributive Foundation of Corrective Justice," ("the legal choice among ... pecuniary remedies is not a matter of legal technicality, but rather requires a choice among varying conceptions of the plaintiff's entitlement. This choice, in its turn, is a normative choice that implicates the prevailing background ethos of the society at issue and is deeply influenced by the society's complex conceptions of self and of community."); Aditi Bagchi, "Distributive Injustice and Private Law" 130 *Hastings L.J.* 105 (2008) (maintaining that "a background of distributive injustice properly informs our understanding of what constitutes responsible conduct, and thus, the scope of otherwise secure legal entitlements." Ibid. at 108).

109 Ernest J. Weinrib, *The Idea of Private Law* 80 (Harvard University Press, Cambridge, MA; 1995) ("As an autonomous form of justice, corrective justice operates on

The view I take here is that neither of the foregoing views is entirely convincing. Consequently, in Chapter 3 I put forward what I term an "interdependent" view of the relationship.[110] This view regards the relationship as a variable one that exhibits the four relations of correlation, subordination, transition and integration introduced earlier.

At the same time, there is considerable complexity to such a view. That is because an interdependent view regards a distributive priority as the law's dominant tendency while also acknowledging corrective justice as the law's subordinate tendency, generating feedback over time for adjustment of the relevant distribution. Such a hybrid view not only reflects state practice but also better accords with the common understanding of distributive justice as "dynamic" and corrective justice as "static."[111]

More fundamentally, perhaps, Rawls's and my views on the nature of community differ. A community may emerge from a Rawlsian "overlapping consensus," but the communitarian theory outlined in this book suggests that the justice which sustains the community is never entirely ideal and encompasses a wide penumbra of dissent, forcing ideas of injustice and change. Moreover, any historic community retains within it a memory of prior inequalities – for instance, about slavery and racial discrimination in the United States or China's humiliation at the hands

entitlements without addressing the justice of the underlying distribution."); Peter Benson, "The Basis of Corrective Justice and Its Relation to Distributive Justice" 77 *Iowa L. Rev.* 515 at 607 (1992) ("The justification of abstract right and of its principles of acquisition does not depend in the least on the prior satisfaction of any distributive requirements of background justice."); Stephen Perry, "On the Relationship between Corrective and Distributive Justice" in Jeremy Horder (ed.), *Oxford Essays in Jurisprudence: Fourth Series* 237 at 247 (Oxford University Press, Oxford; 2000) ("[Corrective justice is] an independent moral principle that operates within the context of distributive justice, but not as part of it.").

110 "The conceptual distinction between distributive and corrective justice seems clear, but their normative relationship is more difficult to pin down." David Miller, "Justice" in *Stanford Encyclopedia of Philosophy* (6 Aug. 2021).

111 Perry, "On the Relationship between Corrective and Distributive Justice" 247 ("if we accept the premise that distributive justice is best understood dynamically rather than statically, corrective justice should be understood as independent moral principle that operates within the context of distributive justice, but not as part of it."). Walt, "Eliminating Corrective Justice" 1317 ("[c]orrective justice's duty of repair is static; it requires compensation for a wrongful harm that has occurred. Distributive justice is dynamic; it is concerned with the distribution of resources and liberties over the entire life of individuals, not at any point within their lives.").

of the Western powers in the nineteenth century – that conditions thinking about the contemporary meaning of equality and fairness.

Another difference between contractarian and communitarian theories of justice lies in their respective approaches to fairness. Rawls's theory of justice was founded on the notion of equality as modified by "justice as fairness" promoting arrangements for the advantage of the least well-off. As part of the communitarian theory put forward in this book, I recognize fairness to be a much more regular and pervasive phenomenon in a community than Rawls's projected. It is not simply undertaken for the benefit of the less well-off.[112]

A further difference between contractarian ideas and a communitarian theory is attention to the specific legal elements involved in realizing justice. As mentioned, Rawls was principally concerned with distributive justice and famously articulated entitlements to his liberty and difference principles in terms of "rights." By contrast, I emphasize the way that a historic community involves both distributive *and* corrective justice as well as obligations *and* rights and therefore mandates some degree of priority between them. As a matter of theory, Rawls was not completely clear about the structure of legal relationships arising in a community.

Finally, Rawls disagreed with the application of his theory of justice as fairness to international law. Instead, he projected a separate "Law of Peoples" in international relations, a particular political conception of right and justice that promotes certain key principles and norms of international law.[113] These would include an ethic of toleration for decently organized peoples. The communitarian theory put forward in this book makes no such distinction. To the extent that a domestic or international community constitutes a community wherein actors hold

[112] It might be argued that Rawls did account for the wider value of fairness in positing the "maximin" as the rational choice rule under conditions of uncertainty. The concept of maximin:

> directs that we play it as safe as possible by choosing the alternative whose worst outcome leaves us better off than the worst outcome of all other alternatives.
>
> (Samuel Freeman, "Original Position" in *Stanford Encyclopedia of Philosophy* (3 Apr. 2019))

I thank Petros Mavroidis for this insight.

[113] John Rawls, *The Law of Peoples* (Harvard University Press, Cambridge, MA; 1999).

things in common, I posit that the same conceptual pairings should be visible in that community's operation as well.

These then are some of the ways in which our respective theories differ, differences which I will elaborate upon in subsequent chapters. At this point I simply suggest that a communitarian theory supplies a more comprehensive and accurate description of what happens under the rubric of "justice" than a purely distributive or contractarian one does, although this should not be taken as a criticism. It might be concluded instead that a communitarian theory "builds out" Rawlsian ideas, supplementing and extending them.[114] That conclusion would be consistent with the view taken here that many Rawlsian positions remain valid.

A distinctive aspect of this theory of law is its treatment of time. Time is a substantive component of the theory, a resource used to generate interdependence and transformation. Time is therefore more central and active a component in this theory than in other theories and accounts of law, which often regard time passively as a sort of background against which other more dynamic factors play out or which proceeds haltingly from one epoch to the next.[115]

Time is inherent in the keystone concept of community, a concept that highlights what actors share and value across time. The community's vision of the good and its value are transformed over time. This is because time transforms perception. Actors within a community are constantly confronted by ideas and views different from their own. They must adapt their ideas and views to those of others. In this way the individual's views are reconciled with those of the community.[116]

[114] For an interpretation of Rawls as a communitarian, see Roberto Alejandro, "Rawls's Communitariansm" 23:1 *Can. J. Phil.* 75 (1993). For an attempt to posit a principle of private responsibility complementary to Rawlsian ideas, see Arthur Ripstein, "The Division of Responsibility and the Law of Tort" 72 *Fordham L. Rev.* 1811 (2004).

[115] In these understandings, time is usually understood statically through a series of political regimes, historical figures or particular thinkers or schools of thought, taken to be representative of law at one particular time. See, for instance, Martti Koskenniemi, *The Gentle Civilizer of Nations* (Cambridge University Press, Cambridge; 2001). See however Priel, "Analytic Jurisprudence in Time" 213 (noting the dominant view within analytic jurisprudence which sees it as aiming to provide an account of the nature of law existing beyond time and place and how this is insufficiently appreciated in the discipline).

[116] "[I]f from a moral point of view cooperation always entails some kind of effacing of one's own interests in deference to others or the group, then from a cognitive point of view,

This working out of the relationship between the individual and the communal happens, however, only over time, the conception of which may differ depending on the particular community.[117] WTO law encompasses two distinct conceptions of time, one which is progressive and dynamic (*chronos*), the other momentary and static (*kairos*). Their combination takes a form that is transcendent, hence the need to regard both justice and law under the WTO Agreement as diachronic.[118]

The communitarian theory introduced above is founded on a number of conceptual pairs: equality/fairness, obligation/right and so forth. John Finnis has argued that one cannot do first-order legal theory without taking a stand on what the important features are that an adequate theory of law must explain.[119] Why then employ these particular pairings to outline a theory?

I focus on these pairs because they appear to describe the most basic conceptual couplets involved in discussions of justice and law and because the individual elements within them are naturally thought of as correlatives and opposites.[120]

This is particularly true of obligations and rights, which are frequently referenced together in constitutive instruments of international and domestic law in ways that suggest their preeminence.[121] In international

cooperative thinking always entails some kind of effacing of one's own perspective in deference to the more 'objective' perspective of others or the group." Michael Tomasello, *A Natural History of Human Thinking* 122 (Harvard University Press, Cambridge, MA; 2014).

117 Carol Ezzell, "Clocking Cultures" in *A Matter of Time* 27 *Scientific American* (Special Edition) 48 (Summer 2018) ("the way various cultures keep time reflects their priorities and even the way they view the world"). See also generally Robert Levine, *A Geography of Time* (Basic Books, New York; 1998).

118 Gabrielle Marceau has observed how much interpretation under international and WTO law according to the Vienna Convention on the Law of Treaties, 8 I.L.M. 679 (1969), is subtly diachronic because of regular reliance on ever-updated dictionary definitions and reference to a wider context that is constantly changing. Gabrielle Marceau, "Evolutive Interpretation by the WTO Adjudicator" 12:4 *J.I.E.L.* 791 (2018).

119 John Finnis, *Natural Law and Natural Rights* 9–15 (Oxford University Press, New York; 1980).

120 In 1917 Wesley Hohfeld put forward his well-known arrangement of jural opposites and correlatives as a means of understanding interests in property. Wesley Hohfeld, *Fundamental Legal Conceptions as Applied in Judicial Reasoning* 36 (1919, rev'd. ed., Lawbook Exchange, Clark, NJ; 2010).

121 See Dworkin, *Law's Empire* 152 ("Legal rights and duties are a familiar part of our legal scene."). William Eskridge has pointed to a need for a balance between these concepts, "Individual rights, without more, are a thin way to express or normalize the relationship

law it is noteworthy, for instance, that among the initial tasks undertaken by then new United Nations International Law Commission (ILC) in the late 1940s was the development of a Draft Declaration on Rights and Duties of States, as if "rights" and "duties" (i.e. obligations) are somehow foundational in the formulation of international law.[122] In domestic legal systems their importance as basic legal elements is beyond question.[123]

Inherent in all the referenced pairs, however, is tension, a tension which is also discerned in biology. What do I mean?

Biology is the study of life and living organisms. It emphasizes the life force (*ζώη*) and interaction exhibited during the life cycle of an organism. Each organism establishes a unique set of relationships between itself and its environment. Internally, living organisms are also unique inasmuch as they possess distinct attributes such as metabolism and the capacity to grow and respond to stimuli that are not displayed by their constituents alone. In sum, they are distinct from their constituent elements and surrounding environments but also dependent upon them.

The trade-off between distinctiveness and dependence is not maintained without effort, however. An organism exerts constant effort to sustain and differentiate itself from the rest of its environment.

A community composed of obligations and rights manifests a similar effort. Out of the resulting push-and-pull, what becomes apparent is that in any single moment the legal system of the community approximates a

of the individual to the community. . . . [the] assumption of responsibility is what separates the full member of the community from the child or the outsider. This conception provides a richer understanding of the relationship between the individual and the community than does liberal theory." William Eskridge, "The Relationship between Obligations and Rights of Citizens" 69 *Fordham L. Rev.* 1721 at 1722 (2001).

122 A/RES/375 (6 Dec. 1949).

123 The phrase "rights and obligations" is also found in Art. 14 of the International Covenant on Civil and Political Rights, 999 U.N.T.S. 171 (1966) in a way that infers it to be portmanteau term for the totality of legal relations between individuals in domestic legal systems ("All persons shall be equal before the courts and tribunals. In the determination of any criminal charge against him, *or of his rights and obligations in a suit at law*, everyone shall be entitled to a fair and public hearing by a competent, independent and impartial tribunal established by law.") The nineteenth-century Chinese constitutional scholar Liang Qichao observed "Defining the *rights and obligations* of the subjects is an essential part of the constitutions of various countries." *Liang Qichao: Anthology of Works on Law by Liang Qichao* (Fan Zhongxin, ed.), p. 9 (1989) [Hein – World Constitutions Illustrated].

"middle way," *via media*, that can be likened to the struggle of an organism to maintain itself between polarities of unity and diversity. The system does so by means of a dialectic.

The dialectic is a process of reasoning dependent upon opposing concepts of thesis, antithesis and synthesis. It has been a regular feature of law and moral philosophy since at least the time of the ancient Greeks. It was famously revived by Hegel, who maintained that mental patterns will manifest themselves over time in pairs of contradictions that ultimately generate a reconciliation.[124]

Such a reconciliation takes place out of the interaction and interdependence among the conceptual pairs I have chosen which, working together, result in transformation. The continual dialectic allows for "integrative thinking," which Roger Martin has described as:

> the ability to face constructively the tension of opposing ideas and, instead of choosing one at the expense of the other, generat[ing] a creative resolution of the tension in the form of a new idea that contains elements of the opposing ideas but is superior to each.[125]

Integrative thinking has four main characteristics. First, it "takes a broader view of what is salient. . . . More salient features make for a messier problem."[126]

Second, integrative thinking is open to considering multidirectional and nonlinear causal relationships. That is because "[s]imple, unidirectional relationships are easier to hold in the mind, but they don't generate more satisfactory resolutions."[127]

Third, integrative thinking does not "break a problem into independent pieces [to be worked on] separately."[128] Instead, the entire problem or system is kept in mind as work proceeds on individual parts. Retention assists in achieving "breakthrough solutions."[129]

Fourth, integrative thinking searches "for creative resolution of tensions, rather than accept unpleasant trade-offs."[130]

[124] Julie Maybee, "Hegel's Dialectics" in *Stanford Encyclopedia of Philosophy* (Fri, 2 Oct. 2020).

[125] Roger Martin, *The Opposable Mind* 15 (Harvard Business School Press, Cambridge, MA; 2007).

[126] The "messiness" of the problem is important to ensuring that no features are edited out that "are necessary to the completion of the problem as a whole." Ibid., p. 41.

[127] Ibid., p. 42.

[128] Ibid., p. 43.

[129] Ibid.

[130] Ibid.

The communitarian theory presented in this book is a product of integrative thinking. It attempts to analyze the conceptual oppositions at work in WTO law from the vantage point of the system as a whole. To that extent, it highlights how ideas of obligations and rights are generated and conditioned within a community.

The theory is also open to considering multidirectional influences in WTO law, particularly from anthropology, evolutionary psychology and biology, mentioned above. Because the theory's implicit frame of reference is system-wide, it does not divide the problem of explaining the nature and shape of WTO law into discrete pieces or cases. Instead, in line with the foundational idea of interdependence, it regards all components of the system as working together.

Finally, the theory's profiling of complexity reveals how the law in operation arrives at a medial point, searching for "creative resolution of tensions, rather than accept[ing] unpleasant trade-offs." This is evident in its identification of "third things" emanating from the operation of a legal system.

As mentioned, a communitarian theory draws heavily upon biology. Law is "bio-mimetic" in that it imitates biology "or is a mimesis of the processes that take place in biological systems."[131]

The particular contribution of biology to the theory is its emphasis on interdependence and evolutionary adaptation. To sustain interdependence in the form of community certain factors need to be adhered to over time, justice and law being among them. Still, conditions and conceptions of the good change, and so consequently there is a need for justice and law to change.

It is common to speak of justice and law as "evolving." However, what I am especially interested in identifying a communitarian theory is the overall direction and content of that change.[132] How exactly do justice and law change over time in the face of interdependence?

Interdependence means that actors may become responsible for acts or effects upon those with whom they do not immediately depend or

[131] E. Donald Elliott, "Law and Biology: The New Synthesis" 41 *St. Louis U. L.J.* 595 at 600 (1997).

[132] Michael Sinclair, "Evolution in Law" 71 *U. Det. Mercy L. Rev.* 31 at 32 (1993) ("It is quite commonplace to talk of law as evolving."). But see Allan Hutchinson, *Evolution and the Common Law* (Cambridge University Press, Cambridge; 2005) (noting that evolution is simply "about change historical change, not normative advancement." Ibid. at 34).

reciprocate. Most evidently, these relationships emphasize obligation. That transformation is visible at the level of justice in the evolution of what is considered right or correct, as in the case of certain transformative outcomes in WTO dispute settlement. It is also visible in the emergence of state responsibility for action that is not, strictly speaking, contrary to any treaty obligation, as indicated for example in the "non-violation" cause of action in GATT/WTO law.[133]

Insight from biology thus promotes a transformative view of the law. The tendency is to see the law either as impermeable, fixed and static, or, alternately, as porous, fluid and dynamic. By contrast, biology tends to emphasize the way law is ultimately adaptive, evolutionary and diachronic. It changes according to the evolving sense of the good. The advantage of this conception is that the law is understood more organically. This is the ultimate product of integrative thinking.

1.5 The Structure of This Book

A few words should be said about the structure of this book. I have intended this opening chapter as an overview of the book's principal themes and ideas. This chapter has provided a summary of the theory and a justification for its three-fold structure.

Chapter 2 examines the WTO Agreement as a community. It sets out a theory of community before furnishing an overview of GATT/WTO arrangements as a community and some idea of the historical background from which they emerged. The chapter makes the point that the WTO Agreement can be understood as a club good belonging to the membership as a whole. A look is taken at the way in which the treaty's cognitive framework is shaped by textual and contextual considerations that lead to a substantial degree of cohesion and unity.

[133] In general, disputes in the WTO involve allegations that a country has violated an agreement or broken a commitment. But in some situations a government can commence a dispute under WTO dispute settlement even when an agreement has *not* been violated. This option is termed a "nonviolation complaint." Non-violation is made out when a government can show that it has been deprived on an expected benefit arising from GATT by action taken by another country outside the treaty. if one government can show that it has been deprived of an expected benefit because of another government's action, or because of any other situation that exists. See GATT Art. XXIII:1(b).

From this set of observations it might be concluded that WTO obligations are integral – that is, they are owed unconditionally – as indeed the text of the WTO Agreement provides. However, a number of additional features suggest that WTO member countries consider their obligations under the treaty to be interdependent. There is an astute appraisal by countries of reciprocal behavior. Countries will commit, but only to the extent that others do so.

A look is then taken at how contemporary perceptions of fairness are causing the club good emanating from the community of the treaty to become uncoupled and evolve into something looser and perhaps less well-defined. Here, the common good of the membership appears at some points to be splintering into bilateral relationships more akin to private goods.

Chapter 3 focuses on the idea of justice and what theories have been put forward to explain it. The chapter introduces a modified Aristotelian theory of justice that explains much of what is observed in WTO dispute settlement. The chapter also illustrates how Aristotelian categories of distributive and corrective justice, classically conceived of as separate and distinct, are in fact interrelated and work together interactively and interdependently to promote transformation. The chapter concludes with a survey of how transformative justice falls short of "ideal justice," thereby instilling a continuing impulse for reform in WTO law.

Chapters 4 to 6 constitute the core of this book. Successive chapters are devoted to explaining WTO law as a law of obligations (Chapter 4), a law of rights (Chapter 5) and as a *sui generis* legal system (Chapter 6). Each chapter opens with some general observations about the law's operation in that mode, followed by more detailed remarks about its workings in four respects. These are: *juridically* in terms of obligations and rights, *structurally* in terms of constitution and contract, *temporally* in terms of future and past, and *rationally* in terms of deduction and induction.

The foregoing framework is reasonably coherent and does a good job of accounting for the nature and structure of WTO law. This raises an intriguing question: to what extent can a communitarian theory be understood as a theory of law in general? The question points to a need to apply and test the theory's operation in other legal systems.

Chapter 7 therefore applies the communitarian theory to international investment law, a body of law chiefly concerned with the protection of investor rights in host countries. Due to this, a communitarian theory would forecast investment law to be preoccupied with corrective justice and to be heavily contractual, retrospective and inductive. The chapter demonstrates how all of these features are confirmed in the shape of contemporary international investment law, and how in light of considerable dissatisfaction with the current regime an impulse is detected toward something more egalitarian, and therefore more obligatory, constitutive, prospective and presumptive.

Finally, Chapter 8 summarizes the ideas put forward in this book. It details how justice under the WTO Agreement is transformative as opposed to corrective but not for that reason entirely unjust. That is because its chief value is solidarity. The chapter also examines the possibility of a communitarian theory serving as a general theory of law. A theory based on these ideas explains a considerable amount in a way that is naturally coherent and fruitful and offers several predictions and prescriptions about the possible future of WTO law.

At the same time, the chapter acknowledges that a communitarian theory is itself incomplete. This is due to abduction, which stresses the tentative, open-ended nature of current knowledge. Presentism suggests there is a danger in thinking about obligations and rights of countries narrowly in the current moment and not in the broader sense of obligations owed to future generations.

1.6 Conclusion

To conclude this opening chapter, it is helpful to say a few words about the wider context in which a communitarian theory will appear.

A theory of WTO law based on ideas about community and justice is likely to provoke reactions from commentators familiar with existing work on the WTO Agreement. There will be the demand to justify the theory outlined above in terms of prior work and to indicate in greater detail what the benefits of identifying such a theory are. Indeed, an acceptable answer to the question posed at the beginning of this chapter – why a theory? – appears to rest implicitly on perceived shortcomings of existing accounts and to promise something better.

To date, the WTO Agreement and its legal system have generated an enormous literature that analyzes the law according to a number of different approaches. I will mention three here.

First, the dominant textual approach to WTO law tracks or reacts to interpretation of the WTO Agreement principally by means of the Vienna Convention on the Law of Treaties (VCLT). That interpretation focuses on the text, context, object and purpose of the treaty.[134] Although textualism has generated significant commentary about the WTO Agreement, it has been unable to offer a coherent theory of WTO law and says little about developments beyond the treaty language itself.

Second, WTO law, as an acknowledged branch of international economic law, might be expected to draw on economics for theoretic insight. However, despite generating substantial commentary about the WTO Agreement, economics also has failed to identify a generally accepted theory of WTO law.[135] In this respect Petros Mavroidis has pointed out:

> The end result is that economic theory has not, as of yet, come up with a comprehensive explanation for the GATT, as we know it . . . What we still lack is an internally consistent theory that we can use as guidance to understand and interpret *all* of the GATT instruments.[136]

This is in addition to the fact that WTO dispute settlement panels and the Appellate Body have been hesitant to engage with economic analysis, treating it for the most part as an "afterthought."[137]

Third, there are power-based approaches to WTO law anchored in ideas about legitimacy. The usual issue in these accounts is why WTO law is lacking in legitimacy or how the law might buttress its legitimacy.[138] That analytical frame normally involves careful analyses of panel and Appellate Body decisions with models of legitimating state authority in mind, an exercise which is inherently problematic given that the WTO is not a state and its organs of dispute settlement are meant to settle disputes, not act as courts. As such, power-based accounts fail to track much of the language employed by the organs

[134] See, for example, Asif Qureshi, *Interpreting WTO Agreements* (Cambridge University Press, Cambridge; 2006); Isabelle Van Damme, *Treaty Interpretation by the WTO Appellate Body* (Oxford University Press, Oxford; 2009).

[135] For a review of economic thinking in relation to the WTO Agreement, see Kyle Bagwell & Robert Staiger, *The WTO: Theory and Practice*, WTO Staff Working Paper ERSD-2009-11 (11 Nov. 2009).

[136] Petros Mavroidis, *Trade in Goods* (1st ed.) 18 (Oxford University Press, Oxford; 2007) [emphasis in original].

[137] Marion Jansen et al. (eds), *The Use of Economics in International Trade and Investment Disputes* 6 (Cambridge University Press, Cambridge; 2017).

[138] On the legitimacy of WTO law, see Joseph Weiler, "The Rule of Lawyers and the Ethos of Diplomats" 35 *J.W.T.* 191 (2001); Robert Howse, "Adjudicative Legitimacy and Treaty Interpretation in International Trade Law" in Joseph Weiler (ed.), *The EU, the WTO and the NAFTA* 35 (Oxford University Press, Oxford; 2000).

of dispute settlement in any systematic way or to explain its content in convincing detail.

Consequently, existing approaches to WTO law offer only fragmentary and limited insight into why the law is as it is. They do not offer a wholesale theory in the sense of an integrated "system of ideas."

Still, the attempt to set out a communitarian theory of WTO law in this book is likely to encounter the objection that the concept of community is too vague a basis for a theory and that WTO law, like the rest of international law, is not traditionally understood as a form of justice.[139] Furthermore, the principal features which I focus on in order to outline a theory have been traditionally understood as countermeasures promoting compliance, not remedies promoting justice.

Nevertheless, I take the view that whatever objections may be raised to my approach, a wholesale theory is merited if previous attempts at theorization fail to say very much in a systematic manner about the arrangement of WTO law. Such a theory is all the more important and pressing if a persistent criticism of WTO arrangements is that they are unjust.

In short, what I have introduced above and will detail in subsequent chapters is the way that a theory of WTO law is justified because it possesses superior explanatory power. Simply put, the theory offers a richer, more complete explanation for the shape of WTO law than other accounts do.

At the same time, the theory put forward in this book will not be easy to assimilate or appreciate. There is, in addition, much in it that on conventional understandings will appear counterintuitive and even nonsensical.

One universal tenet of thinking about justice is corrective, namely that a successful plaintiff is entitled to full recovery for harm. The theory's two-fold response to this principle, namely that corrective justice in most instances is constrained by distributive considerations and is about what is "fair," and beyond that, that justice aims in an overarching sense at transformation, will seem odd and perhaps a little alien.

[139] Frédéric Mégret also notes, however, that there have been sustained efforts recently to identify justice as a basis for international law. Mégret notes that this consists of trying to identify "an intrinsic justice to at least some forms of law," or the idea that justice might arise in "international law based on the commutative exchange of obligations over time" or in "attempts to elucidate international law as based or deserving to be based on a form of deontological or consequentialist morality." Frédéric Mégret, "Justice" in Jean d'Aspremont & Sahib Singh (eds), *Concepts for International Law* 585 at 600–601 (Edward Elgar Publishing, Cheltenham; 2019).

There are other ways that the theory put forward here will be unsettling as well. In the main, what I set out does not engage with cosmopolitan views of global justice or arguments about the priority of human rights.[140] To be sure, core human rights are *jus cogens*, fundamental norms from which no derogation is possible. However, human rights do not operate on the same plane as the rights and obligations in WTO law. As Gabrielle Marceau has pointed out, "there is no perfect coherence between the human rights and WTO systems of law and jurisdiction."[141]Instead, I posit that the justice of WTO law is a distinctive form of justice between member states and an example of what Steven Ratner has termed the "thin justice" of international law.[142] The justice I describe here applies among equals – that is, among countries that have made the necessary trade concessions and commitments to be part of a community. Individuals do not do this. Thus, while some readers may be apt to champion the need for WTO arrangements to forward global justice and to call my description of WTO law as justice a masquerade for continuing injustice, the explanation I prefer for this inconsistency is simply that individuals and countries are different. That difference is a reflection of the fact that justice in sovereign terms is not always the same as justice in human terms.[143]

[140] A cosmopolitan account of justice typically holds that every human being has standing as the ultimate unit of moral concern and is entitled to equal consideration of their interests no matter what other affiliations, especially national affiliations, they might have. See Martha Nussbaum, "Patriotism and Cosmopolitanism" in Joshua Cohen (ed.), *For Love of Country?* 3 (Beacon Press, Boston; 1996) and Thomas Pogge in Thomas Pogge, "Concluding Reflections" in Gillian Brock (ed.), *Cosmopolitanism versus Non-Cosmopolitanism* 294 (Oxford University Press, Oxford; 2013).

[141] Gabrielle Marceau, "WTO Dispute Settlement and Human Rights" 13:4 *E.J.I.L.* 753 at 756 (2002).

[142] Steven Ratner, *The Thin Justice of International Law* (Oxford University Press, Oxford; 2015) (arguing that the standard of international justice is based largely on principles of promotion of interstate peace and respect for basic human rights, with some room for deontological considerations in limited situations beyond these. The "thin" justice of international law is not as thick as that minimally demanded in domestic politics nor is it the limit for justice that should be striven for in the international realm, "but it is justice deserving of the name – one justifiable from an impartial perspective and, indeed, broadly consistent with a cosmopolitan vision of the world." Ibid. at 9).

[143]

> Justice in society in relation to its constituent members is a concept that can only be determined in the context of their socio-juridical status in that society. At a time when slaves were not regarded as legitimate elements of society, the problem of social justice in relation to slaves was not on the conscience of the people. . . . In the context of international society, this would mean that the conception of justice in a given situation could vary depending on whether it was viewed primarily in relation to sovereign states as the constituent

A further objection to the theory will be thus: why focus on "rights and obligations" as the basis for a theory of law? Isn't the landscape of a legal system much richer and more complex than this? What about general principles of law, declarations, soft law and so forth? Don't these merit inclusion and discussion in a theory that aims to be general and comprehensive?

In response I suggest that it is appropriate to focus in the first instance on "rights and obligations" as the foundation for a theory because they reflect a basic understanding of what the law involves. They are backgrounded by consideration of the good and justice and become the nucleus around which other concepts build. Focusing on them to begin with is part of the theory's simplification.[144]

Several years ago Ronald Dworkin observed:

> our intellectuals distrust theory perhaps more than any earlier age has. We hear, wherever we turn, the injunctions and disclaimers of the post-modernists, the pre-structuralists, the deconstructionists, the critical legal students, the critical race scholars, and a thousand other battalions of the anti-theory army. Some say that theory is phony, and others that it is oppression, and many that it is both.[145]

Dworkin's remarks convey the current mood of suspicion and mistrust of theory. A theory can be illuminating and liberating, but it can also be perceived as constraining and "hegemonic."[146]

A theory like the one put forward here is likely to attract particular criticism. One view may be to regard it as presumptuous – in effect,

> members of society in the sense of the community of nations, or in relation to individuals (or groups of individuals) as the real component elements of society in the sense of the global community. In the context of the traditional Westphalian legal order where sovereign states are the basic constituent units of society, justice in international public order as an objective to be realized has always been conceived of primarily in relation to the sovereign states.
>
> (Hisashi Owada, "Some Reflections on Justice in a Globalizing World" 97 *Am. Soc. Int'l L. Proc.* 181 at 188 (2003))

144 There is an entire field of institutional rule-making in the WTO law that often interacts symbiotically with WTO dispute settlement results and which is little referenced here. For a worthy account of WTO rule-making, see Mary Footer, *An Institutional and Normative Analysis of the World Trade Organization* (Martinus Nijhoff, Leiden; 2006).

145 Ronald Dworkin, *Justice in Robes* 57 (Belknap Press, Cambridge, MA; 2006).

146 Philip Allott has described theory's "hegemonic explanatory power": see Allott, *The Health of Nations* 143.

an attempt to do too much. The conventional approach to legal analysis in WTO law and elsewhere is to search for answers provision-by-provision or case-by-case, offering only slim generalizations. A theory of law that identifies broad idea-complexes and their associated relationships at work in WTO law and projects them as a theory of law in general is likely to upset incrementalist orthodoxies and provoke resistance.

In addition, one effect of the increasing interdependence referred to above is a marked bias in many fields of research toward "participation," "inclusiveness" and collaborative development.[147] In light of this preference, nothing – let alone anything as fundamental as a theory of law – is thought to be the product of a single all-encompassing explanation. To the extent that the theory is so, it will be attacked as exclusive and simplistic. Some readers may be tempted to dismiss what is put forward in this book as "Grand Theory."

Another view is likely to criticize the theory as insufficient, in effect doing too little. The apparent novelty of the theory means that it risks being greeted by all sorts of inflated expectations about the insights it will furnish, as the following forecast of a theory of international law implies:

> the theory of international law must take account of law's functions in regime design and maintenance: establishing rules as focal points that provide an equilibrium in situations requiring coordination, where thereafter no participant has an incentive to defect from the rule, providing transparency and monitoring and some sanctioning in ways that make possible the capture of gains from cooperation without excessive cost; embedding international agreements in national law that can have more direct purchase on relevant actors; drawing systemic linkages among otherwise unrelated issues so as to raise the cost of violation; aiding powerful states to make commitments that others have confidence will be adhered to, by enmeshing them in deeper structure of legal obligation.[148]

The foregoing description may appear overwrought – a sort of "kitchen sink" description of a theory – but it is symptomatic of the unstated

[147] Edmund Wilson, *Letters to a Young Scientist* 91 (Liveright Publishing, New York; 2013) ("The conventional wisdom holds that science of the future will be more and more the product of 'teamthink,' multiple minds put in close contact. It is certainly the case that fewer and fewer solitary authors publish research articles in premier journals such as *Nature* and *Science*.").

[148] See Benedict Kingsbury, "The International Legal Order" in Peter Cane & Mark Tushnet (eds), *Oxford Handbook of Legal Studies* 271 at 294 (Oxford University Press, Oxford; 2003).

demand in contemporary legal scholarship that a theory of law should explain *everything*.

Here, I think it is important to keep in mind Thomas Kuhn's observation in 1962 that a theory is useful if it solves "a few problems" recognized as "acute."[149] Among these acute problems is the need to supply an explanation for the kind of justice available under the WTO Agreement and for the peculiar shape of its legal system. Evidently, the theory put forward in this book will not resolve every problem or question of WTO law. To that extent, however, it leaves room for the development of other theories.

[149] Kuhn observed that theories "gain their status because they are more successful than their competitors in solving *a few problems that the group of practitioners has come to recognize as acute.*" Thomas Kuhn, *The Structure of Scientific Revolutions* 23 (University of Chicago Press, Chicago; 1962) [emphasis added].

2

The WTO Agreement as Community

2.1 A Theory of Community

In the previous chapter, I explained how the theory of law put forward in this book is founded on the idea of community. Given that foundation and the way that the theory integrates component theories of justice and law reflective of community, it is useful to begin by setting out a theory of community.

The need to develop a theory of community arises from biology and from the fact that actors are interdependent. They rely on each other. This reliance takes place within communities.

In Chapter 1, I referred to the idea of the WTO Agreement as giving rise to a neo-Grotian community, which "sees the international system on its way to becoming an 'organized state community' with an emphasis on common interests."[1]

However, that very general description of the WTO Agreement does not offer much critical detail about the treaty as a community or how it might be understood in terms of a theory of community. In particular, it leaves unanswered the pivotal question: what is a community and how does it differ from other arrangements *as a matter of law*?[2]

[1] Bruno Simma & Andrea Paulus, "The 'International Community': Facing the Challenge of Globalization" 9 *E.J.I.L.* 266 at 271 (1998).

[2] The subject of community is notoriously vague. As Gerard Delanty has noted, community "is a widely used term in popular and academic discourse, but it is also contested." Gerard Delanty, *Community* (2nd ed.) x (Routledge, New York; 2010). The difficulty of definition is also noted in relation to the "international community." Steven Ratner has observed that "it is frankly hard to know what [international community] means – how, for instance, should it relate to the many national senses of community? – or how should we determine its presence." Steven Ratner, *The Thin Justice of International Law* 59 (Oxford University Press, Oxford; 2015).

An answer is provided by Thomas Franck, who has observed:

> The difference between a rabble or even a primitive association and a developed community is that in the latter members accept specific reciprocal obligations as a concomitant of membership in that community, which is a structured, continuing association of interacting parties. Individuals in a rabble or primitive society do not ordinarily attempt to imagine the reality of those with whom they share a space, nor do they concern themselves with how they may be perceived by those others. There is no expectation that a single, limited transaction will establish a continuing, structured relationship, nor is each such interaction thought to occur within a framework in which many have a stake, including even those not directly involved.[3]

Franck's description stresses certain key features of a community. First, a community creates obligations.[4] Members of a community are prepared to assume obligations because they anticipate repeated transactions with each other concerning something they possess together. One feature is therefore that members of a community will have common obligations.

Second, Franck's description suggests that a community gives rise to two types of obligation. He provides the example of a promissory note made between two actors, A and B, in a community.[5] A wants a pair of shoes but has no money to pay for them, so A issues a promissory note to B, a shoemaker, in exchange for a pair of shoes. The transaction creates reciprocal rights and obligations between A and B in the manner of a contract. The promissory note is evidence of an arrangement between A and B which the law will enforce and which has no immediate consequences for any other party. Hence, one type of obligation in a community is bilateral and contractual.

However, Franck goes on to detail the situation where B transfers the promissory note to C, a leather dealer, in exchange for a shipment of leather. C subsequently transfers the note to another actor, D, in payment

[3] Thomas Franck, *The Power of Legitimacy among Nations* 197 (Oxford University Press, New York; 1990).

[4] "Political association, like family and friendship and other forms of association more local and intimate, is itself pregnant of obligation." Ronald Dworkin, *Law's Empire* 206 (Belknap Press, Cambridge, MA; 1986). Dworkin adds that "the central obligation [of a political association] is that of general fidelity to law." Ibid. at 208.

[5] Franck, *The Power of Legitimacy among Nations* 199.

for some good or service. At the end of the sequence of transactions, the integrity of the promissory note as well as the ability to enforce it become a matter of concern, not only to the ultimate holder of the note but also potentially to every other member of the community. Franck explains:

> ... in due course all parties to all promissory notes within the community will have some degree of interest in sustaining the integrity of such notes in the event of a default. They may institutionalize this interest by establishing a central claim fund by which bad debts are satisfied and to which every drawer or endorser pays a small fee as part of the transaction.[6]

Franck's example illustrates how a network of obligations that is more multilateral and constitutive comes into being and coexists alongside the bilateral and contractual obligations described above. Multilateral and constitutive obligations are of interest to all and stem from the emergence of a common interest.

A third feature of a community that Franck emphasizes is time. To recall, a community is "a *continuing*, structured relationship." Continuity forces members of the community to adapt and adjust their behavior over time so that they can continue to enjoy the benefits of community, typically understood in terms of goods.[7]

[6] Ibid., p. 201.

[7] Ronald Dworkin describes this socialization and its impact on interpretation of the law as follows:

> Every community has paradigms of law, propositions that in practice cannot be challenged without suggesting either corruption or ignorance. Any American or British judge denied that speed regulations were part of the law would be replaced, and this fact discourages radical interpretations. The most powerful influences towards convergence, however, are internal to the character of interpretation. The practice of precedent, which no judges interpretation can wholly ignore, presses towards agreement; each judge's theories of what judging really is will incorporate by reference, through whatever account and restructuring precedent he settles on, aspects of other popular interpretations of the day. Judges think about law, moreover, within society, not apart from it; the general intellectual environment, as well as the common language that reflects and protects the environment, exercises practical constraints on idiosyncrasy and conceptual constraints on imagination. The inevitable conservatism a formal legal education, and to the process of selecting lawyers for judicial and administrative office, adds further centripetal pressure.
>
> (Dworkin, *Law's Empire* 88.)

Still, the distinction made above between obligations owed contractually versus obligations owed constitutionally is a simplification. It is true as a general matter but arises in relation to goods, or that which is considered beneficial. However, the role of goods within communities has more recently revealed a need for finer-grained thinking about them.[8]

In Chapter 1, I mentioned how goods are characterized by different degrees of exclusivity and rivalry.[9] Exclusivity refers to the way in which a good's use may be limited or restricted to some individual or group. Rivalry refers to the way a good's use may diminish its benefits for others.

To recall, the combination of exclusivity and rivalry yields four different types of goods. There are exclusive, rivalrous goods such as real estate; exclusive, nonrivalrous "club" goods such as toll roads; nonexclusive, rivalrous common goods such as natural resources; and nonexclusive, nonrivalrous "public" goods such as public health.[10]

Michael Heller has identified how goods are not simply beneficial but rather, by virtue of their positive (i.e. inclusive) and negative (i.e. exclusive) aspects, have various degrees of realization.[11] He emphasizes how the inclusive character of some goods – such as the environment – may promote a "tragedy of the commons," or depletion of that good, whereas the exclusive character of other goods – such as intellectual property –

[8] For a philosophical discussion of goods, see Patrick O'Riordan, *Global Ethics and Global Common Goods* (Bloomsbury Academic, New York; 2015).

[9] Moya Chin, "What Are Global Public Goods?" 58:4 *Finance & Development* 62 (Dec. 2021).

[10] Ibid.

[11] Michael Heller, *The Gridlock Economy* 41 (Basic Books, New York; 2008). Heller identifies five different property paradigms that highlight the various ways in which the use of goods may be realized or impaired within a community. *Open access*, *group access*, *private property*, *group exclusion* and *full exclusion*. In *open access* anyone has access to the good. Open access encompasses both common goods, which everyone has access to but are rivalrous (i.e. their benefits diminish as they are used), and public goods, which everyone has access to but are nonrivalrous. At the same time, a good's unlimited use can lead to a "tragedy of the commons." As a result, some goods are created and managed by *group access*, wherein use of the good is regulated by a set of actors with a special interest in it. In *private property* a single actor directs use of the good and has exclusive ownership of it. In *group exclusion* a limited number of participants can block each other's use of the good. Finally, in *full exclusion* an unlimited number of participants can block each other's use.

may impair or constrain their use, resulting in what he refers to as "a tragedy of the anticommons," or their underuse.[12]

Heller's identification hints at how the conception of a good is fundamentally a product of community. In some cases the good's use may be realized. In others it may be frustrated. In still others – perhaps the majority of instances – the good's use may be characterized by a combination of these features (i.e. both realization and frustration).

Heller observes:

> when you look closely at any resource, you will see a jigsaw puzzle of commons, private and state ownership, along with elements of anticommons ownership. What's tricky is fitting the pieces together so the resource is reasonably well managed from a social perspective. We need an array of finely honed tools to conserve a single depleting resource or to assemble rights in a newly emerging one.[13]

A related observation is the fact that the conception of a good in a community is not necessarily uniform. On some goods there may be substantial consensus whereas on others there may be very little. The difference of opinion can lead to conflict.[14] In this respect Heller cautions against the elusive aim of seeking a good's "optimal use":

> We don't necessarily require optimal use (not an easy goal because there are genuinely competing conceptions of the term). Instead, the best we may be able to achieve is tolerably good use – avoiding extremes of overuse in a tragedy of the commons and underuse in a tragedy of the anticommons.[15]

In sum, a theory of community suggests that members of a community will possess obligations in relation to goods, some of which are constitutive, others of which are contractual. The obligations will be arranged according to historic use and over time may change as the conception of

[12] Ibid., p. 18.

[13] Ibid., p. 176.

[14]
> The dynamics of [legal] interpretation resist as well as promote convergence, and the centrifugal forces are particularly strong where the professional as well as the larger community is divided over justice. Different judges belong to different and rival political traditions, and the cutting edge of different judges' interpretations will be honed by different ideologies. Nor is this to be deplored. On the contrary, law gains in power when it is sensitive to the frictions and stresses of its intellectual sources.
>
> (Dworkin, *Law's Empire* 88)

[15] Heller, *The Gridlock Economy* 176.

the good changes, not necessarily for optimal use, but as Heller points out, for tolerably good use.

2.2 GATT 1947 and the WTO Agreement

How is the foregoing theory of community manifested in the structure of GATT and operation of the WTO Agreement? To answer this question, some background is necessary.

2.2.1 GATT 1947

The WTO Agreement originates in the General Agreement on Tariffs and Trade of 1947 (GATT 1947), a treaty concluded between twenty-three governments in 1947 that sought to promote stability in international trade relations.

GATT 1947 was originally conceived of as a provisional agreement pending the conclusion of a broader set of negotiations for an International Trade Organization (ITO). When plans for the ITO failed due to US and UK opposition in the early 1950s, GATT 1947 continued as a limited "contractual" engagement among participating governments.[16]

The drafters who designed GATT 1947 foresaw that the most effective way to promote stability in international trade was to oblige countries to "bind" – or fix – their tariffs at individually negotiated levels. The centerpiece of GATT 1947 was therefore the requirement in GATT Art. II that members should not exceed their individual bound tariffs on imports. An additional requirement was the obligation in GATT Art. I for members to extend their best, or "most favored nation" (MFN), tariff or treatment to the remainder of the GATT membership. The obligations in GATT Arts. I and II were complemented by the National Treatment (NT) obligation under GATT Art. III to treat imports no less favorably than domestically produced goods and the obligation in GATT Art. XI to eliminate quantitative restrictions (i.e. quotas) on imports.

The core obligations in GATT Arts. I–III and XI were also supplemented by a range of additional disciplines. These included disciplines on the freedom of transit (GATT Art. V), transparency (GATT Art. X),

[16] Countries participating in GATT 1947 were styled "Contracting Parties," and administrative arrangements for the treaty remained deliberately modest. John Jackson, *World Trade and the Law of GATT* 145 (Bobbs-Merrill, Indianapolis, IN; 1969).

exchange arrangements (GATT Art. XII) and state trading activities (GATT Art. XVIII). Other GATT disciplines pertained to the use by countries of safeguards (GATT Art. XIX), antidumping and countervailing measures (GATT Arts. VI, XVI) and exceptions (GATT Arts. XX–XXI) (see Table 2.1).

The MFN clause of GATT Art. I is vital to understanding the structure of GATT 1947 and, subsequently, the WTO Agreement as goods. The MFN clause requires "any advantage, favour, privilege or immunity" granted by one GATT member country to another country to be extended "immediately and unconditionally" to *all* other GATT member countries.[17] In effect, GATT Art. I renders "public" what is "private" and created a club good, a good that was exclusive to the membership but also nonrivalrous. This semi-public characterization also explains the peculiar shape of dispute settlement that arose under GATT.

[17] A public good is to be contrasted with private goods or property, which were originally described by William Blackstone as "the sole and despotic dominion which one man claims and exercises over the external things of the world, in total exclusion of the rights of any other individual in the universe." Peter Heller defines public goods or common property as:

> shared resources, resources for which there is no single decision-maker. In turn, the commons can be divided into two distinct categories. The first is *open access*, a regime in which no one at all can be excluded . . . The second type of commons has many names, [but it could be called] *group access*, a regime in which a limited number of commoners can exclude outsiders but not each other. If the ocean is open access, then a small pond surrounded by a handful of landowners may be group access.
>
> (Heller, *The Gridlock Economy* 33–34 [emphasis in original])

In the 1970s the idea of global public goods first emerged. See Office of Development Studies, Bureau of Development Policy, United Nations Development Programme, "Global Public Goods: International Cooperation in the 21st Century" (1999). This source notes that the production of global public goods:

> can vary – from a "best-shot" effort (e.g. a disease control effort undertaken by one of the world's leading centres, such as the US Centers for Disease Control) to a "pivotal actors" effort (e.g. forestry preservation by the countries with the world's major forest resources) or a "summation effort" to which all countries and actors have to contribute, on to a "weakest link" effort, which typically depends on even the very last actor's coming on board . . . But, since many actors might indeed be interested in enjoying the benefits of the global public goods, they also have an interest in encouraging all the others, on whose contribution the existence of the good depends, actually to make that contribution. Global public goods thus depend on successful international cooperation.
>
> (Ibid. at 9)

Table 2.1 *The General Agreement on Tariffs and Trade 1947*

GATT Article	Substantive Obligation
I	Most-Favored Nation
II	Tariff Bindings
III	National Treatment
VI	Antidumping and Countervail Action
VII	Customs Valuation
X	Fairness in Administration of Trade Regulations
XI	Prohibition of Quantitative Restrictions
XII	Restrictions for Balance of Payments Purposes
XIII	Nondiscriminatory Application of QRs
XV	Exchange Arrangements
XVI	Subsidies
XVII	State-Trading
XVIII	Government Assistance for Economic Development
XIX	Safeguards
XX	General Exceptions
XXIII	Dispute Settlement
XXIV	Regional Trade Arrangements
XXV	Joint Action by Contracting Parties
XXVIII	Renegotiation of Schedules
XXX	Amendment
XXXI	Withdrawal
XXXIII	Accession
XXXV	Nonapplication of GATT between Contracting Parties
XXXVI–XXXVIII	Trade and Development (1966)

One way in which injury is conceived in international law is *bilaterally*, that is, Country A does damage to Country B. Country B then has a claim against Country A. The injury is discrete – being limited to Country B alone – and implicitly backward-looking.[18] The injured country's loss in the past is made whole by means of reparation.[19]

[18] Peter Drahos, "The Regulation of Public Goods" 7:2 *J.I.E.L.* 321 (2004); Chiedu Osakwe, "Future of the Multilateral Trading System" 10:1 *Asian J. WTO & Int'l Health Law & Pol.* 2 (2015); Petros Mavroidis, "Free Lunches? WTO as Public Good, and the WTO's View of Public Goods" 23:3 *E.J.I.L.* 731 (2012).

[19] As provided for in the Articles on State Responsibility (ARSIWA) Art. 31 on the obligation of reparation in cases of breach and its attendant requirements of restitution (ARSIWA Art. 35), compensation (ARSIWA Art. 36) and satisfaction (ARSIWA Art. 37).

A different operation is called for when the injury is conceived of *multilaterally*, that is, when Country A does damage to a public good belonging to all. In such a scenario it makes no sense to talk about what has been "lost" since any such loss is borne by the community *as a whole*. The classic remedy under international law in that instance is the cessation of wrongful behavior.[20] The remedy must be forward-looking and flexible, with the ultimate recourse being exclusion from the community.[21]

As mentioned, GATT 1947 was originally conceived of as a "contract" and therefore noncompliance under the treaty could be thought of as injuring one country alone. However, the pronounced "public" interest arising from MFN-type obligations meant that GATT dispute settlement evolved differently. The injury done by the noncompliance of one country came to be recognized as an injury occurring to the GATT membership as a whole. As a result, GATT procedures to adjudicate and remedy any breach evolved to be broad and forward-looking.

GATT 1947's dispute settlement process was operationalized under GATT Art. XXIII. Pursuant to that provision, a system of panels arose to determine whether national legislation or other government measures "nullified or impaired" GATT trade commitments. Where a violation of the treaty was found, a panel could make a recommendation of compliance or a ruling on a point of GATT law. A defendant country was then under an obligation to comply, which it normally did by withdrawing the impugned legislation or measure.[22] GATT Art. XXIII:2 also mentions the

See Draft articles on Responsibility of States for Internationally Wrongful Acts, with commentaries, U.N. Doc. A/56/10, 91–107 (2001).

[20] As provided for in ARSIWA Art. 30 on the obligation to cease wrongdoing and provide assurance of nonrepetition. See Draft articles on Responsibility of States for Internationally Wrongful Acts, with commentaries, U.N. Doc. A/56/10, 88–90 (2001).

[21] Oonagh Hathaway & Scott Shapiro, "Outcasting: Enforcement in Domestic and International Law" 121:2 *Yale L.J.* 252 (Nov. 2011).

[22] The Report of the Review Session Working Party on "Organizational and Functional Questions," B.I.S.D. 3rd Supp. 231 at 251 noted that:

> any implication . . . that the provision of appropriate compensation, on the one hand, and the removal of a measure inconsistent with the Agreement, on the other hand, are fully equivalent and satisfactory alternatives would not accord with the intent and spirit of the Article . . . the first objective, if the CONTRACTING PARTIES decided, in the event of a complaint under Article XXIII, that certain measures were inconsistent with provisions of the Agreement, should be to secure the withdrawal of the measures. In such a case, the alternative of providing compensation for damage suffered should be resorted to only if the immediate withdrawal of the measures

possibility of an "injured state" seeking an authorization to suspend the application of concessions against the wrongdoer. However, this retaliatory option proved awkward and was rarely pursued.[23]

On its face GATT dispute settlement appeared – and often operated – in a bilateral fashion "contractually." It usually involved disputes between pairs of countries. Retaliation through selective market closure was possible, although seldom invoked.

At the same time, GATT dispute settlement evolved a practice that did not allow recovery for trade damage in the past – that is, for the period of violation *before* the issuance of a panel report. Instead, the usual remedy was withdrawal of the inconsistent measure. Many GATT disputes also involved significant participation by third countries.[24] These features were more consistent with GATT 1947 as a constitutive and multilateral arrangement.

The bilateral-multilateral tension visible in GATT 1947's dispute settlement system was symptomatic of broader tensions embedded within the treaty itself. As mentioned, the tariff concessions extended by countries under GATT Art. II arose out of reciprocal negotiations.

> was impracticable and only as a temporary measure pending the withdrawal of the measures which were inconsistent with the Agreement.

Similarly, para. 4 of the 1979 Understanding Annex on Customary Practice provides:

> In the absence of a mutually agreed solution, the first objective of the CONTRACTING PARTIES is usually to secure the withdrawal of the measures concerned if these are found to be inconsistent with the General Agreement. The provision of compensation should be resorted to only if the immediate withdrawal of the measure is impracticable and as a temporary measure pending the withdrawal of the measures which are inconsistent with the General Agreement.
>
> (*Agreed Description of the Customary Practice of the GATT in the Field of Dispute Settlement*, GATT B.I.S.D. 26th Supp. 215 (1979))

See also para. ix of the 1982 Ministerial Declaration, GATT Doc. L5424 (29 Nov. 1982).

23 In *U.S. – Dairy Products*, B.I.S.D. 1st Supp. 32 (1953), the Netherlands was authorized by a GATT panel to take counteraction against US restrictions on Dutch dairy exports to the United States. *U.S. – Dairy Products* was the only instance in GATT's forty-eight-year history when such procedures were invoked and applied. See Robert Hudec, *The GATT Legal System and World Trade Diplomacy* 196–197 (Butterworth Legal Publishers, Salem, NH; 1990).

24 Mary Footer, "Some Aspects of Third Party Intervention in GATT/WTO Dispute Settlement Proceedings" in Ernst-Ulrich Petersmann (ed.), *International Trade Law and the GATT/WTO Dispute Settlement System* 211 (Kluwer Law International, Boston;1997); Chi Carmody, "Third Parties under GATT" 18 *Mich. J. Int'l L.* 615 at 618 (1997).

However, the combined effect of GATT Arts. I–III modified reciprocity by diminishing the need for specific reciprocity in which "specified partners exchange items of equivalent value in a specified sequence."[25] Instead, MFN and other nondiscrimination provisions promoted a "diffuse reciprocity" in which, as Robert Keohane explains, "the definition of equivalence is less precise, one's partners may be viewed as a group rather than as particular actors, and the sequence of events is less narrowly bounded."[26] Keohane notes that in diffuse reciprocity "[o]bligations are important. Diffuse reciprocity involves conforming to generally accepted standards of behaviour."[27]

The process of transforming GATT 1947 into "generally accepted standards of behaviour" was also promoted by political and technical considerations. Following the conclusion of GATT in 1947, many former colonies attained independence and a number of new governments were admitted to GATT, with little attention paid to the specific reciprocity they offered.[28] This "free-ridership" provoked debate.

In addition, as tariffs on goods fell GATT negotiations continued in seven successive negotiating rounds that attempted to discipline the misuse of nontariff barriers like safeguards, antidumping and countervailing measures for protectionist purposes. These same disciplines were hard to tie to specific reciprocity. Instead, the general idea emerged that governments should accept them in the form of a series of "side codes"

[25] Robert Keohane, "Reciprocity in International Relations" 40:1 *Int'l Org.* 1 at 4 (Winter 1986).

[26] Ibid., p. 4.

[27] Ibid., p. 4. Ethan Kapstein has offered the following explanation for the promotion of diffuse reciprocity by governments:

> Why would great powers adopt a policy of diffuse or relaxed reciprocity in which they negotiate with and provide a level of benefits to smaller, weaker states that may not be returned in full? The answer is because the resulting international structure is likely to be more robust, more stable, as a result. World politics is full of uncertainty, and at some point small, dissatisfied powers might seek to alter the status quo. Psychological studies of violent behaviour have asserted that "the idea of justice or fairness may be more centrally related to attitudes toward violence than deprivation. It is the perceived injustice underlying the deprivation that gives rise to anger or frustration.

Thus, Kapstein's observation infers that diffuse reciprocity is more stable and aligns with the idea of repeated contact and "community." See Ethan Kapstein, *Economic Justice in an Unfair World* 32–35 (Princeton University Press, Princeton, NJ; 2006).

[28] Robert Hudec, *Developing Countries and the GATT Legal System* 59 (Gower, London; 1987).

entered into on a voluntary, take-it-or-leave-it basis.[29] When some members accepted the side codes but others did not, a pronounced asymmetry arose that later provoked disagreement within the GATT membership.[30]

GATT dispute settlement helped to resolve some of these issues but did so only in a piecemeal fashion and unevenly. Its regular operation was also hampered by decision-making rules. GATT 1947's regular practice of decision-making was one of consensus, a practice that offered a defendant country the opportunity to block an unfavorable panel report when it came up for adoption, thereby pairing GATT's club good character with the possibility of a veto. Approximately one-quarter of all panel reports issued in the GATT 1947 era were so vetoed.[31]

2.2.2 The WTO Agreement

The WTO Agreement was concluded at the end of the Uruguay Round (1986–1994) to address some of the above-mentioned issues and make improvements in the functioning of the GATT system. The new treaty consolidated existing GATT obligations into a "single undertaking,"

[29] The side codes were an attempt to circumvent the GATT 1947's cumbersome amendment procedures, which required approval by at least two-thirds of GATT members. Robert Hudec notes that before the Tokyo Round negotiations (1973–1979) "the GATT had experimented in a few cases with making changes in rules by means of separate side agreements," including an amendment prohibiting export subsidies for nonprimary products in 1954–1955 and the GATT Multi-fibre Arrangement of 1974. See ibid., p. 81. Hudec notes that "[i]n the Kennedy Round negotiations, governments wanting to tighten and refine the discipline on the use of anti-dumping duties . . . resorted, in 1967, to a separate agreement. . . . Although only the major developed countries and a few others signed, the signatories were pleased with the way the code approach had worked." Ibid., p. 82. The nine side codes of the Tokyo Round pertained to subsidies and countervailing measures, technical barriers to trade, import licensing procedures, government procurement, customs valuation, antidumping (replacing the Kennedy Round Antidumping code) and agreements on bovine meat, dairy and trade in civil aircraft. Hudec notes that "[o]f the 65 or so developing countries in the GATT, only a handful signed the Tokyo Round codes." Ibid., p. 88.

[30] For instance, the creation of the Tokyo Round side codes raised the issue of whether "GATT's unconditional MFN obligation required that improvements in trade access granted to other code signatories had to be extended to other GATT members who were not signatories." Hudec notes that "developed country members eventually extended the improved treatment called for by code obligations to all GATT members." Robert Hudec, *Enforcing International Trade Law* 121 (Butterworth Legal Publishers, Salem, NH; 1993).

[31] Ibid., p. 289.

thereby replacing the patchwork that had arisen under GATT 1947 and the side codes, and extended basic GATT disciplines beyond trade in goods to trade in certain services and intellectual property commitments. GATT's dispute settlement system was also streamlined and brought forward, along with a new feature, the possibility of appellate review, designed to ensure consistency and finality in dispute settlement results. Finally, the WTO Agreement was constituted as a stand-alone organization under international law.

The resulting engagement underlines what WTO members share. Specific reciprocity remains formally important within the scheme of the treaty, but with the obligation to extend concessions via MFN to a membership of over 160 countries, reciprocity has lost much of its original significance.[32] The real value of the endeavor lies in all that has evolved, which includes tariff concessions and service and intellectual property commitments as well as a number of practices and procedures – a heritage sometimes referred to as the "WTO *acquis*."[33]

The WTO Agreement is a relatively brief treaty of sixteen articles (Table 2.2). It establishes the WTO as an international organization

[32] During the Uruguay Round, for instance, national delegations "widely but informally accepted that the [negotiating] targets were average [tariff] reductions of one-third for industrial countries and one-fourth for developing countries." However, J. Michael Finger and L. Alan Winters have pointed out that:

> The GATT/WTO members seem to have policed these guidelines rather softly. Interviews with more than a dozen delegations after the round found none that had attempted to calculate the depth of cut by each country, or even for major trading partners. Likewise, no delegation had tabulated concessions received – that is, the coverage of its exports by concessions scheduled by other countries.
>
> (J. Michael Finger & Alan L. Winters, "Reciprocity in the WTO" in Bernard M. Hoekman et al. (eds), *Development, Trade, and the WTO: A Handbook*, Vol. 1, 50 at 55 (World Bank, Washington, DC; 2002))

With respect to disciplines on agriculture – a field that later became the subject of much recrimination and bitterness – Finger and Winters note that "although the [negotiating] guidelines were more precise, either the numbers were checked only casually or disregard of the guidelines was widely accepted" (ibid.). In essence, diffuse reciprocity caused specific concessions negotiated under GATT to evolve into "generally accepted standards of behaviour" under the WTO Agreement.

[33] For use of the term "acquis", see *U.S. – Line Pipe*, WT/DS202/AB/R, para. 174 (15 Feb. 2002) (referring to "the GATT *acquis*"); see also *U.S. – Stainless Steel*, WT/DS344/AB/R, para. 160 (30 Apr. 2008) (noting that "the legal interpretation embodied in adopted panel and Appellate Body reports becomes part and parcel of the *acquis* of the WTO dispute settlement system.") [emphasis in original].

Table 2.2 *The WTO Agreement**

WTO Agreement (16 Articles) +

Annex 1A: Trade in Goods

- **GATT 1994 (GATT 1947** + protocols + certain decisions of GATT + six understandings) + Multilateral Agreements on Trade in Goods (MTAs):
  - Agreement on Agriculture
  - Agreement on Sanitary and Phytosanitary Measures (SPS)
  - Agreement on Textiles and Clothing (ATC)
  - Agreement on Technical Barriers to Trade (TBT)
  - Agreement on Trade-Related Investment Measures (TRIMS)
  - Antidumping Agreement (ADA)
  - Customs Valuation Agreement
  - Agreement on Pre-Shipment Inspection
  - Agreement on Rules of Origin
  - Agreement on Import Licensing Procedures
  - Agreement on Subsidies and Countervailing Measures (SCM)
  - Agreement on Safeguards

Annex 1B: Trade in Services

- General Agreement on Trade in Services (GATS) – a "framework" agreement
  - National commitments +
  - Agreement on Temporary Entry of Natural Persons (1995)
  - Agreement on Basic Telecommunications (1998)
  - Agreement on Financial Services (1995; 1999)
  - Negotiations on maritime services (to continue)
  - Decision on Disciplines relating to the Accountancy Sector (1998)

Annex 1C: Intellectual Property

- Agreement on Trade-Related Aspects of Intellectual Property Rights ("TRIPS")

Annex 2: The WTO Dispute Settlement Understanding ("DSU")

Annex 3: Trade Policy Review Mechanism ("TPRM")

Annex 4: Plurilateral Trade Agreements

- Agreement on Trade in Civil Aircraft
- Agreement on Government Procurement

* Since 1995 the WTO Agreement has been supplemented by two new agreements. The WTO Agreement on Trade Facilitation was concluded in 2013 and entered into force in 2017. The WTO Agreement on Fisheries Subsidies was concluded in 2022 and has not yet entered into force.

(WTO Art. I) and sets out the organization's principal organs (WTO Art. IV), its rules concerning membership (WTO Arts. XII–XIII), voting (WTO Art. IX:1), waivers (WTO Art. IX:2) and amendment (WTO Art. X).

The WTO Agreement's constitutive aspect is perhaps best illustrated by the fact that it is organized as a single instrument with which members are obliged to comply unconditionally (WTO Art. XVI:4). There is, in addition, an express prohibition on reservations (WTO Art. XVI:5).

Appended to the WTO Agreement are four annexes. Annex 1 contains three sub-annexes (Annexes 1A, 1B, 1C) covering trade in goods, services and certain trade-related aspects of intellectual property, respectively. WTO Annex 1A is where GATT 1947 – now reformulated and re-christened "GATT 1994" – is found.[34] Annex 2 provides a common set of rules for dispute settlement in the form of the WTO Dispute Settlement Understanding (DSU). Annex 3 contains a scheme for periodic review of WTO members' individual trade policies known as the Trade Policy Review Mechanism (TPRM). Finally, Annex 4 contains two plurilateral agreements, one on government procurement, the other on trade in civil aircraft.

The treaty's legal character is reinforced by the DSU in WTO Annex 2 (Fig. 2.1). The DSU formalizes and extends the dispute settlement system that arose under GATT 1947. WTO members are required to "have recourse to, and abide by" the DSU in order to resolve differences arising under the treaty (DSU Art. 23).

Three features of the dispute settlement system stand out. First, WTO dispute settlement procedures are automatic and streamlined. Once invoked, they proceed largely by themselves. The practice of consensus decision-making has been carried over into the WTO era and remains the organization's general practice, but the DSU modifies it in important ways. Under the DSU there are four instances where, exceptionally, a "reverse consensus" rule operates.[35] In those instances action is

[34] GATT 1994 incorporates by reference and with some adjustments "the provisions of the GATT 1947." GATT 1994 also includes six Understandings on Articles of the GATT 1947, tariffs and accession Protocols, and GATT decisions adopted between 1948 and 1994 as part of what is often called the "GATT acquis." As a result WTO Art. II:4 provides that the GATT 1994 is "legally distinct" from GATT 1947.

[35] First, a request for the establishment of a panel can be blocked, but only by a consensus against establishment (DSU Art. 6.1). Second, the adoption of a panel report can be blocked, but only by a consensus against adoption (DSU 16.4). Third, the adoption of a report of the Appellate Body can be blocked, but only by consensus against adoption (DSU Art. 17.14). Finally, a request to retaliate can be rejected, but only by a consensus against (DSU Art. 22.6–7).

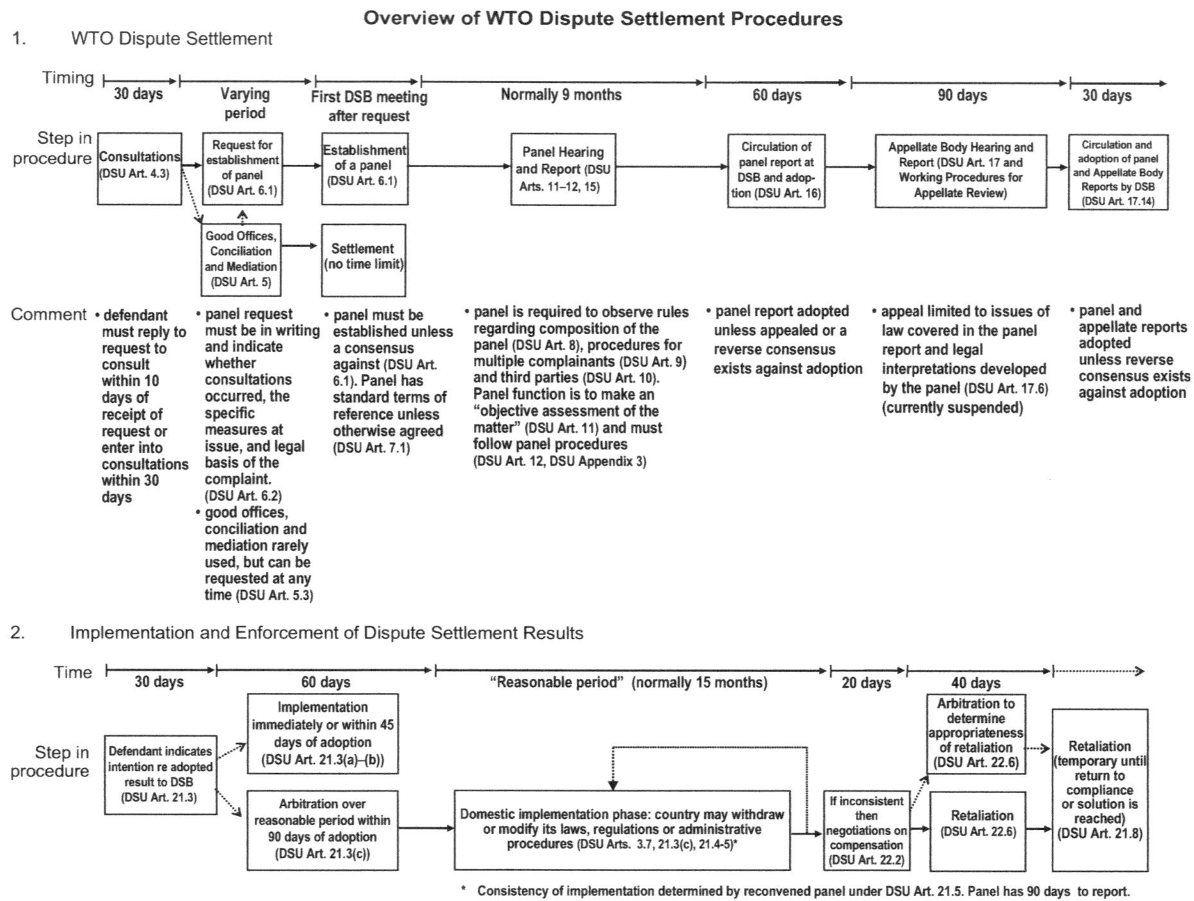

Figure 2.1 The WTO dispute settlement system

considered to be taken unless there is *a consensus against*. The practical effect of these changes means that panel and – and until recently Appellate Body – reports are almost always adopted.

A second feature of the system is its speed. WTO dispute settlement procedures are relatively swift and are designed to conclude in little more than a year. Although delay has become an issue in the system recently, the commitment to prompt settlement tends to underline the idea that the process is conducted for the benefit of the membership as a whole.[36]

A third feature of the system is its inclusivity. WTO dispute settlement continues the tradition of regular third-party participation. Third parties have participated in panel and Appellate Body proceedings in a number of different ways, suggesting that the membership continues to regard the WTO Agreement as having wider public significance to the membership as a club good.[37]

WTO members are able to take each other before dispute settlement panels, as they did under GATT 1947, when there is reason to believe that the domestic law or measure of another member country "nullifies or impairs" benefits accruing under the treaty. Panel proceedings may be

[36] WTO dispute settlement timelines are accelerated and contrast favorably with those of other international dispute settlement mechanisms. A briefing note prepared for the 10th WTO Ministerial Conference in 2015 observed that:

> Compared with other similar international mechanisms for resolving disputes, the WTO's dispute settlement system is very efficient. The average timeframe for a dispute at the WTO, excluding composing of the panel and translation of reports, is about ten months. For the International Court of Justice, it is four years, for the European Court of Justice it is two years and for NAFTA (North American Free Trade Agreement) it is from three to five years.

Some commentators have questioned the speed of WTO dispute settlement. See Arie Reich, "The Effectiveness of the WTO Dispute Settlement System: A Statistical Analysis" EUI Working Papers 11/2017, p. 23 (2017).

[37] DSU Art. 10.1 provides: "The interests of the parties to a dispute and those of other Members under a covered agreement at issue in the dispute shall be fully taken into account during the panel process." Commenting on these rules the panel in *Australia – Apples* noted that "not only have third parties the right to make submissions in a dispute, *but panels have the legal obligation to consider them.*" *Australia – Apples*, WT/DS367/R, para. 7.76 (9 Aug. 2010) [emphasis added]. For commentary, see Marc Busch & Eric Reinhardt, "Three's a Crowd: Third Parties and WTO Dispute Settlement" 58:3 *World Politics* 446 (Apr. 2006); Krzysztof J. Pelc, "Twenty Years of Third-Party Participation at the WTO" in Manfred Elsig et al. (eds), *Assessing the World Trade Organization* 203 (Cambridge University Press, Cambridge; 2017).

followed by an appeal to the Appellate Body. If a violation was identified, a recommendation would normally be made to the defendant country to bring its law "into conformity" with the WTO Agreement.

Conformity is said to involve "a solution mutually acceptable to the parties and consistent with the covered agreements" (DSU Art. 3.7). In the absence of such a solution, the DSU goes on to specify that "the first objective of the dispute settlement system is usually to secure the withdrawal of the measure concerned" (DSU Art. 3.7). The wrongdoer is given a reasonable time to comply, failing which the parties are permitted to negotiate compensation for injury going forward or, as a "last resort," the plaintiff can request authorization to retaliate. Retaliation is described as involving the suspension of "concessions or other obligations under the covered agreements" (DSU Art. 3.7). There are, in addition, a number of procedures and remedies that are specific to certain causes of action and sub-disciplines.[38]

Disputes originate between countries within the WTO Dispute Settlement Body (DSB), an organ composed of the entire WTO membership, and are referred to panels. Panel functions are self-admittedly limited.[39] The dispute settlement system is described as "a central element in providing *security and predictability* to the multilateral trading system," which serves "to preserve" rights and obligations of the membership "and "to clarify" WTO law[40] (DSU Art. 3.2)". Panel procedures may be followed by an appeal to the Appellate Body, and beyond that, where a complaint is made out, multilateral surveillance of implementation in the DSB. However, at the end of 2019 the operation of appellate review was suspended, a development examined further below.

[38] A number of these additional procedures and remedies can be found in appendix 2 of the DSU, which contains special or additional rules and procedures applying to disputes that involve one or more of the Multilateral Agreements on Trade in Goods. They prevail over the DSU in the event of conflict. For instance, Art. 4.7 of the WTO Subsidies Agreement provides that if a measure "is found to be a prohibited subsidy, the panel shall recommend that the subsidizing Member withdraw the subsidy without delay."

[39] The role of panels and the Appellate Body is said to be to "assist" the DSB in discharging its responsibilities with respect to "the *settlement* of disputes" (DSU Art. 1.1). This is also noted in DSU Art. 11, which has been described in greater detail as follows: "[A] panel should make an objective assessment of the facts of the matter before it . . . and make such other findings *as will assist the DSB in making the recommendations or in giving the rulings* provided for in the covered agreements." See *Argentina – Peaches*, para. 7.140, WT/DS238/R (14 Feb. 2003).

[40] [emphasis added].

However, the DSB's surveillance of the implementation of completed cases continues.

WTO dispute settlement has been considered highly successful since it was first activated in 1995.[41] More countries have engaged in WTO litigation than in dispute settlement under GATT 1947, and a number of decisions have prompted the withdrawal or amendment of noncompliant national legislation.[42] In a small number of disputes, immediate compliance has not been possible and interim compensation has been negotiated.[43] In some others, retaliation has been authorized, although

[41] In mid-2023 the WTO website noted that "Since 1995, 617 disputes have been brought to the WTO and over 350 rulings have been issued."

[42] For a list of mutually agreed solutions (MAS), see "Chronological list of disputes cases" on the WTO website. See also see *Overview of the State of Play of WTO Disputes – Annual Report (2014)*, WT/DSB/64/Add.1 (26 Nov. 2014).

[43] As of early 2022 compensation had been negotiated as a temporary measure in seven instances under DSU Art. 22: in *Japan-Alcoholic Beverages II*, WT/DS10 (Japan agreed to modify its Liquor Tax Law and as compensation for its two-year implementation period agreed to eliminate tariff rates on certain products, such as brandy, whisky and vodka). See Mutually Acceptable Solution on Modalities for Implementation, WT/DS10/20 (12 Jan. 1998); in *Turkey – Textiles*, WT/DS34 (Turkey agreed to provide compensation in the form of removing the quantitative restrictions in a staggered manner on imports from India until all quantitative restrictions had been removed). See Notification of Mutually Acceptable Solution, WT/DS34/14 (19 July 2001); in *EC – Hormones*, WT/DS46 (in May 2009 the EC agreed to expanded access in EU markets for US and Canadian hormone-free beef top be phased in three intervals). See *EC – Hormones*, Joint Communication from the European Communities and the United States, WT/DS26/28 (30 Sept. 2009); *U.S.* – Section 110(5) *of the U.S. Copyright Act*, WT/DS160 (the United States agreed to make a payment of $3.3 million to the EC for the period 2001–2004 to a fund to be established for the promotion of authors' rights and provision of general assistance to members of EC performing rights societies. See WT/DS160/18/Add.16); *U.S. – Upland Cotton*, WT/DS267 (the United States in 2010 negotiated payment of $147 million annually to the Brazilian cotton industry in compensation for a WTO finding that US cotton and agricultural export subsidies violated trade rules: "Kind, Blumenauer Reintroduce Bill to End $147 Million Payment to Brazil" 31:17 *Inside U.S. Trade* 18 (26 Apr. 2013). This was later superseded by a single payment of $300 million as part of a comprehensive settlement of the dispute: see "U.S., Brazil Settle WTO Cotton Dispute; Deal Includes $300 Million Payment" 32:39 *Inside U.S. Trade* 1 (3 Oct. 2014)); *China-Publications*, WT/DS363 (China allowed the import of fourteen "enhanced format" (such as 3D or IMAX) films per year from the United States in addition to the twenty films under its existing WTO commitment and the revenue share of US enterprises was increased to 25 percent of gross box-office receipts per film from the previous 13 percent). See Joint Communication from China and the United States, WT/DS363/19 (11 May 2012); *U.S. – Clove Cigarettes*, WT/406 (the United States would give favorable consideration to redesignation of certain Indonesian products as GSP eligible, would not challenge Indonesia's ban on mineral ores exports, would not discriminate against Indonesian cigars or cigarillos and would work with Indonesia to address concerns with respect to

the number of instances where retaliation has actually been invoked by countries remains few.[44]

WTO dispute settlement continues to be popular, and reference is often made to it as a "trade court." However, several DSU provisions suggest that the system is designed to do something more than simply vindicate members' individual trade interests. WTO dispute settlement is styled "dispute settlement," a term which suggests that while the system is tasked with the job of resolving individual "disputes," its ultimate aim is "settlement."

The supplementary and assistive function of panels – and until recently the Appellate Body – is reinforced by DSU provisions and interpretations that have the effect of muting antagonism between the parties. Procedural rules of dispute settlement are described as being "designed to promote, not the development of litigation techniques, but the fair, prompt and effective resolution of trade disputes."[45] Counterclaims are prohibited, something which tends to streamline the proceedings.[46] The system also lacks a mechanism for compulsory discovery.[47]

Indonesia's protection of intellectual property). See Notification of Mutually Agreed Solution, WT/DS406/17 (9 Oct. 2014) and Memorandum of Understanding between the Government of the United States of American and the Government of the Republic of Indonesia (3 Oct. 2014). For discussion, see Yusong Chen & Xiaoling Li, "Constraints of the WTO Compensation Mechanism and Implications from Recent Practice" 49:4 *J. World Trade* 643 (2015).

[44] As of early 2022 retaliation had been authorized in 26 cases among some 612 standard complaints notified and 350 rulings issued under the DSU. Retaliation had only been invoked in five such disputes (some involving multiple requests against a single country): *EC – Bananas III*, WT/DS27; *EC – Hormones*, WT/DS26; *U.S. – Offset Act*, WT/DS217, 234; *U.S. – Upland Cotton*, WT/DS267; *U.S. – Aircraft*, WT/DS353.

[45] *U.S. – FSC*, WT/DS108/AB/R, para. 166 (24 Feb. 2000).

[46] DSU Art. 3.10 provides "[i]t is also understood that complaints and counter-complaints in regard to distinct matters should not be linked." Notwithstanding this, tit-for-tat litigation has been observed in WTO dispute settlement and is not uncommon. See the Brazil–Canada Aircraft cases (WT/DS46, WT/DS70), the EU–U.S. Large Aircraft ("Airbus/Boeing") cases (WT/DS316, WT/DS353), *EC – Commercial Vessels*, WT/DS301/R, para. 7.127 (22 Apr. 2005) (litigation initiated by Korea against EC legislation, the TDM Regulation, making a link between temporal application of the Regulation and the initiation, resolution or suspension of WTO dispute settlement proceeding initiated by the EC against Korea regarding subsidies allegedly provided by Korea to its shipbuilding industry), and the pair of cases *Guatemala – Cement*, WT/DS60/R (19 June 1998) and *Mexico – Steel Pipes*, WT/DS331/R (8 June 2007).

[47] As noted in *Chile – Alcoholic Beverages*, WT/DS87, 110/R, para. 6.26 (15 June 1999).

Antagonism is further diluted by a number of DSU provisions and practices that appear to make WTO dispute settlement a multipolar exercise in achieving a resolution that is acceptable to all parties involved, including to some degree the WTO membership as a whole. This is emphasized by DSU Art. 3.5 which provides:

> All solutions to matters formally raised under the consultation and dispute settlement provisions of the covered agreements, including arbitration awards, shall be consistent with those agreements *and shall not nullify or impair benefits accruing to any Member under those agreements.*

Similarly, DSU Art. 3.6 provides that:

> Mutually agreed solutions to matters formally raised under the consultation and dispute settlement provisions of the covered agreements shall be notified to the DSB and the relevant Councils and Committees, *where any Member may raise any point relating thereto.*

DSU Arts. 3.5–3.6 speak to the general interest that the WTO membership as a whole has in the resolution of disputes. The general interest receives additional confirmation from decisions that have specified that WTO violations are considered to affect "*all members*"[48] and that the dispute settlement system issues "*multilateral* determinations" that are meant to resolve cases "to the benefit of *all* members."[49] Decisions of the dispute settlement system are understood, in some sense, as a proxy for the collective decision of all members.

These features highlight how the tenor of DSU proceedings is more multilateral and less adversarial than might be expected in a "court" and is, at the end of the day, more about reconciling collective and individual impulses within the system and generating interpretations of rights and obligations that are accommodative. In this way the good of the treaty is safeguarded and, consistent with the idea of a "neo-Grotian" community mentioned earlier, the community is sustained.

[48] Thus, DSU Art. 3.8 provides that "there is normally a presumption that a breach of the rules has an adverse impact *on other Members parties to that covered agreement* . . . ." [emphasis added].

[49] *Australia – Salmon*, WT/DS18/AB/R, para. 223 (20 Oct. 1998) citing DSU Art. 21.1 ("Prompt compliance with recommendations or rulings of the DSB is essential in order to ensure effective resolution of disputes *to the benefit of all Members.*") [emphasis added].

2.3 Text and Context

The club good character of the WTO Agreement is reinforced by a number of organizational and other features arising in the treaty's wider context.

One of these is the WTO's institutional arrangements, and in particular, its practice of decision-making. The WTO Agreement is administered by an institutional structure composed of over seventy councils, committees and other bodies (Fig. 2.2). All such bodies are open to all WTO members, although in practice virtually every country's representation is capacity-constrained in some way.[50]

The supreme organ in the organization is the Ministerial Conference (MC), which is composed of national trade ministers and meets bi-annually. Its limited frequency means that the MC is restricted to making only the broadest and most important decisions.[51]

Decisions are more typically taken by the General Council (GC), which is composed of ambassadors and meets monthly, often for several days at a time.[52] The GC also operates on various occasions under different guises as the "Dispute Settlement Body" (DSB) and the "Trade Policy Review Body" (TPRB).

There are, in addition, lower-level councils covering trade in goods, services and trade-related aspects of intellectual property, which report to the GC. They receive reports and administer other, lower-level committees established to oversee individual MTAs or to deal with thematic issues such as trade and the environment.

[50] Mary Footer, *An Institutional and Normative Analysis of the World of the World Trade Organization* 64 (Martinus Nijhoff, Leiden; 2005).

[51] The WTO website notes that the WTO Ministerial Conference is the "topmost" organ of the organization and "can take decisions on all matters under any of the [WTO's] multilateral trade agreements."

[52] The WTO website notes that the WTO General Council "is the WTO's highest-level decision-making body in Geneva, meeting regularly to carry out the functions of the WTO. It has representatives (usually ambassadors or equivalent) from all member governments and has the authority to act on behalf of the Ministerial Conference which only meets about every two years." Negotiating blocs are discernible in its makeup, leading some observers to note it has the makings of a proto-parliament: see Erika Mann, "A Parliamentary Dimension to the WTO: More than Just a Vision?!" 7:3 *J.I.E.L.* 659 (2004); Kobsak Chutikul, "Options for a Parliamentary Dimension of the WTO" (Discussion Paper presented at the Parliamentary Conference on the WTO, 17–18 Feb. 2003), online: Inter-Parliamentary Union www.ipu.org/splz-e/trade03/2c.pdf. For a list prepared by the WTO of negotiating groups within the organization, see www.wto.org/english/tratop_e/dda_e/negotiating_groups_e.htm.

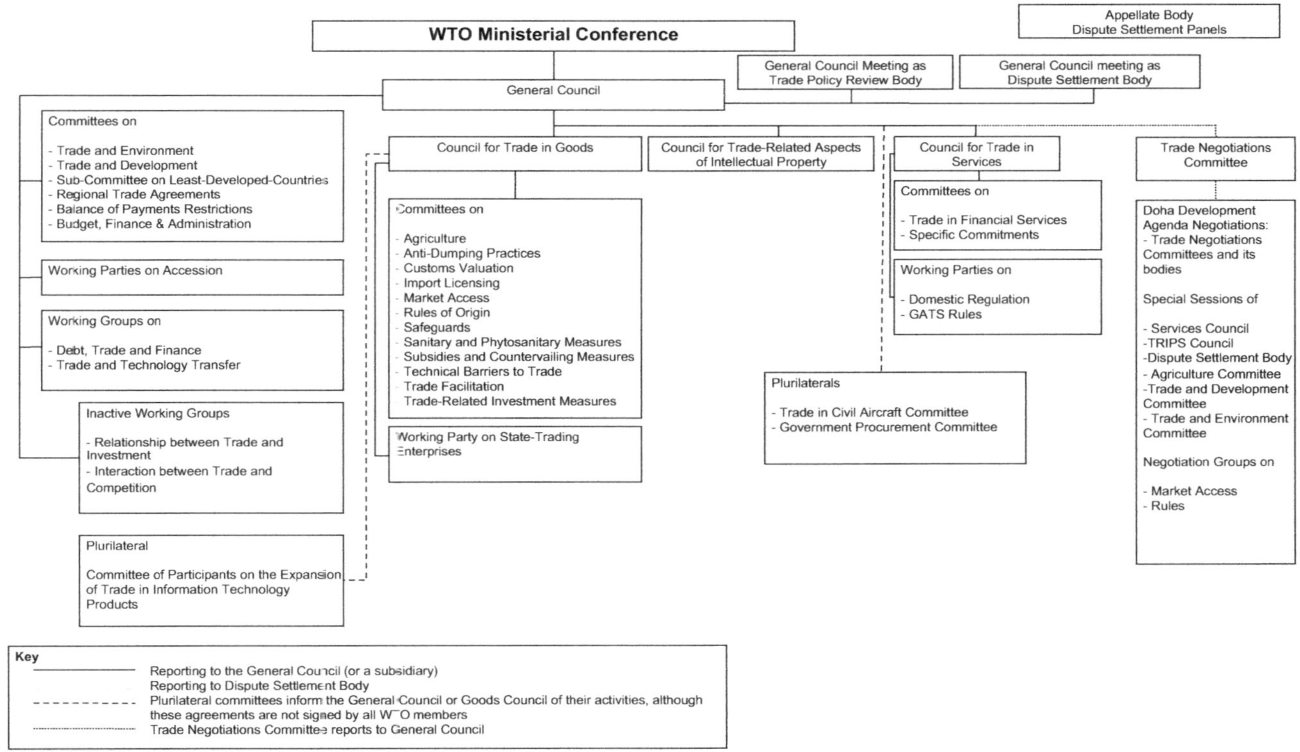

Figure 2.2 WTO organizational structure (as of Nov. 2022)

The WTO's administrative structure is rounded out by a number of other working parties and subsidiary bodies dealing with more specific issues.

The institutional structure of the WTO is administered by a Secretariat headed by a Director-General who serves a five-year term.[53] The current Director-General, Ngozi Okonjo-Iweala, was selected in early 2021 and heads a staff of some 700 at WTO headquarters in Geneva.[54]

Formally speaking, decision-making in the WTO is foreseen to take place by means of voting, but voting rules are rarely invoked and decisions normally occur by consensus.[55] WTO Agreement Art. IX:1 provides that "The WTO shall continue the practice of decision-making by consensus followed under GATT 1947." An accompanying footnote specifies that:

> The body concerned shall be deemed to have decided by consensus on a matter submitted for its consideration, if no Member, present at the meeting when the decision is taken, formally objects to the proposed decision.[56]

Although consensus is often emphasized as a particular attribute of WTO decision-making, the practice is neither rare nor particularly exceptional in the work of international organizations.[57] What distinguishes the role

[53] WTO Agreement Art. IV.

[54] The organization is composed of 17 divisions organized under four Deputy Director-Generals: I (Legal Affairs, Rules, Administration & General Services, Language & Documentation Services), II (Market Access, Intellectual Property, Government Procurement & Competition, Economic Research & Statistics), III (Agriculture & Commodities, Trade & Environment. Trade Policies Review, Human Resources), IV (Development, Institute for Training & Technical Cooperation, Information Technology Solution Division, Knowledge & Information Management, Academic Outreach & WTO Chairs Programme, Accessions).

[55] "In accordance with the wording of Article IX:1 *WTO Agreement*: '[E]xcept as otherwise provided, where a decision cannot be arrived at by consensus, the matter shall be decided by voting.' Implicit in this statement is the notion that consensus is the preferred means for adopting a decision while voting is residual." Footer, *An Institutional and Normative Analysis* 148–149.

[56] Quorum for meetings in the WTO is defined by Rule 16 of the Rules of Procedure for Sessions of the Ministerial Conference and Meetings of the General Council, which provides that a simple majority of the members should constitute a quorum. See WTO Doc. WT/L/28 (31 Jan. 1995). However, several WTO committees have decided to not adopt a quorum rule, meaning that decisions can be taken within certain committees where less than the majority of members are present.

[57] Henry Schermers and Niels Blokker note that "A marked tendency towards decision-making by consensus has been discernible in a large number of international

of consensus in the WTO is the way that it serves as a cover for a variety of positions that mediate between the interests of the organization and individual members.

All WTO members are considered formally equal in law by virtue of WTO Agreement Art. IX:1, which provides that "each Member of the WTO shall have *one* vote." Mary Footer has pointed out how in practice this means that the organization is characterized by a "strong collective action element."[58] Countries must agree, or at the very least not formally object, when a decision is being taken.[59] Consequently, decisions are taken that represent a broad cross-section of opinion and place a premium on agreement. The practice of consensus, while possibly "diluting" decision-making and subjecting it to hold-outs, preserves an important institutional commitment to unity and to the WTO as a "member-driven organization."[60]

At the same time, the veneer of equality projected by consensus obscures its deeper workings. Passivity and capacity constraint allow for action by major interests in the organization even though these may only constitute a subset of the membership. Wenwei Guan has detailed how consensus in the WTO is not necessarily consent in the sense that early decisions taken by minorities of the current membership – some dating back to GATT 1947 – have become "locked in" and often lead to coercive behavior over time.[61]

Footer concludes from this experience that while "one-member, one vote … appears to place all WTO Members on an equal footing and

organizations since the 1960s." Henry Schermers & Niels Blokker, *International Institutional Law* (4th rev'd. ed.) 523 (§772) (Martinus Nijhoff, Leiden; 2003). They go on to note that "The most common explanation for the development of decision-making by consensus is the expansion of membership in international organizations following the years of decolonization. As a result, "the key problem in contemporary international decision-making is the divorce of power from voting majorities."" (ibid., p. 533 (§784)).

58 Footer, *An Institutional and Normative Analysis* 75.

59 Consensus means no negative preference needs to be expressed, thereby avoiding the prospect that the decision-making environment will be poisoned by contrary opinion.

60 The WTO website notes that "The WTO is 'member-driven', with decisions taken by consensus among all member governments." See "Whose WTO Is It Anyway?" (accessed 22 Apr. 2015). See also Footer, *An Institutional and Normative Analysis* 76 (noting that "The WTO characterizes itself as a member-driven organization but the reality is that it is prone to member-domination, due to its institutional structure and the exercise of its executive function by a politically-driven collective membership.")

61 Wenwei Guan, "Consensus Yet Not Consented" 17 *J.I.E.L.* 77 (2014). Practical examples of this "major interests norm" include "WTO+" accession terms and certain TRIPS disciplines.

suggests a degree of egalitarianism in decision-making, it masks the actual practice of decision-making which favours powerful majorities or parity of interest."[62] As a result, attention is often paid to the behavior of major players like the United States, China and the EU with the most at stake in the system.

The exclusive aspect of the veto power, in particular, means that on truly sensitive issues like the WTO Agreement's relationship with regional trade arrangements or agricultural subsidization, the need for consensus has resulted in institutional deadlock.[63] In effect, any WTO member country can veto almost anything, something which occasionally happens and is now particularly evident in the impasse over the Appellate Body.[64]

The resulting paralysis has meant little progress, or in some instances, matters being taken off the negotiating table and resolved elsewhere.[65]

[62] Footer, *An Institutional and Normative Analysis* 157.

[63] For instance, for the period between the WTO Committee on Regional Trade Agreements' (CRTA) establishment in 1995 and the adoption in December 2006 of the Transparency Mechanism for Regional Trade Agreements (TM), the Committee had completed the factual examination of a total of 66 agreements, of which 45 in the area of trade in goods and 21 in trade in services. No report on the examination of any of these agreements has ever been agreed upon in the Committee, for subsequent transmission to the Council for Trade in Goods. See WTO Analytical Index re GATT Art. XXIV. The TM makes no reference to examination of reports. Since that time and probably due to the sensitivity of the task, a regional trade agreement is "considered" by members; examination on the basis of "terms of reference" is not performed anymore. See WTO Analytical Index re GATT Art. XXIV.

[64] The idea of a group access good has a certain similarity to the idea of obligations *erga omnes* identified by the ICJ in *Barcelona Traction*, [1970] I.C.J. Reports, p. 3. This terminology is normally used to denote obligations arising from some interest belonging to the international community as a whole (*erga omnes*) or to a group therein (*erga omnes partes*). The *erga omnes* concept tends to obscure the bounded nature of the "good" arising from inclusion and neglects entirely Heller's obverse anticommons idea of full exclusion. In reality, from a property perspective the WTO Agreement is double-aspected. It is a group access good, but it is also subject to the practice of consensus decision-making, giving it a full exclusion aspect as well. Heller, *The Gridlock Economy* 40. For a discussion of use of the veto to consensus decision making by WTO members, see Patrick Low, "WTO Decision-Making for the Future" WTO ERSD-2011-05 (Economic Research and Statistics Division, World Trade Organization, Geneva; 2011).

[65] Examples of issues "outplaced" from the WTO include the 2007 agreement on aircraft financing negotiated in the OECD and US-EU negotiations over steel production. See Peter Cameron, "The Aircraft Negotiations 2004 to 2007: 'This Will Never Fly!'" in OECD, *Smart Rules for Fair Trade* 190 (2011). See also the work of the OECD Steel Committee, which provides a forum for governments to come together to address challenges facing the steel industry.

A formative element of the WTO Agreement as a club good is interpretation through the dispute settlement system, a process that helps to define the good. As mentioned, all members are required to "have recourse to, and abide by, the rules and procedures of" the DSU (DSU Art. 23). However, with multilateral negotiations having been suspended and the membership reluctant to amend the treaty or issue authoritative interpretations under DSU Art. IX:2, the dispute settlement system has become the "go-to" mechanism for decision-making on a number of issues.

In light of this development, the idea of precedent becomes particularly important. The default position in most international tribunals is that precedent is not binding on countries except to the extent they are parties to a case and in respect of a particular case.[66] This was the original position under GATT 1947.[67]

The same position is formally taken with respect to panel and Appellate Body reports in the WTO. However, in one of its first decisions, *Japan – Alcoholic Beverages*, the Appellate Body observed that while the WTO Agreement reserves the right of definitive interpretation to the MC and GC, adopted panel reports "create legitimate expectations among WTO members, and, therefore, should be taken into account where they are relevant to any dispute."[68] The Appellate Body's statement in that instance was welcomed for the way it skillfully mediated between competing demands of stability and flexibility, and in doing so, effectively established a system of "soft precedent."[69]

Nevertheless, debate has continued over the extent to which Appellate Body interpretations are in fact binding on subsequent panels addressing the same issue.[70] In *U.S. – Stainless Steel*, for example, the Appellate Body dealt with a complaint by Mexico that the US practice of "zeroing" certain

[66] See, for instance, ICJ Statute Art. 59. For a review of precedent in international law, see Ruth Mackenzie et al. (eds), *Manual on International Courts and Tribunals* (Oxford University Press, Oxford; 2010).

[67] The Appellate Body explained in *Japan – Alcohol*: "The generally-accepted view under GATT 1947 was that the conclusions and recommendations in an adopted panel report bound the parties to the dispute in that particular case, but subsequent panels did not feel legally bound by the details and reasoning of a previous panel report." WT/DS8/AB/R, p. 13 (4 Oct. 1996), citing *EC – Dessert Apples*, BISD 36th Supp. 93, para. 12.1 (18 April 1989).

[68] Ibid. [emphasis added].

[69] Adrian Chua, "Precedent and Principles of WTO Panel Jurisprudence" 16 *Berkeley J. Int'l L.* 171 (1998).

[70] For a "hard" view of WTO precedent, see Raj Bhala, "Power of the Past: Towards De Jure Stare Decisis in WTO Adjudication (Part Three of a Trilogy)" 33 *Geo. Wash. Int'l L. R.*

antidumping margins was in violation of the WTO Antidumping Agreement.[71] Panel and Appellate Body decisions had found zeroing to be impermissible in many instances, but the panel in *U.S. – Stainless Steel* departed from previous Appellate Body's decisions and relied instead on panel reports that had allowed the practice and later been reversed. In response, the Appellate Body observed that "WTO Members attach significance to [the] reasoning provided in previous panel and Appellate Body reports" and noted that such reports are often cited by parties in support of legal arguments in dispute settlement. The Appellate Body went on to observe, however, that "the legal interpretation embodied in adopted panel and Appellate Body reports becomes part and parcel of the *acquis* of the WTO dispute settlement system." The Appellate Body concluded that "absent cogent reasons, an adjudicatory body will resolve the same legal question in the same way in a subsequent case."[72] On that basis the Appellate Body reversed a substantial portion of the panel decision. One consequence of the suspension of work by the Appellate Body, to be discussed shortly, is that there is now no way for the particular interpretation generated in a panel decision to be confirmed or overturned, leading to the possibility of interpretative divergence.[73]

The panels' and Appellate Body's work is conducted with a combination of pragmatism and flexibility. Reference is often made by panels and the Appellate Body to Art. 31 of the Vienna Convention on the Law of Treaties[74] (VCLT), which provides that a treaty should be interpreted according to its text, context and purpose. The text obviously enjoys a degree of primacy as an expression of the parties' intent, but textual

873 (2000); for the "soft" view, see James Cameron & Kevin Gray, "Principles of International Law in the WTO Dispute Settlement Body" 50 *I.C.L.Q.* 248 (2001).

[71] *U.S. – Stainless Steel*, WT/DS344/AB/R (30 Apr. 2008).

[72] Ibid., para. 160.

[73] The debate over zeroing furnishes a relevant example of this "splintering" phenomenon. In *U.S. – Stainless Steel*, WT/DS344/AB/R (30 Apr. 2008), the Appellate Body made clear an expectation of consistency by panels with its decision-making. Subsequently, in *U.S. – Continued Zeroing*, WT/DS350/AB/R (4 Feb. 2009), the Appellate Body appeared to call for an end to the lingering debate over the permissibility of zeroing. However, after a suspension of the Appellate Body's work at least one panel has concluded that zeroing remains permissible: *U.S. – Differential Pricing Methodology*, WT/DS534/R (9 Apr. 2019). The report has been appealed but as of this writing there is no functioning Appellate Body to address the panel's interpretation. I thank Joanna Gomula for this insight.

[74] 1155 U.N.T.S. 331 (1969).

silence is not controlling.[75] In addition, panels and the Appellate Body have stressed that interpretation is meant to be a "holistic exercise" in which each component of Art. 31 is analyzed together with the others.[76] The exercise is rounded out by various conceptions that appear to have emerged in the interpretation of WTO law. Here, a number of particular negotiated and practical elements must be appreciated. What are they?

The elements and interpretative techniques in question can be divided into two types: one contractual, the other constitutive. The contractual nature of trade concessions outwardly gives rise to a consciousness of offsetting "rights and obligations" in the WTO legal system. The legal elements are conceived to be in counterpoint with each other, notwithstanding the fact that, due to the operation of MFN and diffuse reciprocity, the original justification for continuing to conceive of them in this way is often difficult to detect.[77] In fact, few WTO legal elements can be described as specifically bargained for anymore, although the language of "rights" and "obligations" persists, including in many situations where nonmember entities, such as panels, are described as possessing them.[78] This usage may simply reflect the fact that there is no other reasonable way of approximating their meaning.

[75] In *U.S. - Carbon Steel*, for instance, the Appellate Body said that "the task of ascertaining the meaning of a treaty provision with respect to a specific requirement does not end once it has been determined that the text is silent on that requirement." *U.S. - Carbon Steel*, WT/DS213/AB/R, para. 65 (28 Nov. 2002). In *Canada - Autos*, WT/DS139, 142/AB/R (31 May 2000) the Appellate Body also observed that "[O]missions in different contexts may have different meanings, and omission, in and of itself, is not necessarily dispositive." Ibid., para. 138. See also Isabelle Van Damme, "The Interpretation of Silence in the WTO Covered Agreements" in Isabelle Van Damme, *Treaty Interpretation by the WTO Appellate Body* 110 (Oxford University Press, Oxford; 2009).

[76] See *EC - Chicken Cuts*, WT/DS269, 286/AB/R, para. 176 (12 Sept. 2005); *China - Audiovisual*, WT/DS363/AB/R, para. 348 (21 Dec. 2009)

[77] Philip Allott has described how a single legal element presupposes the existence of many other legal elements:

> One legal relator's power does not necessarily involve an exactly equivalent loss of power in another legal relator. The benefit and burden may be shared in a complex legal relation, or a complex of legal relations. The burden may not be referable specifically to another legal relator - for example, if the legal power is to make use of natural resources. In such cases, a corresponding loss of power may be widely distributed in society.
>
> (Philip Allott, *Eunomia* 173 (para. 11.20) (Oxford University Press, Oxford; 1990))

[78] For instance, under DSU Art. 13.1 a WTO panel has "the *right* to seek information and technical advice from any individual or body which it deems appropriate." Similarly, in *U.S. - Hot-Rolled Steel*, WT/DS184/R, para. 7.10 (28 Feb. 2001), the panel also observed that it had the freedom to consider any type of evidence.

The outwardly bilateral character of WTO dispute settlement, and of WTO law more generally, tends to emphasize obligations, or somewhat less frequently, the failure to fulfill obligations preliminary to an exercise of rights. In this way, WTO law is often contemplated as a system of obligations to be fulfilled, rather than a bundle of rights to be asserted.[79]

The point is emphasized still further in the occasional reminder by panels and the Appellate Body that countries may yield rights but not obligations.[80] In recent years, the obligatory character of WTO law has been especially apparent to newly acceding countries, which are immediately confronted with the WTO *acquis* as a whole and have little real power to renegotiate it. In general, they have had to accept the treaty as a single undertaking, take-it-or-leave-it, and often their only hope to influence its application is through extended transitional provisions or special status.[81]

Contractualism also generates a conception in which the treaty or parts thereof are understood as a "balance."[82] From this perspective, any violation is easily described as an "imbalance," meaning that remedial action is perceived to "correct" the balance.[83] As mentioned, however, the idea of the WTO Agreement as an equilibrium is mostly fictional, given the imbalance of concessions that went into its making.[84] This is truer still in newer disciplines such as services and intellectual property, where a negotiated quid pro quo is exceedingly problematic to identify

[79] The primacy of obligations in the scheme of the WTO Agreement is indicated by the habitual direction in WTO dispute settlement for a noncompliant member to "ensure that actions it undertakes after the end of the reasonable period of time [for implementation] are consistent with its *obligations*" under the WTO Agreement. See for instance *U.S. - Zeroing (EC) (21.5)*, WT/DS294/RW, para. 342 (17 Dec. 2008).

[80] The Appellate Body has held that "a Member may yield rights and grant benefits, but it cannot diminish its obligations." *EC – Bananas III*, WT/DS27/AB/R, para. 154 (9 Sept. 1997). See also *EC – Poultry*, WT/DS69/AB/R, para. 98 (13 July 1998).

[81] Special status includes designation as a developing or least developed country. Developing country status is claimed by countries individually through self-selection and involves benefits that are primarily procedural. Least developed country (LDC) status is accorded by virtue of countries' being designated as such by the U.N. The sense of obligation is emphasized still further by the recent demand on prospective applicants to agree to "WTO-+" commitments.

[82] See *Argentina – Textiles*, WT/DS56/AB/R, para. 47 (27 Mar. 1997); *Argentina – Footwear*, WT/DS121/R, para. 8.63 (25 June 1999); *U.S. – Wheat Gluten*, WT/DS166/AB/R, paras. 145–146 (22 Dec. 2000); *U.S. – Carbon Steel*, WT/DS213/AB/R, para. 74 (28 Nov. 2002); *Brazil – Aircraft*, WT/DS46/RW/2, n. 131 (26 July 2001).

[83] For WTO violations problematized as "imbalances" *Canada – Continued Suspension*, WT/DS321/AB/R, para. 317 (16 Oct. 2008).

[84] See n. 32 in this chapter.

and where nonquantifiable metrics have had to be devised as proxy.[85] The idea of "balance" is therefore useful chiefly in a metaphoric and political sense. It is at best a description for the entirety of obligations, but it is not wholly accurate as a depiction of the variable concessions and commitments prevailing in the regular operation of the treaty.

Finally, it is understood that member countries are bound only to the extent of their commitments. In this respect, panels and the Appellate Body have been careful to point out that countries are only required to comply with their obligations assumed under the WTO Agreement, the implication being that they retain sovereign freedom beyond this.

A second set of interpretive techniques employed by panels and the Appellate Body is more constitutive. These tend to stress the WTO Agreement as a "single undertaking." According to this understanding, emphasis is placed on a "harmonious" interpretation, with provisions being conceived in relation to each other systematically.[86]

For instance, in *EC – Computer Equipment* the Appellate Body had to deal with whether the panel's reference to the expectations of a single party – in that case the United States – could be used as the defining element for the interpretation of the EC's tariff schedule. The Appellate

[85] See Holger Spamann, "The Myth of 'Rebalancing' Retaliation in WTO Dispute Settlement Practice" 9 *J. Int'l Econ. L.* 31 (2006); Chad Bown & Joost Pauwelyn (eds), *The Law, Economics and Politics of Retaliation in WTO Dispute Settlement* (2010); Chad Bown & Michele Ruta, "The Economics of Permissible WTO Retaliation," WTO Staff Working Paper ERSD-2008-04 (2008); Brendan McGivern, "Seeking Compliance with WTO Rulings: Theory, Practice and Alternatives" 36:1 *The International Lawyer* 141 (2002).

[86]

> We are also well aware that WTO obligations generally apply "cumulatively" and that an appropriate reading of the "inseparable package of rights and disciplines" in these covered agreements must, accordingly, be a harmonious one that gives meaning to *all* the relevant provisions of these three equally binding agreements. See, for example, Appellate Body Report, *Argentina – Footwear (EC)*, paras. 81, 83–84; Panel Report, *Indonesia – Autos*, paras. 14.28 *ff.*
>
> (*U.S. – Cotton*, WT/DS257/R, para. 7.1003 (8 Sept. 2004)).

This interpretation receives direct textual support in Marrakesh Protocol Art. 1 and GATS Art. XX:3. See *EC – Computer Equipment*, WT/DS62/AB/R, para. 109 (5 June 1998) ("the fact that Members' Schedules are an integral part of the GATT 1994 indicates that, while each Schedule represents the tariff commitments made by *one* Member, they represent a common agreement among *all* Members."); [emphasis in original] *U.S. – Gambling*, WT/DS285/AB/R, para. 160 (7 Apr. 2005).

Body observed that "[t]he security and predictability of tariff concessions would be seriously undermined if the concessions in Members' Schedules were to be interpreted on the basis of the subjective views *of certain exporting Members alone*."[87] Instead, the Appellate Body chose to rest its interpretation on the interpretative methodology set out in VCLT Art. 31, the purpose of which the Appellate Body identified as being "to ascertain the *common* intentions of the parties." The Appellate Body went on to note that "[t]hese *common* intentions cannot be ascertained on the basis of the subjective and unilaterally determined 'expectations' of *one* of the parties to a treaty."[88] Instead, it stated that "[t]he legitimate expectations of the parties to a treaty are reflected in the language of the treaty itself. The duty of a treaty interpreter is to examine the words of the treaty to determine the intentions of the parties."[89]

On this basis the Appellate Body went on to identify other sources of common intent. It referred not only to the intentions of exporting countries such as the United States but also to the practice of EC countries as exporters, to that of third parties participating in the case, and to multilateral instruments such as the World Customs Organization's (WCO) Harmonized System (HS) and its Explanatory Notes. Most significantly, the Appellate Body referred to the WCO's classification decisions arising out of disputes between countries other than the EC and the United States, the two disputants in *EC – Computer Equipment*. In other words, the Appellate Body mentioned a wide range of sources in arriving at a meaning of the EC's tariff concession, a meaning that went beyond the expectations of any *one* country in the litigation and ultimately approximated the common intent of all parties to the treaty.

In these instances the usual presumption is also against conflict, with each provision being attributed a distinct meaning, or *effet utile*, that both distinguishes it and complements the others.[90] At the same time, provisions may have varying meaning depending on the particular

[87] The Appellate Body had observed "we disagree with the Panel that the maintenance of the security and predictability of tariff concessions allows the interpretation of a concession in the light of the 'legitimate expectations' of exporting Members, i.e., their *subjective* views as to what the agreement reached during tariff negotiations was": *EC – Computer Equipment*, WT/DS62/AB/R, at para. 82 [emphasis in original].

[88] Ibid. at para. 84 [emphasis in original].

[89] Ibid. at para. 83.

[90] "One of the corollaries of the 'general rule of interpretation' in the VCLT is that interpretation must give meaning and effect to all the terms of a treaty. An interpreter

circumstances in which they are applied.[91] A uniform interpretation is always desirable, but the Appellate Body has underlined the need for a degree of interpretative flexibility:

> WTO rules are not so rigid or inflexible as not to leave room for reasoned judgments in confronting the endless and ever-changing ebb and flow of real fact in real cases in the real world.[92]

The idea of unity achieved through interpretation is also evident conceptually. As part of the "single undertaking," WTO obligations are thought of as applying as an "inseparable package of rights and disciplines"[93] systematically, meaning that countries must abide by them "concurrently and cumulatively."[94] Simultaneous impact increases their normative strength, or weight, and is the source of what may be termed WTO law's "special intensity."

This set of observations also leads to consideration of the way in which WTO law operates as an identifiable system, a subject mentioned in Chapter 1. The word "system" appears frequently in WTO law. The WTO Agreement preamble notes, for instance, the desire to "develop an integrated, more viable and durable multilateral trading *system*." Numerous references have also been made in the case law to the

is not free to adopt a reading that would result in reducing whole clauses or paragraphs of a treaty to redundancy or inutility." *U.S. – Gasoline*, WT/DS2/AB/R, p. 23 (29 Apr. 1996).

91 For instance, the panel discussing references to the concept of discrimination in TRIPS observed:

> Discrimination may arise from explicitly different treatment, sometimes called "de jure discrimination," but it may also arise from ostensibly identical treatment which, due to differences in circumstances, produces differentially disadvantageous effects, sometimes called "de facto discrimination." The standards by which the justification for differential treatment is measured are a subject of infinite complexity. "Discrimination" is a term to be avoided whenever more precise standards are available, and, when employed, it is a term to be interpreted with caution, and with care to add no more precision than the concept contains.
>
> (*Canada – Pharmaceutical Patents*, WT/DS114/R, para. 7.94 (17 Mar. 2000))

92 *Japan – Alcoholic Beverages II*, WT/DS8/AB/R, p. 31 (4 Oct. 1996).

93 *Brazil – Dessicated Coconut*, WT/DS22/R, para. 227 (17 Oct. 1996).

94 *U.S. – Oil Country Tubular Goods Sunset Reviews*, WT/DS268/RW, para. 7.129 (30 Nov. 2006). Similar language has been used in *U.S. – Clove Cigarettes*, WT/DS406/AB/R, para. 91 (24 Apr. 2012); *EC – Sealing Products*, WT/DS400, 401/AB/R, para. 5.121 (22 May 2014) (observing that the TBT and GATT 1994 should be interpreted in a "coherent and consistent manner").

"WTO trading *system*,"[95] "the world trading *system* that is served by the WTO"[96] and the intention of the WTO Agreement's drafters "to create an integrated *system* governing multilateral trade relations."[97] The references suggest that what is perhaps most important about the WTO Agreement in systematic terms is the way that its parts work *together* substantively as a unified whole to modify members' rights and obligations.

Systemic thinking has also generated debate about the relative "closure" or "openness" of WTO law, that is, the degree to which the system is self-referential and impervious to outside influence.[98] An intermediate view forwarded by Ronnie Yearwood is one of "constrained openness," a view that comports with James Crawford's observation that "there cannot be, at the international level, any truly self-contained regime, hermetically sealed against bad weather."[99] In Yearwood's view WTO obligations often "translate" doctrines of public international law, reformulating them in significant ways according to the system's own rationality.[100] In this manner WTO law constitutes a special body of law,

[95] See, for instance, *Canada – Autos*, WT/DS139, 142/AB/R, para. 69 (31 May 2000); *EC – Tariff Preferences*, WT/DS246/AB/R, para. 101 (7 Apr. 2004).

[96] *U.S. – Section 211*, WT/DS176/AB/R, para. 240 (2 Jan. 2002).

[97] *Guatemala – Cement*, WT/DS60/R, para. 7.26 (19 June 1998). See also the description of the WTO Agreement as an "integrated system" in *Brazil – Dessicated Coconut*, WT/DS22/AB/R, p. 11 (21 Feb. 1997).

[98] For the view of WTO law as relatively "open" to outside influence, see Joost Pauwelyn, "The Role of Public International Law in the WTO" 95:3 *Am. J. Int'l L.* 535 (2001). For the opposing view of WTO law as relatively "closed" and self-contained, see Joel Trachtman, "Jurisdiction in WTO Dispute Settlement" in Rufus Yerxa & Brian Wilson (eds), *Key Issues in WTO Dispute Settlement* 132 (World Trade Organization, Geneva; 2005). Trachtman observes:

> When the Appellate Body said in *U.S. – Gasoline* that WTO dispute settlement is not clinically separate from general international law, it did not mean that general international law is fully integrated into WTO dispute settlement. While it is correct to say that the WTO is part of the international law system, it is an error of logic, a non-sequitur, to draw from this proposition the conclusion that general international law is applicable in WTO dispute settlement.
>
> (Ibid. at 136–137)

[99] Daniel Bodansky et al., "The ILC's Articles on Responsibility of States for Internationally Wrongful Acts: A Retrospect" 96 *Am. J. Int'l L.* 874, 880 (2002). See Ronnie R. F. Yearwood, *The Interaction between World Trade Organisation (WTO) Law and External International Law* (Routledge, London; 2012).

[100] See Yearwood, *The Interaction between World Trade Organisation*. Yearwood points out that "only through its own *nomos*, that is, its own descriptions and understandings of the

a body that departs from ordinary consequences of international law and functions as a *sui generis* regime.

A further characteristic of a system is its degree of internal ordering and self-regulation. The great mass of WTO obligations makes some regular hierarchy in WTO law necessary. This order is accomplished in three principal ways. First, the WTO Agreement contains rules that establish an internal hierarchy of norms.[101] Second, the WTO Agreement also contains certain rules about its interaction with other systems of law.[102] Third, dispute settlement is often resorted to where express ordering rules may be lacking.[103] It provides interpretations where the treaty is silent or unclear. In the process, dispute settlement instills consistency and regularity – "security and predictability" – to the tenor of WTO law, reinforcing the idea of its systemic unity as a good.[104]

world can any legal system assess and access the world" (p. 94). He goes on to provide as an example the "reconstruction of precaution" in SPS Art. 5, which "directs a strong inclination towards science, which appears contrary to a precautionary approach, which emphasizes the lack of scientific certainty" (p. 154). Yearwood concludes that "The WTO is not impermeable to external law but the extent that such law may be applicable in the WTO system appears not to be a foregone conclusion" (p. 74).

101 For instance, the Interpretative Note to Annex 1A of the WTO Agreement provides that a conflict between a provision of GATT and the WTO SCM Agreement is to be resolved in favor of the WTO SCM Agreement.

102 Thus, certain rules and determinations under international law are accepted as binding in WTO law. The same is probably also true of the effect of Security Council resolutions under Ch. VII as well as *jus cogens* norms. With respect to the rest of public international law, the relationship appears to be one that is formally left undefined and must be worked out on a case-by-case basis. Finally, with respect to domestic law of member states, WTO Art. XVI:4 requires that member countries bring their laws, regulations and administrative practices into conformity with their obligations under the treaty.

103 *Indonesia – Autos*, WT/DS54/R, para. 14.28 (2 July 1998).

104 *U.S. – Section 301*, WT/DS152/R, para. 7.94 (22 Dec. 1999). The importance of dispute settlement was highlighted in *U.S. – Section 301*, where the panel said:

> . . . the relevance of [DSU] Article 23 obligations for individuals and the market-place is particularly important since *they radiate on to all substantive obligations under the WTO.* If individual economic operators cannot be confident about the integrity of WTO dispute resolution and may fear unilateral measures outside the guarantees and disciplines which the DSU ensures, their confidence in each and every of the substantive disciplines of the system will be undermined as well. The overall systemic damage and the denial of benefits would be amplified accordingly. The assurances thus given under the DSU may, in our view, be of even greater importance than those provided under substantive WTO provisions. For that reason, the preservation of the specific guarantees provided for in Article 23 is of added importance given the spill-over effect they have on all material WTO rights and obligations (ibid. [emphasis added]).

What is the value of understanding WTO law systematically? Here it is useful to consider what the WTO Agreement as a legal "system" actually accomplishes. To recall from Chapter 1, a system *transforms*. In the case of a legal system, the system transforms the regular consequences of legal responsibility by making them *different* from those that would otherwise normally apply under international law.

How exactly does the WTO legal system transform? Most evidently, by altering the nature of legal obligations. As I will show, they are no longer bilateral. Formally, they become integral, although as I will demonstrate shortly, there is considerable evidence that WTO members regard them in practice as functionally interdependent.

The idea of a "system" therefore helps to convey much of what otherwise evades existing accounts of WTO law premised on interpretation under the Vienna Convention on the Law of Treaties (VCLT).[105] These accounts rely heavily on text and tend to regard the WTO system as a set of discrete rules that are not necessarily connected by anything more than the fact of their inclusion in the treaty. Accordingly, it can be difficult to ascertain the normative character of the system and what the system accomplishes.

The counterpoint approach proposed here is more integrated and comprehensive, and therefore more in line with the fact of interdependence. It gives somewhat more prominence to interpretation conducted against the greater background or context of obligations called for in the VCLT. The result is occasionally referred to as the principle of "systemic integration."[106]

Is this "system-ness" so exceptional? No. A number of commentators have observed, for instance, that a similar phenomenon is evident in EU law, where several clauses lay down duties of cooperation, often described as duties of "community solidarity" on member states (*Gemeinschaftstreue*) or on EU organs (*organtreue*).[107] These duties go beyond the normal obligation to fulfill treaties in good faith. EU states and organs must constantly remain aware of the need to act in a general

[105] 1155 U.N.T.S. 331 (1969).

[106] Campbell McLachlin, "The Principle of Systemic Integration and Article 31(3)(c)" 54 *I.C.L.Q.* 279 (Apr. 2005). McLachlin refers to the principle as "an inarticulated major premise in the construction of treaties" having "the status of a constitutional norm within the international legal system." Ibid. at 280.

[107] See John Temple Lang, "Community Constitutional Law: Article 5 EEC Treaty" 27 *Comm. Mkt. L. Rev.* 645 (1990).

way that reinforces the underlying idea of community.[108] Something similar occurs in WTO law, although it is composed of many seemingly unrelated phenomena that so far have received no single doctrinal designation.[109]

2.4 On Interdependence

At the beginning of this chapter, I noted how a community generates two types of legal obligations: one contractual, the other constitutive.

In law the chief consequence of a characterization of obligations as bilateral and contractual means they ordinarily have no consequences for third parties whereas their characterization as multilateral and constitutive means that they do.

WTO arrangements are composed of both contractual and constitutive obligations. They are contractual in that they are negotiated and may be renegotiated and suspended contractually. At the same time, they are also constitutive in that they apply multilaterally via the MFN clause and other nondiscrimination provisions to all other WTO members. This dualism suggests a hybridism and complexity about the characterization of WTO obligations as a matter of law.

The characterization of WTO obligations is important because it appears to have consequences under the Vienna Convention on the

[108] As Jan Klabbers puts it, "Much in the same way as marriage is somehow more than a mere contractual arrangement, so too the creation of an organization is an act which involves not just the normal good-faith duty to give effect to one's commitments, but also a spirit of loyalty, camaraderie and mutual respect." Jan Klabbers, *An Introduction to International Institutional Law* 176 (Cambridge University Press, Cambridge; 2009). Robert Kolb has referred to the same concept in observance of the principle of good faith by members under the U.N. Charter, good faith being a "reminder . . . that they must use a certain degree of restraint and manifest some loyalty to the organization and its common goals when independently interpreting their obligations under the Charter. There is a duty in such cases to take into account the views of the organization' organs and other members, without overly exaggerating the State's individual position." Robert Kolb, *An Introduction to the Law of the United Nations* 43 (Hart, Oxford; 2010).

[109] Evidence of this is discernible from the fact that the WTO dispute settlement system has reserved some of its harshest criticism for situations where legislators have apparently failed to consider the compliance burden on foreigners as opposed to the burden imposed on domestic interests, indicating the modification in *thinking* required by the treaty: see *U.S. – Gasoline*, WT/DS2/AB/R, pp. 28–29 (29 Apr. 1996); *U.S. – Clove Cigarettes*, WT/DS406/R, para. 7.289 (4 Apr. 2012); *EC – Sealing Products*, WT/DS400, 401/AB/R, para. 5.337 (22 May 2014).

Law of Treaties (VCLT)[110] and the International Law Commission's Articles on State Responsibility (ARSIWA),[111] two of the most authoritative documents concerning the interpretation of treaties today. That characterization may also help to explain certain recent developments.

The classification of treaty obligations in international law generally follows the scheme proposed by Gerald Fitzmaurice in the 1950s.[112] Fitzmaurice identified treaties as either *bilateral* or *multilateral* and further classified multilateral treaties as either *reciprocal*, *interdependent* or *integral*, depending on the consequences arising from their breach. Bilateral treaties can be suspended or terminated by either party since they involve a simple exchange of obligations. Subsequent inconsistent treaties are valid subject to appropriate priority rules. The same may be said of multilateral treaties of a reciprocal type. By comparison, multilateral treaties of an interdependent type can be suspended or terminated by any party because they involve "a mutual interchange or benefits between the parties, with rights and obligations for each."[113] Subsequent inconsistent treaties are void. Finally, multilateral treaties of an integral type cannot be suspended or terminated since "the force of the obligation is self-existent, absolute and inherent for each party."[114] Subsequent inconsistent treaties are also void.

The classification of WTO obligations according to the categories set out in the VCLT and ARSIWA has a number of important consequences. The classification of obligations as bilateral, for instance, leads to restrictions on which countries have standing to challenge a breach, to limits on the right of countries to retaliate and to nonentrenched status for the WTO Agreement vis-à-vis other treaties. Their classification as multilateral, on the other hand, leads to something of the opposite result, a result which suggests all treaty members have standing, broad rights of retaliation, and regards the treaty as primate within its own sphere of economic relations.

On its face the WTO Agreement would appear to be composed of obligations that are multilateral and integral in the sense that they apply

[110] 1155 U.N.T.S. 331 (1969).

[111] Draft articles on Responsibility of States for Internationally Wrongful Acts, with commentaries, U.N. Doc. A/56/10 (2001) unanimously endorsed by the U.N. General Assembly in A/RES/56/83 (12 Dec. 2001).

[112] Gerald Fitzmaurice, "Third Report on the Law of Treaties," U.N. Doc. A/CN.4/115, *Yearbook of the International Law Commission* (1958), ii, at 20.

[113] Ibid. at 28, Art. 19.

[114] Ibid. at 27, Art. 18(2).

to member countries regardless of what other countries may do. This identification is confirmed by the wording of WTO Art. XVI:4:

> Each Member shall ensure the conformity of its laws, regulations and administrative procedures with its obligations as provided in the annexed Agreements.

At the same time, as mentioned, there are a number of features that appear to suggest that obligations under the treaty are bilateral and reciprocal, notably in their negotiation, the structure of dispute settlement and the possibility of countermeasures. How is it possible to reconcile the contrast between the necessity of unconditional conformity suggestive of 'constitution' and subsisting bilateralism suggestive of 'contract' in the treaty's design?

I take the position that the most plausible reconciliation of contrasting tendencies under the treaty is to recognize WTO obligations as multilateral but *interdependent*, a hybrid category lying between multilateral reciprocal and absolute obligations. Interdependent obligations would appear to be owed to a *subset of the membership*. They depend upon the general climate or atmosphere prevailing rather than the behavior of any one country or indeed all countries under the treaty.

The classic example Fitzmaurice gave of a treaty composed of interdependent obligations is a disarmament treaty. In that case, the decision by one country – particularly one influential country – to disclaim or breach its obligations introduces general uncertainty that would allow one other member or all members to likewise disclaim or breach theirs. This, in fact, is the outcome foreseen under the VCLT and ARSIWA[115]

WTO obligations appear to conform to their characterization as interdependent obligations reasonably well. As mentioned, all countries have standing to challenge a breach of the treaty. In addition, the WTO Agreement is generally recognized as primary within its own sphere of economic relations. This is in the sense that a number of subsequent treaties and arrangements have been negotiated so as to be structured in deference to it.[116]

[115] Ibid. at 44; see also Gerald Fitzmaurice, "Second Report on the Law of Treaties," A/CN.4/SER.A/1957/Add.l, *Yearbook of the International Law Commission* 54 (1957 II). This is the outcome now provided for in VCLT Art. 60(2)(c) and ASR Arts. 42(b) and 48.

[116] See, for instance, the Kimberly Process for Conflict Diamonds of 2003, where certain WTO member countries agreed to a certification scheme for "conflict diamonds" which

However, one remaining objection to this characterization rests in the fact that both the VCLT and ARSIWA contemplate the option of one *or more countries* suspending or terminating their obligations vis-à-vis the wrongdoer in cases of breach, whereas the DSU only permits *one* country – the complainant – to do so. How to explain this anomaly?

I take the view that while DSU provisions only permit one country in any dispute to invoke countermeasures, it is always possible for another member country beyond the original complainant to complain as well. Where they are successful and unable to negotiate a settlement or compensation, they may invoke countermeasures.[117] Furthermore, it is important to remember that perfect consistency with the VCLT, in particular, is not necessary, given that the exercise that led to the drafting of the VCLT specifically excluded treaties with MFN clauses.[118]

There are also a number of other features of WTO law that appear to reinforce the characterization of WTO obligations as interdependent. First, there is the general idea of "balance," mentioned above, which lingers in the conception of the treaty as an organizing principle in thinking about WTO arrangements generally.[119] The continuing

became the subject of a formal waiver under the WTO Agreement: see WT/L/518 (15 May 2003), and for the most recent extension, see WT/L/1039 (30 July 2018). A second example is the World Health Organization's Framework Convention on Tobacco Control of 2003, 2302 U.N.T.S. 166, where care was taken to address aspects of the global tobacco industry other than international trade such as production, advertising and point-of-sale restrictions. The fact that countries have been so mindful of WTO obligations in crafting other international agreements since 1994 strongly suggests that the WTO Agreement is perceived to be "constitutive" in international law.

117 The language of GATT Art. XXIII:2 appears to contemplate the possibility of multiple states invoking countermeasures ("If the CONTRACTING PARTIES consider that the circumstances are serious enough to justify such action, they may authorize a contracting party *or parties* to suspend the application to any other contracting party or parties of such concessions or other obligations under this Agreement as they determine to be appropriate in the circumstances.") [emphasis added]. This possibility now appears to be precluded by the wording of DSU Art. 22.2, which limits counteraction to "any party *having invoked* the dispute settlement procedures."

118 The MFN clause subsequently became the subject of work by a separate ILC preparatory committee, which submitted the Draft Articles on Most-Favoured-Nation Clauses to the UN General Assembly in 1978: see *Yearbook of the International Law Commission, 1978*, vol. II, Part Two (United Nations, New York; 1979).

119 The metaphor of "balance" is a pervasive one in WTO law – as a shorthand for the arrangement among members generally: *Argentina – Textiles*, WT/DS56/AB/R, para. 47 (27 Mar. 1997); of violations problematized as "imbalances": *Canada – Continued Suspension*, WT/DS321/AB/R, para. 317 (16 Oct. 2008);. Further discussion of the concept of "balance" is provided in Simon Evenett & Richard Baldwin, *Revitalising*

preoccupation with "balance" suggests that member countries are concerned not so much about what *one* country may do as with the general atmosphere of commitment among the membership.

Second, there is also the general environment of compliance under the treaty, an environment that demonstrates substantial flexibility. While WTO law appears to mandate unconditional conformity by virtue of WTO Art. XVI:4, in fact the treaty and state practice suggest that this is an aspiration as opposed to a strict requirement. To begin with, the DSU leaves open the possibility of temporary non-compliance. In addition, a number of settlements of disputes in the system have either been *de jure* or *de facto* non-compliant.[120] Moreover, members' conduct – even with respect to central WTO obligations like MFN – has often departed substantially from treaty requirements. Finally, no single "prosecutor" exists within the legal system, meaning that the question of compliance is addressed unevenly and ad hoc. These factors suggest that while compliance remains a concern, members understand implicitly that the issue of compliance under the treaty is not compliance "at any cost."[121] Hence, a more flexible and permissive compliance environment prevails than one that is, strictly speaking, integral and absolute.

Third, there is the calibrated way in which countries appear to observe their WTO obligations, in effect making them dependent upon the behavior of other members, particularly major players in the system. Whereas a treaty of bilateral or reciprocal obligations is conditioned on what another country does and a treaty of multilateral integral obligations applies regardless of the behavior of any other country, a treaty of

Multilateralism: Pragmatic Ideas for the New WTO Director-General 10–20 (CEPR Press, London; 2020).

120 For example, the settlement reached by Canada and the United States in April 2006 to a series of WTO cases referred to as 'Softwood Lumber IV' established a scheme of border measures to limit the export of Canadian softwood lumber to the United States. The settlement was WTO-inconsistent in the sense that it imposed trade restrictions in violation of free trade commitments. Chi Carmody, "International Decisions – Softwood Lumber Dispute (2001–2006)" 100:3 *A.J.I.L.* 664 (2006).

121 In addition, the Appellate Body in *Mexico – Soft Drinks*, WT/DS308/AB/R (6 Mar. 2006) explained that the burden to demonstrate that a measure is designed to "secure compliance" must focus on the "design of the measure sought to be justified." Ibid. at para. 72. This has been described to mean "to enforce obligations" rather than "to ensure the attainment of the objectives of laws and regulations." Moreover, the Appellate Body clarified that a measure may be considered as securing compliance regardless of whether it is certain to achieve results: "In our view, a measure can be said to be designed 'to secure compliance' even if the measure cannot be guaranteed to achieve its result with absolute certainty." Ibid. at para. 74.

interdependent obligations depends on what those with the most at stake in it do.

The legal consequences of characterizing WTO obligations as interdependent are profound. The most important consequence is that member countries *adjust their behavior to the extent other countries are prepared to do the same.*[122] In this regard, the identification of WTO obligations as interdependent is also illuminating because it infers that there will be a degree of nonobservance – *and perhaps calibrated nonobservance* – particularly as the sense of community and the underlying value of its "good" diminishes.

An examination of recent developments in WTO law lends credence to this view.

2.5 A Great Uncoupling

In Chapter 1 I referred to recent developments that cast doubt on the future of the WTO system. In this section I revisit these developments and explain how they are consistent with the theory of community advanced in this chapter.

The theory posits that obligations within a community emerge from what actors hold in common and value. What actors value they will aim to protect, adjust and transform. It stands to reason that as the sense of the good diminishes, so too will the sense of obligation.

As mentioned, the entry into force of the WTO Agreement in 1994 was a monumental achievement. Its timing was also fortuitous. The Cold War had just ended, and there was a desire for new global arrangements that would allow countries and individuals to develop peacefully under the rule of law.

The WTO Agreement appeared well-suited for this purpose. Its preamble announces several aims including "raising standards of living," "seeking both to protect and preserve the environment" and "expanding the production of and trade in goods and services . . . in accordance with the objective of sustainable development."

[122] For instance, see the incomplete record of notification of industrial subsidies under the WTO Agreement on Subsidies and Countervailing Measures: Terry Collins-Williams & Robert Wolfe, "Transparency as a Trade Policy Tool: The WTO's Cloudy Windows" 9 (4) *World Trade Review* 551 at 564–565 (2010). Without notification, such measures are difficult to challenge in WTO dispute settlement.

In addition, the WTO Agreement's original requirements of nondiscrimination, market access and regulatory harmonization seemed to match the *zeitgeist* by stressing equality of opportunity. In this image, producers and consumers in member countries could be regarded as coming together at a notional global starting line. The implicit assumption was that by adhering to WTO disciplines everyone would be better off.

The successful conclusion of the Uruguay Round also inferred that future rounds of international trade negotiations could likewise be concluded on the basis of a single undertaking embodying this intensive common interest. To further this ambition, the WTO Agreement featured several provisions that automatically expired in 1999 in the hope that expiration would promote the inauguration and eventual conclusion of another round. The Doha Development Round did eventually get underway in December 2001 with an ambitious mandate that foresaw further opening of agricultural and manufacturing markets, expanded coverage of services and new disciplines in intellectual property.

In that era, international trade boomed. Along with this development came improvements in many measures of national economic attainment and improved living standards in WTO member countries.[123]

At the same time, commentators began to point out how much of this growth was not always well distributed. While total numbers were impressive, they masked significant disparities. The growth in international trade was part of a matrix of advantage and disadvantage. On the one hand, the rise of immense virtual networks made it possible to pinpoint economic activity, to identify reliance and to track masses of big data.[124] On the other hand, technical change led to increased corporate

[123] The IMF noted in May 2008 that, "There is substantial evidence, from countries of different sizes and different regions, that as countries "globalize" their citizens benefit, in the form of access to a wider variety of goods and services, lower prices, more and better-paying jobs, improved health, and higher overall living standards. It is probably no mere coincidence that over the past 20 years, as a number of countries have become more open to global economic forces, the percentage of the developing world living in extreme poverty—defined as living on less than $1 per day—has been cut in half." IMF Issue Briefs: "Globalization: A Brief Overview" (08/02 - May 2008)

[124] In many fields the rise of "Big Data" and new forecasting techniques such as "nowcasting" have raised questions about the continuing validity of theory. Some authorities assert that virtually all phenomena can be understood through "data exhaust." A source observes:

> Cheerleaders for big data have made four exciting claims ... that data analysis produces uncannily accurate results, that every single data point

control, the emergence of winner-takes-all-markets, precarious work and environmental degradation.

These developments seemed to accentuate who was winning and who was losing from international trade. Whereas WTO arrangements were originally predicated on a benign view of equality of opportunity *ex ante*, two decades after its conclusion the WTO Agreement came to be associated in a number of quarters with malign views of who had crossed the finish line first, or in other words, the fairness – or unfairness – of outcomes *ex post*.

At the macro level there was also serious reconsideration by policy-makers of the benefits of the unconditional interdependence mandated by the treaty. The massive offshoring and hollowing out of economies linked to globalization since 1990 created a number of supply chain vulnerabilities and emphasized how markets had become over-reliant on a few globally efficient sources of supply. Unconditional interdependence exposed weaknesses in employment, manufacturing, innovation and national defense. In response, certain companies and countries began to "re-shore" or "near-shore" production and examined ways in which supply chains could be secured or nationalized.[125]

Another worrisome phenomenon was the "weaponization" of interdependence.[126] Key countries occasionally began to use their

> can be captured, making old statistical sampling techniques obsolete; that it is passé to fret about what causes what, because statistical correlation tells us what we need to know; and that scientific or statistical models aren't needed because ... with enough data the numbers speak for themselves.
>
> (Tim Harford, "Big Mistake?" *Financial Times* 18 (29–30 Mar. 2014))

The author emphasizes the difference between correlation and causation. For a discussion of nowcasting, a neologism used in both economics and meteorology to describe current conditions and those in the immediate future, see Jeremy Clift, "What Is Nowcasting?" *Finance & Development* 6 (Mar. 2014).

125 Dick Nanto, *CRS Report for Congress: Globalized Supply Chains and U.S. Policy* R40167 (27 Jan. 2010); Rachel Fefer et al., *CRS Report for Congress: Global Value Chains: Overview and Issues for Congress* R46641 (16 Dec. 2020) (noting "Concerns about U.S. value chains and the ongoing COVID-19 pandemic have raised questions about potential risks that GVCs may pose for particular economic sectors, the economy more generally, and, depending on the product and degree of external dependencies, national security"); Isabelle Icso, "Lawmakers Mull Supply Chain Legislation, COVID-19 Response Coordination", 38:25 *Inside U.S. Trade* 19 (19 June 2020).

126 Amrita Narlikar, "As Multilateral as Apple Pie: Managing a World of Weaponized Interdependence" *The Security Times* 34 (Feb. 2020); Henry Farrell & Abraham Newman, "Weaponized Interdependence: How Global Economic Networks Shape

position as critical hubs in supply chains or monopsony power to leverage certain benefits from the chain.

In this contentious atmosphere, there seemed to be growing ambivalence about the net benefits of WTO arrangements. The great sense of commonality and common purpose that marked the early years of the WTO began to fray.

In the WTO itself doubt and difference translated into a divergence of views about the negotiating mandate and proper way forward in the Doha Round, a development which was conveyed in increasingly vague final pronouncements at WTO Ministerial Conferences.[127] The divergence became significant enough that after the 2015 Nairobi Ministerial the Doha negotiations were indefinitely suspended.[128]

The Doha Round's suspension left WTO dispute settlement as the apparent "motor" of the organization. Here too, however, there were a number of difficulties. First, while many panel and Appellate Body reports were well-received, they tended to remove in some degree countries' responsibility to resolve matters cooperatively through negotiation. It was also easy for members dissatisfied with certain decisions to portray what was happening in the organization as a "power grab" by dispute settlement organs.

Second, the preeminence of dispute settlement generated a culture of legalism in the WTO, where relations became heavily conditioned by law,

State Coercion" 44:1 *Int'l Security* 42 (2019). See also Thomas Wright, "Sifting through Interdependence" 36:4 *The Washington Quarterly* 7 (2013).

127 Thus, at the Geneva Ministerial in 2011 Trade Ministers' Elements for Political Guidance in the negotiations recognized "that [WTO] Members need to more fully explore different negotiating approaches." WT/MIN(11)/W/2 (1 Dec. 2011). At the Bali Ministerial in 2013, agreements were announced on trade facilitation and public stockholding for food security purposes but no mention was made of any "single undertaking." WT/MIN(13)/DEC (11 Dec. 2013). At the Nairobi Ministerial in 2015 the Final Communiqué noted that "[m]any Members reaffirm the [Doha negotiations . . .] Other Members do not reaffirm the Doha mandates, as they believe new approaches are necessary to achieve meaningful outcomes in multilateral negotiations. Members have different views on how to address the negotiations." WT/MIN(15)/DEC (21 Dec. 2015). It was after this statement that the Doha negotiations were indefinitely suspended. Finally, at the Buenos Aires Ministerial in 2017 joint initiatives were agreed to on e-commerce, investment facilitation, and micro-, small- and medium-sized enterprises, but there was no Final Communiqué and even a stand-in 'Chairperson's Statement' could not be agreed. WT/MIN(17)/74 (22 Jan. 2018).

128 Ibid. See also Martin Antoine & Bryan Mercurio, "Doha Dead and Buried in Nairobi" 16:1 *J. Int'l Trade & Pol.* 49 (2017).

occasionally to the letter, resulting in a loss of trust and misuse or abuse of provisions that in certain cases amounted to open "lawfare."[129]

Third, in an effort to be conscientious, panel and Appellate Body reports became increasingly lengthy and technical, a factor that introduced significant delays in rendering reports and diminished their accessibility to the global public.[130] Heavy reliance on WTO dispute settlement ultimately overwhelmed the system, which struggled to keep abreast of its workload.

These issues came to a head with the US decision in 2017 to block appointments to the Appellate Body. The Appellate Body had been successful in fulfilling its mandate. However, this success and the results achieved in several dispute settlement outcomes raised fears in Washington about "complexity, delays, lack of transparency, and inter-

[129] DSU Art. 3.10 provides "[i]t is also understood that complaints and counter-complaints in regard to distinct matters *should not be linked.*" [emphasis added]. Notwithstanding this, tit-for-tat litigation has been observed in WTO dispute settlement and is not uncommon. See the Brazil–Canada Aircraft cases (WT/DS46, WT/DS70), the EU-U.S. Large Aircraft ("Airbus/Boeing") cases (WT/DS316, WT/DS353), *EC – Commercial Vessels*, WT/DS301/R, para. 7.127 (22 Apr. 2005) (litigation initiated by Korea against EC legislation, the TDM Regulation, making a link between temporal application of the Regulation and the initiation, resolution or suspension of WTO dispute settlement proceeding initiated by the EC against Korea regarding subsidies allegedly provided by Korea to its shipbuilding industry), and the pair of cases *Guatemala – Cement*, WT/DS60/R (19 June 1998) and *Mexico – Steel Pipes*, WT/DS331/R (8 June 2007). For an early warning of the legalism arising from WTO dispute settlement, see Karen Alter, "Resolving or Exacerbating Disputes? The WTO's New Dispute Resolution System" 79:4 *Int'l Aff.* 783 (2000).

[130] As Arie Reich has observed:

> ... in the early days [of the WTO], most disputes (over 60%) were resolved within 2 years. About 31% were resolved within 2–3 years; and 9% within 3–4 years. No dispute required more than that. In the later period, however, [i.e. 2007–2011] only 32% were resolved in less than 2 years, and 50% required 2–3 years. About 13% required 3–4 years to be resolved and more than 5% required between 4 and 5 years ... Since 2011, the situation is continuing to deteriorate and delays are getting worse ... [the 20 consultation requests in 2013] have produced 8 panel reports, 7 of which went to appeal. The average duration of those 8 cases, from consultations request to adoption was 33.83 months, which is almost 6 months more than the average for 2007–2011. Only one of those cases was adopted within two years of its initiation, three took 2–3 years to resolve, and four took 3–4 years.

(Arie Reich, "The Effectiveness of the WTO Dispute Settlement System: A Statistical Analysis" EUI Working Papers 11/2017 at 24 (2017).)

pretive overreach."[131] The core of US concerns – which had built for some time – was that WTO dispute settlement had become too powerful and risked infringing sovereignty.

In particular, the United States objected to several specific practices of the Appellate Body.[132] In response, a number of reform proposals were made by other members, none of which was successful in allaying US concerns.

Due to the US objections, the Appellate Body's quorum was allowed to run down and the Appellate Body suspended operation in December 2019. Panels continue to hear cases, but at the time of writing there is no final word from the Appellate Body on the outcome of any dispute, something which leaves WTO law in a state of uncertainty and detracts from the treaty's character as a club good.

In response, the EU and a number of other WTO members have agreed to a workaround procedure referred to as the Multi-Party Interim Appeal Arbitration Mechanism (MPIA), which establishes a standing arbitration scheme for appeals under DSU Art. 25. The MPIA essentially duplicates the DSU's appellate structure, where its use is agreed but is not intended to be a permanent replacement for the Appellate Body.[133] Most importantly, perhaps, because of their peculiar

[131] Hannah Monicken, "In First Word on WTO Dispute Settlement, Pagán Seeks 'True Reform Discussion'" 40:17 *Inside U.S. Trade* 1 (29 Apr. 2022).

[132] US concerns with the WTO Appellate Body were summarized in the President's 2018 Trade Policy Agenda. Some have been longstanding while others are relatively new. Leading US concerns were expressed as (1) the Appellate Body's disregard for the ninety-day deadline for appeals contained in DSU Art. 17.5; (2) continued service on the Appellate Body by persons whose terms have expired; (3) the tendency of WTO reports to make findings unnecessary to resolve a dispute or on issues not presented in the dispute; (4) the Appellate Body's alleged review of facts and review of member's domestic law de novo; (5) the Appellate Body's assertion that its reports effectively serve as precedent and that panels are to follow prior Appellate Body reports absent "cogent reasons.". See Office of the United States Trade Representative, *2018 Trade Policy Agenda and 2017 Annual Report of the President of the United States on the Trade Agreements Program* (Mar. 2018).

[133] First, use of the MPIA is to be agreed on a country-by-country basis. In other words, recourse to the MPIA procedure is not automatic and outcomes are not binding on all parties. Second, arbitration under DSU Art. 25 has been little used and results in awards whose legal status is uncertain. The current practice is for panel and Appellate Body reports to be automatically adopted by all WTO members as "rulings and recommendations" of the DSB. In the adoption process, as mentioned, third countries and other WTO members have extensive participatory rights and rights to comment, something they appear to value. Moreover, once adopted, adopted DSB reports enjoy the imprimatur of the organization and may be enforced. Arbitration awards rendered under the

provenance and the fact that they are not "*adopted* rulings and recommendations" of the DSB, MPIA decisions may encounter difficulty being enforced.[134]

As the standoff over the Appellate Body was unfolding, a number of other actions were being taken that seemed to indicate a loss of faith in the organization and the value of interdependence. They frequently occurred in a calibrated way supportive of the idea highlighted above that the obligations in question are interdependent – not one-to-one, but perhaps more accurately, one-to-some. What all of this behavior has laid bare is an arrangement with checkerboard compliance that cannot be traced to any single coherent scheme or principle.

In 2018, for instance, the United States imposed a number of tariffs unilaterally on products from different countries, which were quickly matched by the United States' leading trading partners – not simply in reciprocal fashion against the United States but in some instances against other WTO members more generally.[135] In addition, trade-restrictive action involving safeguards, antidumping and countervailing measures

MPIA procedure are not "rulings and recommendations" of the DSB and would therefore appear to lie somewhat outside WTO law in terms of their legal effect. Third, the possibility of regular recourse to the MPIA procedure for appeals does little to address US-led concerns about a "hegemonic" Appellate Body or the United States' position – which has been the largest user of the dispute settlement system.

134 Jennifer Hillman, "Three Approaches to Fixing the World Trade Organization's Appellate Body: The Good, the Bad and the Ugly?" (Dec. 2018) available at www.law.georgetown.edu/wp-content/uploads/2018/12/Hillman-Good-Bad-Ugly-Fix-to-WTO-AB.pdf. (noting that "the decisions of an arbitration panel would not be formally adopted by the DSB." Because of this "arbitration-appeals would always sit somewhat outside the binding dispute settlement system. While the rules provide that arbitration awards under Article 25 can be subject to the surveillance of the DSB . . . it is not certain exactly what the DSB can do to enforce an unadopted panel report/arbitration appeal.")

135 For instance, in January 2018 the United States imposed tariffs on imports of solar panels and washing machines of 30 to 50 percent and imports and in March 2018 imposed tariffs on steel (25 percent) and aluminum (10 percent) for most countries. On June 1, 2018, these tariffs were extended to the EU, Canada and Mexico. In separate moves, the United States escalated tariffs on goods imported from China, leading to a trade war. The tariffs angered trading partners, who implemented retaliatory tariffs on US goods, and in some cases, on goods coming from third countries, in order to prevent trade diversion. In June 2018, India planned to recoup trade penalties of $241 million on $1.2 billion worth of Indian steel and aluminum, but negotiations delayed these until June 2019 when India imposed retaliatory tariffs on $240 million worth of US goods. Canada imposed matching retaliatory tariffs against US goods on July 1, 2018. China implemented retaliatory tariffs equivalent to the $34 billion tariff imposed on it by the United States. Other countries such as Australia expressed concern over the consequences of a global trade war. The continuing impasse over the Appellate Body also

reached historic highs.[136] In some cases there was also a return to "managed trade" involving export caps, more stringent rules of origin and domestic content requirements.[137] Still another move was frequent recourse to the hitherto rarely invoked "national security" exception under GATT Art. XXI.[138]

prompted certain WTO members to amend or clarify legislation to allow for retaliation before the completion of WTO disputes. For instance, the EU's revised Trade Enforcement Regulation allows the EU to adopt countermeasures against countries that block the conclusion of dispute settlement proceedings under the framework of the WTO or bilateral treaties. See EU Reg. No. 654/2014 as amended by EU Reg. 2021/167. See also Brazil's announcement of similar legislation in January 2022: Bernardo Leite, "Brazil to Apply Unilateral Retaliation in Trade Disputes" Grinberg Cordovil Advogados (18 Jan. 2022).

136 WTO Press Release, "Trade Restrictions among G20 Economies Remain at Historic Highs" (21 Nov. 2019):

> The WTO's new Trade Monitoring Report issued on 21 November shows that G20 economies from mid-May to mid-October 2019 introduced import-restrictive measures covering an estimated USD 460.4 billion worth of traded merchandise. This represents a 37% increase over the previous period going back to mid-October 2018, and is second only to the USD 480.9 billion coverage of import-restricting measures reported between mid-May and mid-October 2018. The report notes that with restrictions accumulating over time, the share of global trade covered by such measures has soared.

137 "Managed trade" is the monicker given to a variety of arrangements requiring strict reciprocity – for example one-to-one or dollar-for-dollar trade in certain products or services – as a condition of liberalization. An example of a managed trade agreement is the 1965 Auto Pact between Canada and the United States, which removed import tariffs on automobiles between the two countries. In exchange auto makers agreed that vehicle production in Canada would not fall below 1964 levels and that they would ensure the same production-sales ratio of domestic to foreign vehicles in Canada. Managed trade arrangements are considered sub-optimal in that they are deemed by classical economics to be less efficient than true free trade agreements. Commentators detect a "managed trade" aspect to the revised Korea-U.S. Free Trade (KORUS) Agreement of 2018 and the USMCA Agreement of 2018, portending a return to managed trade under international trading arrangements more generally: see Gary Clyde Hufbauer & Eujin Jung, "The USMCA, Newly Jeopardized, Was Never a Free Trade Agreement" Petersen Institute Trade and Investment Policy Watch (4 June 2019). See also Jan Piotrowski, "Special Report on Business and the State: Return to Picking Winners" 442:9279 *The Economist* 4 (15 Jan. 2022).

138 See *Russia – Traffic in Transit*, WT/DS512. Ukraine claimed that Russian transit measures are inconsistent with Russia's obligations under GATT Art. V (freedom of transit), Art. X (publication and administration of trade regulations) and with related commitments in Russia's Accession Protocol (para. 7.2). Russia asserted that the measures were necessary for the protection of its essential security interests, which it took in response to the emergency in international relations that occurred between it and

Following the advent of a new US administration in early 2021, there were some indications that certain trade-related tensions would ease. Nevertheless, these developments did not mean a return to business-as-usual and the way forward for the WTO Agreement remained unclear.

According to Simon Evenett and Richard Baldwin, several considerations obscure the prospects for the organization and its mandate in future. There has been criticism of the WTO's over-emphasis on a rule-of-law approach to trade policy and the erosion of trust it has engendered among the membership. Legalism does not necessarily instill confidence.[139] Another criticism is the failure of the Doha Round and the inability to reach deep agreement on perennially problematic issues like intellectual property and agricultural subsidies.[140] Still another criticism is the fact that the institutional concept of "balance" had become unbalanced because relative benefits for developed country members in the system have declined, and these losses have not been matched by corresponding increases in obligations taken on by developing countries.[141] Finally, there is the general sense that existing WTO rules are inadequate to address new types of trade flows, including e-commerce and contentious practices like data localization.[142]

From a US perspective, an additional concern has been the behavior of China, today the world's largest trading nation, which the United States accuses of engaging in market-distorting behavior to beggar its neighbors, conducting massive amounts of strategic trade policy, and undertaking questionable practices like forced labor that violate international norms.[143] All of these practices are said to violate the

Ukraine in 2014. A WTO panel found that WTO panels have jurisdiction to review aspects of a member's invocation of GATT Art. XXI(b)(iii), that Russia had met the requirements for invoking Art. XXI(b)(iii), and, therefore, that the transit bans and restrictions were permissible. The panel rejected Russia's jurisdictional argument that GATT Art. XXI(b)(iii) was totally "self-judging." GATT Art. XXI has also been raised as a defence in several other WTO disputes: *Ukraine - Ammonium Nitrate (Russia)*, WT/DS493; *U.S. - Steel and Aluminium Products (China)*, WT/DS544; *U.S. - Origin Marking (Hong Kong, China)*, WT/DS597.

139 Evenett & Baldwin, *Revitalising Multilateralism* 27.

140 Ibid. at 24.

141 Ibid. at 19–20.

142 Ibid. at 28.

143 See "China's Trade-Disruptive Economic Model – Submission from the United States," WT/GC/W/745 (11 July 2018), "2017 Report to Congress on China's WTO Compliance," WT/GC/W/746 (11 July 2018) and associated discussion in WT/GC/M/173, p. 29ff. (26 July 2018).

"spirit"[144] of the WTO legal order and provide a pretext for the United States to walk away from WTO arrangements, either with respect to China or perhaps more broadly.

In light of these developments "a Great Uncoupling" appears to be underway, and along with it, an evolving appreciation of the value of the WTO Agreement as a community, one which places more emphasis on members' assertion of their rights as opposed to fulfillment of their obligations. This development appears to be taking the form of more reliance on rights-based flexibilities and greater stress on regional agreements under the protective guise of GATT Art. XXIV. As mentioned, the arrangement's club good appears to be evolving or uncoupling into a bundle of discrete bilateral relationships more characteristic of private goods.

Certain actions might be taken to arrest or counter this trend, such as more intensive and regular review of trade protection measures by WTO committees, deeper plurilateral arrangements, and public and private leaders' statements supportive of a rules-based trading system.[145] However, to some degree the existing state of affairs has to be accepted for what it is: an emblem of loss of faith in the value of interdependence. The current result is not optimal use of WTO concessions and commitments but instead something more akin to Heller's idea of "tolerably good use."

These developments do not mean abandonment of the organization but rather an effort to reorient and repurpose it. The adjustment would be for the greater objective of dealing with a number of contemporary challenges, including the aftermath of the COVID-19 pandemic, discipline on trade-distorting subsidies and digital technologies and addressing the "interface" issue between state-sponsored and market versions of

[144] Petros Mavroidis & André Sapir, *China and the WTO* viii (Princeton University Press, Princeton, NJ; 2021) (observing that "China clearly violates the spirit of the WTO").

[145] In addition, more attention might be paid to inclusive growth. See Richard Samans et al., *The World Economic Forum Inclusive Growth and Development Report* (2015), which defines inclusive growth as "output growth that is sustained over decades, is broad-based across economic sectors, creates productive employment opportunities for a great majority of the country's working age population, and reduces poverty." Ibid. at 1. A call for inclusive growth is contained in Salman Ahmed & Rozlyn Engel (eds), *Making U.S. Foreign Policy Work Better for the Middle Class* 3 (Carnegie Endowment for International Peace, Washington, DC; 2020) (noting a need to "revamp the U.S. international trade agenda and ensure it is paired with a domestic policy agenda to support *more inclusive economic growth*" [emphasis added] Ibid. at 3).

capitalism. An additional matter is the urgent need to devote attention to trade-related aspects of climate change.

2.6 Conclusion

This chapter began by outlining a theory of community. A community is based in what actors have in common and value. It is "a structured, continuing relationship" that creates common obligations with respect to goods generated in the community. These obligations are either constitutive or contractual. The ultimate character of obligations with respect to goods is determined by the community's experience over time.

Still, the traditional constitution/contract distinction regarding obligations is insufficient to fully account for the inclusive and exclusive characteristics of goods. Goods may be generated and available within a community, but their full realization depends on decision-making about them. A finer-grained analysis is necessary.

This chapter highlights how arrangements establishing GATT 1947 and the WTO Agreement created a club good. The relevant treaties are composed of trade concessions and commitments that any WTO member is deemed to have an interest in and which any member remains free to assert in the case of breach. In this sense the obligations involved are primarily of a constitutive type.

At the same time, a number of aspects of WTO obligations as a contract linger and the club good character of the arrangement is conditioned by the practice of consensus decision-making, meaning that any member may block the formation of agreement and impede initiative in key instances.

I have suggested that the most plausible reconciliation of these contrasting tendencies is the idea of WTO obligations as functionally interdependent. Several important aspects of the treaty and state practice appear to confirm this conclusion. Simply put, WTO members calibrate their behavior to the extent that other members – particularly major players – are prepared to commit.

In recent years the checking behavior referred to above has become more prominent and appears linked to contemporary doubts about interdependence. In light of the above, the "good" of WTO arrangements has increasingly come to be regarded as less good. As a result, countries are stepping back from their commitments in various ways.

And just as a good comes into being because of what is perceived to be advantageous and therefore worthy of protection, so it may come apart because it is regarded as detrimental and unworthy. That is now what appears to be happening in the "Great Uncoupling" occurring in WTO law. The diminished role of WTO law and dispute settlement needs to be understood in that light.[146]

Despite these developments, there also appears to be recognition of residual worth in the WTO Agreement. WTO arrangements may not fulfill the robust vision of comparative advantage that prevailed in the 1990s, but they continue to allow for it in some degree. That has value and furnishes "tolerably good use."

Recognition of such value comes about in the fact that none of the 164 current members of the WTO has decided to leave the organization, and 23 countries are currently seeking to join.[147] The search is on for some means of evolution and repurposing of the treaty in line with Simma and Paulus' concept of "solidarity between peoples."

Nevertheless, the treaty still needs some way of determining what is right or correct, or in other words, what is just within its community. It is to this subject that I next turn.

[146] "Law cannot flourish as an interpretive enterprise in any community unless there is enough initial agreement about what practices are legal practices so that lawyers argue about the best interpretation of roughly the same data" Dworkin, *Law's Empire* 91.

[147] Evenett & Baldwin, *Revitalising Multilateralism* 9.

3

The WTO Agreement and Justice

3.1 The Nature of Justice

In Chapter 1, I emphasized the importance of interdependence in the form of a community in generating goods. I also stressed how actors will not come together to generate goods in the first place unless they have a reasonable prospect of being better off – or at least no worse off – by doing so, and how that assessment gives rise to a continuing preoccupation in a community with justice.

Consequently, in this chapter I go on to develop a theory of justice that can be linked to the theory of community introduced in the previous chapter.

The outline of a theory of justice is important not only because it sets the background for the theory of WTO law developed in subsequent chapters but also because a persistent criticism of the WTO Agreement is that its arrangements are unjust. Critics have taken aim at the WTO Agreement from a range of perspectives and vantage points.[1] From the view of international human rights, for example, Sarah Joseph has pointed out how WTO commitments can impair human rights due to their uncertain scope, the danger they pose of "regulatory chill," the constraints they introduce on the use of trade sanctions for human rights violations, among other grounds of concern.[2]

Developing a theory of justice in relation to the WTO Agreement is therefore essential because of the need for justification. Without such a

[1] Sundhya Pahuja, "Trading Spaces: Locating Sites for Challenge within International Trade Law" 14:1 *Australian Feminist L.J.* 38 (2000); Philip Alston, "Resisting the Merger and Acquisition of Human Rights by Trade Law: A Reply to Petersmann" 13:4 *E.J.I.L.* 815 (2002); Olga Chyzh, "Dangerous Liaisons: An Endogenous Model of International Trade and Human Rights" 53:3 *J. Peace Research* 409 (2016).

[2] Sarah Joseph, *Blame It on the WTO* 4–5 (Oxford University Press, Oxford; 2011).

developed account, how can we be sure that the treaty and its arrangements have a valid basis?

The theory I develop in this chapter dovetails with what has been developed in earlier chapters and rests on the idea that WTO law is the product of a distinctive community, a community that is composed of countries that have made the necessary concessions and commitments to be part of that community. Individuals do not so concede or commit. Therefore, the resulting arrangement must be understood to generate a distinctive form of justice. The justice of WTO law is primarily concerned with maintaining a club good composed of the equality of competitive conditions between foreign and domestic interests. Only secondarily is it concerned with what is fair for the individual good of member states. Out of the interaction of these goods and their associated forms of justice arises a third, overarching form that emphasizes the generation of transformative solutions needed to reconcile the relevant interests and sustain the community over time.

This combination of forms of justice is different from the justice of international human rights, which often emphasizes certain inalienable fundamental rights of individuals, or from conventional understandings of justice in everyday life, which remains overwhelmingly corrective. My principal point in this chapter is that the WTO Agreement's distinctive good mean that its justice has to be appreciated to some degree on its own terms. This is not to suggest that justice under the WTO Agreement should be analyzed in splendid isolation or that it is necessarily "perfect". Rather, my point is that if we seek to comprehend the justice of WTO law in later chapters, then we must understand it according to the treaty's particular good. It is this understanding which will explain why that community appears to be becoming 'undone' and why, as described in the previous chapter, it is apparently in need of re-purposing.

Justice in WTO law is therefore a challenging subject to theorize both because it is community-specific and because it looks a little alien, at least when compared with the corrective models of justice most readers will be familiar with.

An additional barrier to developing a theory of justice out of WTO law is the fact that in recent decades the discussion of justice has become highly fragmented. Discussion is less likely to take place today concerning "justice" on its own and more likely to involve reference to a number of newly identified variants of justice – "restorative justice",[3] "transitional justice,"[4] "global justice"[5] and the like – without much attention necessarily being paid to how all of these relate or fit together.[6] The result is that the concept of justice as a coherent topic is hard to grasp and difficult to deal with.

A preliminary issue is the lack of a common definition. Many commentators fall back on the definition given in Justinian's *Institutes*, which refers to justice as being a matter of "giving each their due."[7] However, that venerable formulation elides many key questions and is recognized as merely a starting point for thinking about the subject.

[3] Restorative justice is defined as "a way of dealing with victims and offenders by focussing on the settlement of conflicts arising from crime and resolving the underlying problems which cause it." Originating in reactions to the application of Western-style legal systems to Indigenous peoples, restorative justice has been inspired by consensual and communal ways inherent in many Indigenous systems of justice. A key idea is that the traditional Western conception of crime – as a crime against the *state* – needs to be reconceived as a wrong against the *community*. This conceptual shift modifies the focus of justice, which now becomes to resolve the underlying problem. The emphasis is therefore subtly creative, one of "dealing with crime generally in a rational problem-solving way." See Law Commission of Canada, "From Restorative Justice to Transformative Justice: Discussion Paper," Law Commission of Canada Catalogue No. JL2-6 (1999).

[4] Transitional justice is defined as "a range of approaches that societies undertake to reckon with legacies of widespread or systematic human rights abuse as they move from a period of violent conflict or oppression towards peace, democracy, the rule of law, and respect for individual and collective rights." The International Center for Transitional Justice website (accessed 1 July 2008). "What Is Transitional Justice?", available at www.ictj.org/en/tj/.

[5] Global justice inquiries take individual human beings as of primary concern and seek to give an account of what justice among such agents involves. Whereas contemporary political philosophers have focused their theorizing about justice almost exclusively within the state, the last twenty years or so has seen a marked extension of this focus to the global sphere. See Gillian Brock, "Global Justice" in *Stanford Encyclopedia of Philosophy* (6 Mar. 2015). See also Frank Garcia, *Global Justice and the International Economic Law: Three Takes* (Cambridge University Press, Cambridge; 2013).

[6] At base the problem of justice may be interpretative. As Ronald Dworkin notes, "[w]e do not follow shared linguistic criteria for deciding what facts make a situation just or unjust." Ronald Dworkin, *Law's Empire* 73 (1986). He adds, "it is difficult to find a statement of the concept [of justice] at once sufficiently abstract to be uncontroversial among us and sufficiently concrete to be useful. Our controversies about justice are too rich, and too many different kinds of theories are now in the field." Ibid. at 74.

[7] "Justice is the constant and perpetual wish to render everyone his due." Thomas Cooper, *The Institutes of Justinian* 7 (North-Holland, Amsterdam; 1975).

One way forward is to identify some common attributes of justice. Commentators have observed, for example, how justice is first and foremost relational. The phrase "giving each their due" is chiefly of significance among actors who are related to each other. Thus, in 1968 Otto Bird observed:

> Telling the truth, rendering to another person what is due to him, or obeying the law are all actions in which men are involved with other men [*sic*]. Justice, in all three [instances], is conceived of as a guide by which men direct their actions in regard to others.[8]

An initial attribute of justice is therefore that it is *associative*. It is normally a matter of concern among those who are affiliated.

Second, justice is *approbative*. When something is described as "just," it is understood to possess qualities of rightness or correctness. The foundation for this opinion is the conviction that what is just is desirable.

Third, justice is often regarded as *obligatory*. In other words, justice is something to which communal arrangements must conform or at least aspire. This idea is conveyed in Philip Allott's observation that "[j]ustice is present in its presence; and it is present in its absence."[9] Justice is the constant measure of what must be done.

Fourth, justice is distinct from law. Ronald Dworkin has observed:

> Justice is a matter of the correct theory of moral and political rights, and anyone's conception of justice is his theory, imposed by his own political convictions, of what these rights are. Law is a matter of which rights supply a justification for using or withholding the collective force of the state because they are included in or are implied by actual political decisions of the past.[10]

Justice therefore differs from law and may conceivably diverge from it.[11]

[8] Otto Bird, *The Idea of Justice* 10 (Frederick Praeger, New York; 1967).

[9] Philip Allott, *Eunomia* 83 (Oxford University Press, Oxford; 1990).

[10] Dworkin, *Law's Empire* 97.

[11] Although natural law theory maintains that justice is the law's chief aspiration. St. Augustine of Hippo observed that "where there is not true justice, law cannot exist." St. Augustine, *The City of God*, Vol. 2, Book 19, Chapter 21, p. 258 (J. M. Dent & Sons, London; 1931); "the idea and concept of justice demand as the very essence of justice, preexisting rules of law applicable to all alike and impartially applied. If this is not the situation, justice does not exist, nor do laws exist." John Maxcy Zane, *The Story of Law* (2nd ed.) 104 (Liberty Fund, Indianapolis, IN; 1998).

A preliminary description of justice is therefore that it is associative, approbative, obligatory and distinct from law. At the same time, this collection of descriptors does not indicate much about the function or content of justice. Justice is traditionally considered to offer a moral justification for what is observed in the law, yet some commentators describe its function as being to regulate "pleasure and pain,"[12] to distribute "benefits and burdens,"[13] or to arrange "rights and obligations."[14] These catchall phrases do not get directly at the matter of function or content of justice.

To gain further insight into these issues, some additional reflection is necessary.

3.2 Theories of Justice

Many of the issues raised above in relation to justice are complex and have only been resolved – if at all – through the development of theories of justice.

In this section I examine two such theories, those of Aristotle and John Rawls. I focus on Aristotle's theory because Aristotelian ideas are recognized to constitute the "building blocks of legal philosophy"[15] and have served as points of reference for thinking about what is "right" or "correct" in both philosophy and law for centuries.

[12] To say that the rules operate unjustly among nations, however, is to see little about the rules' actual impact on those who matter: the individuals who, unlike states, are capable of pleasure and pain. That this is an inevitable barrier to assessing the *justice* of the international system, however, does not affect our ability to measure quite accurately and usefully the *legitimacy* of those rules.

(Thomas Franck, *The Power of Legitimacy among Nations* 209 (1990) [emphasis in original])

[13] J. R. Lucas, "Justice" 47 *Philosophy* 229 at 235 (1982) ("Justice is really concerned with the distributions of the benefits and burdens of society in a much wider sense.")

[14] Bayo Ogunmupe, "Nigeria: Meaning of Social Justice Today" *Daily Champion* (18 May 2004) ("Justice is a matter of rights and obligations, of gifts and return of gifts.")

[15] Jason Neyers, "The Inconsistencies of Aristotle's Theory of Corrective Justice" 11 *Can. J.L. & Juris.* 311, 313 (1998). See also Izhak Englard, *Corrective and Distributive Justice: From Aristotle to Modern Times* (Oxford University Press, Oxford; 2009). ("Starting in the 1970s, the classic distinction 'conquered' the minds of American legal scholars and literally hundreds of papers, a symposium and many chapters in books, were dedicated to the topic. The vigour of this trend is not yet abating." Ibid. at xii)

I also focus on Rawls's theory of justice because "[n]o political philosopher of the twentieth century has had a great impact on our thinking about justice"[16] and because contemporary theories of justice are often either elaborations of, or responses to, Rawlsian ideas.

Aristotle and Rawls's theories are therefore good places to begin examining the content of justice, although as will be demonstrated, I identify key shortcomings in each theory and therefore go on to develop my own theory of justice later in this chapter.

3.2.1 *Equality and Fairness*

As mentioned, justice depends upon on community and context. The most natural contexts are those in the world around us, an environment that is constantly changing.[17] One way of overcoming this variation is to compare like with like. From this comes a preoccupation with thinking about justice in terms of equality.

The origins of thinking about justice in terms of equality are often attributed to Aristotle, a philosopher who lived in Athens in the fourth century BCE. At that time Athens had undergone substantial political change. The changes culminated in the creation of a democracy, a form of polity emphasizing equality.[18]

Aristotle put forward his theory of justice as part of a broader inquiry into the nature of community, or as he put it, what "holds people

[16] Jack Knight, "Justice and Fairness" 1 *Annu. Rev. Polit. Sci.* 425 at 427 (1998).

[17] "Evolution is change, nothing more or less." "change is a constant feature of the world." "The central challenge, therefore, for any one who wishes to understand or affect the world is to come to terms with change and incorporate its dynamics into any account of how the world or its constituent parts work." Allan Hutchinson, *Evolution and the Common Law* 235 (Cambridge University Press, Cambridge; 2005).

[18] In 510 BCE Spartan troops helped the Athenians overthrow their king. The Spartans put in place a pro-Spartan oligarchy. However, Cleisthenes, with the support of the Athenian middle class and aided by democrats, took over. Cleisthenes's basic reform was to reorganize the entire citizen body into ten new tribes, each of which contained elements drawn from the whole of Attica, and to establish a series of new institutions – an Assembly, a Council and a court system – to administer the city. Through these reforms the Athenians endowed their city with democratic institutions – equal rights for all citizens (though only men were citizens) – and established the institution of ostracism. See Christian Meier, *Athens: Portrait of the City in Its Golden Age* 155–188 (Metropolitan Press, New York; 1998).

together."[19] He observed that what is just is a combination of the "lawful and the fair," and with that in mind, he set out his famous distinction between *distributive* and *corrective justice.*

According to Aristotle *distributive justice* "is found in the distribution of honors or wealth or anything else that can be divided among members of the community who will have a share in the political system."[20] He described distributive justice as "geometrically proportionate" because "all agree that the just in distributions must accord with some sort of worth, but what they call worth is not the same: supporters of democracy say it is free citizenship, supporters of oligarchy say it is wealth, others good birth, while supporters of aristocracy say it is virtue."[21]

Aristotle went on to contrast distributive justice with *corrective justice*, which he described as "numerically proportionate" because it "concerns rectification in transactions." Given that the proportion is unequal, "the judge tries to restore this unjust situation to equality, since it is unequal."[22]

Over time, commentators have struggled to make sense of Aristotle's distinction between the two types of justice.[23] One question seems to be what they apply to. The wording Aristotle used to refer to distributive justice ("honours or wealth or anything else *that can be divided* among members of a community") might suggest that distributive justice applies to private property since, after all, "wealth . . . can be divided." However, other references that Aristotle makes in his discussion of distributive justice, such as "the just in distribution *of common assets*,"[24] are to be contrasted with the operation of corrective justice, which Aristotle

[19] "In reality, this measure is need, which holds everything together; for if people needed nothing, or needed things to different extents, there would be either no exchange or not the same exchange." 1133a28–30; also "Now clearly need holds [a community] together as a single unit, since people with no need of each other, both of them and either one, do not exchange, as they exchange whenever another requires what one has oneself, such as wine, when they allow the export of corn. This, then, must be equalized." 1133b7–11. All references to Aristotle are to the translation of the *Nicomachean Ethics* by Terence Irwin: see Aristotle, *Nicomachean Ethics* (2nd ed.) (Terence Irwin, trans., Hackett, Indianapolis, IN; 1999). I am grateful to Kendall Sharp for bringing the translation to my attention.

[20] Aristotle, *Nicomachean Ethics* 1130b31.

[21] Ibid., 1131a25–29.

[22] Ibid., 1132a7.

[23] For discussion, see Englard, *Corrective and Distributive Justice* at xii.

[24] Aristotle, *Nicomachean Ethics* 1131b29.

describes as involving transactions in items such as shoes and houses, inferring the specific application of corrective justice to private property.[25]

From this identification it is then possible to conclude that distributive justice applies to public property, or what belongs to all, whereas corrective justice applies to private property, or what belongs to one individual.

A further question arising from Aristotle's distinction is the appropriate metric for each type of justice. Aristotle asserted that the metric of distributive justice is variable and proportionate ("but what they call worth is not the same"), whereas the metric of corrective justice is fixed and egalitarian ("the judge tries to restore this unjust situation to equality, since it is unequal"). These metrics are problematic and are an issue I return to below.

Finally, there is the relationship between distributive and corrective justice, which remains an open question. Generally speaking, the relationship can be understood in three different ways.

The first, which I will label a "dependent" view, regards distributive justice as setting out the appropriate distribution and corrective justice working supplementarily to re-establish it. A dependent view is problematic to some commentators, however, because it is said to fail to respect the autonomous character of corrective justice and because at least some corrective operations occur without reference to any pre-existing distribution or its legitimacy.

Hence, a second view of the relationship, which I will label an "independent" view, regards corrective justice as largely autonomous of distributive justice. According to this view, correction happens regardless of the pre-existing distribution. An independent view is also problematic because it does not account for the existence of broad background features that many commentators consider to be distributive in nature and that make correction either less, or occasionally more, than complete.

These two views of the relationship between distributive and corrective justice loom large in contemporary thinking. For this reason, they tend to overshadow a third, less well-known view of the relationship that maintains that the two forms of justice interact. This "interactive" view has received some recognition but on the whole remains little explored or

[25] Ibid. at 1133a23.

understood. Judges and commentators have had difficulty saying much that is specific about how the two forms of justice might plausibly interact.

In general, it may be said that there is a natural intelligibility to the dependent view because it is inherently logical to suggest that justice involves making up *ex post* any upsetting of the *ex ante* distribution.

Still, it is possible to envisage other scenarios where distributive considerations such as need, desert or personal status trump any idea of a return to the original distribution. As such, no one conception of the relationship between distributive and corrective justice universally prevails.

Lingering uncertainty about Aristotle's views and the ultimate justice of his ideas have spurred a quest for alternative theories of justice. One of these is the theory derived by John Rawls. Rawls's theory was motivated by the need to provide an alternative to utilitarianism, or the idea that "the demands of justice as commonly understood correspond roughly to the rules that . . . are most conducive to the greatest happiness."[26] Rawls's concern was that the traditional utilitarian emphasis on aggregates ("the greatest happiness") overlooks disparities and therefore masks injustice.

Rawls's work in *A Theory of Justice* was an attempt to detail how justice might be realized in the context of a prototypical community. Rawls did so for the ultimate purpose of supplying a blueprint for how existing communities might be made more just through fair institutions. In this respect he was not concerned with corrective justice between individuals. Rather, his primary focus was on distributive justice. This has left some question about his views on corrective justice.[27]

Rawlsian ideas identify an "original position," a "public criterion of justice" and a "basic structure of society." In a Rawlsian "original position," individuals who are free and equal, reasonable and rational, come together to determine criteria for justice to be administered in a prototypical community. They do so subject to a "veil of ignorance," which temporarily blinds them to arbitrary facts such as those involving race, class and gender concerning themselves and others. The veil prevents these facts from influencing their ultimate agreement.

Participants then work out a definition of the "liberty principle" and the "difference principle" mentioned in Chapter 1 as part of a communal

[26] S.v. "Justice" in *Stanford Encyclopedia of Philosophy* (26 June 2017) (author: David Miller).

[27] For an attempt to work out what a coherent theory of corrective justice would look like consistent with Rawlsian ideas, see Arthur Ripstein, "The Division of Responsibility and the Law of Tort" 72 *Fordham L. Rev.* 1811 (2004).

exercise in arriving at a composite "public criterion of justice." This working out of the public criterion results in what Rawls termed "justice as fairness," or in other words, "a just arrangement of the major political and social institutions of a liberal society."[28] The core of justice as fairness is described as follows:

> The guiding idea is that since citizens are fundamentally equal, reasoning about justice should begin from a presumption that cooperatively-produced goods should be equally divided. Justice then requires that any inequalities must benefit all citizens, and particularly must benefit those who will have the least.[29]

The motivation for such a fair – as opposed to equal – arrangement comes from what Rawls termed an "overlapping consensus" involving a range of worldviews. In this process of working out the public criterion of justice, "the well-off will recognize that they have the duty to accommodate themselves vis-à-vis those who are less well-off because the well-off have a vested interest in stability, in the way things are, so they will compromise."[30]

With justice as fairness in mind, participants will then proceed through a "four-stage sequence, tailoring these general principles to the particular conditions of the society of the citizens they represent" in an effort to arrive at the "basic structure of society." In this sequence, "the veil of ignorance that screens out information about society's general features gradually becomes thinner, and the parties use the new information to decide on progressively more determinate applications of the principles already agreed upon."[31] Rawls emphasized, however, that a number of remedial mechanisms such as public education, a basic

[28] "John Rawls" in *Stanford Encyclopedia of Philosophy* (9 Jan. 2017) (author: Leif Wenar).

[29] Ibid.

[30] Thomas Pogge, *John Rawls: His Life and Theory of Justice* 36 (Oxford University Press, Oxford; 2007).

[31] "John Rawls" in *Stanford Encyclopedia of Philosophy* (9 Jan. 2017) (author: Leif Wenar).

> The three stages subsequent to the original position are suggested by three kinds of question the citizen will have to face. The first has to do with the justice of legislation – a matter as to which reasonable minds may differ. The second has to do with the justice of the procedures in place to resolve questions about the justice of legislation. And third, the citizen must ask which pieces of legislation are sufficiently just to be binding on her personally. The latter three stages of the four-stage sequence do not strictly correspond to these three questions, but they do suggest the need for a sequential approach.
>
> (William Edmundson, *John Rawls: Reticent Socialist* at 65 (Cambridge University Press, Cambridge; 2017))

minimum income and universal health care would be necessary to ensure that the basic structure could be attained and sustained.

Rawls did not champion any particular idea of the ultimate communal good. Instead, he supposed that a communal idea of the good would emerge from an "overlapping consensus" of individual views about the good.[32]

The reaction to Rawls's ideas of justice has been mixed. Several commentators have noted structural problems with Rawls's position as applied both domestically and internationally. Many have also pointed out that the Rawlsian assumption that actors coming together to decide on certain basic principles *ab initio* and *ex ante* rests on idealism. It does not correspond to real conditions. As David Schmidtz puts it, "[w]e do not start from scratch. We weave our contributions into an existing tapestry of contributions."[33] Reality dictates that "[a]ll principles of justice must answer to social prerequisites of our being able to live good lives together," a condition that Schmidtz and others refer to as respect for "the rule of first possession."[34]

In Schmidtz's view, Rawls's chief shortcoming was to disregard this requirement by positing a model of distributive justice in which a community can be remade *de novo* through a series of fair institutions.[35] Schmidtz observes:

32 Pogge, *John Rawls: His Life* 35. In this respect the institutional order on which the good is premised is "not a fortuitous and transitory product of negotiation and compromise but an enduring structure based on substantive moral consensus among, and genuine moral allegiance by, its participants." Ibid. at 37.

33 David Schmidtz, *Elements of Justice* 151 (Cambridge University Press, Cambridge; 2006).

34 Ibid., 150.

35 It is noteworthy that when Rawls attempted to project his ideas into the international realm, he was much more tentative and circumspect about their application. For instance, in what he referred to as the "Law of Peoples" Rawls attempted to identify how a political conception of right and justice at the international level might be developed out of liberal ideas of justice similar to, but more general than, the idea of justice as fairness. Rawls posited that an international basic structure might be ordered on the basis that peoples are free and independent, that they observe treaties, that they are equal to other peoples, that they have a duty not to intervene, a right of self-defense, an obligation to honor human rights, to observe certain specific restrictions in wartime and to assist other peoples living under unfavorable conditions. These principles would stably order international relations over time. However, Rawls did not maintain that these principles would generate a wholesale liberal international community mirroring what he theorized about prototypic communities in the domestic sphere. See John Rawls, *The Law of Peoples* (Harvard University Press, Cambridge, MA; 1999).

> We start with goods some people have helped to produce and others have not, already possessed and in use by some people as others arrive on the scene. Contractarian thought experiments depict everyone as getting to the table at the same time; it is of central moral importance that the world is not like that.[36]

Thus, even if justice is instituted in a society or community along Rawlsian lines, any move toward the widespread equality he foresaw will be very gradual and limited due to first possession. Moreover, the keystone idea of "justice as fairness" does not get at the central question of why actors might be motivated to strive for – and accept – merely fair as opposed to equal arrangements. More explanation appears necessary to confirm the validity of his views and their operation in the context of actual communities.

Thus, while both Aristotelian and Rawlsian ideas make significant contributions to thinking about justice, on closer examination they leave a number of key questions unanswered. In Aristotle's work the deficiency pertains mainly to clarification of the relationship between distributive and corrective justice. In Rawls's work it involves what implications his ideas about distributive justice might have for historic communities, that is, communities that must engage in distribution and correction on an ongoing basis.

3.2.2 Justice in New Forms

The shortcomings of justice as identified in comprehensive theories by Aristotle and Rawls have given rise to attempts to discern justice in new forms. An additional motivation for this development is the view that while correcting injustice is required to sustain existing relationships, as Tom Campbell has observed:

> most worked-out views as to what constitutes injustice involve a more substantial vision of justice with a positive element that requires action which goes beyond putting right the wrongs that have been done and includes promoting an ideal of just human relationships as part of a harmonious and healthy society.[37]

In this respect some modern understandings of justice have focused on the inclusiveness of the community within which justice is administered

[36] Schmidtz, *Elements of Justice* 112.

[37] Tom Campbell, *Justice* (3rd ed.) 6–7 (Palgrave MacMillian, Basingstoke; 2010).

and operates. This realization has shifted conceptual emphasis away from either distributive or corrective justice toward *social justice*, first identified in literature associated with the Catholic Church in the 1840s. In 1961 social justice was defined as being:

> realized in a particular community when judges and legislators, faced with concrete social problems or conflicts, perform their respective roles so as to give effect to the greatest total of interests or the interests which weigh most in this community with the least sacrifice of the scheme of interests as a whole.[38]

Another form of justice is *transitional justice*, which "is relatively new, emerging in the wake of the Cold War amid euphoria about the 'world order and the possibilities of humanitarianism, human rights and international law.'"[39] The term "transitional justice" "refers to the set of "judicial and non-judicial measures [that have been] implemented in order to redress the legacies of human rights abuses."[40] Such measures include criminal prosecutions, commissions of inquiry, reparations schemes and various institutional reforms. The prime effort in transitional justice is to restore communities, often along more inclusive and equitable lines.

Criminal law has also developed the idea of *restorative justice*. Restorative justice is a response to crime that brings together victims, wrongdoers and the immediate community where the crime happened in order to collectively repair harm in a way that satisfies the communal conception of justice.[41] A key theme in restorative justice is the idea that

[38] Frank Dowrick, *Justice according to the English Common Lawyers* 140 (Butterworths, London; 1961).

[39] Alexander Hinton (ed.), *Transitional Justice* 2 (Rutgers University Press, New Brunswick, NJ; 2010):

> Transitional justice is strongly informed by at least three key streams of experience. One key curret was the post-World War II attempt to deal with the atrocities committed by Nazi Germany and Japan. . . . Second . . . the international community began building a new corpus of international human rights law that went far beyond preexisting laws . . . And, third, transitional justice took shape in the 1980s as a number of countries in Africa . . . and especially Latin America . . . that had been ruled by dictators or military regimes moved toward democratic rule . . .
>
> (Ibid. p. at p. 2–3)

[40] S.v. "Transitional justice," available at https://en.wikipedia.org/wiki/Transitional_justice#.

[41] Ruth Strickland, *Restorative Justice* (Peter Lang, New York; 2004); see also Jennifer Llewellyn & Robert Howse, "Restorative Justice – A Conceptual Framework," Paper Prepared for the Law Commission of Canada (1998).

a crime, traditionally conceived of as a wrong against the *state*, should be reconceptualized as an injury to the proximate *community*, thereby allowing for its localization, specification and particularization.[42]

Experience with restorative justice has in turn encouraged consideration of whether or not restorative justice techniques might be usefully applied in noncriminal fields. Some commentators have noted that the principal issue in private law is whether there is an obvious wrong. In some cases there is, but in others wrongfulness cannot be assumed.[43] As a result, the inherent emphasis in applying restorative justice principles and techniques in private law contexts is on the transformation of relationships between parties to a conflict, hence the identification of a further form of justice in *transformative justice*. One source on transformative justice has observed:

> A transformative approach to conflict resolution would encourage accommodative relationships between groups with competing interests. The conflict situation would be transformed from one in which groups are in competition with one another to one in which groups recognize their mutual interests in arriving at workable solutions.[44]

What does transformative justice transform? The answer lies in *changing or adapting the idea of a legal wrong, and with it, the relevant good.*

42 The conceptual modification places emphasis on resolving the underlying problem. The accent becomes facilitative and creative, one of "dealing with crime generally in a rational, problem-solving way." Restorative justice requires a number of modifications in thinking. The crime, "which is objectified and abstracted from the social context in which it took place," is relocalized. The system of justice, previously adversarial, is made more consensual. Offenders are encouraged to reflect on their acts and appreciate consequences. Victims in criminal proceedings, who traditionally "remain on the outside looking in," are engaged as direct and active decision makers. The immediate community is also involved in reintegrating the offender and in refashioning relationships. Law Commission of Canada, "From Restorative Justice to Transformative Justice."

43

> Of course, in many civil disputes there is an obvious wrong: a person intentionally or inadvertently damages property; a person intentionally or inadvertently breaks a contract; a person intentionally or inadvertently profits from the work or ideas of another. But in other cases, the wrongfulness of a person's behaviour cannot be taken for granted: when children argue about their respective entitlements under a parent's will the dispute is not normally about wrongdoing; when parents disagree about custody and access to children in a divorce case the dispute is normally not about wrongdoing; when creditors make conflicting claims to the property of a bankrupt company, they usually do not accuse one another of wrongdoing.
>
> (Ibid.)

44 Ibid.

Transformative justice can be said to modify the conceptualization of a wrong and how participants are prepared to think about it.

For this reason transformative justice emphasizes the participants' freedom to control the process, to define the boundaries of a conflict and to establish rules about how dispute resolution should unfold. Unlike in the case of restorative justice, there may not always be a requirement to repair harm.[45] Rather, the "goal is to find common ground on which a mutually acceptable resolution be established."[46] One source has observed:

> This is the power of transformative justice: the possibility of using the substance of a conflict as a means of exploring options and establishing responses that are not only acceptable to all parties but *develop and strengthen relationships among those involved.*[47]

The emphasis on developing and strengthening relationships among those involved naturally puts an accent on the good they seek to realize within a community.

These observations suggest that if we seek to go beyond Aristotle's essentially static theory of justice or Rawls's prototypic one to account for the way justice is done in historic communities diachronically then a new theory is needed, one that integrates, or at any rate explains, the transformative impulse identified above, and, moreover, does so in a way that links them to the central ideas underlying a community, here interdependence.

3.2.3 A Communitarian Theory

In this section I put forward a communitarian theory of justice. To recall, a theory is a "system of ideas," with the emphasis being on the "system," or set of relationships, between those ideas.

The theory of justice I forward here is communitarian in that it explains the nature and shape of justice as a reflection of the good pursued within a particular community. If the good is conceived of as more "public," it is likely to be subject to equality and distributive justice,

[45] To do so would unnecessarily handicap the parties and deflect attention from transformative potential by focusing attention on the past as opposed to the future. This speaks to the innate prospectivity of transformative justice.

[46] Law Commission of Canada, "From Restorative Justice to Transformative Justice."

[47] Ibid. [emphasis added].

whereas if it is conceived of as more "private" it is likely to be subject to fairness and corrective justice.

These two poles of analysis are not mutually exclusive, however. The exact characterization of a good is likely to rest on a continuum between public and private whose specific locus can change and is subject to a number of considerations. A parcel of land, for example, can belong to an individual in fee simple, but, depending on the perspective adopted, can also be subject to usufructuary rights that have been leased to a resource company or belong to an Indigenous band by virtue of custom. A single asset may then be subject to competing conceptions as either "public" or "private" and to overlapping claims of distributive and corrective justice that are not wholly reconcilable. In most instances, the job of a decision-maker will be to resolve such claims consistent with the needs of law and justice.

For this reason, what I am concerned with outlining here is not the manifestation of justice in a static community like the one Aristotle contemplated, where the character of goods was considered largely unchanging, or a prototypic one like that of Rawls, where the focus was largely on some initial distribution of public goods. Rather, my aim in this section is to explain how a legal system could be described as effecting justice within a historic community – a community where distribution and correction of goods are ongoing and where the characterization of a good may evolve.[48]

A communitarian theory of justice begins with the idea of fairness. Americo Beviglia Zampetti has noted:

> Fairness is a complex idea with a long history. As Woods put it, "very few ideas are very new", and fairness is certainly not one of them. There is no accepted, uniform, and commonly shared definition of fairness. The notion is strongly associated with such ideas as equality, proportionality, reciprocity, equity, and justice . . . These concepts are entangled and their usage across disciplines and policy areas is far from univocal.[49]

[48] Schmidtz, *Elements of Justice* 112.

[49] Americo Beviglia Zampetti, *Fairness in the World Economy* 26 (Edward Elgar, Cheltenham; 2006). Similarly, Steven Suranovic has written:

> The concept [of fairness] itself overlaps with many other normative principles such as justice, equity, law and even morality. As such, one cannot simply pick up a book or article and quickly discover what fairness means or how to distinguish between the various normative principles. And yet, at the same time, everyone seems to have an inherent sense of what fairness is.
>
> (Steven Suranovic, "A Positive Analysis of Fairness with Applications to International Trade" 23(3) *World Econ.* 283 (2000))

Confusion about fairness mandates some analysis of its meaning. In English usage what is "fair" is taken to be fitting or appropriate in a particular context.[50] We say, for instance, that a specific transaction is "fair," meaning that it is suitable for all concerned. This is not the same as saying that it is optimal. A fair transaction will simply be unobjectionable.

Since 2000 there has been considerable research into the origins and nature of fairness.[51] Both biologists and evolutionary psychologists have sought to determine the particular contribution of fairness to human relations. The research reveals that, generally speaking, fairness is a very human trait. It is not something that is well-developed in our closest genetic relatives.[52] Looking at the way species have evolved differently,

50 "Fair . . . [f]ree from bias, fraud or injustice; equitable, legitimate." J. A. Simpson & E. S. C. Weiner, *The Oxford English Dictionary*, Vol. V (2nd ed.) 671 (1989). Legal dictionaries offer a slightly different definitions. "Fair means . . . 1. impartial; just; equitable; disinterested; 2. Free from bias or prejudice." *Blacks Law Dictionary* (7th ed.) 615 (Brian Garner, ed.) (1999); "Fair means . . . reasonable," Daphne Dukelow, *The Dictionary of Canadian Law* (4th ed.) 474 (2011).

51 Ernst Fehr & Simon Gächter, "Fairness and Retaliation: The Economics of Reciprocity" 14:3 *J. Econ. Perspect.* 159 (Summer 2000); Joseph Henrich et al., "Markets, Religion, Community Size, and the Evolution of Fairness and Punishment" 327 *Science* 1480 (19 Mar. 2010). See also Karla Hoff, "Fairness in Modern Society" 327 *Science* 1467–1468 (19 Mar. 2010); George Akerlof & Robert Schiller, *Animal Spirits* 19–26 (2010). The understanding of fairness developed in this book also parallels in important ways that developed by Louis Kaplow and Steven Shavell in *Fairness versus Welfare* (Harvard University Press, Cambridge, MA; 2002), although the justifications given for it here are somewhat different. Kaplow and Shavell develop a definition of fairness as being primarily nonconsequentialist and as having an *ex post* character. According to their view, fairness is non-consequential because "at least some weight is given to factors that are independent of individuals' well-being" (Ibid., p. 44). They also maintain that "notions of fairness typically are used to reach conclusions based on situational characteristics of events. Furthermore, it is often true – particularly in legal contexts – that an important, indeed central aspect of the events under examination is what in fact has happened. That is, the assessments are usually made from an ex post perspective" (Ibid., p. 48). In my view, rules are imbued with fairness to maintain relationships and are therefore nonconsequential in some degree because they are not only directly tied to the consequences of a legal wrong per se but rather are calibrated to sustain the relation in question, thereby reinforcing community. Fairness is also primarily a matter decided *ex post* because it looks back to determine what needs remedying in order to advance toward whatever the community's current definition of equality entails. I thank Christopher Nicholls for bringing Kaplow and Shavell's work to my attention.

52 "Patience, Fairness and the Human Condition" 385:8549 *The Economist* 67 (Evolution) (6 Oct. 2007); Nicholas Baumard, *The Origins of Fairness* (Oxford University Press, New York; 2016) (developing the idea of fairness as mutual advantage and positing an evolutionary explanation of how the tendency to make such judgments might have arisen

biologists and evolutionary psychologists speculate that fairness is vital to human interaction, and in particular, to the formation of groups.[53]

If these findings are accepted, then it becomes apparent that fairness is important as a component of justice because it is part of a successful evolutionary strategy. Fairness is what has allowed complex human communities involving sophisticated forms of interdependence to arise.

However, fairness cannot be the default metric of justice. While fairness has a stable content in being what is fitting or appropriate, what is fair is inherently variable and therefore tends to erode stability and predictability required to protect expectations over time.

The limits of fairness suggest that in a community where the majority of transactions are impersonal, that is, conducted among strangers who have no continuing relationship, another value becomes important. This is the value of equality.

Equality has long been the ideal of a political community, at least in Western thinking.[54] In a complex community, however, it is of added importance because individuals engage in episodic transactions with strangers to meet most of their needs. That impersonality, in turn, feeds a commitment in terms of justice with the realization of equality since, as explained, individuals foresee no continuing relationship with their transacting counterparts except in the most abstract political sense. However, that commitment can only be partly realized since each instance of realizing equality involves the task of assessing particular circumstances and constitutes, in essence, an instance of fairness.

based on the idea of cooperative markets); Samuel Bowles & Herbert Gintis, *A Cooperative Species* (Princeton University Press, Princeton, NJ; 2011) (altruistic social preferences supporting cooperation outcompeted self-interest due to the development of ways to protect altruistic members, prolonged and elaborate systems of socialization among humans and the advantages enjoyed by cooperative groups over noncooperative ones).

[53] Henrich et al., "Markets, Religion, Community Size, and the Evolution," 327 *Science* 1480 (hypothesizing that market norms evolved from societal evolution to sustain beneficial exchanges where established social relationships were insufficient and showing that among fifteen populations market integration positively covaries with fairness while community size positively covaries with punishment).

[54] Leif Weinar, "Equality" in *Stanford Encyclopedia of Philosophy* (27 June 2007) ("At least since the French Revolution, equality has served as one of the leading ideals of the body politic"); Kenneth Karst, "Why Equality Matters" 17:2 *Ga. L. Rev.* 245 (1983) (noting that "[t]he idea of equality is one of the great themes in the culture of American public life.").

Indeed, many transactions and conditions that will be deemed "equal" are in fact merely fair.[55]

Equality is therefore an ideal and aspirational value, one that contrasts with the realism and pragmatism of fairness. Whereas equality is abstract and generic, fairness is more concrete and particular. Together, the two values function as correlatives in the conception of justice. These conclusions can be distilled into a set of relationships expressed as follows:

$$\text{Justice} = \text{Equality} + \text{Fairness}$$

This equation has the advantage of replicating the definition of justice supplied by a number of legal theorists.[56] The communitarian theory of justice set out above also infers that this basic relationship is accompanied by two provisos. The first is:

$$\text{Equality} \neq \text{Fairness}$$

That is, equality is not the same thing as fairness. The two values serve different functions.

The second proviso is:

$$\text{Equality} > \text{Fairness}$$

This proviso ensures that equality-based considerations take precedence over fairness-based ones. The proviso accounts for the priority that values of equality enjoy in a historic community. In other words, *fairness is inequality that is supplementary and assistive to the dominant task of attaining equality.*

This two-fold arrangement of justice coheres with much-observed behavior. First, a general commitment to equality gives a community something to strive for. As equality should serve as:

[55] This is perhaps the reason why Rawls designated the central part of his theory of justice "justice as fairness." We are constantly doing fairness in an effort to attain justice.

[56] Sanne Taekema observes that the combination of fairness and equality at the core of the concept of justice is also forwarded by Neil MacCormick, *Legal Reasoning and Legal Theory* 73 (Clarendon Press, Oxford; 1978). Fairness as the core of justice is proposed by David Miller, *Principles of Social Justice* (Harvard University Press, Cambridge, MA; 1999). Justice as equal treatment can also be found in Gustav Radbruch, *Legal Philosophy* 278 (Quelle & Meyer, Leipzig; 1932); Herbert Hart, *The Concept of Law* 159 (Oxford University Press, Oxford, 1994), James Harris, *Property and Justice* 171 (Clarendon Press, Oxford; 1996), and Aristotle in the *Nicomachean Ethics*. See Sanne Taekema, *The Concept of Ideals in Legal Theory* 192 n. 31 (Kluwer Law International, The Hague; 2003).

> a standard maxim for free society, which should be familiar to all, revered by all; constantly looked to, constantly labored for, and even though never perfectly attained, constantly approximated.[57]

Lincoln's statement conveys the way that equality is an ideal – perhaps *the* preeminent ideal – of justice, despite the fact that it is never fully or completely realized.[58] It is inherently "public," in contrast to the privateness of fairness.

Second, the supplementary role of fairness in justice can be understood to facilitate the division of labor. With a commitment to fairness, individual actors are free to specialize in particular functions or tasks safe in the knowledge that their contributions will be reciprocated, if not equally, then at least appropriately so that they have no "grounds for complaint."[59] This instills fidelity to communal arrangements.

Third, feedback is observed between equality and fairness. A community cannot be entirely equal otherwise its members would have no need of each other.[60] There must be *some* degree of inequality among them. In certain circumstances, inequality can also spur the desire for equality. Likewise, communal arrangements cannot be entirely fair because the law cannot be tailored to each specific circumstance that fairness demands. Equality and fairness therefore refer back recursively

[57] Doris Kearns Goodwin, *Team of Rivals* 207 (Simon & Schuster, New York; 2005).

[58] The equality of individuals in law is recognized as a matter of international human rights. See International Covenant on Civil and Political Rights, Art. 14(1) ("All persons shall be equal before the courts and tribunals."). The same protection is mentioned in a number of national constitutions. See Constitution of the Federative Republic of Brazil, Art. 5 ("All persons are equal before the law, without any distinction whatsoever."); Constitution of the French Republic, Art. 1 ("France shall be an indivisible, secular, democratic and social Republic. It shall ensure the equality of all citizens before the law."); Constitution of the People's Republic of China, s. 33 ("All citizens of the People's Republic of China are equal before the law."); Constitution of Kenya, s. 27.1 ("Every person is equal before the law and has the right to equal protection and equal benefit of the law.").

[59] Schmidtz, *Elements of Justice* 186.

[60] Aristotle observed that "a *polis* is "composed of unalike elements," that is to say, of individuals who have many different relations to one another – as man and wife, parent and child, soldier and civilian, ruler and ruled – and who engage in many different occupations, "which enables them to serve as complements to one another, and to attain a higher and better life by the mutual exchange of their different services." Aristotle, *The Politics of Aristotle* III, 1274b32, 1277a (Clarendon, Oxford: 1946) cited in Shirley Letwin, *On the History of the Idea of Law* (Noel Reynolds, ed.) at 22 (Cambridge University Press, Cambridge: 2005).

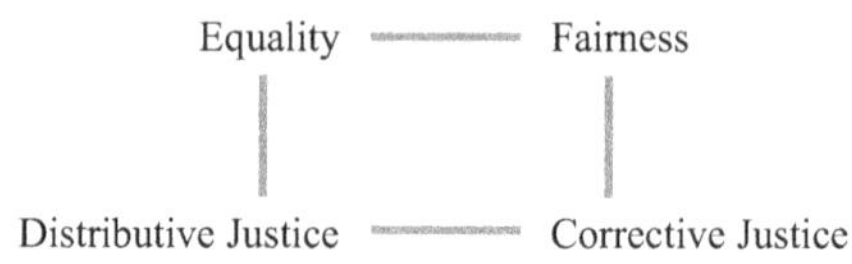

Figure 3.1 The structure of justice

to each other. They might be thought of as two sides of the same moral coin.

What are some benefits to thinking about justice in this way? To begin with, a communitarian theory of justice helps to answer questions arising out of the Aristotelian theory outlined above. To recall, one of these arises from the fact that a traditional understanding of Aristotle is that corrective justice strives to attain equality whereas distributive justice strives to attain fairness. This understanding is troublesome because while the law may call for equal reparation, many corrective operations are evidently unequal.

A communitarian theory infers *the reverse relationship*, namely, that corrective justice seeks to attain fairness – or what is appropriate – and distributive justice seeks to attain equality. The reformulated relationship can be depicted as shown in Figure 3.1.

Support for the reconfiguration is found in several sources.

One is the subsisting idea that the doing of corrective justice conceived of as equality imposes a wider cost that must be borne by the community as a whole. For example, in the context of US common law Jeffrey Standen has noted:

> Full compensation is an appealing goal, but it is not one that the law of remedies must necessarily fulfill. The available remedial means of ensuring full compensation, such as injunction, specific performance and restitution, are issued at a price, not just to the defendant but also to the community, and thus their imposition constitutes a transfer from third parties to the victims of harm.[61]

[61] Jeffrey Standen, "The Fallacy of Full Compensation" 73 *Wash. U. L. Q.* 145 at 225 (1995). See also discussion of compensation for expropriation in German law, wherein "the state must find an 'equitable balance' between the public interest and the interests of those affected [i.e. by the expropriation], reflecting the doctrine of the so-called '*Sozialbindung des Eigentums*' (social function of property)." Imgard Marboe, *Calculation of Compensation and Damages in International Investment Law* (2nd ed.) para. 2.42*ff* (Oxford University Press, Oxford; 2017). From this, the varied national approaches to compensation in cases of expropriation and the lack of a clear standard respecting compensation international investment law, Marboe concludes that "contrary to the

In recognition of this wider communal cost, court rules in many jurisdictions impose sanctions on parties who are unwilling to settle, in effect forcing most plaintiffs to discount their claims.[62]

Another source of support for the reconfiguration is the fact that enforcement of notionally equal awards may be problematic in practice. Intervening change between the time of initial holdings and the time of injury may make it impossible for an impecunious defendant to fully repair the plaintiff's injury. Recognition of this fact has spurred the trend toward fault or insurance schemes, or in some instances, symbolic reparations.

Still another source of support for reconfiguration is the fact that as a matter of behavior many parties do not always seek equal repair, either due to the difficulty of assessing past injury or the need to preserve ties.[63] They may be willing to discount in favor of a continuing relationship, evidence of a bias in favor of interdependence.

widespread general view, the required standard [of compensation] under international law is not 'full compensation' in the meaning of 'full reparation.'" Ibid. at para. 2.53.

62 Rules concerning court costs and settlement offers in a number of jurisdictions are one indication of the discount applied. For discussion of the situation in England and the U.S. see Christopher Hodges, "Settlement and its pitfalls in England and Wales" in Christopher Hodges & Astrid Stadler, *Resolving Mass Disputes* 106 (Edward Elgar, Cheltenham; 2013); Mark Anderson, "Settlement or Roll the Dice?" 28:1 *Litigation* 37 (Fall 2001); William L. Adams, "Let's Make a Deal: Effective Utilization of Judicial Settlements in State and Federal Courts" 72:2 *Or. L. Rev.* 427 (1993); Robert Bone, "To Encourage Settlement: Rule 68, Offers of Judgment, and the History of the Federal Rules of Civil Procedure" 102:4 *Nw U. L. Rev.* 1561 (2008).

63 Stewart Macaulay, "An Empirical View of Contract" 1985 *Wis. L. Rev.* 465 (1985)

> People and organizations bargain, they write documents, and they avoid, suppress, and resolve disputes little influenced by academic contract law. Some cases are taken to court and the formal process begun, although lawyers settle most of them before courts reach final decisions. . . . Business people often do not plan, exhibit great care in drafting contracts, pay much attention to those that lawyers carefully draft, or honor a legal approach to business relationships. There are business cultures defining the risks assumed in bargains, and what should be done when things go wrong. People perform disadvantageous contracts today because often this gains credit that they can draw on in the future. People often renegotiate deals that have turned out badly for one or both sides. They recognize a range of excuses much broader than those accepted in most legal systems.
>
> (Ibid. at 465, 467)

For a similar view of WTO law, see Marc L. Busch & Eric Reinhardt, "Bargaining in the Shadow of the Law: Early Settlement in GATT/WTO Disputes" 24 *Fordham Int'l L.J.* 158 at 163 (2000).

These, then, are key sources of support for a reconfiguration of Aristotelian justice proposed as part of a communitarian theory of justice.

However, there is a further – and very significant – benefit to thinking about justice in terms of a communitarian theory. That is because the theory yields an answer to the unresolved question of the correct normative relationship between distributive and corrective justice. It is embodied in what I will term an "interdependent" view of the relationship drawing heavily on ideas of interactivity.

To recall, a dependent view of the relationship regards corrective operations as aiming to restore, and therefore dependent upon, the original distribution. However, a dependent view runs into difficulty explaining the result in cases where the injury exceeds the distribution or where need, entitlement or natural rights are said to override the distribution.[64] Similarly, an independent view of the relationship has problems accounting for outcomes that are not entirely corrective. This is because there are many instances where recovery is limited or not recognized at all.[65]

Both dependent and independent views have the added shortcoming that they fail to cohere with the generally accepted view of distributive justice as "dynamic" and corrective justice as "static."[66] In particular, the idea inherent in a dependent view that corrective justice reestablishes the

[64] For example natural rights theories of corrective justice have been proposed by Ernest Weinrib, *The Idea of Private Law* 72 (Harvard University Press, Cambridge; 1995) and Peter Benson, "The Basis of Corrective Justice and Its Relation to Distributive Justice" (1992) 77 *Iowa L. R.* 515 at 515-16.

[65] John Murphy refers to a number of wrongs in English tort law, where reparative damages show considerable divergence from the corrective ideal, such as in cases where the only remedies are in the nature of "licence fee" damages (i.e. calculated on the basis of what the defendant obtained), where damages may be expressly forbidden or where injunctive relief is the only remedy available. See John Murphy, "The Heterogeneity of Tort Law" 39 *O.J.L.S.* 455 at 476*ff* (2019).

[66] Stephen Perry, "On the Relationship between Corrective and Distributive Justice" in Jeremy Horder (ed.), *Oxford Essays in Jurisprudence: Fourth Series* 237 at 247 (Oxford University Press, Oxford; 2000) ("if we accept the premise that distributive justice is best understood *dynamically rather than statically*, corrective justice should be understood as independent moral principle that operates within the context of distributive justice, but not as part of it." [emphasis added]). Steven Walt, "Eliminating Corrective Justice" 92:7 *Virginia. L. Rev.* 1311 at 1317 (2006) ("[c]orrective justice's duty of repair *is static*; it requires compensation for a wrongful harm that has occurred. Distributive justice *is dynamic*; it is concerned with the distribution of resources and liberties over the entire life of individuals, not at any point within their lives." [emphasis added]).

original distribution presupposes a fixed distribution and a fixed instance of correction.

To resolve these problems, an interdependent view of the relationship embedded in a communitarian theory maintains that distributive and corrective justice are related to and depend upon each other but not always in the fixed way that either dependent or independent views assert. Instead, the exact relationship between distributive and corrective depends on the conception of the good and the "choice among varying conceptions of the plaintiff's entitlement." As Hanoch Dagan has explained, "this choice ... is a normative choice that implicates the prevailing background ethos of the society at issue and is deeply influenced by the society's complex conceptions of self and of community."[67]

The interdependent view I put forward here draws on ideas of interactivity to suggest that distributive justice sets the general terms on which corrective justice takes place but also maintains that "static" instances of correction prescribe, and reflexively shape, "dynamic" ideas about the appropriate distribution. The pattern of influence observed between the two forms of justice *is therefore reciprocal*. This reciprocity is expressed in relations of correlation, subordination, transition, and integration between justice of both forms. Here some additional explanation is necessary.

First, there is the idea that distributive justice and corrective justice are *correlative*. Where there is one, there will be a perceived need for the other (i.e. Distributive Justice/Corrective Justice).

A second relation between distributive justice and corrective justice is one of *subordination* (i.e. Distributive Justice > Corrective Justice). That is, in the normal course distributive justice will be primary, whereas corrective justice will be secondary. Hence, what will be recouped in any reparative operation will tend to be whatever the community deems is appropriate, not what is necessarily mathematically equal to the plaintiff's loss. The usual inclination is to discount corrective operations in recognition of the communal cost of correction.[68]

A third relation is the notion that at their extremities the idea of equality operationalized through distributive justice tends to *transition* into fairness positions operationalized through corrective justice, and

[67] Dagan, "The Distributive Foundations of Corrective Justice" 140.

[68] See ARSIWA Arts. 34–37; Murphy, "The Heterogeneity of Tort Law" 476*ff.*

similarly, that fairness positions and corrective justice tend to generate momentum toward equality and distributive justice (i.e. Distributive Justice = Corrective Justice). The reason for the transition is that each idea and type of justice, when taken on its own, is wanting and inevitably impels consideration of its opposite. Unification drives fragmentation and vice versa. This contrapuntal movement is evidence conceptually of a "nested opposition."[69]

Finally, a fourth relation arising from a communitarian theory is one of *integration* (i.e. Distributive Justice + Corrective Justice = Transformative Justice). It returns to the idea seen earlier, namely that equality/distributive justice and fairness/corrective justice together culminate in justice that is both transformative and yet imperfect. Justice is imperfect in the sense that it is never completely just. Someone somewhere will perceive what is rendered as "justice" to be unjust. This sense of injustice will promote continuing transformation.

To be sure, within this four-fold set of relations, there is a certain general orientation dictated by distributive priority, or as Neil MacCormick put it, the fact that "what is private is not itself a private question."[70] At the same time, while a dependent or distributive priority may be visible and has natural intelligibility, this is not always so. Certain outcomes may be at odds with it, including those that may appear consistent with an independent view of the relationship. Much turns on the community's conception of the good. Accordingly, cases where the injury exceeds the distribution or where need overrides the original distribution may simply illustrate particularly compelling conceptions of the injury or need linked to the community's current conception of the good. Over time, however, that conception may change.

Once again, it is useful to recall that a communitarian theory of justice suggests that certain kinds of justice are more readily associated with the protection of certain kinds of goods than others. Specifically, distributive justice's egalitarian, inclusive, forward-looking character implies it is

[69] A nested opposition "involve[s] a relation of dependence, similarity or containment between … opposed concepts." Jack Balkin, "Nested Oppositions" 99 *Yale L.J.* 1669 at 1671 (1990). The "nested" character of the opposition implies that the "favored or dominant term bears some form of conceptual dependence to the disfavoured or subordinated term." Ibid., 1676–1677 (1990).

[70] MacCormick, *Legal Reasoning and Legal Theory* 76.

more easily understood as applicable to public goods whereas corrective justice is more easily understood as applicable to private ones.[71]

As mentioned however, that neat division can be criticized as simplistic in the sense that many goods have a hybrid character. For the purposes of legal characterization, most goods can be regarded as both public *and* private and therefore subject to a mix of distributive and corrective applications. This is manifested in the social function of goods. Untangling these to arrive at a single conclusive definition about their just arrangement is often how litigation is triggered and where transformation occurs. A sum of money may be characterized as taxes owed to government or ill-gotten gain. A home might be characterized as an illegally occupied squat or essential to human dignity. A common plant might be characterized as a traditional solvent or a patentable way of controlling invasive species.[72] Hybridism then complicates any analysis of justice in relation to goods for the purposes of a theory.

Hybridism is particularly apparent with respect to club and common goods where the full range of regulatory options is brought to bear on the issue of protecting the good in question.[73] Hybridism is especially on display in the WTO Agreement. There, the dominant aspect of the arrangement as a club good bestows upon it a distributive character associated with the protection of expectations *ex ante*. This is complemented by a subordinate aspect of the arrangement as a series of private

[71] This association is akin to the one identified by Hanoch Dagan. In a survey of US, Jewish and international law jurisprudence on restitution, Dagan's principal point is that "[r]esources are protected to differing degrees because the community regards different resources as variously constitutive of their possessor's identity." Dagan, "The Distributive Foundations of Corrective Justice" 142 (1999).

[72] The African soapberry plant (*Phytolacca dodecandra*) is traditionally cultivated in many parts of Africa as a laundry soap and shampoo. The berries of the plant are lethal to most species of snails. In 1994 the University of Toledo, Ohio, was granted a US patent on a soapberry-based molluscicide with the aim of producing a product to control the zebra mussels which had become a serious invasive species in North America's Great Lakes. An issue was whether the true "proprietors" of the soapberry plant should be justly rewarded, particularly since the discovery that gave rise to the patent took account of centuries of Indigenous knowledge in Africa. The University of Toledo was persuaded to allocate 15 percent of any royalties from the patent for schistosomiasis control in Ethiopia. See Rafi Communiqué, "Endod: A Case Study of the Use of African Indigenous Knowledge to Address Global Health and Environmental Problems" (Mar. 1993).

[73] "Law is not powerful enough by itself to switch a resource from open access to private property. Instead ... survival [of the good] depends on a constantly shifting matrix of strategies – simultaneously public and private, individual and community – and their constant renegotiation." Michael Heller, *The Gridlock Economy* 175–176 (Basic Books, New York; 2008).

goods that bestows upon it a corrective character associated with the adjustment of outcomes *ex post.*

It is the illustration of these ideas and the transformative outcomes they generate in public international and WTO law that are next examined.

3.3 The WTO Agreement and Justice

The communitarian theory of justice put forward above suggests that a legal system will be a combination of equality promoted by distributive justice and fairness promoted by corrective justice. In addition, it suggests that the system will tend to prioritize equality and distributive justice in some degree in recognition of the primacy of equality as a public value or ideal. Ultimately, however, the interaction of equality in the form of distributive justice and fairness in the form of corrective justice will resolve in transformative justice, a justice that seeks to "develop and strengthen relationships among those involved." This is for the greater purpose of sustaining the community.

To illustrate these ideas, I have chosen to focus in this section on justice in public international and WTO law. This focus will be immediately controversial both because international law is not traditionally associated with justice and because the WTO Agreement does not appear to display any explicit connection to justice.[74]

[74] The idea of international relations and law being associated with the exercise of power, not justice, is a longstanding one: Hugo Grotius, *On the Law of War and Peace* (Stephen Neff, ed., Cambridge University Press, Cambridge; 2012) (observing that in international relations "nothing is unjust that is expedient." Ibid., p. 1); Franck, *The Power of Legitimacy among Nations* 210 (noting that "[i]n the international system ... the first task for now, is to build a rule system of such manifest legitimacy as to engender a broad base of uncoerced habitual *compliance*. Lexically, the task of ensuring the *justice* of that rule system is the second, not the first order of business of the urgent, but still largely unfinished, global agenda." [emphasis is original]). Nevertheless, in the UN Charter "justice" is given some – admittedly limited – reference. Rüdiger Wolfrum notes that its express reference in the Charter's Preamble "means something different from international law, and to that extent the Preamble refers to natural law." See Bruno Simma, *The Charter of the United Nations: A Commentary* (2nd ed.) 36 (Oxford University Press, Oxford; 2002). Reference is also made to justice in UN Charter Art. 2(3) in connection with the obligation upon states to peacefully resolve disputes. There Christian Tomuschat has observed that "a tension may exist between the exigencies of law and those of justice." Simma, *The Charter of the United Nations* 111.

Nevertheless, as Frédéric Mégret points out, the fact that:

> [i]nternational law is law, not international justice . . . does not mean that justice does not emerge from states abiding by international law . . . nor does it mean that international law may not be the repository of its own, implicit theory of justice, although that theory is often not expressed as such and remains elusive.[75]

In this section I make an effort to work out what that "elusive" theory looks like, using public international law and the WTO Agreement as prototypical examples thereof. In the main, I will suggest that they reproduce the communitarian theory developed in the previous section.

As mentioned, public international law – of which WTO law is an acknowledged part – is not normally understood to be synonymous with justice. Instead, it has been said that the theory on which the international community is based is one of "social order."[76]

Nevertheless, international law acknowledges an obligation to repair wrongs. The first modern arbitral agreement, the Jay Treaty of 1794, guaranteed the payment by the United States of private debts owed by Americans to British merchants.[77]

This reparative principle was later restated in the *Chorzów Factory* case, a dispute that involved the expropriation of a German-owned fertilizer factor in Poland. In the jurisdictional phase of the *Chorzów Factory* dispute the Permanent Court of International Justice (PCIJ) observed:

> It is a principle of international law that the breach of an engagement involves an obligation to make reparation in an adequate form.

The PCIJ specified that:

> [R]eparation must, as far as possible, wipe out all the consequences of the illegal act and reestablish the situation which would, in all probability, have existed if that act had not been committed.[78]

[75] Frédéric Mégret, "Justice" in Jean d'Aspremont & Sahib Singh (eds), *Concepts for International Law* 585 at 587 (Edward Elgar, Cheltenham; 2019).

[76] Franck, *The Power of Legitimacy among Nations* 211. See also Leah Brilmayer, "International Justice and International Law" 98 *W. Va. L. Rev.* 610 (1996) (maintaining that it is easier for international law to secure international well-being (peace and prosperity) than retributive, corrective and distributive justice because international law is effective at preserving the status quo or moving to a situation that is Pareto superior to it).

[77] S.v. "The Jay Treaty" in *Max Planck Encyclopedia of Public International Law* (Apr. 2013) (author: Katja Ziegler).

[78] *Factory at Chorzów, Jurisdiction* [1927], P.C.I.J., Series A, No. 9, p. 21, para. 55.

The PCIJ held that reparation could be accomplished by restitution in kind, that is, by return of the property, or if restitution was not possible, by compensation, meaning "payment of a sum corresponding to the value which a restitution in kind would bear."[79]

The justice envisioned in *Chorzów Factory* was essentially corrective. It involved compensation equal to the loss sustained by German investors. The wrong was to be righted by correlative gain. The PCIJ's holding was aided by the nature of the good in issue, which was a factory, a private good sharply defined and fixed in time and space. Once compensation was paid, the wrong came to an end.

An associated way of looking at the recovery ultimately achieved in *Chorzów Factory* was that it was merely "fair." Due to delay and legal wrangling between the two state parties, the Court had to estimate the damage based on hypotheticals. Before it could do so, Germany and Poland settled the dispute.[80] In other words, they agreed to a sum that was "appropriate."

About the same time, the case of *The S.S. Wimbledon* came before the PCIJ and highlighted how justice in international law has a distributive aspect as well.[81] The dispute in *The S.S. Wimbledon* involved Germany's refusal to allow passage of an English vessel chartered by the Polish government through the Kiel Canal, thereby potentially breaching a commitment Germany had made to allow passage through the canal

[79] *Factory at Chorzów, Merits* [1928] P.C.I.J., Series A, No. 17, p. 47.

[80] Borzu Sabahi explains that the "full reparation" principle identified in *Chorzów Factory* "was somewhat ambiguous, because it was not clear whether it required putting the aggrieved party where he was before the occurrence of the illegal act (*status quo ante*) or where [the investor] would have been, assuming the injurious act had not occurred (a hypothetical position)." See Borzu Sabahi, *Compensation and Restitution in Investor-State Arbitration* 50 (Oxford University Press, Oxford; 2011). The PCIJ's approach ultimately based on a hypothetical position, which was either (1) that the factory would have remained in the state it was in at the time of expropriation in 1922 or (2) it would have continued its normal development from that moment until the time of an expert opinion. The court finally noted that it intended to compare the results of the two valuations conducted by an expert to ensure that a reasonable value was arrived at. This was necessary, given the relatively long time elapsed between expropriation and the experts' assessment, the transformation of the factory, and the development in the industry. The PCIJ ultimately reserved its judgment on fixing the indemnity, which was to be rendered after it had received the experts' report. Before the experts submitted their report, the parties settled the dispute. For discussion, see Sabahi, ibid., pp. 47–53 (2011).

[81] *S.S. Wimbledon* [1923] P.C.I.J. Series A, No. 1. See James Crawford, *The International Law Commission's Articles on State Responsibility: Introduction, Text and Commentaries* 24 (Cambridge University Press, Cambridge; 2002).

under the Treaty of Versailles. The English vessel was carrying armaments destined for Poland, then at war with the Soviet Union. Germany argued that to allow passage of the vessel would be a violation of its customary right of neutrality, a position the Court rejected. Four countries in the case invoked Germany's responsibility under the treaty even though at least one of them – Japan – had no specific interest in the voyage of the vessel. The Court ultimately agreed that a threat to a purely legal interest, as opposed to an injury to a material one, could give rise to state responsibility under international law.[82] The case reveals a preoccupation with equality in international law in the sense that the decision mandated that Germany return to legality by allowing passage, thereby reestablishing an equal expectation of Germany's lawful behavior among states. That distributive equality is underpinned by the equality of states, which has been labeled "an inference from the basis of international law."[83]

Modern restatements of public international law appear to recognize the existence of both distributive and corrective justice in international law. The International Law Commission's Articles on State Responsibility (ARSIWA) indicate how this duality is manifested.[84] ARSIWA Art. 30, entitled "Cessation and Non-Repetition," provides that:

> The State responsible for the internationally wrongful act is under an obligation (a) to cease that act if it is continuing; (b) to offer assurances and guarantees of non-repetition, if circumstances so require.

The accompanying ARSIWA Commentary indicates that cessation is listed first because it is "relevant to *all* wrongful acts extending in time

[82] *S.S. Wimbledon* [1923] P.C.I.J. Series A, No. 1, para. 19.

[83] Robert Jennings & Arthur Watts (eds), *Oppenheim's International Law* (9th ed.) 339 (Longman, London; 1996).

[84] The ARSIWA are far from being the sole source of insight into the nature of justice under international law – or law generally – but they enjoy a persuasive status. The decades-long manner in which they were drafted, the unanimity attending their adoption and the regard which they have elicited since then among international courts and tribunals are indicative of the respect that they deserve a statement of law and expression of justice. In interpretation of the WTO Agreement, panels and the Appellate Body have generally concluded that the ARSIWA may be "taken into account" in the sense of VCLT Art. 31(3)(c), but strictly speaking, are not binding. See *U.S. – Anti-Dumping and Countervailing Duties (China)*, WT/DS379/AB/R, para. 316 (11 Mar. 2011) ("the relevant provisions of the ILC Articles may be taken into account as one among several interpretative elements.").

'regardless of whether the conduct of a State is an action or omission.'"[85] The statement can be taken as evidence of a prioritization of distributive justice in international law since cessation of wrongdoing allows the reestablishment of an equal expectation of legality.[86] In support of this interpretation, ARSIWA Art. 30 also refers to the offer of "assurances and guarantees of non-repetition," which emphasize the law's prospective character, or in other words, the way its perspective is generalized and future-oriented.[87]

ARSIWA Art. 30 is followed by ARSIWA Art. 31, entitled "Reparation," which provides:

> 1. The responsible State is under an obligation to make full reparation for the injury caused by the internationally wrongful act.
> 2. Injury includes any damage, whether material or moral, caused by the internationally wrongful act.

ARSIWA Art. 31 is referred to in the ILC Commentary as the "*second* general obligation" arising from wrongful behavior and embodies the corrective principle at issue in *Chorzów Factory*. Public international law then contains a commitment to corrective justice operating within the broader frame of distributive justice, as intimated by the ARSIWA Rapporteur's observation that "reparation is usually not the only issue [in disputes between states] and *may not be an issue at all*."[88]

The fact that the task of correction is secondary under public international law is also implied by its conditionality. This subordination can be gleaned from the sequential way in which the various forms of reparation are arranged. These are referred to in ARSIWA Art. 34:

> Full reparation for the injury caused by the internationally wrongful act shall take the form of *restitution*, *compensation* and *satisfaction*, either singly or in combination.

[85] Draft articles on Responsibility of States for Internationally Wrongful Acts, with commentaries, U.N. Doc. A/56/10, p. 88 (2001).

[86] "The responsible State's obligation of cessation thus protects both the interests of the injured State or States and the interests of *the international community as a whole in the preservation of, and reliance on, the rule of law*." Ibid., p. 89 [emphasis added].

[87] See Christian Tams, "Recognizing Guarantees and Assurances of Non-Repetition: *LaGrand* and the Law of State Responsibility" 27:2 *Yale J. Int'l L.* 441 (2002) (by expressly recognizing guarantees and assurances of repetition as a remedy for breaches, the ICJ displayed a new openness toward a future-oriented conception of state responsibility.)

[88] James Crawford, *The International Law Commission's Articles on State Responsibility* 28 (Cambridge University Press, Cambridge; 2002) [emphasis added].

Restitution is defined in ARSIWA Art. 35 and is aimed at reestablishing "the situation which existed before the wrongful act is committed," provided that restitution "is not materially impossible" and "does not involve a burden out of all proportion to the benefit deriving from the restitution instead of compensation."[89] *Compensation* is defined in ARSIWA Art. 36 and involves "an obligation to compensate for damage ... insofar as such damage is not made good by restitution." Compensation is described as covering "any financially assessable damage including loss of profits insofar as it is established."[90] Finally, *satisfaction* is defined in ARSIWA Art. 37 as being available for injury that "cannot be made good by restitution or compensation." Satisfaction may consist of "an acknowledgment of the breach, an expression of regret, a formal apology or another appropriate modality," but "[it] shall not be out of proportion to the injury and may not take a form humiliating to the responsible State."[91] Taken together, the various forms of reparation suggest that what is available in public international law in corrective terms is merely "fair," or whatever is appropriate in the circumstances.

The ARSIWA appear to confirm the communitarian theory of justice set out above. First, the ARSIWA affirm the correlative values of equality and fairness and their link with distributive and corrective justice, respectively. The obligation of cessation referred to in ARSIWA Art. 30 is egalitarian and distributive in the sense that equality can be thought of as the metric of reestablishing bare legality. Second, cessation is also egalitarian because, as the ILC made clear, cessation applies in *all*

[89] The ILC observed that "This applies only where there is a grave disproportionality between the burden which restitution would impose on the responsible State and the benefit which would be gained, either by the injured State or by any victim of the breach." Draft articles on Responsibility of States for Internationally Wrongful Acts, with commentaries, U.N. Doc. A/56/10, p. 98 (2001).

[90] ARSIWA Art. 36(2) and discussion ibid., pp. 98–105. The ILC explained that:

> "any financially assessable damage," that is, any damage which is capable of being evaluated in financial terms. Financially assessable damage encompasses both damage suffered by the State itself (to its property or personnel or in respect of expenditures reasonably incurred to remedy or mitigate damage flowing from an internationally wrongful act) as well as damage suffered by nationals, whether persons or companies, on whose behalf the State is claiming within the framework of diplomatic protection.
>
> (Ibid. at 99).

[91] ARSIWA Art. 37(3). The ILC observed that "satisfaction is not intended to be punitive in character, nor does it include punitive damages." Ibid., p. 107.

situations of legal wrongdoing.[92] All countries have an expectation of legal behavior. Third, by comparison, reparation is an expression of fairness linked to corrective justice in that it seeks to repair injury caused by an internationally wrongful act.[93] Here, justice is particularized and primarily retrospective. While ARSIWA Art. 31(1) insists on equality ("*full* reparation for injury"), its true metric is fairness because corrective operations are conditioned by respect for sovereignty, practicality and proportionality highlighted in ARSIWA Arts. 35–37. This conditioning would appear to confirm the point concerning the prioritization of distributive justice made above (i.e. Equality/Distributive Justice > Fairness/Corrective Justice).

At the same time, the ARSIWA are predicated on the triggering idea of a "wrongful act" as either an act or omission of a discrete or continuing character. Because of this inherently limited frame, it is necessary to look a little more broadly at the nature and structure of public international law to ascertain how the interaction of distributive and corrective features of the system together demonstrate an impulse toward transformation consistent with a communitarian theory.

Commentators have observed how public international law is derived from two leading formal sources: custom and treaties. Custom is defined as the combination of state practice and *opinio juris* and, due to the fact that it is "the oldest and the original source of international law," may be likened to the broad distributive background against which treaties and other sources are interpreted.[94] By contrast, treaties are international agreements

[92] "Cessation is thus relevant to *all* wrongful acts extending in time." Ibid., p. 88.

[93] At the same time, the ILC observed that:

> there is no general requirement, over and above any requirements laid down by the relevant primary obligation, that a State should have suffered material harm or damage before it can seek reparation for breach. The existence of actual damage will be highly relevant to the form and quantum of reparation. But there is no general requirement of material harm or damage for a State to be entitled to seek some form of reparation.
>
> (Ibid., p. 92)

See also comments concerning ARSIWA Art. 48(2)(b), where responsibility is invoked by a state *other than* the injured state. The ILC observed that "[t]his aspect of [ARSIWA] Art. 48(2) involves a measure of progressive development, which is justified since it provides a means of protecting the community or collective interest at stake." Ibid., p. 127.

[94] Robert Jennings & Arthur Watts (eds), *Oppenheim's International Law* (9th ed.) 25–26 (1996).

establishing rules recognized as binding by state parties.[95] These agreements may be likened to compacts attracting corrective justice in the sense that they are often of a bilateral or plurilateral form and "contractual" in character. This two-fold division is further reflected in the nature of international legal rules, only some of which are *jus cogens* (i.e. binding rules) and therefore more customary and distributive versus the fact that most such rules are acknowledged to be *jus dispositivum* (i.e. rules that can be contracted out of) and therefore more treaty-based and contractual.[96]

How then is transformation expressed in the combination of this dual structure? Commentators recognize the way that there is a dynamic process of feedback that occurs between the sources in which instances of practice, as an element of custom, give rise to the need for treaties on various points, which in turn generate state practice, that may be regarded as transformative.[97] In this process the law is altered "by requiring parties to develop a shared understanding of some things or goods about which justice is organized." Illustration of this dynamic process is often made with reference to developments during the twentieth century in the law of the sea.[98]

95 Ibid. at 31.

96 Dire Tladi, "Codification, Progressive Development, New Law, Doctrine, and the Work of the International Law Commission on Peremptory Norms of General International Law (Jus Cogens): Personal Reflections of the Special Rapporteur" 13:6 *FIU L. Rev.* 1137 at 1142 (2019).

97 Pavel Sturma has described:

> the dynamic process of interrelation between codification and development, or custom and treaty … As is well-known, a treaty provision may codify (or be *declaratory* of) a pre-existing rule of customary international law; lead to the *crystallization* of a rule of customary international law; or give rise to (or *generating*) a new rule of customary international law.
>
> (Pavel Sturma, "The International Law Commission between Codification, Progressive Development, or a Search for a New Role" 13:6 *FIU L. Rev.* 1125 at 1133 (2019) [emphasis in original])

98 The law of the sea developed from disputes between coastal states, who sought to expand their control over marine areas adjacent to their coasts. By the end of the eighteenth century, it was understood that states had sovereignty over their territorial sea, generally extending three miles. However, in the early twentieth century, some nations expressed their desire to extend national claims: to include mineral resources, to protect fish stocks and to provide pollution controls. Applying customary international law President Truman in 1945 extended US control to all the natural resources of its continental shelf. This set off a scramble by states to extend maritime claims. Around the same time, litigation occurred pertaining the breadth of the territorial sea (*United Kingdom*

Nevertheless, as Mark Villiger has observed, the dynamic and transformative process of interaction mentioned above "also has its *demerits*: modificatory customary international law arises in a haphazard and unpredictable manner . . . Moreover, the process is slow and difficult to identify, and involves in its early stages much legal uncertainty."[99]

Still, the current structure of international law also prioritizes a desire for agreement or "shared understanding" in many ways. First, there is the machinery of UN Charter, notably in the work of the ILC concerning the progressive development and codification of international law, and the UN Economic and Social Council, which can prepare draft conventions and call international conferences on matters falling within its competence.[100] Second, there is gradual recognition of community interests in "which respect for certain fundamental values is not . . . left to the free disposition of States individually or inter se but is recognized and sanctioned by international law as a matter of concern to all States."[101] Third, there is the related phenomenon of the "constitutionalization" of international law, which by its very emergence suggests that international

v. *Norway* [1951] ICJ 3) and certain other aspects of maritime delimitation (*Germany* v. *Denmark*; *Germany* v. *Netherlands* [1969] ICJ 3), highlighting the need for comprehensive agreement on a variety of points related to the law of the sea. Three UN-sponsored conferences in 1958, 1960 and 1973–1982 culminated in the UN Convention on the Law of the Sea (UNCLOS), 1833 U.N.T.S. 397 (1982), which includes a standard definition of maritime zones. Most of UNCLOS is now generally considered to be a reflection of customary international law, but maritime claims between states continue to proliferate, particularly in the area of straight baselines and coastal state jurisdiction in the EEZ.

99 Mark Villiger, *Customary Law and Treaties* 221 (Kluwer Law International, The Hague; 1997) [emphasis in original]. To address this uncertainty, commentators such as Anthea Roberts have suggested interpretative techniques prioritizing certain sources in specific instances which themselves have been criticized as selective. They depend on the speaker's interpretative choice, not necessarily the objective choices or behavior of states. For discussion see Hugh Thirlway, *The Sources of International Law* 225–229 (Oxford University Press, Oxford; 2014).

100 Claire Breen, "The Necessity of a Role for the ECOSOC in the Maintenance of International Peace and Security" 12:2 *J. Conflict & Security L.* 261 (2007); Thomas Weiss, "ECOSOC and the MDGs: What Can Be Done?" in Rorden Wilkinson & David Hulme (eds), *The Millennium Development Goals and Beyond* 117 (Routledge, New York; 2012).

101 Bruno Simma, "From Bilateralism to Community Interest in International Law" 250 *Recueil des Cours* 217 at 233 (1994).

law has achieved a degree of objectivity in order to limit state sovereignty in ways reminiscent of a classic constitutional order.[102]

Both of these latter developments, in particular, infer that while countries may reach transformative outcomes in the resolution of disputes there will be limits on the degree in which they can do so, notably in the form of *jus cogens* norms and considerations of human rights.[103] These latter sources infer that against the broader distributive background of the common interest there will be played out more limited corrective actions emphasizing individual interests.

Hence, the perennial tension between collective and individual interests identified in a communitarian theory of justice can be said to exhibit in public international law. Perennial relations of correlation are evident in the way that distributive considerations inevitably give rise to corrective ones so that the two exhibit separately in apparent parallel. Similarly, subordination is evident in the way that the maintenance of legality takes priority over efforts at reparation. Transition is also evident in the way that corrective impulses are detected at the outer boundaries or edges of distribution and vice versa. Finally, integration manifests itself in a continuing desire for international law to achieve justice, even if this justice is merely "thin" in Steven Ratner's use of the term and does not fully replicate "thicker" domestic conceptions and accounts.[104]

[102] See Jan Klabbers et al., *The Constitutionalization of International Law* (Oxford University Press, Oxford; 2009).

[103] Furthermore, the relation of transition is visible in the way that specific verdicts or outcomes under public international law can lead to reactions and counter-action against them. For example, in *Kadi* v. *Council and Commission*, C-402/05 P and C-415/05 P (3 Sept. 2008), the issue involved the UN Security Council's imposition of sanctions under Chapter VII of the UN Charter against individuals allegedly associated with Osama bin Laden, the Al Qaeda network and the Taliban. To give effect to the SC resolutions, the EU Council adopted a regulation ordering the freezing of the assets of those on the list, which included Yassin Kadi, a resident of Saudi Arabia with assets in the EU. Kadi argued that his fundamental rights to judicial review were denied by his summary placement on the freeze list. The European Court of Justice allowed Kadi's appeal on the basis that the regulation denied minimal protection of human rights. The European Court of Justice's decision eventually resulted in the creation in 2009 of a Ombuds position for the Security Council Al-Qaida Sanctions Committee, whose mandate has been extended several times. See www.un.org/securitycouncil/ombudsperson. Similar transformative outcomes are visible in the development of international investment law, examined in Chapter 7.

[104] Steven Ratner, *The Thin Justice of International Law* 408 (Oxford University Press, Oxford; 2015) (accepting the continuing centrality of states in the global system, and with this in mind, proposing a standard of global justice that sees international law

Here, however, insight from the communitarian theory developed earlier in this chapter can be illuminating in at least two respects. One is that the incompleteness of justice in international law needs to be understood in light of the specific community and good in question – a community in which corrective justice in the form of reparation "is usually not the only issue and may not be an issue at all."[105]

The other insight is that no system of justice is ever entirely complete or "perfect." Ever-changing conditions and ideas of the good mean that the law must remain open to transformation.

In what follows these same basic ideas are traced in the operation and results of WTO dispute settlement.

3.3.1 Distributive Justice

Under GATT 1947, there was no express remedy for wrongful behavior.[106] GATT Art. XXIII:2 simply states that where there is a finding of "nullification or impairment," the GATT membership can investigate and "make appropriate recommendations to the contracting parties which they consider to be concerned." In addition, where the circumstances are considered "serious enough to justify such action, [the membership] may authorize a contracting party or parties to suspend the application to any other contracting party or parties of such concessions or other obligations under this Agreement as they determine to be appropriate in the circumstances."

What arose in GATT history in situations of a finding of violation was the practice of making a "recommendation" to the offending country to bring its measure "into conformity" with GATT. The formula was vague enough that countries might do a number of things in response.[107] However, the common understanding came to be that a recommendation

norms as just to the extent that they advance peace and do not interfere with basic human rights).

105 Crawford, *The International Law Commission's Articles on State Responsibility* 28.

106 Petros Mavroidis, "Remedies in the WTO Legal System: Between a Rock and a Hard Place" 11:4 *E.J.I.L.* 763 at 774 (2000) (noting that neither GATT 1947 nor the side codes "contained any specific provisions dealing with remedies in cases of violation. This was not an anomaly. . . . it often happens that drafters of a treaty do not regulate this matter. It is left to the discretion of the adjudicating body to recommend the appropriate remedy.").

107 A few GATT panel reports showed considerable creativity in their remedial observations. For instance, in *Jamaica – Margins of Preference*, B.I.S.D. 18th Supp. 183 (2 Feb. 1971), the question was the appropriate date for calculation of Jamaica's margins of preference.

inferred withdrawal of the inconsistent measure.[108] Withdrawal is the equivalent of cessation spelled out in ARSIWA Art. 30 and is fundamentally distributive. Cessation allows for the reestablishment of the expectation of conformity.

Nevertheless, the specific wording of GATT Art. XXIII:2, notably the phrase "*appropriate* recommendations," suggested other potential courses of action, including that of corrective justice identified as part of the obligation of reparation in ARSIWA Art. 31.

In *U.S. – Dairy Products*, for instance, the Netherlands was authorized by a GATT panel to take counteraction against US restrictions on Dutch dairy exports.[109] The counteraction was limited in several ways. First, retaliation was authorized only after time-consuming procedures within GATT that lasted several months and was only prospective, meaning it

GATT Art. 1:4 established a date in April 1947, a time when Jamaica was a colony of Britain. However, Jamaica became independent in August 1962. The panel agreed that:

> it was important to find a solution which, on the one hand, would not lead to a strained interpretation of the General Agreement and which would leave the General Agreement intact, but which, on the other hand, would take into account the uniqueness of the Jamaican case ... The Panel therefore suggests that in the light of the exceptional circumstances the CONTRACTING PARTIES consider taking a decision ... to change with respect to Jamaica the base date referred to in paragraph 1 of Article 4 from 10 August 1947 to 1 August 1962.
>
> (Ibid., para. 13–15)

See also *EEC – Dessert Apples*, B.I.S.D. 36th Supp. 93 (22 June 1989). In that case, Chile sought compensation related to nonviolation nullification or impairment. Chile argued that compensation was appropriate since of the other possible recommendations – withdrawal of the restrictions or retaliatory withdrawal of concessions – one was meaningless as the measures had lapsed and the other was undesirable as a last resort. Chile requested the panel make a finding of retroactive prejudice, something the panel refused to do since there was no straightforward way for the quantum of damage to be determined between the parties. See World Trade Organization, *GATT Analytical Index*, Vol. II (6th ed.) 682–683 (World Trade Organization, Geneva; 1995).

108 Thus, the Report of the Review Session Working Party on "Organizational and Functional Questions" noted that "the first objective, if the CONTRACTING PARTIES decided, in the event of a complaint under Article XXIII, that certain measures were inconsistent with provisions of the Agreement, should be to secure withdrawal of the measures." BISD 3rd Supp. 231, 251, para. 64 (5–7 Mar. 1955). The 1962 panel report on *Uruguayan Recourse to Art. XXIII* observed that: "Where a measure affecting imports is maintained clearly in contradiction with the provisions of the General Agreement ..., the Panel has in all cases recommended that the measure in question be removed." B.I.S.D. 11th Supp. 95, para. 20 (16 Nov. 1962).

109 *Netherlands – Suspension of Obligations*, B.I.S.D. 1st Supp. 32 (1953).

did not cover injury sustained before the authorization. Second, the right to retaliate was restricted to action by the Netherlands, a small market for US agricultural exports. Consequently, the retaliatory impact of the Netherlands' counteraction was minimal.[110] Third, the authorization had to be renewed annually, something that repeatedly exposed the Netherlands to the threat of a US veto.[111] Fourth, the authorization required sectoral correspondence. The Netherlands was only allowed to retaliate against products in the same sector as the dairy products that were the subject of the original complaint.[112] After six years of authorization, the Netherlands' retaliation was allowed to lapse at the first sign of amendment of the US legislation.[113]

The restricted experience with retaliation in *U.S. – Dairy Products* and other cases under GATT 1947 reflects the way the GATT dispute settlement system was predominantly distributive in nature, itself a reflection of the club good that the treaty's concessions created.

Some idea of its dominant distributive orientation was also conveyed in limited experience with attempts at corrective remedies prescribed by certain panels under GATT-era "side codes." Beginning with *New Zealand – Finnish Transformers*, four adopted and four unadopted GATT panel reports examining either antidumping or countervailing duties recommended reimbursement or refund of duties collected.[114]

110 The Netherlands never enforced the quota, likely because of the perception that it would be ineffective in securing removal of the noncompliant US legislation. See Robert Hudec, "Retaliation against Unreasonable Foreign Trade Practices" 59 *Minn. L. Rev.* 461 at 507 (1975).

111 Under GATT rules virtually all decision-making, as a practical matter, was by consensus. The United States could therefore have vetoed the Netherlands' request for authorization. See Robert Hudec, *Enforcing International Trade Law* 8 (Butterworths Legal Publishers, Salem, NH; 1993).

112 Robert Hudec, *The GATT Legal System and World Trade Diplomacy* 181 (Butterworths Legal Publishers, Salem, NH; 1990).

113 Ibid., p. 197.

114 Eight GATT panels involving the examination of either antidumping or countervailing duties considered that it was within their powers to recommend reimbursement or refund of duties collected: see *New Zealand – Electrical Transformers from Finland*, L/5814, B.I.S.D. 32nd Supp. 55 (adopted 18 July 1985); *U.S. – Frozen Pork from Canada*, DS7/R, B.I.S.D. 38 Supp. 30 (adopted 11 July 1991); *U.S. – Softwood Lumber from Canada*, SCM/162, B.I.S.D. 40 Supp. 358 (adopted 27 Oct. 1993); *U.S. – Salmon from Norway*, ADP/87 (adopted 27 Apr. 1994); *Canada – Manufacturing Beef from the EEC*, SCM/85 (issued 13 Oct. 1987) (not adopted); *U.S. – Stainless Steel Hollow Products from Sweden*, ADP/47 (issued 20 Aug. 1990) (not adopted); *U.S. – Gray Portland Cement and Cement Clinker from Mexico*, ADP/82 (issued 7 Sept. 1992) (not adopted); *EC – Audio Tapes in Cassettes Originating in Japan*, ADP/136 (issued 28 Apr. 1995) (not adopted).

However, the panels' directions were only partly corrective since repayment did not undo the damage caused to trade itself. These decisions elicited controversy among the GATT membership and in a number of instances were vetoed by the party to whom they were addressed.[115]

In one further case, *Norway – Toll Collection*,[116] the United States brought a complaint against Norway under the GATT-era Government Procurement Agreement (GPA) for Norway's failure to follow appropriate bid procedures in the award of a toll road construction contract. The essence of the US complaint involved a breach of an opportunity to bid. The panel agreed with the US complaint but felt confined to recommend that Norway "take … measures necessary to ensure that the entities listed in the Norwegian Annex to the [GPA] conduct government procurement in accordance with the above findings [in future]."[117] In giving its reasons, the panel observed:

> The only way mentioned during the Panel's proceedings that Norway could bring the Trondheim procurement [contract] into line with its obligations under the Agreement would be by annulling the contract and recommencing the procurement process. The Panel did not consider it appropriate to make such a recommendation. Recommendations of this nature had not been within customary practice in dispute settlement under the GATT system and the drafters of the Agreement on Government Procurement had not made specific provision that such recommendations be within the task assigned to panels under standard terms of reference. Moreover, the Panel considered that in the case under examination such a recommendation might be disproportionate, involving waste of resources and possible damage to the interests of third parties.[118]

Because the toll road had been built by the time the litigation was complete, there was no effective remedy in simply asking Norway to "withdraw" legal measures. *Norway – Government Procurement* made clear the shortcomings of distributive remedies under the GATT system.

For discussion, see Ernst-Ulrich Petersmann, "International Competition Rules for the GATT/WTO World Trade and Legal System" 27 *J. World Trade* 35 (1993); Edwin Vermulst & Norio Komuro, "Antidumping Disputes in the WTO: Navigating Dire Straits" 31 *J. World Trade* 5 at 25–31 (1997).

115 The United States used its refusal to comply in two instances to press for new, stronger antidumping and countervailing duty disciplines later incorporated in the WTO ADA.

116 B.I.S.D. 40th Supp. 319 (28 Apr. 1992).

117 Ibid., para. 5.2.

118 Ibid., para. 4.17.

Unsatisfactory experience with corrective remedies under GATT 1947 thus had a direct impact on negotiations concerning the WTO DSU. The wording of DSU Art. 19 now reads:

Article 19
Panel and Appellate Body Recommendations

1. Where a panel or the Appellate Body concludes that a measure is inconsistent with a covered agreement, it shall recommend that the Member concerned bring the measure into conformity with that agreement. In addition to its recommendations, the panel or Appellate Body may suggest ways in which the Member concerned could implement the recommendations.
2. In accordance with paragraph 2 of Article 3, in their findings and recommendations, the panel and Appellate Body cannot add to or diminish the rights and obligations provided in the covered agreements.

WTO members wanted to avoid corrective remedies.[119] Consequently, DSU Art. 19 does not indicate any obligation of reparation as specified in ARSIWA Art. 31. Instead, the focus is on a recommendation that "the Member concerned bring the measure *into conformity*." This phrase is understood to require reestablishing legality, thereby fulfilling the obligation of cessation of wrongdoing set out in ARSIWA Art. 30. Accordingly, the remedy inherent in DSU Art. 19 would appear to be primarily distributive.

Other aspects of the DSU confirm this conclusion. Member countries are left in the first instance to determine how they will implement recommendations. It is now a well-established principle that "choosing the means of implementation is, and should be, the prerogative of the implementing Member."[120] However, in a number of instances solutions have been negotiated to disputes, suggesting significant flexibility in

[119] "The bar on awarding retrospective remedies is an enforcement-discouraging device that was installed at the behest of the United States. ... By allowing only prospective remedies under the DSU, the United States could rest assured that it would not need to refund illegally imposed antidumping duties." Thomas Sebastian, "World Trade Organization Remedies and the Assessment of Proportionality: Equivalence and Appropriateness" 48:2 *Harv. Int'l L.J.* 337 at 348–349 (2007). The ultimate form of DSU Art. 19 suggests instead a general concern within the WTO membership about expansive remedies tied to the vision of a forward-oriented, and at the same time relatively constrained, dispute settlement system.

[120] *Korea – Alcoholic Beverages*, WT/DS75/16, para. 45 (4 June 1999); *Canada – Pharmaceutical Patents*, WT/DS114/13, para. 40 (18 Aug. 2000); *Chile – Price Band System*, WT/DS207/13, para. 32 (17 Mar. 2003).

bringing disputes to an end.[121] Because of the passive way in which the WTO dispute settlement system functions, the law and its ascription of wrongdoing frequently remain negotiable in the image of a "contract."

The possibility of negotiated compensation is also provided for in DSU Art. 22.1. It states, "compensation and the suspension of concessions or other obligations are temporary measures available in the event that the recommendations and rulings are not implemented within a reasonable period of time." DSU Art. 22.1 goes on to make clear, however, that "neither compensation nor the suspension of concessions or other obligations is preferred to full implementation" and also that compensation is "voluntary and, if granted, shall be consistent with the covered agreements." The limited experience with compensation under the DSU suggests that it is prospective, that is, going forward from the date of the panel's determination of noncompliance.

Nevertheless, compensation has rarely been negotiated with respect to WTO disputes. It raises troubling issues of calculation and inequality in the sense that only some countries have the means to pay for their breaches. Where compensation has been agreed, it appears to be largely symbolic. In *U.S. – Copyright*, for instance, a panel found that a US law exempting certain small businesses from paying copyright fees contravened TRIPS Agreement Art. 9.1.[122] The complainant EC and United States submitted the question of quantum to arbitration, which determined nullification or impairment of $1.1 million annually. A single three-year payment was made by the United States into a fund run by a European performing rights collective.[123] More recently in *U.S. –*

121 For a partial list of such settlements, see WorldTradeLaw.Net – Summary of Complaints and Resolution, available at www.WorldTradeLaw.Net. See also Joel Trachtman, "The WTO Cathedral" 43 *Stanford J. Int'l L.* 127 (2007) for a discussion of WTO norms as approximating either "property" or "liability" rules. In the case of a property rule, law is considered mandatory and actors are not permitted to violate it. In a liability rule, actors are entitled to violate a rule and incur liability. "The owner of the entitlement that is protected by a mere liability rule cannot object to the action, but must accept the payment of damages." Ibid., pp. 146–147. Trachtman observes that "the WTO legal system is best characterized as employing a liability rule, rather than a property rule." Ibid.

122 WT/DS160/R (15 June 2000).

123 In April 2003, Congress appropriated $3.3 million for a "one-time only, lump-sum payment" to the EU to cover a three-year period of nullification and impairment of benefits in the dispute. See H. Rept. 108–76 at 33, 92. Approval of the payment was intended as a "one-time only" funding measure and the relevant report stated that "[t]here is a long-established practice of using suspension of tariff concessions to resolve trade disputes and the Committee does not intend to appropriate funds to settle these

Upland Cotton, Brazil and the United States agreed to two successive payments of $147.1 million per year in compensation for damage sustained by Brazilian farmers from certain US agricultural subsidies, followed by a one-time payment of $300 million to finally settle the dispute in 2014. As in the *Copyright* case, the payments were made to a private body, a Brazilian agricultural research institute.[124] The beneficiaries in these cases may appear curious. The direction to a nongovernmental organization in each instance may be a way of subtly deflecting state responsibility while minimizing the spectacle of temporary noncompliance.[125]

The possibility of retaliation as a "last resort" is provided for in DSU Art. 22. It allows a successful complainant to selectively close its markets to goods or services from noncompliant defendant countries when noncompliance is determined to continue. Retaliation can be understood as a manifestation of distributive justice with certain corrective overtones in that it functions as a partial exclusion from the community. In essence, the defendant is barred from enjoying the benefit of the WTO Agreement's "good" during the authorized period. Retaliation is supposed to take place in the same sector as the infringement, hence rules on the sectoral correspondence provided for in DSU Art. 22.3. In addition, DSU Art. 22.4 provides that "[t]he level of suspension of concessions or

matters." H. Rept. 108–221 at 65. In addition, the Committee "cautions U.S. negotiators that there should be no commitments made within trade agreements to use funds from the U.S. Treasury that have neither been requested nor appropriated to resolve trade disputes." Ibid. For discussion, see Gene M. Grossman & Petros Mavroidis, "Dispute Settlement Corner: United States – Section 110(5) of the U.S. Copyright Act, Recourse to Arbitration under Article 25 of the DSU: Would've or Should've? Impaired Benefits due to Copyright Infringement" 2(2) *World Trade Review* 233 (2003); Bernard O'Connor & Margareta Djordjevic, "Practice Aspects of Monetary Compensation: The U.S. – Copyrights Case" 8(1) *J.I.E.L.* 127 (2005).

124 For details, see "U.S., Brazil Settle WTO Cotton Dispute; Deal Includes $300 Million Payment" 32:39 *Inside U.S. Trade* (3 Oct. 2014). As part of the settlement, Brazil also agreed to a "peace clause" under which it would refrain from launching new WTO challenges of US cotton subsidy programs through September 2018 and also would not challenge the specific subsidy program in question, known as GSM 102, as long as the United States adhered to the new agreed disciplines for the program.

125 In this respect, they may be considered akin to the payment of certain diplomatic claims made on the basis of *ex gratia* payments without admission of responsibility. For example, the ILC referred to the United States–China agreement providing for an *ex gratia* payment of US $4.5 million, to be given to the families of those killed and to those injured in the bombing of the Chinese Embassy in Belgrade on 7 May 1999, Sean Murphy (ed.), "Contemporary Practice of the United States – State Responsibility for Injury to Aliens: *Ex Gratia* Payment for Bombing of Chinese Embassy in Belgrade" 94:1 *A.J.I.L.* 127 (Jan. 2000). See ILC ARSIWA Commentary, p. 101, n. 533.

other obligations authorized by the DSB shall be *equivalent* to the level of nullification or impairment."

Much attention has been devoted to retaliation under the DSU. The option of retaliatory countermeasures is emblematic of a legal system "with teeth" and has been widely commented upon as a point of comparison and possible imitation by other systems of international law.[126] Still, the general impression from experience with retaliatory action under the DSU is mixed. In almost every case, the amount of retaliation authorized has been considerably below the initial estimates put forward by claimant countries – in essence amounting to "fairness" – and the dispute has been settled.[127] At the same time, compliance with the results of dispute settlement is considered to be reasonably good, meaning the specific contribution of relatively rare instances of retaliation to the system is hard to discern.[128]

Retaliation in WTO law also raises a number of problems. Several commentators have pointed out how its actual workings are unjust by,

126 Georges Abi-Saab, "The WTO Dispute Settlement and General International Law" in Rufus Yerxa & Brian Wilson (eds), *Key Issues in WTO Dispute Settlement: The First Ten Years* 9 (Cambridge University Press, Cambridge; 2005).

127 William J. Davey, "Compliance Problems in WTO Dispute Settlement" 42:1 *Cornell Int'l L.J.* 119 (2009) ("In general, the WTO dispute settlement system has an excellent compliance record. A recent examination of the implementation record of WTO decisions for the first ten years of WTO dispute settlement found a compliance rate of 83%."); Arie Reich, "The Effectiveness of the WTO Dispute Settlement System: A Statistical Analysis," EUI Working Papers Law 2017/11:

> During the time period that was examined (1995–2015) there were 38 suspension requests submitted to the DSB. Using suspension requests as a proxy for noncompliance (based on the reasonable assumption that if a losing member state fails to comply, the prevailing state will submit a suspension request), this indicates a total compliance rate of about 80%. On the one hand, this is not a bad rate and explains why member state have confidence in the system and use it often. On the other hand, 20% non-compliance is not an insignificant percentage, in particular when ... it is not proportionally distributed among all member states.
>
> (Ibid. at 18)

Pavan S. Krishnamurthy, "To Enforce or Manage: An Analysis of WTO Compliance" 32:3 *Emory Int'l L. Rev.* 377 (2018) ("In terms of generalizability, the DSB has been hailed as one of the most successful international legal regimes due to its compliance mechanism.").

128 Bruce Wilson, "The WTO Dispute Settlement System and Its Operation: A Brief Overview of the First 10 Years" in Rufus Yerxa & Bruce Wilson (eds), *Key Issues in the WTO Dispute Settlement: The First Ten Years* 25 (2005); John Magnus, "Compliance with WTO Dispute Settlement Decisions: Is There a Crisis?," ibid. at 242.

for example, being problematic for many small and developing countries with limited capacity to retaliate, by being economically inefficient and inconsistent with trade promotion, by harming innocent parties through trade disruption and diversion, and by allowing for substantial delays in implementation that tend to discourage timely compliance.[129]

Moreover, in at least two high-profile cases, the outcome of retaliation ended in settlements that belied the idea of a clear winner. In *EC – Bananas III* a number of Latin American countries challenged the EC's differential tariffs on imports of bananas, litigation that temporarily authorized countermeasures of $201.6 million by Ecuador against the EC. While the litigation did ultimately benefit the complainants, Ecuador never invoked the authorized countermeasures and the inconsistency of the EU's banana tariff with WTO law continued in various forms until 2017.[130] In *EC – Hormones*, a dispute involving a prohibition on imports of hormone-treated beef, the United States and Canada were authorized

[129] See Bryan Mercurio, "Retaliatory Trade Measures in the WTO Dispute Settlement Understanding: Are There Really Alternatives?" in Hamid Beladi & E. Kwan Choi (eds), *Frontiers of Economics and Globalization (Vol. 6) – Trade Disputes and the Dispute Settlement Understanding of the WTO* 407–410 (Emerald Group Publishing, London; 2009).

[130] The WTO *Bananas* dispute proceeded in several phases. In February 1996, a group of four Central and South American banana exporting countries, together with the United States, requested consultations with the EC over a 1993 EC regulation for the importation, sale and distribution of bananas. The complainants estimated they were losing $147 million annually because of the regulation, which gave preferential access in the EC market to bananas grown in Lomé Convention countries. The dispute resulted in litigation in the WTO, where the 1993 regulation was found to be WTO-inconsistent. As a result, both Ecuador and the United States were eventually authorized to apply countermeasures against the EC in the amounts of $201.6 million and $191.2 million annually, respectively. Ecuador complained that due to the profile of its economy and reliance on many inputs from the EC, it could not successfully apply countermeasures, whereas the United States, with a more varied economy, could and did retaliate. However, in 2001 both Ecuador and the United States settled their differences with the E.U. through a U.S. – EU Banana Agreement in 2009 and waivers of WTO obligations that allowed the EU to reserve a fixed quantity of bananas exclusively for African, Caribbean and Pacific countries (ACP). For the benefits of this outcome for Ecuador and other developing countries, see Chad Bown, *Self-Enforcing Trade: Developing Countries and WTO Dispute Settlement* 59–60 (Brookings Institution Press, Washington; 2009). Nevertheless, due to the persistence of a differential banana tariff in the EU and set-asides for ACP producers, there continued to be dissatisfaction with the EU's import regime. The Agreement introduced a tariff-only EU banana import regime in the period 2009–2017 for ten Latin American countries. In the meantime certain duty- and quota-free access to the EU market by ACP producers continued under EU-ACP preferential agreements covered by GATT Art. XXIV.

to retaliate against the EC in the amount of $116.8 million and $9.7 million per year, respectively, authorizations that ended in settlement, with the parties negotiating to permit continuing noncompliance by the EC. The *Hormones* dispute has been noted for the way that it raised the profile of EU attitudes to hormone-treated meat.[131] As of the time of writing, there are strong indications that the two-decade-long *Airbus–Boeing* dispute over aircraft subsidies between the EC and the United States is headed in the direction of settlement as well.[132]

In addition, in a few notable instances, litigants have engaged in mirror image claims against each other in an obvious bid to secure negotiating leverage toward "stalemate" and eventual compromise.[133] Practice has tended to blunt retaliation as a factor in and of itself so that countries, though authorized to invoke countermeasures, have become reluctant to do so.

As time has gone on and the "last resort" of the dispute settlement system has become less popular, its purpose has become less self-evident. This sentiment was expressed by an arbitral panel in *U.S. – Offset Act (Byrd Amendment)*:

> The DSU does not expressly explain the purpose behind the authorization of the suspension of concessions or other obligations. On the one hand, the general obligation to comply with DSB recommendations and rulings seems to imply that suspension of concessions or other obligations is intended to induce compliance, as has been acknowledged by previous arbitrators. However, exactly what may induce compliance is likely to vary in each case, in the light of a number of factors including, but not limited to, the level of suspension of obligations authorized.[134]

[131] Renée Johnson, "The U.S.-EU Beef Hormone Dispute," *CRS Report for Congress* R40449 (6 Dec. 2010); Cinnamon Carlarne, "From the U.S.A. with Love" 37 *Enviro. L.* 301 (2007).

[132] In June 2021, the United States and EU agreed to a framework that would suspend for five years all tariffs levied in the Airbus-Boeing disputes, establish a trans-Atlantic working group on aircraft, improve subsidy transparency and provide a platform to cooperate on a joint approach to competing against China's aircraft sector. See Hannah Monicken, "U.S., EU Ink Framework on Tariffs, Set up Working Group in Aircraft Dispute" 39:24 *Inside U.S. Trade* 1 (18 June 2021). The transformative aspect of the framework was highlighted: "U.S., UK Set to Launch New 'Atlantic Charter' Touching on Trade" 39:23 *Inside U.S. Trade* 3 (11 June 2021) (noting that leaders of the two countries would "discuss ways of further enhancing our economic relationship, including through a resolution to the civil aircraft dispute.")

[133] See for instance the Canada–Brazil aircraft disputes and the EU–U.S. (Airbus/Boeing) aircraft disputes, WT/DS316, WT/DS317 and 353.

[134] *US – Offset Act (Byrd Amendment)*, WT/234/ARB/CAN, para. 6.2 (31 Aug. 2004).

The result has been that, instead of endless rounds of retaliation, countries have generally sought to settle their differences under the WTO Agreement transformatively, a phenomenon examined later in this chapter.

3.3.2 *Corrective Justice*

The idea of corrective justice is based on correlativity, or in other words, a one-to-one relationship between the injured party and the wrongdoer.[135] Corrective justice is a hard fit in the WTO Agreement, whose structure, as seen, involves obligations undertaken by one member country toward the WTO membership as a whole. This general orientation is underlined by the frequent observation that what the WTO Agreement protects in the main is competitive opportunities in the future, not trade interrupted with specific trading partners in the past.[136]

Nevertheless, the concept of correlativity has important consequences for the nature of corrective justice in WTO law. First, correlatively orients the law toward the past since it is in the past that correlativity can be isolated from the pattern of relationships and the injury can be corrected by means of correlative adjustment. Second, correlatively is associated with fairness since each corrective operation must be tailored to the circumstances yet made harmonious with other such operations in a way that safeguards the integrity of the legal system, hence the subtle limitative aspect of corrective action.[137] Third, correlatively is associated with rights since it is the plaintiff's individual interest that is the primary focus of vindication. This is as opposed to the broader "public" interest and obligations at issue in distributive justice.

135 Weinrib, "Corrective Justice in a Nutshell" LII:4 *U.T.L.J.* 349 at 351 (2002).

136 For example, see *Japan – Alcoholic Beverages II*, WT/DS8/AB/R at p. 16 (4 Oct. 1996); *US – FSC (Art. 21.5 – US)*, WT/DS108/AB/R, para. 215 (14 Jan. 2002).

137
> Full compensation is an appealing goal, but it is not one that the law of remedies must necessarily fulfill. The available remedial means of ensuring full compensation, such as injunction, specific performance and restitution, are issued at a price, not just to the defendant but also to the community, and thus their imposition constitutes a transfer from third parties to the victims of harm ... The question over whether to provide full compensation is not a matter of corrective justice, which is remedial law's concern, but of distributive justice, and ought to be considered as such.
>
> (Standen, "The Fallacy of Full Compensation" 225)

There are two areas of WTO law where a corrective aspect is most visible: WTO rules disciplines (safeguards, antidumping and countervailing duties) and countermeasures under DSU Art. 22. In this section I will deal with these two topics sequentially.

WTO "rules" impose disciplines on member countries' exercise of the right to take action in response to certain trade-related contingencies. These rights are principally the right to counter "emergency" circumstances in trade (as provided for in GATT Art. XIX and the WTO Agreement on Safeguards (SAF)), the dumping of goods (as provided for in GATT Art. VI and the WTO Antidumping Agreement (ADA)), and imports of subsidized goods (as provided for in GATT Arts. VI, XVI and the WTO Agreement on Subsidies and Countervailing Measures (SCM)).

These WTO rules generally require action, injury and the finding of a causal connection between the proscribed act and injury before a market can be closed in response. In normal circumstances the rules mandate an investigation prior to any corrective action.[138] In the case of safeguards, for instance, the investigation must determine whether there are increased imports resulting from "unforeseen developments" and whether there is a causal connection between the imports and the harm complained of according to a standard of "serious injury."[139] In the case of antidumping, the investigation covers the alleged dumping in question, the standard of injury ("material injury") and the fact of causal connection between the act and the injury.[140] In the case of countervailing action, the investigation likewise covers the alleged subsidization in question, the standard of injury ("material injury") and causation between the act and the injury.[141]

Once an investigation by national authorities is complete and assuming all of the necessary requirements have been fulfilled, then a complainant is allowed to take counteraction in the specified form (i.e. a safeguard, an antidumping or a countervailing duty). In each case counteraction is permitted for a limited period up to the amount determined and for the purpose outlined in each area (adjustment, cessation of

[138] Where it does not, the situation in question normally involves an apprehension of injury and temporary closure under provisional measures that must later be justified: see SAF Art. 6, ADA Art. 7 and SCM Art. 17 relating to provisional measures.

[139] SAF Arts. 2 (increased imports), 4.1(a) ("serious injury") and 4.2(b) (causal link).

[140] ADA Arts. 2 (dumping), 3 ("material injury") and 5.2 (causal link).

[141] SCM Arts. 14 (subsidy), 15 ("material injury") and 15.5 (causal link).

dumping or cessation of trade-distorting subsidization).[142] Again, the one-to-one nature of most counteraction speaks to the corrective and "contractual" nature of the law in these instances.

The constrained aspect of corrective action is evident in several respects. First, panels and the Appellate Body have made clear that the exercise of rights contained in WTO rules is predicated on fulfillment of the relevant requirements outlined above. They are preconditions to the invocation of rights. Second, the relevant law features a number of "lesser duty" provisions. Countries are encouraged to impose less than the full amount of the duty if a lesser duty would fulfill the policy purpose of counteraction.[143] Third, WTO rules in each area impose temporal limits. Sunsets and prohibitions on reapplication are common.[144]

At the same time, the empiricism of the law in these areas and the emphasis on metrics are constrained by a number of qualitative features and factors that must be taken into account in decision-making concerning corrective action. For instance, with respect to causation determinations in domestic countervail investigations, the relevant national obligation is described as follows:

> The demonstration of a causal relationship between the subsidized imports and the injury to the domestic industry shall be based on an examination of all relevant evidence before the authorities.[145]

Inevitably, a question that arises in corrective action is the extent to which quantitative factors such as "volumes and prices of non-subsidized imports of the product in question" are to be weighed against qualitative ones such as "developments in technology," "export performance" or "productivity of

[142] SAF Art. 7.1 (application of safeguard measures only for such a period as necessary to prevent or remedy serious injury); ADA Art. 9.1. (imposition to remove injury of dumping in the domestic market); SCM Art. 19.1 (imposition for purposes of withdrawal of subsidies).

[143] See, for instance, SCM Art. 19.2 ("It is desirable that the imposition should be permissive in the territory of all Members, that the duty should be less than the total amount of the subsidy if such lesser duty would be adequate to remove the injury to the domestic industry."), ADA Arts. 8.1, 9.1.

[144] For example, in the case of safeguards the duration of provisional measures is not to exceed 200 days (SAF Art. 6). The duration of definitive safeguards is not to exceed four years, unless extended, and the total period of application of a safeguard measures is not to exceed eight years (SAF Art. 7). In addition, there is a two-year period of nonapplication after any safeguard has expired (SAF Art. 7(5)). Limitations and sunsets are also imposed on countervailing duties and undertakings (SCM Art. 21) and antidumping duties and undertakings (ADA Art. 11).

[145] SCM Art. 15.5.

the domestic industry." Due to the difficulty of assessment, commentators have pointed out that causation in particular is ill-defined.[146]

WTO disciplines on subsidization offer perhaps the most direct illustration of the application of corrective justice. There the requisites of a corrective view of the law are most apparent. WTO law does not prohibit subsidization by governments but rather aims to discipline the use of trade-distorting subsidies by allowing member governments to undertake two sets of policy responses: either (1) countervailing duties on imports of the subsidized product and/or (2) action against prohibited or actionable subsidies.

Under SCM Art. 4, subsidies that are determined to be prohibited due to their basis in export performance or import substitution are subject to specific remedies that differ from the regular requirement in DSU Art. 19.1 to bring measures "into conformity." In this respect SCM Art. 4.7 provides that "If the measure in question is found to be a prohibited subsidy, the panel shall recommend that the subsidizing Member *withdraw* the subsidy without delay." The issue here is whether the withdrawal specified is simply withdrawal *de jure*, that is as a matter of law alone, or whether the obligation extends to withdrawal *de facto*. A requirement to "withdraw" a subsidy in fact has obvious corrective connotations.

SCM Art. 4.10 goes on to permit a complaining member to take "appropriate" countermeasures in cases where the prohibited subsidy is identified and not removed. The standard of "appropriate" countermeasures is qualified by a footnote that clarifies that the term "appropriate . . . is not meant to allow countermeasures *that are disproportionate*." The qualification is notable for the way it suggests a standard of fittingness or appropriateness in line with fairness as the metric of corrective justice, thereby appearing to confirm the workings of a communitarian theory of justice. Several additional points offer further confirmation.

146 The concept of causation was re-introduced as one of a set of tools for distinguishing between acceptable and unacceptable subsidies. Nevertheless, the concept probably defies further meaningful abstract elaboration, as confirmed by the "genuine and substantial" test elaborated by the Appellate Body. As a relatively blunt as opposed to a relatively refined "analytical tool", its (unnecessary) reintroduction in other contexts is a matter of growing concern.

(James Flett, "The Client's Perspective" in Theresa Carpenter et al. (eds), *The Use of Economics in International Trade and Investment Disputes* 83 at 88 (Cambridge University Press, Cambridge; 2017))

First, there has been some discussion of the extent of the obligation of "withdrawal" in SCM Art. 4.7 in WTO case law. In *Australia – Automotive Leather*, for example, a compliance panel disagreed with the view that WTO remedies are purely prospective. The panel felt the need to assign to the term "withdraw" in SCM Art. 4.7 a distinctive meaning when compared with the more general wording of DSU Art. 19.1 to bring measures "into conformity." In light of the interpretative principle of effectiveness, the panel concluded that the term "withdraw the subsidy" did encompass repayment of prohibited subsidies.[147] The decision in *Australia – Automotive Leather* was heavily criticized by a number of WTO member countries.[148] Notwithstanding this reaction, there are subsequent indications of continuing support for a *de facto* withdrawal approach, although most panels have preferred to stress the obligation of withdrawal *de jure* only.[149] That alternative does little to address the concern that limiting the remedy to withdrawal *de jure* effectively immunizes subsidies already granted.

Second, with respect to "appropriate" countermeasures foreseen in SCM Art. 4.10, a preliminary question is the correct metric by which to assess subsidies in determining counteraction. In *Brazil – Aircraft (Art. 22.6)*, for instance, an arbitrator determined that the subsidy in question was the "full amount" of the subsidy. The arbitrator concluded, based largely on the evident difference in terminology between

[147] The panel was adamant in its view. In responding to the question of whether or not partial payment could be sufficient, the panel concluded that there was no basis "that anything less than full payment would suffice" to meet the requirement of withdrawing the subsidy. See *Australia – Automotive Leather*, WT/DS126/RW, para. 6.45 (21 Jan. 2000).

[148] See WT/DSB/M/75 (7 Mar. 2000) (detailing the US position that "The Panel's remedy went beyond that sought by the United States" (p. 5); Australia's view that "the findings as to the 'remedy' involved retrospectivity and were of a punitive nature" (p. 5); Canada's "serious concerns regarding the conclusions of the Panel Report" (p. 7); Japan's view that "the retroactive remedy was inconsistent with the relevant provisions of the DSU and the customary practice under the GATT 1947 and the WTO" (p. 8); the EC's view that "the Panel Report had some important systemic implications" (p. 9); see *contra* the position of Hong Kong, China, that it "welcomed [the panel's] conclusion" (p. 9)).

[149] For instance, in both *Brazil – Aircraft*, WT/DS46, and *Canada – Aircraft*, WT/DS70, panels and the Appellate Body appeared content with specifying *de jure* withdrawal. However, they left open the possibility that SCM Art. 4.7 might require *de facto* withdrawal. See also *U.S. – FSC*, WT/DS108 and *U.S. – Cotton*, WT/DS267 on this point. In *EC – Aircraft*, WT/DS316/AB/R (18 May 2011) the Appellate Body held that "cash extractions" from a company did not result in withdrawal of subsidies within the meaning of SCM Art. 4.7. Due to a lack of evidence, however, the Appellate Body did not go on to determine whether cash extractions "extinguished" prior subsidies: ibid., para. 1416.

"appropriate" countermeasures specified in SCM Art. 4.10 and "equal" countermeasures in DSU Art. 22.4, that when dealing with an export subsidy countermeasures corresponding to the *total amount of the subsidy* rather than its *effect* on the market is "appropriate."[150] However, in two further cases, *U.S. – FSC (Art. 22.6)*[151] and *Canada – Aircraft II (Art. 22.6)*,[152] arbitrators indicated that SCM Arts. 4.10–4.11 do not exclude the possibility of countermeasures based on *either* the amount of the subsidy *or* its trade effects. In the latter case, the amount of the subsidy was used as a starting point for determining the level of appropriate countermeasures.[153] In *U.S. – Upland Cotton (Art. 22.6)* an arbitrator appeared to confirm this interpretation by noting that the term "appropriate . . . entitle[s] the complaining party to countermeasures that *are suited to the circumstances of the case*."[154]

Third, in *Canada – Aircraft II (Art. 22.6)* the arbitrator increased the level of appropriate countermeasure by 20 percent, effectively imposing a punitive award because Canada had indicated it would not withdraw its prohibited subsidy. The increase was imposed in order to "induce compliance."[155] The decision in *Canada – Aircraft II* was criticized in the DSB and has not been followed by subsequent arbitrators.[156]

Taken together, the cases under SCM Art. 4.10 seem to illustrate the highly tailored and ultimately variable nature of fairness consistent with a communitarian theory of justice. The ultimate amount of correction is particularized and heavily dependent on the circumstances and what arbitrators have deemed appropriate rather than strictly equal.

[150] WT/DS46/ARB, para. 3.65 (28 Aug. 2000).

[151] WT/DS108/ARB (30 Aug. 2003).

[152] WT/DS222/ARB (17 Feb. 2003).

[153] Ibid., para. 3.51.

[154] WT/DS267/ARB/1, para. 4.114 (31 Aug. 2009). The arbitrator went on to observe that "the requirements that countermeasures be 'appropriate' and not 'disproportionate' suggest that 'there should be a degree of relationship between the level of countermeasures and the trade-distorting impact of the measure on the complaining Member.'" Ibid., para. 4.135. The arbitrator also said that use of the term "appropriate" infers "a degree of flexibility" in what might be considered to satisfy appropriateness criteria. Again, these comments could be taken to be evidence of an emphasis on fairness in corrective justice.

[155] Ibid., paras. 3.102–3.107.

[156] See WT/M/DSB145, paras. 43–51 (7 May 2003). See *EC – Aircraft (22.6)*, WT/DS316/ARB ("commensurate with: connotes a 'correspondence' between the 'countermeasures' proposed and 'the degree and nature of the adverse effect determined to exist.'" It further observed that "it is generally recognized that WTO remedies are not intended to be 'punitive,' such that, while the phrase does 'not require exact numerical correspondence,' this does not mean that there should also be a punitive element.")

By comparison, under SCM Art. 7 subsidies are determined to be "actionable," where they are having an adverse effect on another member country either because they injure its domestic industry, nullify or impair tariff concessions, or cause serious prejudice to the interests of another member. In those instances SCM Art. 7.8 indicates that the country "granting or maintaining such subsidy shall take appropriate steps *to remove the adverse effects or shall withdraw the subsidy.*" In the event that removal or withdrawal is not possible, SCM Art. 7.10 goes on to foresee arbitration and to specify that "the arbitrator shall determine whether the countermeasures *are commensurate* with the degree and nature of the adverse effects determined to exist."

Like "appropriate" countermeasures in SCM Art. 4.10, the standard of "commensurate" countermeasures in SCM Art. 7.8 has required interpretation. For instance, in *EC – Aircraft (Art. 22.6)* the arbitrator noted that the phrase "commensurate with" as it appears in SCM Art. 7.8 connotes a correspondence of a "*less precise degree of equivalence* than exact numerical correspondence" between the "adverse effects determined to exist" and "countermeasures" proposed.[157] There, the arbitrator had to determine whether a US claim for $10.56 billion in retaliation was "commensurate with" adverse effects calculated to be $7.496 billion. The arbitrator went on to note that "even assuming that the commensurate

[157] *EC – Aircraft (22.6)*, WT/DS316/ARB, para. 5.4 (2 Oct. 2019). In *U.S. – Cotton (22.6)*, WT/DS267/ARB/1 (31 Aug. 2009), the arbitrator noted that the wording "appropriate countermeasures" in SCM Art. 4.10 was different from the equivalence standard spelled out in DSU Art. 22.4 and must be given a distinct meaning. In line with the idea of fairness in a communitarian theory, the arbitrator observed that the term "appropriate" in SCM Art. 4.10 "suggests a degree of flexibility and adaptation to the circumstances of the case that is not found in Article 22.4 of the DSU." Ibid. para. 4.97. The arbitrator went on to note four factors pertaining to this flexibility: first, the absence of any need to demonstrate the effect of prohibited subsidies; second, the inherent flexibility of the language involved ("appropriate"); third, absence of any indication that the drafters "would have intended to endorse a more restrictive standard in SCM Art. 4.10 than those found in SCM Art. 7.9 ("commensurate with") and DSU Art. 22.4 ("equivalent to")." Ibid. para. 4.101; fourth, the cautionary statement in the accompanying footnote that "appropriate countermeasures" is not meant to allow countermeasures that are disproportionate. These factors appear to "confirm that 'appropriate countermeasures' are not limited to a strict quantification of the adverse trade effects on the complainant, and can take into account the entirety of the situation at hand, including the gravity of the breach." Ibid., para. 4.106. The arbitrator concluded that "we read the terms of Article 4.10 of the SCM Agreement as allowing greater flexibility in the context of countermeasures involving prohibited subsidies to take into account the specificities of the situation at hand, but always having regard to the impact of the illegal measure on the complaining Member." Ibid., para. 4.107.

standard permits *some limited degree of discrepancy* between the proposed level and the value of the adverse effects determined to exist," the difference here "would . . . exceed, by far, any permissible degree of discrepancy." The arbitrator was therefore unable to accept the US claim for $10.56 million as the "commensurate" value.[158] The arbitral award appeared to confirm the "discounted" nature of corrective justice in that instance.

Under DSU Art. 22.2, where there is continuing noncompliance and no settlement can be reached or satisfactory compensation agreed, a complainant may request authorization from the DSB to suspend the application to the member concerned of concessions or other obligations under the covered agreements. The option under DSU Art. 22.2 raises some additional issues of corrective justice.

First, the complainant is required to observe certain basic principles and procedures of sectoral correspondence (DSU Art. 22.3).[159] It is also required to ensure that "[t]he level of the suspension of concessions or other obligations authorized by the DSB *shall be equivalent to* the level of the nullification or impairment" (DSU Art. 22.4).

Second, a complainant must specify the amount of proposed countermeasures, which may be objected to by the defendant and subject to arbitration under DSU Art. 22.6. The task of the arbitrator is to determine whether the level of such suspension is equivalent to the level of nullification or impairment. In addition, the arbitrator may also determine if the proposed suspension of concessions or other obligations is allowed under the covered agreement.

It will be recalled that the option to retaliate is premised on continuing noncompliance. Due to this fact and to the arbitrator's need to calculate countermeasures that might be permissibly equivalent, arbitrators have developed a practice of basing the calculation on counterfactuals, that is, "hypothetical scenarios that describe 'what would have happened in terms of trade flows had the responding party implemented the DSB recommendations and rulings.'"[160] The "hypothetical is compared with the actual situation, as of the end of the [reasonable period of time

158 *EC – Aircraft (22.6)*, WT/DS316/ARB, para. 6.508 (2 Oct. 2019).

159 The requisite standard mandates "either that [sectoral correspondence] is 'not practicable' or that it is 'not effective'." At the same time the invoking country need not conclude that same-agreement suspension is both "not practicable" and "not effective," in order to reach the conclusion that it is "not practicable or effective": see *U.S. – Cotton*, WT/DS267/ARB/1, para. 5.70 (31 Aug. 2009).

160 *U.S. – Tuna II (Mexico) (22.6)*, WT/DS381/ARB, para. 4.4 (25 Apr. 2017).

('RPT') for implementation]"[161] to determine the magnitude of equivalent countermeasures.

The task of crafting an acceptable counterfactual is complex. It requires a "reference period," that is, some interval that noncompliance can be benchmarked against. In the appropriate case, it also requires an assessment of the proposal to suspend "other obligations" beyond tariff concessions since the specific wording of DSU Art. 22.2 contemplates this option ("to suspend the application to the Member concerned of concessions *or other obligations*") and member countries have occasionally identified "other obligations" as part of their suspension requests as well.[162]

Practice has evolved considerably in this respect. Early on, arbitrators often simply "split the difference" between complainant and respondent submissions or in several instances were opaque about how they arrived at the specific amount determined to be equivalent.[163] These practices generated criticism that equivalence determinations were essentially arbitrary and, to that extent, appeared to support the view that the real purpose of retaliation is something other than correction or inducing conformity. However, in *U.S. – Offset Act ("Byrd Amendment")* the arbitrator agreed with the claim by the complainant parties that equivalence might be determined by means of a trade effects coefficient, and in subsequent cases such as *U.S. – Upland Cotton* and *U.S. – Washing*

[161] *U.S. – Washing Machines (22.6)*, WT/DS464/ARB, para. 3.7 (8 Feb. 2019). The arbitrator noted that "[g]enerally, arbitrations carried out under Article 22.6 have relied on the 'trade effect' of the inconsistent measure to assess the resulting level of nullification or impairment. However, in *U.S. – 1916 Act (EC)*, the arbitrator looked to the measures' 'economic effect', since no trade had occurred. See Decision by the Arbitrator, *U.S. – 1916 Act (EC) (22.6)*, paras. 5.58–5.63." Ibid., n. 40.

[162] For example in *EC – Bananas III (Ecuador) (Art. 22.6 – EC)*, WT/DS27/ARB/ECU, para. 173(d) (24 Mar. 2000) the arbitrator indicated that the complainant could obtain authorization from the DSB to suspend unspecified obligations "under the TRIPS Agreement" with respect to certain sectors. In *Brazil – Aircraft (Art. 22.6 – Brazil)*, WT/DS46/ARB, para. 4.1 (28 Aug. 2000) the arbitrator authorized both the suspension of tariff concessions and the suspension of "other obligations" including obligations under the Agreement on Textiles and Clothing and the Agreement on Import Licensing Procedures.

[163] "Until relatively recently, when it came to calculating damages or permitting trade retaliation, WTO arbitrators as well as investor-state tribunals would resort to 'splitting the difference' – that is, adding up what the two opposing parties claimed and then awarding half of that amount, rather than using sound economic models and data." Marion Jansen et al., "Introduction" in Marion Jansen et al. (eds), *The Use of Economics in International Trade and Investment Disputes* 5 (Cambridge University Press, Cambridge; 2017).

Machines arbitrators have agreed that equivalence may be determined by formula, lending greater correspondence to any effort at equivalence.

The arbitrator's decision in *U.S. – Washing Machines* is especially illuminating in this respect. As mentioned, corrective justice is classically contemplated to be retrospective and, to that extent, is assessed on the basis of past injury. WTO law modifies this by assessing correction on a prospective basis from the date of the authorization of countermeasures. Arbitral awards under DSU Art. 22.6 have generally adhered to this approach by fixing the assessment on the basis of reference periods *predating* the arbitral award. However, in *U.S. – Washing Machines* Korea challenged the continuing use of certain US antidumping methodologies facially (i.e. "as such").[164] As part of its claim, Korea proposed a counterfactual whereby the United States ceased to use the WTO-inconsistent "as such" measures *in future* antidumping proceedings.

The arbitrator disagreed with Korea's submission but went on to develop a formula "that reflects the economic context of this case and will permit Korea to quantify the trade effect flowing from *the possible future imposition* [i.e. by the US] of inconsistent anti-dumping duty measures, recognizing the range of products and markets that may be covered by such anti-dumping duty measures."[165] While the parties both expressed concerns about a coefficient-based approach, the arbitrator considered that such concerns reflect a "tension" in its mandate between having to determine equivalence and unknown future events.

U.S. – Washing Machines is notable for the way in which the arbitrator attempted an imaginative solution to the inherent problem of static models used in calculating equivalent countermeasures and the question of their application in future. Fixed amounts of retaliation do not reflect the inherent dynamism of markets. By comparison, a formula approach can be made more flexible. To ensure that amounts of retaliation under the formula are in fact equivalent, the arbitrator suggested that Korea notify the DSB of the level of suspension that it calculates and of any adjustment in the level thereafter "for each year during the first quarter of the following year."[166]

[164] *U.S. – Washing Machines (22.6)*, WT/DS464/ARB, para. 4.1 (8 Feb. 2019).

[165] Ibid., para. 4.57. See also *U.S. – Supercalendered Paper*, WT/DS505/ARB (13 July 2022) wherein an arbitrator outlined a methodology for calculating retaliation if the United States at any point reimposed the contested measures.

[166] Ibid., para. 5.3.

Despite these innovations, there are a number of impediments to making WTO law more evidently corrective. First, the WTO Agreement tends to emphasize the importance of diffuse reciprocity, or in other words, the treaty *in operation*. Picking and choosing a single, discrete relationship and trying to ascribe a single value to it for the purposes of counteraction is plainly artificial. It ignores the synergies generate by interdependence.

Second, numbers do not tell the whole story. WTO law is about the potential for trade, *not* actual trade itself. This is something that those advocating the use of "more" economics in WTO law rarely address. It may be that retaliatory models such as the one formulated in *U.S. – Washing Machines* accounting for future noncompliance can be devised. In all probability, however, such retaliatory formula will apply under very limited conditions and subject to the need for constant updating as conditions change.

Third, as Marios Iacovides and Marion Jansen have pointed out, "quantitative evidence can – if scrutinized closely – be easily criticized or disputed based on the assumptions made in order to reach the findings."[167] These same criticisms have not stopped a number of commentators advocating for more quantitative approaches to WTO law. The WTO legal system "is under constant pressure to assimilate economic analysis in a range of areas, including those that raise weighing and balancing issues."[168] At the same time, the selectivity of the models proposed and employed risks introducing distortions. The plain fact is that many corrective concepts in WTO law such as the determination of causation mentioned above are necessarily impressionistic. They cannot be reduced to formulas or raw statistics with definitive accuracy.

Fourth, panels and the Appellate Body are only modestly equipped to meaningfully engage with economic evidence.[169] As mentioned in

[167] Marios Iacovides & Marion Jansen, "Lost in Translation: Communication and Interpretation Challenges Related to Economic Evidence in Trade Disputes" in Marion Jansen et al. (eds), *The Use of Economics in International Trade and Investment Disputes* 164 at 185 (Cambridge University Press, Cambridge; 2017).

[168] Flett, "The Client's Perspective", ibid. at 105.

[169] For instance, Pablo Bentes concludes that a review of the jurisprudence involving "serious prejudice" claims under SCM Art. 6.3(c) "suggests that panels are still reluctant or ill-equipped to meaningfully engage in economic evidence when assessing the trade-distortive effects of subsidies." His general assessment is that:

> Panels have typically eschewed a proper analysis of quantitative evidence, opting instead for a middle-of-the-road approach, or for rejecting such

Chapter 2, there is no formal discovery process in WTO dispute settlement and hence no real way for WTO adjudicators to compare or make choices between regressions or counterfactual models put forward. Of course in a few instances they have had to make such choices, but in a number of others they have not, simply "splitting the difference" mentioned above.[170] It is unlikely that retaliation in WTO law can be reduced to pure econometric forecasting.

Fifth, econometric modeling of WTO action raises a number of issues related to access and availability of economic modeling. The models themselves require economic inputs and insights that take time to assemble and are expensive.[171]

Sixth, retaliation in particular has garnered a substantial amount of commentary and media attention, yet the fact remains that it is relatively

> evidence outright. Instead, panels have prioritized evidence of a qualitative nature and thus have opted for looking at the design, structure, and operation of challenged subsidies – despite the Appellate Body's insistence that the challenged subsidies must be shown to constitute both a "genuine" and a "substantial" cause of trade-distorting effects, and that other non-attribution factors should be fully taken into account. . . . the WTO panels' lack of analytical rigor may render the causation requirement reflected in [SCM] Articles 5 and 6 . . . effectively meaningless, thus creating a right to multilateral remedy even where the existence of trade-distortive effects is equivocal.
>
> (Pablo Bentes, "In Search of a 'Genuine and Substantial' Cause: The Analysis of Causation in Serious Prejudice Claims" in Marion Jansen et al. (eds), *The Use of Economics in International Trade and Investment Disputes* 239 at 259 (Cambridge University Press, Cambridge; 2017))

The fact remains, however, that the WTO Secretariat assigns one or more economists to assist arbitrators in DSU Art. 22.6 decisions and any panel decisions involving economic evidence that usually takes the form of economic modelling. WTO adjudicators also engage in extensive back-and-forth with the parties, especially through written questions posed before and after hearings. The hearings process is not then one in which the panel passively receives models and then has to select one on a take-it-or-leave-it basis. I thank Graham Cook for his insight on this point.

170 See discussion in *U.S. – Washing Machines (22.6)*, WT/DS464/ARB, paras. 3.7–3.12 (8 Feb. 2019).

171 Not all WTO members will have access to the economic assistance necessary to devise or counter such modelling, although it is conceivable that an outside entity such as the Advisory Centre for WTO Law (ACWL) could furnish assistance in appropriate cases. Greater use of econometric models could also promote their "off the shelf" use (i.e. by drawing on them from past cases). Furthermore, access to the numeric inputs necessary for accurate forecasting of the type depends on statistics, something not all WTO member countries may have or be willing to share.

rare. As of early 2022, among 600 or so matters referred to the DSB some 50 requests to suspend were received but suspension itself only invoked in 5 – all of them involving disputes between the United States and the EU.[172] This record suggests that WTO countermeasures embodying corrective justice are an exceptional remedy, designed and operable in the limited circumstances of two major powers of approximately equal economic strength. Law in this instance appears to be "for external display."[173] Its true purpose is something else.

The general impression to be had from a review of efforts at corrective justice under the WTO Agreement is that corrective justice and economic analysis remain restricted, a conclusion consistent with a communitarian theory of justice. Limits arise for a variety of reasons such as the difficulties of calculation, the problem of counterfactuals, and in a legal system designed to promote interdependence, the desire to preserve ties. This is not to suggest that the potential for corrective justice analysis in the WTO Agreement should remain unrealized, only that its application is likely to be restrained to relatively rare circumstances or instances where the law resolves into the neat bilateral form that corrective justice requires.

Pragmatism suggests that in most instances corrective justice is conditioned on broader distributive factors (i.e. Distributive Justice > Corrective Justice) and ultimately subordinate to other considerations. The theory put forward in this book suggests this subordination occurs for the overarching purpose of sustaining community, leading to the need for reconciliation of distributive and corrective impulses through transformation.

3.3.3 Transformative Justice

The concept of transformative justice introduced earlier focuses on the reconciliation of interests. It is accommodative and seeks to promote

[172] As of early 2022, suspension had only been invoked in *EC – Hormones*, WT/DS26; *EC – Bananas III*, WT/DS27; *U.S. – FSC*, WT/DS108; *U.S. – Byrd Amendment*, WT/DS217; *EC – Aircraft*, WT/DS316; and *U.S. – Aircraft*, WT/DS353. In the last two mentioned cases, tariff were suspended in a settlement worked out between the United States and EU in June 2021. See Hannah Monicken, "U.S., EU Ink Framework on Tariffs, Set up Working Group in Aircraft Dispute" 39:24 *Inside U.S. Trade* 1 (18 June 2021).

[173] H. Patrick Glenn, *Legal Traditions of the World* (5th ed.) 74 (Oxford University Press, Oxford; 2014) (writing of how in chthonic legal traditions "[l]aw is for when something goes really wrong, *or for external display.*" [emphasis added]).

interdependence. Fundamentally, it requires actors to transform their legal relationship in light of evolving ideas of the good.

Transformation receives textual support in DSU Art. 3.7, which states that "[t]he aim of the dispute settlement mechanism is to secure a *positive solution* to a dispute." The DSU goes on to state that "[a] solution *mutually acceptable to the parties* to a dispute and consistent with the covered agreements *is clearly to be preferred*."

The exhortation to governments to settle their GATT/WTO disputes in a creative, problem-solving way has a long history. It is detectable in the freewheeling style of many early decisions under GATT 1947, where panels often took the liberty of encouraging parties to arrive at a mutually satisfactory arrangement in a manner that would seem alien – even improper – in the more strictly adjudicative environment of WTO dispute settlement system today.

Thus, in *Australia – Ammonium Sulphate*, a dispute involving competitive conditions in the Australian market between Australian and Chilean fertilizers:

> the working party came to the conclusion that a satisfactory adjustment would be achieved if the Australian Government could consider the possibility of modifying the present arrangements in such a way as to achieve that object while giving to the two types of fertilizers equal opportunity to compete on its market.[174]

In *EC – Oilseeds*, the panel likewise recommended that "the [European] Community should act expeditiously to eliminate the impairment of the tariff concessions – either by modifying its new support system for oilseeds or by renegotiating its tariff concessions for oilseeds under Article XXVIII." The panel added that "[i]n the event that the dispute is not resolved expeditiously in either of these ways, the CONTRACTING PARTIES should, if so requested by the United States, consider further action under Article XXIII:2 of the General Agreement."[175]

And in *Norway – Government Procurement* the panel observed that "it had it had given Norway and the United States full opportunity to develop a mutually satisfactory solution." The panel went on to note that

[174] *Australia – Subsidy on Ammonium Sulphate*, B.I.S.D. 2nd Supp. 188, para. 15 (3 Apr. 1950).

[175] Follow-up on the Panel Report *EEC – Payments and Subsidies Paid to Processors and Producers of Oilseeds and Related Animal-Feed Proteins*, B.I.S.D. 39th Supp. 91, para. 92 (31 Mar. 1992).

"nothing prevented the two governments from negotiating at any time a mutually satisfactory solution that took into account the lost opportunities of United States' suppliers, provided such solution was consistent with their obligations under this and other GATT agreements." The panel concluded that:

> it would be possible for the United States to raise in the [GATT Government Procurement] Committee its concerns of a more general nature . . . The Panel noted that certain proposals for challenge procedures open to suppliers that were under consideration . . . were intended to address the difficulty felt to exist in obtaining effective redress in respect of complaints about specific procurements.[176]

Still, transformation happens over time. The translation of dispute settlement results into transformative outcomes often assumes the form of agreements that take years – often decades – to achieve. It requires memory and a discerning eye.[177]

[176] *Norway – Tendering Procedures on Trondheim Toll Ring Road*, B.I.S.D. 40th Supp. 319, para. 4.27 (28 Apr. 1992).

[177] Some idea of the successive articulation of GATT/WTO law in dispute settlement and then negotiation (and potentially back again) is given by John Weekes. Weekes emphasizes that GATT/WTO dispute resolution, the management of trade relations and trade negotiations need to be clearly seen as part of an integrated and coherent process. For instance, Weekes credits the outcome of *EC – Oilseeds* case, which involved a variable subsidy bestowed by the EC on the production of oilseeds, as something that brought the EC to the negotiating table and set the stage for the conclusion of the Uruguay Round. Likewise, Weekes recounts how several GATT and Tokyo Round Code panels grappled with the terms "serious prejudice" and "more than an equitable share of world trade" in GATT Art. XVI in light of the fact that the complainants had found it difficult to mount sufficient evidence to prove their allegations. Consequently, several delegations sought to ensure that the SCM Agreement provided clearer definitions of key terms and a more operational method of dispute settlement for assessing possible violations. Similar effects on the course and conclusion Uruguay Round were due to GATT-era outcomes in *Canada – Administration of the Foreign Investment Review Act*, B.I.S.D. 30th Supp. 140 (25 July 1983) and *Japan – Restrictions on Imports of Certain Agricultural Products*, B.I.S.D. 35th Supp. 163 (2 Feb. 1988). See John Weekes, "The External Dynamics of the Dispute Settlement Understanding" (23 May 2004) (unpublished manuscript on file with the author). It is also noteworthy that under GATT 1947, the United States held up implementation of several antidumping decisions in order to enhance its negotiating leverage on key antidumping disciplines in the context of negotiations over the new ADA Agreement: *U.S. – Anti-dumping Duties in Grey Portland Cement and Clinker from Mexico*, ADP/82 (unadopted); *U.S. – Anti-dumping Duties on Imports of Stainless Steel Plate from Sweden*, ADP/117 (unadopted). The process Weekes describes continues under the WTO Agreement. At the same time, many of these developments are hidden, or at least obscured. There are many transformative solutions to matters raised in the WTO, but

Perhaps due to the perception that matters raised under the WTO DSU are more complex and that the jurisdiction of panels is circumscribed, explicit emphasis on transformative solutions appears to have become less pronounced in WTO dispute settlement. References to it are more indirect and cryptic. Often, they are left to be inferred negatively, that is, from what is omitted.[178] Thus, in *U.S. – Clove Cigarettes* the Appellate Body stated:

> While we have upheld the Panel's finding that the specific measure at issue in this dispute is inconsistent with Article 2.1 of the *TBT Agreement*, we are not saying that a Member cannot adopt measures to pursue legitimate health objectives such as curbing and preventing youth smoking. In particular, we are not saying that the United States cannot ban clove cigarettes: however, if it chooses to do so, this has to be done consistently with the *TBT Agreement*.[179]

In *U.S. – Clove Cigarettes*, the United States eventually negotiated a wide-ranging settlement of the matter with Indonesia.[180]

Likewise, in *EC – Bananas III* the arbitrators observed that:

> Given the difficulties and the specific circumstances of this case which involves a developing country Member, it could be that Ecuador may find

public knowledge of them is scant and has been obscured by recrimination over the failure to achieve a larger, more visible "agreement" to conclude the Doha Round.

178 It is not uncommon for the Appellate Body to clarify what it has *not* decided in a report. See the Appellate Body reports on *US – Shrimp*, WT/DS58/AB/R, para. 185 (12 Oct. 1998); *Brazil – Aircraft*, WT/DS46/AB/R, para. 187 (2 Aug. 1999); *US – FSC*, WT/DS108/AB/R, para. 179 (24 Feb. 2000); *Canada – Autos*, WT/DS139/AB/R, para. 183 (31 May 2000); *Canada – Patent Term*, WT/DS170/AB/R, paras. 100–101 (18 Sept. 2000); *Canada – Dairy (Article 21.5 – New Zealand and US)*, WT/DS103/AB/RW, para. 103 (3 Dec. 2001); *US – Section 211 Appropriations Act*, WT/DS176/AB/R, para. 362 (2 Jan. 2002); and *US – Softwood Lumber V*, WT/DS264/AB/R, para. 181 (11 Aug. 2004).

179 *U.S. – Clove Cigarettes*, WT/DS406/AB/R, para. 236 (4 Apr. 2012).

180 The settlement reached was a wide-ranging one involving suspension of any potential US challenges to an Indonesian mining product export ban, the qualification of certain Indonesian products for preferential treatment under the US General System of Preferences, and investment disciplines. Pursuant to the terms of the Memorandum of Understanding settling the dispute, the US ban on clove cigarettes imports would remain in place, although the United States agreed that it would not take steps to impede the market access of imported Indonesian cigars and cigarillos, at least not until new regulations "that are non-arbitrary and non-discriminative" could be enacted. For its part, Indonesia agreed to consult with the United States concerning Indonesia's intellectual property regime. See Memorandum of Understanding between the Government of the United States of American and the Government of the Republic of Indonesia (3 Oct. 2014); Victoria Guida, "U.S. Settles WTO Clove Cigarette Case with Indonesia; Keeps Ban in Place" 32:40 *Inside U.S. Trade* 1 (10 Oct. 2014).

> itself in a situation where it is not realistic or possible for it to implement the suspension [of concessions] authorized by the DSB for the full amount of the level of nullification and impairment estimated by us in all of the sectors and/or under all agreements mentioned above combined. The present text of the DSU does not offer a solution for such an eventuality. . . . We trust that *in this eventuality the parties to this dispute will find a mutually satisfactory solution.*[181]

Transformation usually happens through negotiation, litigation or some combinations of these that resolve in the form of a settlement.[182] The corrective impulse and its associated concern with what is fair help to set benchmarks against which settlements can subsequently be negotiated.

A good example of this phenomenon occurred in the *Airbus-Boeing* dispute, the collective name given to a series of complaints involving subsidization of the EU and US large passenger jet industries. These are dominated by Airbus and Boeing, respectively.

The original US complaint against the EU involved the EU's provision of launch aid financing for design and development to Airbus companies and a number of other allegations of benefit, both direct and indirect.[183] The original EU complaint against the United States involved certain US federal, state and local subsidies.[184]

It is apparent from the lockstep way in which the litigation began, eventually involving second complaints as well as authorizations of countermeasures, that there was a degree of parallelism to the proceedings. The litigation was lengthy and protracted, and in each case, the final authorizations for retaliation involved considerably less than the original amounts requested.[185]

[181] WT/DS27/ARB/ECU, para. 177 (24 Mar. 2000) [emphasis added].

[182] Busch & Reinhardt, "Bargaining in the Shadow of the Law" 158 (noting that one little-known fact about GATT/WTO is that fully three-fifths of all disputes end prior to a panel ruling; like dispute settlement under GATT, the success of the WTO system depends on its ability to encourage bargaining in the shadow of weak law). See also Wolfgang Alschner, "Amicable Settlements of WTO Disputes: Bilateral Solutions in a Multilateral System" 13:1 *World Trade Rev.* 65 (2013) (noting that every third dispute brought to the WTO and not withdrawn early is settled amicably through a mutually agreed solution (MAS); MAS favor the instant resolution of disputes but may conflict with third-party interests and collective stakes).

[183] WT/DS316.

[184] WT/DS317, as corrected by WT/DS353. The correction was introduced to account for the addition of thirteen new subsidy programs alleged by the EC to violate WTO law.

[185] In *EC – Large Civil Aircraft*, WT/DS316/ARB (2 Oct. 2019) the United States estimated that the total annualized value of the adverse effects determined to exist was approximately US $10.13 billion. The United States was eventually authorized to retaliate in an

At the same time, it would be wrong to suggest that the ultimate point of the proceedings was retaliation to induce compliance. Instead, as the United States pointed out in the DSB in October 2020, given the porousness of WTO subsidy disciplines what was sought was a "level playing field":

> The United States strongly favours a negotiated resolution of its dispute with the EU over the massive launch aid subsidies it provided to Airbus. The United States has recently provided proposals for a reasonable settlement that would provide a level playing field [for the manufacture of large civil aircraft].[186]

The point, in other words, was not countermeasures per se but use of the amounts authorized to retaliate as benchmarks around which a settlement could be agreed.[187] In this way, corrective and distributive impulses in the system interact and are reconciled.

Settlements detail countries' agreement to exercise their rights and obligations going forward and can be classified as taking three general forms. The first involves some confirmation or clarification of existing bilateral rights and obligations. The second involves the creation of multilateral rights and obligations. The third involves the creation of mechanisms to manage rights and obligations as part of an ongoing relationship.

The first type of transformative arrangement involves the confirmation or clarification of existing bilateral rights and obligations. In *Canada – Tax Exemptions and Reductions*,[188] for instance, the dispute took the form of a complaint by the EC against Canada's lowering of excise duties for Canadian wines while increasing excise duties on imported wine and beer. The settlement detailed how Canada agreed on an MFN basis to

amount of $7.496 billion. Ibid., para. 9.1. In *U.S. – Large Civil Aircraft*, WT/DS353/ARB (2nd Complaint) (13 Oct. 2020) the EU estimated that the total annualized value of the adverse effects determined to exist was approximately US $8.58 billion. It was eventually authorized to retaliate in an amount of $3.993 billion. Ibid., para. 8.1.

[186] "U.S. Regrets EU Move on Tariffs, Seeks Deal on Boeing-Airbus Row: Speech" *Reuters* (26 Oct. 2020).

[187] In connection with this, USTR Ambassador Robert Lighthizer "insisted that resolving the dispute would require not just full compliance from the Europeans, 'but also paying back some element of the subsidy and that's tricky because people don't have the same number.'" Hannah Monicken, "EU: Airbus, Member States in Full Compliance in WTO Dispute" 38:31 *Inside U.S. Trade* 15 (31 July 2020).

[188] WT/DS354/2. See "Notification of Mutually Agreed Solution," G/L/806/Add.1, G/SCM/D72/1/Add.1 (23 Dec. 2008).

remove all applied customs duties on nonalcoholic beer, bulk wine, fortified wines, vermouth and grape must, and to reduce applied customs duties in a two-step process for certain other tariff lines, thereby narrowing – though not completely eliminating – the differential between domestic and foreign products. The amendments to Canadian law were implemented in 2010.

How is the outcome in *Canada – Tax Exemptions and Reductions* specifically transformative? A transformation occurred in legal relations because while the settlement was negotiated with the EU, its benefits were extended multilaterally through the operation of MFN. In this sense, Canada's relationship with the remainder of the WTO community was altered or, in other words, transformed.

The second category of transformative arrangement involves the creation of multilateral rights and obligations. An example is the Doha Declaration on TRIPS and Public Health and the subsequent TRIPS amendment. The Declaration was something arrived at gradually through efforts in many fora, taking final shape in a consensual pronouncement by the WTO membership in November 2001.

Haochen Sun has done a masterful job of tracing the transformation at work in the drafting and adoption of the Declaration.[189] Sun illustrates how a number of developing countries and nongovernmental organizations were concerned about the apparently hard-line approach to pharmaceutical patent protection taken by developed countries in *India – Patent Protection*.[190] This approach was manifested most evidently in response to a proposal by Brazil and South Africa to compulsorily license antiretroviral medication belonging to pharmaceutical manufacturers based in developed countries.

Developing countries and NGOs therefore sought to recast the issue of compulsory licensing as one of human rights by discussing it in the World Intellectual Property Organization, the UN High Commission for Human Rights, the UN Sub-Commission on Human Rights, the World Health Organization and the UN General Assembly.[191] What was involved was an effort to alter the conception of the underlying good from one of pharmaceutical know-how (i.e. private property) to one of fundamental human entitlement (i.e. public property). The discussions

[189] Haochen Sun, "The Road to Doha and Beyond: Some Reflections on the TRIPS Agreement and Public Health" 15 *Eur. J. Int'l L.* 123 (2004).

[190] *India – Patent Protection*, WT/DS50/AB/R (19 Dec. 1997).

[191] Sun, "The Road to Doha and Beyond" 127–32.

had the desired effect. Each body adopted statements broadly supportive of a country's right to compulsorily license in order to protect public health in line with the overarching idea of health as a human right.

Sun also details how litigation launched by branded pharmaceutical companies in South Africa in 1998 and by the United States against Brazil in the WTO in February 2001 effectively backfired because it depicted the branded pharmaceutical companies as profit-driven and the global public in many developing countries as denied the fundamental right to human health.[192] These perceptions were reinforced by the apparently self-interested behavior of certain developed countries in response to an anthrax scare in the fall of 2001 when developed country governments threatened to compulsorily license anthrax antidotes.[193]

The outcome of these events was a certain ripening of the compulsory licensing issue internationally. A transformation of legal relations was required among the WTO membership to better reflect the emerging global consensus on intellectual property protection. New rights and obligations needed to be specified.

The Doha Declaration on TRIPS and Public Health of November 2001 partly achieved this aim by acknowledging that "intellectual property protection is important for the development of new medicines" but also confirmed that "the TRIPS Agreement does not and should not prevent [WTO] Members from taking measures to protect public health."[194] Proceeding from these principles, the Declaration recognized that the flexibility inherent in the TRIPS Agreement allows each member "the *right* to grant compulsory licences and the freedom to determine the grounds on which such licences are granted." The Declaration likewise recognized that "[e]ach Member has the *right* to determine what constitutes a national emergency or other circumstances of extreme urgency," specifically mentioning "those relating to HIV/AIDS, tuberculosis, malaria and other epidemics."

The Declaration established a framework for resolving many issues in a far more comprehensive manner than typically results in WTO dispute settlement. It possessed the added advantage of being interpretative in nature and therefore not necessarily requiring domestic implementation. However, one issue that the Declaration did not resolve was identified in paragraph 6:

192 Ibid., pp. 132–133.
193 Ibid., pp. 133–134.
194 WTO Declaration on TRIPS and Public Health, WT/MIN(01)/DEC/2 (20 Nov. 2001).

> We recognize that WTO Members with insufficient or no manufacturing capacities in the pharmaceutical sector could face difficulties in making effective use of compulsory licences under the TRIPS Agreement.

This statement provided impetus for negotiation and agreement on the Decision on the Implementation of Paragraph 6 in August 2003.[195] The Decision solved the problem of exporting compulsorily licensed pharmaceuticals to countries with little pharmaceutical manufacturing capacity by waiving the requirement in TRIPS Art. 31(f) that "any such use shall be authorized *predominately for the domestic market of the Member authorizing such use.*"[196] The Decision effectively allowed, but did not require, countries to self-identify whether they would be eligible "importing Members," that is, whether they would use the system established by the Decision to import compulsorily licensed pharmaceuticals, or in parallel, whether they wished to be designated as "exporting Members" to produce pharmaceuticals for export to eligible importing WTO members.

In a further development, a proposal was made to modify TRIPS Art. 31(f) in the form of an amendment to the TRIPS Agreement in 2005. The amendment, which creates TRIPS Art. 31*bis* formally incorporating the Decision of August 2003 into TRIPS, received support and ultimately entered into force as a treaty amendment in 2017. Most WTO members have already accepted the amendment but members who have yet to do so currently have until the end of 2023.[197]

What is striking about the Declaration of November 2001, the Decision of August 2003 and the TRIPS amendment in January 2017 is the way in which they transform legal relationships by creating new rights and obligations. First, LDCs, and other WTO members issuing the appropriate notification, may use TRIPS Art. 31*bis* as eligible importers.[198] Second, importing countries are obliged to notify the TRIPS Council of the quantities of products needed and to confirm insufficient

[195] *Decision on the Implementation of Paragraph 6 of the Doha Declaration on the TRIPS Agreement and Public Health*, WT/L/540 (2 Sept. 2003). The three separate elements comprised are: (i) a Ministerial Declaration, (ii) a collective waiver under WTO Art. IX:3, and (iii) a proposed amendment of TRIPS Art. 31 pursuant to WTO Art. X.

[196] The Decision also waives TRIPS Art. 31(h), which provides that in securing a compulsory license for a patented product "the right holder shall be paid adequate remuneration in the circumstances of each case, taking into account the economic value of the authorization."

[197] WT/L/1122 (23 Nov. 2021).

[198] Annex to TRIPS Agreement, Art. 1(b).

manufacturing capacity, and then may proceed to grant compulsory licenses.[199] Exporting countries are likewise obliged to issue compulsory licenses, to indicate how much product is being produced under license, to ensure distinctive packaging and so forth.[200] In this way the ensemble of newly identified rights and obligations agreed to can be seen to transform state behavior multilaterally.

As mentioned, transformative justice does not presume wrongdoing. Instead, it aims to resolve conflicts of interest through the exploration of options and the formulation of acceptable responses. A vital attribute of transformative justice is the fact that it seeks to develop and strengthen relationships among those involved.[201] In the case of the TRIPS amendment, this goal is emphasized by overarching obligations of technical and financial cooperation to prevent the reexportation of compulsorily licensed pharmaceuticals, to develop systems of regional patents and to "cooperate in paying special attention to the transfer of technology and capacity-building in the pharmaceutical sector."[202]

TRIPS Art. 31*bis* is a useful example of what the interaction of rights and obligations under the WTO Agreement can yield. At the same time, it is not a panacea or problem-free. To recall the Appellate Body's statement in *U.S. – Shrimp*, "[t]he location of the line of equilibrium [between community and autonomy] . . . is not fixed and unchanging."[203] This statement suggests that the policy space acknowledged in TRIPS Art. 31*bis* is flexible and may, or may not, be generally acceptable depending upon its ability to reflect varying conceptions of the good and the deeper sense of what is just, including power considerations. In the aftermath of the TRIPS amendment, for instance, there continues to be skirmishing over compulsory licensing apparent in the way that countries have implemented the amendment, the negligible number of specific notifications received from importing countries, and at least so far, limited progress on a waiver for COVID-19-related treatments.[204]

199 Ibid., Art. 2(a).

200 Ibid., Art. 2(b).

201 Law Commission of Canada, "From Restorative Justice to Transformative Justice."

202 *Decision on the Implementation of Paragraph 6 of the Doha Declaration on the TRIPS Agreement and Public Health*, WT/L/540, Art. 7 (2 Sept. 2003).

203 *U.S. – Shrimp*, WT/DS58/AB/R, para. 159 (12 Oct. 1998).

204 In July 2007, Rwanda made the first notification under the Paragraph 6 system when it notified the WTO about the importation of 260,000 doses of TriAvir, a combination antiretroviral, from Canada. See IP/N/RWA/1 (19 July 2007). Canada likewise made a reciprocal notification. See IP/N/10/CAN/1 (8 Oct. 2007). See TRIPS Council, Minutes

A third type of transformation observed in WTO law is one which involves the creation of a framework for *an evolving relationship*, often managed in the form of a "dialogue mechanism." "Dialogue" is the idea of discussion carried on between countries over the nature of their obligations and rights, something identified as significant in studies of compliance.[205] In *EC – Biotech*,[206] for instance, Argentina, Canada and the United States took issue with a moratorium applied by the EC on the approval of biotech products. The complaints also asserted that a number of EC member countries maintained marketing and import bans on biotech products at the national level even though the products had already been approved for import and marketing by EC-level bodies.

Litigation proceeded through WTO dispute settlement in the period 2003–2006 involving all three complainants as well as fifteen third parties. Panel reports were circulated to members in September 2006, following which the EC was given twelve months to comply. At that point the results of the litigation diverged. In the case of the EU–US dispute, the United States threatened retaliation but ultimately suspended

of Meeting WTO Doc IP/C/M/74/Add.1 (held on 10–11 October 2013). Government of Canada, *Report on the Statutory Review of* Sections 21.01 *to* 21.19 *of the Patent Act*, at 32–33 (2007). In May 2021 Bolivia notified the WTO it needed to import 15 million doses of COVID-19 vaccine under TRIPS Art. 31*bis*: IP/N/9/BOL/1 (11 May 2021). In a sign of continuing tension over intellectual property protection, in October 2020 developed countries opposed a proposed waiver of TRIPS disciplines put forward by India and South Africa in the TRIPS Council in relation to COVID-19 prevention, containment or treatment. The waiver would temporarily suspend TRIPS Agreement obligations on copyright, industrial designs, patents and the protection of undisclosed information if members' action were taken for these purposes. In June 2022, a partial waiver was agreed at WTO Ministerial Conference 12 allowing distribution of COVID-19 vaccines but not any true suspension of intellectual property rights. The waiver states that WTO members classified as developing countries may produce and distribute patented vaccines within their own borders "to the extent necessary to address the COVID-19 pandemic." "[T]he proposal originally proposed by India and South Africa would have waived 40 articles of TRIPS related to the granting and enforcement of rights. The final agreement, on the other hand, partially waives only one." See Hannah Monicken, "Industry, Civil Society Groups Frustrated over TRIPS Outcome at 12th Ministerial" 40:25 *Inside U.S. Trade* 9 (24 June 2022). See also "*Ministerial Declaration on the WTO Response to the COVID-19 Pandemic and Preparedness for Future Pandemics*" WT/MIN(22)/31 (22 June 2022).

205 Abraham and Antonia Handler Chayes observe that "the fundamental instrument for maintaining compliance with treaties at an acceptable level is *an iterative process of discourse* among the parties, the treaty organization, and the wider public." Abraham Chayes & Antonia Handler Chayes, *The New Sovereignty* 25 (Harvard University Press, Cambridge, MA; 1995) [emphasis added].

206 WT/DS291, 292, 293.

its request in view of an EU commitment to make biotech approval decisions based on science and without delays.[207] In the case of Canada and Argentina, however, the EU agreed to separate settlements and to establish distinct bilateral dialogue mechanisms on biotech issues of mutual interest.[208]

A further example of a dialogue mechanism was the one achieved in *U.S. – Upland Cotton*.[209] The outcome of the *U.S. – Upland Cotton* dispute resulted in a Framework for a Mutually Agreed Solution between Brazil and the United States in 2010.[210] The Framework was not itself a "mutually agreed solution" under the DSU but set out parameters for discussions on a solution with respect to domestic support programs for US-grown cotton, as well as a process of joint operation reviews regarding US agricultural export credit guarantees. Under the Framework Brazil and the United States agreed to hold regular consultations with the aim of obtaining convergence of views in respect of a comprehensive solution. This commitment resulted in a number of meetings between Brazilian diplomats and the US Congress. The Framework also provided that, upon enactment of successor legislation to the *US Food, Conservation and Energy Act of 2008*, Brazil and the United States would consult with a view to determining whether a mutually agreed solution to the *Upland Cotton* dispute had been reached. In exchange, Brazil agreed not to impose countermeasures authorized by the DSB. A final settlement of the dispute was reached in 2014.[211]

The dialogue mechanisms achieved in *EC – Biotech*, *U.S. – Upland Cotton* and similar cases have been supplemented by mechanisms

[207] More recently, without any apparent modification of the EU's position, the United States appears to have pursued the matter in talks preparatory to the negotiation of a projected US–EU FTA.

[208] In the case of Canada–EU, a bilateral Dialogue on Biotech Market Access Issues was established in 2009 and later became part of the Canada–European Union Comprehensive Economic and Trade Agreement (CETA). EU Commission Press Release, "EU and Canada Settle WTO Case on Genetically Modified Organisms" (15 July 2019). In the case of Argentina–EU, the settlement reached between them in 2010 provided for biannual meetings between EU Commission and Argentine authorities regarding the application of biotechnology to agriculture and related trade issues of mutual interest. See EU Commission Press Release, "EU and Argentina Settle WTO Case on Genetically Modified Organisms" (18 Mar. 2010).

[209] WT/DS267.

[210] See *U.S. – Subsidies on Upland Cotton*: Notification of a Mutually Agreed Solution, WT/DS267/46 (23 Oct. 2014).

[211] See "U.S., Brazil Settle WTO Cotton Dispute; Deal Includes $300 Million Payment" 32:39 *Inside U.S. Trade* 1 (3 Oct. 2014).

formally outside the WTO, notably those between the United States and EU, the United States and China, and China and the EU.[212] To be sure, various WTO organs and committees continue to play an important role in channeling and shaping debate on trade-related topics, yet key WTO members have sought to create dialogue mechanisms going beyond the WTO in recent years. These deal more specifically with issues peculiar to the bilateral or plurilateral relationships in question, providing opportunities to uncover potential problems and head-off recourse to formal dispute settlement before it is invoked. Because of their informality, such mechanisms can also cover overlapping subjects, that is, trade irritants with interdependent causes that are hard to target in WTO dispute settlement, and matters that straddle both WTO and non-WTO obligations. Such developments are emblematic of the ever-greater complexity and interdependence of international economic relations and the importance of transformation in sustaining community.

3.4 Beyond Transformation

The foregoing analysis reveals that a communitarian theory does a relatively good job of accounting for the principal features, practices and outcomes of WTO dispute settlement. Its law and practice appear

[212] The US-EU Transatlantic Economic Council (TEC) was established in April 2007 and is tasked with creating regulatory convergence between the United States and the EU on some forty different public policy areas. The TEC is assisted in shaping its mandate by the Transatlantic Business Dialogue (TABD). The TABD is an informal process, whereby European and American companies and business associations develop joint EU-US trade policy recommendations, working together with the EC Commission and US administration. A second effort at dialogue has been the US–China Strategic Economic Dialogue (SED) established in September 2006. Reflecting the growing relationship between the US and Chinese economies, the dialogue is tasked with examining long-term strategic issues as well as providing coordination among the specialized continuing dialogues. SED's success has given rise to a parallel effort by the EU to institute its own dialogue mechanism with China. The EU–China High Level Economic and Trade Dialogue (HLM) was established in November 2007 and aims to enlarge and deepen cooperation on trade and economic issues between the EU and China. It focused coordination of policy and practice on the most important issues, including energy, trade in high technology, IP protection and trade facilitation. See Iana Dreyer & Fredrik Erixon, "An EU-China Trade Dialogue" *ECIPE Policy Brief* No. 03/2008. For examples of bilateral dialogue efforts, see also Canada-US Regulatory Convergence Council (RCC) and the US–Brazil Commercial Dialogue. On this last see "Nunes Announces Legislation Creating Strategic U.S.–Brazil Dialogue" 31:24 *Inside U.S. Trade* 2 (14 June 2013).

to align reasonably well with the theory's three-fold arrangement of justice as distributive, corrective and transformative.

Still, the culminating idea of transformation raises a number of questions. One of these is the relationship between transformation and "perfect justice," the harmonious reconciliation of all interests. The second concerns the relationship between transformation and global justice, understood as the threshold or ethical minimum that must be adhered to by states in the international community. The third is the question of the relationship between transformative justice and compliance. The fourth concerns the role of transformative justice in efforts to promote WTO law's legitimacy.

3.4.1 Perfect Justice

The idea of transformation as the end product of the interaction of distributive and corrective justice raises the question of why the various transformations achieved in WTO dispute settlement might fall short of perfect justice and how the shortfall can be justified.

I have already mentioned how, according to a communitarian theory, justice is never entirely perfect. That is because justice is never completely done and because transformative justice aims at transformation among interests in the community of the WTO, not the community of all humanity.

The incompleteness of justice was mentioned by Aristotle in the *Nicomachean Ethics* when he observed that "[l]aw belongs to those *among whom injustice is [possible]*."[213] Aristotle's observation suggests that law will not lead to the total elimination of injustice but instead helps keep residual injustice in check.

Residual injustice arises for at least three reasons. The first involves differences over the appropriate idea of the good. As seen in the case of patented pharmaceuticals under the TRIPS Agreement, different views of what good is aimed at can lead to different outcomes, and inevitably, some disappointment that one's preferred vision is not reflected in the law's conception.

The second involves the situated nature of equality and fairness. A communitarian theory accepts that all instances of justice involve fairness passing under the rubric of "equality." However, because not

[213] Aristotle, *Nicomachean Ethics* 1134a31 [emphasis added].

every interest can be taken into account in determining what is deemed equal or fair, some interest is likely to find the transformation achieved to be unjust.

Third, as mentioned, there is the evolving nature of equality and fairness, which are always responding to and "catching up" with what is understood to be just in the present.

These three points underline how justice is never final and how for this reason every community is relatively unjust. That residuum prevents transformation from constituting the ideal of perfect justice.

There continues to be much debate about the ultimate justice of WTO arrangements. Many commentators have found justice under the WTO Agreement wanting. They may also be prompted to describe my threefold arrangement of justice in a communitarian theory to be too felicitous – in effect, too "nice." The examples reveal the results of WTO dispute settlement in perhaps their best light. Many outcomes in WTO dispute settlement are nowhere near as beneficial or accommodative.

Take the situation of Antigua, which has made repeated efforts to settle the *U.S. – Gambling* dispute, a case in which it received the right to levy $21 million in countermeasures against the United States in 2005, an amount too small to pose a retaliatory threat. A series of discussions between Antigua and the United States over the case has gone nowhere.[214] Or the case of Pakistan in *U.S. – Cotton Yarn*, which involved a challenge by Pakistan to a US transitional safeguard on certain imports of cotton yarn from Pakistan. The safeguard expired just as the Appellate Body rendered its report in the dispute, effectively leaving Pakistan without recourse.[215] Or the case of *U.S. – Upland Cotton* mentioned previously, which involved a negotiated settlement between Brazil and the United States and the removal of noncompliant US legislation, only to have it replaced by legislation that is arguably still more trade-distorting.[216] Each of these examples can be pointed to as

[214] WT/DS285. See Tom Miles, "Antigua 'Losing All Hope' of U.S. Payout in Gambling Dispute" *Reuters* (22 June 2018).

[215] See *U.S. – Cotton Yarn*, WT/DS192/AB/R (8 Oct. 2001). The panel and Appellate Body found a number of violations of the WTO Agreement on Textiles and Clothing. The Committee for the Implementation of Textile Agreements directed the US Customs Service to eliminate the limit on imports of combed cotton yarn from Pakistan. See WT/DSB/M/113 (17 Dec. 2001).

[216] Simon Lau & Simon Shropp, "The Role of Economics in WTO Dispute Settlement and Choosing the Right Litigation Strategy – A Practitioner's View" in Marion Jansen et al. (eds), *The Use of Economics in International Trade and Investment Disputes* 55 at 72

evidence of an outcome where justice rendered under the DSU has not worked transformatively to reconcile the interests involved.

More broadly, a number of commentators have pointed out how WTO arrangements as a whole have potential to violate other norms of international law, particularly international human rights. For example, Sarah Joseph has noted how:

> The narrowness of the range of beneficiaries under the WTO gives rise to the danger that [its] beneficiaries are unduly privileged when their interests clash with those of others, such as, for example, local competitors and consumers, in a way that undermines the rights of the latter.[217]

Joseph goes on to detail how under WTO rules "the freedoms of foreign traders are prioritized at the expense of the rights of local traders,"[218] how "part of the point of the WTO is to drive the less advantaged out of business on the basis that they are less efficient than the more advantaged"[219] and how WTO-induced economic adjustments, while creating benefits, also "generate significant social costs."[220]

One response to these shortcomings is to point out how the procedures and outcomes of WTO law as a system of justice are expressions of what sovereign governments have agreed to in their economic relations *inter se*. As part of this agreement, greater efficiency is no wrong. Rather, it is regarded as beneficial. The communitarian theory of justice put forward above highlights how justice is a product of a distinctive community. What is observed in WTO law then can be understood as aimed at a specific conception of the good.

On the specific issue of the conflict between WTO law and international human rights, one response is to recognize the two regimes as separate and distinct.

A number of aspects of the relevant legal systems work to reinforce this difference. One is the fact that "WTO adjudicating bodies cannot formally interpret other [i.e. non-WTO] treaties and customs . . . and thus determine the legal consequences of rights and obligations that

(Cambridge University Press, Cambridge; 2017). Lau and Shropp note that the new "cotton subsidies are more focused on highly subsidized revenue insurance, which is a tool to maintain substantial support even at times of high prices." Ibid., n. 35.

217 Joseph, *Blame It on the WTO* 34.

218 Ibid., p. 38.

219 Ibid., p. 39.

220 Ibid., p. 41.

WTO Members may have under other treaties or by custom."[221] Another aspect is that "WTO Members do not appear to have granted WTO remedies for the enforcement of rights and obligations other than those under the 'covered agreements.'"[222] Furthermore, although "WTO Members in violation of human rights may be liable" for human rights violations, "[state] responsibility [for such violations] cannot be enforced by WTO adjudicating bodies."[223] At the same time, nothing in WTO law expressly requires the violation of human rights or precludes human rights bodies from making findings of violation on their own. These differences and the segregation they imply limit the ability of WTO dispute settlement to harmonize and reconcile all interests.

A further criticism of the WTO Agreement is that the treaty exacerbates inequality. The claim is often made that "[f]ree trade is not working for the majority of the world"[224] and that in the most recent periods of growth in international trade inequality has worsened both between and within countries. WTO rules are said to "have hastened these trends"[225] by promoting foreign investment and making it easier to offshore production. The claim is forwarded that this movement "pulls down wages and environmental standards in developing countries who have to compete globally."[226]

At the same time, evidence also points to international trade under WTO rules making a major contribution to increasing living standards. It appears that many individuals would be poorer if there had been no trade liberalization in the past several decades.[227] How to resolve the conflict between winners and losers in WTO-led globalization?

Here, three points can be made. First, the communitarian theory of justice outlined in this chapter emphasizes the way that justice and law in WTO law are conceived of primarily in distributive and *ex ante* terms. As mentioned, they are the product of the WTO's distinctive community,

[221] Gabrielle Marceau, "WTO Dispute Settlement and Human Rights" 13 *E.J.I.L.* 753 (2002).

[222] Ibid.

[223] Ibid.

[224] "The WTO Is Increasing Inequality," www.wto.org/english/thewto_e/minist_e/min99_e/english/misinf_e/08poor_e.htm

[225] Ibid.

[226] Ibid.

[227] Due in part to trade-induced liberalization in recent decades, there has been "an extraordinary decline in the proportion of people in extreme poverty [worldwide], from 43 percent in 1980 to 10 percent in 2015." Martin Wolf, "COVID-19 Will Hit Developing Countries Hard" *Financial Times* 17 (10 June 2020).

which has created a club good concerned with promoting the equality of competitive conditions going forward. Contemporary criticism of inequality – particularly within developed countries – appears to stem from a desire to regulate outcomes individually and *ex post*. These divergent views – in the treaty and in parts of global public opinion – need to be kept in mind.

Second, under current WTO arrangements, responsibility for redistributing gains from trade *remains with member governments*. The WTO should take the opportunity to periodically remind members that international trade disciplines require a number of strong complementary policies – indexed minimum wages, the promotion of life-long learning, progressive taxation, childcare, digital privacy, public pensions, environmental protection and gender and minority inclusion – in order to spread its benefits.[228] This proposal is in line with contemporary emphasis in development thinking on the idea of "co-responsibility" and the fact that stark differences observed in economic attainment between adjacent countries such as Haiti and the Dominican Republic are partly the result of national value choices.[229] Consequently, development involves an element of national responsibility and a wider range of considerations than simply WTO commitments.

Third, on the specific issue of poverty alleviation, international trade is no longer regarded as a panacea for every country's development challenges. Most mainstream development thinking, as embodied in the UN's Sustainable Development Goals, now adheres to the view that development is multifaceted. The changes that are required for development to take place are likely to occur in a piecemeal fashion, over time, in ways large and small.[230] They will involve many elements working together, of which the WTO Agreement is only one.

[228] Martin Sandbu, *The Economics of Belonging* (Princeton University Press, Princeton, NJ; 2020).

[229] John Tasioulas, "International Law and the Limits of Fairness" 13 *E.J.I.L.* 993 at 1019 (2002).

[230] Development and poverty are multiaspected. Solutions to them must likewise be multiaspected. According to Wendy Smith:

> No single grand plan will end poverty. It will happen in ripples, in fits and starts, and over a fair amount of time. It will resemble parts of the Marshall Plan, the Millennium Development Goals, and top-down and bottom-up aid – which all contribute crucial pieces to the remedy: pro-business policies, universal access to education and health care, mass distribution of humanitarian aid and prevention and treatment of

In assessing the overall balance of negative and positive contributions made by the WTO Agreement to international economic governance and its contribution to attaining justice, it is useful to keep in mind what a forum like the WTO continues to offer. WTO dispute settlement's version of justice-as-transformation may be "thin" and far from perfect, but it provides baseline rules, an adjudicative mechanism and a forum where differences can be worked out. Chantal Thomas has observed:

> In the absence of universal policy directives, an open-ended dialogue may allow for the greatest possible consideration of disparate views and varied sources of information. Although a democratized negotiation procedure in the WTO may be far from ideal, it may nevertheless provide the surest – and perhaps the only – path to decisions that reflect some semblance of distributive justice.[231]

Thomas may be optimistic in her call for a "democratized" negotiating framework, but her instinct for dialogue is sound. Why? Because according to a communitarian theory justice only takes hold where there is common good and value. Dialogue, interaction and interdependence are all required in order to identify the good and arrive at continuing agreement about its value, thereby ensuring a basis for sustainable community.

3.4.2 *Global Justice*

In recent decades discussion of justice at the international level has cleaved into two separate discussions concerning international justice and global justice. The former is conventionally concerned with the

> rampant diseases, and microenterprises free to grow large in an open, pro-business marketplace.
>
> (Wendy Smith, "Extreme Measures for Dire Poverty," Book Review of *The Aid Trap* by R. Glenn Hubbard & William Duggan, 47:1 *Finance & Development* 55 (Mar. 2010))

[231] Chantal Thomas, "The Death of Doha? Forensics of Democratic Governance, Distributive Justice and Development in the WTO" in Chios Carmody et al. (eds), *Global Justice and International Economic Law* 185 at 214 (Cambridge University Press, Cambridge; 2012). The Consultative Board chaired by Peter Sutherland noted in a substantially similar vein in 2004 that the only means through which the WTO can fulfil its mandate is through "the efficient conduct of negotiations and the pursuit of multilateral consensus." Consultative Board to the Director-General Supachai Panitchpakdi, *The Future of the WTO* (World Trade Organization, Geneva; 2004) at para. 269, online: WTO, www.wto.org/english/thewto_e/10anniv_e/future_wto_e.htm [Sutherland Report].

obligations that countries owe to each other, whereas the latter focuses on certain minimum obligations that may be owed by the international community to the less well-off.[232] How does transformative justice align with or depart from this latter concern?

Transformative justice is fundamentally about achieving accommodative solutions to sustain community. By comparison, the starting point for debate about global justice lies in cosmopolitan assertions about the equal moral worth of individuals.[233] The underlying premise of global justice is that many key distinctions observed in international political economy such as citizenship are arbitrary and should play no role in arranging obligations that individuals owe to each other.

One particular position within the cosmopolitan view known as Rawlsian cosmopolitanism goes on to maintain that the well-being of the worst-off representative member of the global society, rather than the domestic community, is the natural basis for assessing inequality.[234]

In taking this position, Rawlsian cosmopolitans differ with Rawls himself, who maintained in *A Law of Peoples* (1999) that his original idea of justice as fairness was worked out for the basic structure of society shared among individuals possessing certain institutions in common. According to Rawls, this requirement limits justice as fairness and any associated duty of redistribution to circumstances found *within* countries.[235]

[232] "Contemporary political philosophers had focused their theorizing about justice almost exclusively within the state, but the last twenty years or so has seen a marked extension to the global sphere." S.v. "Global Justice" in *Stanford Encyclopedia of Philosophy* (6 Mar. 2015) (author: Gillian Brock).

[233] S.v. "Cosmopolitans refuse to differentiate between citizen and stranger. Citizenship is a deep contingency which cannot serve to ground any differentiation in the administration of justice. A variant on this category, Rawlsian cosmopolitanism, regards the well-being of the worst-off representative member of the global society, rather than the domestic, as the starting-point for the justification of inequality." S.v. "Global Justice" in *Stanford Encyclopedia of Philosophy* (6 Mar. 2015) (author: Gillian Brock).

[234] For discussion, see s.v. "International Distributive Justice" in *Stanford Encyclopedia of Philosophy* (4 May 2020) (author: Michael Blake & Patrick Taylor Smith).

[235] Rawls posited that at the international level, a just international regime would involve states agreeing to treat each other fairly without any sort of redistributive obligation. Instead, as part of his "Law of Peoples" Rawls advocated a more limited "duty of assistance" owed to unfortunate states in critical circumstances, a duty which prioritizes both the initial responsibility that individuals owe to their immediate communities and the mutual respect that communities owe each other. "John Rawls" in *Stanford Encyclopedia of Philosophy* (9 Jan. 2017) (author: Leif Wenar).

A number of Rawlsian cosmopolitans have taken issue with Rawls's conclusions in *A Law of Peoples*. In their view Rawls's limitation of justice as fairness to the circumstances of domestic societies is morally illegitimate. A consistent liberal view would require the projection of Rawls's original ideas concerning justice as fairness at a global level.[236]

One advocate of Rawlsian cosmopolitanism in the context of WTO arrangements is Frank Garcia. Garcia's book *Trade, Inequality and Justice* (2003) develops the cosmopolitan argument that the principle of S&DT "could play a central role in satisfying the moral obligations that wealthier states owe poorer states as a matter of distributive justice."[237] Garcia suggests that through enhanced S&DT the WTO as an institution might have a role in reducing global inequality. His proposal forwards a Rawlsian difference principle – which he refers to as an "international difference principle" – through the instrumentality of the WTO.

Garcia premises his position on the idea that social outcomes are "essential to any meaningful concept of justice."[238] His main points can be briefly summarized as follows. First, "allocations of the benefits and burdens of social cooperation must follow the principle of Justice as Fairness, in order that in such allocations, the moral equality of human beings is effectively recognized."[239] Second, through international trade law "states cooperate in international economic relations to create new economic benefits and burdens, and make decisions allocating such benefits and burdens."[240] Third, "international trade law must follow the principle of Justice as Fairness in order that in its allocations of the benefits and burdens of international economic cooperation the moral equality of human beings is effectively recognized."[241]

The communitarian theory of justice put forward in this book regards matters somewhat differently. Without ignoring human rights concerns, it recognizes that the issue of moral equality in WTO law is worked out chiefly among states. As Steven Ratner has pointed out, various actors in

236 Ibid.

237 Franck Garcia, *Trade, Inequality and Justice* 40 (Transnational Publishers, Ardsley, NY; 2003).

238 Ibid., p. 44.

239 Ibid., p. 84.

240 Ibid.

241 Ibid.

international law have "fundamentally different claims."[242] The preeminent duties of states are to refrain from using force, to respect human rights, and to allow various forms of self-determination.[243] This differs from the obligations owed by individuals toward states and toward each other. In addition, international law does not concern itself solely with the standing of individuals nor give their claims greater weight than the claims of other individuals.[244] Consequently, international law cannot be deemed a purely cosmopolitan project.[245] Instead, international law "retains a pro-State bias, one in deep tension with cosmopolitanism" and one that reflects itself in international law's substantive content.[246]

These comments help to preface and foreground certain differences detected between the communitarian theory of justice under WTO law put forward in this chapter and Garcia's idea of an international difference principle based on global justice. To be sure, an international difference principle with a cosmopolitan streak is already visible in WTO arrangements in the form of S&DT. At the same time, from a communitarian perspective Garcia's call for *enhanced* S&DT may go beyond what is necessary to sustain the WTO's community.

To begin with, it appears inaccurate to focus exclusively on the plight of developing countries in the WTO system – to make their betterment, in effect, the *chief* aim of the system – when from a communitarian perspective the principal question is a still greater one: how is this pressing task to be accomplished along with the other tasks that the WTO as a community is supposed to fulfill in order to sustain itself?[247]

A second concern with Garcia's proposal is structural. His proposed difference principle appears to emphasize *ex post* outcomes, whereas a communitarian theory of justice makes clear that a central task of the

[242] Steven Ratner, "From Enlightened Positivism to Cosmopolitan Justice: Obstacles and Opportunities" in Ulrich Fastenrath et al. (eds), *From Bilateralism to Community Interest* 155 at 160 (Oxford University Press, Oxford; 2011).

[243] Ibid.

[244] Ibid., p. 161.

[245] Ibid.

[246] Ibid.

[247] In this respect, questions have been raised about poverty and how this alone is to be the focus of analysis and critique of the international trading system. See Oisin Suttle, "Poverty and Justice: Competing Lenses on International Economic Law," Book Review of John Linarelli (ed.), *Research Handbook on Global Justice and International Economic Law* (2013) and Krista Nadakavukaren Schefer (ed.), *Poverty and the International Economic Legal System: Duties to the World's Poor* (2013) in 15 *J. World Invest. Trade* 1071 (2014).

WTO system is on the reconciliation of *ex ante* expectations with *ex post* outcomes, and in the process facilitatie transformation. True, it may be that over the long run we need to concern ourselves with improving conditions of the disadvantaged. There can be little objection to that worthy aim. But at the very least, any move toward enhanced S&DT requires better identification of exactly who is disadvantaged and who is not. In addition, doing so does not preclude transformative outcomes consistent with global justice – particularly basic human rights – as was evident in the case of the Doha Declaration on TRIPS and Public Health and the subsequent TRIPS amendment.

A third, related concern pertains to implementation. Garcia's proposal for an "international difference principle" overlooks the problem of arriving at a single metric to apply it. To realize such a principle, it would be necessary to have some idea of the particular outcome sought. How big would a "difference" have to be to trigger an associated obligation stemming from an "international difference principle"? Garcia sidesteps this question by asserting that he does not advocate "*absolute* equality of outcomes" so much as an obligation triggered by "*justifiable* inequality."[248] But what is "justifiable"? Perhaps the best answer that might be sought to these questions is some sort of basic minimum entitlement consistent with international human rights in the form of a sufficiency approach.[249] Working this minimum out would appear to require more than consideration of the WTO Agreement, however. It would appear to necessitate a global exercise in determining what equality should be, which a communitarian theory suggests is unlikely, given the very situated nature of equality and fairness.

A few final observations should be made. First, it may be that an enhanced S&DT "could . . . play a central role in satisfying the moral obligations that wealthier states owe poorer states,"[250] account being

[248] "The goal and standard for any egalitarian theory of distributive justice will be a principle of justice by which social organization can be adequately justified in the face of inequality, even if this involves the redistribution of wealth towards, if not absolute equality of outcomes, then *justifiable inequality*." Garcia, *Trade, Inequality and Justice* 115.

[249] "The doctrine of sufficiency holds that it is morally valuable that as many as possible of all who shall ever live should enjoy conditions of life that place them above the threshold that marks the minimum required for a decent (good enough) quality of life." S.v. "Egalitarianism" in *Stanford Encyclopedia of Philosophy* (24 Apr. 2013) (author: Richard Arneson).

[250] Garcia, *Trade, Inequality and Justice* 40.

taken of its acknowledged shortcomings.[251] Second, S&DT has been criticized for being heavily conditional, prone to favoritism and abuse, and subject to caps and phase outs.[252] Third, S&DT also arguably creates unhealthy dependence. A more realistic proposal as a matter of justice might be to phase S&DT out for certain developing countries in order to permit the remaining preferences to be targeted more directly to a limited group of LDCs or to micro-, small- and medium-sized enterprises (MSMEs) that truly need it.

3.4.3 Compliance

An apparent concern in WTO arrangements is with member countries' compliance with the WTO Agreement. This raises the question of how a communitarian theory of justice's emphasis on transformation is to be assessed in light of the task of achieving compliance.

The subject of compliance has "preoccupied international lawyers for almost [three] decades."[253] On the whole, however, it has not been as much of a concern in relation to the WTO Agreement as might be expected.[254] This may be because of the primacy of transformative justice in the scheme of the treaty, and along with it, the law's essential adaptability. Many key WTO norms and standards are vague, and compliance with them is difficult to determine, given the associated treaty framework. I have mentioned several ways in which formal consistency with

251 At the moment, in an era of loss of faith in unconditional interdependence, the ability of certain developing countries to take advantage of the "developing country" designation is under attack by the United States, which is demanding "graduation" for certain LDCs (to developing country status) and aims to end the invocation of developing country status by major countries such as China and India. See B. N. Pandey & Prabhat Kumar Saha, "Special and Differential Treatment in the WTO: Current Anxieties" 61(4) *J. Indian L. Institute* 463 (2019).

252 For criticism of S&DT, see Draft General Council Decision, "Procedures to Strengthen the Negotiating Function of the WTO," submitted by the United States, WT/GC/W/764 (15 Feb. 2019). For discussion see Sonia Rolland, *Development at the WTO* 292–293 (Oxford University Press, Oxford; 2012).

253 Jutta Brunnée & Stephen Toope, *Legitimacy and Legality in International Law* 88 (Cambridge University Press, Cambridge; 2010).

254 Bruce Wilson, "Compliance by WTO members with Adverse WTO Dispute Settlement Rulings" 10:2 *J.I.E.L.* 397 (2007) (noting "[t]he generally positive record of Members in complying with adverse rulings by panels, the Appellate Body or both has been an important factor in the success of the WTO dispute settlement system to date."); Davey, "Compliance Problems in WTO Dispute Settlement" 199 (noting that "[i]n general, the WTO dispute settlement system has an excellent compliance record").

WTO law is not always required or even desirable. Substantial room is left for flexibility, often with the help of "tricks and fictions."[255]

Nevertheless, the significance of compliance in the framework of the treaty invites consideration of the true relationship between transformation and compliance. One set of insights is offered by Peter Gerhart who, in an article surveying compliance with the TRIPS Agreement, attempts to explain how perceptions of the "substantive validity" of rules influence adherence to intellectual property disciplines under the WTO Agreement.[256] According to Gerhart substantive validity is "the issue of whether the obligation in question meets an articulated standard of welfare."[257] A legitimate standard is one that is formalist and process-oriented, whereas a substantively valid standard is one that is "welfare-improving."[258] Gerhart posits that a "statement that a standard is substantively valid is the statement that the standard is just."[259] From this observation it is possible to derive "the common sense notion that people (and states) are more likely to comply with laws they believe to be just than with laws they believe to be unjust."[260]

Gerhart is most directly interested in why compliance with TRIPS has been uneven and what explains the irregular degree of compliance observed. He advances two theses, one a "Coercion Story," the other a "Contract Story." The first "portrays the United States as systematically threatening to close its borders to countries that would not agree to minimum intellectual property standards."[261] The second emphasizes how "the United States, Europe, and Japan 'bought'" TRIPS by "agreeing to liberalize their markets to developing country products further."[262]

While Gerhart admits that there is some truth to both stories, his preference for the latter is based upon its underlying images of reciprocity and consent. In this telling:

> [t]he costs imposed on developing countries by TRIPS [would] be offset by the reciprocal benefits the countries get by being able to sell more textiles and agricultural products in the industrialized world. The pact is,

[255] Glenn, *Legal Traditions of the World* 253.

[256] Peter Gerhart, "Reflections: Beyond Compliance Theory – TRIPS as a Substantive Issue" 32:3 *Case Western Reserve J. Int'l L.* 357 (2000).

[257] Ibid. at 361.

[258] Ibid.

[259] Ibid.

[260] Ibid. at 361.

[261] Ibid. at 368.

[262] Ibid. at 370.

> therefore, substantively valid under a simple exchange rationale; when countries (or people, for that matter) exchange mutually beneficial promises, the outcome of the bargain is substantively valid because the shared gains from trade enhance global wealth.[263]

According to Gerhart the fact that this North–South "deal" was never fully honored after the Uruguay Round – due to China's entry into the organization having taken up much of the enhanced textile access and developed country intransigence on phasing out agricultural support – explains the fact of uneven compliance with TRIPS.

Gerhart's account is both intelligible and plausible. At the same time, it is also true that noncompliance with the WTO Agreement may stem from a range of motives, only one of these being the desire to achieve transformative outcomes. In other instances, continuing noncompliance may not be directly traceable to transformation. It may be, for instance, that standards of compliance have to be worked out progressively. In still other instances, more selfish motives may be at play, such as governments' desire to localize production.[264] In these circumstances, depending on the political constellation and immediate need to address the issue, new rules may have to be worked out transformatively and interim compliance with them will remain tentative and opaque.

In addition, it cannot be automatically assumed that WTO rules themselves are synonymous with justice, and hence, that compliance with them is a form of justice. There is always the possibility that the resistance embodied in continuing noncompliance is regarded by some governments or interests as itself just.[265]

3.4.4 Legitimacy

A final topic of consideration in relation to transformative justice is legitimacy. The subject of legitimacy has featured "heavily in debates about international law and institutions" recently but appears to suffer

[263] Ibid. at 371.

[264] Keith Maskus, "Intellectual Property Rights and Economic Development" 32:3 *Case Western Reserve J. Int'l L.* 471 (2000) (maintaining that strengthened patent protection will lead to greater technology transfer in developing countries). This assertion has been contested. See Rajnish Kumar Rai, "Effect of the TRIPS-Mandated Intellectual Property Rights on Foreign Direct Investment in Developing Countries" 11:5–6 *J. World Intell. Prop.* 404 (2008).

[265] Edward Lee, "Measuring TRIPS Compliance and Defiance" 18 *J. Intell. Prop. L.* 401 (2010–2011).

from a lack of definition.[266] Despite this shortcoming, legitimacy remains undeniably important. Common sense suggests that a legitimate law reflective of justice is more likely to be adhered to than one that does not.

As an initial matter, it might be thought that legitimacy should go hand-in-hand with transformation inasmuch as a legitimate law – one validly made – should aim to sustain community. However, that easy connection is not automatically identified in commentary. A law might be considered legitimate or illegitimate by a variety of actors for numerous reasons that have little to do with its underlying rightness or correctness. Commentators have raised issues of legitimacy primarily in relation to studies of compliance and tend to emphasize its process-oriented character. In one well-known definition, for instance, Thomas Franck has asserted that a rule is legitimate "because the rule or institution has come into being and operates in accordance with generally accepted principles of *right process*."[267]

For this reason, the link between legitimacy and justice is conceived of flexibly and runs the gamut from those who believe the two topics are fundamentally different to those who regard them as essentially the same. It is the differences that matter, however, chiefly because of their ability to highlight distinctions. So in the first instance, I focus here on the work of Thomas Franck since his work on legitimacy is often taken as the starting point for contemporary consideration of the subject and because he is someone who clearly distinguishes between justice and legitimacy.

Franck's position on the relationship between justice and legitimacy could be termed "incrementalist" in the sense that his most developed

266 Legitimacy has been defined as "the justification of the exercise of public authority." S.v. "Legitimacy in International Law" in *Max Planck Encyclopedias of Public International Law* (Mar. 2011) (author: Rüdiger Wolfrum). Many definitions of legitimacy have been employed recently. For instance, Thomas Franck refers to legitimacy as "a property of a rule or rule-making institution which itself exerts a pull towards compliance on those addressed normatively because the rule or institution has come into being and operates in accordance with generally accepted principles of right process." Franck, *The Power of Legitimacy among Nations* 24. Jutta Brunnée and Stephen Toope share some common ground with Franck but focus on legitimacy arising from interaction. For them legitimacy is "the capacity to generate fidelity to the rule of law itself and not merely to specific rules." They posit that "legitimacy is built through broad participation in the construction and maintenance of legal regimes." Brunnée & Toope, *Legitimacy and Legality in International Law* 53. There has been criticism of vague ascriptions of illegitimacy as a standard for measuring international legal behavior. See James Crawford, "The Problems of Legitimacy-Speak" 98 *Proc. Annu. Meet. (American Society of International Law)* 271 (2004).

267 Franck, *The Power of Legitimacy among Nations* 24 [emphasis added].

analysis of the distinction comes at the end of his book *The Power of Legitimacy Among Nations* (1990), in which he brings renewed attention to the topic of legitimacy but also concludes his examination with a postlude entitled "Why Not Justice?." The placement of this query is significant since it suggests that the concept of legitimacy is prefatory and might be regarded as a stepping stone to justice.

Franck excludes justice among factors promoting legitimacy because in his view "justice can only be said to be done to persons, not to such collective entities as states"[268] and because "concepts of justice and legitimacy are related but conceptually distinct."[269] In Franck's view:

> the first task for now [in international relations], is to build a rule system of such manifest legitimacy as to engender a broad base of uncoerced habitual compliance. Lexically, the task of ensuring the justice of that rule system is the second, not the first order of business on the urgent, but still largely unfinished, global agenda.[270]

According to Franck the deeper reason for observing a distinction between justice and legitimacy, however, is structural. The traditional contract theory on which the international community is based does "not claim to be a theory of justice ... but of social order."[271] That order means that "the international rule system is likely to appear more unjust than any nation's legal system, precisely because the structure of the international system is that of a concert of rulers rather than a parliament of humanity."[272] Within that structure "[international] justice would have almost nothing to do with justice as people might understand it, but almost everything to do with the way governments naturally think."[273] A rule of territorial integrity, for instance, would prevail over the claims of a people to self-determination who, absent exigent circumstances, are normally bound to realize their self-determination within the boundaries of an existing state.

According to a communitarian theory, justice depends on the community's vision or idea of the good. Each community will prioritize different goods and will evidence its own mix of distributive and corrective justice in relation to those goods, a difference that manifests

[268] Ibid., 208.
[269] Ibid., 209.
[270] Ibid., 210.
[271] Ibid., 211.
[272] Ibid., 226.
[273] Ibid., 230.

itself in the transformations it is willing to effect. Legitimacy focuses on rules recognizing the good of order, whereas transformative justice involves a wider range of goods whose distribution and correction emanate from a belief in the abiding good of the community.

3.5 Justice: A Communitarian Idea

In the previous chapter I developed a theory of community based on the idea that actors come together in communities to generate goods as a by-product of interdependence. Actors will not come together, however, unless they are reasonably sure that they will be relatively better off by doing so. This further idea – of being better off – normally takes the form of a preoccupation in communal arrangements with justice.

In this chapter, I went on to develop a theory of justice as a complement to the theory of community developed earlier.

To provide an analytical framework I first examined theories of justice put forward by Aristotle and Rawls. Aristotle's theory identified justice in two classic forms, distributive and corrective, with the former being commonly understood to be about the distribution of goods and the latter being understood to involve correction of injury to those goods. Rawls' theory was about how individuals in an original position aiming to establish a prototypical community would employ a public criterion of justice to work out a fair distribution of goods within that community. Both Aristotle and Rawls' theories appear to leave many questions unanswered, notably about how distributive and corrective justice are to be reconciled and integrated withing an actual community.

To answer this question, I went on to develop a communitarian theory of justice based on a reconfiguration of Aristotelian ideas. Unlike many contemporary interpretations, I posited that the most plausible way to understand the relationship between distributive and corrective justice is interactively and interdependently. By "interactive" I meant to suggest that the general pattern of behavior between the forms of justice is reciprocal. Distributive justice sets the general terms on which corrective justice takes place but sequential instances of correction influence ideas about the appropriate distribution which change.

At the same time, I suggested that this interaction is not entirely random. Instead, within the general framework of interactivity can be detected interdependent relations of correlation, subordination, transition and integration. By correlation I mean that where there is distributive justice there will be an associated need for corrective justice. By subordination I mean that distributive justice will tend to be primary whereas corrective justice will be secondary. By transition I mean that at their outer limits both distributive and corrective justice will tend to convert into each other. Finally, by integration I mean that the two forms of justice ultimately merge to create "justice", or in other words, what is considered right or correct in the present.

I posited that this system of ideas is insightful in explaining the shape of WTO dispute settlement and certain recent developments in WTO law. The typical recommendation made in WTO dispute settlement to a wrongdoing country to bring its measures "into conformity" with the WTO Agreement is a direction to re-establish an equal expectation of legality. This remedy identifies the WTO legal system as primarily distributive. A secondary task of WTO dispute settlement is to promote fair adjustment to pre-existing conditions, hence the varying wording of remedies in various WTO rules disciplines and in decisions concerning WTO countermeasures. In these instances, a certain corrective impulse is manifested.

The communitarian theory of justice put forward in this chapter posits that the balance struck between a primarily distributive system and the perceived need to correct trade injury is now having major repercussions for the WTO membership. That is because the failure of corrective justice to adequately protect markets is leading to intense questioning of the need for interdependence – the WTO Agreement's chief "good" - and to the uncoupling of commitments described in Chapter 2. In their place a more individualized idea of the good is emerging. In response some major WTO member countries have undertaken corrective action outside the treaty by engaging in trade wars.

Is the solution stronger, more corrective WTO remedies? Possibly, but a communitarian theory and the practice with WTO countermeasures suggest not. WTO countermeasures are cumbersome and counterproductive. Few WTO members can afford to invoke them successfully.

Instead, what I have suggested in this chapter is that the interaction and interdependence described above produce a *tertium quid*, or "third thing," defined as "something novel, yet also dependent on what went on before." This "new" thing constitutes the core of my position that the forms of justice ultimately go beyond a preoccupation with either distributive or corrective operations to produce justice in a triune form that is transformative. The ultimate goal of the transformation is to sustain the good of the community. In this chapter, I gave several examples of transformative justice in WTO law. In my view this impulse is what is driving current efforts to reform and repurpose the WTO Agreement.

The theory put forward in this chapter also provides a number of additional insights about justice. One is that justice is never "perfect". As such, it never satisfies all interests, a realization that serves as an impetus to ongoing reform. In this respect Frank Garcia has observed:

> It is not meaningful to treat justice as an end-state, because the actual world will never be perfectly, fully just. As long as human nature and social institutions remain their imperfect selves and there are different conceptions of justice at play in the world, there will never be a final moment in which all social allocations are made perfectly according to principles of justice and all improper gain is rectified. . . . We can no more conclude that a particular decision or rule renders the world just in all its outcomes, than we can conclude that a single drink ends our thirst. Instead, we move on to the next decision and the next rule, in which justice is again up for grabs.[274]

Garcia's observation stresses how justice is immediate, being done from moment to moment in a continuing present. Its presentism means it is never entirely consistent or coherent. It can always be criticized as unjust in the next moment or across a series of moments.

Nevertheless, for all the insight offered by a communitarian theory what has been outlined in this chapter is also likely to be perplexing. That is because the justice it describes does not look like the corrective justice familiar from daily life. Instead, it is much more complex, being about how this corrective task is accomplished in light of the need to distribute and re-distribute goods that are shared by members of a community.

A communitarian theory of justice also has limits. What I offer is not a "pure" theory of justice in the sense of excluding consideration of non-normative features such as power.[275] Law and justice are *not* always the product of a purely rational decision-maker. Likewise, interdependence is hardly a neutral value. The three forms of justice identified as part of a communitarian theory – distributive, corrective and transformative – operate together across time and incorporate all that has happened and is happening within a community, including the ability of powerful interests to manipulate the definition of key terms like equality and fairness in pursuit of differing ideas about justice in relation to the good.

[274] Garcia, *Trade, Inequality and Justice* 197–198.

[275] Hans Kelsen, *Pure Theory of Law* (Max Knight, trans., University of California Press, Berkeley; 1967 [Lawbook Exchange, Clark, NJ; rev'd ed., 2005]).

Anatole France's famous dictum about "the majestic equality of the laws, which forbid rich and poor alike to sleep under the bridges"[276] has become iconic precisely because it captures so vividly how law – and equality – can be distorted in apparently "just" settings. The theory accounts for this mismatch by suggesting how, when a consensus develops around an alternative idea of the good, justice may adapt through correlation, subordination, transition and integration to reflect a more appropriate conception of what is just.

[276] Anatole France, *The Red Lily* 95 (John Lane, London; 1922).

4

The WTO Agreement as a Law of Obligations

4.1 Introduction

In the last two chapters, I set out theories of community and justice as a prelude and background to developing a theory of law. In doing so I sought to demonstrate how certain contextual ideas about the "good" of a community and its associated forms of justice work together to condition, and set the stage for, the nature and structure of the law.

In this chapter and the next two chapters, I focus more directly on outlining a theory of law by emphasizing how classic features of the law support and reinforce specific views of the good. The dominant character of the WTO Agreement remains one of a "club good" pursued through distributive justice, a characterization that has definite consequences for the orientation and shape of its legal system.

Earlier I introduced how in pursuit of this good WTO law resolves into two major "idea-complexes," one equality and obligation-based, the other fairness and rights-based. In this chapter I proceed to analyze this first idea-complex of equality and obligation in WTO law by examining each of its constituent elements and their inter-relationship as a coherent whole, that is, the way they align and thread together. As we will see, the WTO Agreement's focus on equality and distributive justice begets an innate emphasis on obligation, which in turn gives rise to a constitutive structure that is prospectively oriented and reasoned deductively.

However, this analysis is preliminary, if only because in operation the law functions in a much more enmeshed and complicated way than described here. There are conceptual counterparts to the above-mentioned ideas of obligation, constitution, prospectivity and deduction that must be accounted for and that will be examined in the next chapter. Beyond that, the operation of a legal system in real-time involves the interaction of innumerable legal elements working together to promote interdependence in the form of *tertia quid*, or "third things", as products of a legal system. All of the complexity involved can impede the identification of a coherent theory.

It is therefore helpful to begin by abstracting and crystallizing the law in the form of its leading idea-complex to illustrate the theory in its initial dominant mode. This is always with the qualification that what I am describing here is not entirely self-contained or exhaustive and that there will be both "noise" and counter-examples that arise in the process of its illustration.

4.2 A Law of Equality

WTO law is chiefly a law of equality. Virtually all the major standards in the treaty – MFN, NT, nondiscrimination, equivalence, harmonization and mutual recognition – can be understood as expressions of equality. They stem from the idea that the prime purpose of the WTO system should be to promote equal access and treatment.

The reason for this primary aim is clear. Equality is the most basic indicator of what is just and constitutes the foundation of international law. Robert Jennings and Arthur Watts have noted:

> Since international law is based on the common consent of states as sovereign communities, the member states of the international community are equal to each other as subjects of international law. States are by their nature certainly not equal as regards power, territory and the like. But as members of the community of nations they are, in principle, equal, whatever differences between them may otherwise exist.[1]

At the same time, the principle of equality does not mean countries necessarily treat each other equally in every respect. Jennings and Watts add:

> Although states are equal as legal persons in international law, this equality does not require that in all matters a state must treat all other states in the same way. There is in customary international law no clearly established general obligation on a state not to differentiate between other states in the treatment it accords to them. The freedom of a state to grant preferential treatment to certain states, or to impose disadvantageous arrangements on others, has long been a valued instrument of policy in the conduct of international relations.[2]

[1] Robert Jennings & Arthur Watts (eds), *Oppenheim's International Law* (9th ed.) 339 (Longman, Harlow: 1996).

[2] Ibid., pp. 376–377.

WTO arrangements attempt to constrain the freedom to discriminate by rendering the behavior of members vis-à-vis each other more uniform and predictable, and ultimately, more equal.

Equality is particularly attractive as an ideal in WTO law because it is something toward which so much thinking instinctively turns. Actors are constantly assessing whether one thing is equal to another, and therefore, whether comparables are commensurate.[3] As such, equality serves as the core of contemporary ideas about justice.[4]

The influence of equality is discernible in WTO law in the recurrent idea that the treaty advances the equality of competitive conditions. By virtue of WTO rules, all economic operators are supposed to have an equal expectation of access to a member country's market.[5] Equality also finds expression in the doctrine of legitimate expectations mentioned in a number of WTO decisions.[6]

[3] On commensurability and the way in which human reasoning "inevitably becomes comparative reasoning," see H. Patrick Glenn, *Legal Traditions of the World* (5th ed.) 47 (Oxford University Press, Oxford; 2014).

[4] See Chapter 3, Section 3.2.1.

[5] Six decades ago John Jackson identified the centrality of expectations under GATT 1947 as follows:

> An important goal of international agreement is *the fulfillment of expectations* of the parties to the agreement. These expectations may have been aroused or engendered by a variety of factors, but one can empirically observe the effect of the practice of the institution upon the expectations of national representatives to that institution and the effects that these expectations have in turn upon national governments. It is clear to anyone who has observed this practice closely that these effects are significant.
>
> (John Jackson, *World Trade and the Law of GATT* 19 (Bobbs-Merrill, Indianapolis, IN; 1969) [emphasis added])

See also Lawrence Ruessmann, "The Place of Legitimate Expectations in the General Interpretation of the WTO Agreements," *K.U. Leuven Institute for International Law Working Paper* No. 36 (Dec. 2002).

[6] In *U.S. – Oil Country Tubular Goods Sunset Reviews*, for instance, the Appellate Body expressed the view that a particular document "has normative value, as it provides administrative guidance and *creates expectations* among the public and among private actors." WT/DS268/AB/R, para. 187 (29 Nov. 2004). Likewise in *China – Audiovisual*, the panel observed that certain administrative guidance of the Chinese government was reviewable under WTO law because it "*creates the expectation* that going forward the government agencies addressed therein will conduct themselves in their administration of foreign investment in the cultural sectors in a manner consistent with the provisions set forth in the Several Opinions." WT/DS363/R, para. 7.198 (12 Aug. 2009). For WTO dispute settlement reports referring to the protection of expectations, see *India – Patent Protection*, WT/DS50/R, paras. 45–62 (5 Sept. 1997); *EC – Computer Equipment*, WT/

Equality and equal expectations are consistent with the stability of the WTO as a legal order. Equality is associated with the "security and predictability" of "reciprocal and mutually advantageous [trade] arrangements." The phrase "security and predictability" appears in DSU Art. 3.2. It has been repeatedly referenced in a line of cases and is now understood to serve as a constitutive idea for the treaty as a whole.[7] Its importance is underlined in decisions that have described the security and predictability of WTO arrangements as the "basic,"[8] "main"[9] or "central"[10] purpose of the WTO Agreement.

Nevertheless, as Colm O'Cinneade has pointed out, "[t]he 'right to equality' has often been interpreted by national and international courts in a narrow and restrained manner."[11] The reason for restraint is uncertainty about how equality should be interpreted. O'Cinneade observes that "'equality' appears to be an open ended and indeterminate concept, capable of giving rise to multiple and often conflicting accounts of its 'proper' meaning." The indeterminacy of equality suggests that:

> [i]t may be better for lawyers, judges and other constitutional actors to refrain from wasting excessive energy on attempts to define in positive terms what equality means [and instead more fruitful] to define the equality principle in negative terms as requiring legal interventions to prevent the occurrence of certain forms of discrimination and demeaning treatment, rather than trying to establish what exactly equality is to abstract moral reasoning.[12]

DS62/AB/R, paras. 83–84 (5 June 1998); *Korea – Alcoholic Beverages*, WT/DS75/AB/R, paras. 125–127 (18 Jan. 1999); *Korea – Government Procurement*, WT/DS163/R, paras. 7.9*ff*, 7.75 (1 May 2000).

7 "We agree with the Panel that the security and predictability of "the reciprocal and mutually advantageous arrangements directed to the substantial reduction of tariffs and other barriers to trade" is an object and purpose of the WTO Agreement, generally, as well as of the GATT 1994." *EC – Computer Equipment*, WT/DS62, 67, 68/AB/R, para. 82 (5 June 1998), see also *EC – Selected Customs Matters*, WT/DS315/R, para. 6.34 and see comments at para. 7.431 (16 June 2006).

8 *Argentina – Textiles*, WT/DS56/AB/R, para. 47 (27 Mar. 1998), cited in *EC – Chicken Cuts*, WT/DS269/R, para. 7.319 (30 May 2005); *China – Automobile Parts*, WT/DS339, 340, 342/R, para. 7.201 (18 July 2008).

9 *China – Automobile Parts*, WT/DS339, 340, 342/R, para. 7.460 and note 955 (18 July 2008).

10 *U.S.* – WT/DS151/R, para. 7.75 (22 Dec. 1999), cited in *EC – Selected Customs Matters*, WT/DS315/R, para. 7.431 (16 June 2006).

11 Colm O'Cinneade, "The Right to Equality" 1 *UCL Human Rights Rev.* 78 (2008).

12 Ibid., p. 79.

The difficulty of defining equality fully and exhaustively explains the popularity of referring to it in a negative way as "non-discrimination," a usage often employed in WTO law.[13] There, nondiscrimination is frequently interpreted as "a requirement that two things should not be distinguished inappropriately."[14]

Still, what is "inappropriate" is hard to assess and the exact content of "non-discrimination obligations are often extremely difficult to apply."[15] As the panel in *Canada – Pharmaceutical Patents* noted:

> The ordinary meaning of the word "discriminate" is potentially broader than ... more specific definitions. It certainly extends beyond the concept of differential treatment. It is a normative term, pejorative in connotation, referring to results of the unjustified imposition of differentially disadvantageous treatment. Discrimination may arise from explicitly different treatment, sometimes called "de jure discrimination," but it may also arise from ostensibly identical treatment which, due to differences in circumstances, produces differentially disadvantageous effects, sometimes called "de facto discrimination." The standards by which the justification for differential treatment is measured are a subject of infinite complexity. "Discrimination" is a term to be avoided whenever more precise standards are available, and, when employed, it is a term to be interpreted with caution, and with care to add no more precision than the concept contains.[16]

The WTO Agreement's emphasis on equality and nondiscrimination manifests itself in a number of separate standards. What is of note in each is the difference in the relevant comparator. In MFN treatment it is treatment granted to the "most favored" trading partner. In NT it is the treatment accorded to nationally produced goods, services and intellectual property. In harmonization it is the convergence of domestic legislation and standards around internationally agreed norms. In equivalence it is governments' recognition of other countries' measures as acceptable so long as an equivalent level of protection is provided. In mutual recognition it is the principle by which members allow goods

[13] "The essence of the non-discrimination obligations is that like products should be treated equally, irrespective of their origin." *EC – Bananas III*, WT/DS27/AB/R, para. 190 (9 Dec. 1997).

[14] William Davey, *Non-discrimination in the World Trade Organization* 56 (Hague Academy of International Law, The Hague; 2012).

[15] Ibid., p. 57.

[16] *Canada – Pharmaceutical Patents*, WT/DS114/R, para. 7.94 (17 Mar. 2000).

that are legally sold in another member state to be sold in their own territory regardless of whether the goods comply with the technical rules of the importing state.

As this listing hints, these standards are far from uniform. Each standard varies across provisions and case law according to a number of differing criteria. With respect to "like" products, for instance, what has to be worked out in jurisprudence are standards of likeness as well as of competitive or substitutable products, of like services and service suppliers, and of similar conditions. In addition, questions arise as to similarity of treatment such as whether there has been "no less favorable" treatment, fair or equitable treatment, arbitrary or unjustifiable treatment, or whether impermissible distinctions in treatment have been made. In all of these varied circumstances, equality and uniformity are difficult to detect.

4.3 A Law of Obligation

4.3.1 A Law of Obligations

What is perhaps most notable about WTO law as a law of equality is the way that it is implemented chiefly by means of obligation. An obligation is usually understood as a "duty," or in other words, a legal relation which "cause[s] conforming willing and acting by the duty-holder."[17] What is emphasized in obligation is "the burden, the order, the universality of the law."[18]

However, the idea of obligation is heavily mediated in WTO law by sovereignty, by the flexibility of the legal order and by the primarily distributive character of the dispute settlement system which, in cases of breach, is followed by a cryptic recommendation to bring measures "into conformity." As mentioned, this plain direction does not invariably result in "conforming willing and acting."

[17] Philip Allott, *Eunomia* 161 (Oxford University Press, Oxford; 1990).

[18] Ibid., p. 160. Four variants of obligation can be distinguished. "A requirement-duty is an affirmative duty, a duty to act in a certain way" (Ibid.). "A constraint-duty is a negative duty, a duty not to act in a certain way" (Ibid.). "A liability-duty . . . limits the willing and acting of the duty-holder to the extent of the power of the right holder" (Ibid.). "A disability-duty is the withholding of a particular right, especially a power-right" (Ibid., p. 162).

The linchpin of the WTO system is the obligation upon member countries in GATT Art. II *to bind* their tariffs. As explained in Chapter 2, this basic obligation is reinforced by the treaty's key substantive provisions in GATT Arts. I, III and XI, as well as a number of other obligations. Even where rights are available, such as in the case of safeguards, countervailing and antidumping action, WTO law often emphasizes the obligations that attend exercise of such rights.[19]

The significance of obligations in the scheme of the WTO Agreement is particularly visible in repeated comments emphasizing obligations in the WTO legal order. As far back as the GATT-era case *U.S. – Sugar*, for instance, the panel noted that:

> [GATT] Article II permits contracting parties to incorporate into their Schedules acts yielding rights under the General Agreement but not acts diminishing obligations under that Agreement.[20]

Similarly, in *EC – Poultry* the Appellate Body observed:

> The ordinary meaning of the term "concessions" suggests that a Member may yield or waive some of its own rights and grant benefits to other Members, but that it cannot unilaterally diminish its own obligations.[21]

These statements indicate the way that obligations take precedence over rights as a jural matter in WTO law (i.e. Obligation > Right).[22] Member

[19] See for example *U.S. – Corrosion-Resistant Steel Sunset Review*, WT/DS244/AB/R, para. 331 (15 Dec. 2003):

> under Article 2.1 of the Agreement on Safeguards, safeguard measures can be justified "only" when, as a result of unforeseen developments and of the effect of obligations incurred, including tariff concessions, a product is being imported in such increased quantities and under such conditions as to cause or threaten to cause serious injury to the domestic industry that produces like or directly competitive products. It is "only" if these pre-requisites set forth in Article XIX:1(a) of the GATT 1994 and the Agreement on Safeguards are shown to exist that the right to apply a safeguard measure arises.

[20] *U.S. – Restrictions on Importation of Sugar*, B.I.S.D. 36th Supp. 331 (1989).

[21] *EC – Poultry*, WT/DS69/AB/R, para. 98 (13 July 1998).

[22] The same priority in observed in the operation of waivers under the WTO Agreement. Waivers can only be obtained upon the identification of "exceptional circumstances." They are accompanied by specific terms and conditions and terminate on a given date. These stringent criteria infer that waivers constitute limited derogations – or "outs" – from the corpus of law, which is otherwise normally conceived of as a regime of obligations. *See* WTO Art. IX:4. *See* also Isabel Feitchner, *The Law and Politics of WTO Waivers* (Cambridge University Press, Cambridge; 2011).

countries may cede rights, but they are otherwise bound by their obligations.

At the same time, the characterization of WTO law as a law of obligations is more complicated than any single description might furnish due to the fact that most WTO obligations are prohibitory, that is, they oblige a country *not* to undertake certain behavior negatively while remaining largely silent as to what a member may do in a positive sense.[23] Such open-endedness makes obligations less than a classic "duty" since considerable freedom is left to members to determine how they will comply.

The negative nature of most WTO obligations means that the "special intensity" of WTO law described in Chapter 2 is qualified in certain ways. It can sometimes be difficult to distinguish between obligations and other legal elements at work in the legal system. This can lead to confusion about what exactly WTO obligations are. Thus, the Appellate Body's careful comments on the distinction between positive obligations and "affirmative defenses" in *Brazil – Aircraft* were phrased as follows:

> Both from its title and from its terms, it is clear that [SCM] Article 27 is intended to provide special and differential treatment for developing country Members, under certain specified conditions. In our view, too, paragraph 4 of Article 27 provides certain obligations that developing country Members must fulfill if they are to benefit from this special and

[23] The WTO Agreement contains relatively few positive obligations, mostly in TRIPS, and these are of mainly of a threshold or minimum character:

> Most of the provisions in the WTO Agreement aim to prevent governments from taking measures that might be harmful to trade and, therefore, concern the existence of legislation requiring governments to act in a way that is inconsistent with the obligations under the WTO Agreement. Thus, if a Member has legislation mandating the executive to act in such a way, it is in breach of its obligations even if that particular legislation has not yet been applied. The TRIPS Agreement is different from other covered agreements in that most of its provisions require Members to take positive action.
>
> (*India – Patent Protection*, WT/DS50/R, para. 7.53 (5 Sept. 1997))

In regard to the negative nature of most WTO obligations, see also *U.S. – Textiles Rules of Origin*, WT/DS243/R, para. 6.24 (20 June 2003). ("By setting out what Members cannot do, these provisions leave for Members themselves discretion to decide what, within those bounds, they can do.")

> differential treatment during the transitional period. On reading paragraphs 2(b) and 4 of Article 27 together, it is clear that the conditions set forth in paragraph 4 are *positive obligations* for developing country Members, *not* affirmative defences. If a developing country Member complies with the obligations in Article 27.4, the prohibition on export subsidies in Article 3.1(a) simply does not apply. However, if that developing country Member does *not* comply with those obligations, Article 3.1(a) *does* apply.[24]

Given the need to distinguish between legal elements, it is to be expected that the tenor of obligations under the WTO Agreement is complex.[25] Some provisions do not impose any substantive obligations but rather set up special rules.[26] Others are "overarching."[27] Elsewhere,

[24] *Brazil – Aircraft*, WT/DS46/AB/R, para. 140 (2 Aug. 1999) [emphasis in original].

[25] Another source of confusion about obligations is their casual reference in WTO discourse. Panels and the Appellate Body have at times ascribed "rights" and "obligations" to nonmembers in the WTO system, such as the Ministerial Conference and councils, without always being clear who the reciprocal rights-holders are. See Frieder Roessler, "Why Only a Small Part of WTO Law Is Enforced through the WTO Dispute Settlement Procedures and Whether Something Should Be Done about This" (unpublished paper available at www.sipa.columbia.edu/wto/html/papers.html (2006)). In the same way, some obligations have been held to apply to panels and the Appellate Body. Thus, in *Thailand – H Beams* the Appellate Body observed:

> [ADA] Articles 17.5 and 17.6 clarify the powers of review of a panel established under the Anti-Dumping Agreement. These provisions place limiting *obligations on a panel*, with respect to the review of the establishment and evaluation of facts by the investigating authority. Unlike Article 3.1, these provisions do not place obligations on WTO Members.
>
> (*Thailand – H Beams*, WT/DS122/AB/R, para. 114 (emphasis added))

It is difficult to imagine how the reciprocal rights in this instance are enforceable. For similar comments, see *EC – Bed Linen*, WT/DS141/AB/R, para. 163 (8 Apr. 2003); *Mexico – HFCS (21.5)*, WT/DS132/AB/RW, para. 36 (22 Oct. 2001).

[26] *Canada – Milk (21.5)*, WT/DS103, 113/AB/RW2, para. 69 (20 Dec. 2002).

[27] Thus, for instance, in *Thailand – H Beams*, WT/DS122/AB/R, para. 106 (12 Mar. 2001), the Appellate Body described ADA Art. 3.1 as "an overarching provision that sets forth a Member's fundamental, substantive obligation in this respect. Article 3.1 informs the more detailed obligations in succeeding paragraphs." See also *EC – AD Duties*, WT/DS219/R, para. 7.225 (7 Mar. 2003). Another reference to overarching provisions takes place in *Japan – Alcoholic Beverages*, WT/DS8, 10, 11/AB/R, p. 18 (4 Oct. 1996) where, in discussing the term "so as to afford protection" in GATT Art. III:1, the Appellate Body observed, "The purpose of Article III:1 is to establish this general principle as a guide to understanding and interpreting the specific obligations contained in Article III:2 and in the other paragraphs of Article III, while respecting, and not diminishing in any way, the meaning of the words actually used in the texts of those other paragraphs."

single provisions may contain two or more obligations.[28] In still other instances, obligations are a specification of more generalized principles.[29]

Because of the density of the arrangement, a single breach can cause a "cascade" of other breaches, as noted in *Canada – Milk*:

> Recalling that Article 8 of the Agreement on Agriculture provides that "[e]ach Member undertakes not to provide export subsidies otherwise than in conformity with this Agreement," we also find that as a consequence of the violations of either Article 3.3 (through Article 9.1) or Article 10.1 . . . Canada has acted inconsistently with its obligations under Article 8.[30]

The assessment of WTO obligations is made still more complex by their *erga omnes partes* nature, or in other words, the fact that they are owed to a plurality of countries. In *U.S. – FSC (Art. 22.6)*, for instance, the arbitrator commented:

> the United States' breach of obligation [of WTO subsidy disciplines] is not objectively dismissed because some of the products benefiting from the subsidy are, e.g., exported to another trading partner. *It is an erga omnes obligation owed in its entirety to each and every Member.* It cannot be considered to be "allocatable" across the Membership. Otherwise, the Member concerned would be only partially obliged in respect of each and every Member, which is manifestly inconsistent with an *erga omnes* per se obligation.[31]

[28] See for instance *EC – Biotech*, WT/DS291/R, p. 309 (29 Sept. 2006). This has important consequences for pleading in WTO disputes, as the Appellate Body observed in *Korea – Dairy*, WT/DS98/AB/R, para. 124 (14 Dec. 1999) ("there may also be situations in which the circumstances are such that the mere listing of treaty articles would not satisfy the standard of Article 6.2. This may be the case, for instance, where the articles listed establish not one single, distinct obligation, but rather multiple obligations."). For similar comments about multiple obligations in the context of the initiation of antidumping proceedings, see *Thailand – H Beams*, WT/DS122/R, para. 7.18 (28 Sept. 2000).

[29] For example, SPS Art. 5.6 has been held to be a specification of the more general obligation in SPS Art. 2.2. See *Japan – Agricultural Products II*, WT/DS76/AB/R, para. 82 (22 Feb. 1999). See also *EC – Hormones*, WT/DS26/AB/R, para. 180 (16 Jan. 1998) discussing SPS Art. 5.1 as a specific application of the basic obligations contained in SPS Art. 2.2. See discussion in *EC – Biotech*, WT/DS291/R, para. 7.1433 (29 Sept. 2006).

[30] *Canada – Milk*, WT/DS103, 110/R, para. 7.134 (17 May 1999).

[31] *U.S. – FSC (Art. 22.6)*, WT/DS108/R, para. 6.10 (30 Aug. 2002) [emphasis added].

At the core of countries' commitments then are obligations implementing a wide array of standards linked to equality. In what follows, I take a look at several such standards. This is not an exhaustive survey. Instead, it is meant to provide some idea of the pluralism inherent in the concept of equality in WTO law.

4.3.1.1 Most Favored Nation (GATT Art. I, GATS Art. II)

WTO members are required to bind their tariffs under GATT Art. II. They are also required to treat goods from all sources as well as like goods from their best, or "Most Favorable," trading partner by virtue of GATT Art. I. This provision requires that "any advantage, favour, privilege or immunity" granted by one WTO member is to be accorded "immediately and unconditionally" to like products originating in other WTO members.[32] The resulting issues of discrimination can be classed into three categories: (1) likeness of the products involved, (2) similarity of treatment and (3) whether differences can be determined to violate the applicable legal standard.

On the issue of likeness under GATT Art. I, for instance, certain GATT-era jurisprudence appears to show considerable deference to governments' tariff classifications.[33] In essence, governments have some latitude to set their tariff schedules such that foreign goods from different sources may be categorized in different tariff categories, and as a consequence, be treated differently.

On the issue of "advantage, favor, privilege or immunity" in GATT Art. I, two possible elements can be used to identify discrimination: intent and effect. As Simon Lester and others note, "[a] finding of discrimination could be based on the existence of *either one* of these two elements, or on the existence of *both* elements."[34] Nevertheless,

[32] In *Canada – Autos*, WT/DS139/AB/R, para. 81 (31 May 2000), the Appellate Body noted the "pervasive character" of the MFN principle and added that apart from GATT Art. I:1, several "MFN-type" clauses dealing with varied matters are found in the GATT 1994. These relate to such matters as internal mixing requirements (Art. III:7), cinema films (Art. IV(b)), transit of goods (Art. V:2, 5, 6), marks of origin (Art. IX:1), quantitative restrictions (Art. XIII:1), measures to assist economic development (Art. XVIII:20) and measures for goods in short supply (Art. XX(j)).

[33] *Japan – SPF Lumber*, B.I.S.D. 36th Supp. 167 (19 July 1989).

[34] Simon Lester et al., *World Trade Law* (2nd ed.) 317 (Hart, Oxford; 2012) [emphasis in original].

WTO case law suggests that intent does not appear to play "any explicit role" in GATT Art. I analysis, at least to date.[35]

With respect to effects, discrimination may take place on a legal (*de jure*) or factual (*de facto*) basis. Discrimination on a *de jure* basis would appear to be a clear violation of GATT Art. I. Thus, a statute making a tariff distinction between goods from Country A and Country B would be enough to contravene GATT Art. I.

The more complex scenario would involve discrimination in fact. In *Canada – Autos* the measure at issue was an import duty exemption for motor vehicles granted if the exporter of the vehicles was affiliated with a manufacturer/importer in Canada.[36] The exemption was limited to exporters linked to manufacturers/importers that had been designated under Canadian regulations. In reality, exporters who benefitted from the scheme were located for historic reasons in a small number of countries. The panel found that the Canadian measure breached GATT Art. I:1. On appeal, the Appellate Body held that by granting an advantage to some products from some members and not to others, the measure in question was inconsistent with MFN. The panel had noted the way in which market data revealed stark differences between the percentages of imports of automobiles from countries that benefited from the zero-rate tariff versus those that did not. On appeal, the Appellate Body agreed with the analysis but found in somewhat more general terms that all of

[35] The Appellate Body has taken a mixed approach to evidence of intent and the weight it should be accorded in the analysis of GATT Art. III. In *Mexico – Taxes on Soft Drinks*, WT/DS308 the panel observed:

> The Appellate Body has cautioned against ascribing too much importance to the subjective legislative intent of legislators and regulators in the drafting of a particular measure, to determine whether the measure is applied so as to afford protection to domestic production, particularly when that declared intent is that protectionism was not an objective. However, the declared intention of legislators and regulators of the Member adopting the measure should not be totally disregarded, particularly when the explicit objective of the measure is that of affording protection to domestic production. Indeed, the Appellate Body has confirmed that statements made by government representatives of a Member, admitting to the protective intent of a measure, may be relevant as part of a number of considerations in reaching the conclusion that a measure is applied so as to afford protection to domestic production.
>
> (Ibid. at para. 8.91 (7 Oct. 2005))

[36] WT/DS139/R.

the evidence pointed to certain countries' automobiles being "more likely" to receive the import duty exemption than other countries' automobiles.[37] In other words, the analysis was holistic, rather than strictly empiric.

Under GATT Art. I an additional issue is the wording of "unconditional" treatment: does it refer to a relatively "narrow" obligation undertaken in the context of some original tariff negotiation with whom the MFN binding was first agreed, or is it a "broader" obligation arising from the fact that *any* "advantage, privilege, favor or immunity" must be offered with *no* conditions that are unrelated to the imported product itself?

In *Indonesia – Autos* the panel held that the unconditional requirement could not be made contingent on a condition such as a private contractual obligation with an Indonesian auto manufacturer whereas in *Canada – Autos* the panel suggested the matter of conditionality should be integrated into the determination of discrimination between like products. "The first approach would mean that a tax or duty exemption based on the use of domestic content [applying] to imports must not discriminate among imports from other Members," whereas "the second approach would hold that domestic content as a condition for a tax or duty exemption would violate Article I:1 regardless of whether there was any discrimination among members."[38]

[37] WT/DS139/AB/R, para. 86 (31 May 2000). An additional issue in *Canada – Autos* involved the "grouping" argument: was the assessment of discrimination to be measured on an individual product basis (i.e. any product) or between groups of products (i.e. group-to-group)? The Appellate Body referred to *de facto* discrimination between "some products" imported from some WTO members when compared with like products originating in all other WTO members, thereby sidestepping the distinction. See Lester et al., *World Trade Law* 321.

[38] Lester et al., *World Trade Law* 324. They go on to note:

> At this point in time, there appears to be a split among panels, and also among Members, as evidenced by the different arguments before these panels as to which approach [concerning the term "unconditional"] is the proper one. The Appellate Body has not yet weighed in. We note that an interpretation prohibiting any conditions, even those that are non-discriminatory, would be a strict one, and is certainly broader than the traditional idea of non-discrimination.
>
> (Ibid.)

In *EC – Seal Products* the Appellate Body clarified the law in the area to some degree by noting that regulatory distinctions may be made by governments so long as those distinctions do not have a detrimental impact:

> as [GATT] Article I:1 is concerned, fundamentally, with protecting expectations of equal competitive opportunities for like imported products from all Members, it does not follow that Article I:1 prohibits a Member from attaching *any* conditions to the granting of an "advantage" within the meaning of Article I:1. Instead, it prohibits those conditions that have a detrimental impact on the competitive opportunities for like imported products from any Member. Conversely, Article I:1 permits regulatory distinctions to be drawn between like imported products, provided that such distinctions do not result in a detrimental impact on the competitive opportunities for like imported products from *any* Member.[39]

One set of authors has noted that:

> A lack of consensus about what is meant by "non-discrimination", combined with the specific wording of the text of [GATT] Article 1:1, has led to an interpretation and application of this provision that is quite complicated.[40]

William Davey has also observed how, on the whole, analysis under GATT Art. I has been relatively uncontroversial.[41] There seems to be fairly broad acceptance that governments have the right to discriminate at the border if their practices remain within recognized limits and do not otherwise constitute an "abuse."

4.3.1.2 National Treatment (GATT Art. III, GATS Art. XVII)

The general purpose of National Treatment in GATT Art. III is avoidance of protectionism "in the application of internal tax and regulatory measures." Broadly stated, the relevant obligation is that WTO members should provide equality of competitive conditions for imports in relation to domestic products. The reason for this requirement is a concern with subversion of tariff commitments.[42] If members could enact legislation

[39] WT/DS400/AB/R, para. 5.88 (22 May 2014) [emphasis in original].

[40] Lester et al., *World Trade Law* 325.

[41] Davey, *Non-discrimination in the World Trade Organization* 94.

[42] *Japan – Alcoholic Beverages II*, WT/DS8/AB/R, p. 16 (4 Oct. 1996): "The intention of the drafters of the Agreement was clearly to treat the imported products in the same way as the like domestic products once they had been cleared through customs. Otherwise

modifying the conditions of competition within the domestic market to the detriment of imports, then much of the value of the commitments undertaken in GATT Arts. I and II would be eroded. The obligation in GATT Art. III is therefore considered to be exceptionally comprehensive, covering both goods that are bound by tariffs and those that are not.[43]

The opening words of GATT Art. III:1 refer to the fact that internal taxes and regulation should not be applied to imported or domestic products "*so as to afford protection* to domestic production." This overarching principle is reflected in several different ways in succeeding paragraphs.[44]

GATT Art. III:2 is a specification of the "so as to afford protection" requirement applied to fiscal measures, whereas GATT Art. III:4 specifies the general obligation of nondiscrimination vis-a-vis regulatory measures. In each case the specific requirement is slightly different, given the distinct wording, context, and object and purpose of each provision.

For instance, the analysis in GATT Art. III:2, first sentence, involves a determination of (1) whether imported and domestic products are "like products" and (2) whether the imported products are tax "in excess of" domestic products.[45] By comparison the analysis in GATT Art. III:2, second sentence, pertains to "similar or substitutable" products and involves a determination of (1) whether imported and domestic products are "similar or substitutable," (2) whether imported products are taxed beyond *de minimus* and (3) whether domestic regulations are applied to imported or domestic products "*so as to afford protection* to domestic production."[46] Yet another analysis and set of considerations apply to cases of regulatory discrimination under GATT Art. III:4.

The determination of likeness criteria in GATT Art. III:2 and elsewhere in WTO law is an important initial issue that has had to be worked out on "a case-by-case basis."[47] Won-Mog Choi has noted that likeness is

indirect protection could be given." Quoting from *U.S. – Taxes on Petroleum*, GATT B.I.S.D. 34th Supp. 136, para. 5.1.9 (5 June 1987).

43 *Japan – Alcoholic Beverages II*, pp. 16–17 (4 Oct. 1996).

44 Ibid., p. 18.

45 *Canada – Periodicals*, WT/DS31/AB/R, pp. 22–23 (30 June 1997).

46 Ibid., pp. 22–23.

47 *Japan – Alcoholic Beverages II*, WT/DS8/AB/R, p. 20 (4 Oct. 1996). The Appellate Body cited Report of the Working Party on *Border Tax Adjustments*, GATT B.I.S.D. 18th Supp. 97, para. 18 (2 Dec. 1970). However, in *Japan – Alcoholic Beverages II* the Appellate Body went on to observe that "The criteria in *Border Tax Adjustments* should be examined, but there can be no one precise and absolute definition of what is 'like'. The concept of 'likeness' is a relative one that evokes the image of an accordion. The

in issue in over fifty WTO provisions.[48] In *Japan – Alcoholic Beverages II* the Appellate Body borrowed from earlier GATT jurisprudence to identify the following factors in determining likeness: (1) the product's end uses in a given market; (2) consumers' tastes and habits; and (3) the product's properties, nature and quality.[49] At the same time, the Appellate Body also suggested the relevance of tariff bindings where they are sufficiently precise and "can therefore provide significant guidance."[50] Nevertheless, the Appellate Body has cautioned that the assessment of likeness must take place on the basis of all the evidence.[51]

The three classic factors in likeness analysis (i.e. end use, consumer tastes, product properties) and, where appropriate, tariff bindings, are merely a point of departure for analysis. In subsequent jurisprudence the Appellate Body has clarified that likeness can also be determined on the basis of "hypothetical" like products where an origin-based distinction is made[52] or where historic market conditions make like products factually unavailable.[53]

In the case of GATT Art. III:2, second sentence, WTO law requires consideration of "directly competitive or substitutable" products that are not similarly taxed. Here the analysis has been interpreted to require assessment of (1) whether imported and domestic products are directly competitive or substitutable, (2) whether they are "not similarly taxed" and (3) whether the dissimilar taxation is "applied ... so as to afford protection to domestic production."[54] The Appellate Body has held that the analysis of "directly competitive or substitutable products" requires

accordion of 'likeness' stretches and squeezes in different places as different provisions of the WTO Agreement are applied." Ibid., p. 21.

48 Won-Mog Choi, *"Like Products" in International Trade Law* ix (Oxford University Press, Oxford; 2003).

49 *Japan – Alcoholic Beverages II*, WT/DS8/AB/R, p. 20 (4 Oct. 1996).

50 Ibid., p. 22 (4 Oct. 1996).

51 *EC – Asbestos*, WT/DS135/AB/R, paras. 101–103 (12 Mar. 2001).

52 In *Indonesia – Autos*, WT/DS54/R (2 July 1998), the panel expressed the view that "an origin-based distinction in respect of internal taxes suffices in itself to violate Art. III:2, without the need to demonstrate the existence of actually traded like products." Ibid., para. 14.113. For similar hypothetical like product analysis, see panel reports in *Korea – Various Measures on Beef*, WT/DS161/R, para. 627 (31 July 2000) (with respect to Art. III:4 of the GATT 1994); *U.S. – Certain EC Products*, WT/DS165/R, para. 6.54 (17 July 2000) (with respect to Art. I:1 of the GATT 1994); *Argentina – Hides and Leather*, WT/DS155/R, paras. 11.168–11.170 (19 Dec. 2000).

53 *Japan – Alcoholic Beverages II*, WT/DS8/AB/R, p. 24 (4 Oct. 1996); *U.S. – Poultry (China)*, WT/DS392/R, paras. 7.424–7.427, and 7.429 (29 Sept. 2010).

54 *Japan – Alcoholic Beverages II*, WT/DS8/AB/R, p. 24 (4 Oct. 1996).

assessment of market competition, which may take the form of references to cross-price elasticities, the market situation in other countries, and latent, extant or potential demand.[55] Beyond these factors a broad range of considerations may be examined. In *Korea – Alcoholic Beverages*, for instance, the panel indicated that it would review "the physical characteristics, end-uses including evidence of advertising activities, channels of distribution, price relationships including cross-price elasticities, and any other characteristics."[56]

An important point in the analysis is the reluctance of WTO adjudicators to rely exclusively on empiric assessment. For example, in *Korea – Alcoholic Beverages* the panel pointed to the "quality" and "nature" of the competition between imports and certain Korean alcoholic beverages in finding that imports were in fact "directly competitive and substitutable." On appeal Korea argued that the panel's reference to the "nature of competition" in its conclusion involved a "vague and subjective element" without foundation in GATT Art. III:2. The Appellate Body disagreed:

> In taking issue with the use of the term "nature of competition", Korea, in effect, objects to the Panel's sceptical attitude to quantification of the competitive relationship between imported and domestic products. For the reasons set above, we share the Panel's reluctance to rely unduly on quantitative analyses of the competitive relationship. In our view, an approach that focused solely on the quantitative overlap of competition would, in essence, make cross-price elasticity *the* decisive criterion in determining whether products are "directly competitive or substitutable."[57]

As for discrimination itself, the standard to be met in various sections of GATT Art. III differs. In GATT Art. III:2, first sentence, the standard is whether taxes on imported products are "in excess of" those on like domestic products, which the Appellate Body has interpreted strictly,[58] whereas in GATT Art. III:2, second sentence, the absence of any direct reference to the keystone idea of "so as to afford protection" infers a more liberal interpretation in which *de minimus* differences in taxation are permissible.[59] At the same time, the fact that some instances of taxation

[55] Regarding latent, extant and potential demand in likeness analysis, see *Korea – Alcoholic Beverages*, WT/DS75/AB/R, para. 117 (18 Jan. 1999).

[56] *Korea – Alcoholic Beverages*, WT/DS75/R, para. 10.61 (17 Sept. 1998).

[57] *Korea – Alcoholic Beverages*, WT/DS75/AB/R, para. 134 (18 Jan. 1999) [emphasis in original].

[58] *Japan – Alcoholic Beverages II*, WT/DS8/AB/R, p. 24 (4 Oct. 1996).

[59] Ibid., pp. 26–27.

are either above or below this threshold makes no difference. WTO members cannot insulate their behavior from responsibility by "averaging" their conduct over a series of instances.[60] Again, this is part of WTO law's "special intensity."

One additional issue that must be determined in the analysis of GATT Art. III:2, second sentence, is whether the dissimilar taxation is "applied . . . so as to afford protection to domestic production." This last requirement involves "a comprehensive and objective analysis of the structure and application of the measure in question on domestic as compared to imported products."[61] What is focused on is the measure's "overall application."[62] In *Japan – Alcoholic Beverages II*, the Appellate Body went on to observe:

> [the] protective application [of a measure] can most often be discerned from the design, the architecture, and the revealing structure of a measure. The very magnitude of the dissimilar taxation in a particular case may be evidence of such a protective application . . . Most often, there will be other factors to be considered as well. In conducting this inquiry, panels should give full consideration to all the relevant facts and all the relevant circumstances in any given case.[63]

Analysis under GATT Art. III:4 is somewhat different again. There the focus is on the potential for regulatory discrimination, a broad category extending beyond the tax and fiscal measures that are targeted in GATT Art. III:2. In *Korea – Various Measures on Beef* the Appellate Body outlined the following three elements of a violation of GATT Art. III:4:

> For a violation of Article III:4 to be established, three elements must be satisfied: that the imported and domestic products at issue are "like products"; that the measure at issue is a "law, regulation, or requirement affecting their internal sale, offering for sale, purchase, transportation, distribution, or use"; and that the imported products are accorded "less favourable" treatment than that accorded to like domestic products.[64]

To begin with, independent assessment of the preambular phrase "so as [to] afford protection to domestic production" is not necessary under

[60] *Canada – Periodicals*, WT/DS31/AB/R, p. 29 (30 June 1997) citing *U.S. – Section 337*, B.I.S.D. 36th Supp. 345, para. 5.14 (7 Nov. 1989).
[61] *Japan – Alcoholic Beverages II*, WT/DS8/AB/R, p. 29 (4 Oct. 1996).
[62] Ibid.
[63] Ibid.
[64] *Korea – Various Measures on Beef*, WT/DS161/AB/R, para. 133 (11 Dec. 2000).

Art. III:4 since Art. III:4 does not specifically refer to Art. III:1. Instead, the "so as to afford" principle has been interpreted to be embedded in the language of Art. III:4 itself.[65] Second, the category of "like products" in Art. III:4 is broader than that of GATT Art. III:2, first sentence, but no broader than the combined scope of GATT Art. III:2, first *and* second sentence.[66] Third, the Appellate Body has pointed out that in the assessment of "less favorable" treatment a WTO member "may draw distinctions between products which have been found to be 'like', without, for this reason alone, according to the group of 'like' imported products 'less favourable treatment' than that accorded to the group of 'like' domestic products."[67] At the same time, identical treatment in all instances could conceivably bestow less favorable treatment.[68]

In terms of the assessment of "less favorable treatment" under GATT Art. III:4, the chief question appears to be the competitive relationship between the products at issue. This focus prompts an expansive and dynamic view of markets and competition. In *Korea – Alcoholic Beverages*, for instance, the panel compared WTO law' focus on competition with classic antitrust law and noted:

> ... trade law addresses the issue of the potentiality to compete. Antitrust law generally focuses on firms' practices or structural modifications which may prevent or restrain or eliminate competition. It is not illogical that markets be defined more broadly when implementing laws primarily designed to protect competitive opportunities than when implementing laws designed to protect the actual mechanisms of competition.[69]

Due to this broad analytical approach, in most instances empirical measurement supplements rather than supplants the law.[70] In *Thailand – Cigarettes (Philippines)* the Appellate Body observed that:

[65] *EC – Bananas III*, WT/DS27/AB/R, para. 216 (9 Sept. 1997).

[66] *EC – Asbestos*, WT/DS135/AB/R, paras. 98–99 (12 Mar. 2001). In *EC – Asbestos*, the Appellate Body also observed that toxicity was a physical difference to be taken into account in the determination of "likeness" and linked this to the criterion of competitive relationship between the products at issue. Ibid., para. 114.

[67] Ibid., para. 100.

[68] *U.S. – Section 337*, B.I.S.D. 36th Supp. 345, para. 5.11 (16 Jan. 1989). See also *Dominican Republic – Cigarettes*, WT/DS302/R, para. 7.182 (26 Nov. 2004).

[69] *Korea – Alcoholic Beverages*, WT/DS75/R, para. 10.81 (17 Sept. 1998).

[70] Wolfgang Alschner, "Aligning Loss and Liability – Towards an Integrated Assessment of Damages in Investment Arbitration" in Marion Jansen et al. (eds), *The Use of Economics in International Trade and Investment Disputes* 283 at 284 (Cambridge University Press, Cambridge; 2017).

> an analysis [of less favourable treatment] under Article III:4 must begin with careful scrutiny of the measure, including consideration of the design, structure, and expected operation of the measure at issue. Such scrutiny may well involve – but does not require – an assessment of the contested measure in the light of evidence regarding the actual effects of that measure in the market. In any event, there must be in every case a genuine relationship between the measure at issue and its adverse impact on competitive opportunities for imported versus like domestic products to support a finding that imported products are treated less favourably.[71]

The method of analysis outlined in *Thailand – Cigarettes (Philippines)* is illustrative of the assessment that ultimately takes place under GATT Art. III and is, to some extent, common to much antidiscrimination analysis in WTO law as a whole. Some attention is paid to "the actual effects" of a measure but more important is the identification of "*a genuine relationship* between the measure at issue and its adverse impact on competitive opportunities." It is the general "structure and design" of a measure, as opposed to its application in any one instance or at a specific point in time, that is at issue.[72]

From all of the above, Lester and others note considerable diversity in the interpretation of GATT Art. III. They conclude that:

> there are a number of basic issues for which the law [on GATT Art. III] seems to be unsettled. It is perhaps surprising that one of the core principles [in the treaty] has not been more clearly defined. In part, the situation is the result of disagreements as to what the law *should* be. In addition, to some extent there may have been an attempt to come up with the judicial language that accommodates different views so as to make all parties happy in the short term because they can see their position reflected, to some extent, in the decision. Whatever the reason, there is still some doubt as to how core concepts like discriminatory intent and effect will be applied in different provisions of Article III.[73]

Furthermore, there are a number of distinct issues pertaining to the burden of proof, "grouping," latent, extant and potential demand, legislative intent and so forth that have been dealt with by panels and the Appellate Body.[74] The foregoing analysis of GATT Art. III is but a

[71] *Thailand – Cigarettes (Philippines)*, WT/DS371/AB/R, para. 134 (17 June 2011).

[72] *Argentina – Hides and Leather*, WT/DS155/R, paras. 11.168–11.170 (19 Dec. 2000).

[73] Lester et al., *World Trade Law* 307–308 [emphasis in original].

[74] For example, regarding the burden of proof in *Japan – Alcoholic Beverages II*, WT/DS8/R (11 July 1996) the panel stated that "complainants have the burden of proof to show first

sampling of some of the many issues that have arisen in its interpretation. Taken together, they illustrate the way a law of equality realized by means of obligation is highly fragmented and difficult to trace to one root concept.

4.3.1.3 Harmonization (TBT Art. 2.4; SPS Art. 3)

MFN, NT and nondiscrimination are basic requirements contained in GATT 1947 and carried over into GATT 1994.

However, there is also concern in international trade law with disguised protectionism. This concern manifested itself in the form of technical barriers and sanitary measures and was an issue under GATT 1947, something which was addressed in the GATT Standards Code of 1980. Still, the GATT Standards Code was only partly successful in achieving the goal of stemming disguised protection. Consequently, an effort was made in the Uruguay Round to deal with disguised protectionism by concluding a WTO Agreement on Technical Barriers to Trade (TBT Agreement) and a separate WTO Agreement on Sanitary and Phytosanitary Measures (SPS Agreement) in 1994.

In some ways these agreements are merely elaborations of GATT rules on nondiscrimination.[75] At the same time, due to the need to respect and take into consideration international norms, TBT and SPS requirements have the potential to go beyond mere nondiscrimination analysis.[76] In essence, both the TBT and SPS Agreements may delve deeply into

that products are like and second, that foreign products are taxed in excess of domestic ones." Ibid., para. 6.14. For latent, extant and potential demand in the analysis of directly competitive and substitutable products in GATT Art. III:2, see *Korea – Alcoholic Beverages*, WT/DS75/AB/R, para. 117 (18 Jan. 1999). Grouping "is almost always necessary in cases arising under Article III:2, second sentence, since generic categories commonly include products with some variation in composition, quality, function and price, and thus commonly give rise to sub-categories." *Korea – Alcoholic Beverages*, WT/DS75/AB/R, paras. 141–144 (18 Jan. 1999). Regarding intent, in *Japan – Alcoholic Beverages II*, WT/DS8/AB/R (4 Oct. 1996) the Appellate Body considered that the subjective intent of legislators and regulators in the drafting and the enactment of a particular measure was irrelevant for determining whether a measure was applied "so as to afford protection to domestic production." In contrast, in *Canada – Periodicals*, WT/DS31/AB/R (30 June 1997) the Appellate Body ascribed some importance to statements made by the government of Canada concerning the policy objectives of the challenged measure: Ibid. at 32.

[75] TBT Art. 2.1; SPS Art. 2.3.

[76] Technical standards and health and safety appear to go "beyond a discrimination-based approach to international trade" and place greater emphasis upon testing as the basis for the justification of national regulations under WTO law. See Andrew Lang & Joanne Scott, "The Hidden World of WTO Governance" 20:3 *E.J.I.L.* 575 at 590 (2009).

domestic jurisdiction, something which makes them inherently controversial. Still, the novelty of TBT and SPS provisions should not be overly emphasized. From the perspective of equality, it should be clear that discrimination analysis shifts from domestic comparators (i.e. "like products") to convergence with international norms.

The TBT Agreement applies to "technical regulations," "standards" and "conformity assessment procedures," while the SPS Agreement applies to "sanitary measures" relating to human or animal health and to "phytosanitary measures" dealing with plant health.

The harmonization requirements set out in the WTO Agreement are contained in several provisions. Generally speaking, harmonization aims to promote convergence of national legislation with internationally agreed norms and prevent discrimination. For instance, TBT Art. 2.4 specifies:

> Where technical regulations are required and relevant international standards exist or their completion is imminent, Members shall use them, or the relevant parts of them, as a basis for their technical regulations.

Similarly, SPS Art. 3.1 specifies:

> Members shall base their sanitary or phytosanitary measures on international standards, guidelines or recommendations, where they exist

To date WTO jurisprudence concerning these provisions is only partially developed. In *EC – Sardines*, for instance, the Appellate Body noted that "something cannot be considered a 'basis' for something else [in TBT Art. 2.4] if the two are *contradictory*."[77] The term "based on" in SPS Art. 3 has been interpreted as a looser standard than "conform to" in the TBT Agreement. In *EC – Hormones* the panel interpreted the wording of

[77] *EC – Sardines*, WT/DS231/AB/R, para. 248 (26 Sept. 2002) [emphasis in original]. In other jurisprudence, a panel has articulated the standard as one of the international standard serving as "a principal constituent or fundamental principle of the . . . [domestic] measures." According to the Panel, the term "based on" "does not require the wholesale adoption of the international standard, guideline or recommendation into the measure of the importing Member" as "this would wipe out any distinction between the scope of coverage of [SPS] Articles 3.1 and 3.2." *U.S. – Animals*, WT/DS447/R, paras. 7.233, 7.239 (24 July 2015). In *Russia – Pigs (EU)* the panel noted that "a challenged measure may be 'based on' the international standard with respect to one element, but not with respect to another element." WT/DS475/R, para. 7.259 (19 Aug. 2016). In that case the panel cautioned that some international standards might be flexible, requiring that account be taken of "the particular nature of the provision of the relevant international standard at issue, in light of the specific facts and circumstances of the dispute."

"conform to" in the TBT Agreement as creating a present obligation to conform. The Appellate Body disagreed, noting:

> that harmonization of SPS measures of Members on the basis of international standards is projected in the Agreement, as a *goal*, yet to be realized *in the future*. To read Article 3.1 as requiring Members to harmonize their SPS measures *by conforming those measures with international standards*, guidelines and recommendations, *in the here and now*, is, in effect, to vest such international standards, guidelines and recommendations (which are by the terms of the Codex recommendatory in form and nature) with *obligatory* force and effect. The Panel's interpretation of Article 3.1 would, in other words, transform those standards, guidelines and recommendations into binding *norms*. But, as already noted, the SPS Agreement itself sets out no indication of any intent on the part of the Members to do so.[78]

In addition, attention must be paid to the treaty text in order to determine the exact nature of the obligation to harmonize. In *EC – Hormones*, for instance, one issue was how to reconcile the obligation in SPS Art. 3.1 that WTO members "*shall base* their sanitary or phytosanitary measures on international standards, guidelines or recommendations" with the right identified in SPS Art. 3.3 that "Members may introduce or maintain sanitary or phytosanitary measures which result in a higher level of sanitary or phytosanitary protection ... if there is a scientific justification." However, the freedom in SPS Art. 3.3 is conditioned by the need to ensure that a different national standard is "not be inconsistent with any other provision of this Agreement." In this respect the Appellate Body observed:

> [SPS] Article 3.3 recognizes the autonomous right of a Member to establish such higher level of protection, provided that that Member complies with certain requirements in promulgating SPS measures to achieve that level. ... merely characterizing a treaty provision as an "exception" does not by itself justify a "stricter" or "narrower" interpretation of that provision than would be warranted by examination of the ordinary meaning of the actual treaty words, viewed in context and in the light of the treaty's object and purpose.[79]

These slim observations do not offer much more than a passing idea of how equality is realized in the context of harmonization obligations.

[78] *EC – Hormones*, WT/DS26/AB/R, para. 165 (16 Jan. 1998) [emphasis in original].
[79] Ibid., para. 104.

Equality suggests uniformity. However, the very situated character of the analysis suggests that the idea of equality expressed in these provisions is greatly fragmented.

4.3.1.4 Equivalence (TBT Art. 2.7; SPS Art. 4)

SPS Art. 4 provides that:

> [m]embers shall accept the sanitary or phytosanitary measures of other Members as equivalent, even if these measures differ from their own or from those used by other Members trading in the same product, if the exporting Member objectively demonstrates to the importing Member that its measures achieve the importing Member's appropriate level of sanitary or phytosanitary protection.

To date little jurisprudence has interpreted this provision. However, an accompanying decision by WTO members in 2004 confirms that "equivalence of sanitary or phytosanitary measures does not require duplication or sameness of measures, but the acceptance *of alternative measures* that meet an importing Member's appropriate level of sanitary or phytosanitary protection."[80]

In other words, a degree of difference appears permissible in what is otherwise denominated "equivalence" provided it meets the importing country's level of SPS protection, again suggestive of flexibility and pluralism.

4.3.1.5 Mutual Recognition (TBT Art. 6.3)

The obligation of mutual recognition requires countries to agree to accept the results of one another's conformity assessment procedures despite the fact that the two sets of procedures might differ. To further this aim, TBT Art. 6.3 encourages WTO members to enter into negotiations with each other for the mutual acceptance of conformity assessment results. Because a high degree of confidence in testing and

[80] Committee on Sanitary and Phytosanitary Measures, *Decision on the Implementation of Article 4 of the Agreement on the Application of Sanitary and Phytosanitary Measures*, G/SPS/19/rev. 2 (23 July 2004) [emphasis added]. The Decision outlines steps designed to make it easier for all WTO members to make use of equivalence. It states in part, "[e]quivalence can be accepted for a specific measure or measures related to a certain product or categories of products, or on a systems-wide basis. Members shall, when so requested, seek to accept the equivalence of a measure related to a certain product or category of products."

certification bodies is a prerequisite for proper functioning of mutual recognition arrangements, TBT Art. 6.1 recognizes that prior consultation may be necessary to arrive at a mutually satisfactory understanding regarding the competence of conformity assessment bodies.

4.3.1.6 Adjudicatively Identified Standards

The idea of equality as underlying WTO arrangements and being in some sense constitutive of them is evident in the way equality and equal treatment serve as defaults under the WTO Agreement. Where the treaty is unclear or silent on the standard to be applied, equality will often appear to supply adjudicative standards such as "even-handedness" or "parallelism." These are obligatory and are attached to conditions that national conduct is required to observe.

An example of the equality "default" at work was evident in *EC – Tariff Preferences.*[81] In that case the measure at issue was the EC's generalized tariff preferences ("GSP") scheme for developing countries and economies in transition. In particular, special arrangements under the scheme to combat drug production and trafficking applied only to twelve countries experiencing certain severe drug problems. India, a nonbeneficiary, asserted that the scheme violated GATT Art. I:1 and the Enabling Clause, a 1979 decision that was carried forward into the WTO Agreement and enables developed countries to treat developing countries more favorably than other WTO members.[82]

The Appellate Body determined that the EC scheme was not justified under the Enabling Clause since the scheme did not set out any objective criteria to determine other developing country beneficiaries. The essence of the dispute was whether the discrimination allowed under the Enabling Clause required equal treatment of *all* developing countries, as India asserted, or permitted residual discrimination *between* developing countries, as the EC asserted.

The Appellate Body observed that it was clear from "the ordinary meanings of 'non-discriminatory' . . . that preference-granting countries must make available identical tariff preferences to all similarly-situated

[81] WT/DS246.

[82] The Enabling Clause introduced differential and more favorable treatment as an integral part of the GATT system, doing away with the need to seek waivers from the GATT for that purpose. It was later incorporated into GATT 1994. See Robert Hudec, *Developing Countries in the GATT Legal System* 85 (Gower, London; 1987).

beneficiaries."[83] At the same time, the Appellate Body observed that the fact that the Enabling Clause "authorizes preference-granting countries to 'respond positively' to 'needs' does not necessarily mean that these needs are 'common or shared by all developing countries.'" Consequently, "[r]esponding to the 'needs of developing countries' may thus entail treating different developing country beneficiaries differently."[84] The Appellate Body concluded that granting different tariff preferences to products originating in different GSP beneficiaries is permitted, provided that the relevant tariff preferences respond positively to a particular "development, financial or trade need" and are made available on the basis of an objective standard to "all beneficiaries that share that need."[85]

EC – Tariff Preferences is a good illustration of the way in which equality – or more broadly nondiscrimination – serves as a default standard in WTO law. Its influence is felt in many situations, both express and implied. In *EC – Tariff Preferences* the premise of equality was express because the Enabling Clause specifically referred to the establishment of GSP schemes involving "*non-discriminatory* preferences."

Elsewhere in the treaty are a number of instances where equality is implied by reference to adjudicatively crafted standards. One of these is "even-handedness." By virtue of GATT Art. XX(g), members are allowed to take measures "relating to the conservation of exhaustible natural resources if such measures are made *effective in conjunction with* restrictions on domestic production or consumption." In *U.S. – Gasoline* the United States was found to have unevenly administered restrictions in the name of conservation. The Appellate Body did not address what relative treatment of domestic and foreign interests was required in order to qualify as "even-handed" regulation but did say that if there is a restriction on foreign production or consumption but none on its domestic equivalent, the export restrictions cannot be even-handed.[86]

An obligation of even-handedness has also been identified in the obligation on WTO members to conduct an "objective examination" in

[83] WT/DS246/AB/R, para. 154 (7 Apr. 2004).
[84] Ibid., para. 162.
[85] Ibid., paras. 163–172.
[86] *U.S. – Gasoline*, WT/DS2/AB/R, p. 21 (29 Apr. 1996).

determinations of injury mentioned in WTO Antidumping Agreement Art. 3.1 and elsewhere.[87] In that circumstance the Appellate Body has observed that:

> If an examination is to be "objective," the identification, investigation and evaluation of the relevant factors must be even-handed. Thus, investigating authorities are not entitled to conduct their [antidumping] investigation in such a way that it becomes more likely that, as a result of the fact-finding or evaluation process, they will determine that the domestic industry is injured.[88]

A second egalitarian standard is that of "balance." Balance is a common metaphor in WTO law and is often associated with the structure of the treaty as a reciprocal exchange of legal commitments, discussed in Chapter 2. In this conception it is relatively uncontroversial to characterize breaches of the WTO Agreement as "imbalances" and to conceive of either countermeasures or compliance as "righting" the balance, thereby returning to notional equality.[89]

Finally, the egalitarian concept of "parallelism" is derived from the parallel language used in the first and second paragraphs of Art. 2 of the WTO Agreement on Safeguards (SAF).[90] Under SAF Art. 2.1 WTO members are allowed to apply safeguard measures to increased imports of a product where imports cause or threaten to cause serious injury to the domestic industry. However, under SAF Art. 2.2 "[s]afeguard measures shall be applied to a product being imported *irrespective of its source*." The combined effect of these provisions denotes an obligation of parallelism in the investigation and application of safeguard measures.[91]

[87] See also SCM Art. 15.1.

[88] *U.S. – Hot-Rolled*, WT/DS184/AB/R, para. 196 (24 July 2001).

[89] The metaphor of "balance" is a pervasive one in WTO law and serves as a shorthand for the arrangement among members generally: *Argentina – Textiles*, WT/DS56/AB/R, para. 47 (27 Mar. 1997); *Argentina – Footwear*, WT/DS121/R, para. 8.63 (25 June 1999); *U.S. – Wheat Gluten*, WT/DS166/AB/R, paras. 145–146 (22 Dec. 2000); *U.S. – Carbon Steel*, WT/DS213/AB/R, para. 74 (28 Nov. 2002); *Brazil – Aircraft*, WT/DS46/RW/2, n. 131 (26 July 2001); of violations problematized as "imbalances": *Canada – Continued Suspension*, WT/DS321/AB/R, para. 317 (16 Oct. 2008); of "prompt settlement" of disputes as essential to the maintenance of a proper balance between rights and obligations: *Canada – Continued Suspension*, WT/DS321/AB/R, para. 317 (16 Oct. 2008); *EC – Hormones*, WT/DS26/15-13, para. 26 (29 May 1998).

[90] *U.S. – Line Pipe*, WT/DS202/AB/R, paras. 179, 181, 194.

[91] In *Argentina – Footwear (EC)*, for example, the EC contested a safeguard measure applied by Argentina to imports of footwear but continuing to permit entry of footwear from Argentina's MERCOSUR partner countries. The Appellate Body observed:

There are many other adjudicatively developed standards referencing equality in WTO law. Together they suggest the abiding influence of equality in the operation of the WTO Agreement. Nevertheless, the great diversity of equality-based standards makes it difficult to say much conclusively about its persistent significance, except perhaps the obvious point that an exhaustive definition of equality is elusive.

4.3.1.7 GATS and TRIPS

The WTO Agreement is composed of disciplines on goods contained in GATT 1994. However, an important aspect of the WTO Agreement's expansion and consolidation of rules of international trade concerns trade in services (under the General Agreement on Trade in Services (GATS)) and trade-related aspects of intellectual property (under TRIPS). Although most of the early jurisprudence of WTO dispute settlement has arisen out of disputes concerning trade in goods, it is useful to examine how a concern with equality and equal treatment is also manifested under GATS and TRIPS for the purposes of comprehensiveness.

GATS and TRIPS were negotiated with the preexisting structure and experience of GATT in mind and are therefore heavily influenced by GATT's basic architecture and reasoning. This includes an emphasis in many key instances on equality. Under GATS, for instance, members are required to extend "treatment no less favourable than that accorded to like services and services suppliers of any other country" immediately and unconditionally to services or services suppliers of other WTO members (GATS Art. II).[92] They are also required to fulfill obligations of transparency by publishing all measures of general application and to establish national inquiry points to respond to other members'

> we find that Argentina's investigation, which evaluated whether serious injury or the threat thereof was caused by imports from *all* sources, could only lead to the imposition of safeguard measures on imports from *all* sources. Therefore, we conclude that Argentina's investigation, in this case, cannot serve as a basis for excluding imports from other MERCOSUR member States from the application of the safeguard measures.
>
> (*Argentina – Footwear (EC)*, WT/DS121/AB/R, para. 113 (14 Dec. 1999) [emphasis in original])

[92] These are accompanied by a number of derogations that take the form of GATS Art. II exemptions. The exemptions are subject to review and should in principle not last longer than ten years.

information requests. In addition, members must observe market access commitments (GATS Art. XVI) and a national treatment requirement (GATS Art. XVII) ensuring that conditions of competition are not modified in favor of a member's own service industries.

At the same time, the emergent nature of GATS and disciplines on trade in services recognizes that service supply may not be entirely analogous to the consumption of goods, hence GATS distinguishes between four modes of service supply on the basis of which national commitments are made and allows certain limits on market access by foreign service providers. These are critical restrictions that derogate from the idea of equality of competitive conditions and equal access.

To the extent that issues of discrimination arise in relation to services, it appears that they are to be analyzed in a similar manner to that found under GATT with a few modifications. On the issue of likeness, for instance, the panel in *Canada – Autos* observed that "to the extent that the service suppliers concerned supply the same services, they should be considered 'like' for the purpose of this case."[93] As to the degree or extent of similarity necessary for services or service suppliers to be considered "like," this will vary among GATS provisions. Because the determination of likeness of services and service suppliers is a determination of the nature and extent of competitive relationships, the question can only be determined on a case-by-case basis.[94]

Still, the Appellate Body has cautioned that due to the specific wording of "services and service suppliers" in GATS Arts. II:1 and XVII, "the assessment of likeness of service suppliers should not be undertaken in isolation from considerations relating to the likeness of the services they provide." It added:

> Because the "likeness" analysis serves to assess the competitive relationship of the "services and service suppliers" at issue, the particular features of that competitive relationship, in the circumstances of any specific case, will determine the relative weight to be accorded in the analysis of "likeness" to considerations relating to the service and the service supplier, respectively.[95]

In comparison to the method of analyzing "likeness" in GATT, which involves the four classic criteria mentioned earlier in the discussion of

[93] *Canada – Autos*, WT/DS139/R, para. 10.248 (11 Feb. 2000).

[94] *Argentina – Financial Services*, WT/DS453/AB/R, para. 6.26 (14 Apr. 2016).

[95] Ibid.

GATT Art. III:2, the Appellate Body has observed that "these [same] criteria may be employed also in assessing 'likeness' in the context of trade in services, provided that they are adapted as appropriate to account for the specific characteristics of trade in services."[96] That adaptation may involve, for instance, taking into account the fact that service disciplines are committed under different modes of supply and consideration of how this might affect likeness.[97]

To date WTO dispute settlement has interpreted only a few GATS provisions. For instance, it has agreed that the MFN obligation in GATS Art. II:1 encompasses both *de jure* and *de facto* discrimination.[98] With respect to interpretation of the term "treatment no less favorable" in GATS Arts. II:1 and XVII, the Appellate Body has also commented that both provisions share the character of antidiscrimination disciplines and that therefore the interpretation of one provision should be pertinent in interpretation of the other. In:

> substance, the concept of "treatment no less favourable" under both the most-favoured-nation and national treatment provisions of the GATS is focused on a measure's modification of the conditions of competition. This legal standard does not contemplate a separate and additional inquiry into the regulatory objective of, or the regulatory concerns underlying, the contested measure.[99]

[96] Ibid., para. 6.31. The Appellate Body went on to elaborate:

> For example, the characteristics of services and service suppliers or consumers' preferences in respect of services and service suppliers may be relevant for determining "likeness" under the GATS. We note that, in this vein, the panel in *EC – Bananas III* considered the "nature and the characteristics" of the service transactions at issue, which may be seen as an adaptation of the original criterion in *Border Tax Adjustments* – namely, properties, nature and quality. Furthermore, with respect to the criterion of tariff classification, the classification and description of services under, for instance, the UN Central Product Classification (CPC) could be relevant. The panel in *China – Electronic Payment Services* undertook another such adaptation in considering evidence that the service suppliers at issue "describe[d] their business scope in very similar terms," and that this suggested that "these suppliers compete[d] with each other in the same business sector." This may be seen as adaptations of the criteria of "properties, nature and quality," "end-use," and/or "consumer preferences."
>
> (Ibid., para. 6.32)

[97] Ibid., paras. 6.33.

[98] *EC – Bananas III*, WT/DS27/AB/R, paras. 231–234 (9 Sept. 1997).

[99] *Argentina – Financial Services*, WT/DS453/AB/R, paras. 6.105–6.106 (14 Apr. 2016).

In general, however, there is the idea of greater flexibility under GATS, and hence, less necessarily equal treatment. In *Argentina – Financial Services*, for instance, the Appellate Body observed that its analysis of the phrase "no less favorable treatment" in GATS accords a considerable degree of flexibility to WTO members in service regulation since GATS commitments are contemplated as legitimately serving a wide variety of policy objectives. GATS therefore involves a balance of rights and obligations different from that under GATT:

> Through these flexibilities and exceptions, the GATS seeks to strike a balance between a Member's obligations assumed under the Agreement and that Member's right to pursue national policy objectives. A Member's right to pursue national policy objectives is recognized in the preamble of the GATS, including the third and fourth recitals. The term "national policy objectives" in the preamble, which is general and undefined, may cover a wide array of objectives, and Members retain various means to pursue these objectives. To begin with, measures pursuing national policy objectives may be taken outside the sectors or supply modes covered by GATS Schedules. Furthermore, a Member may pursue a wide range of policy objectives while acting consistently with its obligations or commitments assumed under the GATS. Indeed, a Member's commitments under the GATS could in some cases serve to further its national policy objectives. Where measures are found to be inconsistent with a Member's obligations or commitments under the GATS, the GATS provides for various mechanisms, such as Article XIV, which take account of policy objectives underlying such measures. This balance, too, reinforces the established legal standard for "treatment no less favourable" under the non-discrimination provisions of the GATS, that is, whether a measure modifies the conditions of competition to the detriment of like services or service suppliers of any other Member. Where a measure is inconsistent with the non-discrimination provisions, regulatory aspects or concerns that could potentially justify such a measure are more appropriately addressed in the context of the relevant exceptions. Addressing them in the context of the non-discrimination provisions would upset the existing balance under the GATS.[100]

In the same case the Appellate Body emphasized that the "analysis [of 'no less favourable treatment'] does not suggest that any evidence relating to the regulatory aspects must a priori be excluded." According to the Appellate Body:

> Consistent with the established approach to assessing "less favourable treatment" under the GATT 1994, an assessment of whether a measure

[100] Ibid., paras. 6.114–6.115.

> modifies the conditions of competition to the detriment of like services or service suppliers of any other Member "must begin with careful scrutiny of the measure, including consideration of the design, structure, and expected operation of the measure at issue." In such assessment, to the extent that evidence relating to the regulatory aspects has a bearing on the conditions of competition, it might be taken into account, subject to the particular circumstances of a case.[101]

The emphasis on specific conditions ("subject to the particular circumstances of a case") suggests that assessment of less favorable treatment in the realm of services will be highly individuated, and again, less necessarily equal.

The parameters of MFN and NT protection under TRIPS are also distinct from that of GATT. TRIPS is an agreement largely designed to reinforce disciplines on national treatment contained in preexisting intellectual property conventions, along with certain additions and modifications. It applies to the rights to intellectual property possessed by "nationals," not products. In addition, "[l]ike GATT 1994, [TRIPS] Article 3.1 [concerning National Treatment] refers to 'no less favourable' treatment . . . but it does not refer to likeness."[102]

The focus in any analysis under TRIPS is then on the treatment accorded to members' *nationals* in their efforts to maintain their intellectual property rights. Because of this individual-oriented focus, there is naturally more uniformity, and TRIPS disciplines are arguably more rigorous than those found elsewhere in the WTO Agreement. As under GATT Art. III, formal identity of treatment is not dispositive. Instead, what is in issue is whether or not nationals enjoy "effective equality of opportunity" in the protection of their intellectual property.[103] This, in turn, requires:

> close scrutiny of the "fundamental thrust and effect of the measure itself." This examination cannot rest on simple assertion, but must be founded on a careful analysis of the contested measure and its implications in the marketplace. At the same time, the examination need not be based on the actual effects of the contested measure.[104]

[101] Ibid., paras. 6.127.

[102] *EC – Trademarks and Geographical Indications*, WT/DS290/R, para. 7.181 (15 Mar. 2005).

[103] *US – Section 211 Appropriations Act*, WT/DS176/R, para. 8.131 (15 Mar. 2005) quoting from *U.S. – Section 337*, B.I.S.D. 36th Supp. 345, para. 5.11 (16 Jan. 1989).

[104] *EC – Trademarks and Geographical Indications*, WT/DS290/R, para. 7.186 (15 Mar. 2005). See also *Korea – Various Measures on Beef*, WT/DS161/AB/R, para. 142 (11 Dec. 2000).

For instance, in *US – Section 211 Appropriations Act* the measure at issue was a US provision that prohibited those with an interest in trademarks or trade names related to certain businesses or assets confiscated by the Cuban government from registering or renewing such trademarks or names without the original owner's consent. Cubans and their successors-in-interest were prevented from having their rights recognized, enforced or validated in US court, whereas US and non-Cuban-foreign nationals were only prevented from doing so when they were successors-in-interest to Cubans. The Appellate Body held that less favorable treatment for Cubans vis-à-vis US nationals violated the NT obligation, while less favorable treatment for Cubans as compared to non-Cuban-foreign nationals violated the MFN obligation.

Where the extent of TRIPS disciplines was particularly noted was in counter-arguments made by the United States in attempting to rebut the determination of discrimination. This included arguments that Cuban original owners could consent to the assertion of their rights, which the panel found was not the case because the Cuban original owner might not be deemed the original owner of the same or similar Cuban trademark under US law. They also included the argument that a Cuban original owner of a trademark could be "unblocked" under US asset control regulations, which did not eventuate in every instance, and in any event, constituted an additional barrier that US original owners were not required to meet.[105]

The Appellate Body's comments in *US – Section 211 Appropriations Act* appear to highlight the way that TRIPS imposes uniform obligations that are more embracing and far-reaching than that of GATT or GATS because they are based on a uniform legal concept, that of a rights-holder.

4.3.2 A Constitutive Law

The idea of WTO law as a "law of obligation" foreshadows how WTO law and the WTO Agreement can be thought of structurally as a constitution.

[105] *US – Section 211 Appropriations Act*, WT/DS176/AB/R, para. 286–290 (2 Jan. 2002).

A constitution is an order of obligations. References to "governing" and "organization" in the definition of a constitution in both domestic and international law highlight the way a constitution is directive.[106] A constitution directs the arrangement of the community through obligation since in the first place it is through obligations that the aims of the constitution are achieved. A constitution does this by distributing powers, by defining relations among powers and by providing recourse against those powers. A constitution may also provide a mechanism for amendment and the ordering of conflicts that arise from the relationship with powers outside the community.[107] In all of the senses, a constitution is implemented chiefly by means of duties.

At the same time, a constitution is almost always more than written text. The difficulty of amending a constitutive instrument means that it differs from ordinary law and is foreseen to apply in many and varied circumstances across time. Consequently, constitutional norms are often general, or at least generally expressed. A constitution is a visionary instrument oriented toward the future.[108]

106 In terms of international organizations, Henry Schermers and Niels Blokker have written that "[t]he constitution sets the pattern for the legal order of the international organization. Further rules develop from the operation of its organs. The power of these organs to take decisions stems from the constitution." Henry Schermers & Niels Blokker, *International Institutional Law* (6th rev'd. ed.) 756 (Brill Nijhoff, Leiden; 2018). In domestic law constitutions are often identified as the supreme law. For example, the Constitution of the People's Republic of China is self-described as "the fundamental law of the state and has supreme legal authority." Constitution of the People's Republic of China, Preamble (1982); South Africa's Constitution is described as adopted "as the supreme law of the Republic so as to heal the divisions of the past and establish a society based on democratic values, social justice and fundamental human rights …" Constitution of the Republic of South Africa, Preamble (1996); the US Constitution is described as being established "to form a more perfect Union, establish Justice, insure domestic Tranquility, provide for the common defense, promote the general Welfare, and secure the Blessings of Liberty to ourselves and our Posterity." Constitution of the United States of America, Preamble (1789). Philip Allott has observed, "it may be said that the constitution is the structure-system of a society which enables social power to be applied to make the transformations which enable a society to create itself from its possibilities." Allott, *Eunomia* 152.

107 The ILC has defined "constitution" as including "all legal rules establishing and regulating the organization." See Report of the International Law Commission, G.A.O.R. 17th Sess., Supp. No. 9 (A/5209), at 7. See also Schermers & Blokker, *International Institutional Law* 758–765 (identifying classic characteristics of the constitution of an international organization as involving the creation of a legal person, limits on reservations, provisions for withdrawal, and where necessary, tacit renewal).

108 "A constitution is framed for ages to come, and is designed to approach immortality as nearly as human institutions can approach it." *Cohens* v. *Virginia*, 19 U.S. (6 Wheaton)

The WTO Agreement is most evidently constitutive in the way that it binds adherents to a single undertaking in which obligations apply "concurrently and cumulatively."[109] This application is the product of the MFN clause, various nondiscrimination requirements, and the standards of harmonization, equivalence and mutual recognition discussed above, as well as the independent obligation specified in WTO Art. XVI:4 that each WTO member shall conform its laws with its obligations in the WTO Agreement. These requirements, taken together, impose a "unity" of obligation upon members.

Several features of the treaty work to reinforce this idea. First, members' obligations themselves must be appreciated within the context of a legal order that is generally difficult to modify or amend. The WTO Agreement foresees only three express options for such action: waivers of obligation under WTO Art. IX:3, multilateral interpretations under WTO Art. IX:2, and formal amendments under WTO Art. X.

Waivers of obligation are contemplated to be "specific and exceptional" instruments under the treaty that are only granted upon justification, with prior approval, and for a limited duration.[110] Multilateral interpretations are possible and may be likened to "subsequent agreements" among members under VCLT Art. 31(3)(a). However, to date no such

264 at 387 (1821). "A constitution . . . is drafted with an eye to the future. Its function is to provide a continuing framework for the legitimate exercise of governmental power." *Hunter* v. *Southam Newspapers*, [1984] 2 *Sup. Ct Rep.* 145 at 155 (Can.).

[109] *U.S. – Oil Country Tubular Goods Sunset Reviews*, WT/DS268/RW, para. 7.129 (30 Nov. 2006).

[110] A list of waivers granted by the General Council in 2021, as well as waivers previously granted and still in force, was available in WTO document WT/GC/W/840 (17 Dec. 2021). The document lists 24 waivers, some of which have since expired. The total number is relatively small and contrasts markedly with practice under GATT 1947 when waivers were frequent under GATT 1947. In an effort to comply with the spirit of a single undertaking, GATT-era waivers lapsed or were not carried over into the WTO Agreement. In *EC – Bananas III (21.5)*, WT/DS 27/AB/RW2/ECU, para. 382 (26 Nov. 2008) the Appellate Body noted that:

> the function of a waiver is to relieve a Member, for a specified period of time, from a particular obligation provided for in the covered agreements, subject to the terms, conditions, justifying exceptional circumstances or policy objectives described in the waiver decision. Its purpose is not to modify existing provisions in the agreements, let alone create new law or add to or amend the obligations under a covered agreement or Schedule.

For this reason, the Appellate Body held that a waiver could not be likened to a "subsequent agreement" pursuant to VCLT Art. 31(3)(a).

interpretation has been agreed.[111] Finally, formal amendments may be made pursuant to WTO Art. X, but so far only one such amendment – involving TRIPS Art. 31*bis*, discussed in Chapter 3 – has been adopted.[112] Limited options for modification and amendment are testament to the relatively fixed nature of the treaty. To that extent, they reference its entrenched character.

Second, the attitude developed by panels and the Appellate Body toward the interpretation of WTO law has been exclusivist and generally wary of external influence. This is an important aspect of its operation as a "system." While WTO law is undoubtedly part of public international law, the treaty is interpreted in dispute settlement in a relatively self-contained and systematic fashion in the manner of a constitution.[113] WTO adjudicators appear to take seriously the obligation to supply acceptable interpretations and answers to legal questions. Until recently, the unified structure of dispute settlement and the way that WTO members commit to "have [exclusive] recourse to, and abide by" the DSU means that little room has been left to develop alternative, conflicting interpretations. Interpretative pluralism is therefore limited. A single,

[111] In *EC – Bananas III (21.5)* the Appellate Body noted that:

> multilateral interpretations are meant to clarify the meaning of existing obligations, not to modify their content. ... We consider that a multilateral interpretation pursuant to Article IX:2 of the WTO Agreement can be likened to a subsequent agreement regarding the interpretation of the treaty or the application of its provisions pursuant to Article 31(3)(a) of the Vienna Convention, as far as the interpretation of the WTO agreements is concerned.
>
> (Ibid., WT/DS27/AB/RW2/ECU, para. 383 (26 Nov. 2008))

[112] The effort to amend occurred in 2005 in connection with the Decision on Paragraph 6, when certain members introduced a protocol to formalize the arrangement by proposing an insertion of TRIPS "Art. 31*bis*" and an Annex governing its application. See discussion in Section 3.3.3. A Revision of the WTO Agreement on Government Procurement was successfully concluded and entered into force in 2014. The WTO Agreement on Trade in Civil Aircraft was amended in 2001 and again in 2015 to align the relevant portions of the Agreement with Harmonized System updates.

[113] Nico Krisch notes that:

> WTO law claims for itself the right to define status vis-à-vis other regimes: we have seen this in the panel report in *Biotech*, but it is also on display in the decisions of the Appellate Body which refers quite frequently to other international legal rules, but does not necessarily accord them much interpretive weight.
>
> (Nico Krisch, *Beyond Constitutionalism* 201 (Oxford University Press, Oxford; 2010))

all-encompassing vision of the law is projected – as befits an integrated instrument such as a constitution.

Third, the WTO Agreement appears to prevail over subsequent inconsistent instruments involving the same subject matter. As mentioned in Chapter 2, the treaty permits member countries to enter into regional trade agreements (RTAs) between themselves under GATT Art. XXIV but also contains an approvals mechanism under GATT Art. XXIV:7 that has become gridlocked and to date, apart from rare instances, has never worked as intended. Instead, the system of approvals under GATT Art. XXIV has continued to operate via the diplomatic fiction of simply "taking note" of notifications made by countries concerning the RTAs they are entering into.[114] Despite this, on a number of occasions panels and the Appellate Body have made it clear that it is not open to member countries to unilaterally modify their WTO rights and obligations by concluding deals *inter se*.[115] In other words, members cannot "contract out" of their WTO commitments without multilateral approval, a requirement which appears to confirm that in WTO law the broad constitutive character of the treaty takes precedence over narrower contractual ones (i.e. Constitution > Contract).

Fourth, objective and dynamic interpretation of the WTO Agreement by panels and the Appellate Body is another indication of the constitutive nature of WTO arrangements. Constitutional interpretation is chiefly distinguished by being teleologic and purposive, and to that extent, prospective in character.[116] It is contrasted with contractual

[114] The *WTO Analytical Index* notes that:

> For the period between the Committee's establishment and the adoption in December 2006 of the Transparency Mechanism for Regional Trade Agreements, the Committee had completed the factual examination of a total of 66 agreements, of which 45 in the area of trade in goods and 21 in trade in services. No report on the examination of any of these agreements has ever been agreed upon.
>
> (*WTO Analytical Index* – GATT Art. XXIV: WTO Practice, p. 14 (June 2020))

[115] "In our view, however, a bilateral agreement between two Members . . . does not alter the legal nature of the measures at issue or the applicability of the relevant GATT/WTO provisions." *Turkey – Textiles*, WT/DS34/R, para. 9.178 (31 May 1999); *EC – Bananas III*, WT/DS27/AB/R, paras. 164–170 (9 Sept. 1997) (the Appellate Body, in examining the Lomé Convention, concluded that unless explicitly authorized by a waiver, provisions of the Convention could not alter rights and obligations of WTO members).

[116] "Scholars have sought to distinguish between a contractarian versus constitutional approach to the GATT/WTO system. Contractual interpretation tends to look at the

interpretation, which is largely static and retrospective and which takes its implicit point of reference the time at which the contract was concluded. The trend toward dynamic interpretation in many – though admittedly not all – instances of WTO treaty interpretation is an important indicator of the WTO Agreement's fundamentally constitutive character.[117]

Fifth, notwithstanding the "contractual" origins of the WTO Agreement, recent additions to the treaty and those potential additions now under negotiation largely evade quantification and therefore underline the idea that the WTO Agreement, in a real sense, escapes measurement and must be constitutive and integral. That is because, in an environment where quantification assumes a diminished role, countries do not bargain for strict reciprocity but rather engage in diffuse reciprocity. Their motivation is the greater benefit they foresee receiving from WTO arrangements over the long-term.

All of these features illustrate the way that WTO arrangements can be thought of as constitutive or a constitution. However, to describe the WTO Agreement as constitutive or something more than this is to consciously rely on domestic models and experience of constitutionalism. Controversy persists about the appropriateness of doing so.

In the early years of the WTO Agreement, substantial commentary was devoted to the "constitutionalization of the WTO."[118] Commentators

intent of the parties at the time of the signing of the agreement. Constitutional lawyers vary in their approach." Jeffrey Waincymer, *WTO Litigation* 400–401 (Cameron May, London; 2002); "To a considerable degree, the interpretation of treaties establishing international organizations is governed by the principle of effectiveness." S.v. "Interpretation in International Law" in *Max Planck Encyclopedias of International Law*, para. 40 (Mar. 2013) (author: Matthias Herdegen).

117 Gabrielle Marceau, "Evolutive Interpretation by the WTO Adjudicator" 21:4 *J.I.E.L.* 791 (2018).

118 For the extensive literature on WTO law as a constitution, see Deborah Cass, *The Constitutionalization of the World Trade Organization* (Oxford University Press, Oxford; 2005); Ernst-Ulrich Petersmann, *Constitutional Functions and Constitutional Problems of International Economic Law* (Westview Press, Boulder; 1991); Jeffrey Dunoff, "Constitutional Conceits: The WTO's Constitution and the Discipline of International Law" 17:3 *E.J.I.L.* 647 (2006); Thomas Cottier & Randall Hertig, "The Prospects of 21st Century Constitutionalism" 7:1 MaxPlanckUNYB 261 (2004); Sungjoon Cho, "A Bridge Too Far" 7 *J.I.E.L.* 219 (2004); Laurence Helfer, "Constitutional Analogies in the International Legal System" 37 *Loy. L.A. L. Rev.* 193 (2003); Robert Howse & Kalypso Nicolaides, "Legitimacy and Global Governance" in R. B. Porter et al. (eds), *Efficiency, Equity and Legitimacy* 227 (Brookings Institution Press; Washington, DC; 2001); Neil Walker, "The EU and the WTO: Constitutionalism in a New Key" in Grainne de Búrca & J. Scott (eds), *The EU and the WTO* (Hart, Oxford; 2001); Deborah

such as John Jackson focused on the organization's institutional architecture as a basis for the claim that the treaty is a constitution.[119] The claim relied at least in part on analogy with the experience of the EC/EU, which had gradually evolved a sophisticated form of transnational constitutionalism largely through the jurisprudence of the European Court of Justice (ECJ).[120] Some commentators forecasted that the WTO's then-new binding dispute settlement system might cause the organization to follow a parallel constitutional path.[121]

Nevertheless, a number of commentators noted that this traditional "vertical" conception of constitution – as a top-down instrument outlining a separation of powers, a system of checks and balances, and buttressing individual rights – was largely missing in WTO law. Jeffrey Dunoff points out, for instance, how there is no express announcement in the WTO Agreement of a world trade "constitution."[122] The treaty also does not explicitly set out any real system of checks and balances.[123] Furthermore, only a handful of WTO disputes have addressed institutional issues, and of these, exceedingly few have commented at any length – and with exceeding caution – about the treaty's division of

Cass, "The 'Constitutionalization' of International Trade Law" 12 *E.J.I.L.* 39 (2001); John McGinnis & Mark Movsesian, "The World Trade Constitution" 114 *Harv. L. Rev.* 511 (2000); John Jackson, "The WTO 'Constitution' and Proposed Reforms" 4 *J.I.E.L.* 67 (2001); Ernst-Ulrich Petersmann, "The WTO Constitution and Human Rights" 3 *J.I.E.L.* 19 (2000); Ernst-Ulrich Petersmann, "The WTO Constitution and the Millennium Round" in Marco Bronckers & Reinhard Quick (eds), *New Directions in International Economic Law* 111 (Martinus Nijhoff, Leiden; 2000); Gail Evans, *Lawmaking under the Trade Constitution* (Kluwer Law International, London; 2000); Ernst-Ulrich Petersmann, "Constitutionalism and International Organizations" 17 *Nw. J. Int'l L. & Bus.* 398 (1997); Arie Reich, "From Diplomacy to Law" 17 *Nw. J. Int'l L. & Bus.* 775 (1997).

119 John Jackson, *The World Trade Organization* 6 (Routledge, New York; 1998) (referring to "the 'constitution' of the WTO, in the broad meaning of the word 'constitution'. That is, it will consider the institutional structure of the WTO, including the structure of the organization, its treaty basis, its very important procedures for dispute settlement, and the relation of these to GATT, its predecessor.").

120 For a comparison of EU/WTO constitutionalism, see Walker, "The EU and the WTO" 31.

121 Peter Holmes, "The WTO and the EU" in Grainne de Búrca & Joanne Scott (eds), *The EU and the WTO* 59 (Hart, Oxford; 2001); Ernst-Ulrich Petersmann, "European and International Constitutional Law" in Grainne de Búrca & Joanne Scott (eds), *The EU and the WTO* 81 (Hart, Oxford; 2001).

122 Dunoff, "Constitutional Conceits" 647.

123 Ibid. at 657.

competences.[124] In this respect, the development of a WTO constitution in the image of the EU seems unlikely.[125]

These limitations prompted considerable soul-searching about alternative ways to understand constitutionalism in the WTO. One way put forward by Robert Howse and Kalypso Nicolaidis suggests that rather than EU-style constitutionalism, the WTO Agreement could aspire to subsidiarity, or the principle that "a central authority should have a subsidiary function, performing only those tasks which cannot be performed at a more local level."[126] Subsidiarity would be based on concepts of institutional sensitivity, political inclusiveness and top-down empowerment. Institutional sensitivity would "involve[] sensitivity to the superior credentials that other institutions of governance may have in addressing ... substantive value trade-offs."[127] Political inclusiveness would involve enhanced participatory opportunities in WTO dispute settlement and the WTO's ability to enhance transnational inclusiveness in domestic rulemaking.[128] Top-down empowerment would involve the WTO playing a role "in enhancing ... domestic processes by helping create local political spaces for local actors or NGOs who might have been hitherto dis-empowered in their domestic context (women,

[124] For example, Jeffrey Dunoff notes how in *India – Quantitative Restrictions*, WT/DS90, the Appellate Body explicitly and unequivocally rejected an "invitation to adopt a theory of separation of powers, or to articulate anything approaching a constitutional theory concerning the relationships between the WTO's 'political and judicial organs'." From this Dunoff concludes that "[t]he AB does not understand – or at least declare – itself to be articulating a constitutional vision of the relationships among coordinate branches of an overarching institution or to be policing the jurisdictional lines that separate these coordinate branches." Ibid. at 658.

[125] The Treaty establishing a Constitution for Europe was an unratified international treaty intended to create a consolidated constitution for EU. It would have replaced the existing EU treaties with a single text, given legal force to the Charter of Fundamental Rights, and expanded qualified majority voting into policy areas which had previously been decided by unanimity among member states. The Treaty was signed on 29 October 2004 by representatives of the then twenty-five EU member states. It was later ratified by eighteen member states. However, the rejection of the document by French and Dutch voters in May and June 2005 brought the ratification process to an end. Following a period of reflection, the Treaty of Lisbon was created to replace the Constitutional Treaty. This contained many of the changes that were originally placed in the Constitutional Treaty but was formulated as amendments to the existing treaties. The Lisbon Treaty entered into force in December 2009.

[126] Robert Howse & Kalypso Nicolaidis, "Enhancing WTO Legitimacy?" 16:1 *Governance* 73 (2003).

[127] Ibid. at 87.

[128] Ibid. at 88–89.

children, unions, migrants)," in effect rebalancing their domestic representation at a global level. According to Howse and Nicolaidis, "top-down empowerment, alongside indirect accountability, could go a long way in addressing the 'global democratic deficit.'"[129]

While Howse and Nicolaidis's ideas are provocative and find some reflection in WTO practice, little of their promise has been realized in the interim. In the years since Howse and Nicolaidis made their proposals, reliance on nonstate participation in WTO dispute settlement has been negligible and other formal participatory opportunities by nonstate actors in the WTO system are limited.[130] WTO dispute settlement, in particular, continues to focus on the immediate tasks at hand, which is to settle disputes between member states, leaving open the possibility of transformative solutions acceptable to the membership.

Partly for this reason, Anne Peters and others have asserted the need to understand what is happening in the WTO and other international fora as involving a distinctive "reconstructed constitutionalism." In this process, traditional legitimating factors of international governance such as state sovereignty and the effective exercise of power are "gradually being complemented (if not substituted) by other guiding principles, notably the 'global common interest' and/or 'rule of law' and/or 'human security.'"[131] In a complementarity scenario the relationship between international and national law is not described as either hierarchy or subsidiarity.[132] Instead, domestic and international norms operate together as a network in a form of complementarity.[133] Peters indicates that this reconception manifests itself in a number of legal developments

[129] Ibid. at 90.

[130] Gabrielle Marceau & Mikella Hurley, "Transparency and Public Participation at the WTO" 4 *Trade L. & Dev.* 19 (2012). For a review of the subject, see Yves Bonzon, *Public Participation and Legitimacy in the WTO* (Cambridge University Press, Cambridge; 2014) (noting that the institutional structure of the WTO and the contractual nature of its negotiations result in a lack of meaningful participatory opportunities for nonstate actors). The WTO Public Forum is currently the WTO's largest annual outreach event, providing an opportunity for participants to discuss recent developments in world trade and to propose ways of enhancing the multilateral trading system. In addition, in June 2023 the WTO Director-General established two advisory groups involving representatives from civil society and industry respectively to provide a mechanism for the Director-General to receive views from outside the WTO: see "Okonjo-Iweala establishes WTO business, civil society advisory groups" 41:26 *Inside U.S. Trade* 21 (30 June 2023).

[131] Peters, "Global Constitutionalism Revisited" 11 *Int'l Leg. Theory* 39 at 49.

[132] Ibid. at 51.

[133] Ibid. at 50–51.

on the international plane, such as the gradual erosion of consent, the development of objective legal orders, changes in the concept of statehood and recognition, and growing participation by nonstate actors.[134]

Peters suggests that these ideas might provide a framework for a "constitutionalist reconstruction" of international law by serving as a guideline for the interpretation of textually open norms, referencing procedural developments in lawmaking and reinforcing the idea of good governance.[135] The reconstruction will help move the international legal regime toward a genuine global constitutionalism, "which is apt to compensate for national constitutions' growing deficiencies."[136] At the same time, Peters acknowledges that there are important arguments against such a reconstruction, notably the fact that, given the realities of international power politics, regimes such as the WTO must content themselves with a more or less "symbolic constitutionalization."[137] In reality, the use of constitutional language in international contexts such as the WTO conscripts a highly value-laden term such as "constitution" to profit from its positive connotations and promote the institution's purposes.

In the end, whether one accepts a vertical, subsidiarity or complementarity view of constitutionalism, current experience appears to confirm rather than deny the continuing constitutive impulse at work in WTO arrangements. The challenge appears to be to make sense of it at a time of acute differences over the treaty's "good" mentioned in earlier chapters and its ability to encompass different economic systems.[138]

[134] Ibid. at 51–54.

[135] Ibid. at 64–66.

[136] Ibid., p. 67.

[137] Ibid., p. 66.

[138] For example, In January 2020 the United States, the EU and Japan released a detailed joint statement outlining proposed changes to the SCM to address industrial subsidies, particularly those contributing to overcapacity. The three argue that the SCM should ban more industrial subsidies and place the burden of proof on members to justify their subsidy programs. See "Joint Statement of the Trilateral Meeting of the Trade Ministers of Japan, the United States and the European Union" (14 Jan. 2020). Hannah Monicken, "Shea: WTO Reform a Priority 'at the Highest Levels' in the U.S." 38:10 *Inside U.S. Trade* (2 Mar. 2020).

> The U.S. proposal would "reaffirm" that the WTO is intended to promote market principles. Accordingly, it outlines several conditions the United States says members must meet to be considered market-oriented, including allowing prices, investment and other business decisions to be based on the market and not subject to "significant" government interference.
>
> ("China: U.S. Proposal Merely 'Scene-Setting' for Desired Subsidy Rules" 38:10 *Inside U.S. Trade* 1 (6 Mar. 2020))

4.3.3 *A Law of the Future*

Prevailing law is typically a product of the past. As such, it inevitably bears the imprint of prior attitudes, practices and reasoning. Pastness may be acceptable when a community is fixed and relatively static. However, when a community begins to change or when its conditions are fundamentally altered, the pastness of the law becomes an impediment.

GATT 1947 was designed to respond to the problem of pastness. The treaty was assembled by its drafters during the mid-1940s, a time when policymakers were looking for something new to govern international economic relations.[139]

In response, the centerpiece of GATT 1947 became a system of national tariff bindings complemented by obligations of MFN, NT and the prohibition on quantitative restrictions. These commitments, taken together, were designed to promote equality of opportunity in the future

Equality and futurity have certain consequences. One is that the inherently prospective gaze of the law implies an activist conception of time, a conception that emphasizes power and agency.[140] Time is a resource to be used to construct a better future.

Another consequence is the way in which the law inclines forward and is apodictic, or all-encompassing.[141] A dynamic and fluid perspective takes hold. In the process the future becomes more important than the past (i.e. Future > Past).

This dynamic perspective was evident in *U.S. – Cotton Yarn*, where the dispute involved the WTO-consistency of a safeguard invoked by the United States under the WTO Agreement on Textiles and Clothing (ATC). ATC Art. 6.2 permitted safeguard action to be taken in order to

See also Brett Fortnam, "Former USTRs: Next DG Will Have to Take Risks to Get WTO Back on Track" 38:30 *Inside U.S. Trade* 21 (24 July 2020); Hannah Monicken, "U.S., China Spar at WTO over 'Market-Oriented Conditions,'" 38:31 *Inside U.S. Trade* 16 (24 July 2020).

139 For a review of interwar trade policies, see League of Nations, *Commercial Policy in the Interwar Period: International Proposals and National Policies* (League of Nations, Geneva; 1942).

140 Glenn, *Legal Traditions of the World* 26–27 (noting how the conception of time introduces an idea of change and how in Western thinking there is "a concept of time within which human rationality can be seen as effecting change, making a difference.")

141 Ibid., p. 50.

protect a domestic industry from serious damage (or actual threat thereof) caused by a surge in imports, provided the domestic industry was identified as the industry producing "like and/or directly competitive products" to imports. For this reason, the Appellate Body had to analyze the meaning of the term "competitive." The Appellate Body observed:

> According to the ordinary meaning of the term "competitive," two products are in a competitive relationship if they are commercially interchangeable, or if they offer alternative ways of satisfying the same consumer demand in the marketplace. "Competitive" is a characteristic attached to a product and denotes the capacity of a product to compete *in a current or a future situation*. The word "competitive" must be distinguished from the words "competing" or "being in actual competition." It has a wider connotation than "actually competing" and includes also the notion of a potential to compete. It is not necessary that two products be competing, or that they be in actual competition with each other, in the marketplace at a given moment in order for those products to be regarded as competitive. Indeed, products which are competitive may not be actually competing with each other in the market place at a given moment for a variety of reasons, such as regulatory restrictions or producers' decisions. Thus, a static view is incorrect, for it leads to the same products being regarded as competitive at one moment in time, and not so in the next, depending on whether or not they are in the marketplace.[142]

Due to this future-oriented inclination, the body of WTO law is also given to a degree of idealism and abstraction, already noted in its preoccupation with equality. Thus, in *Colombia – Ports of Entry*, a dispute involving Colombian restrictions on entry of goods from Panama, the panel asserted that "a thorough examination of trade effects would be unnecessary and unwarranted due to the inherent difficulty in interpreting trade statistics, in which a wide variety of economic and other factors complicate the picture." It continued:

> The Panel will base its assessment on the terms of the measure as opposed to any previous or ongoing effect on the level of imports, in terms of volume or value. In light of this approach, Colombia cannot rely on evidence of an increase in imports to rebut arguments of a restriction on importation. Similarly, Panama cannot point solely to evidence demonstrating a decline in the level of imports to establish the existence of a restriction on importation or exportation.[143]

[142] *US – Cotton Yarn*, WT/DS192/AB/R, para. 96 (8 Oct. 2001) [emphasis in original]. See also *Korea – Alcoholic Beverages*, WT/DS75/AB/R, paras. 114, 120 (18 Jan. 1999).

[143] *Colombia – Ports of Entry*, WT/DS366/R, para. 7.256 (27 Apr. 2009).

The reason for this abstract methodology is essentially the same as that seen above in connection with the analysis of GATT Art. III. Figures do not always reveal the state of play, and even when they do, attribution of nullification or impairment by means of numbers alone is fraught with uncertainty. Instead, the law is conceived of as applying to something in a constant state of flux. This ever-evolving "thing," composed of constant tides of economic activity, is in fact reified in the epithet "expectations" conceived of in a single instant or moment.

An inference to be drawn from this approach is that things are always potentially other than they seem. The law manifests a healthy skepticism about what appears to exist. It retains in mind the image of something better. Consequently, reliance on facts is suspect. Whereas many commentators have criticized panels' and the Appellate Body's apparent aversion to statistical analysis, the failure to do so, or at least to place decisive emphasis on metrics, is explainable by reference to the idea that numbers may not provide an accurate assessment of what is actually taking place.[144]

In *U.S. – Lamb*, for instance, the Appellate Body noted that "[a]s facts, by their very nature, pertain to the present and the past, the occurrence of future events can never be definitively proven by facts."[145] Similarly, in

[144] Petros Mavroidis, *Trade in Goods* (1st ed.) 55–56 (Oxford University Press, Oxford; 2007). It has long been recognized that trade effects are of diminished importance in the ascription of state responsibility under GATT 1947 and the WTO Agreement due to the treaty's general emphasis on the protection of expectations of trade, not specific amounts of trade itself. This, in the 1949 *Working Party Report on Brazilian Internal Taxes* noted that the Working Party:

> the absence of imports from contracting parties during any period of time that might be selected for examination would not necessarily be an indication that they had no interest in exports of the product affected by the tax, since their potentialities as exporters, given national treatment, should be taken into account. These members of the working party therefore took the view that the provisions of the first sentence of Article III, paragraph 2, were equally applicable whether imports from other contracting parties were substantial, small or non-existent.
>
> (GATT/CP.3/42, B.I.S.D. II Supp. 181 at 185, para. 16 (adopted 30 June 1949))

Similarly in *U.S. – Taxes on Petroleum*, B.I.S.D. 34th Supp. 136, it was noted that "Article III:2, first sentence, cannot be interpreted to protect expectations on export volumes; it protects expectations on the competitive relationship between imported and domestic products." Ibid., para. 5.1.9.

[145] WT/DS177, 178/AB/R, para. 136 (1 May 2001).

Brazil – Tyres, the Appellate Body was critical of the panel's heavy reliance on statistics and effects-based reasoning in finding that a ban on retreaded tires made a "material contribution" to the necessity of Brazil's defense under GATT Art. XX(b). The Appellate Body noted:

> In order to justify an import ban under Article XX(b), a panel must be satisfied that [the ban] brings about a material contribution to the achievement of its objective. Such a demonstration can of course be made by resorting to evidence or data, pertaining to the past or the present, that establish that the import ban at issue makes a material contribution to the protection of public health or environmental objectives pursued. This is not, however, the only type of demonstration that could establish such a contribution. Thus, a panel might conclude that an import ban is necessary on the basis of a demonstration that the import ban at issue is apt to produce a material contribution to the achievement of its objective. This demonstration could consist of quantitative projections in the future, or qualitative reasoning based on a set of hypotheses that are tested and supported by sufficient evidence.[146]

Inherent in prospectivity and potentiality is the concept of latency, or the delay experienced in the manifestation of some phenomenon. There is, in other words, the unspoken expectation that some better counterfactual would eventuate if WTO member countries fulfilled their obligations under the treaty.

An example of this latency was furnished in *Korea – Various Measures on Beef*.[147] There the measure at issue was a dual retail system for meat that South Korea had established, following initial attempts to liberalize its economy in the 1980s and its removal of import restrictions.[148]

The dual system required foreign beef to be sold through a specially designated system of shops devoted solely to this purpose. In 1997 Australia and the United States brought claims against Korea concerning the system and its related measures, asserting that they treated imported beef less favorably than domestic beef. The panel observed that "under a dual retail system, the only way the imported product can get on the shelves is if the retailer agrees to substitute it, not only for one but for all existing like domestic products. This is clearly an added burden on the imported product in principle."[149] The additional

146 WT/DS332/AB/R, para. 151 (3 Dec. 2007).

147 *Korea – Various Measures on Beef*, WT/DS161–169/AB/R (11 Dec. 2000).

148 Dukgeun Ahn, "Korea in the GATT/WTO Dispute Settlement System" 6:3 *J.I.E.L.* 597 at 603 (2003).

149 *Korea – Various Measures on Beef*, WT/DS161–169/R, para. 632 (31 July 2000).

burden, combined with other burdens imposed by the system, led the panel to find that the dual retail system treated imported beef less favorably than domestic beef.[150] There was little direct reference to statistics.[151]

On appeal Korea contested the panel's analysis as "seriously flawed, [and as] relying largely on speculation rather than factual analysis."[152] The Appellate Body agreed "that a more direct, and perhaps simpler, approach"[153] to analysis of the dual retail system was merited and differed with the panel as to the relevance of several alleged grounds of discrimination. However, the Appellate Body reasoned that the introduction of the dual system in 1990 "meant, in direct practical effect . . . the sudden cutting off of access to the normal . . . distribution outlets," a "central consequence" of which was "the imposition of a drastic reduction of commercial opportunity to reach, and hence generate sales to, the same consumers served by the traditional retail channels for domestic beef."[154] The Appellate Body chose to confirm its decision by referring to statistics, not of trade volumes but retail operations.[155]

The reference to current statistics might appear to undercut the argument about WTO law's idealism as a "law of the future." However, several points militate against such a conclusion. First, the nature of the Korean regulatory shifty was dramatic. The regulatory change at a single point in time appeared to support what the panel and Appellate Body had hypothesized. Second, the statistical reference essentially confirmed the Appellate Body's conclusion, rather than constituted the basis of it. The statistics were taken as circumstantial evidence as opposed to direct proof. Third, the Appellate Body was careful to confine its analysis to "the present case."[156] There is, in other words, a reluctance to base legal analysis on empiric considerations alone, to make them the central factor

[150] Ibid., para. 639.

[151] "the jurisprudence on Article III makes it clear that no consideration needs to be given to the effects of any less favourable treatment or the impact of such discriminatory regulation on trade volume." Ibid., para. 637.

[152] *Korea – Various Measures on Beef*, WT/DS161–169/AB/R, para. 140 (11 Dec. 2000).

[153] Ibid., para. 142.

[154] Ibid., para. 145.

[155] Thus, it observed that "the much smaller number of specialized imported beef shops (approximately 5,000 shops) as compared with the number of retailers (approximately 45,000 shops) selling domestic beef." Ibid.

[156] Ibid., para. 142.

in the assessment of market conditions. Instead, these are assessed in an immanent perspective oriented toward what is to come.

4.3.4 A Deductive Law

Law is normative and it is often described as being so because law is distinguished from fact. At a minimum it involves the rights and obligations of actors in a legal system whereas facts involve "something that actually exists."[157]

The difference between law and fact means that the law must have a way of identifying, organizing and analyzing the facts. The totality of these methods is referred to as the law's *rationality*. Rationality infers that the law is rational, that is, within a given frame of reference it is subject to defensible reasoning.

Law is classically understood to be reasoned according to two types of logic: deductive and inductive reasoning.[158] Deductive reasoning "entails establishing a framework and then applying the framework to a problem."[159] A deductive argument might run as follows:

1. Every human will die someday.
2. Jones is a human.
3. Jones will die someday.[160]

The most common form of legal device embodying deductive reasoning is a presumption. A presumption is a legal rule that either prohibits or dispenses with the need for further proof.[161] Presumptions can be

[157] Bryan Garner (ed.), *Black's Law Dictionary* (7th ed.) 610 (West Group, St. Paul, MN; 1999).

[158] For example, J. S. Covington, Jr., *The Structure of Legal Argument and Proof* (William S. Hein; Buffalo, NY; 1993) who observes that "[t]here are two forms of reasoning and therefore two forms of argument." Ibid., p. 2.

[159] Roger Martin, *The Opposable Mind* 144–145 (Harvard Business School Press, Cambridge, MA; 2007).

[160] Paraphrase of an example used by Covington, Jr., *The Structure of Legal Argument and Proof* 7–8.

[161] "A presumption is an inference in favour of a particular fact and would also refer to a conclusion reached in the absence of direct evidence." *Argentina – Footwear*, WT/DS56/R, para. 6.38 (25 Nov. 1997). In that case the panel went on to observe that:

> Inference (or judicial presumption) is a useful means at the disposal of international tribunals for evaluating claims. In situations where direct evidence is not available, relying on inferences drawn from relevant facts of each case facilitates the duty of international tribunals in determining

rebuttable or irrebuttable. Deductive reasoning can also take the form of inferences, which are conclusions about facts reached "by considering other facts and deducing a logical consequence from them."[162] Generally speaking, presumptions pertain to the law, whereas inferences are more likely to be drawn about specific facts.[163] Thus, in international law and the law of many domestic systems, a presumption of innocence operates but a court or tribunal may draw inferences separately from certain factual conditions.[164]

WTO law is oriented toward deductive logic for several reasons. First, WTO law is idealistic and aims primarily at the abstract goal of non-discrimination. Abstraction is important because numbers may not adequately convey the real effects of government measures.

Second, the broad, forward-looking orientation of the WTO system as constitutive[165] and as a "law of the future" means that it is intensely

> whether or not the burden of proof has been met. It would therefore appear to be the prerogative of an international tribunal, in each given case, to determine whether applicable and unrebutted inferences are sufficient for satisfying the burden of proof.
>
> (Ibid., para. 6.39)

162 Garner, *Black's Law Dictionary* 781.

163
> Theoretically, the difference between legal presumptions and [inferences] are clear. Legal presumptions express the state of the law, whereas inferences express the state of the facts. Moreover, legal presumptions are usually general and do not need proof as to their logic and reasonableness; rather, their applicability as to a specific situation needs to be proven. [Inferences], on the contrary, are related to specific situations and their reasonableness is subject to the discretion of the tribunal. Nonetheless, because of the absence of statutory legal presumptions in international law, the border between legal presumptions and [inferences] is narrow.
>
> (Mojtaba Kazazi, *Burden of Proof and Related Issues* 260 (Kluwer Law International, The Hague; 1996))

164 For example, Art. 14(2) of the International Covenant on Civil and Political Rights, 999 U.N.T.S. 171 (1966) specifies that "Everyone charged with a criminal offence shall have the right to be presumed innocent until proved guilty according to the law."

165 On the connection between constitution and deduction, see *McCulloch* v. *Maryland*, 17 U.S. (4 Wheaton) 316 at 407 (1819):

> A Constitution, to contain an accurate detail of all the subdivisions of which its great powers will admit, and of all the means by which they may be carried into execution, would partake of the prolixity of a legal code, and could scarcely be embraced by the human mind. It would probably never be understood by the public. Its nature, therefore, requires, that only its great outlines should be marked, its important objects designated, and the minor ingredients which compose *those objects be deduced from the nature of the objects themselves*. That this idea was entertained by the

concerned with the maintenance of the equality of competitive conditions and hence with threats to potential trade. Some means are needed to establish apprehension of injury, and as we will see, this normally happens through the operation of presumptions and inference.

Third, WTO law places a special priority on automaticity, that is, on the ability to do things relatively quickly and without much investigation into detail. Consequently, many matters have to be assumed or presumed.

Fourth, WTO dispute settlement has limited fact-finding ability. In a number of cases, outcomes have been heavily dependent on what countries choose to disclose, meaning there is a need for presumptions and inferences that can operate in the absence of concrete evidence.

An important presumption in the WTO system is that countries are considered to comply with their obligations in good faith in line with VCLT Art. 26.[166] In this way, a veneer of normalcy is maintained about the treaty's operation even though there may be considerable noncompliance in practice.[167]

When a measure is challenged before the WTO dispute settlement system, the system applies a further presumption embodied in DSU Art. 3.8, which provides that:

> In cases where there is an infringement of the obligations assumed under a covered agreement, the action is considered *prima facie* to constitute a case of nullification or impairment.

> framers of the American Constitution, is not only to be inferred from the nature of the instrument, but from the language.
>
> ([emphasis added])

166 VCLT Art. 26 provides that "[e]very treaty in force is binding upon the parties to it and must be performed by them in good faith." For discussion, see *Brazil – Aircraft*, WT/DS46/RW/2, para. 5.124 (26 July 2001). See also Marion Panizzon, *Good Faith in the Jurisprudence of the WTO* (Hart, Oxford; 2006). In WTO law, the presumption of members' compliance has been noted in several cases: *Argentina – Peaches*, WT/DS238/R, para. 7.142 (14 Feb. 2003); *Brazil – Aircraft*, WT/DS46/RW/2, para. 5.124 (26 July 2001) (observing that "when the executive branch of a Member is not required to act inconsistently with requirements of WTO law, it should be entitled to a presumption of good faith compliance with those requirements.").

167 For example, in its September 2018 concept paper on WTO modernization the European Commission noted a "lack of comprehensive information on subsidies provided by Members [as] one of the biggest shortcomings in the application of the current system." See EU Concept Paper on WTO Reform (18 Sept. 2018). For further discussion of tacit noncompliance, see Gregory Schaffer et al., "Can Informal Law Discipline Subsidies?" 18 *J.I.E.L.* 711 (2015).

DSU Art. 3.8 goes on to observe that: "This means that there is normally a *presumption* that a breach of the rules has an adverse impact on other Members parties to that covered agreement, and in such cases, it shall be up to the Member against whom the complaint has been brought to rebut the charge."[168] The presumption lies at the heart of the WTO legal system inasmuch as it conditions when state responsibility will be triggered.

The case law concerning the presumption in DSU Art. 3.8 has generally upheld the principle, first identified under GATT 1947, that while the presumption is formally rebuttable, in practice, it had "operated as an irrefutable presumption."[169] This conclusion followed from a number of GATT cases wherein nullification or impairment was found even for measures that had no demonstrable trade effect.[170] Thus, in *Turkey – Textiles*, the panel assessed Turkey's argument that quantitative restrictions imposed on imports from India had had no real effect on trade. The panel concluded that:

> even if Turkey were to demonstrate that India's overall exports of clothing and textile products to Turkey have increased from their levels of previous years, it would not be sufficient to rebut the presumption of nullification and impairment caused by the existence of WTO incompatible import restrictions. Rather, at minimum, the question is whether exports have been what they would otherwise have been, were there no WTO incompatible quantitative restrictions against imports from India.[171]

The panel also noted that the fact that nonfulfillment of quotas could not be determinative of nullification or impairment of the WTO Agreement because the existence of quotas could lead to increased transaction costs and create uncertainties which would affect investment plans. Given its continuing application of quotas, Turkey had failed to rebut the presumption.

These presumptions and others in WTO law are noteworthy for the way that they are linked to obligation and its associated ideas of the

[168] Emphasis added.

[169] See *U.S. – Taxes on Petroleum*, 34th B.I.S.D. Supp. 156–157, para. 5.1.7 (17 June 1987).

[170] For instance, in *Japan – Leather*, 31st B.I.S.D. Supp. 94 (15–16 May 1984) it was noted that "the panel wished to stress that the existence of a quantitative restriction should be presumed to cause nullification or impairment not only because of the effect it had on the volume of trade but also for other reasons e.g., it would lead to increased transaction costs and would create uncertainties which would affect investment plans." Ibid., paras. 55–56.

[171] *Turkey – Textiles*, WT/DS34/R, para. 9.204 (31 May 1999).

"burden, the order, the universality of the law."[172] Jeffrey Waincymer has noted a presumption against conflict within the treaty,[173] a presumption of consistent usage,[174] a presumption of differential usage[175] and a presumption against retroactivity.[176] Upon reflection, however, it becomes apparent how presumptions operate to quietly stress the nature of WTO law as *a body of law*, that is, a regime of obligation. If a country accepts the WTO *acquis*, that is, the accrued body of law and practice under the treaty, then it is presumed to be obliged to the extent of the law.

In addition to presumptions, substantial use is also made of inferences in WTO law, particularly in WTO dispute settlement. Inferences are fact-based determinations drawn from other facts, another indication of deductive reasoning. Inferences can be important where countries are reluctant to fully disclose. Disclosure and notification have become serious issues in WTO practice recently.[177]

A good example of inference occurred in *Saudi Arabia – IP Rights*.[178] There Qatar contested Saudi Arabia's compliance with certain provisions of the TRIPS Agreement in connection with Saudi Arabia's efforts to strip a Qatar-based media group of its broadcast rights in the kingdom. The deprivation occurred in conjunction with a cessation of diplomatic relations between Saudi Arabia and Qatar.[179]

172 Allott, *Eunomia* 160.

173 Waincymer, *WTO Litigation* 465–466.

174 Ibid., p. 468.

175 Ibid., p. 469.

176 Ibid., p. 477.

177 Notification is particularly problematic with respect to subsidy notifications under the SCM. In September 2018 the EU observed that "Although the SCM Agreement already requires Members to notify their subsidies, the level of compliance is poor and has deteriorated in recent years, to the extent that as of end of March 2018 over half of the membership (90 Members) had not made any notification." EU Concept Paper on WTO Reform (18 Sept. 2018). See also G/SCM/W/546/Rev.9. In addition, in May 2018 the United States for the first time submitted a counter notification in the WTO Committee on Agriculture (COA) on India's market price support for wheat and rice. See "United States Issues First-Ever WTO Counter Notification against India's Market Price Support," US Department of Agriculture Press Release No. 0101.18 (5 May 2018). For discussion see Schaffer et al., "Can Informal Law Discipline Subsidies?" 711.

178 WT/DS567/R (16 June 2020).

179 In June 2017 Saudi Arabia severed diplomatic ties with Qatar. Saudi Arabia took the decision due to what it termed Qatar's "embrace of various terrorist and sectarian groups aimed at destabilising the region." Patrick Wintour, "Gulf Plunged into Diplomatic Crisis as Countries Cut Ties with Qatar" *The Guardian* (8 June 2017). As part of the rupture, Saudi Arabia closed its border to Qatar and imposed a blockade in concert with

The panel proceedings were marked by unfriendly behavior by Saudi Arabia which indicated that "it would not interact, or have any direct or indirect engagement, with Qatar in any way in this dispute."[180] The refusal left a number of discrete factual issues in limbo, which had to be resolved via inference. Among them was the fact that both Qatari and foreign license holders in the Saudi market were unable to secure legal representation concerning the deprivation by Saudi law firms. Another issue was the lack of any criminal or other enforcement by Saudi authorities of unauthorized broadcast activities. A further issue was Saudi authorities' alleged promotion of public gatherings for screenings of unauthorized broadcasts.

In resolving these issues, the panel observed that "[w]hile WTO-inconsistent conduct may not be lightly presumed, and must always be supported by sufficient evidence, the applicable evidentiary standard of proof in WTO dispute settlement proceedings is closer to that of the balance of probabilities, and is not a standard of certainty or proof beyond a reasonable doubt." Thus, "panels may make findings of *fact based on inferences and circumstantial evidence*."[181]

On all three of the issues outlined above, the panel inferred its conclusions from basic facts. Thus, with respect to the Qatari (and foreign) inability to secure legal representation, the panel found it "difficult to conceive of any plausible explanation [for such behaviour] ... if not some form of government instruction, direction or guidance."[182] Second, with respect to the lack of criminal enforcement activity, the fact that unauthorized broadcasts were undertaken by Saudi nationals or entities allowed the panel to find that Qatar had established a presumptive case that the activities complained of were undertaken by individuals or entities subject to Saudi criminal jurisdiction.[183] Third, the panel found that in response to Qatari evidence of the unauthorized broadcasts, Saudi Arabia had in fact promoted public gatherings with the aim of securing attendance at such broadcasts.[184] On these bases the panel found that Saudi Arabia had acted inconsistently with TRIPS Art. 42 by preventing Qatari entities from obtaining Saudi counsel to enforce their IP rights

the United Arab Emirates, Bahrain and Egypt. The dispute was resolved and diplomatic relations were restored in early 2021.

[180] WT/DS567/R, para. 1.10 (16 June 2020).

[181] Ibid., para. 7.39 [emphasis added].

[182] Ibid., para. 7.72.

[183] Ibid., para. 7.155.

[184] Ibid., para. 7.163.

and TRIPS Art. 61 by failing to provide criminal procedures and penalties in response to the unauthorized broadcasts.[185]

Apart from their evidentiary use in specific cases, presumptions and inferences also act as important stabilizers in the WTO system. On the one hand, it might be thought that presumption and inference would almost *always* conduce to findings of responsibility, as the results of WTO dispute settlement appear to suggest.[186] On the other, one presumption in particular – the presumption against conflicts both within the WTO Agreement and beyond it – is supremely important in maintaining a key fiction in WTO law and generally "keeping the peace."

A general assumption in international law is that countries do not normally intend to incur conflicting obligations.[187] The assumption is behind the practice of harmonious interpretation of the WTO Agreement.[188] At the same time, the presumption is also been invoked in a broad, constitutive manner in relation to agreements or commitments formally outside of WTO law. Thus, in *U.S. – Shrimp* the listing of seven recognized species of sea turtles in the Convention on International Trade in Endangered Species of Wild Fauna and Flora (CITES) was used to determine that sea turtles constitute "exhaustible natural resources" for purposes of interpreting Art. XX(g) of the GATT 1994.[189] At the same time, the presumption has not been applied in other situations where external (i.e. non-WTO) obligations do not exhibit the same overlapping membership.[190]

Still, the presumption is a powerful impetus to harmonization efforts, especially with respect to subsequent treaties that could potentially

185 Ibid., paras. 7.197–199, 7.214–221.

186 Simon Lester has calculated that as of mid-March 2020, almost 90 percent of WTO cases had resulted in at least one finding of violation. See https://ielp.worldtradelaw.net/2020/03/us-wins-and-losses-in-wto-disputes.html.

187 Thus, VCLT Art. 31(3)(c) states that "There shall be taken into account, together with the context [of a treaty] . . . [a]ny relevant rules of international law applicable in the relations between the parties." See Campbell McLachlan, "The Principle of Systemic Integration and Article 31(3)(c) of the Vienna Convention" 54 *I.C.L.Q.* 279 (Apr. 2005).

188 See, for example, *Canada – Periodicals*, WT/DS31/AB/R, p. 19 (30 June 1997). The practice is reinforced by the idea of the WTO Agreement as a "single undertaking." See Waincymer, *WTO Litigation* 466.

189 WT/DS58/AB/R, para. 134 (12 Oct. 1998).

190 Thus, in *EC – Approval and Marketing of Biotech Products*, WT/DS291/R (29 Sept. 2006) the panel refused to apply the precautionary principle found in the Cartagena Biosafety Protocol to the UN Convention on Biodiversity to interpret the extent of the EC's WTO obligations due to the fact that the complainant United States was not a signatory to the protocol. Ibid., para. 7.75.

violate the WTO Agreement. The presumption that these treaties are harmonious – or at least not inconsistent with – the WTO Agreement is an important element in legitimizing state behavior. Thus, as explained, WTO members continue to conclude a wide range of RTAs whose consistency with the WTO Agreement is uncertain. However, due to political gridlock, the mechanism foreseen for approvals under GATT Art. XXIV has been only minimally operative. The *status quo* has allowed hundreds of regional arrangements to be concluded and entered into. On its own it constitutes one of the great fictions of the WTO system.

Clear conflict between the WTO Agreement and subsequent inconsistent treaties was contemplated in *Turkey – Textiles.*[191] There the Appellate Body held that Art. XXIV did not justify the adoption of quantitative restrictions unless these were "necessary" for the regional arrangement's formation and had been introduced at the time of the arrangement's formation.[192] At the same time, the Appellate Body noted the specific wording of the Preamble of GATT Art. XXIV:5 ("the provisions of this Agreement *shall not prevent*, as between the territories of contracting parties, the formation of a customs union or of a free-trade area"). In addition, subsequent decisions appear to de-emphasize the "necessity" standard articulated in *Turkey – Textiles* either because of some feature of the particular regional agreement or because of a perception that there is no need to decide the matter of inconsistency.[193]

[191] WT/DS34/AB/R (22 Oct. 1999).

[192] The Appellate Body observed:

> [I]n a case involving the formation of a customs union, this "defence" is available only when two conditions are fulfilled. First, the party claiming the benefit of this defence must demonstrate that the measure at issue is introduced upon the formation of a customs union that fully meets the requirements of sub-paragraphs 8(a) and 5(a) of Article XXIV. And, second, that party must demonstrate that the formation of that customs union would be prevented if it were not allowed to introduce the measure at issue. Again, both these conditions must be met to have the benefit of the defence under Article XXIV.
>
> (Ibid., paras. 45–46)

[193] See, for instance, *Peru – Agricultural Products*, WT/DS457/AB/R, para. 5.119 (20 July 2015) ("the Panel did not err in declining to make findings as to whether an FTA modified the WTO rights and obligations between Peru and Guatemala because the FTA was not in force."); *India – Iron and Steel Products*, WT/DS518/R, para. 7.72 (6 Nov. 2018) ("no indication here that the measure resulted in regional or local authorities engaging in any GATT-inconsistent conduct, such that [certain obligations under GATT Art. XXIV] did not arise here").

The conclusion to be drawn from all of the above is that deductive reasoning is vitally important to the WTO legal system and would appear to predominate over the need for proof (i.e. Deduction > Induction). Singularly small and apparently insignificant, many presumptions within the legal system reinforce the idea that the law adheres to ideals, standards that may not be visible in the present but are to be achieved in the future. Presumption and inference also serve in important ways to consolidate the treaty and stress its coherence and unity, even when this may not be entirely warranted.

4.4 Conclusion

In this chapter, I have profiled the way in which the conception of justice as equality is realized in WTO law through obligation, constitutive structuring, a prospective perspective and deductive reasoning.

At the same time, a theory is more than simply a random collection of ideas. It is a "system" or a set of relationships, and so to illustrate the theory I have highlighted the relationships between these ideas in two ways.

First, I have demonstrated how each of the ideas profiled as part of the idea-complex examined in this chapter is predominant. It assumes a preeminence in defining what the law is.

The second way in which I have emphasized relationships is to describe how the ideas involved are threaded together *inter se* in the manner of an "idea-complex." Throughout the chapter, I have highlighted how associated ideas of obligation, constitution, prospectivity and deduction align, and how they call upon and reinforce one another. I have described how an emphasis on equality begets obligation, how an order of obligations is constitutive, how inherent in a constitution is a vision of the future and how so much in an unknown future must be presumed or assumed. As an explanation for the shape of the law, these coordinate ideas are "naturally reliable, naturally coherent, naturally fruitful."[194] They merge into a single overarching explanation for the shape of the law. The law is dynamic, an idea encapsulated in the oft-repeated observation that WTO law is noninstrumental and for the most part eschews measurement.

At the same time, each of these keystone ideas comes under strain. To begin with, a law of equality examined closely is a plural standard. It is

[194] Allott, *Eunomia* 31.

splintered and, in so being, is at odds with the idea of WTO law as a "unity." The various equality-derived standards implemented by means of obligation are in fact heterogeneous. They are difficult to make sense of together or trace to a common root.

In addition, the imposing nature of equality as an ideal, its demanding character, requires that it be conceptualized in less rigorous terms as "non-discrimination," a formulation that tends to dilute and distance the law from equality per se. Equality as an ideal is constantly offset and mediated by real conditions. Rarely is absolute equality *the* legal standard. Departures from it are contemplated in *de minimus* flexibilities and other allowances.

There is also trouble conceptually and factually in conceiving of the WTO's legal order as compulsive and constitutive, or perhaps more formally, as a "constitution." The WTO Agreement and its legal system do not meet all the classic criteria of a constitution. Consequently, commentators have searched for ways to understand the treaty as something else, possibly as subsidiary or complementary to state sovereignty. Factually too, the idea of the WTO Agreement as constitutive is challenged since while WTO members are not allowed to conclude side-deals to alter their WTO obligations, the proliferation of regional trade arrangements and a host of other agreements concluded without multilateral approval means that in practice members do conclude such agreements.[195] Constitutionalism's coherence then coexists uneasily with fragmentation.

WTO law is also future-oriented and assumes an open-ended quality. It is concerned not with what is but with realizing the potentiality of what may be in times to come. This causes the law to adopt an *ex ante* perspective, which views matters on broad, and at times seemingly impressionistic, lines. The law is said to protect expectations or the equality of opportunity. Consequently, there is reluctance to make empirical measures the decisive or pivotal consideration in legal analysis. Still, the characterization of the law as future-oriented is also tested,

[195] Debate has erupted in the WTO over the consistency of ongoing plurilateral negotiations with essential WTO disciplines. A majority of members, both developing and developed, participate in at least one of the plurilateral negotiations, also known as Joint Statement Initiatives (JSIs), begun in Dec. 2017 but a few members have opposed such talks as detrimental to the WTO and legally inconsistent with its rules. See Hannah Monicken, "Brazilian Ambassador: WTO Must Choose 'Fragmentation or Irrelevance'" 39:39 *Inside U.S. Trade* 3 (1 Oct. 2021); Jane Kelsey, "The Illegitimacy of Joint Statement Initiatives and Their Systemic Implications for the WTO" 25:1 *J.I.E.L.* 2 (Mar. 2022).

if only because of the constant tug of the past, of precedent, and of the way things are.

Finally, WTO law is deductive in the sense that it relies heavily on presumptions and inference. That reliance is dictated by the law's extension into an unknowable future in which its ideal standards are to be realized. The law cannot require proof of everything to ascribe responsibility. Proof would be too time-consuming to obtain, and in any event, WTO dispute settlement is ill-equipped to supply it. Nevertheless, this rationality is confronted with an opposing rationality that relies on induction and demands certainty.

So WTO law as a law of equality and obligation comes up short and encounters objections. In the next chapter, I examine the extent of those objections and their manifestation in the form of a competing and counterpart idea-complex.

5

The WTO Agreement as a Law of Rights

5.1 Introduction

In the previous chapter, I examined how WTO law is primarily a reflection of justice-as-equality implemented by means of obligation. In this chapter, I go on to examine how WTO law is secondarily a reflection of justice-as-fairness implemented by rights.

A communitarian theory of law posits that equality and equal treatment are the principal purpose of WTO law. However, that purpose is accomplished in varying conditions, conditions that make it difficult to regularly attain the consistency and coherence that an egalitarian and obligatory conception of the law assumes. No country – or individual – lives up to expectations all the time.

Consequently, in addition to seeking ideal standards such as those of equality and nondiscrimination implemented by means of obligation, the WTO legal system must also accommodate need for fairness that arises in the treaty's operation and can be linked to the assertion of rights.

Rights emphasize "competing, rather than unified, positions"[1] and are therefore fundamentally about accommodation. Their aim is to accommodate individuality. That accommodation cannot be limitless, however. As discussed in Chapters 2–3, a legal system cannot accommodate *every* individual interest or aspiration otherwise it risks losing the commonality that is the foundation of community. The accommodation must be restricted, hence the theme of constraint that recurrently emerges in a law of rights.

The unifying element that brings all of the diversity encountered together in a law of rights is what might be termed "realities." Their

[1] Peter Gerhart, *Property Law and Social Morality* 10 (Cambridge University Press, Cambridge; 2014).

common thread is what is *real*, or in other words, things as they *actually are*, as opposed to what *is expected* in a law of equality and obligation.[2] Realities justify departures from the norm.

As I will show, there is perennial controversy over the "realities" accounted for in WTO law. Many commentators have noted the way that exceptions in the system are relatively limited and seemingly arbitrary. They do not display coherence, except perhaps in the fact that they originate in the legislative experience of certain WTO members.[3] There have been calls for the WTO legal system to accommodate greater flexibility and to allow more bases of exception.[4]

As I will also show, however, there is more commonality in a law of rights than first meets the eye. Rights manifest themselves in a number of paradigmatic ways. They manifest themselves in the form of various claims, freedoms, powers and immunities, in the law's tendency to be structured consensually in the form of a "contract," in its orientation toward the past and *ex post* perspectives (i.e. after the event), and in inductive reasoning.

Such tendencies outline an image of the law that is in many ways the diametric opposite of the one examined in the previous chapter. Whereas

[2] A philosophical division between the idea and the real has been observed in Western thinking since the time of the ancient Greeks. The ideal is a mental construct of the world as it should be. By contrast, the real is the world as it is. Robert Skidelsky describes the difference as follows: "Idealism is the doctrine that reality is mental. Idealism is contrasted with Realism, the belief that reality exists independently of our perception of it. To Realists, belief do not construct reality, but picture it." Robert Skidelsky, *John Maynard Keynes* 74 (Macmillan, London; 1992).

[3] See, for instance, Robert Hudec, "Mirror, Mirror, on the Wall: The Concept of Fairness in United States Trade Policy" in Robert Hudec, *Essays on the Nature of International Trade Law* 227 at 261 (Cameron May, London; 1999), noting that:

> . . . there is no way to know whether the playing field is level to begin with. That being so, there is no way to know whether any particular government measure produces an unfair advantage. A single advantage, like a subsidy, is unfair only if one assumes that all other factors are equal . . . Critics of unfair trade laws welcome this demonstration of the normative incoherence of such laws, but advocates for liberal trade policy take no comfort in its unpleasant corollary – the fact that it is also impossible to prove that any instance of foreign competition is fair.

[4] Timothy Meyer, "The Political Economy of WTO Exceptions" 99:4 *Wash. U. L. Rev.* 1299 at 1362 (2022).

a law of obligation is compulsive and therefore stresses "the burden, the order, the universality of the law," a law of rights is about consent and therefore stresses "the benefit, the protection, the assurance, the individuality of the law."[5]

This individualism is problematic and often sits in acknowledged tension with the categories and doctrines highlighted in a law of obligation. Yet the balance struck between the narrow individualism inherent in rights and the broader collectivism inherent in obligations is not an all-or-nothing proposition. Ultimately it is a relative matter, one of reconciliation and community.[6]

5.2 A Law of Fairness

As mentioned, a key component of a communitarian theory is the idea that the law implements justice in the form of equality and fairness. What follows is a need to explain how the law manifests a secondary preoccupation with fairness, amid a primary preoccupation with attaining equality.

Awareness of the need for fairness has tempered GATT/WTO arrangements from the outset. In 1945 the United States observed in its original proposals for an International Trade Organization (ITO) that:

> No government is ready to embrace "free trade" in any absolute sense. . . . Every country has its own kind of [trade] restriction, adapted to its own situation, and can hardly be expected to throw off its armor unless the other kinds of armor, employed by other countries, are thrown off at the same time. What is needed is a broad and yet detailed agreement, among many nations, dealing at one time with many different sorts of government restrictions upon trade, reducing all of them at once on a balanced and equitable basis, and stating rules and principles with which the restrictions permitted to remain should be administered.[7]

[5] Philip Allott, *Eunomia* 159–160 (Oxford University Press, Oxford; 1990).

[6] As the Appellate Body has observed, "The location of the line of equilibrium [between individual and multilateralism in the WTO Agreement] is not fixed and unchanging; the line moves as the kind and the shape of the measures at stake vary and as the facts making up specific cases differ." *U.S. – Shrimp*, WT/DS58/AB/R, para. 159 (12 Oct. 1998).

[7] See "Statement by President Truman and Prime Minister Attlee" (6 Dec. 1945), reprinted in XII *Department of State Bulletin* 905, 915 (9 Dec. 1945).

A fundamental idea behind GATT 1947 and later the WTO Agreement was that rules concerning trade liberalization would be tempered by adjustments that took into account real conditions. As the US proposals noted, no country was willing to "embrace 'free trade' in any absolute sense." Instead, the best that could be hoped for was some recognition of the need for "rules and principles with which the restrictions permitted to remain should be administered."

Rules thus appear in GATT 1947 and the WTO Agreement that allow members to respond to certain realities arising in the course of trade as a matter of fairness. These include a range of permissible exceptions such as those found in GATT Arts. XX and XXI; disciplines on safeguards, subsidies and antidumping in GATT Arts. XIX, VI and XVI; and the possibility of invoking countermeasures in GATT Art. XXIII. Many commentators have recognized the way that these flexibilities and responses serve as temporary exits or "outs" from the treaty, and in so doing, build support for trade liberalization. In that way the larger project of free trade is able to move forward.[8]

Virtually all of these flexibilities and responses can be accommodated under the broad rubric of justice as fairness discussed in Chapter 3. There, I explained the idea of fairness as involving the tailoring of legal disciplines to individual circumstances appropriately.

There are a number of references to fairness in the WTO Agreement itself that help to confirm this characterization.

First, there are several preambular references to fairness. For example, the preamble of the WTO Import Licencing Agreement (ILA) mentions the "*fair* and equitable application and administration" of import licensing procedures. Import licensing procedures normally take place in the context of a discrete encounter between an importer and a national customs administration where the possibility of inappropriate behavior arises. The ILA attempts to limit the potential for this sort of behavior by requiring governments to publish sufficient information so that traders can know how and why import licenses are granted. ILA Art. 1(3) also provides that "rules for import licencing

[8] "It is agreed that trade remedies will be provided to 'correct' certain highly visible claims of unfairness, in exchange for the business community's acceptance of a generally liberal trade policy, and with the reservation that fairness claims will not be allowed to threaten the main contours of that liberal policy" Hudec, "Mirror, Mirror, on the Wall" 279.

procedures shall be neutral in application and administered in a *fair* and equitable manner." Similarly, the preamble of the WTO Agreement on Agriculture (AoA) mentions an abiding objective of negotiations on international trade in agriculture being "to establish a *fair* and market-oriented agricultural trading system." This reference must be understood in light of the perceived inequities of the current global framework for agriculture in which developed countries continue to subsidize production, thereby suppressing potential exports by developing countries.[9] Fairness in this context arises about an issue (continuing agricultural support) between subsets of the WTO membership (i.e. developing versus developed countries).

Second, there are a number of procedural references to fairness made in the context of administrative proceedings. For example, fairness is often in issue in antidumping cases where, depending on the specifics, national authorities' comparison of export prices versus normal value in a producer's home market may be in controversy. Thus, the ADA Art. 2.4. ADA mandates that in the calculation of dumping margins "[a] *fair* comparison shall be made between the export price and the normal value." Fairness here requires national authorities to ensure that assessments of prices are made that accurately reflect comparable conditions. This concern has been particularly salient in disputes involving the practice of "zeroing."[10] In *EC – Bed Linen* a WTO panel commented on the obligation to conduct a fair comparison in the following terms:

> Read in light of the obligation in [ADA] Article 2.4 to make a fair comparison, the specific requirements to make comparisons at the same level of trade and at as nearly as possible at the same time, and the obligation to make due allowance for differences affecting price

[9] Rafael Cedro & Bruno Vieira, "John Rawls' Justice as Fairness and the WTO" 3:2 *Law & Dev. Rev.* 122 (2010).

[10]
> Zeroing refers to the practice, conducted in some jurisdictions, of replacing the actual amount of dumping calculated for model or sales comparisons that yield negative dumping margins … with a value of zero prior to the final calculation of a weighted-average margin of dumping for the product under investigation. Zeroing, thus, has the effect of overstating dumping margins by denying the full impact of non-dumped or negatively dumped models/export sales on the dumping margin for the product as a whole.

(Edwin Vermulst & Daniel Ikenson, "Zeroing under the WTO Anti-Dumping Agreement: Where Do We Stand?" 2:6 *Glob. Trade Cust. J.* 231 (2007).

> comparability, the use of the word comparable in Article 2.4.2 indicates to us that investigating authorities may insure comparability either by making necessary adjustments under Article 2.4, or by making comparisons for models which are, themselves, comparable.[11]

The panel's reference to "a fair comparison" being "at the same level of trade and at as nearly as possible at the same time" speaks to the approximating character of fairness. Fairness is proportionate as opposed to identical and a particular as opposed to a generalized value. In ADA Art. 2.4, the treaty requires that the comparison must be tailored to circumstances that are as close as reasonably possible to original conditions in the country of production without them necessarily being the same.

Fairness also arises as a procedural issue in the varied circumstances of WTO disputes themselves.[12] Like the duty of fairness in English and continental systems of administrative law, these involve situations where specific rights are in play and where the decision in question has some particular importance to one WTO country as opposed to another.[13] Thus, WTO dispute settlement, which takes place largely according to a bilateral matrix involving a single complainant and a single respondent, or clusters of these, has been described as aimed at providing "*fair*, prompt and effective resolution" of trade disputes.[14]

[11] *EC – Bed Linen*, WT/DS141/R, para. 6.117 (30 Oct. 2000) [emphasis added].

[12] Marion Panizzon, "Good Faith, Fairness and Due Process in WTO Dispute Settlement Practice" in Julian Chaisse & Tiziano Balmelli (eds), *Essays on the Future of the World Trade Organization (Vol. II – The WTO Judicial System: Contributions and Challenges)* 26 (Editions interuniversitaires suisses, Geneva; 2008).

[13] In surveying this law of rights/law of fairness, it is useful to keep in mind that there is an analogous body of jurisprudence in English law and the law of other common law jurisdictions concerning the "duty of fairness" in administrative proceedings: see Robert Riggs, "Legitimate Expectation and Procedural Fairness in English Law" 36 *Am. J. Comp. L.* 395 (1988). See also William Wade & Christopher Forsyth, *Administrative Law* (10th ed.) 402 (Oxford University Press, Oxford; 2009); David Jones & Anne S. de Villars, *Principles of Administrative Law* (5th ed.) 253 (Carswell, Toronto; 2009). The same point has been made by other commentators who have referred to similar fairness principles developed in the context of European and EU administrative law. See, for instance, Stephan Schill, "Fair and Equitable Treatment under Investment Treaties as an Embodiment of the Rule of Law," IILJ Working Paper 2006/6 (2006).

[14] *U.S. – FSC*, WT/DS108/AB/R, para. 166 (24 Feb. 2000) [emphasis added].

Within these proceedings, the WTO Appellate Body has also referred to a requirement of due process. Due process, in turn, has been described as "fundamental to ensuring a *fair* and orderly conduct of [WTO] dispute settlement proceedings."[15] In *Canada – Continued Suspension* due process was described as guaranteeing "that the proceedings are conducted with *fairness* and impartiality, and that *one* party is not *unfairly* disadvantaged with respect to *other parties in a dispute.*"[16] Similarly, in *Chile – Price Band System* the Appellate Body observed that "[a] panel will fail in the duty to respect due process if it makes a finding on a matter that is not before it, because it will thereby fail to accord to a party a *fair* right of response."[17] In *Canada – Continued Suspension* the Appellate Body also observed that the allocation of the burden of proof in compliance proceedings was, among other considerations, a matter of "procedural *fairness.*"[18] And in *Chile – Price Band System* an arbitrator assessing the reasonable period of time (RPT) for implementation by Chile noted that the RPT "will *fairly* balance the legitimate needs of the implementing Member against those of the complaining Member."[19] Once more, a recurrent theme in fairness determinations involves characteristics of specific relationships among members and between tribunals and litigating parties. It is particularistic and situated as opposed to the generalizing impulse detected in a law of equality and obligation examined in the previous chapter.

A third set of fairness references and considerations is substantive. These involve the "fairness" of WTO arrangements or the "fittingness" or "appropriateness" of their outcomes. As discussed in Chapters 2–3, there is much debate about the ultimate justice of the WTO Agreement. Fairness considerations are normally regarded as being embodied in the text of the treaty itself. They are part and parcel of negotiated arrangements between member countries. For example, S&DT arrangements have traditionally been associated with the fairness of the WTO

[15] *Thailand – H-Beams*, WT/DS122/AB/R, para. 88 (12 Mar. 2001) [emphasis added].

[16] *Canada – Continued Suspension*, WT/DS321/AB/R, para. 433 (16 Oct. 2008) [emphasis added].

[17] *Chile – Price Band System*, WT/DS207/AB/R, para. 176 (23 Sept. 2002) [emphasis added].

[18] *Canada – Continued Suspension*, WT/DS321/AB/R, para. 361 (16 Oct. 2008) [emphasis added].

[19] *Chile – Price Band System (Art. 21.3)*, WT/DS207/13, para. 37 (17 Mar. 2003) [emphasis added].

system in as much as they attempt to redress the "development divide" noted in the international economic system.[20]

There are a number of additional situations where it is deemed necessary that WTO law should be tailored so that outcomes are more "fitting" or "appropriate" than they otherwise might be. One of these involves the invocation of formal exceptions or flexibilities to WTO rules, such as those found in GATT Arts. XX and XXI. Under GATT Art. XX members have the right to depart from WTO requirements in the pursuit of certain defined policy objectives, such as measures "necessary to protect public morals" (GATT Art. XX(a)) or "necessary to protect human, animal or plant life or health" (GATT Art. XX(b)).

Second, there are the traditional "rules disciplines" involving the application of safeguards, countervailing and antidumping duties, where members may take action in specific conditions involving the application of trade policy measures. For instance, a member may decide that it needs to apply a safeguard to protect its domestic industry from "serious injury" caused by increased imports in situations of "unforeseen developments." Another member's challenge of these measures or their application in WTO dispute settlement can question whether these were fair or "appropriate" in the circumstances.

Third, the application of countermeasures under DSU Art. 22 raises analogous issues.

Fourth, there are certain instances under the TBT and SPS Agreements where countries must meet a standard of ensuring that rules are "necessary," which inevitably raise considerations of fittingness in the circumstances.

Taken together, what do these varied references about the nature of fairness in WTO law reveal? First, the context of fairness is highly circumstantial. It involves particular circumstances as opposed to the general ones encountered in a law of equality and obligation. Such individuation is not always entirely idiosyncratic. In many instances it simply refers to some consideration or interest pertaining to less than the whole membership. An example arose in *EC – Tariff Preferences*.[21] There, as mentioned, the Appellate Body had to determine whether preferential

[20] "The Continued Relevance of Special and Differential Treatment in Favour of Developing Members to Promote Development and Ensure Inclusiveness," WT/GC/W/765/Rev. 2, para. 1.2 (4 Mar. 2019).

[21] WT/DS246/AB/R (7 Apr. 2004).

treatment extended by the EC to some developing countries but not others was a violation of the general nondiscrimination principle under GATT Art. I:1. The Appellate Body took an intermediate view. It recognized that developing country members had collective as well as individual and plurilateral interests:

> We are of the view that the objective of improving developing countries' "share in the growth in international trade," and their "trade and export earnings," can be fulfilled by promoting preferential policies aimed at those interests that developing countries have in common, *as well as* those interests shared by sub-categories of developing countries based on their particular needs.[22]

The Appellate Body therefore determined that collective, individualized and plurilateral preference schemes were permissible under WTO arrangements, provided that in the case of individualized schemes preference-granting countries "ensure that identical treatment is available *to all similarly-situated . . . beneficiaries*."[23] The EC's tariff preference scheme did not meet this last condition and was therefore held to be nonconforming.

Second, considerations of fairness are likely to involve situations that are exceptional in some way, or in other words, that are at odds with the idea of equality.[24] They arise outside of or in the pattern of legitimate trade and must be responded to in some manner. The reason motivating this response is that they are not a part of the ideal normative order and, as such, may be thought of as "unequal." In the particular circumstances of international trade, this inequality might involve a surge of imports that threatens to cause serious injury to a domestic industry, or subsidized goods that disrupt international markets, or sales of imports at less than fair value. In each instance WTO members must have the ability to respond to the particular contingency. The circumstances will demand a "fair" – not necessarily equal – response.

Third, as comments above have suggested, the desire for fairness can be linked to "appropriateness," often thought about in terms of the legal

[22] Ibid., para. 169 [emphasis in original].

[23] Ibid., para. 173 [emphasis added].

[24] Joost Pauwelyn, "Defenses and the Burden of Proof in International Law" in Lorand Bartels & Frederica Paddeu (eds), *Exceptions in International Law* 88 (Oxford University Press, Oxford; 2020).

doctrine of proportionality. The reason for proportionality as opposed to equality has to do with the strong desire in a law of fairness to tailor the law to the circumstances, a desire which, as explained in Chapter 3, manifests itself in a tendency to keep the demand for fairness within reasonable bounds, thereby reflecting the theoretic relationship Equality > Fairness. For example, countermeasures in international law are to be merely "*commensurate* with the injury suffered, taking into account the gravity of the internationally wrongful act and the rights in question."[25] This commitment to proportionality is limited by the ILC *to countermeasures*, but as I will demonstrate below, it is to some extent characteristic of virtually all rights-related action in WTO law.

Fourth, the interests being asserted in claims of fairness must be ascertainable otherwise there is no justification for using them as a basis for departing from the treaty's general requirements. Thus, in conjunction with the circumstantial character of fairness, there is a notable propensity in WTO law as a law of fairness to require proof, although this need is at times difficult to satisfy and involves a mix of both quantitative and qualitative factors that make it difficult to present the application of fairness as an "exact science."

All of the above suggests that it is possible to identify a "stable content" to fairness. Fairness is something that is contextual, exceptional, proportionate and proof-oriented, and, in so being, is likely to be subjective. And because it is subjective and particularistic, it is also likely to be static. That is, the conception of time and matter within it is held still. As such, fairness is about the past and *ex post* perspectives and is more a matter of momentary time (*kairos*) than ongoing time (*chronos*).

A closer examination of these features in WTO law is undertaken in the next section.

5.3 A Law of Right

5.3.1 A Law of Rights

As mentioned, the law of fairness discussed above is closely associated with the exercise of rights under the WTO Agreement.

A right is usually understood as a "claim," or in other words, a legal relation that "enables the right-holder to invoke the law to obtain certain

[25] ARSIWA Art. 51.

willing and acting from another person."[26] As noted, what is emphasized by means of rights is "the benefit, the protection, the assurance, the individuality of the law."[27]

Nevertheless, the influence of a right is limited. Those limits recognize the fact that a right is exercised within the broader environment of a community and, if unrestrained, has the potential to undermine the rights of others.[28]

WTO law features many rights as well as their Hohfeldian variants in the form of freedoms, powers and immunities.[29] For example, WTO member countries have the right to impose safeguards in certain circumstances. They have the right to form free trade areas. They also have the right to invoke dispute settlement for breaches of the treaty.

In each instance, however, what becomes apparent is the way in which the relevant right is restricted. Thus, member countries may impose safeguards but in doing so must ensure that there is present or incipient "serious injury," that there is prior notice of the safeguard to trading partners, that the requirement of "unforeseen circumstances" is fulfilled, and that the safeguard is extended "only ... to the extent and for such time as necessary to prevent or remedy" the associated injury. What is evident in the example is the way that the rights in question are qualified by the need to satisfy certain conditions prior to, or concurrent with, its exercise.

[26] Allott, *Eunomia* 161.

[27] Ibid., p. 160.

[28] "An abusive exercise by a Member of its own treaty right thus results in a breach of the treaty rights of the other Members and, as well, a violation of the treaty obligation of the Member so acting." *U.S. – Shrimp*, WT/DS58/AB/R, para. 158 (12 Oct. 1998).

[29] Allott, *Eunomia* 161. For instance, all WTO members have the *right* to expect equal treatment for their exports under GATT Art. I. Correlatively, WTO members are under an *obligation* to accord this level of treatment to imports from all members. Similarly, every WTO member is allowed the *freedom* to set its own "appropriate level of protection" (ALOP) against human, animal or health diseases or risks under the WTO SPS Agreement. WTO members have *no right* to challenge the appropriate level of protection selected. Furthermore, a number of WTO bodies such as the MC, GC or the WTO Balance of Payments Committee have the *power* to make decisions binding on the membership, and members are likewise subject to a *liability* to comply with them. Finally, WTO members are *immune* from decisions taken under parts of the WTO Agreement that they have not acceded to, such as the WTO Agreement on Government Procurement (AGP), but are unable, or "*disabled*," from raising claims under the AGP against nonsignatories. See Wesley Hohfeld, *Fundamental Legal Conceptions as Applied in Judicial Reasoning* 36 (1919, rev'd. ed., Lawbook Exchange, Clark, NJ; 2010).

This qualification contrasts sharply with the generalized and plenary nature of obligations highlighted in Chapter 4. The contrast is still starker when it considered that "[g]enerally speaking, all Members benefit from all WTO rights."[30] In other words, WTO law appears to lack the idea of a purely subjective right – a right belonging to one country exclusively – although this idea is reasonably qualified by a number of instances wherein one WTO member *is* entitled to take certain action alone, such as in the case of authorized countermeasures.

The apparent generality of rights in WTO law is emphasized in a number of other ways. First, in *EC – Hormones* the Appellate Body affirmed the principle of a restrictive interpretation of treaty obligations (*in dubio mitius*) in deference to state sovereignty.[31] Conversely, it might be assumed that members' rights should be interpreted broadly or at least correspondently to align with this idea. Second, the Appellate Body has also made clear that there is no doctrine of restrictive interpretation of exceptions in WTO law.[32] Exceptions, which often involve assertions of rights, have been interpreted in several instances to merit the same interpretation as obligations. They are to be interpreted according to "the normal rules of treaty interpretation."[33]

Yet when examined in closer detail, the exercise of rights in WTO law *is* more particularized and nuanced than that of obligations. Like the construction of a tall building in a large city, many requirements need to be satisfied in order to assert rights under the WTO Agreement. These have the evitable effect of constraining what countries do. Rights must be exercised carefully and judiciously, mindful of others. The result is, in most instances, calibrated or proportionate behavior consonant with the idea of life in a community.

In the ordinary course, the assertion of rights assumes a restrained form that naturally highlights the idea of their opposite: obligations. Interestingly, this restraint tends to confirm the relationship highlighted in the previous chapter (i.e. Obligation > Right). It also confirms the idea

[30] *EC – Bananas III*, WT/DS27/R/USA, para. 7.91 (22 May 1997).

[31] *EC – Hormones*, WT/DS26/AB/R, para. 165, n. 154 (16 Jan. 1998). Notwithstanding this interpretation, it has been noted that "[n]either the VCLT nor the recent jurisprudence of the ICJ and of other international tribunals supports [*in dubio mitius*] as a generally operable presumption." S.v. "Interpretation in International Law" in *Max Planck Encyclopedias of International Law*, para. 29 (Mar. 2013) (author: Matthias Herdegen).

[32] *EC – Hormones*, WT/DS26/AB/R/USA, para. 104 (18 Aug. 1997).

[33] Ibid.

of *trace* mentioned in Chapter 1, that is, the way that absent concepts are retained in the operation of opposing concepts illustrative of transition (i.e. Obligation = Right).[34] This obligatory restraint is most prominently and regularly identified in the operation of three rights-related doctrines: conditionality, proportionality and mutuality.

5.3.1.1 Conditionality

To condition something is to make it dependent upon something else. The conditional nature of many, if not all, WTO rights is evident in the attachment of requirements to their exercise. In the main, these conditions relate to notification and transparency, exercise, and termination.

First, WTO rights are conditioned on notification and transparency. WTO members have obligations to keep other members informed of actions they propose to take or to implement. This requirement is often attached to duties to consult, leaving room for "sunshine methods" and moral suasion by others that may serve to modify or change views about ongoing or intended action.[35]

For instance, WTO members in receipt of a petition for the initiation of a countervailing duty investigation are required to provide an opportunity to other members to consult about the projected investigation:

> Members the products of which may be subject to such investigation shall be invited for consultations with the aim of clarifying the situation . . . and arriving at a mutually agreed solution.[36]

Notification also allows for planning and the formation of legitimate expectations concerning future behavior. In this way the conditionality requirement instills a degree of discipline.

Second, WTO rights often indicate the extent of permissible behavior in the course of a right's exercise. In so doing they define what the limits of the right are. For example, SCM Art. 19.4 provides that in the case of countervailing action taken against subsidized imports:

> No countervailing duty shall be levied on any imported product *in excess of the amount of the subsidy* found to exist, calculated in terms of subsidization per unit of the subsidized and exported product.

[34] Jack Balkin, "Nested Oppositions" 99 *Yale L.J.* 1669 at 1676 (1990).

[35] "The essential power of transparency . . . is that deviations from prescribed conduct can be observed and the actor called to account." Abraham Chayes & Antonia Chayes, *The New Sovereignty* 136 (Harvard University Press, Cambridge, MA; 1995).

[36] SCM Art. 13.1.

In mandating this limit, the text of the SCM recalls the point made earlier that rights imply a peripheral obligation not to go beyond the extent of the right in question.[37] Limitation offers further illustration of the theoretic relationship of transition (i.e. Right = Obligation) embedded in a communitarian theory in the sense that one element (i.e. an obligation) is encountered at the outer limits of the other (i.e. a right).

The last set of general conditions applicable to rights relates to timing. Most rights in WTO law are temporary, a limitation that tacitly emphasizes the plenary nature of obligations in the WTO system, another example of the relationship of transition (i.e. Obligation = Right). Thus, ADA Art. 11.1 provides that:

> An anti-dumping duty shall remain in force *only as long as* and to the extent necessary to counteract dumping which is causing injury.[38]

Time limits imply that there are restrictions on the exercise of rights and that the desired end-state is a return to the notional equality of all member states observing their obligations under the law. The phenomenon of "graduation" of LDCs to developing country status[39] and the broader

[37] Allott, *Eunomia* 162:

> ... rights necessarily involve constraint and duties necessarily involve empowering. Rights may protect a certain area of willing and acting but they protect *only that area* of willing and acting. The limits of a right are as significant as its content. The limits of a right amount to a peripheral duty ... not to exceed those limits. To exceed those limits gives rise to rights of all kinds in other rights-holders, either the coming into existence of new rights or the actual exercise of existing rights.
>
> ([emphasis in original])

[38] ADA Art. 11.1 [emphasis added].

[39] LDCs are accorded special treatment in the WTO, including exemption from the requirement of reciprocity. A general principle is the idea that nonreciprocity should be reserved for those countries that need it. When these needs cease, a country should be "graduated" from LDC to developing country status, thereby losing LDC-specific benefits. Graduation from the LDC category is an overarching objective of the UN Istanbul Programme of Action for the LDCs for the Decade 2011–2020 (IPoA). IPoA has the aim of enabling half of all LDCs to meet the criteria for graduation by 2020. The issue has assumed special significance with a quarter of the LDCs on the path to graduation and the associated loss of benefits tied to this status. See Alexander Keck & Patrick Low, "Special and Differential Treatment in the WTO: Why, When and How?" WTO Staff Working Paper ERSD-2004-03 (May 2004); World Trade Organization, EIF Executive Secretariat, *Trade Impacts of LDC Graduation* (World Trade Organization, Geneva; 2020).

debate about the limitation or possible termination of S&DT status are examples of this phenomenon.[40]

5.3.1.2 Proportionality

A second doctrine limiting the exercise of rights in WTO law is proportionality. Proportionality can be understood to refer to a broad requirement "to balance[e] competing *rights*, values, or other objectives" and a narrower one addressing the requisite relationship between action and counteraction.[41]

Andrew Mitchell explains that the assessment of proportionality in international law today often draws upon a three-step test for proportionality developed by the ECJ:

1. whether the measure is suitable to achieve its objective
2. whether the measure is necessary by determining whether less restrictive alternatives could be used to achieve the same aim
3. whether the benefits of the measure are not disproportionate to the interests or rights curtailed ("proportionality *stricto sensu*")[42]

At the same time, Mitchell points out how "no universal rule or test embodies this principle [of proportionality]."[43]

In WTO law the requirement of proportionality takes several forms. To the extent they vary, however, it is noteworthy that proportionality is often associated with the exercise of rights.[44] A concern with proportionality and the exercise of rights is chiefly detected in four instances: (i) in the invocation of general exceptions (GATT Art. XX), (ii) in the exercise

[40] Communication from the United States, "An Undifferentiated WTO: Self-Declared Development Status Risks Institutional Irrelevance," WT/GC/W/757/Rev. 1 (14 Feb. 2019).

[41] Andrew Mitchell, *Legal Principles in WTO Disputes* 182–183 (Oxford University Press, Oxford; 2008). Mitchell notes that while proportionality has no textual basis in the Communities' treaties "[o]ne of the reasons that the principle was so easily incorporated into the law of the European Communities was that it was already well established in the jurisprudence of the European Court of Human Rights and in the domestic laws of many of its Member States." Ibid. at 188.

[42] Ibid. at 189.

[43] Ibid. at 190.

[44] Meinhardt Hilf observes that while there is no textual reference to "proportionality" found in the WTO Agreement, "the basic idea of proportionality, i.e. *reconciling competing rights*, is reflected several times in WTO agreements." Meinhardt Hilf, "Power, Rules and Principles – Which Orientation for WTO/GATT Law?" 4 *J.I.E.L.* 111 at 121 (2001) [emphasis added].

of rights by members under the TBT and SPS Agreements, (iii) in permissible counteraction under WTO rules disciplines (safeguards, countervailing and antidumping duties), and (iv) in the invocation of countermeasures under the DSU.

GATT Art. XX First, WTO members have the right to take action inconsistent with their obligations under GATT 1994 by virtue of the language of GATT Art. XX, which provides that, subject to certain requirements, members may apply nonconforming measures for ten distinct policy purposes. These include the protection of public morals, the protection of human life or health, the necessity to secure compliance with the law, and so forth. Proportionality is in issue in connection with virtually every one of these purposes since WTO members are required to regulate in conformity with their WTO obligations. Therefore, the essential task in proportionality analysis under GATT Art. XX is one of balancing competing rights: the right of a WTO member to regulate versus the rights of other WTO members to expect a member's conformity with its WTO obligations.

In *U.S. – Gasoline* the Appellate Body clarified that the correct interpretative method for analysis of GATT Art. XX is, first, to determine whether or not the measure meets the terms of the provisional justification in the relevant exception and, second, to assess whether the defending country has applied the measure consistent with the terms of GATT Art. XX's preamble.[45]

An important point is that several exceptions provided for in Art. XX employ different introductory terminology suggestive of different degrees of proportionality. In GATT Art. XX(a), (b) and (d), for instance, the phrase "necessary to" is employed whereas in Art. XX(c), (e) and (g) it is "relating to." Commenting on this difference in *U.S. – Gasoline* the Appellate Body observed:

> It does not seem reasonable to suppose that the WTO Members intended to require, in respect of each and every category, the same kind or degree of connection or relationship between the measure under appraisal and the state interest or policy sought to be promoted or realized.[46]

Through jurisprudence the Appellate Body has identified a test for proportionality that is similar to the ECJ test set out earlier. However,

[45] *U.S. – Gasoline*, WT/DS2/AB/R, p. 22 (29 Apr. 1996).
[46] Ibid., p. 17.

due to textual and conceptual differences, the WTO test consists of a plurality of discrete tests that vary incrementally from provision to provision. For the purposes of keeping the discussion here within manageable bounds, I will only examine the jurisprudence developed with respect to GATT Arts. XX(b) and XX(g).

The jurisprudence involving GATT Art. XX(b) originates in its text which reads:

> nothing in this Agreement shall be construed to prevent the adoption or enforcement by any contracting party of measures: ... (b) *necessary* to human, animal or plant life or health;

With respect to the term "necessary," the Appellate Body has observed that its many interpretations of that term can be distilled as follows:

> an assessment of "necessity" involves "weighing and balancing" a number of distinct factors relating both to the measure sought to be justified as "necessary" and to possible alternative measures that may be reasonably available to the responding Member to achieve its desired objective.[47]

Generally speaking, the applicable test of proportionality in cases invoking GATT Art. XX(b) is conducted in a three-step sequence:

> [first] "The process begins with an assessment of the 'relative importance' of the interests or values furthered by the challenged measure"; [second] "Having ascertained the importance of the particular interests at stake, a panel should then turn to the other factors that are to be 'weighed and balanced'"; and [third] "A comparison between the challenged measure and possible alternatives should then be undertaken."[48]

Despite this sequence, the Appellate Body has also stressed that the test of proportionality itself is a "holistic operation that involves putting all the variables of the equation together and evaluating them in relation to each other after having examined them individually, in order to reach an overall judgment."[49] In the analysis the elements from each step may overlap.[50]

[47] *China – Publications and Audiovisual Products*, WT/DS363/AB/R, para. 239 (21 Dec. 2009).

[48] As summarized by the Appellate Body in *China – Publications and Audiovisual Products*, WT/DS363/AB/R, para. 240 (21 Dec. 2009). In that instance the Appellate Body drew heavily from its decision in *U.S. – Gambling*, WT/DS285/AB/R, para. 306 (7 Apr. 2005) concerning the interpretation of GATS Art. XIV(a), which also refers to "measures *necessary* to protect public morals or to maintain public order" [emphasis added].

[49] *Brazil – Retreaded Tyres*, WT/DS332/AB/R, para. 182 (3 Dec. 2007).

[50] *Colombia – Textiles*, WT/DS461/AB/R, para. 5.76 (7 June 2016).

The first analytical factor involves assessment of the "relative importance" of the interests or values furthered by the challenged measure. Additionally, a panel must also assess the extent of the measure's contribution to the goal pursued. Generally, "[t]he greater the contribution, the more easily a measure might be considered to be 'necessary.'"[51] At the same time, the Appellate Body has observed:

> there is no "generally applicable standard requiring the use of a predetermined threshold of contribution in analysing the necessity of a measure under Article XX of the GATT 1994." Since a measure's contribution is only one component of the necessity calculus under Article XX, the assessment of whether a measure is "necessary" cannot be determined by the degree of contribution alone, but will depend on the manner in which the other factors of the "necessity" standard inform the analysis.[52]

Moreover, the Appellate Body has also been reluctant to highlight any one component of the necessity analysis under GATT Art. XX(b) as determinative and so far has eschewed any attempt to set "predetermined thresholds in respect of any particular [necessity] factor." It has commented:

> If the level of contribution alone cannot determine whether a measure is necessary or not, we do not see that mandating in advance a predetermined threshold level of contribution would be instructive or warranted in a necessity analysis.[53]

The calculation of "necessity" will therefore depend "on the nature, quantity, and quality of evidence, and whether a panel's analysis is performed in quantitative or qualitative terms."[54] Reference to evidence in this instance is an indicator of the way the law in this mode is particularly concerned with proof.

The second factor in proportionality analysis under GATT Art. XX(b) is the trade restrictiveness of the measure. A measure that is less trade restrictive is more likely to be found "necessary" than one that is more trade restrictive.[55] In connection with this analysis, the Appellate Body

[51] Ibid., para. 5.72.

[52] Ibid.

[53] *EC – Seal Products*, WT/DS401/AB/R, para. 5.215 (22 May 2014).

[54] Ibid.

[55] "[a] measure with a relatively slight impact upon imported products might more easily be considered as 'necessary' than a measure with intense or broader restrictive effects." *Korea – Various Measures on Beef*, WT/DS161/AB/R, para. 163 (11 Dec. 2000).

has noted that "a panel must seek to assess the degree of a measure's trade-restrictiveness, rather than merely ascertaining whether or not the measure involves some restriction on trade."[56]

A third analytical factor is reasonably available alternative measures. Any alternative policy instrument proposed must be "reasonably available" in the sense that it must not be purely theoretical or impose an undue burden on a member.[57] At the same time, a member is not able to establish "undue burden" simply by indicating that a potential alternative exists. Instead, such an assertion must be supported "with sufficient evidence."[58]

In comparison with the analysis of GATT Art. XX(b), proportionality analysis in GATT Art. XX(g) is distinct. The prime source of the distinction is the language involved. GATT Art. XX(g) provides that:

> nothing in this Agreement shall be construed to prevent the adoption or enforcement by any contracting party of measures ... (g) *relating to* the conservation of exhaustible natural resources if such measures are made effective in conjunction with restrictions on domestic production or consumption.

The familiar elements of suitability, connection and alternatives under GATT Art. XX(g) do emerge, but they do so in a different context marked by the more permissive opening phrase ("relating to"). In *Korea – Various Measures on Beef* the Appellate Body summarized its jurisprudence on GATT Art. XX(g) as follows:

> We note that, under the more flexible "relating to" standard of Article XX (g), we accepted in *United States – Gasoline* a measure because it presented a "*substantial* relationship," (emphasis added) i.e., a close and genuine relationship of ends and means, with the conservation of clean air ... In *United States – Shrimp* we accepted a measure because it was "*reasonably related*" to the protection and conservation of sea turtles.[59]

"Substantial" and "reasonably related" are not necessarily consistent or reconcilable. Thus, the jurisprudence of suitability adopts different formulations in line with the idea of "flexibility" in a law of fairness and rights.

[56] *Argentina – Financial Services*, WT/DS453/AB/R, para. 6.234 (14 Apr. 2016).

[57] *U.S. – Gambling*, WT/DS285/AB/R, para. 308 (7 Apr. 2005).

[58] *China – Publications and Audiovisual Products*, WT/DS363/AB/R, para. 327 (21 Dec. 2009).

[59] *Korea – Various Measures on Beef*, WT/DS161/AB/R, n. 129 (11 Dec. 2000) [emphasis in original].

An additional issue that arises in the interpretation of GATT Art. XX (g) is whether the measures are made effective *in conjunction* with domestic measures, a term which the Appellate Body has interpreted as imposing a "*requirement of even-handedness* in the imposition of restrictions."[60] I examined the requirement of even-handedness in Chapter 4 in relation to its manifestation of an equality standard, something which could be taken to demonstrate the subsisting influence of equality in a law of fairness, and to that extent, of *trace*. At the same time, the Appellate Body made clear in *U.S. – Gasoline* that the "requirement of even-handedness" in Art. XX(g) does not amount to a requirement of "identity of treatment."[61]

A further issue in proportionality analysis is that of causation, which arises in GATT Art. XX(g) since measures on imports are to be "made effective" in conjunction with restrictions on domestic production or consumption. The question then is whether there is or should be an "empirical effects test" to measure the degree of making effective. Perhaps because of the looser introductory language, the Appellate Body has demurred on this point:

> We do not believe ... that the clause "if made effective in conjunction with restrictions on domestic production or consumption" was intended to establish an empirical "effects test" for the availability of the Article XX (g) exception. In the first place, the problem of determining causation, well-known in both domestic and international law, is always a difficult one. In the second place, in the field of conservation of exhaustible natural resources, a substantial period of time, perhaps years, may have to elapse before the effects attributable to implementation of a given measure may be observable. The legal characterization of such a measure is not reasonably made contingent upon occurrence of subsequent events. We are not, however, suggesting that consideration of the predictable effects of a measure is never relevant. In a particular case, should it become clear that realistically, a specific measure cannot in any possible situation have any positive effect on conservation goals, it would very probably be because that measure was not designed as a conservation regulation to begin with. In other words, it would not have been "primarily aimed at" conservation of natural resources at all.[62]

In the absence of a concrete effects test, the Appellate Body seemed to contemplate a minimalist one in its place ("a specific measure *cannot in*

[60] *U.S. – Gasoline*, WT/DS2/AB/R, p. 20 (29 Apr. 1996).
[61] Ibid., p. 21.
[62] Ibid.

any possible situation have any positive effect on conservation goals").[63] Veering between extremes is not a recipe for satisfactory jurisprudence. At the same time, the evolving law in the area appears not to require any assessment of reasonable alternatives, as in the analysis of GATT Art. XX(b).

TBT/SPS In both the TBT and SPS Agreements, proportionality is in issue where a member adopts either technical regulations and standards (in the case of the TBT Agreement) or sanitary or phytosanitary measures (in the case of the SPS Agreement). TBT Art. 2.2 provides:

> Members shall ensure that technical regulations are not prepared, adopted or applied with a view to or with the effect of creating *unnecessary* obstacles to international trade.

Again, the test developed for assessing "necessity" under the TBT appears virtually identical to that developed under GATT Art. XX(b) in being a three-step test involving consideration of (1) the degree of contribution made by the measure to a legitimate objective, (2) the trade restrictiveness of the measure, and in most cases (3) possible alternatives. What differs in the assessment under TBT Art. 2.2. is consideration within the third factor of the risks at issue and the gravity of consequences that would arise from nonfulfillment of the objectives pursued through the measure.[64] The difference appears to stem from the more directly technical nature of the regulations and standards at issue, many of which address specific risks.

There are some additional differences in the analysis of necessity under TBT Art. 2.2. First, TBT Art. 2.2 specifies a nonexhaustive list of legitimate objectives that members may pursue. In addition, the sixth recital of the TBT Agreement preamble provides that, subject to certain qualifications, a member is not to be prevented from taking measures necessary to achieve its legitimate objectives "at the levels it considers appropriate." As a result of the language of legitimate objectives and the express sovereign freedom to regulate referenced in the preamble, a certain ethos of flexibility pervades necessity analysis under the TBT Agreement. For instance, in measuring the first factor – the "degree of contribution" of the measure toward the achievement of a legitimate objective – the Appellate Body has pointed out that:

[63] Ibid.

[64] *U.S. – Tuna II (Mexico)*, WT/DS381/AB/R, para. 318 (16 May 2012).

> The degree or level of contribution of a technical regulation to its objective is not an abstract concept, but rather something that is revealed through the measure itself. In preparing, adopting, and applying a measure in order to pursue a legitimate objective, a WTO Member articulates, either implicitly or explicitly, the level at which it pursues that objective. Thus, a panel adjudicating a claim under [TBT] Article 2.2 must seek to ascertain – from the design, structure, and operation of the technical regulation, as well as from evidence relating to its application – to what degree, if at all, the challenged technical regulation, as written and applied, actually contributes to the achievement of the legitimate objective pursued by the Member.[65]

Here too, questions of the appropriate "threshold" or degree of contribution have arisen, which the Appellate Body has refused to set a fixed standard for.[66]

Second, the order of analysis of factors involved in the proportionality test is recognized to be somewhat more flexible under the TBT than in GATT Art. XX. Thus, in *Australia – Tobacco Plain Packaging* the panel observed that no set order of analysis must be followed. Instead, "the appropriate order of analysis will depend on the circumstances of the case at hand."[67]

Third, due to the fact that mandatory regulations may only have effects visible over the medium or long term, the evidence presented "may need to be understood in the light of that possibility."[68]

Fourth, on the issue of trade restrictiveness, a number of comments have been made about appropriate supporting evidence. For example, in *Australia – Plain Packaging* the panel observed that "the way in which trade restrictiveness is demonstrated to exist will depend on the circumstances of a given case." The panel added that the demonstration:

> could be based on qualitative or quantitative arguments and evidence, or both, including evidence relating to the characteristics of the challenged measure as revealed by its design and operation.[69]

65 *U.S. – COOL*, WT/DS384/AB/R, para. 373 (29 June 2012).

66 Thus, the Appellate Body has expressed the view that it is not found or implied that "in order for a measure to comply with [TBT] Article 2.2, it must meet some minimum threshold of fulfilment." *U.S. – COOL*, WT/DS384/AB/R, para. 461 (29 June 2012).

67 *Australia – Tobacco Plain Packaging (Indonesia)*, WT/DS467/R, para. 7.420 (28 June 2018).

68 Ibid., para. 7.940.

69 Ibid., para. 7.1076.

In addition, the panel observed that:

> there is no need for a complaining party to demonstrate the existence of a trade-restrictive effect on the trade of all WTO Members in all products that are subject to the technical regulation. Thus ... a Member could demonstrate the existence of a trade restriction on a particular product in which it trades, even if the trade(s) of other Member(s) has increased.[70]

Do modifications of the conditions of competition caused by technical regulations and standards demonstrate a limitative effect on international trade? In *Australia – Tobacco Plain Packaging* the Appellate Body held that "in 'assessing the trade-restrictiveness of a technical regulation under Article 2.2 ... [a] demonstration of a limiting effect on competitive opportunities in qualitative terms *might suffice in the particular circumstances of a given* case.'"[71] Nevertheless, while panels have determined that a measure modifying the conditions of competition for imported products as a group vis-à-vis domestic producers as a group is sufficient for the purposes of indicating that a technical regulation is trade restrictive under TBT Art. 2.2, the Appellate Body has observed that "evidence of actual trade effects may also be probative" to a panel's determination of trade restrictiveness and, while "a detrimental modification of competitive opportunities may be self-evident in respect of certain *de jure* discriminatory measures, ... supporting evidence and argumentation of actual trade effects might be required to demonstrate the existence and extent of trade-restrictiveness in respect of *non-discriminatory* internal measures." Thus, a showing of a reduction in the competitive opportunities of imported products is only relevant to the assessment of trade restrictiveness to the extent that it reveals a limiting effect on international trade. For instance, where a measure is shown to reduce the competitive opportunities of *imported products* as a group, from a Member, vis-à-vis competing *domestic products*, that would suffice for a panel to conclude that the measure is indeed trade-restrictive.[72]

At the same time, the Appellate Body has rejected the view that a higher standard of evidence such as factual proof is necessary to prove discrimination by nondiscriminatory measures as opposed to

[70] Ibid., para. 7.1078.

[71] *Australia – Tobacco Plain Packaging (Honduras)*, WT/DS435/AB/R, para. 6.385 (9 June 2020).

[72] Ibid., paras. 6.385–6.386 [emphasis in original].

discriminatory ones under TBT Art. 2.2. In this way, "actual trade effects" are *not* always required in order to demonstrate the trade restrictiveness of a nondiscriminatory measure.[73] In this connection the Appellate Body has repeatedly asserted that "it is appropriate for panels to take into account all relevant evidence adduced by the parties before concluding on the degree of trade restrictiveness."[74]

Fifth and finally, there has been significant jurisprudence on the issue of proposed alternative measures in the TBT context. There is no need for the alternatives to achieve a degree of contribution "*identical* to that achieved by the challenged technical regulation."[75] Instead, "it is the *overall degree of contribution* that the technical regulation makes to the objective pursued that is relevant, rather than any individual isolated aspect or component of contribution."[76] However, in *Australia – Tobacco Plain Packaging* the panel observed that:

> [i]t would ... need to be demonstrated that a proposed alternative measure would *not only be less trade-restrictive than the challenged measures*, but also that it would make *at least an equivalent contribution* to the objective being pursued through the challenged measure, and be "reasonably available" to the Member as an alternative to the challenged measures.[77]

In addition, the case law suggests that the risk of nonfulfillment of the legislative aim under any alternative is also a consideration.

In connection with this "comparative analysis," a number of further issues arise, notably the broader regulatory background in which the challenged measures operate and how they function together with other measures to achieve the desired objective,[78] as well as the risks that nonfulfillment of the technical regulation's objective would create, the nature of the risks, and the gravity of any consequences that nonfulfillment would present.[79]

[73] Ibid., para. 6.391.
[74] Ibid., para. 6.393.
[75] *U.S. – COOL (Art. 21.5 – Canada and Mexico)*, WT/DS384/RW, para. 5.215 (18 May 2015) [emphasis in original].
[76] Ibid., para. 5.126.
[77] *Australia – Tobacco Plain Packaging (Indonesia)*, WT/DS467/R, para. 7.1364 (28 June 2018) [emphasis added].
[78] Ibid., para. 7.1391.
[79] Ibid., para. 7.1722.

The SPS Agreement also features a necessity test in SPS Art. 2.2:

> Members shall ensure that any sanitary or phytosanitary measure is applied only to the extent *necessary* to protect human, animal or plant life or health, is based on scientific principles and is not maintained without sufficient scientific evidence.

In *Japan – Agricultural Products II* the Appellate Body noted that SPS Art. 2.2 requires a "rational connection" between the SPS measure and the scientific justification used to sustain it:

> [W]e agree with the Panel that the obligation in Article 2.2 that an SPS measure not be maintained without sufficient scientific evidence requires that there be a rational or objective relationship between the SPS measure and the scientific evidence. Whether there is a rational relationship between an SPS measure and the scientific evidence is to be determined on a case-by-case basis and will depend upon the particular circumstances of the case, including the characteristics of the measure at issue and the quality and quantity of the scientific evidence.[80]

To date much less has been said about SPS Art. 2.2 than its counterpart provision in the TBT Agreement.

Counteraction Proportionality emerges as a prominent theme in permissible counteraction under the SAF, SCM and ADA Agreements. Under these agreements, WTO member countries have rights to take permissible counteraction against either "serious injury" caused by imports (in the case of the SAF) or "material injury" caused by subsidized or dumped imports (in the case of the SCM or ADA, respectively). Proportionality is emblematic of the individuation called for in justice as fairness and the exercise of rights.

In practice, proportionate counteraction calls for a calibrated response that generally expresses a preference for *lesser* reaction than the triggering fact. This is in line with the idea mentioned earlier that proportionality aims at what is merely "fitting" or "appropriate" as opposed to what is necessarily equivalent. A concomitant of this preference is the tendency toward constraint.

For example, with respect to safeguards a WTO member is entitled under SAF Art. 5.1 to "apply safeguard measures *only to the extent necessary* to prevent or remedy serious injury and to facilitate adjustment." Commenting on this provision in *U.S. – Line Pipe*, the

[80] *Japan – Agricultural Products II*, WT/DS76/AB/R, para. 84 (22 Feb. 1999).

Appellate Body cited the ILC's definition of proportionality in ARSIWA Art. 51 in support of the idea that "countermeasures *must be commensurate* with the injury suffered, taking into account the gravity of the internationally wrongful act and the rights in question."[81] For this reason the Appellate Body concluded that "the phrase 'only to the extent necessary to prevent or remedy serious injury and to facilitate adjustment' in [SAF] Article 5.1, first sentence, must be read as requiring that safeguard measures may be applied only to the extent that they address serious injury attributed to increased imports."[82] SAF Art. 3.1 goes on to specify that if a quantitative restriction is imposed on imports, such a restriction shall not reduce the quantity of imports below the average level of imports during the last three representative years "unless clear justification is given that a different level is necessary." There are a number of additional notification, consultation, substantive and temporal requirements that further constrain the right to apply a safeguard.[83]

Constraint is also apparent in the right to take countervailing action against subsidized goods or antidumping action to counter dumping. As mentioned, in advance of both actions a determination must be made (a) that either subsidization or dumping is occurring, (b) that the domestic industry producing the like product in the importing country is suffering material injury, and (c) that there is a causal link between the subsidization/dumping and the material injury. In addition to substantive rules governing the determination of dumping, injury and causal link, the agreements in question also set forth detailed procedural rules for the initiation and conduct of investigations, the imposition of measures, and the duration and review of measures. All of these provisions also work to restrict exercise of the rights in question.

The theme of constraint likewise appears in the preference expressed in the SCM and ADA agreements for the imposition of lesser duties. For example, SCM Art. 19.2 specifies:

> It is desirable that the imposition [of countervailing duties] should be permissive in the territory of all Members, that *the duty should be less*

[81] *U.S. – Line Pipe*, WT/DS202/AB/R, para. 259 (15 Feb. 2002) [emphasis added].

[82] Ibid., para. 260.

[83] For instance, SAF Art. 7.1 specifies that the duration of a safeguard "shall not exceed four years" unless it is determined that the safeguard "continues to be necessary to prevent or remedy serious injury," in which case SAF Art. 7.3 specifies that "[t]he total period of application of a safeguard measure . . . shall not exceed eight years."

> *than the total amount of the subsidy if such lesser duty would be adequate to remove the injury to the domestic industry*, and that procedures should be established which would allow the authorities concerned to take due account of representations made by domestic interested parties whose interests might be adversely affected by the imposition of a countervailing duty.[84]

The inclusion of a reference to "domestic interested parties whose interests might be adversely affected by the imposition of a countervailing duty" highlights the interests of those who might be natural allies in the effort to constrain the exercise of such rights as well.

A number of WTO decisions have also stressed the general theme of fairness inherent in rights and proportionality in other ways. For instance, in *U.S. – Lead and Bismuth II* the panel noted that there must be "*a clear nexus* between the imposition of a countervailing duty, and the existence of a (countervailable) subsidy."[85] The panel added, "we consider that a countervailing duty may only be imposed on an imported product if it is demonstrated that a (countervailable) subsidy was bestowed directly or indirectly on the manufacture, production or export of that merchandise."[86] In *China – Broiler Products* the panel emphasized that the investigating authority "was obligated to accurately determine the per unit subsidy amount and not impose countervailing duties exceeding that amount."[87] The panel added that the investigating authority has "an obligation to ascertain the precise amount of subsidy attributed to the imported products under investigation. This requires more effort on the part of an investigating authority than simply accepting data and using it."[88] Furthermore:

> authorities charged with conducting an inquiry or a study – to use the treaty language, an "investigation" – "must actively seek out pertinent information" and may not remain "passive in the face of possible shortcomings in the evidence submitted." Thus, [China's investigating authority] needed to ensure that it had calculated the correct subsidy amount, rather than simply accept the information submitted by respondents,

84 Emphasis added. For equivalent language with respect to antidumping disciplines see ADA Art. 8.1.
85 WT/DS138/R, para. 6.52 (23 Dec. 1999) [emphasis added].
86 Ibid., para. 6.57.
87 WT/DS427/R, para. 7.258 (2 Aug. 2013).
88 Ibid., para. 7.261.

> particularly as the respondents had alerted [China's investigating authority] that they may have misunderstood the question and provided incorrect data.[89]

A further indicator of fairness arises in use of the general term "appropriate" in key provisions involving permissible counteraction. This usage stands in sharp contrast to the insistence on equivalence in, for example, DSU Art. 22.4.

For example, SCM Art. 19.3 refers to countervailing duties being levied "*in the appropriate amounts* in each case, on a non-discriminatory basis," language which has been interpreted to prohibit concurrent application of countervailing and antidumping duties to address the same situation of subsidization.[90] Likewise, ADA Art. 9.2 provides that "When an anti-dumping duty is imposed in respect of any product, such anti-dumping duty shall be collected *in the appropriate amounts* in each case." Use of the suffix term "in each case" has been interpreted to mean that "'appropriate amounts' implies *a certain tailoring of the amounts according to circumstances*"[91] and is evidently suggestive of the particularity of fairness.

This set of observations leads to another abiding theme in fairness: the need for individuation. This need is especially evident in antidumping

[89] Ibid.

[90] *U.S. – Anti-Dumping and Countervailing Duties (China)*, WT/DS379/AB/R, paras. 552–553 (11 Mar. 2011). The Appellate Body noted that relevant dictionary definitions of the term "appropriate" include "proper," "fitting" and "specially suitable (*for, to*)"; and that:

> ... what is "appropriate" is not an autonomous or absolute standard but rather something that must be assessed by reference or in relation to something else. They suggest some core norm – "proper," "fitting," "suitable" *and at the same time adaptation to particular circumstances*. Within Article 19.3, the circumstance-specific quality of "the appropriate amounts" is further reinforced by the immediate context provided by the words "in each case"; that "appropriate amounts" implies a certain tailoring of the amounts according to circumstances ...
>
> (para. 552, emphasis added)

The Appellate Body concluded that "considering that each agreement sets forth a standard of appropriateness of the amount and establishes a ceiling for the respective duties, it should not be possible to circumvent the rules in each agreement by taking measures under both agreements to counteract the same subsidization" (para. 572). See also *U.S. – Supercalendered Paper*, WT/DS505/R, para. 7.263 (5 July 2018) ("'appropriate,' *in the sense of fitting or suitable*").

[91] *U.S. – Anti-Dumping and Countervailing Duties (China)*, WT/DS379/AB/R, para. 553 (11 Mar. 2011) [emphasis added].

practice, where the proscribed behavior – dumping – is carried out by individual economic operators. ADA Art. 9.2 provides that "The authorities *shall name the supplier or suppliers* of the product concerned." ADA Art. 9.2 goes on to specify that:

> If, however, several suppliers from the same country are involved, and it is impracticable to name all these suppliers, the authorities may name the supplying country concerned. If several suppliers from more than one country are involved, the authorities may name either all the suppliers involved, or, if this is impracticable, all the supplying countries involved.

Disputes have arisen over the extent of the obligation of individuation, particularly where it is not "impracticable" but simply "ineffective" to name specific suppliers.[92]

Dumping margins may also be imposed through the imposition of an "all others" rate, that is, a presumptive dumping margin that applies to all producers within a given country who have otherwise supplied the necessary information, subject to certain exclusions listed in ADA Art. 9.4. In that situation the treaty "provides for a 'ceiling' for such a rate and establishes two 'prohibitions' on the use of certain margins in the calculation of the 'all others' rate: (i) zero or *de minimis* margins and (ii) margins established on the basis of best facts available."[93]

Finally, the panel in *U.S. – Supercalendered Paper* observed that in the case of residual or "all others" rates of dumping assessed against non-investigated exporters:

> countervailing duty rates established for investigated exporters will generally be "*appropriate*," *in the sense of fitting or suitable*, for non-investigated exporters, since the subsidization available to investigated exporters generally constitutes a reasonable proxy for the amount of subsidization that may have been available to non-investigated exporters.[94]

[92] In *EC – Fasteners (China)* WT/DS397/AB/R (15 July 2011) the Appellate Body observed that "the notion of 'ineffective' is not included in the notion of 'impracticable' . . . the notion of 'ineffective' is concerned with bringing about or producing an effect or result, which is absent from the notion of 'impracticable,' which describes the action itself." Ibid., para. 347. On the basis of this distinction and the clear wording of the treaty, the Appellate Body determined that an assertion of "ineffectiveness" did not meet the threshold for application of a country-wide duty.

[93] *US – Hot-Rolled Steel*, WT/DS184/AB/R, para. 116 (24 July 2001).

[94] *U.S. – Supercalendered Paper*, WT/DS505/R, para. 7.263 (5 July 2018) [emphasis added].

The panel went on to observe that this approach would not always be suitable, however, particularly when the antidumping rate is calculated on the basis of facts available, as "the non-investigated exporters or producers are similarly treated as being non-cooperative, even though there has been no finding of non-cooperation in their regard, and even though they may have been willing to participate fully in the investigation."[95] Hence, the panel considered "that the appropriate amount of subsidization determined in respect of investigated exporters may serve as the ceiling for applying countervailing duties on non-investigated exporters."[96]

It is also important to observe that although the law on an "all others" antidumping rate is silent concerning a number of critical details pertaining to the exercise of this right by member countries, silence does not imply that there are *no* obligations for WTO members to follow. In *U.S. – Zeroing (Art. 21.5 – EC)* the Appellate Body dealt with a situation where all calculated margins of dumping fell into excluded categories for the purposes of assessing the "all others" rate. These total exclusions did not mean that the US Department of Commerce had unlimited discretion in calculating an "all others" rate:

> [T]he fact that all margins of dumping for the investigated exporters fall within one of the categories that Article 9.4 directs investigating authorities to disregard, for purposes of that paragraph, does not imply that the investigating authorities' discretion to apply duties on non-investigated exporters is unbounded. The lacuna that the Appellate Body recognized to exist in Article 9.4 is one of a specific *method*. Thus, the absence of guidance in Article 9.4 on what particular methodology to follow does not imply an absence of any obligation with respect to the "all others" rate applicable to non-investigated exporters where all margins of dumping for the investigated exporters are either zero, *de minimis*, or based on facts available.[97]

Again, the case law suggests that the exercise of rights implies attendant obligations stressing limitation.

Countermeasures Proportionality has received perhaps its most extensive interpretation of countermeasures under the SCM Agreement. I have

[95] Ibid., para. 7.266.
[96] Ibid., para. 7.271.
[97] *U.S. – Zeroing (EC) (Art. 21.5 – EC)*, WT/DS294/AB/RW, para. 453 (14 May 2009) [emphasis in original].

already introduced the discussion of countermeasures in Chapter 3. Under the SCM Agreement particular rights to take countermeasures arise that are strongly suggestive of proportionate – as opposed to strictly equal – action against noncompliance.

The SCM defines two categories of subsidies: *prohibited* and *actionable.*[98] *Prohibited subsidies* are subsidies that require recipients to meet certain export targets or to engage in import substitution. They are prohibited because they are especially likely to distort international trade. Such subsidies can be challenged in WTO dispute settlement procedures, where they are handled under an accelerated timetable, and if found to be prohibited, must be withdrawn immediately. If the subsidy is not withdrawn, then under SCM Art. 4.10 "the DSB shall grant authorization to the complaining Member to take *appropriate countermeasures.*" SCM footnote 9 specifies that the term "appropriate countermeasures . . . is not meant to allow countermeasures that are disproportionate in light of the fact that the subsidies dealt with under these provisions are prohibited."

By comparison, *actionable subsidies* under SCM Arts. 5–6 are subsidies that are determined to have an adverse effect on another country's interests. The SCM defines three types of damage these subsidies can cause. First, one country's subsidies can injure the domestic industry in an importing country. Second, subsidies granted by one country can hurt rival exporters from another country when the two compete in third markets. Third, subsidies in one country can hurt exporters trying to compete in the subsidizing country's domestic market. If it is determined that a domestic subsidy has an adverse effect, the subsidy must be withdrawn or its adverse effect must be removed. Where the member granting the actionable subsidy has not taken appropriate steps to remove the adverse effects of the subsidy or has failed to withdraw the subsidy, then under SCM Art. 7.9 the complaining member may take countermeasures "*commensurate with* the degree and nature of the adverse effects determined to exist."

These distinctive remedies – of "appropriate countermeasures" in SCM Art. 4.10 and "commensurate" countermeasures in SCM Art. 7.9 – must be considered in connection with the obligation to "withdraw" subsidies discussed previously. This obligation appears to

[98] The SCM originally contained a third category: nonactionable subsidies. This category existed for five years, ending on December 31, 1999, and was not extended. It pertained to permissible subsidies for environmental, research, and regional development purposes.

go beyond the usual prescription in DSU Art. 19.1 to bring measures "into conformity," which is distributive and traditionally understood to be purely prospective in nature. The language involved in these distinctive remedies under the SCM seems to indicate a desire to do something more evidently corrective than simply mandating a requirement to remove a subsidy *de jure*. The different qualifying language means that the possibility of removal *de facto* cannot be ruled out.

Generally speaking, arbitrators examining the issue of withdrawal of prohibited or actionable subsidies have not made any distinction between *de jure* and *de facto* withdrawal. At the same time, at least one arbitrator has noted that "to continue to make payments under an export subsidy measure found to be prohibited is not consistent with the obligation to 'withdraw' prohibited export subsidies, in the sense of 'removing' or 'taking away.'"[99] More directly, in *Australia – Automotive Leather II (Art. 21.5 – U.S.)* the arbitrator noted that "an interpretation of 'withdraw the subsidy' that encompasses repayment of the prohibited subsidy seems a straightforward reading of the text of the provision." In that case the arbitrator went on to note that "[a]n interpretation of [SCM] Article 4.7 . . . which would allow exclusively 'prospective' action would make the recommendation to 'withdraw the subsidy' under Article 4.7 indistinguishable from the recommendation to 'bring the measure into conformity' under Article 19.1 of the DSU, thus rendering Article 4.7 redundant."[100] For that reason, the arbitrator interpreted the language as requiring Australia to withdraw the subsidy *de facto*. The issue of the extent of any general duty to recover subsidies *de facto* has not been definitively settled in subsequent jurisprudence.[101]

99 *Brazil – Aircraft (Art. 21.5 – Canada)*, WT/DS46/AB/RW, para. 45 (21 July 2000).

100 *Australia – Automotive Leather (Art. 21.5 – US)*, WT/DS126/RW, paras. 6.27–6.31 (21 Jan. 2000). More recently, this issue has arisen in the Airbus–Boeing dispute, where the issue of whether the obligation of withdrawal encompasses both de jure *and* de facto elements is ongoing. In connection with this, USTR Ambassador Robert Lighthizer "has insisted that resolving the dispute would require not just full compliance from the Europeans, 'but also paying back some element of the subsidy and that's tricky because people don't have the same number.'" Hannah Monicken, "EU: Airbus, Member States in Full Compliance in WTO Dispute" 38:31 *Inside U.S. Trade* 15 (31 July 2020).

101 In *EC and certain member States – Large Civil Aircraft (Art. 21.5 – EU)*, WT/DS316/RW2 (2 Dec. 2019) the panel found that "the life of a subsidized loan may come to an end in either of two situations: when the financial contribution and the benefit have been removed; or when only the benefit is removed." Ibid., para. 7.202. In addition, the panel in *EC and certain member States – Large Civil Aircraft (Art. 21.5 – EU)* indicated that although "a Member has no compliance obligation under Article 7.8 with respect to expired subsidies," the repayment of a loan on subsidized terms does not necessarily

More generally, arbitrators have had to grapple with the specific meaning of the term "appropriate countermeasures" in SCM Art. 4.10 in light of the duty to comply. Their comments have closely tracked what is projected by a communitarian theory in its forecasting of a concern with particularism and specificity in the exercise of rights.

Thus, in *Brazil – Aircraft (Art. 22.6 – Brazil)* the arbitrator observed:

> the relevant dictionary definitions of the word "appropriate" are "specially suitable; proper." However, they point in the direction of meeting a particular objective. . . . We conclude that a countermeasure is "appropriate" *inter alia* if it *effectively* induces compliance.[102]

In *U.S. – FSC (Art. 22.6 – U.S.)* the arbitrator observed that:

> Based on the plain meaning of the word ["appropriate"], this means that countermeasures should be *adapted to the particular case at hand.* The term is consistent with an intent not to prejudge what the circumstances might be in the specific context of dispute settlement in a given case. To that extent, there is an element of flexibility, in the sense that there is thereby an eschewal of any rigid *a priori* quantitative formula. But it is also clear that there is, nevertheless, an objective relationship which must be absolutely respected: *the countermeasures must be suitable or fitting by way of response to the case at hand.*[103]

One additional question is the exact content of "appropriate countermeasures" in SCM Art. 4.10. As mentioned, the wording of SCM Art. 4.10 is manifestly different from that found in the equivalence standard articulated in DSU Art. 22.4. Some particular meaning must be ascribed to the difference by virtue of the interpretative principle of

mean that the subsidy has expired and it does not "remove," "return" or "withdraw" the subsidized loan. For both a grant and a subsidized loan, "the life of the subsidy will depend upon the extent to which the recipient is continuing to use the subsidy for its originally intended purposes . . . without having repaid at least the remaining value of the benefit associated with the original financial contribution on a prospective basis." Ibid., para. 7.203. These statements are not definitive since the EU has appealed the compliance panel's report and the appeal remains in limbo as a result of the Appellate Body's suspension of work in December 2019.

102 *Brazil – Aircraft (Art. 22.6 – Brazil)*, WT/DS46/ARB, paras. 3.42–3.44 (28 Aug. 2000) [emphasis in original].

103 *U.S. – FSC (Art. 22.6 – U.S.)*, WT/DS108/AB/RW, para. 5.12 (30 Aug. 2002) [emphasis added]. See also *U.S. – Upland Cotton (Art. 22.6 – U.S. I)*, WT/DS267/ARB/1, para. 4.47 (31 Aug. 2009).

effectiveness. In this respect the arbitrator in *Brazil – Aircraft (Art. 22.6 – Brazil)* noted:

> We are mindful of the fact that, from the point of view of a textual interpretation, "equivalent" and "appropriate" should not be given the same meaning. Interpreters are not permitted to assume such a thing. What we mean is that the term "appropriate," read in the light of [SCM] footnotes 9 and 10, may allow for more leeway than the word "equivalent" in terms of assessing the appropriate level of countermeasures. A countermeasure remains "appropriate" as long as it is not disproportionate, having also regard to the fact that the measure at issue is a prohibited subsidy.[104]

In *U.S. – FSC (Art. 22.6 – U.S.)* the arbitrator added:

> rather than there being any requirement to confine "appropriate countermeasures" to offsetting the effects of the measure on the relevant Member, there is a clear rationale exhibited that reinforces our textual interpretation that the Member concerned is entitled to take countermeasures that are tailored to neutralizing the offending measure qua measure as a wrongful act. The expression "appropriate countermeasures," in our view, would entitle the complaining Member to countermeasures which would at least counter the injurious effect of the persisting illegal measure on it. However, it does not require trade effects to be the effective standard by which the appropriateness of countermeasures should be ascertained. Nor can the relevant provisions be interpreted to *limit* the assessment to this standard. Members may take countermeasures that are not disproportionate in light of the gravity of the initial wrongful act and the objective of securing the withdrawal of a prohibited export subsidy, so as to restore the balance of rights and obligations upset by that wrongful act.[105]

These comments suggest that there are several possible bases on which to found "appropriate countermeasures" – the trade effects of the subsidy, the amount of the subsidy, or benefit conferred by the subsidy as well as the gravity of the initial wrongful act and the objective of securing the withdrawal – and that the precise amount of "appropriate countermeasures" may vary from case to case. There is substantial evidence of variation displayed in existing case law, as mentioned by the arbitrator in *U.S. – Upland Cotton (Art. 22.6 – U.S. I)*:

[104] *Brazil – Aircraft (Art. 22.6 – Brazil)*, WT/DS46/ARB, n. 51 (28 Aug. 2000).

[105] *U.S. – FSC (Art. 22.6 – U.S.)*, WT/DS108/AB/RW, para 5.41 (30 Aug. 2002) [emphasis in original].

> In *Brazil – Aircraft (Art. 22.6 – Brazil)*, the full payments made under the programme were used a basis for the calculation. In *U.S. – FSC (Art. 22.6 – U.S.)*, the calculation was based on the annual expenditure by the U.S. Government. Finally, in the *Canada – Aircraft (Art. 22.6 – Canada)* case, the amount of the subsidy was calculated on the basis of the benefit conferred by the loan, which was found to correspond to "the difference between the amount Air Wisconsin pays on the loan from EDC and the amount Air Wisconsin would pay on a comparable commercial loan which that company could actually obtain on the market."[106]

The arbitrator also discussed the "amount of the subsidy" approach:

> The use of the "amount of the subsidy" in prior cases does not imply, however, that the arbitrators in these earlier cases necessarily considered that the "amount of the subsidy" was the only basis on which "appropriate countermeasures" might have been calculated. In fact, as we understand it, the arbitrators in these cases took into account the fact that the legal standard embodied in Article 4.10 of the *SCM Agreement* allows greater flexibility than those under Article 22.4 of the DSU or Article 7.9 of the *SCM Agreement* to tailor the countermeasures to the specific circumstances of the case at hand, but did not exclude trade effects as a relevant consideration. In fact, in these decisions, some form of consideration was given to the trade effects of the measure on the complaining Member.[107]

The arbitrator went on to note, however, that:

> This Arbitrator is not convinced, however, that an "amount of subsidy" approach, of itself and without adjustment, will always be consistent with the legal standard embodied in Article 4.10 of the SCM Agreement. Actually, we think that in most cases such an approach will not be "appropriate," notwithstanding its convenience, from a calculation perspective, and its literal attraction, from a "withdraw the subsidy" perspective. As we have determined above, a consideration of the "appropriateness" of countermeasures, and in particular the requirement for the countermeasures not to be "disproportionate," *suggests that there should be a degree of relationship between the level of countermeasures and the trade-distorting impact of the measure on the complaining Member*. . . . the amount of the subsidy may in fact be lower than its trade effects, and apportioning it would ordinarily exacerbate that likelihood. This amount therefore does not seem to us to be a priori appropriate, nor is it necessarily proportionate to the extent to which the trade of the Member concerned is adversely affected. In these circumstances, it cannot be assumed that the total amount of the

106 *U.S. – Upland Cotton (Art. 22.6 – U.S. I)*, WT/DS267/ARB/1, n. 181 (31 Aug. 2009).
107 Ibid., para. 4.133.

subsidy is an appropriate measure of its trade effects, or even that it is necessarily a relevant "proxy" for those effects.[108]

On this basis the arbitrator made the following statement of principle consistent with the idea of fairness:

> We recall in this context our interpretation of "appropriateness" in the case of countermeasures against prohibited subsidies, in particular its less precise quantitative constraints. In particular, we note our previous observation that a range of factors can be presented to an arbitrator, together with a number of calculation methods. The arbitrator need not calculate direct equivalence, but instead may accept what the arbitrator feels to be within the bounds of what is appropriate in the circumstances of the case.[109]

In contrast with "appropriate countermeasures" called for in SCM Art. 4.10, SCM Art. 7.9 provides that "the DSB shall grant authorization to the complaining Member to take countermeasures, *commensurate with* the degree and nature of the adverse effects determined to exist." In *U.S. – Upland Cotton (Art. 22.6 – U.S. II)* the arbitrator elaborated upon the "commensurate with" standard in SCM Art. 7.9, carefully linking it to greater concern with the trade effects of an actionable subsidy, as follows:

> [W]ithin the context of the SCM Agreement, the terms of Article 4.10 contrast with those of Article 7.9, which foresees, in relation to actionable subsidies, countermeasures "commensurate with the degree and nature of the adverse effects determined to exist." Here too, the terms of Article 7.9, through this reference to the "degree and nature of the adverse effects determined to exist," point to *a single specific benchmark as reference, and require the countermeasures to be "commensurate" with this benchmark, which is carefully defined in relation to the specific adverse effects that form the basis of the underlying findings.* These elements distinguish the terms of Article 7.9 from the terms of Article 4.10. This difference can be understood in the broader context of the SCM Agreement, where actionable subsidies may only be challenged to the extent that they result in certain enumerated adverse effects for other WTO Members. By contrast, prohibited subsidies are prohibited independently of any demonstration of adverse effects. In such cases, no specific "adverse effects" will have been "determined to exist" prior to the request for authorization to apply countermeasures, and therefore there are none that could be referred to.[110]

[108] Ibid., para. 4.135 [emphasis added].
[109] Ibid., para. 4.137.
[110] *U.S. – Upland Cotton (Art. 22.6 – U.S. I)*, WT/DS267/ARB/1, para. 4.98 (31 Aug. 2009) [emphasis added].

More specifically, in *U.S. – Upland Cotton (Art. 22.6 – US II)* the arbitrator interpreted the term "commensurate" as follows:

> Dictionary definitions of this term include: "equal in measure or extent: coextensive" and "corresponding in size, extent, amount, or degree: proportionate," "of equal extent, coextensive." In light of these elements, we agree that the term "commensurate" essentially connotes a "correspondence" between two elements. In the context of Article 7.9, the "correspondence" is between the countermeasures and the "degree and nature of the adverse effects determined to exist." ... We agree that the term "commensurate" does not suggest that exact or precise equality is required, between the two elements to be compared, i.e. in this case, the proposed countermeasures and the "degree and nature of the adverse effects determined to exist." To that extent, *we agree that the term "commensurate" connotes a less precise degree of equivalence than exact numerical correspondence*. Nonetheless, the term "commensurate" does indicate, in our view, a relationship of correspondence and proportionality between the two elements.[111]

The arbitrator noted in addition:

> The exact nature of the correspondence at issue will further be informed by the identification of what exactly the proposed countermeasures are required to be "commensurate" with. This is defined through the terms "the degree and nature of the adverse effects determined to exist."[112]

In this respect SCM Art. 7.10 specifies that an arbitrator is to determine whether the proposed countermeasures are commensurate "with the degree and nature of the adverse effects determined to exist." Regarding the terms "degree and nature" the arbitrator in *U.S. – Upland Cotton (Art. 22.6 – U.S. II)* observed:

> We agree that the reference to both the "degree" and the "nature" of the adverse effects determined to exist suggests that the correspondence that is required to exist, between the proposed countermeasures and the "degree and nature of the adverse effects," may encompass both quantitative and qualitative elements. The "degree" of the effects could be understood as a

[111] WT/DS267/ARB/2, paras. 4.36–4.39 (31 Aug. 2009) [emphasis added]. The arbitrator in *EC and certain member States – Large Civil Aircraft (Art. 22.6 – EU)*, WT/DS316/ARB (2 Oct. 2019) further clarified that the "commensurateness" standard may not require exact equivalence between the level of the proposed countermeasures and the adverse effects found to exist. Ibid., para. 6.508. At the same time, the arbitrator cautioned that "this does not imply that countermeasures commensurate with the adverse effects determined to exist may or should incorporate any punitive element." Ibid., para. 5.4.

[112] *U.S. – Upland Cotton (Art. 22.6 – U.S. II)*, WT/DS267/ARB/2, para. 4.39 (31 Aug. 2009).

> quantitative element, whereas the reference to the "nature" of the adverse effects seems to point to something more qualitative. . . . We agree that the reference to the "nature" of the adverse effects may be understood to refer to the different "types" of adverse effects that are foreseen in Articles 5 and 6, and that this therefore invites a consideration of the specific type of "adverse effects" that have been determined to exist as a result of the specific measure in relation to which countermeasures are being requested. These effects could manifest themselves in a variety of ways, each reflecting a specific type of trade distortion.[113]

5.3.1.3 Mutuality

A third doctrine limiting the exercise of rights consistent with fairness in WTO law is mutuality. Mutuality refers to the shared quality of things, in this case the fact that all rights in WTO law are mirrored in the reciprocal rights of others. Mutuality infers that the assertion of rights by WTO members needs to be constrained in order not to undermine those other rights. This idea is frequently embodied in the doctrine of abuse of rights (*abus de droit*). The doctrine provides that no right may be exercised "in an excessive and unreasonable manner which is contrary to the requirements of good faith."[114]

The doctrine of abuse of rights is civilian in origin.[115] It is a singularly collective and protective doctrine. It is imposed in furtherance of an

[113] *U.S. – Upland Cotton (Art. 22.6 – U.S. II)*, WT/DS267/ARB/2, para. 4.43 (31 Aug. 2009).

[114] For a general requirement of good faith, see Civil Code of Québec Art. 6 ("Every person is bound to exercise his civil rights in accordance with the requirements of good faith."). For its specification see Quebec Civil Code Art. 317: "The juridical personality of a legal person may not be invoked against a person in good faith so as to dissemble fraud, *abuse of right* or contravention of a rule of public order."

[115] The traditional thinking in English common law is that rights are limitless, which is suitable to a system of law without a universalizing aspiration and marked by an "interstitial rationality." See H. Patrick Glenn, *Legal Traditions of the World* (5th ed.) 246, 251 (Oxford University Press, Oxford; 2014) ("The common law was held in check by its originators. Its courts did not lay claim to large areas of exclusive jurisdiction."; "the notion of subjective right . . . played little or no role in the history of the common law in England. The existence of rights in English law was denied well into the twentieth century.")

> [I]n eschewing, until recently at least, the systematics of Gaius, the English judges have invested the individual with remedies capable of finding their starting point at best only in the notion of "duty" – a notion that lends itself to analysis as an "objective juridical situation" rather than a "subjective right" – and at worst in some vague notion of freedom and liberty.
>
> (Geoffrey Samuel, "'Le droit subjectif' and English Law" 46 *Cambridge L.J.* 264 at 286 (1987))

adjudicative sense of communal order and evidences an overarching concern with balance between individual and collective interests.

Writing in 1983 Ian Brownlie observed that "it is not unreasonable to regard the principle of abuse of rights as a general principle of law." At the same time Brownlie noted that "whilst it is easy to sympathize with exponents of the doctrine, the delimitation of its function is a matter of delicacy." Brownlie cited Hersch Lauterpacht for the proposition that there is no legal right "which could not, in some circumstances, be refused recognition on the ground that it has been abused." Brownlie concluded that "the doctrine is a useful agent in the progressive development of the law, but that, as a general principle, it does not exist in positive law."[116]

Brownlie went on to describe abuse of rights as the "alter ego" of nondiscrimination.[117] In the crowded and intensive legal landscape of the WTO Agreement containing several versions of the nondiscrimination

[116] Ian Brownlie, *System of the Law of Nations – State Responsibility (Part 1)* 52 (1983).

[117] Ibid., p. 70. Where abuse of rights receives clear expression in international law is in situations of shared resources. As Alexandre Kiss observes:

> States sharing a natural resource will often enter into bilateral and multilateral conventions for the purposes of utilizing the resources to mutual advantage. In a sense, treaty clauses providing for the application and implementation of measures agreed in good faith could be considered as involving the prohibition of any abuse of the rights which those treaties confer upon the contracting parties.
>
> (Alexandre Kiss, "Oxford Public International Law – Abuse of Rights" para. 15 (Dec. 2006))

Thus, a number of treaties provide for specific prohibitions such as in the case of Art. 2 of the 1958 Convention on the High Seas, which qualifies the various aspects of freedom of the high seas with the condition that such freedoms "are to be exercised by all States with reasonable regard to the interests of other States." More recently, UNCLOS Art. 300 specifies that "States Parties shall fulfill in good faith the obligations assumed under this Convention and shall exercise the rights, jurisdictions and freedoms recognized in this Convention in a manner which would not constitute *an abuse of right*." [emphasis added] Thus, it is noteworthy that the doctrine appears to arise most prominently in situations of neighborliness – from which the doctrine arose in Roman law – where, by implication, the parties share some connection or interest. There is then a need to regulate the exercise of rights in order to protect the common good or thing. At the same time, rights contain limits. However, the extent of those limits is rarely predefined. For this reason, some commentators have expressed the view that any determination of abuse of rights would involve an uncomfortable amount of judicial discretion and would have to meet a very high standard, likely one amounting to "bad faith." See Son Tan Nguyen, "The Applicability of Comity and Abuse of Rights in World Trade Organisation Dispute Settlement" 35 *U. Tas. L. Rev.* 95 at 128 (2016).

principle, the prohibition on abuse of rights can be considered a requirement. Its presence reflects the density of the legal order.

This point was emphasized in *U.S. – Shrimp*, where the issue was the right of the United States to invoke the exception in GATT Art. XX(g) involving conservation measures.[118] The United States raised GATT Art. XX(g) as a defense to its violation of GATT Art. XI:1, the prohibition on quantitative restrictions, since the US legislation in issue effectively prohibited imports of shrimp that were not caught in a "turtle-friendly" manner.

The Appellate Body agreed that the United States had met the terms of the exception but then went on to analyze whether it had fulfilled the conditions of the preamble, or "chapeau," of Art. XX:[119]

> *Exercise by one Member of its right to invoke an exception, such as Article XX(g), if abused or misused, will, to that extent, erode or render naught the substantive treaty rights in, for example, Article XI:1, of other Members.* Similarly, because the GATT 1994 itself makes available the exceptions of Article XX, in recognition of the legitimate nature of the policies and interests there embodied, the right to invoke one of those exceptions is not to be rendered illusory. The same concept may be expressed from a slightly different angle of vision, thus, a balance must be struck between the *right* of a Member to invoke an exception under Article XX and the *duty* of that same Member to respect the treaty rights of the other Members. *To permit one Member to abuse or misuse its right to invoke an exception would be effectively to allow that Member to degrade its own treaty obligations as well as to devalue the treaty rights of other Members. If the abuse or misuse is sufficiently grave or extensive, the Member, in effect, reduces its treaty obligation to a merely facultative one and dissolves its juridical character, and, in so doing, negates altogether the treaty rights of other Members.* The chapeau [of GATT Art. XX] was installed at the head of the list of "General Exceptions" in Article XX to prevent such far-reaching consequences.[120]

A similar observation was made in *U.S. – Line Pipe*, where the dispute involved the United States' right to impose safeguards against imports of steel pipe from Korea. The Appellate Body observed:

[118] *U.S. – Shrimp*, WT/DS58/AB/R (12 Oct. 1998).

[119] The preamble to GATT Art. XX provides that "Subject to the requirement that such measures are not applied in a manner which would constitute a means of arbitrary or unjustifiable discrimination between countries where the same conditions prevail, or a disguised restriction on international trade, nothing in this Agreement shall be construed to prevent the adoption or enforcement by any contracting party of measures."

[120] *U.S. – Shrimp*, WT/DS58/AB/R, para. 156 (12 Oct. 1998) [emphasis added in part].

> There is, therefore, a natural tension between, on the one hand, defining the appropriate and legitimate scope of the right to apply safeguard measures and, on the other hand, ensuring that safeguard measures are not applied against "fair trade" beyond what is necessary to provide extraordinary and temporary relief. A WTO Member seeking to apply a safeguard measure will argue, correctly, that the *right* to apply such measures must be respected in order to maintain the *domestic* momentum and motivation for ongoing trade liberalization. In turn, a WTO Member whose trade is affected by a safeguard measure will argue, correctly, that the *application* of such measures must be limited in order to maintain the *multilateral* integrity of ongoing trade concessions. The balance struck by the WTO Members in reconciling this natural tension relating to safeguard measures is found in the provisions of the Agreement on Safeguards. This natural tension is likewise inherent in two basic inquiries that are conducted in interpreting the Agreement on Safeguards. These two basic inquiries are: *first*, is there a right to apply a safeguard measure? And, *second*, if so, has that right been exercised, through the application of such a measure, within the limits set out in the treaty?[121]

The Appellate Body's statements in *U.S. – Shrimp* and *U.S. – Line Pipe Safeguards* illustrate the fact that the WTO Agreement as a law of rights involves action that is conditioned and contextualized, and that exists within a larger matrix of rights *and* obligations. Where rights are exercised, their use comes with concurrent obligations that are limitative.

The body of WTO law then exhibits a preoccupation with the limitation of rights, consistent with the theoretic relation Obligation > Right. The jurisprudence reveals how "rights are as much a constraint as they are an empowering."[122] Constraint is necessary to further the purposes of the system. It is a reflection of community.

5.3.2 *A Contractual Law*

A second feature of WTO law in a fairness and rights idea-complex is its generally contractual structure. In many legal systems a contract is understood to be an agreement among parties that binds their mutual relations only to the extent agreed and without any consequences for third parties.[123] A contract stresses the voluntary aspect of the law.

[121] *U.S. – Line Pipe*, WT/DS202/AB/R, paras. 83–84 (15 Feb. 2002) [emphasis in original].

[122] Allott, *Eunomia* 160.

[123] "A contract is an agreement in which a party undertakes to do, or not to do, a particular thing." *Sturges* v. *Crowninshield*, 17 U.S. (4 Wheat) 122, 143 (1819); "The regime of contract law, which respects the dispositions individuals make of their rights, carries to

There are numerous mentions of "contract" in GATT/WTO law. The WTO Agreement is the successor to GATT 1947, an informal arrangement among governments with notable contractual features. GATT's original members were formally referred to as "*Contracting Parties*," and countries participating in the arrangement were accorded important rights to renegotiate their tariff concessions, which continue to exist under the WTO Agreement.

Despite the "constitutionalization" of WTO law introduced by the WTO Agreement, various metaphors related to contractualism remain popular, a popularity that is no doubt due to the flexibility they imply. Thus, in the WTO's 2019 Annual Report it was noted that:

> At [the heart of the international trading system] are the WTO agreements, negotiated and signed by the bulk of the world's trading nations ... *They are essentially contracts*, binding governments to keep their trade policies *within agreed limits*.[124]

In a contractual conception members retain substantial freedom to modify their obligations under the treaty and to fulfill them in the manner they see fit. As such, the consensualism implied by a contract is both politically convenient and attractive.

The associated idea of GATT and WTO arrangements as an "incomplete contract" has also been popularized by some commentators who regard the phrase as a prudent description for what has emerged from the treaty's apparently unfinished features.[125] The same commentators appear to mistrust or regard as troublesome the undeniably constitutive aspects of WTO law referenced in the previous chapter. Thus, in addition to being consonant with certain historic attributes of the WTO Agreement, the moniker of "contractualism" offers a degree of safety and intelligibility.

its natural conclusion the liberal premise that individuals have rights." Charles Fried, *Contract as Promise* 1 (Oxford University Press, Oxford; 1981). Article 1.1 of the UNIDROIT Principles of International Commercial Contracts emphasizes the rights-based nature of contracting in noting that "[t]he parties are free to enter into a contract and to determine its content."

124 WTO Annual Report 2019 (2019) [emphasis added]. The same statement appeared in every WTO Annual Report in the period 2010–2018.

125 See, for example, Petros Mavroidis, *Trade in Goods* (1st ed.) 30, n. 71 (Oxford University Press, Oxford; 2007) ("In *an incomplete contract*, like the WTO, linear evolution of case-law is quite an important factor in securing predictability as to transaction costs (legal security)." [emphasis added]); Henrik Horn et al., "The GATT/WTO as an Incomplete Contract" (2005) (unpublished paper).

The idea of WTO law as contractual receives additional support from WTO jurisprudence. In *Japan – Alcoholic Beverages*, the Appellate Body referred to the WTO Agreement as "a treaty – the international equivalent of a *contract*"[126] – and in *U.S. – Line Pipe* the panel observed that "WTO members have *contracted* a package of rights and obligations."[127] These references are often made in connection with provisions in the treaty that appear to allow countries to modify their obligations. They include treaty amendment, renegotiation and the freedom to conclude RTAs. In assessing this aspect of WTO arrangements, it is useful to consider how "contractual" the WTO Agreement really is.

First, as noted, there is the possibility of counteraction under WTO rules disciplines, and to that extent, a limited form of "contractualism" appears to prevail in the sense that countries may engage in bilateral rebalancing in certain proscribed circumstances.

Second, there are WTO provisions that allow for waivers, definitive interpretations and amendment of the WTO Agreement, although so far each of these devices has been used sparingly or not at all. WTO members have therefore adopted the expedient of occasionally negotiating "around" existing commitments, sometimes in apparent disregard of WTO arrangements.[128] The results are "contractualist" in the sense that they affirm the subsisting power of the membership to freely negotiate.

Third, both GATT and GATS contain renegotiation provisions. In the case of GATT, members are allowed under GATT Art. XXVIII:1 to renegotiate their concessions on a three-year cycle, a requirement originally designed to provide a modicum of stability and predictability to tariff concessions. Second, under GATT Art. XXVIII:4, renegotiation may take place upon approval of the membership "under special circumstances." Third, under GATT Art. XXVIII:5, renegotiation can take place at any time provided that a member makes a reservation to this effect at the beginning of the three-year cycle contemplated in GATT Art. XXVIII:1.

[126] *Japan – Alcoholic Beverages*, WT/DS8/AB/R, p. 15 (4 Oct. 1996).

[127] *U.S. – Line Pipe*, WT/DS202/R, para. 7.40 (29 Oct. 2001).

[128] In three instances – for example, the Access to Medicines Case, the Basic Telecoms Case and the Trade Facilitation Case – negotiations skirted formal WTO amendment procedures. See also See Hannah Monicken, "Brazilian Ambassador: WTO Must Choose 'Fragmentation or Irrelevance'" 39:39 *Inside U.S. Trade* 3 (1 Oct. 2021); Jane Kelsey, "The Illegitimacy of Joint Statement Initiatives and Their Systemic Implications for the WTO" 25:1 *J.I.E.L.* 2 (Mar. 2022).

To simplify potentially complex renegotiations, renegotiation is to be conducted pursuant to GATT Art. XXVIII with the country that possesses "initial negotiating rights" (INR), that is, the member with which the concession in question was originally granted, as well as with the member possessing the "principal supplying interest," that is, the member that over time has become the largest supplier of the product(s) in question. Furthermore, GATT Art. XXVIII specifies a duty to consult with any country having a "substantial interest," or in other words, any member with a significant share in exports of the product(s) concerned. Renegotiation is also made subject to the requirement expressed in GATT Art. XXVIII:2 that the parties involved "shall endeavor to maintain a general level of reciprocal and mutually advantageous concessions no less favourable to trade than ... prior to such negotiations." Where such reciprocity is not maintained, then it is possible for the renegotiating parties to withdraw substantially equivalent concessions.[129]

In practice, countries' behavior in renegotiations has exhibited considerable flexibility and informality.[130] This may be understood as tacit acknowledgment that renegotiation requires significant give-and-take. As proof, Anuwarul Hoda cites the fact that during the period 1958–1994, there were only three cases of retaliatory withdrawal under GATT Art. XXVIII:2, a record Hoda attributes to the general success of renegotiation proceedings, the desire to avoid "chains" of retaliatory withdrawals, and the existence of the MFN clause.[131] At the same time, this record should not be taken to mean that such renegotiations were straightforward. Hoda observes that a number of renegotiations took several years to conclude, and in one particular instance, more than two decades. Renegotiations triggered in the case of EC/EU enlargement have always been problematic.[132] This complexity has meant that some

[129] GATT Art. XXVIII:3(a)–(b) ("any contracting party determined ... to have a principal supplying interest and any contracting party determined ... to have a substantial interest shall then be free ... to withdraw ... substantially equivalent concessions initially negotiated with the applicant contracting party.")

[130] The WTO Analytical Index observes in this regard that:

> "the [WTO] Secretariat's records show that at least 42 GATT contracting parties initiated roughly 300 renegotiations between 1951 and 1994." See WTO Analytical Index GATT Art. XXVIII - Practice: 1.6 GATT 1947 practice under Article XXVIII.

[131] See Anwarul Hoda, *Tariff Negotiations and Renegotiations under the GATT and WTO* 95 (Cambridge University Press, Cambridge; 2001).

[132] Hoda notes the complexity of renegotiation proceedings carried on due to successive rounds of EC enlargement in 1972, 1981 and 1986. Ibid., pp. 99–107.

countries decided to have "recourse to waivers and special authorization more than once."[133]

In the WTO era renegotiation has become rarer still. Rarity is likely related to a decline in the importance of tariffs as an instrument of trade policy, the difficulty of finding quantitative equivalents for nonquantitative disciplines, as well as the inherent complexity of renegotiating concessions and commitments with more than 160 other members.[134]

A fourth feature of subsisting "contractualism" in the WTO Agreement is the possibility of members concluding or acceding to bilateral or regional RTAs under GATT Art. XXIV or its GATS equivalent.[135] As mentioned, GATT Art. XXIV:5 specifies that nothing is to prevent the formation of a customs union or free trade area so long as certain conditions are met. First, in the case of a customs union, the arrangement must eliminate "duties and other restrictive regulations of commerce . . . with respect to substantially all the trade between the constituent territories of the union or at least with respect to substantially all the trade in products originating in such territories" (GATT Art. XXIV:8(a)); and in the case of a free trade area "the duties and other restrictive regulations of commerce . . . are eliminated on substantially all the trade between the constituent territories" (GATT Art.

[133] Ibid, p. 98.

[134] The WTO Analytical Index observes:

> A factual report released in 2020 by the Secretariat indicated that there had been 48 renegotiations under Article XXVIII of the GATT 1994 since 1 January 1995. Of these, eight requests had been withdrawn; one request had not been authorized by the Council for Trade in Goods; 24 renegotiations had been concluded and formally certified; five had been concluded and draft changes submitted under the 1980 Procedures; and 10 renegotiations remained ongoing.
>
> (See G/MA/W/123/Rev.6 (6 Mar. 2020) and G/MA/W123/Rev.6/Corr.1 (3 June 2020). WTO Analytical Index GATT Art. XXVIII – Practice (consulted 11 July 2022))

[135] The WTO Analytical Index observes:

> As of 31 December 2020, 305 of the 496 RTAs notified to the GATT/WTO remained in force (counting goods and services separately). 271 of the 496 notifications have been made under Article XXIV of the GATT 1947 or the GATT 1994, 61 under the Enabling Clause and 164 under Article V of the General Agreement on Trade in Services (GATS). In addition, 32 RTAs notified to the WTO at the end of 2020 were due to enter into force at the beginning of 2021. Each of these notifications was made under Article XXIV of the GATT 1994, and 13 were made under both Article XXIV of the GATT 1994 and Article V of the GATS.
>
> (WTO Analytical Index GATT Art. XXIV – Practice (consulted 11 July 2022))

XXIV:8(b)). Second, because "the purpose of a customs union or of a free-trade area should be to facilitate trade between the constituent territories and not to raise barriers to the trade of other contracting parties" (GATT Art. XXIV:4); where such barriers arise, members have an obligation to negotiate compensatory adjustments with the affected members (GATT Art. XXIV:6). Third, GATT Art. XXIV features procedural requirements obliging countries to notify their RTAs to the WTO Committee on Regional Trade Agreements (CRTA), which is empowered to make recommendations concerning the RTAs reviewed to the countries involved and to the WTO membership more generally, which may approve proposals for non-conforming arrangements by a two-thirds majority.

The difficulty with this structure, as previously discussed, is that it has not worked in practice. Both under GATT 1947 and the WTO Agreement, the CRTA has largely failed to make the recommendations foreseen and thus meaningful discipline of RTAs has been avoided.[136] By default, what failure permits is significant flexibility to members who tacitly "contract out" of their WTO obligations.[137]

The failure of the WTO as an organization to constrain regionalism is well-known. It has led in many instances to MFN obligations constituting a "ceiling" rather than a "floor" and to the establishment of a *système à plusieurs vitesses* under the nominal umbrella of a "single undertaking." Jagdish Bhagwati and others have seized on this phenomenon to lament

[136] Joanna Langille observes that:

> For most of the 124 RTAs that were formed during the GATT era, an ad hoc working party was formed. Of those, no RTA was ever judged to be in violation of GATT Article XXIV; the working parties "merely articulated issues raised … without arriving at any firm conclusions." All other working parties ended without any agreement. Enforcement of GATT Article XXIV provisions through this mechanism was therefore nonexistent. After the WTO was established, member states unsuccessfully attempted to fix this ineffective system for monitoring RTAs. Over 300 RTAs have been notified to the WTO, but the CRTA has never come to a consensus. Further, members often refrain from notifying their RTAs to the WTO or notify after they are already implemented, thereby "avoiding examination and discussion."
>
> (See Joanna Langille, "Neither Constitution nor Contract: Understanding the WTO by Examining the Legal Limits on Contracting Out Through Regional Trade Agreements" 86 *N.Y.U. L. Rev.* 1482, 1505–1506 (2011).)

[137] "The fact that Article XXIV is largely moribund and that the original review mechanism is ineffective means that extensive contracting out is tacitly accepted by the WTO regime." See ibid., p. 1516.

the creation of a "spaghetti bowl" of trade obligations.[138] Other commentators have regarded it as healthy, the by-product of an arrangement that has grown too large for meaningful reciprocity and a reflection of pragmatism.[139] Contractualism continues to provide impetus in plurilateral negotiations that have been underway for some time on trade in services, green goods and fisheries subsidies, although as has pointed out, "[h]ow these agreements would be implemented, should they be successful, has not yet been determined."[140]

At the same time, panels and the Appellate Body have continued to assert that as a matter of law, countries cannot simply negotiate out of their WTO commitments by cutting deals among themselves.[141] Organs

[138] See Jagdish Bhagwati, who has expressed concern about the "spaghetti bowl" effect of governments' rush to conclude RTAs. See Jagdish Bhagwati, "U.S. Trade Policy: The Infatuation with Free Trade Agreements" in Jagdish Bhagwati & Anne Kreuger (eds), *The Dangerous Drift to Preferential Trade Agreements* 2 (AEI Press, Washington, DC; 1995).

[139] For positive views of regionalism, see Richard Baldwin, "The Causes of Regionalism" 20:7 *World Econ.* 865 (2002) (noting that "North-South preferential arrangements may be an excellent way of promoting liberalisation in developing nations" at p. 885); Sam Laird, "Regional Trade Agreements: Dangerous Liasons?" 22:9 *World Econ.* 1179 (1999), noting that:

> RTAs have brought a number of benefits to world trade, not least because of the political and security factors behind many agreements. Even on a narrower, economic basis for evaluation, RTAs appear to be welfare enhancing overall. Although on some analyses, they may divert trade from third countries, the risk of trade diversion is offset by the apparent dynamism that RTAs seem to have imparted to world trade, including with nonparticipants.
>
> (Ibid. p. 1198)

See also Robert Z. Lawrence, *Regionalism, Multilateralism, and Deeper Integration* (Brookings Institution, Washington, DC; 1996).

[140] Debra Steger, "Strengthening the WTO Rulemaking Function" in *Modernizing the World Trade Organization: A CIGI Essay Series* 97 at 99 (Centre for International Governance Innovation, Waterloo, Ontario; 2019). Since 1995 the WTO Agreement has been supplemented by two new agreements. The WTO Agreement on Trade Facilitation was concluded in 2013 and entered into force in 2017. The WTO Agreement on Fisheries Subsidies was concluded in 2022 and has not yet entered into force.

[141] *Turkey – Textiles*, WT/DS34/R, para. 9.178 (31 May 1999) ("In our view, however, a bilateral agreement between two Members ... does not alter the legal nature of the measures at issue or the applicability of the relevant GATT/WTO provisions"); *EC – Bananas III*, WT/DS27/AB/R, paras. 164–170 (9 Sept. 1997) (the Appellate Body, in examining the Lomé Convention, concluded that unless explicitly authorized by a waiver, provisions of the Convention could not alter rights and obligations of WTO members).

of dispute settlement have maintained that they have a right to review RTAs in dispute settlement and, in a limited and piecemeal fashion, they have done so.[142] In a number of disputes, they have also held that RTAs cannot be used as a defense against various claims of trade-related discrimination.[143]

This uneasy sense of disorder and difference of opinion would not prevail unless there were some latent impulse in the system for uniformity and constitutionalism. The impulse would appear to confirm the point of theory that the concept of the WTO Agreement as constitutive prevails over the idea that it is only contractual (Constitution > Contract). State behavior also suggests that members are not always at ease with the idea of subsisting contractualism and with being denied the benefit of deals cut between pairs of countries in practice.[144] At best, the WTO Agreement as a "contract" is a *modus vivendi* hinting at something more substantial.

5.3.3 *A Law of the Past*

Much of WTO law is oriented toward what *will be* in the future. A requirement of nondiscrimination, for instance, is likely to rely on a standard of what is to be attained in more ideal times to come.

However, this is not the universal outlook of WTO law. To a degree, things must be dealt with as they are, or perhaps more accurately as they were, since they already exist and need to be accounted for. In addressing this, WTO law becomes a "law of the past."

Throughout the WTO Agreement, there are instances where WTO law casts a retrospective gaze at things as they were. Pastness and an *ex post* perspective is particularly evident in WTO rules disciplines, where a look is taken at conditions as they were in order to determine if a country has fulfilled its WTO obligations in exercising its rights.

142 *Turkey – Textiles*, WT/DS34/AB/R, paras. 42–63 (22 Oct. 1999).

143 *U.S. – Line Pipe*, WT/DS202/AB/R, paras. 198–199 (15 Feb. 2002).

144 Wolfgang Alschner, "Amicable Settlements of WTO Disputes: Bilateral Solutions in a Multilateral System" 13:1 *World Trade Rev.* 65 (2013) (noting that every third dispute brought to the WTO and not withdrawn early is settled amicably through a mutually agreed solution (MAS); MAS favor the instant resolution of disputes but may conflict with third-party interests and collective stakes. Where WTO members use their MAS to contract out of WTO law the multilateral trading system may be at risk); Kelsey, "The Illegitimacy of Joint Statement Initiatives" 2 (the justifications for JSIs rely on tenuous interpretations of WTO rules and the preferred mode of implementation involves a misuse of trade in services schedules; precedent set by JSIs would license future rule making by self-selecting groups of WTO members on a potentially limitless range of subjects).

An illustration is offered by the case of safeguards. As mentioned, safeguards are only applicable to the extent that they are necessary "to prevent or remedy serious injury or to facilitate industrial adjustment." Under SAF a WTO member can only exercise the right to impose a safeguard to the extent it can prove that "serious injury" has arisen or that industrial adjustment is needed. Proof requires evidence. For example, the definition of "serious injury" in SAF Art. 4.2(a) specifies:

> In the investigation to determine whether increased imports have caused or are threatening to cause serious injury to a domestic industry under the terms of this Agreement, the competent authorities shall evaluate all relevant factors of *an objective and quantifiable nature* having a bearing on the situation of that industry.

The definition of a "threat of serious injury" – also a cause of action under SAF in certain circumstances – is even more fact-oriented. In this regard SAF Art. 1(b) specifies:

> "threat of serious injury" shall be understood to mean serious injury that is clearly imminent ... [a] determination of the existence of a threat of serious injury shall be based *on facts and not merely on allegation, conjecture or remote possibility.*

In *U.S. – Wheat Gluten*, the panel determined that since the examination of increased imports in any safeguard investigation is necessarily based on the most recent imports, a finding of "serious injury" should be based in evidence related to the recent past:

> [A]ny determination of serious injury must pertain *to the recent past.* This flows from the wording of the text of Article XIX:1(a) of the GATT 1994 and [SAF] Article 2.1, which requires an examination as to whether a product "is being imported" "in such increased quantities ... and under such conditions as to cause or threaten serious injury...." The use of the present tense of the verb in the phrase "is being imported" in that provision indicates that it is necessary for the competent authorities to examine *recent imports.* It seems to us logical that if the increase in imports that the investigating authorities must examine must be recent, so also must be any basis for a determination by the authorities as to the situation of the domestic industry. Given that a safeguard measure will necessarily be based upon a determination of serious injury *concerning a previous period,* we consider it essential that current serious injury be found to exist, up to and including the very end of the period of investigation.[145]

[145] *U.S. – Wheat Gluten*, WT/DS166/R, para. 8.81 (31 July 2000) [emphasis added].

At the same time, in *U.S. – Lamb* the panel emphasized that the most relevant evidence in a "threat of serious injury" claim under the SAF would be drawn from the most recent past:

> In our view, due to the future-oriented nature of a threat analysis, it would seem logical that occurrences at the beginning of an investigation period are less relevant than those at the end of that period. While the [SAF] does not specify the appropriate duration of the time-period to be considered in an investigation, the Panel and Appellate Body in *Argentina – Footwear* both considered this issue to some extent. Both concluded that (for an *actual* serious injury finding) the most recent data were clearly the most relevant.[146]

The same preoccupation with pastness is evident in the SCM and ADA. For example, in *EC – Large Civil Aircraft*, the dispute involved allegations of more than 300 instances of subsidization spanning four decades. The measures complained of by the United States included "launch aid" and EC member state financing, loans from the European Investment Bank, infrastructure and infrastructure-related grants, as well as corporate restructuring measures, and research and technological development funding. The US claim was that each of the challenged measures was a "specific subsidy" within the meaning of the SCM Arts. 1–2 and that, in particular, several "launch aid" and member state financing measures were prohibited export subsidies under SCM Art. 3.

Similarly, in *U.S. – DRAMS from Korea*, the measure at issue involved US antidumping duties on Korean computer memory chips. The chips in question were assembled by a Korean company, Hynix, that was alleged to have received substantial Korean government support. The US Department of Commerce levied antidumping duties on the Hynix chips after making a determination that the Korean government had pursued a policy of preventing the financial collapse of Hynix, held control or influence over groups of Hynix creditors, and pressured certain Hynix creditors into participating in the company's restructuring.[147] All of these allegations could only be ascertained by evidence from the past.

The law's focus on the past in these instances means that it is more susceptible to individuation. The situations pointed out above are illustrative of the way that the law "picks" individual instances out of the

[146] *U.S. – Lamb*, WT/DS177/R, para. 7.192 (21 Dec. 2000) [emphasis in original].

[147] *U.S. – DRAMS from Korea*, WT/DS296/AB/R, para. 152 (27 June 2005).

pattern of economic activity and holds them up to scrutiny. This is to be contrasted with the generality of the law emphasized in the previous chapter. Particularism and the stasis it infers also cause the law in this mode to be a law of discrete transactions wherein time is understood at a given instant, consistent with an *ex post* perspective and the idea of *kairos*, or singular decisive moment.

A good example of stasis is encountered in the implementation of countermeasures under DSU Art. 22. There, a specific "reference period" must be chosen for the purposes of determining the level of nullification or impairment that may be used as a basis for determining the amount of suspension of concessions or other obligations. The "reference period" constitutes the interval for calculating any definitive amount of countermeasures.

For example, in *U.S. – Tuna II (Mexico) (Art. 22.6 – US)* the dispute involved US measures setting out conditions under which tuna products sold in the United States could be labeled "dolphin-safe." After the initial determination in the dispute, the United States amended its tuna labeling measures. The Appellate Body found that the amended measure modified the competitive conditions to the detriment of Mexican tuna products inconsistently with GATT Arts. I:1 and III:4 and was not saved by the exceptions in GATT Art. XX. The Arbitrator had to determine the appropriate time-frame for the calculation of the level of nullification or impairment. The arbitrator observed:

> There is no rule in the DSU prescribing the time-frame for the determination of the level of nullification or impairment. Past Article 22.6 arbitration decisions indicate that the period of time for the arbitrator's determination of the level of nullification or impairment is usually the period that follows the end of the [reasonable period of time for compliance]. . . . In our view, the impact of the withdrawal of the Measure would be best captured in the period immediately following the withdrawal. Developments in the long-run would be less likely to be linked to withdrawal.[148]

In other cases the specific frame of certain years has been identified as constituting the appropriate time-frame.[149]

[148] *U.S. – Tuna II (Mexico) (Art. 22.6 – U.S.)*, WT/DS381/ARB, para. 4.14 (25 Apr. 2017).

[149] For example, in *U.S. – Washing Machines (Art. 22.6 – U.S.)*, WT/DS464/ARB (8 Feb. 2019) the appropriate time-frame was determined to be calendar year 2017, which was the end of the reasonable period for implementation. Similarly in *U.S. – Anti-Dumping Methodologies (China) (Art. 22.6 – U.S.)*, WT/DS471/ARB (1 Nov. 2019) when

5.3.4 *An Inductive Law*

I have already described the way in which the WTO Agreement as a law of fairness and rights looks retrospectively at the conditions within which rights are being exercised. Those conditions already exist. As such, they are fixed and can be determined according to available proof. The need for proof is emblematic of inductive reasoning.

In Chapter 4 I noted how WTO law can be said to be characterized in the first instance as being reasoned according to deductive reasoning – the reasoning of what "will be."[150] This is expressed in WTO law's heavy reliance on presumption and inference. However, in a second instance WTO law can be characterized by inductive reasoning – the logic of what "is" or "was" – based on proof.

Inductive reasoning begins with data or evidence from the past that is accumulated to support a conclusion. The data or evidence points to a conclusion that makes the conclusion probable. However, an inductive conclusion "is not inescapable, as it may be in deductive argument."[151] An inductive argument might run as follows:

1. Able drives his car into an intersection with a traffic light.
2. Able's car collides with Baker's car.
3. The following facts are led at a criminal trial:
    1. There are long skid marks behind Able's car.
    2. A pedestrian witness says Able ran a red light.
    3. Baker testifies that he (Baker) entered the intersection on a green light.
    4. Able denies that he (Able) entered the intersection on a red light.[152]

At the trial, favorable evidence points to a hypothetical conclusion, namely, that Able did indeed run the red light. Nevertheless, some evidence supports the conclusion and some denies it. "Since it is impossible to prove what happened in the past to a certainty, the jury decides whether the hypothetical conclusion is more likely than not, based on the evidence. 'More likely than not' conclusions to inductive arguments are

the reasonable period of time for the United States to implement expired in August 2018, the parties used calendar year 2017 as the reference period.

150 Roger Martin, *The Opposable Mind* 144–145 (Harvard Business School Press, Boston; 2007).

151 Ibid., p. 4.

152 Ibid., p. 8.

probable conclusions."[153] They converge at a result that makes that conclusion *likely*.

The most common form of inductive reasoning is proof.[154] Proof will be subject to the *burden of proof* – the question of which party has the obligation to provide proof in a given instance[155] – and weighed according to the *standard of proof*, the question of what degree of probability the proof must satisfy in order to conclusively sustain a legal point.[156]

As mentioned in Chapter 4, the standard of proof in WTO dispute settlement is the "preponderance of the evidence," which "requires panels to be convinced that the proposition at issue is at least more likely than not to be true."[157] The standard has been described as "closer to that of the balance of probabilities, and is not a standard of certainty or proof beyond a reasonable doubt."[158] It requires disputing parties to put forward what is commonly termed a *prima facie* case. Once the evidence has been received from both sides and arguments made, panels are in the position of asking "themselves whether that evidence supports a conclusion that the proposition advanced is . . . more likely than not to be true."[159]

The evidentiary process in WTO dispute settlement may appear strange and somewhat artificial, at least from a domestic law perspective, where pretrial disclosure is often important in resolving claims. That is because, apart from consultations, WTO dispute settlement lacks a pretrial discovery phase of proceedings where the parties exchange information. In addition, during panel proceedings it is usual that there are no witnesses, no experts, nor any jury. Instead, as Michelle Grando has

[153] Ibid., p. 9 [emphasis in original].

[154] "When evidence is capable of demonstrating a fact, it can be said that it constitutes 'proof' of that fact." Michelle Grando, *Evidence, Proof and Fact-Finding in WTO Dispute Settlement* 6 (Oxford University Press, Oxford; 2009). "Positive evidence" has been defined as relating "to the quality of the evidence upon which the authorities may rely in making a determination. The word 'positive' may be understood as meaning that the evidence must be of an affirmative, objective and verifiable character, and that it must be credible." *EC – Pipe Fittings*, WT/DS219/R, para. 7.226 (7 Mar. 2003).

[155] Grando, *Evidence, Proof and Fact-Finding* 70.

[156] Ibid., p. 86.

[157] Ibid., p. 357.

[158] *Saudi Arabia – IP Rights*, WT/DS567/R, para. 7.39 (16 June 2020), citing Panel Report, *Thailand – Cigarettes (Philippines) (Art. 21.5 – Philippines)*, WT/DS371/RW, para. 7.777 (12 Nov. 2018).

[159] Grando, *Evidence, Proof and Fact-Finding* 136.

pointed out, the process of fact-finding is "unitary" in the sense that there are no intermediate rulings on evidence and also "dynamic" in that fresh evidence may be admitted until fairly late in the panel process.[160] Panels also have broad power under DSU Art. 13 "to seek information and technical advice from any individual or body which it deems appropriate." Finally, the parties have a duty to collaborate in providing evidence.[161]

These possibilities suggest that it is not enough for a complainant in WTO dispute settlement simply to state its case and allow for the various presumptions mentioned in Chapter 4 to kick-in in order to prevail. Both complainants and defendants must provide both claims and arguments to buttress their positions, as well as supporting evidence.[162] Even in the case of uncontested claims, a panel is still bound to make an objective assessment of the measure and its operation before making its findings.[163]

As a result, parties engaged in WTO dispute settlement must furnish proof. Once again, the demand for proof is particularly noticeable in WTO rules disciplines in connection with the exercise of rights. In most instances, the inquiry is conducted in order to properly assess whether a national investigating authority has complied with the WTO Agreement in making its findings and, by extension, whether the country has acted properly in exercising attendant rights.

This fixed frame of reference – set in the past – allows the law to be concrete and precise. The relevant disciplines are heavily marked by the desire to objectify. Thus, SAF Art. 4.2(a) specifies that in assessing "serious injury" to a domestic industry, the competent authorities "shall evaluate all relevant factors *of an objective and quantifiable nature* having a bearing on the situation of that industry." In *U.S. – Lamb* the Appellate

160 "[O]wing to the fact that neither the DSU nor the Standard Working Procedures of Appendix 3 establish time limits for the submission of evidence to a panel, panels and the Appellate Body have been reluctant to decline to admit evidence during the second stage of the proceedings which could have been submitted earlier." Ibid., p. 52.

161 *EC – Hormones*, WT/DS26,48/AB/R, para. 11 (12 July 1999).

162
> [I]t is incumbent upon a party to identify in its submissions the relevance of the provisions of legislation – *the evidence* – on which it relies to support its arguments. It is not sufficient merely to file an entire piece of legislation and expect a panel to discover, on its own, what relevance the various provisions may or may not have for a party's legal position.
>
> (*Canada – Wheat Exports and Grain Imports*, WT/DS276/AB/R, para. 191 (30 Aug. 2004) [emphasis added].)

163 See *U.S. – Shrimp/Sawblades*, WT/DS422/R, paras. 7.5–7.7 (8 June 2012).

Body observed that the requirement of objectivity applies not only to relevant factors but also to data:

> We note that no provision of the Agreement on Safeguards specifically addresses the question of the extent of data collection, and in particular, whether competent authorities must have before them data that is representative of the domestic industry. However ... competent authorities are obliged to "evaluate" all relevant factors of an "objective and quantifiable" nature ... We recognize that the clause "of an objective and quantifiable nature" refers expressly to "factors," but not expressly to data. We are, however, convinced that factors can only be "of an objective and quantifiable nature" if they allow a determination to be made, as required by Article 4.2(b) of the Agreement on Safeguards, *on the basis of "objective evidence." Such evidence is, in principle, objective data.* The words "factors of an objective and quantifiable nature" imply, therefore, an evaluation of objective data which enables the measurement and quantification of these factors.[164]

Similar empiric requirements are found in the ADA and SCM and in the associated case law.[165] For instance, in ADA 3.7 it is noted that "a threat of material injury *shall be based on facts and not merely on allegation, conjecture or remote possibility.*" Identical wording is contained in SCM Art. 15.7.

Use of inductive reasoning is particularly visible in relation to questions of nonattribution and causation. All three major WTO rules disciplines require national investigating authorities not to attribute injury to imports that cannot be so attributed. The determination of this matter depends heavily on empiricism. Debate has ensued as to whether the causation test is satisfied *only* when increased imports, considered in isolation, are causing injury, or when they merely make "a contribution" toward all factors causing injury. In *U.S. – Wheat Gluten*, the Appellate Body took an intermediate position on the issue, holding that there must be "a *genuine and substantial relationship* of cause and effect" between increased imports and injurious effects.[166]

[164] *U.S. – Lamb*, WT/DS/177/AB/R, paras. 129–130 (1 May 2001) [emphasis added].

[165] For discussion of the standard in case law, see *U.S. – Hot Rolled*, WT/DS184/AB/R, para. 192 (24 July 2001), *Thailand – H Beams*, WT/DS122/R, para. 7.143 (28 Sept. 2000) (defining "positive evidence" as "formally or explicitly stated; definite, unquestionable *(positive proof)*") [emphasis in original]. Particularism is also noted in the standard of "special care" required by SCM Art. 15.8. See *U.S. – ITC Lumber*, WT/DS277/R, para. 7.53 (22 Mar. 2004).

[166] *U.S. – Wheat Gluten*, WT/DS166/AB/R, para. 69 (22 Dec. 2000).

In terms of causation, one key question is whether quantification and the use of econometric models are necessary to satisfy the legal standard. The panel in *U.S. – Steel Safeguards* observed:

> We note, first, that the text of the Agreement on Safeguards does not require quantification. However, in the Panel's view both the [SAF] and relevant jurisprudence anticipate that quantification may occur.
>
> In addition, the Panel considers that quantification may be particularly desirable in cases involving complicated factual situations where qualitative analyses may not suffice to more fully understand the dynamics of the relevant market. In support, we note that [SAF] Article 4.2(a) . . . refers to "factors of [a] quantifiable nature." As explained . . . we consider that Articles 4.2(a) and 4.2(b) must be read together and in a mutually consistent fashion. Therefore, the factors referred to in Article 4.2(a) must be taken into consideration in undertaking the non-attribution exercise (in addition to any other factors that may be relevant). In addition, the requirement in Article 4.2(a) that evaluated factors be of a "quantifiable nature" implies that at least some of the factors assessed in the non-attribution exercise will be quantifiable and, in those circumstances, should be quantified.[167]

The panel further noted an obligation on competent authorities to establish nonattribution explicitly on the basis of general duty to provide a "reasoned and adequate" explanation for their determination:

> the Panel considers that quantification may, in certain cases, be entailed in the obligation on competent authorities to establish non-attribution "explicitly" on the basis of a reasoned and adequate explanation. In this regard, the Panel recalls that . . . WTO Members are expected to interpret and apply their WTO obligations in good faith. Moreover, in light of the obligations imposed on competent authorities to consider all plausible alternative explanations submitted by the interested parties, *we believe that a competent authority may find itself in situations where quantification and some form of economic analysis are necessary to rebut allegedly plausible alternative explanations that have been put forward.* While the wording of the provisions of the Agreement on Safeguards does not require quantification in the causal link analysis per se, the circumstances of a specific dispute may call for quantification.[168]

[167] *U.S. – Steel Safeguards*, WT/DS252/R, paras. 10.336–10.337 (11 July 2003).

[168] Ibid., paras. 10.339–10.340 [emphasis added].

At the same time, the panel in *U.S. – Steel Safeguards* was quick to point out that any such quantification is not controlling:

> Having said that quantification may be desirable, useful and sometimes necessary depending on the circumstances . . . the Panel recognizes that quantification may be difficult and is less than perfect. Therefore, the Panel is of the view that the results of such quantification *may not necessarily be determinative. . . .*[169]

The panel added:

> We consider that an overall qualitative assessment that takes into account all relevant information, must always be performed. Nevertheless, in the Panel's view, even the most simplistic of quantitative analyses may yield useful insights into the overall dynamics of a particular industry and, in particular, into the nature and extent of injury being caused by factors other than increased imports to a domestic industry.[170]

The foregoing statements would appear to emphasize the way that a qualitative assessment based on deductive reasoning is required ("*must always* be performed") whereas a quantitative assessment based on inductive reasoning, while desirable, "may be difficult and is less than perfect" and therefore "may not necessarily be determinative." These comments strongly suggest the way that deductive reasoning takes precedence over inductive reasoning and appears to confirm the theoretic relation, Deduction > Induction.

The great difficulty with inductive reasoning and a purely proof-based approach in WTO law is the constrained nature of disclosure and fact-finding in WTO dispute settlement. As mentioned, parties are expected to cooperate in the production of evidence, an expectation that they occasionally fulfill with reluctance. This attitude has led panels and the Appellate Body to develop substantial jurisprudence concerning adverse inferences that may be drawn against a member where they fail to furnish evidence they might otherwise be expected to provide.[171] It is also tacitly at issue in recent controversy over the failure of many WTO members to notify subsidies and, in response, potential for expanded use of "counter notifications."[172]

[169] Ibid., para. 10.341 [emphasis added].

[170] Ibid., para. 10.341.

[171] See, for example, *Turkey – Rice*, WT/DS334/R, paras. 7.106–7.107 (21 Sept. 2007).

[172] Counter notifications allow factual determinations on the basis of evidence presented by a second party. Agreement on Agriculture Art. III:5 specifies that "[a]ny Member may counter-notify any measure taken by another Member which it considers affects the operation of the Agreement." In May 2018 the United States for the first time submitted a counter notification in the WTO Committee on Agriculture (COA) on India's market

5.4 Nonviolation

The great majority of disputes arising under the DSU are brought under GATT Art. XXIII:1(a) and involve claims of "nullification or impairment." The basis of such a claim is the fact that a member has failed to carry out its obligations under the WTO Agreement. Claims are more rarely brought under GATT Art. XXIII:1(b) – the so-called nonviolation clause – which allows action to be brought against a measure "whether *or not* it conflicts with" the treaty.

The nonviolation cause of action has long stood out as a puzzling anomaly in the GATT/WTO system. The WTO Agreement is a treaty and its consensual origins mean that in the normal course one would expect responsibility under international law to arise only in situations foreseen under the treaty. Consequently, commentators have struggled to understand how such a clause triggering responsibility for actions *outside* the treaty could have found its way into the WTO Agreement and have advanced a range of explanations for it. Some commentators have regarded nonviolation as a means of reinforcing treaty disciplines.[173] Others regard it as an expression of the more general duty of good faith.[174] Still others have concluded nonviolation to be superfluous and called for its elimination.[175]

I examine nonviolation here because it is most often associated with an assertion of rights, and to that extent, it is properly analyzed as part of a "law of rights." A communitarian theory is helpful in piecing together the

price support for wheat and rice. See "United States Issues First-Ever WTO Counter Notification against India's Market Price Support," US Department of Agriculture Press Release No. 0101.18 (5 May 2018).

[173] For work on nonviolation claims, see Sungjoon Cho, "GATT Non-Violation Issues in the WTO Framework" 39 *Harv. Int'l L. J.* 311 (1998); Thomas Cottier & Krista Schefer, "NVNI Complaints in WTO/GATT Dispute Settlement: Past, Present and Future" in Ernst-Ulrich Petersmann (ed.), *International Trade Law and the WTO/GATT Dispute Settlement System* 145 (Kluwer, The Hague; 1997); Marc Busch & Eric Reinhardt, "Bargaining in the Shadow of the Law" 24 *Fordham Int'l L. J.* 158 (2000); Robert Hudec, *Enforcing International Trade Law* (Butterworth Legal Publishers, Salem, NH; 1993); John Jackson, *World Trade and the Law of GATT* (Bobbs-Merrill, Indianapolis, IN; 1969); Andrew Mitchell, "Good Faith in WTO Dispute Settlement" 7 *Melbourne J. Int'l L.* 339 (2006).

[174] Marion Panizzon, *Good Faith in the Jurisprudence of the WTO* (Hart, Oxford; 2006).

[175] Frieder Roessler & Petina Gappah, "A Reappraisal of Non-Violation Complaints under the WTO Dispute Settlement Procedures" in Patrick McCory et al. (eds), *The World Trade Organization: Legal, Economic and Political Analysis* 1371 (Springer, New York; 2005).

puzzle of the nonviolation cause of action referred to above because it provides an idea of the broader background against which nonviolation claims are made as well as a specific place to locate them within. That background and place are ones that emanate from the law's intensely "systemic" aspect, its dislike of uncertainty and an emphasis on extended and indirect effects. As a result, a wide range of action is considered to give rise to breach. In short, a nonviolation cause of action can be thought of as embodying an anticircumvention principle.

Anticircumvention is critical to the integrity of the WTO system. It works to reinforce the requirements of WTO law and to sustain its legitimacy. The same function makes anticircumvention unusual. In most cases the established law should be enough to ascribe responsibility. To pursue responsibility beyond that should be considered extraordinary. Panels examining nonviolation claims have confirmed this view.[176]

The particular way in which a right constitutes a "claim" and the way it stresses "the benefit, the protection, the assurance, the individuality of the law" are helpful to understanding how nonviolation claims unfold and in explaining why they assume the peculiar form they do. Action for nonviolation requires an assertion by a member that its legitimate expectations have been breached. Case law has specified that such an action lies where three criteria are met:

(1) There is some benefit under the WTO Agreement.
(2) A member applies a nonviolating measure beyond or outside the treaty, for example, an income tax.

[176] In *Japan – Film*, WT/DS44/R (31 Mar. 1998) the panel observed:

> Although the non-violation remedy is an important and accepted tool of WTO/GATT dispute settlement and has been "on the books" for almost 50 years, we note that there have only been eight cases in which panels or working parties have substantively considered Article XXIII:1(b) claims. This suggests that both the GATT contracting parties and WTO Members have approached this remedy with caution and, indeed, have treated it as an exceptional instrument of dispute settlement . . . The reason for this caution is straightforward. Members negotiate the rules that they agree to follow and only exceptionally would expect to be challenged for actions not in contravention of those rules.
>
> (Ibid., para. 10.36)

(3) There is nullification or impairment of the negotiated benefit by the nonviolating measure.[177]

These criteria emphasize nonviolation's concern with the circumvention of treaty disciplines. The basic fear is that a WTO-consistent measure – such as an income tax – could be used indirectly to erode WTO concessions, commitments or benefits.

The substantive requirements of nonviolation are accompanied by certain procedural peculiarities. Under DSU Art. 26.1(a), "the complaining party shall present *a detailed justification* in support of any complaint." Under DSU Art. 26.1(b) there is "no obligation to withdraw the measure" but in such instances "the panel or Appellate Body shall recommend that the Member concerned make a mutually satisfactory adjustment." In addition, under DSU Art. 26.1(c) any arbitration over the reasonable period of time for implementation of dispute settlement results "may include a determination of the level of benefits which have been nullified or impaired." Finally, under DSU Art. 26.1(d) it is specified that "compensation may be part of a mutually satisfactory adjustment as final settlement of the dispute."

These requirements can be traced to nonviolation's roots in the assertion of rights. As explained in Chapter 2, the primary interest protected by WTO law is expectations of governments' trade-related behavior. In essence, all WTO member countries are supposed to enjoy the same expectation of trade with a given member. In a nonviolation claim, however, the basis of claim is the breach of expectations belonging to *one* particular country. A nonviolation claim, therefore, is meant to vindicate its particular expectations, or rights.

Additional proof of this point comes from the fact that like in the law of rights generally, the perspective in nonviolation cases is backward-looking and to that extent matters under consideration – including expectations – are taken to be "fixed."

Thus, in *Japan – Film* the panel questioned the US expectation of market access for American-made photographic film in Japan. It queried the US assertion that the US expectation of market access had not changed since Japan's concession on certain types of photographic film, originally made in 1964 and updated in 1979 and 1994:

> where the United States claims that it did not know of a measure's relevance to market access conditions in respect of film or paper, we would

[177] *Japan – Film*, WT/DS44/R, para. 10.41 (31 Mar. 1998).

> expect the United States to clearly demonstrate why initially it could not have reasonably anticipated the effect of an existing measure on the film or paper market and when it did realize the effect. Such a showing will need to be tied to the relevant points in time (i.e., the conclusions of the Kennedy, Tokyo and Uruguay Rounds) in order to assess the extent of the United States' legitimate expectations of benefits from these three Rounds.[178]

Notwithstanding its query, the panel determined that the US expectation of market access had been set as of certain fixed dates and was not affected by interim change.[179]

The same concern with individual rights explains nonviolation's broad scope. An anticircumvention provision applied in limited circumstances should be conceived liberally, and indeed, that is the way Art. XXIII:1(b) has been interpreted. For instance, in *EC – Asbestos* the Appellate Body held that a nonviolation claim founded in some violation outside the treaty could be made out "even if the measure 'conflicts' with some substantive provisions of the GATT 1994."[180] Similarly, the Appellate Body rejected the contention that a country might have "legitimate expectations" only with respect to commercial matters arising from tariff concessions and held that such expectations could arise from nontrade measures as well. Nonviolation linked to an assertion of rights is an ample concept because it is supplementary and assistive to obligations as the foundation of the normative order.

These statements, as well as the unconventional form and character of nonviolation claims, continue to perplex commentators. At base the

[178] Ibid., para. 10.80.

[179] There is, of course, an evident tension in reconciling the doctrine of fixity with ever-changing circumstances. In *EC – Asbestos*, WT/DS135, for instance, the panel held that Canada had failed to plead nonviolation with sufficient certainty and dismissed the claim. However, it also observed that:

> the accumulation of international and Community decisions concerning the use of asbestos, even if it did not necessarily make it certain that the use of asbestos would be banned . . . could not do other than create a *climate* which should have led Canada to anticipate a change in the attitude of the importing countries, especially in view of the long-established trend towards ever tighter restrictions on the use of asbestos.
>
> (Ibid., para. 8.297 (18 Sept. 2000) [emphasis in original])

In other words, Canada's reasonable expectations of market access derived from tariff negotiations in the 1970s could be anticipated to have changed as international attitudes about the safety of asbestos changed.

[180] WT/DS135/AB/R, para. 187 (12 Mar. 2001).

concern appears grounded in the search for justifiable limits to the concept. Perhaps for this reason many commentators have pointed to nonviolation's close connection with the principle of good faith, a connection highlighted in *Korea – Government Procurement*.[181] In that case the issue was incomplete answers given by Korean negotiators to US counterparts during negotiations over the extent of commitments under the WTO Government Procurement Agreement. The commitments later became an issue in the construction of a new international airport in South Korea for which US contractors were unable to bid. The panel found the absence of a negotiated commitment by Korea and hence no violation.[182] Nevertheless, the panel indicated a willingness to consider the US claim "flowing in part from the panel's belief that nonviolation should be interpreted against the backdrop of customary international law and, in particular, the principle that treaty commitments must be performed in good faith."[183] Robert Staiger and Alan Sykes conclude from the case that "the function of non-violation claims is to address deceit and other forms of opportunistic behaviour."[184]

The theory put forward in this book suggests a somewhat broader role for nonviolation than simply the promotion of good faith. Case law infers that an ordinary violation of WTO law is not itself bad faith. Something additional is required to vindicate a claim of bad faith, possibly intent.[185]

Anticircumvention as the foundation for nonviolation claims is ultimately grounded in the exercise of rights. As in the case of abuse of rights, anticircumvention is fundamentally concerned with whether a country misuses its rights, either knowingly or not. To that extent, it is an objective as opposed to a subjective concept.

This realization infers that a continuing search for limits to nonviolation may be unnecessary and even counterproductive. Nonviolation

181 WT/DS163/R (1 May 2000).

182 Ibid., para. 7.119.

183 Robert Staiger & Alan Sykes, "Non-Violation" 16:4 *J.I.E.L.* 741 at 752 (2013).

184 Ibid., at 753.

185 See *US – Offset Act (Byrd Amendment)*, WT/DS217/AB/R, para. 298 (16 Jan. 2003). "Nothing, however, in the covered agreements supports the conclusion that simply because a WTO Member is found to have violated a substantive treaty provision, it has therefore not acted in good faith. In our view, it would be necessary to prove more than mere violation to support such a conclusion." See also *Korea – Government Procurement*, WT/DS163/R, para. 7.99 (1 May 2000).

must continue to have a degree of flexibility in order for it to remain able to respond to many and varying misuses of rights that may take place in future. Its contours will remain justifiably ill-defined and vague.[186]

5.5 Implementation

In the section "Countermeasures" above I examined the exercise of rights that arises in the context of countermeasures under DSU Art. 22. This exercise involves compliance with the *obligation* to implement DSB recommendations and rulings. At the same time, implementation also inevitably involves the exercise by members of their sovereign *rights* in the sense that defendants must determine when and how they will implement.

There are three determinations that are linked to implementation:

(1) the decision of an arbitrator concerning the reasonable period of time (RPT) for implementation under DSU Art. 21.3
(2) the decision of an arbitrator concerning compliance at the end of the RPT under DSU Art. 21.5 (with the possibility of an appeal)
(3) the decision of an arbitrator concerning the level of proposed countermeasures under DSU Art. 22.6

The last of these determinations I have already examined above as it pertains to countermeasures. The first two involve implementation by defendants. Each of these determinations is varied and invokes "fairness" considerations.

Following adoption by the DSB of a panel or Appellate Body report, the defendant member has an obligation of prompt compliance under DSU Art. 21.1. At the same time, "[i]f it is impracticable to comply immediately . . . the Member concerned shall have a reasonable period of time in which to do so" under DSU Art. 21.3, a matter which, in the absence of agreement, is to be determined by arbitration.

[186] For example, under TRIPS Art. 64.2 a temporary moratorium on nonviolation was agreed and continues. The moratorium recognizes the controversial nature of many TRIPS commitments. At least two WTO members (the United States and Switzerland) maintain that nonviolation cases should be allowed under TRIPS in order to discourage members from engaging in "creative legislative activity" that would enable them to get around their TRIPS commitments. Most members would like to see the moratorium continued or made permanent. Some members have suggested additional safeguards to prevent circumvention of TRIPS commitments.

For example, in *US – Washing Machines (Art. 21.3(c))* the arbitrator interpreted "prompt compliance" under DSU Art. 21.1 and "a reasonable period" under the chapeau of DSU Art. 21.3 to mean a member shall comply in as short a period as possible.[187] Moreover, in assessing the interval of what is "reasonable" the arbitrator in *EC – Sugar (Art. 21.3(c))* identified three relevant "governing principles" to guide a determination:

1. The reasonable period of time should be the shortest period of time possible within the legal system of the implementing member.
2. The implementing member must utilize all the flexibility and discretion available within its legal and administrative system in order to implement within the shortest period of time possible.
3. The "particular circumstances" of the case must be taken into account in determining the reasonable period of time.[188]

In *Canada – Pharmaceutical Patents (Art. 21.3(c))*, the Arbitrator defined "particular circumstances" in DSU Art. 21.3 determinations as those that can influence what the shortest period possible for implementation may be within the legal system of the implementing member:

> The "particular circumstances" mentioned in Article 21.3 are, therefore, those that can influence what the shortest period possible for implementation may be within the legal system of the implementing Member. Conceivably, several such "particular circumstances," depending on the facts, could be relevant to a case such as the one before me.
>
> . . . There may well be other "particular circumstances" that may be relevant to a particular case. However, in my view, the "particular circumstances" mentioned in Article 21.3 do *not* include factors unrelated to an assessment of the shortest period possible for implementation within the legal system of a Member. Any such unrelated factors are irrelevant to determining the "reasonable period of time" for implementation. For example . . . any proposed period intended to allow for the "structural adjustment" of an affected domestic industry will not be relevant to an assessment of the legal process. The determination of a "reasonable period of time" must be a legal judgement based on an examination of relevant legal requirements.[189]

A wide range of such factors has been canvassed by arbitrators.[190]

[187] WT/DS464/RPT, para. 3.7 (13 Apr. 2017).

[188] *EC – Sugar (Art. 21.3(c))*, WT/DS265/33, para. 61 (28 Oct. 2005).

[189] *Canada – Pharmaceutical Patents (Art. 21.3(c))*, WT/DS114/13, paras. 48 and 52 (18 Aug. 2000) [emphasis in original].

[190] These include the need to implement through legislative action versus administrative decisions, requirements to comply with other WTO obligations or decisions of other

With respect to compliance itself, the arbitrator in *U.S. – Tuna II (Mexico) (Art. 22.6 – U.S.)* noted, "It is well established that it is for the responding party to choose how to implement DSB recommendations and rulings. Consequently, there is no prescribed manner of complying; the responding party may choose to withdraw the measure at issue in its totality or appropriately modify its WTO-inconsistent aspects."[191]

The particular "mechanics" of withdrawal or modification are for the implementing country to determine:

> [T]he non-conforming measure is to be brought into a state of conformity with specified treaty provisions either by withdrawing such measure completely, or by modifying it by excising or correcting the offending portion of the measure involved. Where the non-conforming measure is a statute, a repealing or amendatory statute is commonly needed. Where the measure involved is an administrative regulation, a new statute may or may not be necessary, but a repealing or amendatory regulation is commonly required.[192]

The legal machinery in the implementing country is also considered distinct from the underlying economic, social or other circumstances that constitute the broader background against which the legislation in question is applied:

> Compliance within the meaning of the DSU is distinguishable from the removal or modification of the underlying economic or social or other conditions the existence of which might well have caused or contributed to the enactment or application of the WTO-inconsistent governmental measure in the first place. Those economic or other conditions might, in certain situations, survive the removal or modification of the nonconforming measure; nevertheless, the WTO Member concerned will have complied with the DSB recommendations and rulings and with its obligations under the relevant covered agreement. To my mind, it is inter alia for the above reason that the need for structural adjustment of the industry or industries in respect of which the WTO-inconsistent measure was promulgated and applied, has generally been regarded, in prior arbitrations under Article 21.3(c) of the DSU, as not bearing upon the determination of a "reasonable period of time" for implementation.[193]

international organizations, natural disasters, complexity of implementation, and measures fundamentally integrated into other policies. See WTO Analytical Index entry for DSU Art. 21 (Jurisprudence) (consulted 7 July 2022).

191 *U.S. – Tuna II (Mexico)*, WT/DS381/ARB, para. 4.4 (25 Apr. 2017).

192 *Argentina – Hides (Art. 21.3(c))*, WT/DS155/10, para. 40 (31 Aug. 2001).

193 Ibid., para. 41.

At the same time, in the absence of a "solution mutually acceptable to the parties," the DSU expresses a preference for "withdrawal" of the measures concerned. Consequently, withdrawal of measures has commonly been used as the metric in the selection of counterfactuals against which non-compliance is determined.[194]

In addition, in *EC – Sugar (21.3(c))* it was noted that the right to implement is not entirely unfettered:

> the implementing Member does not have an unfettered right to choose any method of implementation. Besides being consistent with the Member's WTO obligations, the chosen method must be such that it could be implemented within a reasonable period of time in accordance with guidelines contained in Article 21.3(c). Objectives that are extraneous to the recommendations and rulings of the DSB in the dispute concerned may not be included in the method if such inclusion were to prolong the implementation period. Above all, it is assumed that the implementing Member will act in "good faith" in the selection of the method that it deems most appropriate for implementation of the recommendations and rulings of the DSB.[195]

Review of compliance may occur under DSU Art. 21.5. The review is limited to measures taken to comply.[196] This will include measures that are identified as "inextricably linked" and "clearly connected" to the measure(s) taken to comply.[197]

[194] Counterfactuals have been used in several WTO arbitration proceedings. In *EC – Bananas III*, the arbitrator compared the value of relevant EC imports from the United States under the actual banana import regime with their value under a hypothetical WTO-consistent regime. *EC – Bananas III (US) (Art. 22.6 – EC)*, WT/DS27/ARB, para. 7.1 (9 Apr. 1999). In *Canada – Aircraft (Art. 22.6 – Canada)* the arbitrator noted how prior arbitrators had used a "counterfactual approach" by comparing the existing situation with that which would have occurred "had implementation taken place as of the expiration of the reasonable period of time." *Canada – Aircraft (Art. 22.6 – Canada)*, WT/DS222/ARB, para. 3.21 (17 Feb. 2003). Similarly, in *EC – Hormones* the arbitrator based its analysis on what the complaining party's exports of the relevant product to the respondent would have been had the latter withdrawn the measure at the end of the reasonable period of time for implementation. *EC – Hormones (Canada) (Art. 22.6 – EC)*, WT/DS27/ARB/ECU, paras. 166–170 (24 Mar. 2000). In *US – COOL* arbitration the arbitrator also decided to use a counterfactual that assumed that the COOL measure was withdrawn at the end of the reasonable period of time. *US – COOL (Art. 22.6)*, WT/DS384, para. 6.32 (7 Dec. 2015).

[195] *EC – Sugar (Art. 21.3(c))*, WT/DS265/33, para. 69 (28 Oct. 2005).

[196] *U.S. – Softwood Lumber IV (Art. 21.5 – Canada)*, WT/DS257/AB/RW, para. 66 (5 Dec. 2005).

[197] *Colombia – Textiles (Art. 21.5 – Colombia)/Colombia – Textiles (Art. 21.5 – Panama)*, WT/DS461/RW, para. 7.81 (27 Nov. 2015).

The obligation to comply with recommendations and rulings continues until measures taken to comply are fully consistent with a WTO member's concessions and commitments. As indicated by the panel in *U.S. – FSC (Art. 21.5 – EC – II)*, "[t]hese [recommendations and rulings] remain operative through compliance panel proceedings under Article 21.5 of the DSU *until the 'problem' is entirely 'fixed'* "[198]

5.6 Conclusion

This chapter has examined WTO law as a law of rights expressing justice-as-fairness. A communitarian theory of justice posits that fairness is essentially a matter of what is "fitting" or "appropriate." The central question in virtually every instance of fairness in WTO law is, has a member country exercised its rights fittingly or appropriately? The language and jurisprudence of "appropriate" countermeasures in SCM Art. 4.10 and "commensurate" countermeasures in SCM Art. 7.9 appear to offer particularly striking confirmation of this abiding idea.

Another way of asking the same question is, has a WTO member met the preconditions necessary to exercise the relevant right? I have illustrated how the law in this idea-complex is heavily preoccupied with conditionality, proportionality and mutuality, all being qualifications that contrast starkly with the plenary and unconditional nature of WTO law as a law of equality implemented through obligations. Justice as-fairness promotes a law of specific circumstances.[199] Its associated themes are those of particularity, constraint and limitation. In short, rights are recognized interstitially through fairness for the greater purpose of achieving equality (i.e. Equality > Fairness).

198 *U.S. – FSC (Art. 21.5 – EC II)*, WT/DS108/RW2, para. 7.36 (30 Sept. 2005) [emphasis added].

199 For example, in *U.S. – Gasoline*, WT/DS2/AB/R (29 Apr. 1996) the Appellate Body observed how analysis of GATT Art. XX is effected through a case-by-case reconciliation of obligations with rights: "The relationship between the affirmative commitments set out in, e.g., Articles I, III and XI, and the policies and interests embodied in the 'General Exceptions' listed in Article XX, can be given meaning within the framework of the General Agreement and its object and purpose by a treaty interpreter *only on a case-to-case basis.*" Ibid., p. 16 [emphasis added]. There is, in other words, a circumstantial aspect to fairness. Justice is only done from instance to instance, as noted in Chapter 1.

What is perhaps most notable in law of this type is its tremendous fragmentation and specification. In so being, the law naturally gives rise to a demand for unity. Commentators have observed, for instance, how the tremendous variety of outcomes in rules determinations, in retaliation and in the array of RTAs in existence today gives rise to inconsistency and calls for further unifying discipline.

Could fairness and a law of rights be generalized, in effect becoming the dominant mode in WTO law? They could, but experience suggests that their operation would be problematic, as appears to be evident from the immediate experience of WTO law. As mentioned in Chapter 2, the prevailing environment of WTO law is one in which rights claims are being asserted with vigor, a vigor that threatens the viability of the system and erodes its community.

At the same time, it is useful to remember that the current preoccupation with fairness – or unfairness – of WTO arrangements may not be so unprecedented. A similar impulse was observed under GATT 1947.

In 1990 Robert Hudec examined the context of fairness claims in US foreign trade policy.[200] Hudec was writing from the vantage point of the late 1980s, an era when many traditional US industries were under attack from overseas manufacturers, notably those in Japan. Hudec tied fairness claims in international trade to domestic US concerns about ensuring a "level playing field."

The nub of the concern with fairness at that time, as Hudec saw it, was that:

> the rhetorical image of a level playing field is somewhat fanciful to the extent that it portrays competitors grappling for commercial success in some pristine environment free of external influences. The modern world has never known such a government-free state of nature. Government is everywhere.[201]

Hudec therefore attacked the notion of fairness in international trade law as selective and politically motivated. Conceptually, he suggested it was bereft of meaning.

At the same time, Hudec was also clear that fairness can be politically advantageous since it highlights an important *quid pro quo*:

> It is agreed that trade remedies will be provided to "correct" certain highly visible claims of unfairness, in exchange for the business community's

[200] Hudec, "Mirror, Mirror, on the Wall" 227.
[201] Ibid., p. 258.

> acceptance of a generally liberal trade policy, and with the reservation that fairness claims will not be allowed to threaten the main contours of that liberal policy.[202]

Hudec observed – presciently it appears – how "[t]he greatest danger posed by the current attachment to fairness concepts in international trade policy is the possibility that those concepts *will be used to attack almost all foreign trade*."[203] This eventuality appears to have happened in the recent past in a number of developments: in the growth of contingent protection, a return to "managed trade," in the retreat into regionalism, and the proliferation of defenses invoking the ill-defined "national security" exception of GATT Art. XXI.[204]

In his own time, Hudec concluded resignedly:

> The fairness debate goes on. As long as trade policy continues to worship at the shrine of fairness, trade policy advocates will try to satisfy the relentless demands for proof that trade is fair. The fact that fairness concepts make no sense in international trade matters will not excuse the need to employ them.[205]

In this chapter and book, I have taken a somewhat different view of fairness than Hudec did. I agree with him that fairness is heavily subjective, but I do not agree that "fairness makes *no sense* in international trade matters."

Instead, as part of the theory of justice, I posit that fairness lies at the heart of what is just and that it *is* possible to identify a core meaning of the term. Fairness has a "stable content," a content that though often subjective in expression is a matter of what is fitting or appropriate

202 Ibid., p. 279.

203 Ibid., p. 263 [emphasis added].

204 GATT Art. XXI was never formally invoked in dispute settlement under GATT. In response to its widespread use as a justification for trade measures taken against Argentina during the Falklands/Malvinas War of 1982, the GATT Contracting Parties adopted a "Decision Concerning Article XXI of the General Agreement" which laid out procedural guidelines for its invocation. See GATT Doc. L/5426, B.I.S.D. 29th Supp. 23 (1982). *Russia – Traffic in Transit*, WT/DS512, constitutes the first time that the exception has been formally considered in WTO dispute settlement. See the exception's invocation in *Ukraine - Ammonium Nitrate (Russia)*, WT/DS493; *U.S. - Steel and Aluminium Products (China)*, WT/DS544; *U.S. - Origin Marking (Hong Kong, China)*, WT/DS597.

205 Hudec, "Mirror, Mirror, on the Wall" 278.

traceable to the assertion of rights, to contractual structures, to a retrospective and *ex post* perspective, and to inductive logic. For that reason it is worth paying attention to. Claims of unfairness are really about responding fittingly or appropriately how things are – or were – in a manner consistent with community.

6

The WTO Agreement as a *Sui Generis* Legal System

6.1 Introduction

As mentioned, time is an active element in a communitarian theory of WTO law. Across the passage of time, the idea-complexes of obligations and rights identified in previous chapters interact in their pursuit of justice-as-equality and justice-as-fairness, bringing about law in a third overarching idea-complex. This takes the form of a *sui generis* legal system generating transformation.

In Chapter 3 I pointed out how this triune form of justice is never "perfect" but instead constitutes the best present estimate of equality and fairness. These ideals work together for the purpose of promoting interdependence and sustaining community.

Interdependence then is the ultimate product of the law.[1] It is inherent in its arrangement. As explained, the foundation of the WTO Agreement

[1] Interdependence originates in our biology and is a factor that has been pointed to by theorists and commentators of international law. Emmerich de Vattel observed in *The Law of Nations* (Carnegie Institute of Washington, Washington, DC; 1916 [1758]):

> Such is man's nature that he is not sufficient unto himself and necessarily stands in need of the assistance and intercourse of his fellows, whether to preserve his life or to perfect himself and live as befits a rational animal . . . From this source we deduce a natural society existing among all men. The general law of the society is that each member should assist the others in all their needs, as far as he can do so without neglecting his duties to himself - a law which all men must obey if they are to live comformably to their nature and to the designs of their common Creator; a law which our own welfare, our happiness, and our best interests should render sacred to each of us. Such is the general obligation we are under of performing our duties; let us fulfil them with care if we would work wisely for our greatest good.
>
> (Ibid., p. 5, quoted in Philip Allott, *The Health of Nations* 414, n. 6 (Cambridge University Press, Cambridge; 2002))

as a legal system rests in members' interdependent obligations and rights. One legal element – an obligation – is the correlative of another – a right (i.e. Obligation/Right).[2]

Still, WTO law has difficulty accommodating interdependence. That is because in specific instances, obligations and rights tend to be analyzed separately or through the lens of various principles or doctrines that implicitly isolate them, neatly stripping away the broader systemic context. Only rarely are they considered together.

If the conventional approach to legal analysis is set aside, however, then a more coordinated and intelligible image emerges, one which recognizes the role of the legal elements involved as working in tandem. The image is one that, like the warp and weft of a textile, comes together from one moment to the next as justice is done in an ongoing process of transformation. In that process the fundamental relation between "the

In the 1920s and 1930s, commentators such as Georges Scelle, Alfred Verdross and Louis Le Fur mentioned "solidarity," "justice" and "interdependence" as part of sociologic theories of international law. See, for instance, Georges Scelle, *Précis de Droit des Gens* 2–3 (Recueil Sirey, Paris; 1932). For an account, see Martti Koskenniemi, *The Gentle Civilizer of Nations* ch. 4 (Cambridge University Press, Cambridge; 2001). Interdependence has also been recognized at a political level by leading statespersons: see, for instance, Kofi Annan, "The Meaning of the International Community," UN Press Release, SG/SM/7133, PI/1176 (15 Sept. 1999) ("Ours is a world in which no individual, and no country, exists in isolation. All of us live simultaneously in our own communities and in the world at large ... We are connected, wired, interdependent."); Tony Blair, "What I've Learned" 383:8531 *The Economist* (2 June 2007) (referring to interdependence as "the defining characteristic of the modern world"); The White House, "Remarks on a New Beginning" made to students at Cairo University (4 June 2009) (Barack Obama observing that "Given our interdependence, any world order that elevates one nation or group of people over another will inevitably fail. So whatever we think of the past, we must not be prisoners to it. Our problems must be dealt with through partnership; our progress must be shared.").

2 I have already mentioned some qualification to this keystone idea in WTO law, notably in the evolving WTO habit of referring to certain organs and bodies as having obligations and powers without it being entirely clear who holds the corresponding rights or liabilities. A number of commentators in domestic law have also questioned this neat correlation and pointed out that, in certain instances, legal relations give rise to irregular relationships unforeseen in strict Hohfeldian terms. See Peter Jaffey, "Hohfeld's Power-Liability/Right-Duty Distinction in the Law of Restitution" 17:2 *Can. J. L. & Jurisprudence* 295 (2004); Stephen Smith, "A Duty to Make Restitution" 26 *Can. J. L. & Jurisprudence* 157 (2013) (arguing that rather than imposing duties to make restitution rules governing impaired transfers in restitution impose only liabilities, in particular liabilities to judicial orders on judgments).

One and the Many"[3] is worked out, and the sum of all relations displays its design in the fabric of a legal system.

Philip Allott has noted:

> A society interacts with itself in all of its socially organized becoming . . . Such an organizing is, in social consciousness, an endless cycle of interaction, every aspect interacting with every other, modifying every other, all of them interacting with the rest of reality-made-by-consciousness, including all the words and ideas and theories and values of the given society.[4]

The interaction Allott describes culminates in "a self-creating structure-system for the socializing of [right] and obligation."[5] It is this structure that must be assembled out of the elements examined in previous chapters.

6.2 A Just Law

The interaction of justice-as-equality and justice-as-fairness together results in a law that is just. As mentioned, this is not "perfect" justice nor is it necessarily consistent with justice as it is usually understood correctively. Rather, in this mode justice is what will sustain interdependence.

However, interdependence is not an unalloyed good or problem-free. It has both positive and negative aspects. On the one hand, the supply and value chains that are facilitated by WTO rules are undeniably productive. As a result of globalization in the past few decades, the international economy has grown as never before.[6] On the other hand, experts have noticed a recurrent feature. This is the fact that as supply and value chains mature and their outputs become subject to greater

[3] Philip Allott has referred to "the One and Many" as a shorthand for the dilemma of power: "A person and a society *are one and many*. The dilemma of power is the struggle to create a systematic relationship between the one and the many . . . Consciousness synthesizes as readily as it analyzes, generalizes as readily as it particularizes, integrates and unifies as readily as it separates and multiplies." Philip Allott, *Eunomia* 60–61 (Oxford University Press, Oxford; 1990) [emphasis added].

[4] Ibid. at 51.

[5] Ibid. at 52.

[6] The World Bank GDP statistics indicate that worldwide GDP per capita increased 73 percent from US $8,926 in 1990 to US $15,469 in 2017. See https://ourworldindata.org/economic-growth (GDP per capita table).

competition, power shifts to the end of the chain.[7] Stuart Macauley observes:

> Continuing relationships are not necessarily nice. The value of arrangements locks some people into dependent positions. They can only take orders. The actual lines of bureaucratic structure may be much more extensive than formal ones. Seemingly independent actors may have little real freedom and discretion in light of the costs of offending dominant parties. Once they face some costs and comfortable patterns, the possibility of command rather than negotiation increases.[8]

The impact of what Macauley describes is significant. The increased specialization and interchangeability of labor have given rise in many countries to a "gig" economy and to a precariat exposed to shifting tides of economic fortune.

More recently, considerable attention has focused on interdependence opening up possibilities for monopolistic behavior, and in some instances, monopsony, the scenario of a single buyer who can dictate terms that impact the rest of the supply chain. Intensive interdependence also creates opportunities for its "weaponization."[9]

WTO dispute settlement provides numerous descriptions of the material changes wrought by the ever-greater interdependence promoted by WTO arrangements. In *U.S. – Underwear*, for example, the panel described the overseas extension of the US textile and clothing industry during the early 1990s as follows:

> In the course of the last six years, there has been a significant change in the US cotton and manmade fibre underwear manufacturing industry which has significantly switched from producing and assembling underwear domestically to producing components in the United States for assembly in other countries and subsequent return to the same enterprises

[7] William Copacino, *Supply Chain Management* 42 (St. Lucie Press, Boca Raton, FL; 1997).

[8] Stewart Macaulay, "An Empirical View of Contract" 1985 *Wis. L. Rev.* 465 at 469 (1985).

[9] "The fact that production is integrated through global supply chains means that certain advantaged states can use their positions in crucial hubs of networks to 'extract informational advantages vis-à-vis adversaries,' and they can also 'cut adversaries off from network flows'." See Amrita Narlikar, "A Grand Bargain to Revive the WTO" in Oonagh Fitzgerald (ed.), *Modernizing the World Trade Organization: A CIGI Essay Series* 93 at 94–95 (Centre for International Governance Innovation, Waterloo, Ontario; 2020). Narlikar cites from Henry Farrell & Abraham L. Newman, "Weaponized Interdependence: How Global Economic Networks Shape State Coercion" 44:1 *Intl Security* 42 (2019).

> in the United States for marketing. This pattern of co-production has enabled the companies in this industry to maintain their share of the US market by making use of the labour force available outside the country while at the same time controlling the source of raw materials, the production timetable, the types and amounts of underwear to be produced and the marketing of the final product. Moreover, these co-production operations were consistent with the policies of the United States, which was encouraging investment and production in Mexico and the Caribbean Basin.[10]

Likewise in *Mexico – Telecoms* the panel observed that:

> basic telecommunications services supplied between Members do require, during the delivery of the service, a high degree of interaction between each other's networks, since the service typically involves a continuous, rapid and often two-way flow of intangible customer and operator data. The interaction results in a seamless service between the originating and terminating segments, which suggests that the service be considered as a single, cross-border service.[11]

At a substantive level, interdependence has a profound impact on how actors and interests are conceived. Unity is all-important. The underlying matter is thought about as one, as was evident in *EC – Bananas III*. There, the EC objected to US participation in the retaliation phase of a dispute about the EC's discriminatory banana tariff on the grounds that the United States lacked an export interest in bananas. In dismissing the EC's objection the arbitrator observed:

> Indeed, with the increased interdependence of the global economy, which means that actions taken in one country are likely to have significant effects on trade and foreign direct investment flows in others, Members have a greater stake in enforcing WTO rules than in the past since any deviation from the negotiated balance of rights and obligations is more likely than ever to affect them, directly or indirectly. Since the United States is likely to be affected by the EC regime, it would have an interest in a determination of whether the EC regime is inconsistent with the requirements of WTO rules. Thus, in our view a Member's potential interest in trade in goods or services and its interest in a determination of rights and obligations under the WTO Agreement are each sufficient to establish a right to pursue a WTO dispute settlement proceeding.[12]

[10] *United States – Underwear*, WT/DS24/R, para. 2.1 (8 Nov. 1996).

[11] *Mexico – Telecommunications Services*, WT/DS204/R, para. 7.38 (2 Apr. 2004).

[12] *EC – Bananas III*, WT/DS27/R/USA, para. 7.50 (22 May 1997). See also *Korea – Dairy*, WT/DS98/R, para. 7.14 (12 Jan. 2000).

Inherent in the arbitrator's position is the view that WTO obligations are owed to all, become the property of all, and therefore may be protected by all. It suggests that, as in biology, a purely reductivist approach to analysis focused on the interests of a single actor means something vital is lost.[13]

At the same time, there have been exhortations by panels and the Appellate Body concerning the change in outlook necessary for intensive interdependence, or in other words, the way it requires a shift in thinking. For example, in *U.S. – Gasoline* the Appellate Body observed that while the introduction of baseline emission requirements for "clean" gasoline was considered unfeasible in the domestic context, there was "nothing in the record to indicate that [the U.S.] did other than disregard that kind of consideration when it came to foreign refiners." The Appellate Body concluded that "[t]he resulting discrimination must have been foreseen, and was not merely inadvertent or unavoidable."[14] Likewise in *U.S. – Clove Cigarettes*, the panel noted that "[i]t seems to us that the effect of banning cigarettes with characterizing flavours other than menthol is to impose costs on producers in other Members, notably producers in Indonesia, while at the same time imposing no costs on any U.S. entity."[15] These criticisms can be understood as a call to governments to consider more than their own interests in setting trade policy.[16]

Expansive pronouncements dictated by the fact of growing interdependence can be contrasted with certain provisions in the WTO

[13] Marjorie Grene & David Depew, *The Philosophy of Biology* 311 (Cambridge University Press, Cambridge; 2004) (noting the view of many prominent biologists that "something important about complex wholes is lost if they are conceived solely in terms of their least parts.").

[14] WT/DS2/AB/R, p. 28 (29 Apr. 1996).

[15] WT/DS406/R, para. 7.289 (2 Sept. 2011).

[16] Indeed, as part of WTO arrangements, they are now in many instances required to do so. For instance, TBT Art. 2.9 includes obligations requiring notification and comment in national standard-setting "[w]henever a relevant international standard does not exist or the technical content of a proposed technical regulation is not in accordance with the technical content of relevant international standards." Likewise, SPS Art. 3.4 provides that "Members shall play a full part, within the limits of their resources, in the relevant international organizations and their subsidiary bodies, in particular the Codex Alimentarius Commission, the International Office of Epizootics, to promote within these organizations the development and periodic review of standards, guidelines and recommendations with respect to all aspects of sanitary and phytosanitary measures."

Agreement that restrict its recognition since interdependence is potentially limitless. The restriction is especially notable in relation to the assertions of rights, in particular *who* may assert rights.

An example is the case of safeguards. Whereas the WTO Safeguards Agreement contains a relatively broad definition of who can initiate and participate in a safeguard investigation, it restricts consideration of the effects of serious injury to effects on producers of like or directly competitive products.[17]

Another example where interdependence is problematic is in "pass-through" analysis conducted in the context of investigations aimed at potential countervail action. The aim of such investigations is to determine whether subsidies have bestowed a benefit on an imported product. The particular issue in "pass-through" analysis is to assess whether there has been a passing through of benefit in situations of either a change of ownership of an enterprise or the use of subsidized inputs "passed through" to downstream users of a product. In both situations current WTO law holds that no presumption of "pass-through" applies. Instead, in line with the assertion of rights, proof appears necessary.[18]

[17] The WTO Safeguards Agreement does not establish specific standards for the decision to initiate a safeguard. SAF Art. 3.1 provides that "[a] Member may apply a safeguard measure only following an investigation by the competent authorities ... This investigation shall include reasonable public notice *to all interested parties* and public hearings or other appropriate means in which importers, exporters and other interested parties could present evidence and their views." In *Ukraine – Passenger Cars*, WT/DS468/R (26 June 2015) the panel observed that SAF Art. 3 "does not define the term 'interested parties'. Nevertheless, it makes clear that the term 'interested parties' at a minimum includes importers and exporters. In addition, it refers to 'other interested parties', without qualification." Ibid., para. 7.403.

[18] *U.S. – Lead and Bismuth II*, WT/DS138; *U.S. – Softwood Lumber IV*, WT/DS257/AB/R, para. 143, noting that:

> Where the input producers and producers of the processed products operate at *arm's length*, the passthrough of input subsidy benefits from the direct recipients to the indirect recipients downstream cannot simply be presumed; it must be established by the investigating authority. In the absence of such analysis, it cannot be shown that the essential elements of the subsidy definition in Article 1 are present in respect of the *processed product.*
>
> ([emphasis in original])

Consideration of interdependence is also restricted in the case of countermeasures under DSU Art. 22. Arbitrators reviewing proposed amounts of retaliation for the purposes of countermeasures "equivalent to the level of nullification or impairment" have limited the effects they will take into account in their assessment of proposals for equivalent retaliation.[19]

Given these contrasting attitudes in the treaty and associated references to interdependence, it is not surprising that the institutional response to it in the WTO is mixed. To some extent the organization speaks for the membership as a whole, a fact might be taken to reflect an interest in promoting interdependence.

A reflection of this interest is the WTO Secretariat's launch of a "Made in the World Initiative" (MIWI) in 2010. The basic concept behind MIWI is to provide a better evaluation of the contribution of international trade to national economies as well as the contribution of services to trade and improved assessments of "value added." MIWI's kick-off crystallized in the form of a report, *Trade Patterns and Global Value Chains in East Asia*.[20]

The central premise of MIWI and the *Trade Patterns* report is that national borders do not matter as much as they once did. The report observes "that much of [international] trade these days comprises components or intermediate goods and services that pass from economy to economy before becoming part of a final traded product." The report notes that:

> The distinction between "them" and "us" that has traditionally defined our way of thinking about imports and exports is increasingly outmoded. Products are no longer "made in Japan," or "made in France"; they are truly "made in the world."[21]

[19] *EC – Bananas III (US) (Art. 22.6 – EC)*, WT/DS27/ARB, para. 6.12 (9 Apr. 1999):

> We are of the view that the benchmark for the calculation of nullification or impairment of US trade flows should be losses in US exports of goods to the European Communities and losses by US service suppliers in services supply in or to the European Communities. However, we are of the opinion that losses of US exports in goods or services *between the US and third countries* do not constitute nullification or impairment of even indirect benefits accruing to the US under the GATT or the GATS for which the European Communities could face suspension of concessions.
>
> ([emphasis in original])

[20] See IDE-JETRO, *Trade Patterns and Global Value Chains in East Asia* (World Trade Organization, Geneva; 2010) [hereinafter *Trade Patterns*].

[21] Ibid., p. 3.

According to the report, this diversity of sources "redefines the nature of trade relations that are now characterized by a much closer inter-relationship." Consequently, "we need to promote a conceptual and statistical shift in the way trade is most commonly perceived in policy debates."

Trade Patterns does a worthy job of providing an introduction to the phenomenon of interdependence in the international trading system, but the report also emphasizes how interdependence challenges many members' preconceptions of economic sovereignty. Since the report's release, the organization has struggled to accommodate this phenomenon and appears to be unsure of its place in a state-centric system. Institutionally, the WTO as an organization has had a difficult time driving home the idea that production has become so thoroughly globalized that trade balances and other classic indicia of national economic well-being are no longer as important as in the past.

The MIWI agenda is an uncertain one of symposia and studies, but as yet little in the way of specific policy prescriptions for the organization or its legal system. At the moment most of the MIWI agenda's focus appears to be statistical and empiric, rather than normative, with some attention being paid to preferential trade agreements.[22] MIWI's agenda must also contend with the fact that several countries have sought to "weaponize" their place in supply and value chains in order to secure advantages.[23] If interdependence is now so pervasive and if it

[22] See, for example, Michele Ruta, "Preferential Trade Agreements and Global Value Chains: Theory, Evidence, and Open Questions" in The World Bank, *Global Value Chain Development Report 2017* 175 (2017) (noting that "changing expectations for the course of policy could lead to a reversal and result in an inferior equilibrium where production is progressively renationalized and trade agreements undone." Ibid. at 183).

[23] McKinsey Global Institute, *Risk, Resilience and Rebalancing in Global Value Chains: Report* (6 Aug. 2020) (noting that intricate production networks were designed for efficiency, cost and proximity to markets but not necessarily for transparency or resilience. Now they are operating in a world where disruptions are regular occurrences); Rachel Fefer et al., "Global Value Chains: Overview and Issues for Congress," Congressional Research Service Report R46641 (16 Dec. 2020) (discussing how recent events had highlighted the potential risks and vulnerabilities of global value chains, particularly those that are concentrated in a particular region or reliant on a single supplier); Daniel Drezner, *The Uses and Abuses of Weaponized Interdependence* (Brookings Institution Press, Washington, DC; 2021) (noting growing concern that some countries will use their position in globalized networks to gain undue influence over other societies through their dominance of information and financial networks).

challenges a state-centered model based on obligations and rights, it is also unclear to many governments whether it provides a net benefit or "good."[24]

This conflicting sentiment was particularly evident during the COVID-19 pandemic beginning in 2020. The pandemic, which spread worldwide quickly due to networks of interdependence, highlighted how the reliance that interdependence fosters can also expose critical vulnerabilities.[25]

6.3 A Legal System

The transformations wrought by interdependence are reflected in the emergence of transformative justice.

To transform is to change substantively. It is a modification of both the shape *and* content of the law in response to changes in conceptions of the good. As mentioned, this is for the purposes of sustaining community. In the process the law is no longer characterized by an exclusive focus on individual obligations *or* rights. Rather, it is manifested in their integrated form as an operative legal system.

A legal system emerges because, as Allott has observed, "[l]egal reality is a network of infinite intensity and complexity in which everything, without exception, *is subject to countless legal relations.*"[26] Allott adds that "the relationship between two legal persons can be analysed in many different ways and ... an analysis in terms of one

[24] In his Inaugural Address in January 2017, US President Donald Trump said:

> From this day forward, a new vision will govern our land. From this day forward, it's going to be only America first. America first. ... Every decision on trade, on taxes, on immigration, on foreign affairs will be made to benefit American workers and American families. We must protect our borders from the ravages of other countries making our products, stealing our companies and destroying our jobs. Protection will lead to great prosperity and strength.
>
> (Inaugural Address of President Donald Trump (20 Jan. 2017))

[25] See for example Karen Sutter et al., "COVID-19: China Medical Supply Chains and Broader Trade Issues", Congressional Research Service Report R46304 (23 Dec. 2020) (discussing China's role as a global supplier of personal protective equipment during the COVID-19 pandemic and associated US vulnerabilities).

[26] Allott, *The Health of Nations* 85 [emphasis added].

particular legal relation always *implies the existence of many other supporting legal relations.*"[27]

A legal system conditions the relationships of actors within it. That conditioning is achieved by means of many elements and components – principles, doctrines and so forth – that are commonly encountered and are generic. For instance, a constitution is commonly recognized to be an ordering structure for governance. Today every state in the international community is considered to possess one.[28]

At the same time, a legal system will also be *sui generis* – "of its own type" – because it represents a unique combination of obligations and rights, an arrangement that, due of its own past, present and future, is both the same as, and different from, the combination embodied in other legal systems.[29] Out of the combination, a series of "third things" emerge.

6.3.1 A Sui Generis *Legal System*

In Chapter 2 I discussed the idea of WTO law as a distinctive legal system when assessed against the system of public international law. Here, a closer look is taken at what the system generates.

Gabrielle Marceau makes a point that WTO law "is the system of law (rights and obligations) that provides for effective remedies in case of their violation."[30] She adds that "[a]s a 'self-contained regime', WTO law is a subsystem which is 'intended to exclude more or less totally the application of the general legal consequences of wrongful acts, in particular the application of countermeasures normally at the disposal of an injured party.'"[31] Marceau cautions, however, that this label of "self-contained regime" must be treated with care since it could imply that

[27] Allott, *Eunomia* 162 [emphasis added].

[28] Zachary Elkins et al., "Constitute: The World's Constitutions to Read, Search and Compare" 27 *Web Semant.* 10 (2014). Available online at constituteproject.org.

[29] S.v. "*sui generis*" in *Black's Law Dictionary* (6th ed.) 1434 (1990). In the context of intellectual property (IP) protection, for example, it has been noted that "[w]hat makes an IP system a *sui generis* one is the modification of some of its features so as to properly accommodate the special characteristics of its subject matter, and the specific policy needs which led to the establishment of a distinct system." WIPO, "Elements of a *Sui Generis* System for the Protection of Traditional Knowledge," WIPO/GRTKF/IC/4/8, p. 14 (30 Sept. 2002).

[30] Gabrielle Marceau, "WTO Dispute Settlement and Human Rights" 13 *E.J.I.L.* 753 at 766 (2002).

[31] Ibid. See also Bruno Simma, "Self-Contained Regimes" 16 *Neth. Yearbook Int'l L.* 111 (1985).

WTO law is a "hermetic system, and we all know that it is not; the WTO is not in clinical isolation from public international law."[32] Instead, she describes WTO law as "a system of *lex specialis*."[33]

What are some of the elements of this "special law"? First, the system generates specific obligations and rights. As mentioned, WTO law is conceived of as a distinct package of obligations and rights entered into without reservation.

Second, there are specific causes of action under GATT Art. XXIII relating to violation, nonviolation and "situation" complaints. As Marceau explains, these complaints are limited to making a finding of consistency with the WTO Agreement. They are not to be used to interpret non-WTO norms such as the Cartagena Biosafety Protocol or the Paris Agreement on Climate Change except to the extent that those other norms are directly relevant to the interpretation of WTO norms themselves.[34]

Third, complaints concerning WTO obligations and rights can only be brought before panels and the Appellate Body in accordance with the DSU.[35] Their distinctiveness is reinforced by dispute settlement organs whose mandates are limited and whose conclusions are, for the most part, restricted to making a finding of consistency or inconsistency with a country's obligations under the WTO Agreement.

In particular, Marceau notes that the powers of panels and the Appellate Body "extend only to interpreting and applying WTO law, not deciding all aspects of a dispute."[36] With respect to human rights violations, for instance, she observes that:

> WTO adjudicating bodies do not appear to have the competence either to reach any formal conclusion that a non-WTO norm has been violated, or to require any positive action pursuant to that treaty or any conclusion that would enforce a non-WTO norm over WTO provisions.[37]

[32] Marceau, "WTO Dispute Settlement and Human Rights" 766.

[33] This is within the meaning of ARSIWA Art. 55, which provides that "the [ARSIWA] do not apply where and to the extent that the conditions for the existence of an internationally wrongful act or its legal consequences are determined by special rules of international law. It reflects the maxim *lex specialis derogat legi generali*." See Draft articles on Responsibility of States for Internationally Wrongful Acts, with commentaries, U.N. Doc. A/56/10, p. 140 (2001).

[34] Marceau, "WTO Dispute Settlement and Human Rights" 767.

[35] Ibid., p. 768.

[36] Ibid., p. 766.

[37] Ibid., p. 756. With respect to *jus cogens* norms in particular, Marceau adds that "[s]-ituations of pure conflicts between WTO provisions and jus cogens are ... difficult to

Marceau's observations intimate how a degree of difference is to be discerned between WTO law and other bodies of law, and therefore, how the law is "of its own type," (i.e. *sui generis*) reflecting its own distinctive community.

Fourth, the DSU adapts many general rules of international law "to its specific needs, especially with regard to remedies."[38] Marceau notes, for instance, that "[i]n providing explicitly what can be done in addition to cessation and non-repetition, the system of regulation of remedial actions for WTO violations can be read as excluding certain remedies under international articles on state responsibility."[39] Thus, in case law "the Appellate Body seems to have concluded that, once the challenged measure has been removed (i.e. cessation [of de jure wrongdoing]), no further remedial action is possible; the standard [WTO] remedy (to 'bring your measure into conformity') would not include the possibility, for instance, of obtaining financial compensation for lost trade opportunities."[40]

Fifth, Marceau also observes that "[i]n addition to imposing [a requirement of] immediate cessation, the DSU specifically regulates the consequences of wrongful acts or violation of WTO provisions, including numerous aspects of members' remedial actions."[41] The calibrated nature of countermeasures under DSU Art. 22 is an example of this regulation.

Sixth, the covered agreements cannot be modified or amended without accessing the WTO's specific amending procedures.[42] Again, with respect to international human rights protections, Marceau adds:

> It is difficult to conceive of situations where a panel would set aside a WTO provision in favor of another treaty or a customary provision claimed to have superseded the relevant WTO provision, without changing the relevant covered agreement . . . at least between two disputing states. Generally, those human rights and WTO rights and obligations would be cumulatively binding, but enforceable in different jurisdictions and under different systems of state responsibility.[43]

conceive. In most, if not all, cases, the strong presumption against a violation of jus cogens will lead to an interpretation of WTO law which avoids such a violation." Ibid.

[38] Ibid., p. 769.
[39] Ibid.
[40] Ibid.
[41] Ibid., p. 770.
[42] Ibid., p. 771.
[43] Ibid.

Finally, there is the fact that the WTO Agreement is a single undertaking.[44] For this reason, as mentioned, there is added emphasis on interpreting the WTO Agreement in a "coherent and harmonious" manner. This interpretative practice "reinforces the idea that members wanted to set up an international system of rules and obligations specific to their trade relations, a system that would be coherent in itself and within which rights, obligations and related state action would be the result of an overall balance of concessions."[45]

From all of the above Marceau, like several other commentators, concludes that WTO law is a law of "limited 'domain.'"[46] Marceau asserts that "[t]here is nothing pejorative in having a *lex specialis* regime. On the contrary, the qualification of the WTO as a *lex specialis* regime – far from being insensitive and unreceptive to general international law – is evidence of a high-level of legal sophistication in regulating and adapting general norms of the rules on state responsibility."[47] She goes on to note:

> [a] self-contained regime does not imply that a subsystem of law would "suffice" in itself. Rather, it refers to specific *rights and obligations* that provide for *effective remedies* in the case of their *violation*. In the WTO, these three variables are specifically regulated. Thus, it is not unreasonable to suggest that the WTO is a specific system [of international law].[48]

Marceau's conclusion is a comprehensive and yet limited one. WTO law is a "specific system" of international law because it provides for specific obligations and rights and effective remedies. My own conclusion goes somewhat beyond this. I take the view in this book that WTO law's total operation brings about much more extensive and profound modifications to legal relations between members. As a result, governments' entire cosmovision is transformed. It is for this reason that I characterize

44 Ibid., p. 772.
45 Ibid., p. 773.
46 Ibid. See also Pieter-Jan Kuijper, "The Law of GATT as a Special Field of International Law – Ignorance, Further Refinement or Self-Contained System of International Law" 25 *Neth. Yearbook Int'l L.* 227 (1994). Marceau also notes that "[t]he ILC itself seems to have considered the WTO as a self-contained regime ... After suggesting that there is a presumption against the creation of whole self-contained regimes in the field of reparations, James Crawford added: "There are, no doubt, to a greater or lesser degree, elements of *lex specialis* in the work of the Dispute Settlement Understanding of the World Trade Organization, the focus of which is firmly on cessation rather than reparation."" Marceau, "WTO Dispute Settlement and Human Rights" 774.
47 Marceau, "WTO Dispute Settlement and Human Rights" 774.
48 Ibid., p. 774 [emphasis in original].

the law's outcome as generating a *sui generis* system rather than mere *lex specialis* regime, which is a more restricted designation usually employed to denote individual deviations from a general legal benchmark.[49]

The changes wrought by WTO law have been profound. They involve novel law on many points that cast a series of reflections both within WTO law and beyond it.[50] A useful way to understand the sum of these changes and the way that they cumulatively transform the substance of the law has been put forward by Ronnie Yearwood. One of the outstanding questions posed by the operation of the WTO Agreement is the degree to which it remains "open" or "closed" to outside law. Yearwood, drawing on the work of Niklas Luhmann, posits a thesis of the "constrained openness" of WTO law.[51]

According to Yearwood, a legal system is considered to be "cognitively open," that is, presumptively receptive to "outside" (i.e. nonsystemic) norms and ideas. However, the system is also "operatively closed" in the way it differentiates its operation from other systems. Closure is a

[49] The ILC defined *lex specialis* in ARSIWA Art. 55 as "special *rules* of international law," thereby suggesting that *lex specialis* pertains to specific rules as opposed to general legal consequences generated by a wholesale system. However, in commentary the ILC goes on to note that "[i]t will depend on the special rule to establish the extent to which the more general rules on State responsibility set out in the present articles are displaced by that rule. In some cases, it will be clear from the language of a treaty or other text that only the consequences specified are to flow." The ILC gave as an example of this instance DSU rules as they relate to certain remedies. Draft articles on Responsibility of States for Internationally Wrongful Acts, with commentaries, U.N. Doc. A/56/10, p. 140 (2001).

[50] For example, José Alvarez has pointed out how developments in WTO law will have far-reaching effects on doctrine and general principles of public international law:

> While much of what the DSB does will continue to be seen as *lex specialis* (that is, applicable only to the trade regime), particularly to the extent its panels and Appellate Body reach for public international law principles, those principles themselves will be developed by what it does. WTO dispute settlers' interpretations of the *non ultra petita* principle, *compétence de la compétence*, fundamental evidentiary rules demanded by equality of arms or other principles of fairness, other rules contained in the [VCLT], canons of interpretation derivable from the rules of treaty interpretation or the principle of effectiveness, and the requirements of state responsibility . . . will have an impact on these "non-trade" rules.
>
> (José Alvarez, *International Organizations as Law-Makers* 496 (Oxford University Press, Oxford; 2005))

See also Donald McRae, "The Contribution of International Trade Law to the Development of International Law" 260 *Recueil des Cours* 103 (1996).

[51] Ronnie R. F. Yearwood, *The Interaction between World Trade Organisation (WTO) Law and External International Law* (Routledge, London; 2012).

metaphor for the fact that closed systems recognize "no norms other than those which they produce as being valid."[52] In the case of the WTO Agreement, closure allows the WTO system to "reconstruct" the law through the development of an "internal point of view" by WTO adjudicating bodies, reformulating certain norms of international law in a way that, taken together, generates a *sui generis* system.

Yearwood provides several examples of the "constrained openness" of WTO law, notably in relation to the precautionary principle. The principle embodies the idea of "caution in advance."[53] It is an expression of the need to anticipate harm before it occurs.

At the international level, the precautionary principle was originally endorsed in the World Charter for Nature in 1982 and first implemented in the 1987 Montreal Protocol.[54] It is also contained in the 1992 Rio Declaration. Principle 15 of the Rio Declaration provides:

> In order to protect the environment, the precautionary approach should be widely applied by states according to their capabilities. Where there are threats of serious irreversible damage, lack of full scientific certainty shall not be used as a reason for postponing cost-effective measures to prevent environmental degradation.[55]

The particular "translation" that the precautionary principle has received in WTO law is not conclusive. There is no direct reference to such a principle as an overarching premise of WTO law. In *EC – Hormones*, for instance, the Appellate Body observed that although the precautionary principle has not been written into the SPS Agreement as a ground for justifying SPS measures that are otherwise inconsistent with members' obligations, the principle "finds reflection"[56] in SPS Art. 5.7. That article provides:

> In cases where relevant scientific evidence is insufficient, a Member may provisionally adopt sanitary or phytosanitary measures on the basis of available pertinent information, including that from the relevant international organizations as well as from sanitary or phytosanitary measures

52 Ibid., p. 76.

53 Andrew Jordan & Timothy O'Riordan, "The Precautionary Principle: A Legal and Policy History" in Marco Martuzzi & Joel A. Tickner (eds), *The Precautionary Principle* ch. 3 (World Health Organization, Copenhagen; 2004).

54 Montreal Protocol on Substances that Deplete the Ozone Layer, 1522 U.N.T.S. 3 (1989) was the first international treaty to address a global environmental regulatory challenge and the first to embrace the precautionary principle in its design for science-based policymaking.

55 Adopted at the UN Conference for the Environment and Development, U.N. Doc. A/CONF.151/5/Rev.1 (13 June 1992).

56 *EC – Hormones*, WT/DS26/AB/R, para. 124 (16 Jan. 1998).

> applied by other Members. In such circumstances, Members shall seek to obtain the additional information necessary for a more objective assessment of risk and review the sanitary or phytosanitary measure accordingly within a reasonable period of time.

In *EC – Hormones* the Appellate Body added that SPS Art. 5.7 does not exhaust the relevance of the precautionary principle in WTO law since the principle also finds reflection in other SPS provisions – notably the sixth paragraph of the SPS preamble and SPS Art. 3.3.[57] At the same time, the Appellate Body upheld the panel's determination that the precautionary principle did not override the provisions of SPS Arts. 5.1–5.2 concerning the need for a risk assessment and the taking into account of scientific evidence in a government's formulation of its own SPS standards.[58] Consequently, it might more accurately be said that there is limited recognition in WTO law of a "precautionary *approach*."[59]

From the example of its modest translation of precaution and other norms, Yearwood concludes that although "the WTO does not incorporate external international law . . . [it] is cognitively open to that law and through its own operations."[60] The combined effect of these norms *operating together* creates a *sui generis* system.

In all of the above ways, then, legal relations between countries are transformed. That transformation may not always be acknowledged, but it is nonetheless real. Its practical effect is to make the international economy more productive. This is due to the fact that the system emphasizes interdependence. Justice as reflected in law then becomes a condition of greater interdependence.

6.3.2 A Contractual Constitution

In conjunction with the interdependence of obligations and rights, WTO law simultaneously exhibits both constitutional and contractual impulses. These combine structurally in what I term a "contractual constitution."

The designation of a "contractual constitution" inverts a term borrowed from international environmental law – a "constitutional contract" – which is used to describe "an agreement setting forth an interlocking system of behavioural prescriptions expected to remain operative

[57] Ibid.
[58] Ibid.
[59] Ibid., para. 122; *EC – Biotech*, WT/DS293/R, para. 7.3065 (29 Sept. 2006).
[60] Yearwood, *The Interaction between World Trade Organisation* 174.

over an indefinite period."[61] Commentators in the environmental context stress its interdependent and durable quality. "Constitutional contracts" endure because they are "sets of rights and rules that are expected to govern subsequent interactions."[62]

I invert the term here to stress how the WTO Agreement is designed in the first place to provide "security and predictability" in international trade relations consistent with a constitutional impulse. The dominant constitutive aspect of the WTO Agreement is reinforced by several points made earlier, namely, that the renegotiation of trade concessions and commitments is now infrequent and procedures for amendment make the overall arrangement difficult to modify. In broad outline the treaty is essentially fixed.

Nevertheless, a subordinate contractual aspect to WTO arrangements persists. Acceding countries continue to negotiate individual "tickets of admission," and both counteraction and retaliation, though rare, remain possible. Members have also skillfully exploited the ambiguity present in the treaty's relationship with RTAs to conclude outside arrangements without much fear of negative repercussions.[63] Beyond this, they continue negotiations on a variety of trade-related subjects, some of which may be included in the treaty in future. In these many ways, a degree of harmony is maintained between the idea of WTO Agreement as a "holistic settlement"[64] reach at one point in time and something more open and flexible evolving across time.

[61] Oran R. Young & Gail Osherenko, *Polar Politics* 2 (n3) (Cornell University Press, Ithaca, NY; 1993). Catherine Redgwell has written that the term "constitutional contract," refers to the dynamic force of negotiated treaties, treaties that are not one-off events but dynamic and evolve over time. The "constitutional contract" is relational rather than discrete. See Catherine Redgwell, "Multilateral Environmental Treaty-Making" in Vera Gowland-Debbas (ed.), *Multilateral Treaty Making* 91 (Martinus Nijhoff, The Hague; 2000).

[62] John Ikenberry, *After Victory* 14–15, n. 24 (Princeton University Press, Princeton, NJ; 2001), quoting Oran Young, "Political Leadership and Regime Formation: On the Development of Institutions in International Society" 45:3 *Int'l Org.* 281 (Summer 1991).

[63] Thus, the WTO Analytical Index for GATT Art. XXIV (April 2020) notes at p. 14 that:

> [f]or the period between the Committee's establishment and the adoption in December 2006 of the Transparency Mechanism for Regional Trade Agreements, the Committee had completed the factual examination of a total of 66 agreements, of which 45 in the area of trade in goods and 21 in trade in services. No report on the examination of any of these agreements has ever been agreed upon in the Committee, for subsequent transmission to the Council for Trade in Goods.

[64] Nico Krisch, *Beyond Constitutionalism* 304 (Oxford University Press, Oxford; 2010).

What does this combined structure amount to? One way of understanding the WTO's contractual constitution is to consider the work that is quietly and patiently accomplished in the organization far from the glare of specific disputes. Andrew Lang and Joanne Scott highlight how proceedings in WTO committees reveal a "hidden world" of trade governance.[65] For instance, the SPS Committee serves as a forum where many problems can be detected and raised early. As Nico Krisch has described it:

> [F]rom 1995 to 2008, more than 7,500 SPS measures were notified to the [SPS] Committee, and 277 "specific trade concerns" were raised. A significant number of these concerns – about one-third – was wholly or partly resolved through broader information, better mutual understanding, capacity-building, and/or the adjustment or withdrawal of the measures in question. Moreover, cooperation in the Committee helps to concretize rules and align normative expectations so that member states can anticipate, avoid, or solve potential problems early on.[66]

In a similar vein, Mary Footer has observed of the Working Party on Professional Services' drafting of a set of voluntary Guidelines for Mutual Recognition Agreements or Arrangements in the Accountancy Sector ("MRA Guidelines") issued in 1997:

> The important point about the *MRA Guidelines* is that they consist of a series of recommendations to the Members on the form and coverage of mutual recognition agreements, which could be applied not only to the accountancy sector but also, due to their general and more abstract nature, to other services sectors in order to deal with "differences in education and examination standards, experience requirements, regulatory influence and various other matters, all of which make implementing recognition on a multilateral basis extremely difficult."[67]

The ultimate product of this contractual constitution then is a body of work that mediates between the interests of member states and the common interest. The continuous tension in this hybrid structure might appear peculiar except that it is characteristic of many legal relations, including those at the level of the EU where constitutions have been

[65] Andrew Lang & Joanne Scott, "The Hidden World of WTO Governance" 20:3 *E.J.I.L.* 575 (2009).
[66] Krisch, *Beyond Constitutionalism* 212.
[67] Mary Footer, *An Institutional and Normative Analysis of the World Trade Organization* 285 (Martinus Nijhoff, Leiden; 2006).

understood "as contracts or compromises"[68] and vice versa. In other words, there is a degree of porousness and oscillation between the anchor concepts consistent with the theoretical relationship of transition (i.e. Constitution = Contract).

That still leaves the question of how this contractual constitution is to be understood beyond itself. The identification of WTO law as embodying a *sui generis* system and of WTO law as primarily "constitutive" strongly infers that WTO law claims for itself the right to define its status vis-à-vis other regimes. As such, it should be interpreted in classic constitutive terms. However, the issue of the WTO's place in hierarchy vis-à-vis the rest of international law is left largely undefined, and in any event, as I suggested in Chapter 4, international constitutionalism may differ significantly from its domestic analogue.[69]

Krisch has put forward an alternative view of the WTO arrangement as existing within a wider international landscape that is legally "pluralist." A pluralist account regards that terrain as subject to a "competition of different collectives for ultimate law-making authority"[70] typically reflective of "processes of resistance."[71] An example would be the scenario profiled in Chapter 2 involving the settlement reached on patented medicines culminating in TRIPS Art. 31*bis*. The ultimate form of the settlement in that instance was the result of action in multiple international fora, which managed to recharacterize the good in issue as less a matter of private property protection involving obligations and more a matter of public property involving baseline human rights.

As Krisch describes it, "a key dimension on which pluralism and constitutionalism differ is the degree of hierarchy: while constitutionalism

[68] Günter Frankenberg, "The Return of the Contract: Problems and Pitfalls of European Constitutionalism" 6 *Eur. L.J.* 257 (2002); Richard Bellamy, *Liberalism and Pluralism: Towards a Politics of Compromise* (Routledge, London; 1999).

[69] The WTO Agreement contains no equivalent of UN Charter Art. 103, which specifies that "In the event of a conflict between the obligations of the Members of the United Nations under the present Charter and their obligations under any other international agreement, their obligations under the present Charter shall prevail." Instead, the position taken in this book is that while WTO obligations are in fact interdependent and subsequent inconsistent treaties are void, member countries have taken action in many instances to ensure the consistency of other international arrangements such as the Kimberley Process Certification Scheme and the WHO Framework Convention on Tobacco Control with their WTO concessions and commitments. At the same time, the consistency of a number of regional trade arrangements with the WTO Agreement remains untested due to "gridlock" over the application of GATT Art. XXIV.

[70] Krisch, *Beyond Constitutionalism* 197.

[71] Ibid., p. 227.

presupposes a fully determined framework that sets out relationships of super- and subordination, pluralism operates with relations of sub-orders that leave ultimate hierarchies open."[72] This openness creates possibilities for contestation.

To be sure, contestation is an issue *within* WTO law. A common perception of WTO law is that it is relatively "fixed" but in fact the law changes over time. This is true because WTO law is more than simply the product of dispute settlement. It also involves the work of negotiators, diplomats, administrators as well as nongovernmental interests that together fashion its legal outputs and results through a dense web of conferences, councils, committees and other bodies. Within and beyond this machinery, there is intense competition for authority, as witnessed, for example, in the tug-of-war in 2000 between the Appellate Body and the General Council over the admission and treatment of *amicus briefs* in Appellate Body proceedings.[73] Internal decisions and rule-making can also be used to shape – even circumvent – the formal law.[74] Consequently, WTO law is not entirely "stable." It adapts and evolves as the constellation of interests involved in its making and observance change.

There is also contestation occurring *beyond* WTO law that presents a challenge to it. The examples of the Biosafety Protocol to the Convention on Biological Diversity and the UNESCO Convention on Cultural Diversity are cases in point. In both instances, the EU, in concert with some other countries, mounted an effort to alter WTO norms and enjoyed at least some success in doing so.[75] The contestation possible

[72] Ibid., p. 235.

[73] In *EC – Asbestos* the Appellate Body developed a special procedure for the submission of amicus briefs, which was objected to by certain WTO members in the General Council, who claimed that the procedure encroached upon their own authority under WTO Agreement Art. V:2 "to make appropriate arrangements for effective cooperation with other intergovernmental organizations." Subsequently, all submissions made under the procedure were rejected and the special procedure has never been used since. See *EC – Asbestos*, WT/DS135/AB/R, paras. 50–57 (12 Mar. 2001). In *U.S. – Certain EC Products*, WT/DS165/AB/R, para. 92 (11 Dec. 2000) the Appellate Body observed that "it is certainly not the task of either panels or the Appellate Body to amend the DSU." For coverage, see World Trade Organization, "Briefs in a Twist" 357:8200 *The Economist* 85 (9 Dec. 2000).

[74] For other examples of intra-regime contestation, see *U.S. – Clove Cigarettes*, WT/DS406/AB/R, paras. 210–212 (4 Apr. 2012), where the Appellate Body held that a decision adopted by WTO members other than under the formal procedures of WTO Art. IX:2 could constitute a "subsequent agreement" for the purposes of VCLT Art. 31(3)(a). This effectively circumvented the WTO Agreement's formal amending procedure.

[75] The Biosafety Protocol to the 1992 Convention on Biological Diversity (CBD) was adopted in 2000 by the 176 nations that are CBD parties. The United States participated

in this pluralist environment arises from what, as Krisch points out, are differences of values that work to shape the contours of the WTO's contractual constitution.

6.3.3 *A Law of the Present*

The interdependence of obligations and rights in the form of a *sui generis* system generates an intensive emphasis in legal thinking on the present (i.e. *eo instante*). That moment is important because it is the moment of

in the negotiations of the Protocol as an observer but did not vote on its adoption. US hesitance to full participation was prompted in part by the Protocol's recognition of precaution, which US officials feared could prevent the development and use of innovative biotechnology such as genetically modified organisms [GMOs]. Krisch concludes from this that:

> [c]ooperation on GMOs is unlikely to happen – because significant constituencies within the EU regard the issue as one of culture and values: an issue with an absolute baseline, not to be traded off against other gains. This points to the non-exchangeable character of the goods involved here, and it suggests that the costs of cooperation simply outweigh its benefits, making a stable equilibrium impossible to achieve.
>
> (Krisch, *Beyond Constitutionalism* 221)

See also Robert Faulkner, "Regulating Biotech Trade" 76:2 *International Affairs* 299 (2000); Grant Isaac & William Kerr, "The Biosafety Protocol and the WTO: Concert or Conflict?" in Robert Faulkner (ed.), *The International Politics of Genetically Modified Food* 195 (Palgrave Macmillan, Basingstoke; 2007). The UNESCO Convention on Cultural Diversity (CCD) was concluded in 2005 in response to the open-endedness of many WTO provisions on liberalization and nondiscrimination as well as of the WTO dispute settlement system. This gave rise to concern that the WTO Agreement would erode national sovereignty in many areas, including culture. The immediate response to this threat was an initiative led by Canada and France in UNESCO to better define cultural protection in international law. The initiative took the form of the CCD, which made clear the connection between cultural protection and human rights and affirmed the right of countries to "adopt measures to protect and promote the diversity of cultural expressions." The Convention also specified an obligation for countries to "foster mutual supportiveness between this Convention and other treaties," to take account of the Convention in the interpretation of other treaties, and to ensure the Convention's "complementarity and non-subordination" vis-à-vis other international obligations. The CCD was perceived as a direct challenge to the United States, which had quit UNESCO some years before and which returned post-haste in 2002 in an unsuccessful effort to head-off the Convention. Since then, the United States and the forces behind the UNESCO Convention have skirmished over the issue of cultural protection globally. See Gilbert Gagné, *The Trade and Culture Debate: Evidence from US Trade Agreements* (Lexington Books, Lanham, MD; 2016).

action, or in legal terms, the "moment of decision"[76] – in particular, the moment when responsibility crystallizes. In that moment the *ex ante* perspective of a law of obligation and the *ex post* perspective of a law of rights merge in a continuing present. The law becomes apodictic, all-encompassing. It constitutes *the law* – part of the recognized order of things and a condition of continuing interdependence.

WTO law reveals itself to be a law of the present in several ways. First, there is general recognition of the way in which WTO obligations have a continuing character. In *China – Audiovisual*,[77] for instance, the Appellate Body justified its decision to interpret certain terms in China's schedule of service commitments in a generic fashion, noting "that GATS Schedules, like the GATS itself and all WTO agreements, constitute multilateral treaties with *continuing obligations* that WTO Members entered into for an indefinite period of time, regardless of whether they were original Members or acceded after 1995."[78]

In another case, *EC – Sardines*,[79] the issue was a trade description of canned sardines imposed by the EC. The panel found that the EC standard did not reproduce the relevant international standard without contradiction and therefore violated the TBT Agreement. The panel reminded the parties that TBT Art. 2.4, which mandates that WTO members "shall use" international standards "is not a static obligation; there is an *ongoing* obligation to reassess technical regulations in light of international standards."[80]

Second, another aspect of WTO law's temporality is its innately presentist perspective. In *Korea – Alcoholic Beverages*, for example, a panel had to deal with the sensitive issue of how far into the future WTO adjudicators might look as part of determining a reasonable expectation of market access under GATT Art. III:2. The panel observed:

> We will not attempt to speculate on what could happen in the distant future, but we will consider evidence pertaining to what could reasonably be expected to occur *in the near future* based on the evidence presented. . . . If one is dealing with products that are experience based

[76] H. Patrick Glenn, *Legal Traditions of the World* (5th ed.) 20 (Oxford University Press, Oxford; 2014). See also references to "the primacy of the present" in Western legal thinking. Ibid. at 27.

[77] *China – Audiovisual Products*, WT/DS363/AB/R (21 Dec. 2009).

[78] Ibid., para. 396 [emphasis added].

[79] *EC – Sardines*, WT/DS231/R (29 May 2002).

[80] Ibid., para. 7.80.

> consumer items, then trends are particularly important and it would be unrealistic and, indeed, analytically unhelpful to attempt to separate every piece of evidence and disregard that which discusses implications for market structures in the near future.[81]

Legal analysis in many instances segues into an attempt to construct a "present" based on an appreciation of all the facts, a sort of abstraction that collects and brings together all considerations at one moment in time. Thus, in *U.S. – Clove Cigarettes* the panel observed that "in the case of a de facto discrimination claim . . . a panel must base its determination on the totality of facts and circumstances before it, including the design, architecture, revealing structure, operation, and application of the technical regulation at issue."[82]

Third, there is an observed tendency for legal interpretation to dwell in a fictive present, even though evidence can only be about the past or make presumptions about the future. In *U.S. – Cotton Yarn*, for instance, the issue was whether or not evidence compiled by the US Department of Commerce concerning an alleged "threat of material injury" was adequately grounded in fact. The dispute raised the intriguing issue of the degree to which *past* evidence could be used to determine projected, but unrealized, *future* injury. The Appellate Body stated:

> The demonstration by a Member that a particular product is being imported into its territory in such increased quantities as to cause serious damage (or actual threat thereof) to the domestic industry can be based only on facts and evidence which existed at the time the determination was made. The urgent nature of such an investigation may not permit the Member to delay its determination in order to take into account evidence that might be available only at a future date. Even a determination on the existence of threat of serious injury must be based on projections extrapolating from *existing* data.[83]

The use of the present voice ("*existing* data") is indicative of the presentness of the analysis, notwithstanding the essentially retrospective nature of the investigative exercise. In indicating its awareness of this paradox – of constructing a picture of the present about the past and projecting it into the future – the Appellate Body referred to its prior decision in *U.S. – Lamb*:

[81] *Korea – Alcoholic Beverages*, WT/DS75, para. 10.50 (17 Sept. 1998) [emphasis added].
[82] *U.S. – Clove Cigarettes*, WT/DS406/AB/R, para. 206 (4 Apr. 2012).
[83] *U.S. – Cotton Yarn*, WT/DS192/AB/R, para. 77 (8 Oct. 2001) [emphasis in original].

> As facts, by their very nature, pertain to the present and the past, the occurrence of future events can never be definitively proven by facts. There is, therefore, a tension between a future-oriented "threat" analysis, which, ultimately, calls for a degree of "conjecture" about the likelihood of a future event, and the need for a fact-based determination. Unavoidably, this tension must be resolved through the use of facts *from the present and the past* to justify the conclusion *about the future*, namely that serious injury is "clearly imminent."[84]

Still another example of "presentness" occurred in *U.S. – Upland Cotton*, where the panel had to assess how the existing regulatory structure for agricultural loans in the United States would influence planting decisions by US agricultural producers. In determining a plausible production scenario, a compliance panel considered that:

> it is reasonable to conclude that the fact that US cotton producers know that they will receive marketing loan payments whenever the adjusted world price is below the marketing loan rate continues to be an important factor affecting the level of acreage planted to cotton (and thus the level of production), even when, as in [Marketing Year] 2006, the expected market price for upland cotton at the time of planting is higher than the marketing loan rate.[85]

This quote indicates how the divergent temporal perspectives taken by the law – past and future – are woven together in practice. The quote focuses on knowledge in an unmentioned present ("producers *know*") about information that can only be gleaned from the immediate past ("adjusted world price") and its influence with respect to future expectations ("*expected* market price"). In essence, the analyses contribute to a conclusion that is located in the present.

A final area where the "presentness" of the law is evident is in relation to countermeasures and retaliation. In Chapters 3 and 5 I detailed how WTO countermeasures and retaliation are most often a retrospective exercise and how, in so being, they are aspects of a "law of the past." In certain cases, however, there has been an effort to update retaliation more regularly, and in a few disputes, arbitrators have adverted to the possibility of variable retaliation that tracks actual nullification or impairment closer to its actual present course.[86]

[84] *U.S. – Lamb*, WT/DS177, 178/AB/R, para. 136 (1 May 2001) [emphasis added].

[85] *U.S. – Upland Cotton*, WT/DS267/RW, para. 10.81 (18 Dec. 2007).

[86] *U.S. – Offset Act (Byrd Amendment)*, WT/DS217/ARB/EEC (31 Aug. 2004) the arbitrator agreed with the claim by the complainant parties that equivalence might be determined

Thus, in *U.S. – 1916*,[87] the arbitrator noted that:

> we do not consider that the European Communities' right to suspend obligations *must be frozen in time as of the date it made its request under DSU Article 22.2.* The existence and maintenance of the 1916 Act as such violates the rights of the European Communities, and each application of the Act – i.e. if a court in the United States were to issue an award of damages against an EC entity, or if EC entities enter into agreements to settle claims under the 1916 Act – increases the level of nullification or impairment sustained by the European Communities as a result of the Act.[88]

The Arbitrator went on to observe that "each application of the Act, as indicated above, would entitle the European Communities to increase concomitantly the level of its suspension of obligations."[89]

Commentators have been noncommittal about this continuing presence of the present. Lothar Ehring has observed about this methodology in the context of nondiscrimination analysis that:

> It examines the configuration of imports and domestic products at one point in time in order to explore whether the measure at issue modifies the competitive relationship between imports and like domestic goods, both taken as a whole, to the detriment of the former. It does not attempt to measure the significance of actual trade effects by comparing the levels of trade volumes at two points, or in fact any point in time. Neither does it exclusively take account of actual trade flows; on the contrary, potential imports are of paramount importance.[90]

Is all acceptable about this intensely presentist perspective? Obviously not. Beneath the law's objective countenance, there is much that cannot be reconciled with any single temporal perspective, any uniform set of settled explanations determined as of a single point in time. As Patrick Glenn has observed, "[n]o tradition can exercise full control, in its particular social context, of the capture of present information."[91]

by means of a trade effects coefficient, and in subsequent cases such as *U.S. – Upland Cotton*, WT/DS267/ARB/1-2 (31 Aug. 2009) and *U.S. – Washing Machines*, WT/DS464/ARB (8 Feb. 2019) arbitrators have agreed that the equivalence determination may be determined by formula, lending greater transparency and consistence to the exercise.

87 *U.S. – Anti-Dumping Act of 1916 (21.3(c))*, WT/DS136/ARB (24 Feb. 2004).

88 Ibid., para. 6.14 [emphasis added].

89 Ibid., para. 6.17.

90 Lothar Ehring, "De Facto Discrimination in WTO Law," *Jean Monnet Working Paper* 12/01, p. 32 (2001).

91 Glenn, *Legal Traditions of the World* 15.

What an *eo instante* perspective does do, however, is to remain subtly forward-looking. Prospectivity, in turn, leaves room for a number of things. Chief among them is the deferral of a number of key questions to the future, including the all-important question of how countries will adjust their sovereignty to comply with WTO law.

At the same time, this incompleteness may be something appealing and desirable. Rather than striving for finality and concreteness in the present, the legal system is wisely left open to subsequent modification and adjustment. Glenn observes:

> The undefined or incomplete nature of all [legal] traditions thus rests ultimately on the difficulty of concluding as to the existence of absolute or irrefutable knowledge within a tradition, given the ongoing process of exchange. Information exists only alongside other information, available in one form or another; it is always in this sense contingent and comparable.[92]

It is the contingency of present knowledge and the fact that the legal system based on it must be left open to revision that are key.

6.3.4 An Abductive Reasoning

As mentioned, legal reasoning is characterized by two types of logic: deduction and induction. Traditionally, deduction and induction have been regarded as exclusive and exhaustive. Together, they admit of no other forms of logic.[93]

However, some commentators have recognized a third, triune form of logic in abduction. Abductive reasoning is thought to have been first identified by Charles Saunders Pierce and is "a form of logical inference which goes from an observation to a theory which accounts for the

[92] Ibid., p. 23.

[93] For example, J. S. Covington observes that "[t]here are two forms of reasoning and therefore two forms of argument." He goes on to refer to abductive logic in an accompanying footnote as follows:

> Some writers include a third form of reasoning called "abduction." Abduction is similar to induction, since it results in their creation of new hypotheses, but abduction does so on one datum [i.e. data set]. It is an intelligent guess on very limited information about what a hypothesis may be, and the guess leads to the search for data to confirm the new hypothesis.
>
> (See J. S. Covington, Jr., *The Structure of Legal Argument and Proof* 2, n. 1 (John Marshall, Houston, TX; 1993))

observation, ideally seeking to find the simplest and most likely explanation." It is often called "an intelligent guess"[94] and is "equated with inference to the best explanation."[95]

Abductive reasoning is "a guess because it is tied to an incomplete body of evidence. As new evidence comes in [across time], the guess could be shown to be wrong."[96] Abductive reasoning emphasizes the tentative, open-ended nature of knowledge. It is the best explanation *right now*. In contrast to deductive reasoning, the logic of what "will be," or inductive reasoning, the logic of "what is" or was, abductive reasoning is sometimes referred to the logic of what "might be."[97]

An example of abductive reasoning originally supplied by Pierce runs as follows:

> The Four Horseman Example
>
> I once landed at a seaport in a Turkish Province; and as I was walking up to the house which I was to visit, I met a man upon horseback, surrounded by four horseman holding a canopy over his head. As the governor of the province was the only person I could think of who would be so greatly honoured, I inferred that this was he. This was an hypothesis.[98]

Abductive reasoning is therefore hypothetical reasoning subject to revision as new information becomes available.

Authorities have noted the role of abductive logic in the law of evidence. John Henry Wigmore employed the following illustration of abductive reasoning in law:

> The fact that before a robbery someone had no money, but after had a large sum, is offered to indicate that by robbery he became possessed of the large sum of money. There are several other possible explanations – the receipt of a legacy, the payment of a debt, the winning of a gambling game, and the like. Nevertheless, the desired explanation rises, among other explanations, to a fair degree of plausibility, and the evidence is received.[99]

[94] Ibid.

[95] Douglas Walton, *Abductive Reasoning* 4 (University of Alabama Press, Tuscaloosa; 2004).

[96] Ibid., pp. 3–4.

[97] Roger Martin, *The Opposable Mind* 144–146 (Harvard Business School Press, Boston; 2007).

[98] Ibid., p. 5.

[99] Wigmore's example originally appeared in John H. Wigmore, *A Treatise on the Anglo-American System of Evidence*, vol. 1 (3rd ed.) (Little, Brown, Boston; 1940). It is reproduced in Walton, *Abductive Reasoning* 25.

Despite its potential for application, the importance of abductive reasoning in law is rarely recognized. Generally speaking, it remains little understood.[100]

Philosophers disagree about the exact relationship between deduction, induction and abduction.[101] In this book I take the position that, like the other conceptual pairings and the *tertia quid* they generate in a *sui generis* system, deduction and induction together generate abductive reasoning. As in the case of inductive reasoning, abduction is based on evidence collected in the past, but like deductive reasoning it projects a hypothesis into the future. It is the best explanation available *at a given time*, though the explanation may change. For this reason it is tentative and provisional. Its flexibility is behind the opinion that "[abduction] sound[s] highly intuitive and creative, even instinctive in nature."[102]

100 Walton observes that:

> Wigmore's use of abductive inference in his analysis of legal evidence suggests emphatically that the abductive model is highly applicable to legal reasoning. In the past, the notion of abduction has not been widely known to experts on legal logic and legal evidence, and much of their work has centered on deductive and inductive models of rational argument. But even a glimpse of Wigmore's work on evidence shows the enormous potential of abduction as applied to the logical structure of reasoning in legal evidence.
>
> (Walton, *Abductive Reasoning* 25–26)

Abduction as a blend of deduction and induction is regularly recognized in science. In 1937 the physicist Paul Dirac observed: "The successful development of science requires a proper balance to be maintained between the method of building up from observations and the method of deducting by pure reasoning from speculative assumptions." Paul Dirac, 119 *Nature* 1001–1002 (untitled supplement) (June 1937) cited in Graham Farmelo, *The Strangest Man* 290 (Faber & Faber, London; 2009). For recent work that may be indicative of the pervasiveness of abductive reasoning, see Adam Grant, *Think Again* (Viking, New York; 2021) (an invitation to let go of views that are no longer working well and prize mental flexibility over consistency).

101 Walton notes that the relationship between the three modes of logic is open: "Should one of these variously named types fit in as the third kind of inference contrasting with the other two? Or should all of them fit into that category?" He concludes that "[t]he situation is complicated, and the terminology is unsettled." Walton, *Abductive Reasoning* 1–2. Atocha Aliseda, *Abductive Reasoning* 33 (Springer, Dordrecht; 2006) (noting that "For C.S. Peirce … 'deduction', 'induction' and 'abduction' formed a natural triangle – but the literature in general shows many overlaps, and even confusions.") See also Dan Hunter, "No Wilderness of Single Instances" 48:3 *J. Legal Educ.* 365 at 384–391 (1998) (discussing abductive and retroductive inference).

102 Walton, *Abductive Reasoning* 9.

What this "combined" understanding of abductive reasoning suggests is that we should not expect to see abductive logic displayed in the operation of any *one* legal device in WTO law – either presumption *or* proof – but rather in *their combination* over time. The two traditional forms of reasoning – deduction and induction – support each other *in a continuing present.*

This point is particularly noted in questions related to the burden of proof. In general, the burden of proof rests "upon the party, whether complaining or defending, who asserts the affirmative of a particular claim or defence."[103] In matters of pleading, for instance, a party must adduce evidence sufficient to raise a *prima facie* case. Beyond that, a presumption arises that the burden is met and must be countered by the opposite party.[104] Presumption and proof thus work together.

For example, in *Japan – Agricultural Products II* the Appellate Body reviewed findings by the panel that the United States had adduced sufficient evidence to raise a presumption that a Japanese testing requirement as applied to apples, cherries, nectarines and walnuts violated SPS Art. 2.2 but had furnished insufficient evidence to raise such a presumption with respect to apricots, pears, plums and quince.[105]

In other cases the interaction of presumption and proof suggestive of abduction is less automatic and more subtle. In *U.S. – FSC*, for instance, a compliance panel had to determine whether certain amounts "otherwise due" as US taxes were "foregone" for the purposes of the definition of a subsidy in SCM Art. 1.1(a)(1)(ii).[106] The panel observed that determining what was "otherwise due" was not only ascertainable "where a purely mechanical exercise of inspection was feasible" since this would give a defendant country "every reason to ensure that there was no automatic or explicit link to the situation of what would otherwise be due."[107] For this reason the panel refused to be limited to a strictly inductive inquiry, that is, examining what countries had done in the past concerning amounts "otherwise due."

[103] *U.S. – Shirts and Blouses*, WT/DS33/AB/R, p. 14 (25 Apr. 1997).

[104] Michelle Grando, *Evidence, Proof, and Fact-Finding in WTO Dispute Settlement* 105–106 (Oxford University Press, Oxford; 2009).

[105] *Japan – Agricultural Products II*, WT/DS76/AB/R, para. 136 (22 Feb. 1999).

[106] SCM Art. 1.1(a)(1)(ii) provides that for the purposes of the SCM "a subsidy shall be deemed to exist if . . . (ii) government revenue that is otherwise due is foregone or not collected (e.g. fiscal incentives such as tax credits)."

[107] WT/DS108/RW, para. 8.14 (20 Aug. 2001).

At the same time, the panel noted that a purely deductive approach would be undesirable as well. The panel concluded that it would be impossible "simply to assert that revenue is otherwise due in the abstract. It cannot be *presumed*."[108] An intermediate approach "grounded *in the actual way* in which the U.S. tax regime functions"[109] was called for, one that looked "at the overall situation as *an integrated whole*."[110] Based on an abductive approach focused on the present, the panel was able to conclude that treating the overseas income of certain US manufacturers as nontaxable led to "the foregoing of revenue otherwise due," a key element in the finding of a subsidy under the SCM.[111]

Another example of abduction occurred in *Brazil – Tyres*.[112] There, the EC brought a challenge against a ban on tire imports maintained by Brazil for environmental purposes. The ban prohibited tire imports generally but made an exception for tires from MERCOSUR countries. Brazil defended its differential treatment under GATT Art. XX(b) as "necessary to protect human, animal or plant life or health." The panel noted that MERCOSUR imports did not appear to have been significant and therefore concluded that their differential treatment did not amount to "unjustifiable discrimination," as prohibited by the preamble of GATT Art. XX. The panel backed this opinion up with reference to Brazil's foreign trade statistics.[113] Its analysis was essentially inductive.

On appeal, the Appellate Body faulted the panel for its interpretation of the exception as not amounting to "unjustifiable discrimination," complaining that the panel's analysis was too empiric. The Appellate Body stated:

> analyzing whether discrimination is "unjustifiable" will usually involve an analysis that relates primarily to the cause and rationale of the discrimination. By contrast, the Panel's interpretation of the term "unjustifiable" does not depend on the cause or rationale of the discrimination but, rather, is focused exclusively on the assessment of the *effects* of the discrimination.[114]

[108] Ibid., para. 8.17 [emphasis added].
[109] Ibid., para. 8.25 [emphasis added].
[110] Ibid., para. 8.23 [emphasis added].
[111] Ibid., para. 8.26.
[112] WT/DS332/R (12 June 2007).
[113] Ibid., para. 7.288.
[114] WT/DS332/AB/R (3 Dec. 2007) [emphasis in original].

The Appellate Body concluded:

> The Panel's approach has no support in the text of Article XX and appears to us inconsistent with the manner the Appellate Body has interpreted and applied the concept of "arbitrary or unjustifiable discrimination" in previous cases.[115]

The Appellate Body went on to allude to the need for a hybrid quantitative *and* qualitative approach to the assessment of discrimination, noting that effects are merely "a relevant factor [in discrimination analysis], among others."[116] A similar hybrid method analysis of qualitative *and* quantitative considerations suggestive of abduction is observed in a number of other WTO disputes.[117]

[115] The Appellate Body observed:

> ... we recognize that in certain cases the effects of the discrimination may be a relevant factor, among others, for determining whether the cause or rationale of the discrimination is acceptable or defensible and, ultimately, whether the discrimination is justifiable. ... Taking into account as a relevant factor, among others, the effects of the discrimination for determining whether the rationale of the discrimination is acceptable is, however, fundamentally different from the Panel's approach, which focused exclusively on the relationship between the effects of the discrimination and its justifiable or unjustifiable character.
>
> (Ibid., para. 230)

The Appellate Body later added that the panel's "quantitative approach – according to which discrimination would be characterized as unjustifiable only if imports under the MERCOSUR exemption take place in such amounts that the achievement of the objective of the measure at issue would be 'significantly undermined' – is flawed." Ibid., para. 247.

[116] WT/DS332/AB/R, para. 230 (3 Dec. 2007).

[117] For instance, in *Korea – Alcoholic Beverages*, WT/DS/AB75/R (18 Jan. 1999), the Appellate Body eschewed a rigid quantitative analysis. It specifically noted that "an approach that focused solely on the quantitative overlap of competition would, in essence, make cross-price elasticity *the* decisive criterion in determining whether products are 'directly competitive and substitutable.'" Ibid., para. 134 [emphasis in original]. It also observed, "we share the Panel's reluctance to rely unduly on quantitative analyses of the competitive relationship." Ibid. In *Chile – Alcoholic Beverages*, WT/DS87/R (13 Dec. 1999) the panel examined similar factors and noted, that "when a product is being marketed in ways that suggest that it is in competition with the most upmarket imported distilled products, this is evidence of at least potential competition with those imports." No quantification of this "potential" was provided. Similarly, in *Philippines – Distilled Spirits*, WT/DS396/R (15 Aug. 2011) the panel found that the products in question, certain imported spirits, were both like and competitive with domestic Philippine products. As part of its analysis, the panel examined several studies put forward by the parties but noted the difficulty of using econometric studies with limited historical price data. More broadly, on the issue of the protective application of a measure, as prohibited

What is noteworthy is a blend of deductive and inductive approaches to the reasoning of WTO law. Inductive logic is used to confirm or supplement hypotheses arrived at by deduction. The two functioning together constitute abduction.

6.4 Transforming the Law

In Chapter 1 I explained how a theory is a "system of ideas" with the emphasis being on the "system," or set of relationships, between those ideas.

In the last few chapters, I alluded to certain theoretic relationships exhibited in WTO law at specific points, but only episodically. In this section I go on to examine more systematically how the evidence of these theoretic relationships offers proof of the theory of law outlined in this book.

To begin with I focus on the modifications effected *horizontally*, that is, between elements in the *same* conceptual pair. Subsequently, I focus on the modifications effected *vertically*, that is, between the elements of *different* conceptual pairs, so that they may be confirmed in the form of distinct idea-complexes.

These relations and their transformative modifications are a reflection of efforts in the WTO system to do justice for the purpose of sustaining

by GATT Art. III:1, in *Japan – Alcoholic Beverages*, WT/DS8/AB/R (4 Oct. 1996), the Appellate Body held that:

> [the] protective application [of a measure] can most often be discerned from the design, the architecture, and the revealing structure of a measure. The very magnitude of the dissimilar taxation in a particular case may be evidence of such a protective application, as the Panel rightly concluded in this case. Most often, there will be other factors to be considered as well. In conducting this inquiry, panels should give full consideration to all the relevant facts and all the relevant circumstances in any given case.
>
> Ibid. at 29.

The Appellate Body labelled this approach a "comprehensive and objective analysis." (Ibid.) Similarly, in *Chile – Alcoholic Beverages*, WT/DS87/AB/R, para. 71 (13 Dec. 1999), the Appellate Body added in a broad-brush way that "a measure's purposes, objectively manifested in the design, architecture and structure of the measure, *are* intensely pertinent to the task of evaluating whether or not that measure is applied so as to afford protection to domestic production." Ibid. [emphasis in original]. Noteworthy in all these examples is the way the analysis attempts to be as comprehensive as possible (e.g. "all the relevant facts and all the relevant circumstances"). The mode of reasoning is based on what is known in the present.

the community. To recall, they consist of the four classic relationships of correlation, subordination, transition and integration.

How are these relationships visible in the workings of WTO law?

6.4.1 Correlation

The relationship of correlation designates a correspondence among concepts.

A correlation between obligations and rights in WTO law arises from the basic observation that to speak in any worthwhile sense of having a right in WTO law there must be a correlative obligation. This is apparent not only from text of the WTO Agreement, which frequently references the two concepts together, but also from the way in which panels and the Appellate Body regularly do so and the more generalized concern expressed in dispute settlement about adding to or diminishing WTO members rights and obligations.[118] Furthermore, a relationship of correlation is evident in continuing awareness of the importance of "balance" in the treaty.[119] In essence, members recognize that the WTO Agreement must achieve a continuing equilibrium composed of corresponding obligations and rights that express interdependence.

The relationship of correlation is likewise visible in the structural concepts of constitution and contract. Correspondence is to be inferred from continuing debate about whether the WTO Agreement is essentially arranged as either one structure or the other. As seen, there is support for both views, with the conclusion being that they must correspond in some degree. In addition, where one structural concept (i.e. the WTO as constitution) has waned, the other (i.e. the WTO as contract) has appeared to wax. It is not beyond contemplation that over long

[118] Thus, in DSU Art. 3.2 it is provided that "[r]ecommendations and rulings of the DSB cannot add to or diminish the *rights and obligations* provided in the covered agreements." Likewise in DSU Art. 19.2 it is mandated that "in their findings and recommendations, the panel and Appellate Body cannot add to or diminish the *rights and obligations* provided in the covered agreements." In early 2020 the US Trade Representative was critical of the Appellate Body on this very point, observing that "[t]he Appellate Body's persistent overreaching *has also taken away rights and imposed new obligations* through erroneous interpretations of WTO agreements." United States Trade Representative, "Report on the Appellate Body of the World Trade Organization," p. 2 (Feb. 2020) [emphasis added].

[119] See discussion of the abiding significance of the concept of "balance" in Chapter 2.

periods of time the reverse tendency (i.e. from contract to constitution) might be observed, indicating oscillation and connection between them.

Similarly, correlation is visible in the temporal concepts of future and past. Again, as seen, both the treaty text and panels and the Appellate Body have appeared to mandate reference to the immediate past as a means of making determinations about an unknown future. To have a past is likewise to have a future.

Finally, correlation is visible in the logical concepts of deduction and induction. Their correlation is indicated by the way that deduction and induction are classically understood to occupy the entirety of the logical spectrum, as manifested in WTO rules on the burden of proof. Deduction and presumption serve as "initial premises of legal reasoning."[120] The requirements of inductive logic and proof apply beyond them.

6.4.2 *Subordination*

The relationship of subordination is visible between obligations and rights in WTO law in the fact that member countries can cede their rights but not their obligations.[121] Subordination is also to be inferred from the fact that all WTO members are subject to an overarching duty to comply with WTO law (WTO Art. XVI:4) and the way in which observance of most WTO obligations is unconditional, whereas assertions of rights normally depend, as explained, on conditionality, proportionality and mutuality.

Subordination is likewise visible between the structural concepts of constitution and contract in the sense that WTO members are required

[120] C. F. Amerasinghe, "Presumptions and Inferences in Evidence in International Litigation" 3 *Law & Prac. Int'l Cts. & Tribunals* 395 at 396 (2004).

[121] *EC – Poultry*, WT/DS69/AB/R, para. 98 (13 July 1998). Steven Ratner has suggested three reasons why obligations enjoy primacy as elements in the international legal system. First, a focus of the system on obligations is a natural by-product of the law's authority. That authority is grounded in the "right to impose duties." Second, law as a sociologic phenomenon inevitably leads to questions about what the law requires and by whom. If an actor has a right, we inevitably look for a duty holder "to ensure that the right is realized." Third, as Ratner observes, in international law legality is often assessed through the prism of state responsibility. From that vantage point, the chief issue is whether a state has acted in breach of its international obligations. Steven Ratner, *The Thin Justice of International Law* 51–52 (Oxford University Press, Oxford; 2015).

to ensure that most arrangements concluded voluntarily between individual members and trenching on those members' WTO concessions and commitments must be consistent with the WTO Agreement.[122] This ordering would appear to infer that the WTO "constitution" is entrenched and takes precedence over its "contracts." A number of features of WTO dispute settlement reinforce this view, including the wording of DSU Arts. 3.5–3.6. At the same time, the ambiguity of the treaty's relationship with other arrangements – RTAs as well as a number of others – introduces a note of uncertainty and open-endedness in this characterization.

Similarly, subordination is visible in the temporal concepts of future and past in the way that WTO law is not entirely fixed and therefore does not remain as it was in the past, but instead is open to change. The ongoing reality of change in WTO law suggests that the future prevails over the past.

Finally, subordination is visible in the logical concepts of deduction and induction, a relationship apparent from the way in which certain key aspects of deductive reasoning in WTO law such as the presumption in DSU Art. 3.8 are essentially fixed and irrefutable. This contrasts with inductive reasoning where requirements for proof fluctuate, as expressed in the Appellate Body's well-known dictum in *U.S. – Woven Wool Shirts and Blouses* that the "kind of evidence will be required to establish [a] presumption *will vary* from measure to measure."[123]

6.4.3 *Transition*

Transition indicates movement from one concept to the other. It occurs when one concept is logically exhausted and gives rise to a need for the other.

A relationship of transition is discerned between obligations and rights in the way that WTO members are regularly bound by their obligations but only to the extent of those obligations, not beyond.[124] Conversely, WTO members may exercise their rights, but those rights are

[122] *Turkey – Textiles*, WT/DS34/R, para. 9.178 (31 May 1999); *EC – Bananas III*, WT/DS27/AB/R, paras. 164–170 (9 Sept. 1997).

[123] WT/DS33/AB/R, p. 14 (25 Apr. 1997) [emphasis added].

[124] For instance, WTO Art. XVI:4 makes clear that "Each Member shall ensure the conformity of its laws, regulations and administrative procedures with its obligations as provided in the annexed Agreements." The implication to be drawn from this phrase is that members are only bound to the extent of their "obligations," not beyond. See also *U.S. – FSC*, WT/DS108/AB/R, para. 90 (24 Feb. 2000) (noting that a WTO member is

conditioned by inherent obligations such as the obligation upon members not to abuse their rights (*abus de droit*).[125] This doctrine suggests the existence of a frontier between the two elements. Where obligations end, they give way to rights and vice versa.

The relationship of transition is similarly visible in the observation that where the WTO as constitution ends the possibility of contracting begins. Where a constitution as an order of obligations is exhausted, the possibility of contracting through rights-based arrangements emerges. Likewise, where there is a plurality of contracts, there is often an in-built tendency, or desire, for more uniformity and standardization in a constitutive form.[126]

The relationship of transition is also visible in the temporal concepts of future and past. Viewed from the perspective of the present, it might be said that where there is nothing new, then existing WTO law – a form of the past – prevails.[127] In this way the future becomes assimilated into or is a version of the past. However, in WTO law there is also evidence that the past transitions into the future. This movement is apparent in the

free to tax or not tax any particular category of revenues "[b]ut, in both instances, *the Member must respect its WTO obligations.*"). This is also the case with autonomous rights recognized in WTO law, such as the ability of a country to set its own "appropriate level of protection" (ALOP) in relation to sanitary and phytosanitary matters. See *EC – Hormones*, WT/DS26/AB/R/USA, para. 104 (18 Aug. 1997) (noting that SPS Art. 3.3 recognizes the autonomous right of a WTO member to establish such higher level of protection, provided that that member complies with certain requirements in promulgating SPS measures to achieve that level).

125 As Philip Allott has observed, "[t]he limits of a right amount to a peripheral duty . . . not to exceed those limits." Allott, *Eunomia* 162. See *U.S. – Shrimp*, WT/DS58/AB/R, para. 156 (12 Oct. 1998).

126 See, for instance, Thomas Cottier & Marina Foltea, "Constitutional Functions of the WTO and Regional Trade Agreements" in Lorand Bartels & Federico Ortino (eds), *Regional Trade Agreements and the WTO Legal System* 43 at 44 (Oxford University Press, Oxford; 2006) (noting how from a functional point of view WTO principles and rules assume the role of overriding, constitutional disciplines which structure the shape and contents of preferential agreements with a view to supporting trade creation).

127 This observation is at the heart of debate about precedent in WTO law, or in other words, the degree to which panels should be bound by previous Appellate Body reports. See *U.S. – Stainless Steel*, WT/DS344/AB/R, para. 160 (30 Apr. 2008). In recent criticism of the Appellate Body the US Trade Representative has noted that "[a]llowing the Appellate Body to create binding precedent has profound implications for the WTO system and the rights of WTO Members. Panels and the Appellate Body increasingly resolve disputes not by reference to the carefully negotiated and agreed-upon texts, but by reference to interpretations found in prior Appellate Body reports." United States Trade Representative, "Report on the Appellate Body" 7.

way that the law changes – a form of the future – thereby modifying the past and altering the law's total content.[128]

Finally, the relationship of transition is visible in terms of logic in the way that the demand for proof becomes a presumption. Inductive reasoning transitions into its correlative opposite in the form of deduction. An example occurs in the establishment of an "all others" anti-dumping rate under ADA Art. 6.10. There, the general rule is that in antidumping investigations "[t]he authorities shall, as a rule, determine the individual margin of dumping *for each known exporter or producer concerned*."[129] The rule mandates an empiric exercise in the determination of an individual margin for entities that are alleged to dump. However, ADA Art. 6.10 goes on to provide:

> In cases where the number of exporters, producers, importers or types of products involved is so large as to make such a determination impracticable, the authorities may limit their examination either to a reasonable number of interested parties or products by using samples which are statistically valid.

This paragraph describes the establishment of an "all others" rate, which, as pointed out in Chapter 5, can be understood as a *presumptive* rate characteristic of deductive logic. There has been litigation over the extent to which the presumption should apply.[130]

Several cases have referred to inductive measures – in essence, numbers – to reinforce deductive conclusions.[131]

128 For example, Donald McRae has expressed the view that WTO dispute settlement "provides the basis for the development of international trade law through judicial decision making. The interpretation of the WTO Agreement is an active, law-creating process." Donald McRae, "The WTO in International Law" 3(1) *J.I.E.L.* 27 at 30 (2000). Jeffrey Waincymer has similarly noted that "most observers would acknowledge that GATT/WTO adjudication has developed many worthy principles that might not have been possible through a strict negotiation format." Jeffrey Waincymer, *WTO Litigation* 391 (Cameron May, London; 2002). In recent criticism the US Trade Representative has noted a number of ways in which the Appellate Body has allegedly modified WTO law: See United States Trade Representative, "Report on the Appellate Body" 2.

129 Emphasis added.

130 See, for instance, *Argentina – Poultry Anti-Dumping Duties*, WT/DS241; *Mexico – Anti-Dumping Measures on Rice*, WT/DS295; *U.S. – Shrimp (Viet Nam)*, DS404/R.

131 In *India – Patents*, for instance, the panel noted the uncertainty created by India's vague legislative basis for a "mailbox" system of patent registrations. The panel confirmed this conclusion by referring to evidence that "*a number* of United States pharmaceutical companies do not believe that India has established a mailbox application system, and consequently have not filed applications for patent protection." WT/DS50/R, para. 7.39 (5 Sept. 1997) [emphasis added]. See also *Argentina – Footwear*, WT/DS56/R, para. 6.65 (25 Nov. 1997); *U.S. – Clove Cigarettes*, WT/DS406/R, para. 7.276 (2 Sept. 2011).

6.4.4 *Integration*

The relationship of integration involves the idea that the two concepts working together generate something new, or as mentioned elsewhere, a *tertium quid.* This "third thing" is not entirely *de novo* but instead depends "on what went on before."[132]

A relationship of integration is visible jurally in WTO law in the way that obligations and rights come together as a *sui generis* legal system. I have discussed how the interaction and interdependence of obligations and rights in WTO law ultimately gives rise to a legal system "of its own type." This is not only with respect to obligations and rights and the remedies available for their breach but also an array of legal features that modifies the total viewpoint of WTO members. As a result, both public and private thinking are changed.

A relationship of integration is also visible in the device of a "contractual constitution," which offers perhaps the most plausible explanation for the hybrid structure of WTO arrangements. A contractual constitution is not entirely fixed or flexible. However, without the relative fixity of the treaty's basic constitutive structure, there would be an unattractive degree of flexibility that might deter countries from concluding trade agreements at all. Member countries rely on its basic framework to pursue further elaborations of both this framework and others.[133]

Likewise, integration is visible in the way that the past and static aspect of WTO law combines with the future and dynamic aspect of WTO law in a diachronic present. The law is reasoned in the present (i.e. *eo instante*) and, generally speaking, legality is determined as of that time.

A sign of this presentism is the varied practice of treaty interpretation in WTO law. If the WTO Agreement were merely a "contract" it would be interpreted according to the usual rules of treaty interpretation, this being the understanding of the parties at the time of its conclusion. However, as discussed in Chapter 4 and has been noted by commentators, an objective method of treaty interpretation has been adopted by WTO adjudicators in a number of instances if the terms involved are

[132] Alan Brudner & Jennifer Nadler, *The Unity of the Common Law* (2nd ed.) 2 (Oxford University Press, Oxford; 2013).

[133] See, for instance, Cottier & Foltea, "Constitutional Functions of the WTO" 43 (discussing the constitutive function of WTO arrangements in relation to RTAs).

sufficiently generic. This is *not* invariably the same as a teleological method of interpretation, the method that would be expected if the WTO Agreement was considered purely constitutive. Instead, a combination of interpretative techniques is employed consistent with the treaty's hybrid character as a contractual constitution applicable in the present.[134]

Finally, integration is visible logically in the way that deduction and induction combine. Together in real-time, the two modes of logic work compositely so that the law reasons abductively. It looks back at facts in the past to form a hypothesis about the future – an "intelligent guess" – but always in the present, and always contingently and provisionally, and therefore in most cases incrementally.[135] Likewise, the law presumes, and where the presumption cannot be sustained in the face of evidence, it relies on proof. Abduction then is, in fact, the overarching mode of reasoning in WTO law.

[134] Gabrielle Marceau, "Evolutive Interpretation by the WTO Adjudicator" 12:4 *J.I.E.L.* 791 (2018) (identifying four categories of evolutive interpretation in relation to (1) generic terms, (2) specific or technical terms, (3) physical or technical transformations and evolutions and (4) changes to related and relevant rules of international law. The use of ever-evolving dictionary definitions and the reading of "context" in VCLT Art. 31 to include the contemporary ordinary meaning of the terms in their social or semantic context by WTO adjudicators leads to a clear dynamism in the process of WTO interpretation).

[135] For example, Dan Hunter depicts how abductive reasoning explains the tendency of incremental change in English common law:

> The view of abduction held by [Charles Saunders] Peirce and [Nicholas] Rescher is useful in legal domains for another reason. It is somewhat puzzling that practitioners should know how the law is changing. Yet I would suggest that the better practitioners are always aware of subtle shifts in the attitude of courts to previous untenable arguments. . . . For change to occur in law, attorneys must present arguments that the court adopts in its decision, and these arguments must be novel yet within the scope of acceptable change. So practitioners must be able to see the way courts are moving, and they make arguments in this direction in favor of their clients, which the courts subsequently accept. . . . Thus it must be that attorneys have some ability to read the way the law is going. I am loath to ascribe some mystical sixth sense to practitioners; but it remains that attorneys can tell which way the law is going, and this premonition is consistent among practitioners. Though not exactly predictable, the anticipated outcomes will fall within a fairly narrow range. Peirce/Rescher's view of abduction explains how this might be so.
>
> (Hunter, "No Wilderness of Single Instances" 387–388).

6.4.5 *Transformation and Idea-Complexes*

In Chapter 1, I introduced the concept of "idea-complexes" at work in WTO law and in Chapters, 4–5 I detailed how they interact between correlative elements of the same pair, that is, *horizontally*. However, that description did not focus on or explain how they operate *vertically* between correlative elements of *different pairs*, in other words how they function as true complexes by integrating those pairs in a particularly close way.

To recall, in justice- as- equality the law is conceived of principally as a regime of obligations. The normative order is compulsive. It takes the form structurally of a constitution that is prospective in nature and that is reasoned deductively. In justice-as-fairness the law is conceived of principally as a regime of rights. The normative order is consensual. It takes the form of a contractual structure that is retrospective and reasoned inductively.

In the real-time workings of a legal system, of course, there are many situations that obscure these idea-complexes, obstructing their visibility.[136] The law in operation is not so tidy as their neat arrangement into corresponding idea-complexes might infer. This calls for proof of their structure.

There are several indications that the components of justice-as-equality do in fact form a distinctive idea-complex in WTO law. The first of these is the equality of WTO members in law. All members are equal and are described as assuming certain basic obligations. This suggests that, as a

[136] We can immediately think of contracts as being concluded to protect obligations or constitutions enshrining bills of rights as counterexamples to the framework I have proposed. Many legal systems now allow claims for continuing or future damages due to some failure to perform in the past. To that extent, the law will depart from a strictly retrospective view of liability suggested by the theory. Nevertheless, future-oriented damages are a relatively recent development in many legal systems, and their award is normally attended by many limitative considerations – expectations, certainty, proof and so forth – that tend to confirm the restrictive tenor of rights. Conversely, a constitution is an order of obligations in the sense that, as explained, a constitution will be composed mainly of obligations. Constitutional law talk today often emphasizes the idea of rights – bills of rights, charters and so forth – that are enshrined in constitutions, another example of a potential complication to the alignment suggested by a communitarian theory of law. However, it is generally acknowledged that rights – individual rights in particular – are included in constitutions as a counterweight to the tremendous force of obligations within them. See Steven Calabresi et al., "State Bills of Rights in 1787 and 1791: What Individual Rights Are Deeply Rooted in American History and Tradition" 85 *S. Cal. L. Rev.* 1451 (2011–2012).

minimum, a chief aim in doing justice through WTO law must be to sustain equality, whatever that might mean. A straightforward connection is thus observed between equality and obligation.

A connection is also observed between equality, obligation and constitution in the sense that the WTO Agreement as a constitution, or at least as constitutive, is fundamentally about what states are required to do. And since a constitution is often described as an instrument "for the future," there is also a link between equality, obligation, constitution and the future involving a prospective outlook that is reasoned before the event (i.e. *ex ante*).[137] Moreover, this reasoning is chiefly by means of deductive logic.[138]

At the same time, however, there are a number of indications that the components of justice-as-fairness also form a distinctive idea-complex in WTO law. The first of these is the demand for fairness in WTO law evident in a number of specific instances. These can be traced to assertions of rights.

A connection is also identified between fairness, rights and contract in the sense that the WTO Agreement as a "contract" places emphasis on what states are permitted to do. And since a contract is analyzed retrospectively in terms of what parties undertook to do at the time the contract was concluded, there is a link between fairness, rights, contract and the past involving a retrospective outlook that is reasoned after the event (i.e. *ex post*). Moreover, this reasoning is chiefly by means of inductive logic.

Out of the above two idea-complexes, however, I also posited the emergence as a matter of theory of a *third* idea-complex involving justice whose value is transformation.

[137] "Obligation is necessity before the event . . . Necessity gives rise to order, resisting order's tendency to decline into disorder. If the physical world acts as a system, it is due to necessity. If the physical world is governed by necessity, it can act as a system." Allott, *Eunomia* 45, para. 3.17.

[138] Connections are often observed between equality and deductive logic in the sense that equality is referred to as being presumptive. See s.v. "Equality" in *Stanford Encyclopedia of Philosophy* (27 June 2007) (noting that "[m]any conceptions of equality operate along procedural lines involving a *presumption of equality*." [emphasis in original] (author: Stefan Gosepath). The presumption is one observed in the system of public international law. See Robert Jennings & Arthur Watts (eds), *Oppenheim's International Law*, vol. 1, 339 (Longman, Harlow; 1996) (referring to "equality [as] an inference from the basis of international law"). The practical consequence of the presumption or inference is that "[t]he burden of proof lies on the side of those s.v. "Equality" in *Stanford Encyclopedia of Philosophy* ibid.

This transformation is accomplished through the machinery of a *sui generis* legal system, a system "of its own type," involving obligations and rights. They operate together in the form of a contractual constitution reconciling a mix of coercive and consensual impulses that is reasoned in the present (i.e. *eo instante*) by means of a combination of deductive and inductive devices.

There are thus alignments in WTO law's operation, which provide considerable support for the structures outlined as part of a communitarian theory. At the same time, there are counterexamples. For instance, constitutions often enumerate rights, and likewise, contracts are frequently described as embodying the parties' obligations. To that extent, the theory may appear internally inconsistent and incomplete.

Still, a degree of inconsistency and incompleteness need not be stigmatized. As Thomas Kuhn pointed out, "a theory must seem better than its competitors, but it need not, and in fact never does, explain all the facts with which it can be confronted."[139] I will return to this idea in the final chapter.

6.5 Conclusion

This chapter has examined what arises out of the WTO Agreement as a *sui generis* legal system. It is a process driven by the transition to evermore intensive interdependence, although that interdependence – at least in an unconditional form – is now being reassessed.

I have posited that over long periods of time, the law will oscillate back and forth between the idea-complexes of compulsion and consent, sometimes being more equality- and obligation-oriented, at other times being more fairness- and rights-oriented, in its pursuit of a particular vision of justice for the purpose of promoting "the good." The general tendency is *toward* equality and *away from* fairness, but there are also counter-tendencies. Rarely will the law fall neatly into one or the other idea-complex. Instead, it momentarily occupies some midpoint on the spectrum between the two.

The emergent idea of oscillation also infers that over time the two complexes work together to produce a third thing. At the level of justice, this third thing is something transformative that sustains the community as ideas about the good, as well as equality and fairness in relation to it, change.

[139] Thomas Kuhn, *The Structure of Scientific Revolutions* 17–18 (University of Chicago Press, Chicago; 1962).

The changes induced by such modifications are profound. They demand that actors pay attention to interests other than their own. They also demand that actors conceive of and conform their behavior in light of collective interests. In WTO law this interest coexists uneasily with the sovereignty of states so that there is a persistent tension between individual member interests and the collective interest of the membership. WTO disputes often manifest this basic tension.

Interdependence also induces changes in the conception of law. The law is traditionally understood through a bilateral lens in which norms are conceived of principally in terms of individual transactions between specific actors.[140] Through interdependence, however, another understanding arises that stresses the collective of all transactions between *any* actor. Law and adherence to it for the purposes of attaining justice then become a condition of life in community.

[140] Christine Chinkin makes clear that the point of departure for the conception of international law is bilateral:

> The international legal system has been described as a series of bilateral consensual relationships within which rights, commitments, and obligations are formulated, and values are allocated between parties inter se. In the words of International Law Commission Special Rapporteur on the subject of state responsibility, Roberto Ago:
>
> "The correlation between legal obligation on the one hand and the subjective right on the other admits of no exception; as distinct from what is said to be the situation in municipal law, there are certainly no obligations incumbent on the subject which are not matched by an international subjective right of another subject or subjects, or even . . . of the totality of the other subjects of the law of nations".
>
> These serial bilateral relationships are created both by treaties and the operation of rules of customary international law. A multilateral treaty may be broken down into a series of bilateral relationships. "It is as if each contracting party were bound by as many bilateral treaties as there are other contracting parties." (See Christine Chinkin, *Third Parties in International Law* 1 (Oxford University Press, Oxford; 1993))

7

A Communitarian Theory and International Investment Law

7.1 Introduction

The communitarian theory of WTO law outlined in previous chapters works reasonably well as a description of key features of WTO law. Its "fit" with the existing law raises the possibility of the theory serving wider applications.

That possibility is likely to be canvassed perhaps most insistently in relation to international investment law, the body of law pertaining to the protection and treatment of foreign investment by host states. International investment law has come of age roughly at the same time as GATT/WTO law and is often compared with it.[1] For this reason it makes an intriguing subject of study and potential confirmation of the theory.

Superficially, both WTO and international investment law appear to have much in common. Both are concerned with the protection and treatment of economic interests. In WTO law this assumes the form of an emphasis on maintaining the equality of competitive conditions among goods, services and intellectual property regardless of origin, whereas in international investment law it assumes the form of an emphasis on the protection and treatment of individual foreign investors and investments in host countries. Both WTO and international investment law feature similar standards of MFN, NT and nondiscrimination, but beyond them, international investment law has evolved distinctive standards of fair and equitable treatment (FET), full protection and security (FPS) and denial of justice as specifications of the

[1] See, for instance, Nicholas di Mascio & Joost Pauwelyn, "Nondiscrimination in Trade and Investment Treaties" 102 *Am. J. Int'l L.* 48 (2008); Friedl Weiss, "Trade and Investment" in Peter Mulchinski et al. (eds), *The Oxford Handbook of International Investment Law* 182 (Oxford University Press, Oxford; 2008); Jürgen Kurtz, *The WTO and International Investment Law* (Cambridge University Press, Cambridge; 2016).

customary international minimum standard of treatment (IMS). Both bodies of law are also heavily committed to adjudication. In WTO law the commitment takes the form of an integrated dispute settlement system, whereas in international investment law it typically takes the form of ad hoc investor-state arbitration.

There are also a number of differences between the two regimes. Perhaps the most important of these is with respect to their normative bases. As seen, WTO law is sourced in a single set of treaty instruments whose provisions are interpreted "concurrently and cumulatively"[2] in an effort to find "order."[3] Its coherence is reinforced by a unified dispute settlement system whose structure – at least until recently – has been successful at generating a single expression.

By contrast, international investment law is sourced in customary international law supplemented by thousands of bilateral investment treaties, few of which are exactly the same. Arbitrations occur under most investment treaties on an ad hoc basis, with different arbitrators deciding different cases. This loose structure leaves considerable room for divergence.

Another difference is the nature of the underlying good, or "thing," protected by the law. As mentioned, in WTO law the "good" is a club good arising out of obligations belonging to the WTO membership as a whole. It is the sum of all concessions and commitments made by WTO members. Notwithstanding recent developments, there appears to be widespread consensus about its subsisting value. The arrangement is "public" and nontransferable, and in so being, is structured primarily according to distributive justice.

In international investment law, by comparison, the "good" is normally conceived of as the protection of specific investments composed of rights to something – to land, assets, or, more controversially, intangibles such as intellectual property,[4] profits[5] or

[2] *U.S. – Oil Country Tubular Goods Sunset Reviews*, WT/DS268/RW, para. 7.129 (30 Nov. 2006).

[3] *U.S. – Continued Zeroing*, WT/DS350/AB/R, para. 306 (4 Feb. 2009).

[4] Claims for intellectual property in international investment law have been relatively rare until recently. See Henning Grosse Ruse-Khan, "The Protection of Intellectual Property and International Investment Law" 19:1 *J.I.E.L.* 87 (2016). For discussion, see Susy Frankel, "Interpreting the Overlap of International Investment and Intellectual Property Law" 19:1 *J.I.E.L.* 121–143 (2016).

[5] Irmgard Marboe, *Calculation of Compensation and Damages in International Investment Law* (2nd ed.) 111–116 (Oxford University Press, Oxford; 2017).

goodwill.[6] It also frequently involves standards of treatment. These pertain to something "private" that in many instances is transferrable and therefore attracts the application of corrective justice. Investment law's focus on individual rights and the way that those rights naturally "emphasize competing rather than unified positions"[7] means that the law embodies much less agreement about its value.[8]

These differences have led to starkly different outcomes. Whereas the WTO Agreement and its dispute settlement mechanism have come to be regarded as lynchpins in promoting the "security and predictability" of the multilateral trading system, international investment law elicits much less consensus. There continues to be significant debate about the benefits of foreign investment.[9] Arbitrators occasionally interpret investment standards differently, and there is disagreement on a number of key doctrinal points. Partly as a result, some commentators have called for the investment regime's reform, if not its wholesale abolition.[10]

In response, in recent years certain countries – notably the United States and Canada – have curtailed or withdrawn from investment protection disciplines.[11] A few countries have even withdrawn from the

[6] Ibid., p. 201.

[7] Peter Gerhart, *Property Law and Social Morality* 10 (Cambridge University Press, Cambridge; 2014).

[8] For discussion José Alvarez, *The Public International Law Regime Governing International Investment* 16–24 (Hague Academy of International Law, Leiden; 2011) (noting for instance that although "most Governments now accept in principle that they need foreign capital to thrive, they continue to have a love-hate relationship with it. FDI has prompted strikingly similar concerns in a wide range of contexts, irrespective of whether the host of FDI is a developed economy, a poor developing country, or a State that finds itself somewhere in between." Ibid. at 21). Steven Ratner has observed that international investment law's "diversity of rules – different treaties may regulate the same issue in highly different ways – along with the fluid nature of interpretation, raises distinct challenges to a moral appraisal of the body of law as a whole." Steven Ratner, "Survey Article: Global Investment Rules as a Site for Moral Inquiry" 27:1 *J. Polit. Philos.* 107 at 108 (2019).

[9] See discussion in Alvarez, *The Public International Law Regime Governing International Investment* 18–24.

[10] See Public Statement on the International Investment Regime (31 August 2010) (recommending that "States should review their investment treaties with a view to withdrawing from or renegotiating them in light of . . . concerns . . . [and] should take steps to replace or curtail the use of investment treaty arbitration."). Available at www.osgoode.yorku.ca/public-statement-international-investment-regime-31-august-2010.

[11] NAFTA ch. 11 allowed investors of a NAFTA country to bring proceedings directly against the government of another NAFTA party for alleged breaches of its investment

keystone instrument for dispute settlement in the field, the International Centre for the Settlement of Investment Disputes (ICSID) Convention.[12] A lingering question has to be why?

In this chapter I posit that the explanation is traceable to the distinctive nature of international investment law's good. Simply put, there is little or no clear agreement about the benefit – or value – of international investment protection, and beyond that, little appreciation of the advantage to be derived from foreign investment in host states.

This difference means that the starting point for theoretical reflection – the sense of what is common, or "community" – is diluted and harder to discern in international investment law than it is in WTO law. Rather than functioning as an integrated "system," international investment law is often described as constituting a diffuse "framework" or "regime."[13]

obligations under the treaty. NAFTA ch. 11 developed arbitral jurisprudence that was heavily cited and influential. However, given growing controversy about international investment protection raised by civil society and certain academics, the United States and Canada – traditional champions of investment protection – decided not to carry over investment protection provisions into the successor treaty, the USMCA. Instead, under the USMCA Ch. 14 investor-state arbitration is limited to the United States and Mexico and in a more restricted form than previously. Investor-state arbitration between Canada and Mexico proceeds under the Comprehensive and Progressive Agreement for Trans-Pacific Partnership (the "CPTPP").

[12] The ICSID Convention was withdrawn from by Bolivia in May 2007, by Ecuador in July 2009 and by Venezuela in January 2012. The withdrawals were regarded as an expression of dissatisfaction by countries with elements of the "Washington Consensus," of which investor-state arbitration is popularly considered to be one element. See Rodrigo Polanco Lazo, "Is There a Life for Latin American Countries after Denouncing the ICSID Convention?" 11:1 *TDM* 1 (2014).

[13] There has been much speculation about whether it is appropriate to refer to international investment law as a "system". See Christoph Schreuer & Matthew Weiniger, "A Doctrine of Precedent?" in Peter Muchlinski et al. (eds), *The Oxford Handbook of International Investment Law* 1188 at 1189 (Oxford University Press, Oxford; 2008) (noting that "[t]he system, if it can even be called a system, of investment treaty arbitration is not unitary in the sense of each tribunal sitting under the same source of jurisdiction."). See also Alvarez, *The Public International Law Regime Governing International Investment* 359 (noting Charles Brower's suggestion that "if one expects BITs and FTAs to produce a 'system' and not merely an ambiguous 'regime' or merely a 'framework', even a small handful of inconsistent arbitral rulings, especially arising in the context of comparable or identical treaty language and comparable facts … is a source of serious concern").

In previous chapters, I explained how WTO law can be thought of chiefly as a law of equality and obligation. This is because most of its major standards are expressions of equality and its dispute settlement system is understood, at least notionally, to reestablish the "equality of competitive conditions." The body of law is primarily constitutive in that it sets out broad norms of behavior. In the main it is also prospective in stressing what countries must do in future, in adopting an *ex ante* perspective and in being reasoned deductively.

International investment law presents the opposite of these concepts in many respects. It is chiefly a law of fairness and rights. What the law is concerned with is the protection of those rights. When the law seeks to correct an injury done to an investor, it is implicitly making amends for the past and adopts an *ex post* perspective. The correction might be thought of as warranting compensation equal to the injury suffered. However, because of the time value of money, litigation costs and pressure to settle, there is often a discount in investment awards so that the actual amount recovered by investors is simply "fair," or what is appropriate. International investment law is likewise considered "contractual" in the sense that it emanates chiefly from bilateral agreements between countries. Finally, the law is reasoned inductively and requires proof.

International investment law is therefore intriguing because it assumes an opposing yet correlative form to that of WTO law. In a number of ways, it might be taken to be WTO law's alter ego. That opposition, which aligns with the idea-complexes outlined in earlier chapters, presents substantial confirmation of the theory's structure.

Nevertheless, little of the foregoing explains how international investment law has come to be as it is. To furnish some idea of its development, it is necessary to review how contemporary international investment law has emerged and evolved.

7.2 An International Law of Investment

The origin of international investment law lies in the law of diplomatic protection. Under international law traditionally a home state was allowed to intervene on behalf of its nationals with investments in a host state.[14] This power was recognized for the purpose of avoiding

[14] For an overview of the evolution from diplomatic espousal to investor claims, see Andrew Newcombe & Lluis Paradell, *Law and Practice of Investment Treaties* 1–73 (Wolters Kluwer Law & Business, Austin, TX; 2009).

discrimination against a home state's nationals and the possibility of prejudice in host state courts. The power to intervene had shortcomings, however, notably in the requirement of diplomatic espousal. According to this requirement, a home state had to take up a claim with the host state, meaning that specific claims were sometimes deferred or denied for the sake of the greater state-to-state relationship.[15]

During the nineteenth century, some investor claims did proceed and a modest body of case law pertaining to investor claims emerged.[16] In the usual instance, an investor would pursue action against a host state before an arbitral tribunal alleging breach of the IMS. Over time, countries began to dispense with the requirement of espousal. The result was a direct right of action by foreign investors against host governments. In such cases the host state was the respondent, never a claimant. The host state's conduct was judged according to the IMS sourced in international law, not by the law of any national system.[17]

The IMS is customary and therefore vague and fluctuating.[18] In time the need for certainty – in WTO parlance "security and predictability" – prompted countries to begin negotiating bilateral investment claims procedures, which were eventually formalized in bilateral investment agreements. These agreements increased substantially in number after 1959.[19] In 1966 the ICSID, an arm of the World Bank, was established to provide a common framework for investment arbitration.[20] Proceedings

[15] Ibid. at 7–8.

[16] Ibid.

[17] Campbell McLachlin et al., *International Investment Arbitration: Substantive Principles* 5 (Oxford University Press, Oxford; 2007).

[18] Ibid., p. 21, 205*ff*; Newcombe & Paradell, *Law and Practice of Investment Treaties* 236.

[19] As Andrew Newcombe and Lluis Paradell note, "Germany is commonly cited as the first state to develop a BIT program and to sign the first BIT, with Pakistan, in 1959. The Treaty between the Federal Republic of Germany and Pakistan for the Promotion and Protection of Investments (Germany-Pakistan (1959)) contains many of the substantive provisions that have become common in subsequent BITs." Newcombe & Paradell, *Law and Practice of Investment Treaties* 41. As of 2022 UNCTAD indicated that there were 2,231 bilateral investment agreements in force and 335 other treaties with investment provisions in them: UNCTAD, UNCTAD Investment Policy Hub (visited 17 Aug. 2022).

[20] ICSID was established by multilateral treaty in 1965 to provide facilities for conciliation and arbitration of investment disputes between contracting states and individuals and companies that qualify as nationals of other contracting states. ICSID does not conciliate or arbitrate investment disputes itself. Instead, this task is left to individual conciliation

under ICSID were slow to begin but by the early 2000s had become popular and were a source of regular recourse for major foreign investors against host states.[21]

Christoph Schreuer has pointed out how bilateral investment treaties have a certain orientation in the sense that they:

> are designed to provide guarantees for foreign investors from the respective countries. They do not normally address obligations of investors, although some BITs provide that investments, in order to be protected, must be in accordance with the host State's law. The idea of including duties for investors, such as certain human rights, environmental, and labour standards are only beginning to be reflected in treaty practice.[22]

Today the typical clauses of an investment agreement provide a definition of "investments" and "investors," the admission of investments, guarantees of fair and equitable treatment ("FET"), full protection and security ("FPS"), guarantees against arbitrary and discriminatory treatment, national treatment (NT) and most favored nation (MFN) treatment, guarantees against expropriation, commitments regarding free transfer of payments, and provisions on dispute settlement.[23] Schreuer notes that "[a]lthough many BITs display similarities, they are by no means identical. In some respects, BITs display significant variations. Therefore, each BIT must be examined on its own terms."[24] This variety and the fact that most bilateral agreements are negotiated individually give investment law a heavily "contractual" aspect.

The popularity of bilateral investment treaties in recent decades has promoted a "treatification" of law in the field, yet as José Alvarez has

commissions or arbitral tribunals, most of which have been appointed ad hoc. As of mid-2023 165 countries had signed and/or ratified the ICSID Convention. Since 1978 ICSID also administers certain proceedings between states and nationals of other states *outside* the scope of the Convention under a set of procedures known as the Additional Facility Rules.

21 UNCTAD noted that the total count of known investor–state dispute settlement cases had reached 1,190 at the end of 2021. See UNCTAD, *International Investment Agreements Issues Note* (July 2022).

22 S.v. "Investments, International Protection" *Max Planck Encyclopedia of Public International Law* para. 7 (June 2013) (author: Christoph Schreuer).

23 S.v. "Investments, International Protection" *Max Planck Encyclopedia of Public International Law* para. 8 (June 2013) (author: Christoph Schreuer).

24 S.v. "Investments, International Protection" *Max Planck Encyclopedia of Public International Law* para. 9 (June 2013) (author: Christoph Schreuer).

pointed out, custom remains a valid and technically distinct source of international investment law.[25] In addition, treaties and custom are supplement by nonbinding standards in the form of guidelines and codes of conduct. Doctrines of state responsibility and international rules on the nationality of individuals may also be applicable. In some instances, a further source of law is contained in specific concessionary agreements concluded between individual investors and host states.[26]

In most cases international investment disputes are resolved by means of arbitration, which is often made subject to rules under a given arbitral mechanism. Many disputes are subject to ICSID rules or rules adopted by the UN Commission on International Trade Law (UNCITRAL). Difficulties can occur where a contract provides for dispute settlement through domestic courts while an applicable treaty provides for international arbitration. For this reason, umbrella clauses extending treaty coverage to all undertakings of investors are sometimes included in investment agreements, although the extent of such clauses continues to be controversial.[27]

If a breach of a bilateral investment treaty is found, typical remedies take the form of restitution, compensation or satisfaction. A common feature of bilateral investment agreements is that the choice of principal remedy – restitution or compensation – is left to the host state but almost always involves compensation.[28] In addition, in complaints concerning a breach of the standard of treatment, the arbitrator is often prohibited from ordering the repeal, cessation or modification of the treatment concerned.[29]

[25] Alvarez, *The Public International Law Regime Governing International Investment* 228.

[26] S.v. "Investments, International Protection" *Max Planck Encyclopedia of Public International Law* para. 24 (June 2013) (author: Christoph Schreuer).

[27] S.v. "Investments, International Protection" *Max Planck Encyclopedia of Public International Law* para. 31 (June 2013) (author: Christoph Schreuer).

[28] See, for instance, EU Commission, TTIP proposal – Investment, Resolution of Investment Disputes and Investment Court System, published on 12 November 2015, online: http://trade.ec.europa.eu/doclib/docs/2015/november/tradoc_153955.pdf. Céline Lévesque, "The European Commission Proposal for an Investment Court System: Out with the Old, In with the New?" CIGI Investor-State Arbitration Series Paper No. 10, p. 4 (Sept. 2016).

[29] See ibid. For discussion of the dislike of ordering specific performance against a state see Roslyn Higgins, "The Taking of Property by the State", 176 *Recueil des Cours* 259, 315–317 (1982). See also Borzu Sabahi et al., *Investor-State Arbitration* (2nd ed.) 708–713 (2019).

Arbitrators generally recognize that "[r]eliance on past decisions is a fundamental feature of any orderly decision-making process" and that such reliance "strengthens the predictability of decisions and enhances their authority."[30] At the same time, arbitrators and commentators have had difficulty describing what has arisen in the associated jurisprudence as strict precedent and have instead tended to describe it as more akin to the *jurisprudence constante* of civil law.[31]

A typical investment dispute involves a claim as to whether the IMS has been breached. In an earlier era the IMS was defined largely in terms of nationalizations and expropriations involving specific "takings" – that is, the taking of property. As government behavior has become more wide-ranging and sophisticated, however, there has been pressure for the IMS to evolve. The outcome is a more fragmented, less conceptually coherent IMS involving a number of distinct sub-standards, especially since the focus of international investment law in recent decades has shifted from a concern with the protection of property to a more general concern with investor treatment.[32]

Investors and investments are entitled to the IMS, but what the IMS consists of in any given instance has to be worked out on a case-by-case basis with reference to the treaty text and case law.[33] The IMS' contextual character is an important aspect of the law's overall attention to fairness and rights.

The accepted standards of protection are FET, FPS, guarantees against arbitrary and discriminatory treatment, NT, MFN, and in certain instances, a separately recognized standard of denial of justice. Some investment tribunals interpret the sub-standards as related to one another. FET, in particular, has been regarded by some arbitrators as

[30] Schreuer & Weiniger, "A Doctrine of Precedent?" 1188 at 1189.

[31] The primary difference between *jurisprudence constante* in the civil law and precedent in common law systems is that in the common law controlling authority may be given to a single decision whereas in the civil law it is not. See Eva Steiner, *French Law* 74 (Oxford University Press, Oxford; 2018).

[32] Ioana Tudor, *The Fair and Equitable Treatment Standard in the International Law of Foreign Investment* 2 (Oxford University Press, Oxford; 2008) (noting that in the early 1980s "[t]he focus of . . . international rules shifted from the protection of investment to the treatment of investment").

[33] Andrew Newcombe and Lluis Paradell note that "The substantive content of the minimum standard . . . is usually not specified in any detail." They go on to note that "the content . . . has been and remains contentious." Newcombe & Paradell, *Law and Practice of Investment Treaties* 233.

an overarching sub-standard that embraces others. As Schreuer notes, however, "[t]he better view, subscribed to by a majority of tribunals, is to see the [sub-]standards [of the IMS] as analytically distinct even though there may be a certain degree of overlap among them."[34] A brief review of the sub-standards helps to provide some idea of their respective role.

7.2.1 Fair and Equitable Treatment (FET)

FET is currently the leading standard in investment law and is commonly said to be an expression of the principle of good faith.[35] FET is noncontingent and may be violated even if the investor receives national treatment. Schreuer notes that a number of principles have come to be recognized as included in FET. These include transparency, consistency, stability, the protection of the investor's legitimate expectations, compliance with contractual obligations, procedural propriety and due process, and freedom from coercion and harassment.[36]

FET first emerged in the 1960s to cover behavior that the IMS was not thought to cover. References to "*fair* and equitable" treatment give it a highly circumstantial quality in line with the idea of fairness developed as part of a communitarian theory in previous chapters.[37]

[34] Christoph Schreuer, "Investments, International Protection" Oxford Public International Law para. 50 (June 2013).

[35] Peter Muchlinski, "Caveat Investor – The Relevance of the Conduct of the Investor under the Fair and Equitable Treatment Standard" 55:3 *Int'l & Comp LQ* 527 at 530 (2006).

[36] S.v. "Investments, International Protection" *Max Planck Encyclopedia of Public International Law* para. 52 (June 2013) (author: Christoph Schreuer).

[37] To recall, fairness-derived rules are said to respond to the need to deal with "a near infinitude of particulars which have to be sorted out case by case." Sean Carroll, *The Serengeti Rules* 10 (Princeton University Press, Princeton, NJ; 2016). José Alvarez has noted, for instance, that there is an emerging consensus among arbitral decisions that FET "is a fact specific, flexible, and contextual standard *whose application turns on the circumstances of each case.*" Alvarez, *The Public International Law Regime Governing International Investment* 206 [emphasis added]. Similarly, Ioana Tudor observes that "[s]ince the FET is a standard, it is natural that it has variable content *that depends on the circumstances of the case.*" Tudor, *The Fair and Equitable Treatment Standard* 155. In *Rumeli Telekom A.S. and Telsim Mobil Telekomunikasyon Hizmetleri A.S.* v. *Kazakhstan* (2008), ICSID Case No. ARB/05/16, the tribunal noted that the FET standard in treaties is "intentionally vague in order to give tribunals the possibility to articulate the range of principles to achieve the treaty's purpose *in particular disputes.*" Ibid., para. 583 [emphasis added].

Specific applications of FET pertain to the treatment of investors by host state courts and administrative bodies, in situations of government decision-making, and under legislation. In terms of treatment by host state courts and administrative bodies, "FET requires host States to provide a fair and efficient system of justice."[38] In such circumstances, a host state may be responsible for procedural shortcomings as well as "clear and malicious misapplication of the law."[39]

With respect to governmental acts, "the use of power for improper purposes as well as coercion and harassment by State officials are self-evident and severe violations of the FET standard."[40] Here, FET has been held to require a stable – though not necessarily fixed – business environment, the honoring of the investor's expectations, and transparency in the host state's decision-making. Nicolas Angelet observes that the legitimacy of the investor's expectations is considered as of the time the investment entered into and on the basis of specific representations made to the investor.[41] The legitimacy of the investor's expectations is also dependent on the investor's own behavior.[42]

The gravity of the behavior necessary to find breach of the FET standard is uncertain. Some arbitrators have found a plain breach by the host state to be sufficient, whereas others have required something more serious such as "an outright and unjustified repudiation of the transaction" or an exercise of public authority to be required.[43] Finally, with respect to legislative acts, an issue in FET analysis is whether the domestic legal framework exhibits sufficient stability, consistency and transparency, and accords with the investor's legitimate expectations. The investor cannot typically expect that the legal framework will be

[38] S.v. "Fair and Equitable Treatment" *Max Planck Encyclopedia of Public International Law* para. 17 (Mar. 2011) (author: Nicolas Angelet).

[39] *Azinian* v. *Mexico*, ICSID Case No. ARB (AF)/97/2, para. 103 (1 Nov. 1999).

[40] S.v. "Fair and Equitable Treatment" *Max Planck Encyclopedia of Public International Law* para. 20 (Mar. 2011) (author: Nicolas Angelet).

[41] S.v. "Fair and Equitable Treatment" *Max Planck Encyclopedia of Public International Law* para. 23 (Mar. 2011) (author: Nicolas Angelet).

[42] Yulia Levashova, "Fair and Equitable Treatment and Investor's Due Diligence under International Investment Law" 67 *Neth. Int'l L. Rev.* 233 (2020).

[43] S.v. "Fair and Equitable Treatment" *Max Planck Encyclopedia of Public International Law* para. 25 (Mar. 2011) (author: Nicolas Angelet).

"frozen" since that framework "can always evolve and be adapted to changing circumstances, but neither is [FET] a question of whether the framework can be dispensed with altogether when specific commitments . . . have been made."[44]

FET's relationship with the IMS remains uncertain. Three models of relationship can be envisaged between them. First, FET can be regarded as being the same as the IMS (i.e. an identity standard). Second, FET can be regarded as containing some elements of treaty obligations, the IMS, state practice and general principles of law, but not necessarily all of them (i.e. an overlap standard). Third, FET can be regarded as possessing an independent meaning over and above the IMS (i.e. a supplementary standard).

An identity standard might be contemplated if attention is paid to treaty references making FET correspondent with customary international law or some treaty referencing the IMS.[45] An overlap standard might be contemplated if attention is paid to attempts to harmonize FET obligations with other treaty standards and the remainder of international law.[46] Finally, a supplementary standard might be contemplated if attention is paid to FET's distinct textual basis.[47] In practice, none of

44 *CMS Gas Transmission Co* v. *Argentina (Decision on Jurisdiction)*, ICSID Case No. ARB/01/8, paras. 276–277 (12 May 2005).

45 For example, in *Saluka* the tribunal observed "the difference between the Treaty standard [of FET] . . . and the customary minimum standard, when applied to the specific facts of the case, may well be more apparent than real." *Saluka Investments* v. *Czech Republic*, (Partial Award), PCA Case No. 2001-04, para. 291 (17 Mar. 2006).

46 Support for an overlap standard comes from an UNCTAD study, which concludes that "[f]air and equitable treatment is not synonymous with the international minimum standard. Both standards *may overlap significantly* with respect to issues such as arbitrary treatment, discrimination, and unreasonableness, but the presence of a provision assuring fair and equitable treatment in an investment instrument does not automatically incorporate the international minimum standard for foreign investors." UNCTAD, *Fair and Equitable Treatment* 40 (1999) (emphasis in original).

47 As Ioana Tudor notes, "if States and Investors believed FET was entirely interchangeable with the IMS, they would have indicated this clearly in their investment instruments. The absence of such an explicit link between the two standards shows, according to the UNCTAD Secretariat, that most States and Investors do not believe FET is implicitly the same notion as the IMS." Tudor, *The Fair and Equitable Treatment Standard* 66. Tudor lists the principal arguments for a diversity approach as follows. First, the main problem of equalizing FET with the IMS is that equalization limits the scope of FET. The IMS provides for action only in extreme cases. In contrast, FET offers the foreign investor more generous guarantees designed to be operational. Second, the IMS was intended to function in a state-to-state context, not in an investor-state context. Third, references to the IMS do not yield any additional clarification on the meaning of the FET. Fourth, the

these interpretive options holds exclusive sway. Instead, the interpretation of FET appears to involve various outcomes that are, at one time or another, a combination of all three.[48]

The diversity of approaches appears to be appropriate when account is taken of FET's variable character. Commentators generally acknowledge that FET's application "will always remain a highly case specific exercise."[49]

7.2.2 Full Protection and Security (FPS)

The basic meaning of FPS is that the host state is required to take measures to protect the investment from adverse effects. The requirement to grant physical protection and security applies in relation to conduct by both state organs and private actors in the host state. FPS is understood to be noncontingent.

Traditionally, protection extended under FPS was considered to cover physical violence. More recently, FPS has been extended to protections against infringements of the investor's legal rights.[50] A host state is not required to afford absolute protection to the investor but merely to observe standards of due diligence.[51]

IMS ensures a minimum standard of treatment that is only a minimum, while the FET is designed to go beyond it. Fifth, the IMS remains a customary international law standard whereas FET is conventional. Ibid., pp. 67–68.

[48] Thus, Campbell McLachlin and others have suggested that:

> [a dichotomous view of the relationship between the IMS and FET] is misguided, and the dichotomy presented by the opposing views is a false one on a number of levels. It takes an overly simplistic view of differences in formulation of the right in different treaties. It suggests that the only choice open to a tribunal is between a complete discretion to determine whether particular conduct is 'unfair and inequitable' on the one hand, and the application of a conception of customary international law "frozen in amber."
>
> (McLachlin et al., *International Investment Arbitration* 203)

McLachlin and others conclude that "the fair and equitable standard gives modern expression to a *general principle of due process* in its application to the treatment of investors." Ibid., p. 205 (emphasis in original).

[49] Gebhard Bücheler, *Proportionality in Investor-State Arbitration* 3 (Oxford University Press, Oxford; 2015).

[50] S.v. "Investments, International Protection" *Max Planck Encyclopedia of Public International Law* para. 54 (June 2013) (author: Christoph Schreuer).

[51] Ibid., para. 56.

7.2.3 *Arbitrary or Discriminatory Behavior*

Many investment treaties offer protection against arbitrary or discriminatory behavior. Arbitrary behavior has been defined by the ICJ as "not so much something opposed to a rule of law, as something opposed to the rule of law. It is a willful disregard of due process of law, an act which shocks, or at least surprises, a sense of judicial propriety."[52] Arbitrary behavior has been held to arise in situations where "it inflicts damage on the investor without serving any apparent legitimate purpose"; where "it is not based on legal standards but on discretion, prejudice, or personal preference"; where "[a] measure [is] taken for reasons that are different from those put forward by the decision-maker"; and where "it is taken in willful disregard of due process and proper procedure."[53]

Intent does not appear necessary for a finding of arbitrary behavior. For example, the standard has been held to be violated because of the "very confusion and lack of clarity that resulted in some form of arbitrariness [in decision-making], even if not intended."[54]

In a number of cases, tribunals have dealt with the prohibition on unreasonable or arbitrary measures in conjunction with claims concerning FET. Schreuer notes that this tendency is particularly pronounced with tribunals applying the former NAFTA, which did not contain a separate provision on arbitrary or discriminatory treatment.[55] However, even tribunals applying treaties that expressly mention FET as well as protection from arbitrary or discriminatory measures do not always distinguish between the two standards.[56]

With respect to discriminatory behavior, the most frequent issue involves discrimination on the basis of nationality. Not every distinction

[52] *Elettronica Sicula S.P.A. (ELSI)*, I.C.J. Reports 1989 at para. 128.

[53] *EDF* v. *Romania*, ICSID Case No. ARB/05/13, paras. 302–306 (8 Oct. 2009); *Lemire* v. *Ukraine*, ICSID Case No. ARB/06/18, para. 262 (14 Jan. 2010); *Toto* v. *Lebanon*, ICSID Case No. ARB/07/12, para. 157 (7 June 2012); *TRACO* v. *Poland*, paras. 224–227 [Partial Award of 5 Sept. 2012].

[54] *Occidental* v. *Ecuador*, LCIA Case No. UN3467, para. 163 (1 July 2004).

[55] S.v. "Investments, International Protection" *Max Planck Encyclopedia of Public International Law* para. 63 (June 2013) (author: Christoph Schreuer); *Waste Management Inc* v. *United Mexican States* [Award of 30 Apr. 2004], para. 98.

[56] *Saluka Investments* v. *Czech Republic*, (Partial Award), PCA Case No. 2001-04, para. 460 (17 Mar. 2006); *GEA Group AG* v. *Ukraine*, ICSID Case No. ARB/08/16, paras. 325–331 (31 Mar. 2011). Other tribunals stressed the difference between the two standards: *LG & E* v. *Argentina*, ICSID Case No. ARB/02/1, paras. 162–163 (3 Oct. 2006).

based on nationality is a violation, but most BITs contain specific standards of nondiscrimination. These are reflected in provisions that guarantee NT and MFN. Frequently, both standards are found in the same provision. Arbitrators have held that the discriminatory effect of a measure is what is of chief concern, although discriminatory intent may be relevant.[57]

7.2.4 National Treatment (NT)

An NT principle is found in many bilateral investment treaties and is contingent. What is at issue in an NT claim is how the host state treats its own nationals. Most NT clauses apply only once a business is established (i.e. postentry NT), although some investment treaties, especially those concluded by the United States and Canada, also include provisions concerning a right of access to a national market on the basis of NT (i.e. preentry NT).

US bilateral investment treaties, including the former NAFTA, make reference to "a like situation" or to "like circumstances." One arbitrator interpreting NAFTA Art. 1102 commented with respect to the basis for comparison in analyzing an NT standard:

> In evaluating the implications of the legal context, the Tribunal believes that as a first step, the treatment accorded a foreign owned investment protected by Article 1102(2) should be compared with that accorded domestic investments in the same business or economic sector. However, that first step is not the last one. Differences in treatment will presumptively violate Article 1102(2) unless they have a reasonable nexus to rational government policies that (1) do not distinguish, on their face or de facto, between foreign-owned and domestic companies, and (2) do not otherwise unduly undermine the investment liberalizing objectives of NAFTA.[58]

In the context of finding the appropriate basis of comparison or "like circumstances," Schreuer notes that some investment tribunals have adopted standards from jurisprudence developed under GATT 1947 and the WTO Agreement.[59]

[57] *LG & E* v. *Argentina*, ICSID Case No. ARB/02/1, paras. 146, 148 (3 Oct. 2006).

[58] *Pope & Talbot Inc* v. *Canada* para. 78 [Award on the Merits of Phase 2 of 10 Apr. 2001].

[59] S.v. "Investments, International Protection" *Max Planck Encyclopedia of Public International Law* paras. 69–70 (June 2013) (author: Christoph Schreuer).

7.2.5 MFN Treatment

Because MFN is not required under customary international law, it is provided for in virtually every bilateral investment treaty. Specific MFN clauses vary and the standard itself is contingent. It will depend on the benefits enjoyed by third states and their nationals.

As seen in previous chapters, the role of MFN in WTO law is pivotal. By comparison, the role of MFN in international investment law is more limited. This is due to the fact that most investors today perceive greater benefit from asserting claims pursuant to noncontingent standards such as FET and FPS.[60]

Generally speaking, the application of MFN clauses to substantive standards has been unobjectionable. Arbitrators have held, for instance, that MFN clauses would attract the application of an FET clause in a third-party treaty,[61] a more favorable standard for assessing compensation,[62] and the requirement to provide effective means of asserting claims and interests.[63]

Where sharp differences are observed is with respect to the extension of procedural benefits. Investors have attempted to use MFN to access both substantive and procedural benefits contained in third-party treaties. In *Maffezini* v. *Spain*, for instance, the advantage involved sidestepping an eight-month waiting period for bringing action.[64] In *Salini* v. *Morocco*, the advantage involved sidestepping the previous attornment to jurisdiction to domestic courts in order to proceed with arbitration.[65] In both instances, reliance on MFN was permitted.

In *Plama* v. *Bulgaria*, on the other hand, the tribunal highlighted doubts as to the parties' intentions if certain procedural advantages were to be accessed by means of an MFN clause. The *Plama* tribunal noted that "it is one thing to add to the treatment provided in one treaty more favorable treatment provided elsewhere. It is quite another thing

[60] Tudor, *The Fair and Equitable Treatment Standard* 2. S.v. "Investments, International Protection" *Max Planck Encyclopedia of Public International Law* para. 90 (June 2013) (author: Christoph Schreuer).

[61] *Bayindir* v. *Pakistan*, ICSID Case No. ARB/03/29, paras. 231–232 (Decision on Jurisdiction of 14 Nov. 2005).

[62] *CME* v. *Czech Republic*, UNCITRAL, para. 500 [Final Award of 14 Mar. 2003].

[63] *White Industries* v. *India* [Final Award of 30 Nov. 2011] paras. 11.2.1–11.2.9.

[64] *Maffezini* v. *Spain*, ICSID Case No. ARB/97/7 (13 Nov. 2000).

[65] *Salini* v. *Morocco*, ICSID Case No. ARB/00/4 (31 July 2001).

to replace a procedure specifically negotiated by parties with an entirely different mechanism."[66] In particular, the tribunal criticized the liberal approach taken in *Maffezini* as an "inappropriate basis for analysis." The tribunal opined that automatic *Maffezini*-type extensions could lead to a "chaotic situation – actually counterproductive to harmonization [of investment disciplines]," which would not be consistent with the state parties' intent. Adopting a restrictive approach, the *Plama* tribunal decided to give precedence to the intentions expressed by the state parties by limiting the investor to procedures contained in the base treaty. Applying *Plama*, an arbitrator in *Telenor* v. *Hungary* went on to note that "the effect of wide interpretation of the MFN clause is to expose the host State to treaty shopping by the investor." A wide interpretation of MFN "generates both uncertainty and instability." Thus, "what has to be applied is not some abstract principle of investment protection in favor of a putative investor who is not a party to the BIT ... but the intention of the States who are the contracting parties."[67]

Experience with MFN in international investment law emphasizes how the underlying structure of the law – here bilateral obligations – conditions its interpretation. In WTO law the MFN obligation is central to the formation of broad-based collective expectations by the membership that take the form of a "club" good. By comparison, in international investment law MFN has been regarded as potentially destabilizing, at least procedurally. An MFN clause can be the source of undesirable international obligations that run counter to expectations of the signatory countries and give rise to free-ridership. As a result, some countries have expressly sought to limit MFN's application in the investment context, a reflection of the underlying good's essentially "private" character.[68]

[66] *Plama* v. *Bulgaria*, ICSID Case No. ARB/03/24 (8 Feb. 2005). In *Plama* the tribunal rejected ICSID jurisdiction under the MFN clause in the 1987 Bulgaria-Cyprus BIT which, according to the investor, applied to "all aspects of treatment" and, consequently, to the dispute settlement clauses in Bulgaria's other BITs such as that between Bulgaria and Finland. The tribunal's analysis involved a detailed evaluation of the MFN clause specifically included in the Bulgaria-Cyprus agreement. In *Plama* the tribunal observed that *Maffezini* was an inappropriate basis for analysis and could lead to "a chaotic situation – actually counterproductive to harmonization." Ibid. at para. 219.

[67] As cited in *Telenor* v. *Hungary*, ICSID Case No. ARB/04/15, para. 95 (13 Sept. 2006).

[68] For instance, Art. 4, Annex III of the Canadian Model BIT now seeks to condition MFN by noting that it "shall not apply to treatment accorded under all bilateral and multilateral agreements in force or signed prior to the date of entry into force of this Agreement." Pia

7.2.6 Expropriation

Originally, international investment law dealt in most instances with "takings" in the form of specific expropriations of property. Today arbitrations tend to identify expropriation only where the taking "is total or substantial."[69] As Schreuer notes, "[e]ven a grave interference will not amount to an expropriation if it leaves a measure of control in the hands of the investor."[70]

Over time the IMS has evolved to cover behavior that might fall short of an outright taking but still impair an investor's rights to property in some way – what is now commonly referred to as "indirect" expropriation.

Contemporary jurisprudence identifies three different bases for a claim of indirect expropriation.[71] First, the sole effects doctrine predicates indirect expropriation on the effects of government action. The essential question is whether enjoyment of property has been neutralized or in some cases whether there has been a "substantial deprivation" of property rights. Second, the police powers doctrine emphasizes the purpose of the measure being complained of. It asks what the purpose and goal of the particular measure is, bearing in mind that a general regulatory measure in the public interest cannot give rise to a claim for expropriation. Third, the mitigated police powers doctrine takes into account both the effect of the measure on the investment and the public purpose for which it was adopted. Here, the purpose and character of governmental action are relevant if state measures exceed a certain threshold of severity.

The law with respect to indirect expropriation reveals a gradual shift away from a pure effects-based test to one that is somewhat more deferential to sovereign decision-making. Attention continues to focus on the impairment of rights. However, a claim of indirect expropriation is not recognized unless the impairment is of a certain gravity. In *Glamis Gold*, for example, the arbitrator held that the effect of the measure must

Acconci, "Most-Favoured-Nation Treatment" in Peter Mulchinski et al. (eds), *The Oxford Handbook of International Investment Law* 363 at 403 (Oxford University Press, Oxford; 2008).

69 S.v. "Investments, International Protection" *Max Planck Encyclopedia of Public International Law* para. 87 (June 2013) (author: Christoph Schreuer).

70 Ibid.

71 For an overview of the law relating to indirect expropriation, see Bücheler, *Proportionality in Investor-State Arbitration* 124–133.

be "*radically* to deprive [the investor] of economic use and enjoyment of its investments, *as if the rights thereto ... had ceased to exist.*"[72]

7.2.7 Necessity and Fundamental Change of Circumstances

The doctrine of necessity has been referred to by the ILC as the situation prevailing in "exceptional cases where the only way a State can safeguard an essential interest threatened by a grave and imminent peril is, for the time being, not to perform some other international obligation of lesser weight or urgency."[73] The defense is suspensory in the sense that once the peril has ended the original obligations revive. The defense was successfully invoked by Argentina in a number of investment disputes stemming from the Argentine financial crisis in 1999–2001.[74] Commentators have divided on the merits of these decisions.[75] In addition, it is theoretically possible for a country (or pair of countries) to declare a fundamental change of circumstances (*rebus sic stantibus*) in relation to an investment treaty between them with suspensive effect, as mentioned in VCLT Art. 62(3), thereby entirely precluding action by claimants.[76]

[72] *Glamis Gold*, Award, para. 357 (8 June 2009) [emphasis added], citing *Tecmed*, Award, ICSID Case No. ARB(AF)/00/2, para. 115 (29 May 2003).

[73] *Report of the International Law Commission on the Work of Its Fifty-Third Session*, U.N. Doc. A/56/10 p. 80 (2001).

[74] In four disputes (*CMS* v. *Argentina*, ICSID Case No. ARB/01/8; *LG&E* v. *Argentina*, ICSID Case No. ARB/02/1; *Enron* v. *Argentina*, ICSID Case No. ARB/01/3; *Sempra* v. *Argentina*, ICSID Case No. ARB/02/16) US-based companies asserted that Argentina's emergency measures violated the FET, umbrella, nondiscrimination, and expropriation guarantees of the Argentina-US bilateral investment treaty. In each case arbitrators found a violation of FET and umbrella clauses, and awarded significant amounts of compensation. Each award was later annulled pursuant to ICSID Art. 52.

[75] For commentary see Alvarez, *The Public International Law Regime Governing International Investment* 247*ff*.

[76] VCLT Art. 62(3) provides that "If ... a party may invoke a fundamental change of circumstances as a ground for terminating or withdrawing from a treaty it may also invoke the change as a ground for suspending the operation of the treaty." The government of Canada threatened to invoke a parallel provision, VCLT Art. 58.1, to support its projected suspension of NAFTA ch. 11 in relation to three lumber companies contemplating action against the US government in 2005. The government's action was necessary to settle the *Softwood Lumber IV* dispute. See "Ontario Groups Sue U.S., Canada for Suspending NAFTA Lumber ECC," 24:20 *Inside U.S. Trade* (19 May 2006).

7.2.8 Appraisal

Despite the foregoing definitions, the dominant impression left by the sub-standards of international investment law is one of flux and uncertainty. There has been significant criticism that the sub-standards themselves are vague and that the law on many points lacks stability. To overcome this problem, various solutions have been proposed, some of which will be discussed later.

In the meantime, a law of international investment has emerged and continues to evolve in ways that do not always accord with what would be suggested by the continuing bilateralism of treaty-making. Considered on their own, bilateral investment treaties would infer a body of law that is relatively limited and self-contained, with each treaty generating its own entirely distinctive interpretation. To some degree this is true, but the total corpus of international investment law appears to have effects that are broader than this.[77]

Earlier I mentioned the characterization of international investment law as a "framework" or "regime." What has intrigued commentators in this respect is the ordered and systematic nature of the law, the commonalities arising in its interpretative processes and the concomitant need to protect investor expectations in line with the relationship of subordination introduced in Chapter 1 (i.e. Obligation > Right).[78]

[77] McLachlin et al., *International Investment Arbitration* 15 (noting that "investment treaties are not self-contained regimes"). José Alvarez has observed:

> conclusions that BITs or FTAs are *lex specialis*, are not "legislative", or lack common content, present artificially constrained black/white choices that bear little resemblance to the complexities of the interactions between treaty and nontreaty sources of law or the international legal process. These are not qualities subject to a dichotomous on/off switch. There are aspects of BITs that are *lex specialis*: that is, intended to exclude the application of any general rules to the contrary. This seems to be the case, for example, with respect to particular procedural conditions required by each of these treaties for the initiation of investor-State dispute settlement. . . . On the other hand, there are other provisions in such treaties that explicitly or implicitly relying on general international law or reflect intent by the drafters to affirm such traditional principles.
>
> (Alvarez, *The Public International Law Regime Governing International Investment* 197–198)

[78] Rudolph Dolzer & Christoph Schreuer, *Principles of International Investment Law* 128 (Oxford University Press, Oxford; 2008).

7.3 Law and Investment

A number of features of international investment law tend to confirm a communitarian theory of law in the sense that they align reasonably well with at least one of its idea-complexes: that of fairness, rights, contractualism, retrospectivity and inductive logic.

Before examining this alignment, however, it is useful to glean some idea of international investment law's community and commitment to justice in terms of the theories of community and justice developed earlier as a means of explaining this orientation.

As mentioned, Simma and Paulus have suggested how the international community may be described as either Hobbesian, Kantian or Grotian. Based on these descriptions, I posited in Chapter 2 how the WTO Agreement is most accurately thought of as creating a "neo-Grotian" community. This is in the sense that its structure is "on its way to [creating] an 'organized state community' with an emphasis on common interests, the development of common values, and the creation of common institutions."[79]

By comparison, the identification of community in international investment law is more evidently Kantian. The community "sees at work in international politics a potential community of mankind" whose systemic value is corrective justice. Intriguingly, Simma and Paulus describe a Kantian community justifying "intervention for *the protection of individuals against their own state*."[80] In the case of international investment law – in a slight modification of that description – the community's intervention aims to protect individuals against *another* state.

The type of good protected in this Kantian community of international investment protection is private property. However, the definition of private property varies from jurisdiction to jurisdiction.

Most treaties covering investment deal with the issue of property rights according to the treaty's own definition of "investment," which usually takes as its basis of reference the law of the host state. Ursula Kriebaum and Christoph Schreuer have pointed out, however, that most arbitral tribunals have rejected total deference to a host state's own definition of

[79] Bruno Simma & Andrea Paulus, "The 'International Community': Facing the Challenge of Globalization" 9 *E.J.I.L.* 266 at 271 (1998).

[80] Ibid. at 270 [emphasis in original].

investment in order to avoid the possibility of a government auto-defining the rights in question and minimizing responsibility.[81] Instead, many tribunals have held that domestic law is only concerned with the legality of the investment (i.e. that it was made legally).[82] This position means that "the object of protection remains determined, in principle, by international standards."[83]

Legal and interpretative variation in the definition of property introduces a degree of pluralism in the investment regime that can be significant. An example helps to illustrate the point.

International law recognizes the possibility of an indirect taking but debate persists about whether property exists in intangible interests such as shareholdings. *Lauder* v. *Czech Republic*, for instance, involved a claim under the US–Czech Republic BIT for the taking of a television station.[84] The investment was held by the investor in the form of shares. The shares themselves remained untouched. Because there was no interference with the shares themselves, the *Lauder* tribunal dismissed the claim. Conversely, in *CME* v. *Czech Republic*, a parallel proceeding involving the very same investment under the Netherlands-Czech Republic BIT, the tribunal agreed that an arm of the Czech state had interfered with the investment regardless of the physical integrity of the shares.[85]

[81] Ursula Kriebaum & Christoph Schreuer, "The Concept of Property in Human Rights Law and International Investment Law" at 4 in Stephan Breitenmoser et al. (eds), *Human Rights, Democracy and Rule of Law: liber amicorum Luzius Wildhaber* (Dike; Nomos, Zürich, Baden-Baden; 2007).

[82] Ibid.

[83] Ibid. But see Zachary Douglas, "Property, Investment and the Scope of Investment Protection Obligations" in Zachary Douglas et al. (eds), *The Foundations of International Investment Law* 373 (Oxford University Press, Oxford; 2014). ("The test for whether or not the claimant has property is supplied by the law of the host state and it is then for the definition of an investment in the treaty to determine whether that property is an investment.")

[84] *Lauder v. The Czech Republic*, IIC 205 (2001) 3 Sept. 2001 (Final Award).

[85] *CME* v. *Czech Republic*, 14 Mar. 2003 (Final Award). In this respect, many commentators have noted that the issue of definition of property depends largely on how property itself is conceived. Under a rights' approach, an investment is simply a "bundle" of rights. Depending on the degree of impairment of those rights, a violation may be found. Under a totality-of-the-enterprise approach, by comparison, an investment is considered "frequently [as] a rather complex operation, composed of various interrelated transactions, each element of which, standing alone, might not in all cases qualify as an investment." Different claims stress different aspects of these approaches. No single or uniform conception of rights or interests prevails. See Zachary Douglas, "Property, Investment and the Scope of Investment Protection Obligations" in Zachary Douglas et al. (eds), *The*

This sort of divergent outcome can contribute to the impression that the "good" in question in an international investment dispute is not a "good" but simply whatever some arbitrator says it is. That, taken together with interpretative heterogeneity concerning the sub-standards of treatment, uncertainty about whether treaty protections do in fact encourage foreign investment, and the loosely "networked" nature of the system, all contribute to dissensus about international investment law and the extent to which corrective justice should correct. The result is continuing debate about the justice and legitimacy of the regime.

These background considerations structure and shape international investment law as it evolves.

7.3.1 Doing Fairness

An indicator of the particular orientation of international investment law in terms of theory is its emphasis on fairness. Fairness is integral to international investment law because so much of the decision-making occurs case-by-case, agreement-by-agreement, and therefore by definition must be "fitting" or "appropriate" to particular circumstances.

I have already discussed the relevance of fairness in the jurisprudence of the FET standard. There, its influence appears most evidently in the way it imbues the law with contextualism. Decisions on FET are recognized to be highly specific.

Jeff Waincymer concurs in this view by pointing out how fairness in international arbitration "connotes the justice *of a situation*."[86] As a concept fairness has two distinct aspects: procedural and substantive. Procedurally, fairness can be broken down into "general principles of due process, equality of treatment, and providing each party with a sufficient opportunity to present its case."[87] Substantively, the view is sometimes

Foundations of International Investment Law 369–380 (Oxford University Press, Oxford; 2014), quoting from *CSOB* v. *Slovakia*, Decision on Jurisdiction, ICSID Case No. ARB/97/4, para. 72 (24 May 1999). See also Kriebaum & Schreuer, "Concept of Property in Human Rights Law and International Investment Law" 18.

[86] Jeff Waincymer, *Procedure and Evidence in International Arbitration* 12 (Kluwer Law International, Alphen aan den Rijn; 2012) [emphasis added].

[87] Ibid., p. 14.

taken that "[w]hatever outcome is reached by a fair process is in that sense seen to be a fair outcome."[88]

At the same time, fairness in international investment law can also be highly nuanced, involving considerations "based on the technical application of law, or the most equitable solution, or the one that seems to conform more closely with the true intent or reasonable expectations of the parties."[89] In addition, in specific circumstances Waincymer notes that there can be considerations of fairness that go beyond the arbitral award alone to encompass its effect on the parties' business activities. Further considerations include "the need for peace-keeping, consensus building and preserving contractual relationships."[90]

Waincymer concludes that "[b]ecause there are differing views on the nature of arbitration and the methodologies leading to particular solutions, there can be differences in view as to what makes for a just outcome."[91] What is noteworthy in international investment law is the way that considerations of fairness so often appear to be the sum total of justice. In a very real sense, fairness *is* justice in this context.

Because of the preeminence of fairness considerations in international investment law, the value of equality is less naturally visible. It is emphasized in the formal equality of the parties in arbitral proceedings and in a continuing concern with ensuring that arbitral decision-making is the same, or at least not *too* divergent. Commentators often engage in deep apologetics about the unwarranted flexibility of international investment arbitration.[92] That reaction would appear to confirm the theoretic relationship of correlation (i.e. Equality/

88 Ibid.

89 Ibid.

90 Ibid.

91 Ibid.

92 Thus, Jeffrey Waincymer mentions that "[w]hichever form of fairness is being considered, it can also be looked at from the perspective of consistency and certainty. It is highly desirable that procedural determinations are consistent and predictable." Waincymer, *Procedure and Evidence in International Arbitration* 19. There is, in other words, a perennial tension between certainty and flexibility, and by extension, equality and fairness: "Flexibility is an important value in ensuring that proper attention is given to the nuances of individual cases. Yet finding an appropriate trade-off between flexibility and certainty is difficult." Ibid. at pp. 19–20. This would appear to confirm the way in which fairness transitions into equality in international investment law, hence the third theoretic relationship (i.e. fairness = equality).

Fairness). In other words, where fairness is a concern an egalitarian impulse is also detected.

As for the second theoretic relationship – that of subordination (i.e. Equality > Fairness) – this is harder to identify in investment law due to the regime's inherent fragmentation. So often the law is rendered "at retail" and, hence, prioritizes equality only in a superficial manner.

The priority of equality is evidenced perhaps most pointedly in relation to the doctrine of precedent. Formally, no doctrine of precedent exists in international investment law, and yet predictability is often sensed to be what the law is all about. Thus, Gabrielle Kaufmann-Kohler has observed that arbitrators apply a *de facto* doctrine of precedent.[93] Similarly, August Reinisch has referred to the emergence of a "kind of de facto case-law system whereby tribunals routinely rely upon previous decisions."[94] And Gilbert Guillaume has written about arbitration tribunals referencing precedent "more frequently than in the past."[95]

The arguments for equality embodied in the form of precedent are many. Precedent is consistent with general expectations. It makes the law more coherent and easier to access. It bolsters the law's authority and legitimacy.

Nevertheless, some voices have been heard against the idea of equality embodied in precedent, or at least the notion of complete consistency in arbitral case law. Thomas Schultz makes the argument that while "consistency and the rule of law are perceived as some of the most widely accepted ideals," the international rule of law is fundamentally a "neutral act-type from a perspective of political morality." As such, "striving for consistency is not inherently, by necessity, a moral positive. Put bluntly, it is not more important for a rule to be settled than it is to be settled right."[96]

93 Gabrielle Kaufmann-Kohler, "Arbitral Precedent: Dream, Necessity or Excuse?" 23:3 *Arbitr. Int.* 357 (2007).

94 August Reinisch, "Investment Arbitration – The Role of Precedent in ICSID Arbitration" in Ch. Klausegger et al. (eds), *Austrian Arbitration Yearbook 2008* 495 at 508 (2008).

95 Gilbert Guillaume, "The Use of Precedent by International Judges and Arbitrators" 2:1 *J. Int'l Dispute Settlement* 5 at 17 (2011).

96 Thomas Schultz, "Against Consistency in Investment Arbitration?" in Zachary Taylor et al. (eds), *The Foundations of International Investment Law* 297 at 298 (Oxford University Press, Oxford; 2014).

Schultz's arguments are built around the assertion that arbitral decision-making in international investment law is heavily fact-specific and was never meant to be imbued with complete consistency. Arbitration is designed "to satisfy the interests of the instant parties" and "to impartially and competently apply the proper legal rules to the relevant facts, to take into consideration all the particulars of the case and to grant the parties appropriate due process." As such:

> The aim is to provide the parties with the fairest, most just decision given their particular case, for that is the primary legitimate interest of parties in adjudicative procedures. There is no reason here why there must be obiter dicta or references to prior cases, at least not in the context of investment arbitration.[97]

Schultz's position is based on the characterization of investment arbitration as being about the protection of investors and certainty of contracts, the ultimate end being to promote investment. The implicit paradigm is one of private law.[98] In Schultz's view, an "ossified, consistent, predictable"[99] jurisprudence embodying equality accentuates certain negative features of the investment regime and should instead try to pursue an approach that is more sensitive to whether consistency is indeed beneficial. This would, Schulz admits, "open up a whole new, and welcome, set of arguments about the 'good' and 'bad' of investment arbitration."[100]

The difficulty with Schultz's position is certain fundamental assumptions. Many commentators argue that arbitral awards made under bilateral investment agreements are not about "contracting" per se but rather have important – perhaps even predominant – public law features.[101]

97 Ibid. at 305.
98 Ibid. at 306.
99 Ibid. at 313.
100 Ibid. at 315.
101 Gus Van Harten argues that a number of features of international investment law render investor-state arbitration public law disputes because (1) it allows corporations to challenge governmental regulations and not merely commercial contracts with the host state; (2) typical provisions in bilateral investment treaties require a host state to give its irrevocable consent to arbitration by any investor of the other state; (3) there is the possibility of substantial damage awards against host states; (4) the absence of any need under bilateral investment treaties for investors to institute arbitration without first attorning to domestic courts; and (5) the widespread enforceability for arbitral awards. See Gus Van Harten, *Investment Treaty Arbitration and Public Law* 95*ff* (Oxford University Press, Oxford; 2007).

Schulz's position appears to be an outlier, but illustrative of the power of underlying fairness concerns.

Uncertainty about a doctrine of precedent in international investment law leaves equality to be expressed in other forms. It is especially evident in debate about "full" versus "fair" reparation in international investment law.

Many BITs adopt the so-called "Hull Formula" standard of "prompt, adequate and effective" compensation. Others refer to "fair market value" in the case, for example, of expropriated assets. Because of "frequent assimilation between the Hull Formula and the fair market value formula, the majority of commentators believe that the two formulas are equivalent and that the terms 'fair' and 'adequate' refer to full compensation."[102] However, this easy equivalence belies certain subtleties highlighted by a communitarian theory.

First, "fair" and "adequate" do not mean "full." Rather, their meaning may be taken to connote what is appropriate or sufficient. Tension over the difference plays itself out in various considerations that make "full reparation" merely fair. One is for arbitrators to take into account all relevant circumstances when calculating compensation. This reformulation of the rule on reparation obliges arbitrators to go beyond fair market value and consideration of purely financial factors in general. For example, in the case of expropriation, the valuation of a taking could involve "the current and past use of the property, the history of its acquisition, the fair market value of the property, the purpose of the expropriation, the extent of past profits made by foreign investors through the investment, and duration of the investment."[103]

Second, the availability of full reparation in international investment law is often indexed to the lawfulness of the taking. Traditionally, a distinction is observed between lawful takings, which entitle the investor to the traditional standard of "prompt, adequate and effective"

[102] Suzy Nikièma, *Compensation for Expropriation Best Practices Series* 10 (Mar. 2013). See also Irmgard Marboe, "Assessing Compensation and Damages in Expropriation versus Non-expropriation Cases" in Christina Beharry (ed.), *Contemporary and Emerging Issues on the Law of Damages and Valuation in International Investment Arbitration* 111 at 122 (Brill Nijhoff, Leiden; 2018).

[103] This wording is taken from section 6.2 of the SADC Model Bilateral Investment Treaty (2012).

compensation or "fair market value," and unlawful takings, which are understood to entitle the investor to something more.[104] The implication to be drawn here is that in garden-variety takings case done legally, full compensation actually means something less than full recovery.

Third, restitution alone may not provide full reparation because of interim events after the date of the wrongful act.[105]

Fourth, a few commentators have questioned the application of the full reparation standard in international investment law because the ARSIWA appear to contemplate full reparation in the law of *state-to-state* responsibility,[106] whereas a typical investment claim involves the obligation of a state *toward individual investors*. This modification militates in favor of a different – possibly lesser – standard of responsibility and recovery.[107]

[104] Pursuant to the *Chorzów Factory* formula, the victim must be restored, in the event of a lawful act – e.g., a lawful expropriation – to the status quo ante. The PCIJ in that case clarified that a restoration to the status quo ante is insufficient and unjust in a case involving an unlawful act: in such situations, the aggrieved party must receive something more.

(Borzu Sabahi, *Compensation and Restitution in Investor-State Arbitration* 59 (Oxford University Press, Oxford; 2011))

[105] Sabahi, *Compensation and Restitution in Investor-State Arbitration* 60.

[106] See Zachary Douglas, "Hybrid Foundations of Investment Treaty Arbitration" 74 *B.Y.I.L.* 151 at 189 (2003) (recommending that transplantation of a secondary rules of state responsibility into investor-state arbitration should take place with due caution). See also Martin Endicott, "Remedies in Investor State Arbitration" in Philippe Kahn & Thomas Wälde (eds), *New Aspects of International Investment Law* 531, 531–532 (Martinus Nijhoff, Leiden; 2007). At the same time, ARSIWA Art. 33(1) makes clear that the scope of the content of international obligations depends "in particular on the character and content of the international obligation and on the circumstances of the breach." The associated ARSIWA Commentary adds that the ARSIWA "do not deal with the possibility of the invocation of responsibility by persons or entities other than States" and specifies that "It will be a matter for the particular primary rule to determine whether and to what extent persons or entities other than States are entitled to invoke responsibility on their own account."

[107] Why a lesser standard? For that matter, why not a greater one? My argument here is that a higher standard is owed to a state – and by implication, a lesser standard is owed to other actors – because a state is the supreme possessor of rights and obligations in international law. As the ICJ indicated in the *Reparation for Injuries* Case, other entities only possess rights and obligations according to "the needs of the international community." For discussion, see Irmgard Marboe, "Assessing Compensation and Damages in Expropriation versus Nonexpropriation Cases", in Christine Beharry (ed.), *Contemporary and Emerging Issues on the Law of Damages and Valuation in International Investment Arbitration* 111 at 115 (Brill Nijhoff, Leiden; 2018).

This lesser standard is also directed by the conditionality of the forms of reparation – restitution, compensation, satisfaction – highlighted in the discussion of ARSIWA in Chapter 3.

In the case of restitution, for example, restitution is only available to the extent it is not materially impossible and does not involve a burden out of all proportion to the benefit to be derived. For this reason, Borzu Sabahi has pointed out that restitution is awarded less often in international investment law than the scheme of the ARSIWA might infer.[108]

The difficulties of restitution militate in favor of compensation, by far the most popular remedy in international investment law. However, as mentioned, there continue to be a number of uncertainties with respect to the Hull Formula and Fair Market Value, which appear to indicate more of a fairness metric. Debate also continues over whether the applicable standard is one of "adequate" versus "appropriate" compensation, a position advanced by developing countries as part of the New International Economic Order in the 1960s.[109] Nevertheless, whether one adopts "adequate" or "appropriate" as the applicable standard of compensation, both are notable for the way in which they suggest a compensatory obligation that amounts to less than full reparation.[110]

Fifth, a specific issue with respect to compensation is the wording of ARSIWA Art. 36(2), which specifies in particular that "The

[108] Sabahi, *Compensation and Restitution in Investor-State Arbitration* 189.

[109] Thus, in the 1960s and 1970s there were influential resolutions of the UN General Assembly that called for the payment of "appropriate" compensation: see U.N.G.A. Res. 1803 (XVII) (14 Dec. 1962) (Permanent Sovereignty over Natural Resources); U.N.G.A. Res. 3281, 14 I.L.M. 251 (1975) (Charter of Economic Rights and Duties of States). For commentary see Karl Sauvant, *Yearbook on International Investment Law & Policy* 679–681 (Oxford University Press, New York; 2010–2011). "'Appropriate' compensation is a more subjective standard than a requirement that compensation be 'adequate and effective.'" McLachlin et al., *International Investment Arbitration* 317.

[110] The influential Restatement of Foreign Relations Law (3rd) provides that a state is responsible under international law for injury from a taking where the taking is not for a public purpose, is discriminatory, or is not accompanied by provision of "just compensation." See section 185. The Restatement refers to both the "adequate" and "appropriate" standards of compensation. See section 188. At the same time, section 188 specifies that "[u]nder ordinary conditions . . . the amount must be *equivalent to the full value* of the property taken." [emphasis added]. Such a direct reaffirmation of the equivalence standard of compensation needs to be tempered to the fact that even under US law compensation for takings is not always equivalent, the need to accommodate varying conceptions of property if the Restatement's "just" standard of compensation is to serve as an international one, and general appreciation that the principle of absolute respect for alien property may not be appropriate in all circumstances. See the Reporters' Notes to section 188.

compensation shall cover any financially assessable damage *including loss of profits* insofar as it is established." This wording might be taken to mandate a view of compensation as including loss of profits (i.e. a *lucrum cessans* standard). At the same time, the conditional wording of the ARSIWA Commentary suggests otherwise. The Commentary states that "Paragraph 2 of article 36 recognizes that *in certain cases* compensation for loss of profits *may be appropriate*." It goes on to mention several cases where loss of profits was awarded, inferring that lost profits are not awarded in *all* cases.[111] The Commentary's survey of the jurisprudence concludes with the statement that "lost profits have not been as commonly awarded in practice as compensation for accrued losses," adding that "[t]ribunals have been reluctant to provide compensation for claims with inherently speculative elements." It adds:

> When compared with tangible assets, profits (and intangible assets which are income-based) are relatively vulnerable to commercial and political risks, and increasingly so the further into the future projections are made. In cases where lost future profits have been awarded, it has been where an anticipated income stream has attained sufficient attributes to be considered a legally protected interest of sufficient certainty to be compensable.[112]

The Commentary's carefully hedged wording on loss of profits suggests there is a considerable degree of fairness-derived contingency attached to their award. In aiming to achieve the equality of full reparation, fairness then becomes the *de facto* standard.[113]

111 See also Marboe, *Calculation of Compensation and Damages in International Investment Law* 111–116. Marboe points out that rejection of claims for lost profits in international investment law generally occurs on the basis that profits are too speculative, that claims often arise out of termination of contract, which in some national legal systems disentitles a party to claim damages of any type, or that claims originate in assertions of force majeure, which frees both parties from liability for failure to perform.

112 Draft Articles on Responsibility of States for Internationally Wrongful Acts, with commentaries, U.N. Doc. A/56/10, p. 104 (2001). The Commentary refers to the example of the fourth installment of "E3" claims before the United Nations Compensation Commission involving the Iraqi invasion of Kuwait, where the panel expressed the view "that in order for such claims to want a recommendation [i.e. of compensation] it is necessary to demonstrate by sufficient documentary and other appropriate evidence a history of successful (i.e. profitable) operation, and a state of affairs which warrants the conclusion that the hypothesis that there would have been future profitable contracts is well-founded." Ibid., n. 567.

113 As Marjorie Whiteman noted in her 1943 work, *Damages in International Law*:

> There is apparently no clear-cut demarcation between the allowance of damages for prospect of profits in tort as distinguished from contract

In all of the above, it is perhaps harder to see the two further relationships inferred by a communitarian theory, those of transition (Equality = Fairness) and integration (Equality + Fairness = Justice). With respect to transition, transition is arguably discernible in the way that mere fairness is deemed to satisfy the standard of full reparation (i.e. equality) in many instances. Several practicalities confirm the point. One reason is the difficulty of forecasting.[114] Another is the crippling effect of large awards of profits on sovereignty, the source of an informal proviso invoked by some investment tribunals to limit awards of profits to what is "reasonable."[115] Yet another is preference for an evidence-based standard in line with the need apparently felt by tribunals for certainty in calculation.[116] Furthermore, many recent awards pertain to greenfield investments with little history of profitability that predispose them to reliance-based measures of recovery.[117]

> cases. Prospective profits are allowed or disallowed, not on the basis of whether a particular case is a contract or tort case, except in rare instances, but rather on the basis of whether the expected profits for which damages claimed were reasonably to be expected from the state of affairs existing at the time of the respondent government's wrongful act.
>
> See Sabahi, *Compensation and Restitution in Investor-State Arbitration* 46.

The multiple reference to expectations is a notable example of the way that expectations are "threaded" throughout international law.

[114] For example, the ARSIWA Commentary notes that the obligation to pay compensation in ARSIWA "is delimited by the phrase 'any financially assessable damage,' that is, any damage which is capable of being evaluated in financial terms." See ARSIWA Commentary, A/56/10, p. 99 (2001). The Commentary goes on to note that "Claims for lost profits are also subject to the usual range of limitations on the recovery of damages, such as causation, remoteness, evidentiary requirements and accounting principles, which seek to discount speculative elements from projected figures." See ARSIWA Commentary, A/56/10, p. 105 (2001).

[115] "Tribunals can be reluctant to award compensation for lost profits as this can oblige an often impecunious State to pay a large sum to a wealthy foreign investor. The tensions between awarding the full measure of compensation and not wishing to award a sum that is so large (even if it is not) punitive rather than compensatory lie behind many of the more contentious awards . . ." McLachlin et al., *International Investment Arbitration* 319.

[116] For example, the ARSIWA Commentary notes with respect evaluation techniques that "although income-based methods have been accepted in principle, there has been a decided preference for asset-based methods." See ARSIWA Commentary, A/56/10, p. 104 (2001).

[117] For example, the ARSIWA Commentary notes to *AAPL* v. *Republic of Sri Lanka*, ICSID Case No. ARB/87/3 (27 June 1990), where a claim for lost profits by a newly established business was rejected for lack of evidence. See ARSIWA Commentary, A/56/10, p. 105 (2001). See also McLachlin et al., *International Investment Arbitration* 327 ("a number of tribunals have refused to award DCF-based compensation to enterprises lacking a proven record of profitability.").

All in all, it is hard to escape the conclusion that despite calls for a *lucrum cessans* standard of compensation, in practice the most popular standard is the more limited extra-contractual one of *damnum emergens*.[118] Fairness then *becomes* equality – equality in those specific circumstances. At the same time, because the two measures – equality and fairness – appear to work together, the relation of integration (i.e. Equality + Fairness = Justice) is detected here as well.

7.3.2 Rights Redux

I have previously mentioned the way that international investment law is chiefly a law of rights. The claims process commences with a claim that certain investor rights to property or interests inherent in a standard of treatment have been infringed. The logical inference is that duties rest upon a host state. This conclusion would appear to confirm the theoretic relationship of correlation (i.e. Obligation/Right).

As Steven Ratner points out, however, the correlation of rights with obligations is frequently regarded today as unbalanced in international investment law and therefore at the root of legitimacy concerns. The point is often made that international investment law is nonreciprocal because it creates only rights for investors and imposes obligations on states.[119] This view would appear to contravene the theoretic relation of subordination (i.e. Obligation > Right).[120]

Due to this objection, there have been some indications of a desire to recalibrate the regime's jural balance. The recalibration has come about

[118] The same two approaches to compensation – *lucrum cessans* and *damnum emergens* – are also apparent in violations of investment protections other than expropriation. Thus, a NAFTA tribunal in *S.D. Myers* v. *Canada* noted that most investment treaties lack any provision regarding calculation for violations of investment protections beyond expropriation. The tribunal proceeded to award compensation for a breach of FET just as it would in a case of expropriation. See *S.D. Myers* v. *Canada* (Second Partial Award) (21 Oct. 2002).

[119] Ratner, "Survey Article" 107 at 109. At the same time, Thomas Wälde has noted that "essentially, any rule of international law . . . is a restriction on sovereignty." Thomas Wälde, "Interpreting Investment Treaties: Experience and Examples" in Christina Binder et al. (ed.), *International Investment Law for the Twenty-First Century* 724 at 735 (Oxford University Press, Oxford; 2009).

[120] Thus, Steven Ratner observes that "[t]o protect investors, [international investment law] places deep obligations on states, far exceeding the rules of international trade." Ratner, "Survey Article" 107.

chiefly in the form of greater attention to investor conduct. With respect to FET, for instance, Peter Mulchinski notes that investor duties are being accepted in relation to the avoidance of unconscionable conduct, the reasonable assessment of investment risk in the host country, and a duty to operate an investment reasonably.[121] These requirements are leading to new limits upon FET that in Mulchinski's estimate can be encapsulated in a doctrine of "Caveat Investor."

Still, other commentators have pointed out that the recalibration – or at least reorientation – of systemic concern away from state behavior and toward that of investor behavior in international investment law is conceptually problematic. That is because international law holds state behavior to a good faith standard, whereas the standard of behavior expected from private actors is merely one of ordinary commercial conduct. To expect complete equality between investor claimants and state defendants is unrealistic.

What therefore seems to be emerging in international investment law is a *sui generis* standard of conduct for investors that is distinct from considerations of good faith in international law. The threshold is set by the expectation that corporations "should be good corporate citizens and respect the emergent principles of international corporate social responsibility"[122] informed by informal standards such as the OECD Guidelines for Multinational Enterprises and the UN Global Compact, as well as corporate and industry codes, and any binding treaties in the field.[123] Here, human rights discourse has played a role in supplementing existing law through an increasing emphasis on corporate social responsibility for overseas operations as well as the need for corporate behavior to respect human rights extraterritorially.

These developments highlight the theoretic relationship of transition (i.e. Obligation = Right). That is, beyond a state's particular obligations to an investor the state must have the ability to exercise sovereign rights, and conversely, that beyond certain rights conferred by virtue of custom

[121] Muchlinski, "Caveat Investor" 527.

[122] Ibid. at 535.

[123] Organisation for Economic Cooperation and Development (OECD), OECD Guidelines for Multinational Enterprises (27 June 2000) (the Guidelines are recommendations addressed by governments to multinational enterprises providing for voluntary principles and standards for responsible business conduct consistent with applicable laws); United Nations Global Compact: The Ten Principles. [online] Available at www.unglobalcompact.org/AboutTheGC/TheTenPrinciples/index.html.

and treaty, investors have an obligation to obey the law of the host state.[124]

The specific issue of sovereign rights to regulate has become a contentious one. In some degree it is recasting the jural relationship from one of obligation-right (i.e. investor rights versus state obligations) to one of competing rights (i.e. the investor right to protection versus sovereign right to regulate), a recasting that appears to be an astute move inasmuch as conflicts of competing rights are universally recognized as contentious and, absent any prioritization, do not suggest straightforward resolution.[125]

The right to regulate and the associated need to prioritize between rights also raises the issue of proportionality, a recurrent topic in international investment arbitration. In Chapter 5 I described how proportionality in international law often draws upon the three-step test developed by the ECJ involving considerations of suitability, use of the least restrictive means, and proportionality *stricto sensu* (i.e. weighing and balancing of different stakes).

As Gebhard Bücheler has observed, however, application of proportionality at an international level depends on the legal setting in which it is being applied.[126] In international investment claims, that setting is exceptionally varied. Hence, application of proportionality in the context of FET claims can make "the reasoning of tribunals more transparent and enhance the probability that all the relevant factors will be taken into account."[127] In the case of exceptions, it may serve as "a transparent and efficient tool for resolving conflicts between competing interests at stake."[128] Finally, in the case of a defense like necessity, proportionality analysis may help to clarify that invocation of the defense involves certain

124 Rahim Moloo & Alex Khachaturian, "The Compliance with the Law Requirement in International Investment Law" 34 *Fordham Int'l L.J.* 1473 (2011); Athina Fouchard Papaefstratiou & Tejas Shiroor; "Investors' Obligation to Comply with Domestic Law" *TDM* 4 (2019).

125 Jeremy Waldron, "Rights in Conflict" 99:3 *Ethics* 503 (1999).

126 Bücheler, *Proportionality in Investor-State Arbitration* 178. See also Caroline Henckels, *Proportionality and Deference in Investor-State Arbitration* (Cambridge University Press, Cambridge; 2015) (arguing that "proportionality analysis represents a tried and tested method of review for regulatory disputes involving competing public and private interests, and that it is a rational and coherent means of determining state liability ... preferable to other methods employed by investment tribunals such as review for reasonableness or other approaches that give arbitrators overly broad discretion.")

127 Bücheler, *Proportionality in Investor-State Arbitration* 208.

128 Ibid., p. 303.

residual duties on states and that governments "are under an obligation to pay damages for acts justified by necessity, albeit not necessarily to the same degree as for internationally wrongful acts."[129]

At the same time, both Bücheler and Caroline Henckels betray a certain caution toward express acceptance of proportionality analysis in international investment law. This is because international investment agreements do not explicitly call for it, there is no guidance as to what factors and interests should be weighed against each other as part of it, and it is not entirely clear that proportionality is a recognized constitutive value in international law.[130] There is, in addition, the concern that "investment tribunals are not institutionally well placed to engage in the proportionality *stricto sensu* stage of analysis."[131] Despite this, the salience of proportionality analysis in international investment law is noteworthy for the way it confirms investment law's rights-based orientation.

The combination of rights and obligations is understood to culminate in integration in the form of a *sui generis* legal system (i.e. Obligation + Right = *Sui Generis* System). Perhaps because of the ill-defined idea of system in international investment law and because neither custom nor convention seeks to oust the jurisdiction of domestic or international law, commentators have preferred to describe international investment law in somewhat more limited terms as *lex specialis*. Alvarez, for instance, has warned that:

> conclusions that BITs or FTAs are *lex specialis*, are not "legislative", or lack common content, present artificially constrained black/white choices that bear little resemblance to the complexities of the interactions between treaty and non-treaty sources of law or the international legal process. These are not qualities subject to a dichotomous on/off switch. There are aspects of BITs that are *lex specialis*: that is, intended to exclude the application of any general rules to the contrary . . . On the other hand, there are other provisions in such treaties that explicitly or implicitly rely on general international law or reflect intent by the drafters to affirm such traditional principles.[132]

[129] Ibid.

[130] Ibid., p. 85.

[131] Henckels, *Proportionality and Deference* 193.

[132] Alvarez, *The Public International Law Regime Governing International Investment* 197–198.

In a similar vein, Anthea Roberts has written of the international investment regime being caught between concurring paradigms of public and private law litigation and being relegated to crafting *sui generis* solutions. With respect to amicus participation, for instance, Roberts notes:

> On an ad hoc level, we can already see "between the poles" solutions developing in the participation of amici in investment treaty arbitrations. In a relatively short period of time, the system moved from having no amicus interventions (based on a commercial arbitration paradigm) to permitting some amicus interventions (based on public law and international public law paradigms).[133]

Roberts adds, however, that the shift to a purely public law model in investment arbitration "is unlikely to be complete because, in contrast to most international and domestic courts, the cost of paying for the arbitrators' time is borne by the disputing parties alone rather than the treaty parties as a whole or the community at large."[134] Consequently, the final outcome will likely be hybridized. In her view, "participants need to move past the singular paradigms [of public versus private law litigation] to begin theorizing about the more complicated platypus-like nature of the investment treaty system."[135]

Instead of taking positions on whether international investment law effects limited changes in the form of a *lex specialis* or generates one-off hybridized solutions, some commentators have also asserted that the world is witnessing the emergence of a "common law of investment protection."[136] A common law would provide a relatively strict doctrine of precedent and a hierarchy of decision-making, or perhaps less systematically, a civil law-style *jurisprudence constante* in which "a line of decisions being made in the same way ... should determine the outcome of future cases."[137]

133 Anthea Roberts, "Clash of Paradigms: Actors and Analogies Shaping the Investment Treaty System" 107:1 *Am J. Int'l L.* 45 at 92 (2013).

134 Ibid.

135 Ibid. at 93.

136 Matthew C. Porterfield, "An International Common Law of Investor Rights?" 27:1 *U. Pa. J. Int'l Econ. L.* 79 (2006); Wälde, "Interpreting Investment Treaties" 724 at 780 (2009) (asserting that "[t]he ultimate aim [of interpretation] should be to facilitate the emergence of an international common law of investment arbitration – as if a world investment code existed"); Laurence Shore & Robert Rothkopf, "For Better or Worse, Is There a Common Law of Investment Arbitration?" in 7 Arthur W. Rovine (ed.), *Contemporary Issues in International Arbitration and Mediation* 292 (Brill Nijhoff, Leiden; 2013).

137 Ibid. at 293.

Commentators have divided on the merits of such a development. For example, Frédéric Sourgens maintains international investment law is developing a common law method "not principally because of the weight given to prior cases, . . . but because of the manner in which prior cases are employed. Counsel focus intensively on the similarity of facts at bar to the facts of prior decisions."[138]

Other commentators differ. Laurence Shore and Robert Rothkopf note, for instance, that in almost two decades of arbitral practice in the field "no . . . *jurisprudence constante* is emerging. Instead, tribunals continue to issue diametrically opposed decisions on major issues of investment treaty protection." They refer to divergent jurisprudence on key doctrinal points such as cooling-off periods, MFN, and cost awards as outcomes that "will provide meagre guidance as to the likely outcome of future disputes."[139] The conclusion requires users of the system to accept that investment protection case law will continue to be disordered in some measure. For commentators such as Shore and Rothkopf, and Schulz above, that reality coheres with the origins of the investment arbitration system which was designed to resolve individual cases as opposed to generating a coherent body of jurisprudence.[140]

7.3.3 A Contractual Ethos

International investment law is sourced largely in bilateral treaties concluded between pairs of countries that bear resemblance to contracts. The treaties are concluded between defined parties. They are understood to create rights and obligations for the parties alone, or perhaps more accurately, for host states and third-party investors who are their prime beneficiaries. Moreover, these arrangements may be amended or terminated according to their terms. In all of these respects, investment treaties place emphasis on the text as an expression of will.

Contractualism shapes the traditional style of investment agreement interpretation. Thomas Wälde has pointed out how "most of the arbitrators (and counsel) in investment disputes have been drawn from the international arbitration community"[141] and how "[t]he essence of international commercial arbitration culture is to provide an effective

[138] Frédéric Sourgens, *A Nascent Common Law* 334 (Brill Nijhoff, Leiden; 2015).
[139] Ibid.
[140] Ibid. at 298.
[141] Wälde, "Interpreting Investment Treaties" 724 at 725 (2009).

resolution of dispute [sic] between the parties – and nothing further. That culture brings a strong focus on the facts rather than on the law."[142] In addition, "the culture of commercial arbitration comes with a great focus on the text – irrespective of context, purpose, and history – of specific contracts between international parties considered to be professionally competent, interacting on a level of presumed equality."[143]

The will-driven aspect of the law is not simply evident at the level of treaties and their interpretation. It is also apparent among those who pursue arbitration under them. Private parties have substantial flexibility in crafting their claims, a freedom that contributes substantially to the shaping of the law. As José Alvarez notes, "who is entitled to bring claims … matters a great deal with respect to the intensity with which issues may be pursued, the prospect of annulment or enforcement challenges or for settlement, and the likelihood that litigants will raise 'political' or other extraneous issues in the course of adjudication."[144]

The result is an autonomy that is at times disquieting, as Alvarez observes:

> The intrusive nature of many of these [investment] claims – involving challenges to environmental regulations, to the way States conduct administrative proceedings at all levels of government, or to national measures taken to handle a financial crisis – is exacerbated by the unpredictability of the resulting awards. And the prospect of more arbitral precedents seem all the more troubling when these involve the application of vague standards such as fair and equitable treatment by ad hoc panels of three that only come together to resolve one dispute at the time with no prospect of an appeal.[145]

[142] Ibid., p. 724 at 725–726. An example of this relatively restrained interpretive style is the award in *Eastern Sugar* v. *Czech Republic*, SCC Case No. 088/2004, where the tribunal had to determine if a decreased sugar quota constituted a breach of the Netherlands-Czech BIT. The award contains many procedural details. However, the crux of its reasoning – namely that the reduction did in fact constitute a breach of FET – is minimal. There is little legal analysis of the standard or its application. There is also little discussion of other cases, of alternatives to the decision arrived at, or awareness of the decision itself constituting a precedent. Instead, the arbitrators essentially indicate, "we think this is a breach and so determine. You need to trust us because you have chosen us to make such a decision." See Wälde, "Interpreting Investment Treaties" 724 at 727 (2009).

[143] Wälde, "Interpreting Investment Treaties" 724 at 727 (2009).

[144] Alvarez, *The Public International Law Regime Governing International Investment* 56.

[145] Ibid. at 56.

The unconstrained freedom – even license – of international investment law has provoked questioning about the basic contractual assumptions underpinning the regime and given rise to a number of developments that may be characterized as "constitutive." These provide a greater framework against which the contractual features of the law can be contextualized. In these ways a correlation is observed between the two concepts (i.e. Constitution/Contract).

First, there has been greater acknowledgment recently of international investment law's link to public international law. Wälde and others point to the growing recognition of international investment agreements as part of international law and therefore more properly influenced by interpretive approaches based upon canons of international law.[146] This recognition necessarily begins to import into the interpretation of international investment law constitutive-type methods such as those found in the VCLT. They involve greater consideration of the treaty's context (VCLT Art. 31(1)), the international law and background drawn from treaty-practice (VCLT Art. 31(3)) and recognition of the need to assign special meaning to treaty terms that depart from well-established treaty-practice (VCLT Art. 31(4)).

At the same time, application of the VCLT is haphazard and approximate. Many arbitrators are not international lawyers and the commercial, and to some extent national, aspect in decision-making remains strong. Thus, as Wälde notes, "[w]hile at least lip-service to [the VCLT] is now *de rigueur*, it is rare to find a systematic application of Articles 31 to 33 of the Vienna Convention."[147]

Second, there is a tendency to regard certain awards or "lines" of awards as setting down, or at least reflective of, customary international law that may be interpreted as constitutive. Traditionally, it was relatively easy to characterize investment treaties as creating *lex specialis* among the parties to them. By doing so, the parties were taken to have "contracted out" of international law. A more modern view is to regard this practice as taking place against the background of the broad corpus of international law and to recognize the intertwined nature of conventional and customary sources. Thus, Alvarez observes that:

> [i]t may be misleading to state, as a leading case does, that BITs "[a]s *lex specialis* between the parties ... supersede any inconsistent customary

[146] Wälde, "Interpreting Investment Treaties" 724 at 725.
[147] Ibid., p. 724 at 729.

> international law and embrace or exclude any incipient norms ... The language of most BITs welcomes or even requires the residual application of customary international law ... it is much harder to point to concrete instances where such treaties explicitly exclude it."[148]

Third, wariness of easy contractual analogies has important consequences for the sources of international investment law. Whereas many commentators appear to assume that the proliferation of investment treaties is leading to wholesale "treatification," that is, a kind of takeover of the field by conventional sources, some question this opinion. This is for the reason mentioned above that treaties themselves are interpreted against a greater constitutive background of custom. More reference to treaty interpretation means that "[r]ecourse to non-treaty sources is [likewise] more prevalent than ever before."[149] Such development infers that what is happening is a "mestization" of sources.[150] Alvarez maintains that "unless treaty parties explicitly provide to the contrary, treaty interpreters should not presume that a treaty dispenses with the application of fundamental rules of customary international law (such as the principle requiring exhaustion of local remedies)."[151] For this reason, "Treatification, at least in this regime, does not, contrary to the expectations of some, suggest the 'twilight of customary international law.'"[152]

All of these developments might appear to subtly highlight a relationship of subordination (i.e. Constitution > Contract) in the sense that a constitutive impulse anchored in custom can be detected behind the regime's superficially contractual aspect. Still, there are good reasons to continue treating international investment agreements as grounded in consent and not to overstate the role of custom.

First, custom is famously vague. To the extent it is hard to determine, it serves as an imprecise basis for expectations about the normative framework, and, ultimately, the arrangement of rights and obligations. Arbitrators will tend to shy away from it regardless of doctrinal purity.

148 Alvarez, *The Public International Law Regime Governing International Investment* 116, n. 213.

149 Ibid., p. 230.

150 Thus, Alvarez suggests that the way international investment law has handled FET means that "treaty, [customary international law] and general principles *are inexorably intertwined and hard to disentangle*." Alvarez, *The Public International Law Regime Governing International Investment* 235 (emphasis added).

151 Alvarez, *The Public International Law Regime Governing International Investment* 237.

152 Ibid. at 238.

Second, many existing investment agreements were concluded in an era when concluding such agreements was considered by governments the "thing to do" from a political or reputational standpoint.[153] There was little sense that such agreements were *legally* binding. For this reason, a measure of interpretive restraint may be in order. That realization translates most directly into respect for the agreements' consensual origins. Arbitrators should be particularly conscious of the standard form analogy, that is, the fact that investment agreement models were offered by certain influential *demandeur* countries in response to which developing countries had little input. Indeed, this realization could be used to support a principle of treaty interpretation *contra preferentum.*[154]

Third, a related point is that states parties to investment treaties are "communities." As such, their policy preferences often reflect those of governments, which are entitled to a measure of deference or a margin of appreciation in law- and policy-making. International investment law exhibits awareness of this idea, which, I suggest, is subsumed within the doctrine of proportionality, discussed above.

Perhaps for all of these reasons, certain commentators have shied away from identifying a true constitutional impetus at work in the international investment regime. They prefer instead the vaguer, more fluid and possibly less threatening formula of a "common law of investment."[155] To that extent, however, transition is observed between complementary concepts of constitution and contract (i.e. Constitution = Contract).

Where mention of constitutionalism and constitutional discourse is perhaps most noted in international investment law is in contrasting

[153] "Today's treaties follow (and largely copy) standard language that was developed in the late 1950s and 1960s when such treaties were in practice in effect more political goodwill statements than legally binding and enforceable treaties." Wälde, "Interpreting Investment Treaties" 724 at 737 (2009).

[154] "The *contra proferentem* rule has not frequently been invoked in investment disputes, possibly because it is rather a rule for interpreting contracts drafted by one party (also unilateral declarations) and more or less imposed or accepted without much questioning by the other side." Wälde, "Interpreting Investment Treaties" 724 at 741. Wälde suggests the rule could be invoked to counter ambiguity in certain instances but also observes that "is not that easy as we have here a tri-partite situation (home State, host State, and private claimant) rather than the usual bi-partite situation where the *contra proferentem* rule originated." Ibid.

[155] Ari Afilalo, "Towards a Common Law of International Investment" 17 *Geo. I.E.L. Rev.* 51 (2004); Porterfield, "An International Common Law of Investors Rights" 79; McLachlin et al., *International Investment Arbitration* 18.

strands of scholarship, which emphasize the regime's evidently public character. For instance, Stephan Schill has noted how the current framework of international investment law constitutes a relatively coherent multilateral framework akin to that of the WTO Agreement. In Schill's telling, bilateral investment treaties have a common historic background, aim to establish reciprocal rules for both developing and developed countries, and contain standard guarantees that put all foreign investors on the same plane. These features are not only beneficial for foreign investors. They have important spillover effects for good governance in host countries generally.[156] In addition, in legal terms, "most investor-state arbitrations rely on interpretative approaches consistent with a multilateral legal framework, that is, they tend to avoid reliance on treaty-specific negotiation history, privilege systematic over treaty-specific interpretations of commonly accepted legal provisions, and make extensive use of arbitral precedents, whether or not involving the specific treaty at issue."[157] Out of this reliance emerges an underlying "unity" in the law, and from it, a "system" that serves a "constitutional function" insofar as it restricts state action.

A more wary attitude to international investment rules is taken by Gus Van Harten.[158] Like Schill, Van Harten recognizes that international investment arbitration represents a distinctive development of international commercial arbitration, a "paradigm-shifting event" that removes home states from diplomatic espousal but also bestows considerable law-making capacity on arbitrators. Inevitably, the bestowal involves the elaboration of common standards that "serve a 'constitutional' function attuned to a particular market ideology."[159]

However, whereas Schill regards these developments as emerging from, and also driving, economic globalization in a constructive sense, Van Harten forwards a critique of what is perceived to be "hegemonic international law."[160] The critique is based on the view that there is little

156 Stephan Schill, *The Multilateralization of International Investment Law* (Cambridge University Press, Cambridge; 2009).

157 José Alvarez, "Book Review of *The Multilateralization of International Investment Law*" 105 *Am. J. Int'l L.* 377 at 379 (2011).

158 Van Harten, *Investment Treaty Arbitration and Public Law.*

159 Alvarez, "Book Review of *The Multilateralization of International Investment Law*" 377 at 380.

160 For a comparison of views, see Stephan Schill, "The Multilateralization of International Investment Law" 2 *Trade L. & Dev.* 59 (2010); Gus Van Harten, "Five Justifications for Investment Treaties" 2 *Trade L. & Dev.* 19 (2010).

evidence supporting the idea that investment treaties actually encourage foreign direct investment, that investment treaties are both underinclusive (by extending access to international adjudication to a narrow class of private actors) and over-inclusive (by failing to account for situations where domestic courts offer justice to a foreign investor), that investment arbitration fails to incorporate key institutional safeguards of judicial independence, that in many instances governments do not carry out sophisticated cost-benefit analyses prior to committing themselves to the investment treaty system, and that certain aspects of investment treaties appear to undermine democratic choice. As a result, Van Harten's conclusion is that governments should exercise greater care when considering concluding international investment agreements or, more likely, when they amend or renew existing treaties, and that governments consider options for reform.

In sum, Schill tends to regard the constitutionalization of international investment law as stabilizing and beneficial, whereas in Van Harten's view it is constraining and detrimental. As will be discussed, this difference of opinion has had important consequences in recent debates about the legitimacy of the international investment regime. On the whole, these opposing perspectives underline the view that competing conceptions of constitution and contract are at the heart of the law and constitute a hybrid structure, one which some regard as a "contractual constitution" while others might prefer to see it as a "constitutional contract" (i.e. Constitution + Contract).

7.3.4 *Looking Back*

Under the typical investment treaty, an investment claim arises when a host state fails to protect an investment or to accord the necessary standard of treatment. By definition, therefore, an investment claim deals with events in the past and is inherently backward-looking.

"Pastness" is vital to appreciating the temporal orientation of international investment law. The factual orientation toward the past helps to fix the interests in issue. They become well-defined, discrete and unitary. The injury can be sharply delineated in time and space. As a result, they are more naturally amenable to corrective justice.[161]

[161] These circumstances correspond to the five basic ideas around which corrective or compensatory justice is organized: (1) that the event producing the injury is both discrete and unitary, (2) that the injury is sharply defined in time and space, (3) that the defendant's conduct has clearly caused the harm suffered, (4) both plaintiff and

Pastness and corrective justice also cohere with the pattern of relationships underlying international investment law. Investment treaties are concluded between countries to promote investment and development between them, but their prime beneficiaries are foreign investors. A common assumption of international investment law is that if one investor or investment does not work out, then another one can be attracted or substituted in its place. In other words, the relationship is terminable. Unlike WTO law, no ongoing relationship is foreseen.

The particular nature of the interests involved in this retrospective perspective means that international investment law is substitutive. The law seeks to compensate for breaches that have already happened. Both treaty law and custom are clear that a government has the sovereign right to take certain action.[162] What the law requires in response, however, is reparation, which in most instances means fair compensation. As mentioned, there is no general requirement to amend or withdraw legislation.[163]

These comments, taken together, might infer the primacy of the past in international investment law, and indeed, there is much to support that view. It is reinforced by the attitude that arbitrators are reluctant to

defendant are easily identifiable, and (5) apart from the goal of compensation, existing rights are held constant. The law is not to engage in any kind of social reordering or social management except in so far as those functions are logically entailed by the principle of compensation. Cass Sunstein, *The Partial Constitution* 319 (Harvard University Press, Cambridge, MA; 1993).

162 Andrew Newcombe and Llius Paradell note that:

> International expropriation law mediates between two general principles of international law: (i) that states exercise permanent sovereignty over their territories and natural resources; and (ii) that states must respect the acquired rights of foreigners. The exercise of permanent sovereignty means that private property is not inviolable. Subject to specific commitments to the contrary, states have a right to regulate and tax property as well as to expropriate it.
>
> (Newcombe & Paradell, *Law and Practice of Investment Treaties* 321.)

163
> Unlike WTO authorized tariff retaliation, which … is relatively rare and considered something of a defeat for a regime that seeks to achieve lower trade barriers, the sometimes considerable damage awards rendered in the course of investor state arbitration are not seen as a regrettable defeat for the system but as its vindication. … investment treaties do not say, as the relevant WTO commitments do, that States are supposed to remove offending measures. Nonetheless, a host State that is obligated under an investor-State arbitral award to pay millions of dollars to an investor is bound to get the same message just as quickly if not more so than under the WTO.
>
> (Alvarez, *The Public International Law Regime Governing International Investment* 55)

quantify anything too speculative.[164] The future is unknown and, as mentioned above in relation to recovery of profits, largely speculative.

Nevertheless, an oft-remarked aspect of investment treaties is that they are meant to spur investment and general business conditions going forward. As Schreuer explains, "[t]he desire attract foreign investment has led most countries, especially developing countries, to adopt policies that are designed to create a favourable investment climate" in the future.[165] For this reason the future cannot but be a complement to the past, thereby providing evidence of a correlative relationship (i.e. Future/Past).

There is also persistent awareness of change in the investment regime. Schill points out, for example, how waves of expropriations and takeovers in many countries in the 1950s spurred efforts to give greater precision to hitherto ill-defined customary investment norms. This took the form of the Abs-Shawcross Draft of 1958 followed by the OECD Draft Convention on the Protection of Foreign Property of 1967. Both documents proposed schemes of comprehensive protection of foreign investment.[166] When these and other early attempts at investment protection failed, countries began to conclude bilateral investment agreements. The sub-standards contained within them have developed significantly since. This historical awareness infers that just as international investment law has changed in the past, so must it continue to change and evolve in the future, inferring the priority of the future over the past (Future > Past).[167]

[164] Bias toward the past is evident in statements of the type that, for example, in estimating damages in international investment law "[o]bjective historical data should in case of doubt be given rather greater weight than inherently speculative forecasts." Thomas W. Wälde & Borzu Sabahi, "Compensation, Damages, and Valuation" in Peter Muchlinski et al. (eds), *The Oxford Handbook of International Investment Law* 1052 at 1072 (Oxford University Press, Oxford; Sept. 2012).

[165] S.v. "Investments, International Protection" *Max Planck Encyclopedia of Public International Law* para. 5 (June 2013) (author: Christoph Schreuer).

[166] Schill, *The Multilateralization of International Investment Law* 36. Another example of change is given by Thomas Wälde, who notes that

> [t]he ICSID Convention was conceived simply as a tool to facilitate arbitration agreements between investor and host State and did not introduce, by itself, the modern treaty-based direct investor-State arbitration method; but the ICSID Convention, the associated discussions, and appreciation of the difficulties for investors of negotiating a contract-specific arbitration agreement have probably encouraged the search for and development of the modern investor-State arbitration method by way of investment treaty.
>
> (Wälde, "Interpreting Investment Treaties" 724 at 729)

[167] For instance, in 2014 Karl Sauvant and Federico Ortino put forward a series of options for improving international investment law. They noted that there continues to be debate about the purpose of the international investment regime, that questions persist

In the meantime, however, where standards do not change, the existing interpretation of a standard identified in the past will continue to serve as law in the future or at least a reference point for it (Future = Past).

The final temporal relationship forwarded by the theory – of the abiding presence of the present *eo instante* – is manifested in the repeated insistence that international investment law should be applied in each instance *de novo* in order to resolve the immediate difference at issue. Here, future and past merge in a continuing present (i.e. Future + Past = Present). Wälde notes in this respect:

> The essence of international commercial arbitration culture is to provide an effective resolution of dispute *between the parties – and nothing further*. That culture also brings a strong focus on the facts rather than on the law; that is most visible in the style of reasoning that is meant to assuage the losing party rather than to show in depth and detail how the law is applied and developed.[168]

7.3.5 Induction and Empiricism

International investment law is fact-intensive and therefore highly inductive.[169] In the normal course of an investment dispute, investors must prove their claims.[170]

about the scope of foreign investment and when an investor is "foreign"; temporal and other exclusions from international investment agreements; the problem of relatively open sub-standards; the balance between investment protection and the right to regulate; investment liberalization; and disciplines on home countries and foreign investors. Their ultimate conclusion is the need for an international investment consensus-building process. See Karl Sauvant & Federico Ortino, *Improving the International Investment Law and Policy Regime* (Ministry for Foreign Affairs of Finland, Helsinki; 2014).

[168] Wälde, "Interpreting Investment Treaties" 724 at 725–726 (2009) [emphasis added]. See also Jan Paulsson, "Avoiding Unintended Consequences" in Karl Sauvant & Michael Chiswick-Patterson (eds), *Appeals Mechanism in International Investment Disputes* 241 (Oxford University Press; New York; 2008).

[169] One study of international arbitration estimates that about 60–70 percent of cases turn on facts, rather than the application of principles of law. See Nigel Blackaby et al., *Redfern and Hunter on International Arbitration* (5th ed.) 384 (Oxford University Press, New York; 2009). The authors suggest that in the vast majority of remaining cases, the outcome is based on a combination of factual and legal issues. Only in a very small number of cases are factual determinations not required.

[170] "In investor-state arbitration case, each party has the burden of producing the evidence required to prove its case." Frédéric Sourgens et al., *Evidence in International Investment Arbitration* 175 (Oxford University Press, Oxford; 2018).

The requirement of proof is variable.[171] Parties normally deal with the uncertainty "through extensive production of documents, when possible, and detailed presentation of facts." Borzu Sabahi explains, "The basic rule of thumb is: given that the applicable principles of international law and treaties are somewhat vague, it is better to be precise and full on the facts to help the tribunal apply them more easily."[172]

In most instances the evidence presented is tested by an adversarial process. The process is described as follows:

> valuation experts usually present their assessments of what a particular enterprise or investment is worth or how the losses should be valued in the form of expert witness statements. These assessments may take into account a variety of data obtained from market and from other sources, including the parties. The assessments, however, ultimately require the exercise of judgment by the valuers. The opposing parties' valuers usually provide diverging forecasts about the value of investment at issue. Cross-examination of valuation experts helps to highlight the strong and weak points of the expert's assessments, particularly by testing the assumptions that valuers make on forecasting future profits of the business.[173]

On the basis of the evidence put forward, arbitrators arrive at a reasonable estimate of the damage. An award of compensation follows.

The standard of proof is the degree of proof necessary to convince a tribunal of the veracity of facts. Because rules about the standard have not been clearly formulated in international law and jurisprudence, "[i]nternational judges and arbitrators seem to silently apply concepts from both common-law and civil-law jurisdictions,"[174] these being either proof beyond a reasonable doubt from the common law or a standard of judicial appreciation from the civil law.[175]

At the same time, the requirement of a preponderance of evidence can become a serious hurdle when the question involves specific practical

[171] Sabahi notes that "it is not clear what amount of evidence should be produced to satisfy a particular burden." Sabahi, *Compensation and Restitution in Investor-State Arbitration* 184.

[172] Ibid.

[173] Ibid.

[174] Sergey Ripinsky & Kevin Williams, *Damages in International Investment Law* 163 (British Institute of International and Comparative Law, London; 2008).

[175] Given the subjectivity of the civil law standard, Sergey Ripinsky and Kevin Williams note that "[c]ommentators tend to support 'preponderance of evidence' as a prevalent standard in international arbitration." Ibid.

issues such as lost profits. Consequently, "international law has followed the lead of most legal systems, which 'relax the standards of proof and are satisfied if the profits would have been *probable* in light of the circumstances.'"[176] "In different cases, arbitral tribunals have held the future losses must be proved with 'sufficient (degree of) certainty,' 'sufficient degree of probability,' 'some level of certainty' or 'comparative likelihood' and that they must be 'probable and not merely possible.'"[177] This view coheres with the more general standard elucidated in the *Chorzów Factory* case that "reparation must . . . re-establish the situation which *would, in all probability, have existed* if that [wrongful] act had not been committed."[178] In the same vein, "[i]t is sufficient to convince a tribunal, on the basis of available evidence, that lost profits are more probable than not . . . [However] [t]he impossibility of fixing with mathematical precision the degree of certainty that is required by law leaves room for arbitrators' subjective judgment in each particular case."[179]

It might appear then that international investment law is largely inductive. That impression would seem to be reinforced by the commonly stated rule of evidence in international investment arbitration: that of free appreciation of evidence by the arbitrator.[180]

Yet here and there deductive devices in the form of presumptions and inferences do emerge.[181] Given the nature of investment law, it is not surprising that most presumptions and inferences are heavily fact-oriented and confined to specific points of practice. Their source is uncertain.[182] For instance, in the context of international arbitration,

[176] Ibid. at 164 [emphasis added].

[177] Ibid.

[178] Ibid. at 165.

[179] Ibid.

[180] Sourgens et al., *Evidence in International Investment Arbitration* 3.

[181] According to Sourgens and others, presumptions arising in the investment context are evident in jurisdiction, merits and remedies phases. See Sourgens et al., *Evidence in International Investment Arbitration* 124–134.

[182] On this point Sourgens notes that:

> the jurisprudence of investor-state tribunals has established a canon of legal presumptions in ICSID and other investor-state disputes. This raises the question whether the jurisprudence in its own right has created legal presumptions for application in investor state-arbitration. The question of the status of investor state determinations in future disputes remains an issue of debate. As a practical matter, however, a determination of the

Nathan O'Malley has noted that "[t]he majority of the well-known international arbitration rules omit reference to a tribunal's right to draw on adverse inference from the failure of a party to produce evidence."[183] Nevertheless, it has been held that an arbitrator's power to take notice of, and draw adverse inferences from, a party's failure to produce evidence is considered inherent to its right to assess the evidence and render a decision.[184] The determination of an adverse inference "is in practice reserved for the final award and is part of the tribunal's process of weighing the evidence."[185]

Waincymer also observes that as a purely practical matter "[e]fficiency requires many presumptions in adjudicatory processes, absent assertions to the contrary. For example, a claimant does not need to prove that a request for arbitration was served. It is for respondent to challenge adequate notice."[186] This sort of statement would appear to sustain the theoretic relationship of correlation (i.e. Deduction/Induction). It would also appear to sustain the relation of subordination (i.e. Deduction > Induction) in the sense that presumptions operate as background factors that condition the need for proof.[187] Moreover, there are indications of a relation of transition (Deduction = Induction) in certain evidentiary requirements for judicial presumptions to arise at all.[188]

The interrelated way that proof and presumption work together in investor-state arbitration is explained by Frédéric Sourgens and others, who observe that:

> existence of a legal presumption by an investor state tribunal is an *indicium* that a potentially applicable legal presumption may exist.
>
> (Sourgens et al., *Evidence in International Investment Arbitration* 123)

183 Nathan O'Malley, *Rules of Evidence in International Arbitration* (2nd ed.) 224 (Informa, London; 2019). Sourgens and others take the view that "[a]ll judicial presumptions functioning arise out of the legal presumption of good faith," a principle of international law. This involves honesty-in-fact and reasonableness. Sourgens et al., *Evidence in International Investment Arbitration* 117.

184 O'Malley, *Rules of Evidence in International Arbitration* 225.

185 Ibid., p. 225; see IBA Rules Art. 9.1.

186 Waincymer, *Procedure and Evidence in International Arbitration* 110.

187 For instance, in *Quiborax* v. *Bolivia* the claimant submitted that the registration of shares was evidence of acquisition of the shares in question. Entry into the share registry created a presumption that the transaction had legal effect as of the date of registration. The arbitrator held that the state could rebut this presumption by specific evidence negating it. *Quiborax* v. *Bolivia*, ICSID Case No. ARB/06/2 para. 85 (Decision on Jurisdiction 27 Sept. 2012).

188 Sourgens et al., *Evidence in International Investment Arbitration* 119.

> The use of presumptions is ubiquitous in investor-state arbitrations, as it is in other domestic and international disputes. The reason for this is intuitive: legal claims typically assert that one or both parties to a dispute deviated from relevant general practices to which both parties ought to adhere or frustrated reasonable background expectations . . . To rely upon or rebut the presumption requires a two-step process . . . First, it is necessary to prove that a general practice or relevant circumstance exists. This first step can be satisfied by proving a legal presumption by reference to the law applicable to the dispute. Alternatively, this first step can be satisfied through proof of fact that certain general practices or circumstances exist. Secondly, it is necessary to relate that general practice or relevant circumstance to the situation at bar. This second step requires a showing that the relevant question in dispute is a specific instance that would typically be governed by the general practice or circumstance proved as part of the first step.[189]

This description appears to confirm the operation of abductive logic in international investment arbitration as well. It is restated in the observation that that "Prima facie evidence and presumptions may alleviate the burden of proof."[190] Deductive and inductive logic then work together in the normal course of arbitral decision-making, resulting in abductive reasoning (Deduction + Abduction = Induction).

For instance, international investment arbitration generally recognizes the rule that *prima facie* evidence is required in order to establish a contention on the balance of probabilities. In this process, inductive reasoning in the form of evidence is required to raise a presumption, a hallmark of deduction.[191] The same combination is also observed in the drawing of adverse inferences. Thus, the jurisprudence of the Iran-US Claims Tribunal has also held that "a party seeking [the drawing of an] adverse inference must provide prima facie evidence of the facts supporting its claim."[192]

7.4 A Lesser Unification

The overview provided above reveals that international investment law conforms in some degree to the theoretic model of a

[189] Ibid., p. 112.

[190] ICC Case No. 7365, para. 15.2 (1997) (unpublished), cited in O'Malley, *Rules of Evidence in International Arbitration* 220, n. 69.

[191] *Marvin Feldman Karpa* v. *Mexico*, ICSID Case. No. ARB 99/01, Final Award, para. 177 (2002).

[192] Jeremy Sharpe, "Drawing Adverse Inferences from the Non-production of Evidence" 22:4 *Arbitration International* 549 (2006); see also O'Malley, *Rules of Evidence in International Arbitration* 226–230.

communitarian theory put forward in earlier chapters. However, it does so in a way that is in many respects the reverse of WTO law. While WTO law is primarily equality- and obligation-oriented, international investment law is primarily fairness- and rights-oriented.

At the same time, the body of international investment law is complicated, even messy. Generally speaking, this has provoked two reactions. One seeks to improve the regime by introducing broad reforms that might be labeled "constitutive." The other aims to limit the regime or possibly do away with it altogether.

Gebhard Bücheler has grouped current discontent with the international investment regime into six categories.[193] First, there is the perceived pro-investor bias of most arbitrators. The argument is that once they are appointed, many arbitrators are anxious to find a violation in order to confirm their professional worth. Second, traditionally arbitral proceedings are considered "private" and accessible only to the parties directly involved. There has been concern expressed about the need to promote transparency in arbitral proceedings and results, given that these can have demonstrably public consequences. Third, international investment agreements appear to impose obligations principally upon states. A more balanced idea of the jural relationship between host states and investors implies that the latter should have obligations as well. Fourth, the international investment regime lacks methods to ensure consistency in decision-making. Arbitral awards do diverge, making it difficult for governments and parties to establish reasonable expectations. Fifth, concern is sometimes expressed about the potential threat posed by arbitrators to democracy. The fear is that they may exceed their jurisdiction in rendering awards and thereby infringe legitimate democratic decision-making. Sixth, awards can impose limits on the regulatory flexibility of states in a phenomenon known as "regulatory chill." A further concern centers on the fact that, as mentioned, many international investment agreements were concluded when they were the "thing to do" politically. As a result, the argument is sometimes made that investment treaty provisions should not be interpreted with complete seriousness, and their interpretation and enforcement should be tempered.

[193] See Bücheler, *Proportionality in Investor-State Arbitration* 6.

In the face of these criticisms, the body of international investment law has not stood still. There is a powerful strand of thinking that regards it as reformable.

With respect to transparency, for instance, major standards under the ICSID Convention and its associated Rules of Procedure traditionally require tribunal hearings to be closed if either party objects to a public hearing.[194] Similarly, both the ICSID Convention and the UNCITRAL Arbitration Rules provide that awards cannot be published without party consent. Nevertheless, with the adoption of the UNCITRAL Rules on Transparency in 2013 and the UN Convention on Transparency in Treaty-Based Investor-State Arbitration in 2014 transparency of proceedings and awards now has become the default.[195] A number of bilateral agreements now replicate these same standards.[196]

Countries have also clarified or amended their investment agreements to ensure that the sovereign right to regulate is safeguarded. Thus, the 2012 U.S. Model BIT contains the following wording:

> (b) Except in rare circumstances, non-discriminatory regulatory actions by a Party that are designed and applied to protect legitimate public welfare objectives, such as public health, safety, and the environment, do not constitute indirect expropriations.[197]

Similarly, with respect to more consistent interpretation of FET, certain countries have made efforts to tie FET to the customary international minimum standard of treatment or to clarify that FET means nothing more than that standard, although arbitrators recognize that "the

[194] ICSID Arbitration Rules (as amended 10 Apr. 2006), ICSID Convention, Regulations and Rules (Washington, Apr. 2006) 99. See Rule 32(2) (hearings), 48(5) (awards); UNCITRAL Arbitration Rules, General Assembly Resolution 109, 68 GAOR vol. 1 at 829, UN Doc. A/68/462 (2013), UN Doc. A/462/465 (2010). See Arts 28(3) (hearings) and 34(5) (awards).

[195] UNCITRAL Rules on Transparency, G.A. Res. 109, 68 GAOR vol. 1 at 829, U.N. Doc. A/68/462 (2013), Art. 6(1) (hearings), Art. 3(1) (awards); UN Convention on Transparency in Treaty-Based Investor-State Arbitration, General Assembly Res. 116, 69 G.A.O.R. vol. 1 at 883, U.N. Doc. A/69/496 (2014).

[196] At least two signatories to the UN Convention have acted to provide for transparency in ISDS proceedings. Canada's 2004 Model BIT mandates public headings of tribunals (Art. 38(1)) and requires documents submitted to, or issued by, tribunals to be publicly available unless the parties otherwise agree and subject to the protection of confidential information (Art. 38(3)). Similarly, the 2012 U.S. Model BIT provides for public hearings (Art. 29(2)) and the publication of documents (Art. 29(1)), again subject to requirements of confidentiality.

[197] See 2012 U.S. Model BIT, Annex B.4.

customary international law [standard] ... is not static and that the minimum standard of treatment does evolve."[198]

An ambitious idea to help systematize arbitral jurisprudence is a proposal made by the EU in 2015 for a multilateral investment court (MIC).[199] The EU proposal foresees the establishment of a two-tiered tribunal to hear investor-state disputes and would involve a Tribunal of First Instance and an Appeal Tribunal. The proposal is in many ways historic in that it departs from a private law conceptualization of international investment dispute settlement by providing for rules on transparency, third-party participation, protection of the right to regulate, and an increased emphasis on predictability and consistency in decision-making.

The EU proposal was the basis for bilateral investment court systems in recently negotiated international investment agreements between the EU and a number of key countries which, in addition to efforts at UNCITRAL, are designed to serve as "stepping stones" to a full-fledged MIC.[200]

Nevertheless, these constitutive-type changes have failed to quiet the chorus of criticism from those who are concerned that a MIC and other recent changes will not address in any fundamental way persistent objections to the international investment regime.

In this respect Won Kidane argues that international investment arbitration imposes "severe restrictions on sovereign or democratic

198 *Waste Management* v. *Mexico (Number 2)*, ICSID Case No. ARB(AF)/00/3, para. 92 (30 Apr. 2004).

199 The proposal was made in the context of EU–US negotiations over a Transatlantic Trade and Investment Partnership. See EC Press Release, "Commission proposes new Investment Court System for TTIP and other EU trade and investment negotiations" (16 Sept. 2015).

200 Multilateral talks started in late 2017 under the auspices of the Working Group III of the UN Commission on International Trade Law (UNCITRAL). The talks have been divided in three phases: identifying the concerns regarding international investment dispute settlement, assessing the desirability of reforms; and if so, recommending action and reform options to the UNCITRAL Commission. The working group has identified concerns pertaining to three categories: consistency, coherence and predictability of international investment dispute settlement; criteria for appointment and conduct of arbitrators and decision-makers; guidelines concerning the cost and duration of cases. For all these concerns the UNCITRAL working group concluded that multilateral reforms are desirable. The talks are now in the third phase recommending action and reform. The UNCITRAL Secretariat has issued three documents, which summarize the proposals and give reform directions. These are a Code of Conduct for Adjudicators, an appellate mechanism and enforcement, and guidelines on the selection and appointment of international dispute settlement tribunal members.

control" and notes that "deference to private actors without meaningful checks and balances has nurtured a culture of condescension."[201]

A more radical position still is to propose limits on international investment protection. Thus, Gus Van Harten has written:

> Foreign investor protections have been made into an exceptionally powerful component of international law that constrains governments to insulate the wealthy from sovereign choices designed to protect others. In turn, they disadvantage those whose life and future are rooted in one place. No one besides owners of high-value cross-border assets has a realistic prospect of using the protections, yet most people (as voters, taxpayers, or property owners) must assume the risks and the costs. Removing these protections from international law is a feasible, important, and perhaps necessary step to stem the concentration of wealth and reinvigorate state institutions that are needed to confront pressing concerns of humanity.[202]

Van Harten and others point to the vagueness of the applicable international investment law sub-standards, the weaknesses of evidence that bilateral investment treaties spur foreign investment, the fact that investment standards appear to offer protections for the wealthy, the allegedly intertwined nature of the arbitral bench and bar, and the fact that investment law "hamper[s] sovereign action to respond to urgent social and environmental priorities."[203] In Van Harten's view, a solution could be for arbitrators to "moderate the treaties' pro-investor design and show restraint when reviewing legislatures and governments."

Beyond this Van Harten proposes a more radical solution still: "[t]o free sovereigns in the short term requires countries to agree to amend or terminate their treaties."[204] In a few instances, this course of action now appears to be occurring.[205]

[201] Won Kidane, *The Culture of International Arbitration* 285 (Oxford University Press, New York; 2017).

[202] Gus Van Harten, *The Trouble with Foreign Investor Protection* 133 (Oxford University Press, Oxford; 2020).

[203] Ibid., p. 135.

[204] Ibid., pp. 136–137.

[205] For instance in the period 2007–2012, Bolivia, Ecuador and Venezuela withdrew from the ICSID Convention, and in 2018 Canada and the United States agreed that investment protection would be left out of their reformulated bilateral relationship under the USMCA, the successor treaty to NAFTA. Under NAFTA ch. 11 investors could commence arbitration proceedings against the host state where the host state had violated the investment protection obligations agreed to. The USMCA provides much more limited recourse to arbitration, and no independent arbitration right at all in the case

In turn, moves to restrict or terminate investor-state protection have triggered a further set of countercharges from those who, on the whole, are supportive of the international investment regime as it is. In the main, those views assert that international investment law constitutes a coherent and defensible body of law,[206] that international investment disciplines promote investment even if their effects are not always measurable,[207] that divergence in arbitral results is both warranted and kept within reasonable bounds,[208] that breaches found by arbitrators in many instances are egregious and have little to do with assertions of regulatory flexibility or the need for policy space,[209] that there is little clear evidence of "regulatory chill,"[210] and that the amount of compensation in most arbitral awards is consistent with their being nuisance claims as opposed to onerous judgments.[211] In addition, on a number of practice points like the need for diversity in arbitrator selection,[212] ethical standards,[213] and

of investors from, or in, Canada. Mexican and US investors continue to have recourse to investor-state arbitration under USMCA ch. 14 (Annex 14-D), though in a diluted fashion. Mexican investors in Canada and Canadian investors in Mexico have recourse to investor-state arbitration provisions under the Comprehensive and Progressive Trans-Pacific Partnership (CPTPP) treaty.

206 Schill, *The Multilateralization of International Investment Law* 18 (claiming that "investment protection constitutes a multilateral system").

207 Jonathan Bonnitcha et al., *The Political Economy of the Investment Treaty Regime*, pp. 49, 159, 166, 179, 218 (Oxford University Press, Oxford; 2015); Joachim Pohl, "Societal Benefits and Costs of International Investment Agreements: A Critical Review of Aspects and Available Empirical Evidence," *OECD Working Papers on International Investment*, 2018/01, pp. 9–10, 28–29, 32, 55–57, 62–65 (2018).

208 See, for instance, Sourgens, *A Nascent Common Law* 352–354 (noting that divergence in arbitral decision-making is "one of the happy incidents of the lack of hierarchy between [investment] tribunals . . . a single courageous tribunal may, if the parties choose, serve as a laboratory and try novel legal approaches to social and economic problems." Ibid. at 353); Schreuer & Weiniger, "A Doctrine of Precedent?" 1189.

209 Charles Brower & Sadie Blanchard, "What's in a Meme? The Truth about Investor-State Arbitration" 52:3 *Colum. J. Transnat'l L.* 689 (2014); Ursula Kriebaum, "Evaluating Social Benefits and Costs of Investment Treaties" 33 *ICSID Rev.* 14 (2018).

210 Ratner, "Survey Article" 107 at 124 (observing that "the economic research is woefully incomplete – with no systematic evidence of regulatory chill by states that enter into investment treaties").

211 Wälde & Sabahi, "Compensation, Damages, and Valuation" 1052 (2012) (noting that with respect to the law and practice of compensation, investment arbitrations "have moved cautiously and as a rule rejected 'speculative elements.'" Ibid. at 1114).

212 Chiara Giorgetti, "Who Decides Who Decides in International Investment Arbitration?" 35:2 *U. Pa J. Int'l L.* 431 (2013).

213 Malcolm Langford et al., "The Revolving Door in International Investment Arbitration" 20:2 *J.I.E.L.* 301 (2017).

transparency,[214] these same commentators point to reforms that they maintain are responsive to contemporary concerns about the regime.

The differences of opinion outlined above appear reflective of the absence of a strong consensus on the good underpinning international investment law. In an effort to bridge the gap between divergent positions, Karl Sauvant and Federico Ortino note an acute need for an international investment consensus-building process that could involve intensive fact-finding about the regime; efforts at dialogue between business and civil society; consensus-building working groups on substantive and procedural issues; the development of model investment instruments; specific mechanisms to improve the regime (e.g. in the form of an FDI investment protectionism observatory, an advisory center on international investment law, and/or a recourse mechanism for a wider set of stakeholders); and establishing the desirability of a multilateral investment framework.[215]

Steven Ratner has observed that "[b]oth the critiques and defenses of [international investment law] reflect certain assumptions about those effects."[216] Broadly stated, the prevailing assumption among supporters of the regime is that international investment law is beneficial whereas among critics the dominant assumption is that it is detrimental. Intriguing from the point of view of a communitarian theory is the fact that the assumption pertaining to the evaluative question (i.e. does international investment law make a positive contribution to international political economy?) is essentially the same question that is the focus of the theory (i.e. is international investment law a "good" that is adequately defined and worthy of protection?). On both sets of questions, the problem at the moment appears to be the need for more empiric research.

What does a communitarian theory contribute to all of the ongoing debate? A communitarian theory rests on the idea of goods and of justice as arranged to realize the goods' ever-evolving distribution and

[214] Joachim Delaney & Daniel Barstow Magraw, "Procedural Transparency" in Peter Muchlinski et al. (eds), *The Oxford Handbook of International Investment Law* 752 (Oxford University Press, Oxford; 2012). See also UNCITRAL Rules on Transparency in Treaty-Based Investor-State Arbitration (2014) followed by the UN Convention on Transparency in Treaty-Based Investor-State Arbitration, U.N. Reg. 54749 (2017).

[215] See Sauvant & Ortino, *Improving the International Investment Law and Policy Regime* 145–146.

[216] Ratner, "Survey Article" 107 at 113.

correction as well as transformation in the goods themselves. The extent to which justice will operate to fulfill these functions depends on underlying consensus about the good of foreign investment. Right now to many observers that consensus is unclear, which is why the regime appears to be in need either of unification, modification or perhaps abolition.

Given the pluralism of the contemporary investment regime and continuing debate about its 'good', it appears likely that the impetus for reform will come from different directions. Host state responsibility may be leavened by various forms of residual state flexibility under international law and by appreciation of the coercive nature of the regime. Investors may be held to account by sources other than international investment law, such as the possible exercise of extraterritorial jurisdiction by home states or the development of codes of corporate social responsibility.

7.5 Conclusion

In this chapter I demonstrated how the communitarian theory of law put forward in earlier chapters and abstracted from WTO law does a relatively good job of explaining the nature, shape and current tensions observed in international investment law. The focus of international investment law is on the protection of investments and the treatment of investors. Because of this, it is primarily rights-oriented.

That orientation helps to explain why the body of international investment law is so contested and problematic. Rights are subjective and in being subjective they manifest a lack of agreement. This shortcoming is visible in many ways. It is evident in the lack of a clear doctrine of precedent. It is evident in unanticipated consequences of legal standards such as FET and MFN. It is also evident in the remedy of compensation, which more often than not falls short of the international law standard of "full reparation." In sum, the cohesion and coherence expected of an integrated legal system seem to be missing.

To be sure, the public image of international investment law is one of agreement. Countries are concluding new investment agreements all the time. This pattern of behavior is frequently pointed to as evidence of the investment regime's legitimacy.

At the same time, the visceral reactions elicited by the international investment regime today underline how all of this "agreement" is, to some extent, fictive. Diverse reactions appear to confirm the point made in Chapter 2 that more than "agreement" about goods is necessary to truly achieve justice, and by extension, sustainable community. What is necessary in addition is value.

Almost everywhere one looks in international investment law at the moment, it is clear that actors in the regime do not ascribe the same value to it. In this respect the record of international investment law differs significantly from that of WTO law, where the good's value continues to be recognized, if perhaps somewhat less evidently than in the past.

At least some of the difference in assessments of value arise because of perceptions that the current regime of international investment law appears unbalanced.

In Chapter 1, I explained how a communitarian theory suggests that obligations are primary whereas rights are secondary (i.e. Obligation > Right) and how this subordination is reproduced in other aspects of the law. The theory suggests that international investment law arouses so much antipathy because the regime appears to run counter to this abiding orientation by maintaining that investor rights are *superior to* obligations (i.e. Rights > Obligations). Indeed, what has troubled many commentators as the international investment regime has matured and a vigorous rights culture taken hold is the apparent lack of a corresponding sense of investor obligation.[217] Most current efforts to modify the regime – by restating traditional duties owed by investors to host or home states or possibly introducing new duties through human rights protections or corporate social responsibility – can be understood as an attempt to rebalance it and instill a greater sense of community.

It is not yet clear what form this rebalancing will take. However, a "system of ideas" inherent in a theory is instructive for the way that it explains this and much else about a particular community, the community of international investment law.

[217] Sabahi, *Compensation and Restitution in Investor-State Arbitration* 55 (noting that "[r]ules of international law, however, which may impose responsibility on investors ... such as those relating to corporate social responsibility, do not seem to have fully formed nor exist in a concrete form at present"). Instead, the contours of obligation have been left to gradual elaboration through corporate social responsibility frameworks such as the United Nations' Guiding Principles on Business and Human Rights, HR/PUB/11/04 (2011). For an overview and discussion of the backlash against international investment protection generated, in part, by the perceived lack of corresponding investor obligations, see Alvarez, *The Public International Law Regime Governing International Investment* 340*ff.*

8

Some Concluding Thoughts

In this book, I have outlined a communitarian theory of WTO law and suggested how it might provide a "system of ideas" for thinking about law and legal systems.

In this closing chapter, I summarize the theory's principal points and certain aspects of its nature as a theory. I also examine its potential to serve as a general theory of law, its application to some unanswered questions, its role in an era of ever-intensifying concern about climate change, certain predictions and prescriptions for the WTO Agreement, and a few final remarks.

8.1 A Substantive Theory

In Chapter 1, I made an initial attempt to define and contextualize the theory outlined in this book. That definition is not easy to arrive at, given that the theory is a three-fold theory of community, justice and law, and that it synthesizes and integrates much that is contained in the traditional semantic theories. At a glance, it might appear to be likened to a "Theory of Everything."

With the benefit of intervening explanation, however, it should now be clear that what I have put forward is a substantive theory. This is in the sense that its foundations lie in the substance of the law, as opposed to text or economics or politics. I have posited that that substance is located, first and foremost, in correspondent obligations and rights.

The theory's principal theoretical points can be summarized as follows:

1. Interdependence gives rise to goods. A theory of law must therefore incorporate constituent theories of interdependence in the form of community and justice that serve to shape the conception of those goods within communities.

2. The theory of community I put forward in this book emphasizes how interdependence gives rise to goods within a community.
3. The associated theory of justice I put forward emphasizes the structure of what is considered "right" or "correct" in relation to those goods.
4. Classic Aristotelian ideas posit that justice comes in two forms: distributive and corrective. Distributive justice regulates the distribution of goods and is about fairness, whereas corrective justice regulates the correction of wrongdoing in relation to those goods and is about equality.
5. The theory of justice I put forward in this book suggests that in reality the values visible in the operation of justice should be the reverse of what Aristotle projected: namely, that the distribution of goods aims to achieve equality, whereas the correction of wrongdoing aims to achieve fairness. The reversal is mandated by the need to account for wider communal priorities in the operation of justice, including the communal cost of correction and changes in the conception of the good over time.
6. The theory of justice also posits that where the good is "public" it is more likely to be amenable to distributive justice, whereas when the good is "private" it is more likely to be amenable to corrective justice.
7. Conventional accounts of the relationship between distributive and corrective justice suggest either a distributive priority view (i.e. correction acts to restore the original distribution) or an independent view (i.e. correction is autonomous of distributive justice), but I have posited that reciprocal influences between the two types of justice suggest it is more accurate to adhere to an interactive and interdependent view exhibiting variation.
8. That variation consists of four relations understood in light of the theories set out above. First, there is the relation of *correlation*: where there is equality and distributive justice there will be a demand for fairness and corrective justice, and vice versa. Second, there is the relation of *subordination*: equality and distributive justice are primary whereas fairness and corrective justice is secondary. Third, there is the relation of *transition*: at the outer edges of both equality/distributive and fairness/corrective justice, there is observed movement in the direction of their correlative opposite. Fourth there is the relation of *integration*: in integration the values and two forms of justice – distributive

and corrective – ultimately merge, creating a "third thing" in transformative justice.

9. The overarching aim of transformative justice is to sustain the community. Nevertheless, transformative justice is not "perfect" justice, hence a subsisting impulse in all efforts at justice of reform.
10. The four relations of correlation, subordination, transition and integration are likewise identified in a theory of law. They are manifested "horizontally" between conceptual pairs of obligation and right, constitution and contract, future and past, and deduction and induction. Their combined operation generates a *sui generis* legal system structured as a "contractual constitution," apprehended *eo instante*, and reasoned abductively.
11. In addition, "vertical" relationships are visible between concordant elements of *different* conceptual pairs, thereby creating distinct "idea-complexes." In one such complex the law is about attaining equality and is characterized by obligations, constitutive arrangements, an *ex ante* perspective and deduction. In the other complex the law is about fairness and is characterized by rights, contractual arrangements, an *ex post* perspective and induction. These idea-complexes describe the law in a single moment but in fact work together. Over time oscillation is observed between them.

I applied the above points to explain current developments in relation to the WTO Agreement as follows:

12. When the WTO Agreement was established in 1994, there was a relatively strong consensus about the benefits of unconditional interdependence as a good.
13. The WTO Agreement responded to this by creating a "club" good belonging to WTO members whose orientation is chiefly *ex ante* and which is characterized by the operation of distributive justice. In this conception the law is primarily concerned with safeguarding the good composed of the trade concessions and commitments of all WTO members. It therefore makes little sense to talk about what has been "lost" in cases of injury since any such loss is borne by the membership as a whole.
14. A secondary task of justice under the WTO Agreement is more *ex post* and aims to protect the private good belonging to single

members. Justice seeks to correct injury arising in the past. This is particularly evident in certain WTO rules disciplines, in nonviolation cases, and in decisions concerning countermeasures.

15. The WTO Agreement applies over time. If a long-term view of what WTO law is taken, it can generally be said that the treaty's overarching purpose is to promote interdependence. The protection of expectations and the correction of injury, as well as their associated remedies, tend to facilitate interaction. In doing so the treaty acts transformatively to modify thinking about both the common and individual interests.
16. Transformative justice is observed in a number of settlements achieved through WTO dispute settlement.
17. There are exceptions and counter-indications to all the above points. As a result, the theory should be regarded as identifying WTO law's chief tendencies, rather than its certainties.
18. The unconditional interdependence promoted by the WTO Agreement has been beneficial but has also been disruptive, promoting backlash and exposing critical vulnerabilities. Consequently, the good of the treaty is no longer regarded as unreservedly positive.
19. Growing concern about unconditional interdependence is expressed in WTO members' behavior under the treaty, which appears to be oscillating away from an equality and *ex ante*-driven focus based on expectations and toward a preoccupation with the fairness or unfairness of certain *ex post* outcomes.
20. The oscillation might be taken to suggest parallel movement toward greater corrective justice under the WTO Agreement except that the treaty is ill-designed for this purpose. Instead, in many instances correction has occurred in the form of unilateral trade action taken by certain member countries and a continuing impasse over the WTO Appellate Body.
21. The diminished nature of the good under the WTO Agreement hints at a more modest role for the WTO, not as a Kantian "trade enforcer," but as a setting within which transformation and common positions can achieved, with some attention paid to law. Ultimately, what matters is sustaining a "Neo-Grotian community," which aims to realize common values and interests.
22. The record of transformation under WTO law is to be contrasted with that of international investment law, which is more evidently

rights-based and corrective, but wherein there is even less agreement on the underlying good. As a result, theoretically speaking, there is some indication that the investment regime appears to be oscillating in the opposite direction to that of WTO law toward a more integrated framework that stresses obligation, constitutive structures, an *ex ante* perspective and deduction.

23. Taken together, the two legal systems examined in this book – WTO law and international investment law – infer that a legal system will exhibit distributive and corrective characteristics but that the system's overall nature will be transformative. Although a communitarian theory is perhaps most clearly exhibited in legal systems based on equality, the theory may serve as a template for thinking about the nature of legal systems generally.

These points need further contextualization in order to be fully appreciated.

Andrei Marmor and Alexander Sarch have identified four categories of contemporary legal theory.[1] The first takes jurisprudence to be a form of conceptual analysis along the lines pursued by Herbert Hart in his influential book, *The Concept of Law* (1961).[2] A second category offers a reductivist account of law by distilling the law into key categories or components in "an explanatorily powerful way."[3] A third category consists of theories based on a prescriptive view, that is, on the best or most desirable conception of the law. Finally, a fourth category of theories is interpretative and, like the work of Ronald Dworkin, offers "a constructive interpretation of legal practice."[4]

The theory outlined in this book is perhaps most accurately described as reductivist. It reduces the law to foundational categories based on either equality or fairness and explains how the law seeks to attain these ideals through relationships among idea-complexes. I have pointed out, however, how it is a mistake to see the law as falling into one of these complexes exclusively and how in reality the law is most accurately

[1] Andrei Marmor & Alexander Sarch, S.v. "The Nature of Law" *Stanford Encyclopedia of Philosophy* (7 Aug. 2015).

[2] In that book Hart posited that law is the union of primary rules consisting of rules of conduct and secondary rules consisting of empowering rules.

[3] Marmor & Sarch, S.v. "The Nature of Law".

[4] Ibid.

described as a combination of them. Its underlying good is an ever-evolving hybrid.

What is perhaps most noteworthy about the theory's account of the law is its emphasis on equality. Ideas about equality have been present in Western thinking for a long time. They continue to resonate powerfully in developments almost everywhere, including in international law where there is now a presumption of equality among states.[5] WTO law reproduces and extends that presumption in important ways.

At the same time, equality is acknowledged to be "a loaded and 'highly contested' concept" with "a rhetorical power rendering it suitable as a political slogan."[6] The experience of WTO law suggests that equality is so varied, so pliant, so kaleidoscopic, as to have "no unified meaning" or possibly to be "devoid of meaning."[7]

The emptiness of equality was highlighted by Peter Westen in 1982.[8] Westen asserted that the durability of equality in Western thinking is attributable to its vacuity and to the fact that it is politically opportune. Equality can be – and often is – conscripted and misused for a variety of purposes. In WTO law, for instance, the "equality of competitive conditions" is a catchphrase that underpins the treaty's broad political acceptability. This focus is to be contrasted with the fact that in most contexts competitive conditions remain highly unequal for many economic operators.[9]

For equality to have meaning, Westen argued, it must incorporate external values that determine correspondence. Once those criteria are

[5] See Robert Jennings & Arthur Watts (eds), *Oppenheim's International Law* (9th ed.) Vol. 1, 339 (Longman, Harlow; 1996) (referring to "equality [as] an inference from the basis of international law").

[6] S.v. "Equality" *Stanford Encyclopedia of Philosophy* (rev'd. 27 June 2007).

> What must be particularly noticed is that the idea of equality has been extensively used as a moral and political weapon. Ever since the eighteenth century radical social and political thinkers and activists criticised the prevailing social, economic and political arrangements as *unjust*, partly on the grounds that these favoured in certain respects some classes of the population at the expense of others ... These considerations ... suggest that there is an intuitive, if obscure, connection ... between *political inequality* and *injustice* and so between *political equality* and *justice*.
>
> (Polyvios Polyviou, *The Equal Protection of the Laws* 6 (Duckworth, London; 1980) [emphasis in original])

[7] S.v. "Equality" *Stanford Encyclopedia of Philosophy* (rev'd. 27 June 2007).

[8] Peter Westen, "The Empty Idea of Equality" 95 *Harv. L. Rev.* 537 (1982).

[9] "U.S., WTO Officials: Better Data Needed to Advance Gender Equality in Trade" 40:17 *Inside U.S. Trade* 20 (29 Apr. 2022).

selected, equality is spent. Its retention causes confusion. As a result, the rhetoric of equality should be abandoned.

I have suggested a somewhat more redemptive and constructive view of equality in this book. I maintain that equality continues to be useful for the way in which it serves as a cover for a variety of positions that are often unequal but not for that reason alone unjust. Instead, what matters is that no actor has "cause for complaint."

Many actors now do appear to have "cause for complaint" in relation to the WTO Agreement. The treaty has become a lightning rod for dissatisfaction with globalization and neo-liberalism and yet it is not clear that all of the blame for the resulting ills can be placed at its feet. I have suggested that at least some of the responsibility has to be borne by WTO member governments, who in many cases have failed to distribute the benefits of interdependence broadly enough and who have not always followed the policy prescriptions necessary to achieve inclusive growth.

Beyond this, the WTO remains an important forum for discussion and a place where settlements can be worked out. It has a transformative value.

8.2 A General Theory?

One remaining question in this book is the degree to which a communitarian theory might serve as a theory of law in general. This question is implicitly linked to a very broad set of claims, namely that a general theory of law is possible and that WTO law is representative enough of legal systems to act as a "source" system for such a theory.

In 2009 a leading theorist of law, Joseph Raz, asked the question "can there be a theory of law?"[10] His question evidenced the current mood of frustration and resignation concerning the possibility of ever successfully identifying a general theory. In many legal systems, the law has come to be regarded as too substantial and complex to be capably reduced to a general theory, that is, a theory "necessarily true of the law wherever and whenever it is to be found."[11]

[10] Joseph Raz, "Can There Be a Theory of Law?", ch. 2 in Joseph Raz, *Between Authority and Interpretation: On the Theory of Law and Practical Reason* (Oxford University Press, Oxford; 2009).

[11] Ibid. at 18.

I have taken issue with this view in preceding chapters by suggesting that a theory of law *is* possible but that its identification requires the acknowledgment of certain limits. That is because the essence of a theory lies in simplification. In the process of simplification, some aspects of the law inevitably are excluded.

There is likely to be some irritation caused by this last point. Many commentators will assert that the sweeping terms and categories used to assemble the theory in this book – "community," "justice," "law" – as well as their component categories – "goods," "equality," "fairness," "obligations," "rights" etc. – are too broad-brush to say very much of consequence about outstanding issues in WTO law or about exactly when legal obligations will arise in a given legal system. Regardless of the observation made in Chapter 1 that a theory should solve "a few problems that the group of practitioners has come to recognize as acute,"[12] there will always be pressure for it to do more, and perhaps justifiably, some disappointment that it cannot.

A related objection will be that while all theory involves simplification, what I have presented in this book simplifies too much. Consequently, it does away with the law's sophistication, and by extension, much of the complexity and nuance that has come to pervade commentary about it. Some commentators may search in vain for the specific ideas they are interested in here. As a result, they may be tempted to conclude that a communitarian theory fails the test of generality, or at least of general application.

A further objection will arise from the observation that a communitarian theory is abstracted chiefly from the experience of WTO law. It must therefore successfully overcome the "parochialism" argument Raz adverted to, that is, the idea that it is simply a theory of WTO law alone.[13] While in previous chapters I made an effort to demonstrate how the theory displays in at least one other legal system, some readers may find that effort insufficient. They will argue that a theory grounded in the workings of WTO law cannot be effortlessly transposed to explain the law elsewhere.

They will point out, for example, that few legal systems are as ambitious as WTO law in mandating the "equality of competitive conditions." Instead, many legal systems aim merely to put the plaintiff back in the position they were in before the wrongful conduct or injury. In the usual

12 Thomas Kuhn, *The Structure of Scientific Revolutions* 23 (University of Chicago Press, Chicago; 1962).

13 Raz, *Between Authority and Interpretation* 32–36 (2009).

case, principles of corrective justice imply that "[t]he law is not to engage in any kind of social reordering or social management."[14]

How then to understand the theory in terms of the aspiration to serve as a general theory of law? There are at least three ways for it to do so.

First, the fact that the theory does not explain everything is acknowledged to be only partly dispositive of its ability to serve as a general theory. As Peter Cane has observed in relation to the English private law:

> it is not a valid objection that a legal theory cannot explain all the relevant data – even if the theory is claimed to be 'immanent' in a body of law – because there is no reason to think that areas of the law developed by many agents over a long period of time will instantiate an 'immanent rationality' perfectly.[15]

To the extent that a legal system is assembled and maintained by the kind of open-sourcing Cane refers to, the fact that a given system does not adhere perfectly to the outline presented in a communitarian theory cannot be determinative of the theory's generality.

Second, the fact that the theory offers an incomplete or deficient account of the law in a given legal system should not be the basis on which it is judged. Rather, its deficiencies should be measured against the shortcomings of other theories. Thus, as Thomas Kuhn observed, "a theory must seem better than its competitors, but it need not, and in fact never does, explain all the facts with which it can be confronted."[16]

My point here is that a communitarian theory does a better job than competitor theories based in text, economics or politics at explaining a range of phenomena in WTO law, and moreover, does so in a "coherent, naturally fruitful" way.[17] In addition, with some allowance, its basic structure can be identified in the operation of other legal systems so that

[14] Cass Sunstein, *The Partial Constitution* 319 (Harvard University Press, Cambridge, MA; 1993).

[15] Peter Cane, "The Anatomy of Private Law Theory: A 25th Anniversary Essay" 25:2 *O.J.L.S.* 203 at 207 (2005). Ronald Dworkin observes, "[g]eneral theories of law, like general theories of . . . justice, must be abstract because they aim to interpret the main point and structure of legal practice, not some particular part or department of it." Ronald Dworkin, *Law's Empire* 90 (Belknap Press, Cambridge, MA; 1986). Dworkin adds, "No conception need justify every feature of the political practices it offers to interpret: like any interpretation, it can condemn some of its data as a mistake, as inconsistent with the justification it offers for the rest, and perhaps propose that this mistake be abandoned in . . . its postinterpretive stage." Ibid. 99.

[16] Kuhn, *The Structure of Scientific Revolutions* 17–18.

[17] Philip Allott, *Eunomia* 31 (Oxford University Press, Oxford; 1990).

a communitarian theory can be regarded as offering a more detailed and intelligible account of the law than other recognized shorthands for theory such as "justice as fairness" or "law as integrity."[18] Hence, in pointing to the theory's shortcomings, its flaws and imperfections, due regard must be had for the shortcomings, flaws and imperfections of other theories. On that score a communitarian theory appears to do rather well.

A third way of understanding a communitarian theory of law as a general theory is to recognize how it can be appreciated as provisionally supplying a "core" understanding of the law, even if that understanding does not supply an exhaustive explanation of the law in every instance. It works at a very basic level.

Here, analogy can be made with the history of biology. Gregor Mendel was a Bohemian monk who in the 1860s conducted hybridization experiments with pea plants (*Pisum sativum*). Mendel discovered that when he crossed a white flower pea plant with a purple flower pea plant all offspring in the first generation were purple-flowered, but in the second generation (i.e. fertilized from the first) a purple-to-white flower ratio emerged of 3:1. From this ratio Mendel deduced the existence of "factors" – now called "genes" – which determine variations in organisms' color characteristics.

What Mendel did not realize, and what initially caused early geneticists to doubt his findings, was the fact that *Pisum sativum* expresses the trait of "complete dominance," that is, it regularly features either purple- *or* white-colored flowers, not both. Lack of awareness of its genetic simplicity presented problems when later geneticists sought to replicate Mendel's results in other more complex plants such as hawkweed (*Hieracium*).[19]

In time, geneticists came to realize that the pattern of genetic inheritance in most sexually reproducing organisms is more intricate than "complete dominance." Genes can influence genetic expression in several ways including a blend of the two traits (incomplete dominance), simultaneous expression (codominance) or polygenic expression (i.e. influence

[18] In legal philosophy law as integrity is a theory of law put forward by Ronald Dworkin which claims that a legal interpreter first arrives at a set of moral principles that fit the institutional legal materials and puts them in their best light. Subsequently, using those principles the interpreter establishes the applicable rights and obligations. See T. R. S. Allen, "Review: Dworkin and Dicey: The Rule of Law as Integrity" 8:2 *O.J.L.S.* 266 (1988).

[19] Ernest Mayr, *The Growth of Biological Thought* 723 (Belknap, Cambridge, MA; 1982).

by more than one gene).[20] Dominance, in other words, is not a "law."[21] Nevertheless, Mendel's ideas were recognized to be generally valid despite the fact that they are obscured in many organisms by intervening layers of genetic complexity.

These qualifications reveal the way that Mendel's ideas were originally postulated about the "simple case." They are not universally true but their binary dominant-recessive character might serve – and today have come to be recognized as serving – as the foundation for understanding the rest of the genetic structure.

Similarly, in this book, I have suggested that a communitarian theory of law based on the correlation of obligations and rights in WTO law might serve as a foundation on which to lay a general understanding of justice in relation to goods. To be sure, I do not assert that *every* legal relationship can be distilled and conceptualized in the same binary way. I also do not assert that law invariably reproduces perfect justice. Rather, my point is that correlative obligations and rights constitute a "nucleus," or kernel, around which other types of legal relationships and ideas about justice take hold in pursuit of the good.[22]

To be sure, there are undoubtedly many more exotic variants of legal relationships beyond these. However, obligations and rights can be regarded as a sort of minimum requirement for these others to arise. Substantial evidence was provided in this book that these same basic relations can be identified in at least one other legal system. Like in Mendel's case, however, a final conclusion about the generality of the theory can only be reached when the results of detailed analysis from the most diverse legal systems are available.[23]

[20] Angelo Collins & James Stewart, "The Knowledge Structure of Mendelian Genetics" 51:3 *Am. Biol. Teach.* 143 (1989).

[21] Mayr, *The Growth of Biological Thought* 722.

[22] See, for example, Peter Jaffey, "Hohfeld's Power-Liability/Right-Duty Distinction in the Law of Restitution" XVII:2 *Can. J. L. & Jurisprudence* 295 (2004) (arguing that "in some cases confusion has resulted from the mistaken characterization of a power-liability relation as a right-duty relation"); Stephen Smith, "A Duty to Make Restitution" XXVI:1 *Can. J. L. & Jurisprudence* 157 (2013). For mention of this "core" thesis – that is the idea that rights and obligations constitute the simple core around which the remainder of a legal system takes shape – see Andrew Halpin, "Correlativity and Its Logic" 32:1 *Can. J. L. & Jurisprudence* 83 at 84–85 (2019). See also David Frydrych's description of Hofeldian correlativity as a starting point for exploring the correlativity of normative positions. David Frydrych, "Rights Correlativity" in Shyam Balganesh et al. (eds), *Wesley Hohfeld A Century Later: Edited Work, Select Personal Papers, and Original Commentaries* 112 (Cambridge University Press, Cambridge; 2021).

[23] Mayr, *The Growth of Biological Thought* 724.

8.3 Some Unanswered Questions

The communitarian theory in this book answers key questions that are of perennial interest in legal theory, but it also generates several questions of its own. It is worthwhile considering what some of these are in order to highlight the theory's limits and potential avenues for further work.

The first of these questions involves "windfall" cases, where the plaintiff recovers compensation *greater* than the amount of the injury sustained. A communitarian theory emphasizes a tendency for corrective justice to operate at a discount, that is, to award plaintiffs less than they are entitled to (i.e. Distributive Justice > Corrective Justice). The discount is imposed for a number of collective reasons, including the desire to foster settlement and conserve judicial resources.

Nevertheless, there are a few cases in WTO law and in international investment law where the plaintiff stands to recover *more than* the amount of injury. For instance, in WTO dispute settlement an arbitrator assessing retaliation by Brazil in *Canada – Aircraft* imposed a 20 percent premium on the amount of countermeasures the Brazil would be authorized to invoke after Canada admitted that it had no intention of withdrawing the noncompliant subsidy at issue.[24] Similarly in international investment law, some cases and commentators adhere to the view that unlawful expropriation entitles a successful claimant to recover profits, which in the normal course is a speculative exercise likely to enrich the claimant beyond any loss they have sustained.[25]

How are windfalls to be reconciled with the remainder of the theory? In most instances recoveries of a windfall sort are rare. Thus, the punitive increment imposed in *Canada – Aircraft* is exceptional and was subject to strong criticism in the DSB.[26] To date it has not been followed. Likewise in international investment law, recovery for lost profits is unusual in light of the speculative aspect involved in their assessment

[24] WT/DS267/ARB/1, paras. 3.102–3.107 (31 Aug. 2009).

[25] "Some authors argue that the difference between lawful and unlawful expropriation should be reflected in the compensability of lost profits." Imgard Marboe, *Calculation of Compensation and Damages in International Investment Law* (2nd ed.) para. 3.84*ff* (Oxford University Press, Oxford; 2017). See also Konstantin Christie & Rodica Turtoi, "Compensation for Expropriation" *Lexology* (27 Apr. 2020) ("tribunals' decisions awarding higher damages and lost profits in the case of unlawful expropriation have been considered to represent a deterrent effect against the unlawful conduct of states akin to punitive damages.").

[26] WT/M/DSB145, paras. 43–51 (7 May 2003).

and discomfort at the possibility of awarding the claimant more than they are entitled to.[27]

The rarity of windfalls in all of these situations suggests that they are uncommon, and although available as a practical possibility, such premiums are awarded for reasons that straddle the divide between idea-complexes identified by a communitarian theory. These involve considerations of compensation for private injury with a public expression of distaste for the injury, its nature or extent. For that reason, they must be regarded as a special case of the theory.

A second unanswered question arising from the theory involves the contrast of "transition" versus dilution of the good. In previous chapters I outlined how the relationship of transition, or movement back and forth from one idea complex to another, is one of four classic relationships discernible between conceptual pairs identified in a communitarian theory. This contrapuntal movement is dictated by the tendency for unified positions inherent in obligation to fragment, and conversely, by the fact that rights, which emphasize "competing, rather than unified, positions,"[28] tend to generate contradiction, thereby promoting unity.

Thought about mechanically, it might be supposed that this reversible behavior constitutes a "closed loop," which could go on indefinitely.

Nevertheless, there is another possibility. Inherent in competition among rights is the possibility of dilution of the good to the point where that good becomes indistinct, or in extreme cases, no good at all. The phenomenon of dilution is visible, for instance, in the English common law in relation to amatory torts, that is, civil actions that could be brought for the end or disruption of a romantic or marital relationship. England

[27] In international investment law the investor must demonstrate a causal link between the breach by the state of an investment protection instrument and the lost profits claimed with "a sufficient degree of certainty." *Autopista Concesionada de Venezuela* v. *Bolivarian Republic of Venezuela*, ICSID Case No. ARB/00/5, para. 352 (23 Sept. 2003). This means that the arbitrator will likely reject any claim for compensation of purely speculative profits and will tend to reject lost profits for projects that were only in their early stages of completion or operation. In *Stati* v. *Kazakhstan* it was held that the standard of proof to establish lost profits should be high, and investors must generally show that "their project either has a track record of profitability rooted in a perennial history of operations, or has binding contractual revenue obligations in place that establish the expectation of profit at a certain level over a given number of years." *Anatolie Stati* v. *The Republic of Kazakhstan*, SCC Case No. V 116/2010, para. 1688 (19 Dec. 2013).

[28] Peter Gerhart, *Property Law and Social Morality* 10 (Cambridge University Press, Cambridge; 2014).

abolished such torts, apart from actions for loss of consortium, by statute in 1970.[29]

This example demonstrates the way that the idea of a good can change over time. I discuss further observations on this idea in relation to the WTO Agreement below.

A third unanswered question arising from the theory involves legal issues structured in a nonegalitarian way. While equality is one measure of justice, it is far from the only one. There are many legal questions that do not involve, or cannot be reduced to, issues of equality.

For example, in many legal systems questions of jurisdiction often are not amenable to equality analysis, except perhaps in the idea that one decision should follow the reasoning of another similar one. In cases deciding such matters, much will depend on particular facts.

Another example is the fact that in many jurisdictions today child custody and access disputes are resolved on the basis of the "best interests of the child."[30] Case law suggests that these disputes are not determined with special attention given to equality between parents.[31] Instead, judges focus solely on the well-being of the child and on protecting them from any harm when deciding which party or parent should be awarded custody or access.

Similarly, in bankruptcy and insolvency scenarios, legislation often mandates special priorities. In English law, for instance, the property of an insolvent company is to be distributed according to the priorities identified in the current version of the Insolvency Act, not equally among creditors.[32]

29 Jane Larson has noted, for instance, that "[a] new general of female reformers came to equate the seduction action with antiquated values threatening to the interests of emancipated women and men." Jane Larson, "Women Understand So Little, They Call My Good Nature 'Deceit': A Feminist Rethinking of Seduction" 93:2 *Columbia L.R.* 374 at 393 (1993).

30 Art. 3(1) of the UN Convention on the Rights of the Child specifies that "In all actions concerning children, whether undertaken by public or private social welfare institutions, courts of law, administrative authorities or legislative bodies, the best interests of the child shall be a primary consideration."

31 *ZH (Tanzania) (FC)* v. *Secretary of State for the Home Department*, [2011] UKSC 4 ("the best interests of the child must be a primary consideration. This means that they must be considered first. They can, of course, be outweighed by the cumulative effect of other considerations.")

32 Until the 1980s, the usual outcomes for an over-indebted company in the UK was a receivership initiated by a secured creditor and usually ending in liquidation of the company. The Insolvency Act, 1986 (UK) provided for administration, a form of rescue allowing the ongoing operation of a business under the protection of a moratorium and

My response to these examples is to acknowledge that a communitarian theory is premised on the distinction between justice-as-equality and justice-as-fairness. This is not the only distinction about justice that could be made.[33] At the same time, I suggest that the distinction on which a communitarian theory rests is a particularly illuminating one, one which cleaves to an important conceptual distinction visible in many legal systems. It does not explain everything, but it explains many things.

A fourth and final question is whether the theory supplies any answer or insight into the "interface problem" currently bedeviling the WTO. That problem has been described as a "clash of capitalisms, a clash of power, and a clash of values"[34] between China and the United States that has led the United States, in particular, to tacitly step back from the organization and become "the wrecking ball" of the world trading system.[35] US behavior has been motivated by the perception that the current Chinese leadership's authoritarian turn and its enhancement of the role of the state and the Communist Party in China's economy pose a threat to the United States and other countries. Current WTO rules are inadequate to address it.

One prominent chronicle of the problem recently put forward by Gregory Schaffer has suggested "rebalancing within a multilateral framework" whereby the two countries would be allowed to decouple their economies from each other in some degree while preserving the overall multilateral system.[36] Where bilateral agreement to resolve outstanding

guardianship. Equal treatment across classes was not guaranteed. Passage of the Corporate Insolvency and Governance Act 2020 transformed the restructuring regime still further, introducing a new stand-alone moratorium process, restrictions on certain termination rights of contractual counterparties, and the possibility of restructuring plans permitting cross-class cramdown wherein restructuring plan can be used to bind a nonconsenting class of stakeholders. Karen McMaster et al., "The Insolvency Review: United Kingdom – England & Wales" in Donald Bernstein (ed.), *The Insolvency Review* (9th ed.) (Law Business Research, London; 17 Oct. 2021).

33 David Miller has pointed out how, in addition to the distinction between distributive and corrective justice, the topic might also be divided into contrasting categories of conservative versus ideal justice, procedural and substantive justice, and comparative versus non-comparative justice. S.v. "Justice" *Stanford Encyclopedia of Philosophy* (6 Aug. 2021) (author: David Miller).

34 Gregory Schaffer, "Governing the Interface of U.S.-China Trade Relations" 115:4 *A.J.I.L.* 622 (2021).

35 Ibid. at 628.

36 Ibid. at 623.

issues is impossible, each country would be permitted to "adjust and respond unilaterally to protect itself," but such action would have to be proportionate to the harm caused.[37]

A communitarian theory offers some insight into this problem, and more particularly Schaffer's proposal, by noting that a China-US decoupling and rebilateralization of their relationship is an extreme example of what the theory predicts is to be observed over the long-term as the WTO membership oscillates from multilateralism to bilateralism and potentially back again. On its current trajectory that oscillation should see more limited trade agreements being concluded that are fairness-based, rights-oriented, contractual, retrospective and inductive. These respond to the diminished nature of the WTO Agreement as a good and are something I will have more to say about shortly.

8.4 Theory in the Anthropocene

The correlativity on which the theory in this book rests is founded in reciprocity among equals – in this instance states.[38]

That frame, however, is implicitly anthropocentric in that it takes as its premise and starting point for analysis obligations and rights among individual states *inter se* and not necessarily the broader ecosystems that they are part of. The same frame tends to obscure the fact of actors' critical reliance on natural elements. It also tends to neglect the way in which the concept of common property (*res communis*) so central to any identifiable notion of community is rooted in broader biological and

[37] Ibid. at 631.

[38] Mohammed Bedjaoui, *Towards a New International Economic Order* 239 (UNESCO, Paris; 1978) (observing that the state is "only a community of men" and that "international society is only a community of peoples"). The International Law Commission relies on the same idea as a basis for establishing responsibility under international law:

> The State is a real organized entity, a legal person with full authority to act under international law. But to recognize this is not to deny the elementary fact that the State cannot act of itself. An "act of the State" must involve some action or omission by a human being or group: "States can act only by and through their agents and representatives."
>
> (Draft articles on Responsibility of States for Internationally Wrongful Acts, with commentaries, *Yearbook of the International Law Commission, 2001* Vol. II, Part Two, p. 35 (2001))

ecological considerations.[39] To that extent, the communitarian theory outlined in this book may be regarded as deficient.

In recent decades, growing environmental consciousness and emphasis on the need for sustainability have caused some commentators to identify a transition in geologic epoch from the current Holocene to a projected Anthropocene.[40] The idea of an emergent Anthropocene, together with growing evidence of significant environmental stress in many parts of the world, has triggered forecasts of impending environmental and human collapse.[41] Partly for this reason and conscious of the load that trade-induced consumption is imposing on the global environment, efforts have been made to "Green the GATT" and now the WTO Agreement.

When the WTO Agreement came into existence in 1994, an attempt was undertaken to emphasize its environmental credentials by referencing the fact that countries undertook their WTO commitments

[39] For a history of the concept of "global commons," see Nico Schrijver & Vid Prislan, "From Mare Liberum to the Global Commons: Building on the Grotian Heritage" 30:1 *Grotiana* 168 (2009).

[40] The Anthropocene is a proposed epoch dating from the commencement of significant human impact on earth's geology and ecosystems, including, but not limited to, anthropogenic climate change. In that epoch current generations would be the first people considered to live in an age defined by human choice in which the dominant risk to survival is human activity.

[41] "[T]here is a strong, credible body of evidence, based on multiple lines of research, documenting that climate is changing and that these changes are in large part caused by human activities": National Research Council, *America's Climate Choices: Panel on Advancing the Science of Climate Change* (The National Academies Press, Washington, DC; 2010) at 1; David Wallace-Wells, "Can You Even Call Deadly Heat 'Extreme' Anymore?" *New York Times* Subscriber Newsletter (17 May 2022). Moreover, commentators such as Jared Diamond have pointed out how this prospect is not simply speculative. At various points in history peoples in very different places and at very different times – the Anasazi of the American Southwest; the Indigenous peoples of Easter, Pitcairn and Henderson Islands; the Maya of Central America; and the original Norse inhabitants of Greenland – developed complex, highly sophisticated cultures through interdependence, only to see those cultures suddenly vanish due to the failure to align their relationships with the environments around them. Diamond notes that "human societies and small groups may make disastrous decisions for a whole sequence of reasons: failure to anticipate a problem, failure to perceive it once it has arisen, failure to attempt to solve this after it has been perceived, and failure to succeed in attempts to solve it." Jared Diamond, *Collapse* 438 (Viking, New York; 2005). Diamond also notes that "[t]wo types of choices seem … to have been crucial in tipping [societal] outcomes towards success or failure: long-term planning and willingness to reconsider core values." Ibid., p. 522.

in light of the objective of "allowing for the optimal use of the world's resources in accordance with the objective of sustainable development."[42] Although this preambular phrase was not binding, and, moreover, was not accompanied by any express environmental commitments that members took as a concomitant of their obligations to liberalize trade, much was also made of the possibility that WTO dispute settlement might provide a way to reconcile trade and environmental objectives.

In particular, the wording of VCLT Art. 31(3)(c) specifies that in the process of treaty interpretation "[t]here shall be taken into account, together with the context ... (c) *any relevant rules of international law* applicable in the relations between the parties."[43] This principle of "systemic integration" appears to mandate that interpretation of WTO provisions should occur with other international commitments in mind, notably those pertaining to the environment as found, for example, in the World Charter for Nature, the UN Convention on Biological Diversity and the Paris Agreement on Climate Change.

Thus, for example, in the *U.S. – Shrimp* case the Appellate Body examined a US import ban on shrimp caught without "turtle-friendly" certification.[44] The United States relied in its defense on GATT Art. XX(g), which provides an exception to GATT requirements for measures "relating to the conservation of exhaustible natural resources." One issue raised in the litigation was whether sea turtles could constitute an "exhaustible natural resource." The US position was that they could. By contrast, the position of the complainants – India, Pakistan and Thailand – was that the term "exhaustible" referred to "finite resources such as minerals, rather than biological or renewable resources."[45]

In its decision the Appellate Body made reference to provisions of the UN Convention on the Law of the Sea, the Convention on Biological Diversity, and the Convention on International Trade in Endangered Species to hold that the sea turtles involved did constitute "exhaustible natural resources" for purposes of invoking the exception in GATT Art.

[42] Preamble, WTO Agreement.

[43] Campbell McLachlan, "The Principle of Systemic Integration and Article 31(3)(C) of the Vienna Convention" 54:2 *I.C.L.Q.* 279 (Apr. 2005).

[44] WT/DS58/AB/R (12 Oct. 1998).

[45] Ibid., para. 127.

XX(g).[46] A few other WTO disputes have also involved environmental questions.[47]

Nevertheless, the selectivity of these disputes emphasizes the way that WTO dispute settlement proceeds case-by-case. Few disputes raise environmental issues in a systematic way. Consequently, the WTO dispute settlement system's ability to respond to broader environmental concerns appears constrained.

For this reason, some commentators have suggested reforming WTO law in order to make the legal regime more identifiably biocentric. There are a number of problems with this ambition.

First, there is no enshrined environmental commitment in the WTO Agreement. Instead, as of mid-2021 the WTO website specified that "While there is no specific agreement dealing with the environment, under WTO rules members can adopt trade-related measures aimed at protecting the environment provided a number of conditions to avoid the misuse of such measures for protectionist ends are fulfilled." In other words, a right exists under the treaty for members to legislate for environmental purposes in derogation of WTO commitments, subject to their fulfilling the terms of specified exceptions such as the one highlighted in *U.S. – Shrimp*. Thus, any environmental right is constrained in the manner of the relationship identified previously (Obligation > Right) and subject to the requirement of proportionality expressed in the relevant exception ("necessary to"; "relating to" etc.).[48]

Second, the trade-related logic of the understanding and enforcement of the right to regulate for environmental purposes can be criticized as anthropocentric. It implicitly prioritizes trade at the expense of the environment. Instead, an interpretative approach is required that goes beyond "preventing and remedying only those environmental problems that directly affect humans" and is more "biocentric [in recognizing] the intrinsic value of nature and [valuing] all life equally."[49]

How might the goal of biocentricism be achieved? Again, the focus on obligations and rights highlighted by a communitarian theory is instructive. The environmental right identified in the WTO Agreement could be

[46] Ibid. at para. 134.

[47] See *U.S. Gasoline*, WT/DS2, *EU – Asbestos*, WT/DS135.

[48] Nathalie Bernasconi-Osterwalder et al., *Environment and Trade: A Guide to WTO Jurisprudence* 76 (Earthscan, London; 2006).

[49] Joshua Bruckerhoff, "Giving Nature Constitutional Protection: A Less Anthropocentric Interpretation of Environmental Rights" 86 *Tex. L. Rev.* 615 at 617–618 (2008).

made less evidently anthropocentric by interpreting the exceptions more broadly – for instance, by allowing members to take measures to protect "a biologically diverse environment – rather than just an adequate, pollution-free environment."[50] Other grounds of exception could include the protection of biodiversity that provides cultural benefits to certain groups such as Indigenous peoples. In addition, there could be recognition of measures broadly structured to promote biodiversity goals by encouraging sustainable development. A further option might be an exception for measures taken to provide citizens with a "healthy" – as opposed to merely an "adequate" – environment within which to live.[51]

The difficulty with all these options, however, is that they are highly subjective and clash with the reciprocal structure of the WTO Agreement. They could be invoked for a wide variety of protective purposes that risk upsetting the balance struck between obligations and rights in the treaty. In all probability, they would have to be subject to some sort of protocol designed to prevent their misuse or abuse. In addition, they would rely on the adequacy of rights which, as mentioned, are apt to be interpreted in a constrained manner.

An alternative approach would be to reconceptualize the relevant environmental element as involving obligations rather than rights, as has happened under certain domestic constitutions.[52] This would involve a degree of constitutionalization of environmental norms along with certain legal accessories such as a presumption expressing some version of the precautionary principle.

[50] Ibid. at 625.

[51] Ibid.

[52] Bruckerhoff mentions Art. 225 of the Constitution of Brazil, which provides both a right and a duty: "All have the right to an ecologically balanced environment, which is an asset of common use and essential to a healthy quality of life, and both the Government and the community *shall have the duty* to defend and preserve it for present and future generations." [emphasis added] The Constitution of Brazil goes on to place an affirmative duty on the government, stating that the government must:

> preserve and restore the essential ecological processes and provide for the ecological treatment of species and ecosystems; ... preserve the diversity and integrity of the genetic patrimony of the country[; and] protect the fauna and the flora, with prohibition, in the manner prescribed by law, of all practices which represent a risk to their ecological function, cause the extinction of species or subject animals to cruelty.
>
> (See ibid. at pp. 634–635)

These possibilities entail the need for agreement on environmental rights vis-à-vis the WTO Agreement, one possibly achieved *outside* the WTO but linked to it hierarchically in some way. The link could either be a subordinate one, wherein the environmental obligation is subordinated to trade concerns, as is now the case; or a complimentary and coordinate one where, like in the UNESCO Convention on Cultural Diversity, an effort is made to stress the nonsubordination of environmental and trade goals;[53] or an enhanced one where environmental goals take precedence over trade goals.

The problem of tinkering with obligations and rights under WTO law to promote environmental sustainability, however, is that it amounts to just that: tinkering. Selective or small-scale action does not address the broader issues that need to be dealt with promptly in a move toward broad-based sustainability. Ultimately, unless environmental rights are prioritized *ahead of* trade concerns, there will be little action toward a desirable environmental future.

Minimally, this action could involve certain environmentally friendly interpretative strategies applied in relation to the WTO Agreement.[54] Somewhat more intensively, it could involve the phasing out of fossil fuel and harmful agricultural and fishing subsidies, the elimination of tariffs on green goods and measures to encourage eco-labeling.[55] However, in an era of impending – if not actual – climate emergency, it seems increasingly likely that meaningful action to promote sustainability would have to be in the form of an agreement of some – or better still

[53] The UNESCO Convention on the Protection and Promotion of the Diversity of Cultural Expressions, 2440 UNTS 311 (2005), offers one example of the way in which trade and nontrade disciplines are to be reconciled. The Convention makes clear the connection between cultural protection and human rights and affirms the right of countries to "adopt measures to protect and promote the diversity of cultural expressions" (CCD Art. 5). The Convention also specifies an obligation for countries to "foster mutual supportiveness between this Convention and other treaties," to take account of the Convention in the interpretation of other treaties, and to ensure the Convention's "complementarity and non-subordination" vis-à-vis other international obligations (CCD Art. 1).

[54] Bruckerhoff, "Giving Nature Constitutional Protection" 615.

[55] For example, under the planned Agreement on Climate Change, Trade and Sustainability (ACCTS), the five countries involved (Costa Rica, Fiji, Iceland, New Zealand and Norway) would slash barriers to trade in environmental goods and services, phase out their fossil fuel subsidies, and encourage the promotion and application of voluntary eco-labelling programs and mechanisms. The countries envisage ACCTS to be a "living agreement" that can be updated and take on additional issues.

all – WTO members concerning carbon emissions, linked in some way to WTO arrangements.

Given the above, it is hard to escape the impression that WTO Agreement's sensitivity to environmental concerns is oblique. In the meantime, the precise balance of obligations and rights stressed in a communitarian theory highlights the deficiencies of current WTO arrangements. Consideration needs to be urgently given to alternatives. One of these could be a global cap-and-trade system.

Currently, the centerpiece of global efforts to address greenhouse gas (GHG) emissions is the 2015 Paris Agreement on Climate Change[56] negotiated within the UN Framework Convention on Climate Change.[57] Under the Paris Agreement, countries voluntarily commit to setting Nationally Determined Contributions (NDCs) for GHG emission reductions. However, considered opinion has come to recognize that national commitments made to date "collectively fall far short of what is needed to achieve the goals of the Paris Agreement."[58]

These developments have spurred calls for accelerated decarbonization. At the same time, mindful of domestic impacts, national climate responses are increasingly divergent. In this context, fresh attention is being given to the possibility of a limiting "carbon leakage" – that is, the incentive for covered emitters to leave a jurisdiction to avoid or evade program compliance costs by exporting from noncompliant jurisdictions – through trade measures such as carbon taxes applied to imports. There is also concern about "potential reactions by trading partners worried about disguised protectionism, whether in the form of disputes through the WTO or other trade-related retaliation."[59] Still, there remains a worry whether anticircumvention measures of this type can really be effective at encouraging greater environmental action from trading partners, as opposed to heightening trade tensions.[60]

[56] 3156 UNTS 79 (Registration No. 54113) (12 Dec. 2015; entry into force 4 Nov. 2016).

[57] *United Nations Framework Convention on Climate* Change, 8 Sept. 1992, 1771 UNTS 107, 31 ILM 849 (1992).

[58] Andrew Prag, "The Climate Challenge and Trade: Would Border Carbon Adjustments Accelerate or Hinder Climate Action?" OECD Round Table on Sustainable Development 4 (25 Feb. 2020).

[59] Ibid.

[60] In the field of climate change, the principle of common but differentiated responsibilities (CBDR) acknowledges that all states have a shared obligation to address environmental depletion. In the case of CBDR, the designation of "common ... responsibilities" is complemented by "differentiated responsibilities" and, more recently, by "respective

The point to be taken from all of this is that the ultimate response to current concerns about a deteriorating global environment requires a profound change of mindset. It requires greater recognition of the global environment as a good. To this end there must be more serious and abiding attention in WTO arrangements to sustainability and to countering the threat of climate change.[61] This imperative is only modestly profiled by a communitarian theory, whose chief contribution is to highlight the respective role of obligations versus rights in the existing legal matrix, hinting at what lies beyond.

In the interim something else is important to remember. Time is running out.

8.5 WTO: Predictions and Prescriptions

A theory should be able to forecast.[62] For instance, Dimitri Mendeelev's arrangement of atomic elements in the form of the Periodic Table in 1869 projected with great accuracy the existence of additional elements discovered decades later.[63] To that extent, accepted theories are guides. They offer an accurate prediction of what is to come.

capabilities" (i.e. CBDR-RC) in gradual acknowledgement of the fact that developed countries have contributed more to environmental depletion and should have greater responsibility to address it than developing countries. Christopher Stone, "Common but Differentiated Responsibilities in International Law" 98 *Am. J. Int'l L.* 276 (2004); Tuula Honkonen, "The Development of the Principle of Common but Differentiated Responsibilities and Its Place in International Environmental Regimes" in Tuomas Kuokkanen et al. (eds), *International Environmental Law-Making and Diplomacy* 159 (Routledge, Milton Park; 2016).

61 Evenett and Baldwin suggest that such a move could address the WTO's "relevance imperative," that is, the organization's need to remain current in international policy-making circles: "Given that so many senior policymakers around the globe appear determined to take steps to address climate change, and to speed up the implied transition in related energy sectors, the absence of any meaningful multilateral cooperation on this matter is likely to relegate the WTO from the first division of international organisations." Simon Evenett & Richard Baldwin, *Revitalising Multilateralism: Pragmatic Ideas for the New WTO Director-General* 33 (Centre for Economic Policy Research, London; 2020).

62 "A scientific theory's claim to forward our understanding of nature is therefore, in the last resort, dependent on its power *to predict* what will occur." Herbert Hart, *The Concept of Law* (2nd ed.) 188 (Oxford University Press, Oxford; [1961] 1994) [emphasis added].

63 In the early 1860s, there were fifty-six known elements, with new elements being discovered at the rate of approximately one per year. Scientists had previously identified the periodicity of elements, that is, the recurring variations in elemental properties with increasing atomic number. Dmitri Mendeelev's basic idea was that elements could be

What does a communitarian theory portend for the future of WTO law?

In previous chapters, I detailed the way that the conclusion of the WTO Agreement in 1994 was a great unifying moment. It was probably inevitable that countries would begin to chafe under its disciplines and seek to test the bounds of its flexibilities. This testing was particularly apparent in relation to WTO dispute settlement where, after an initial period of familiarizing themselves with the new dispute settlement system, a number of member countries – though still a minority – engaged in vigorous lawfare.[64]

Despite this behavior, there was an abiding sentiment at the outset that something of value had been created – a good – which was worth protecting and promoting. All members had subscribed to a "single package" of obligations and by complying with them, unconditional interdependence would be allowed to do its beneficial work.

Twenty-five years on, much of that general feeling seems to be forgotten, or perhaps is taken for granted. The conception of interdependence has changed. The good inherent in WTO arrangements is no longer regarded as unreservedly good.

That change has prompted the unified sense of community embodied in the WTO Agreement to fray.[65] Energy and attention have been redirected elsewhere.

arranged according to their atomic weight and exhibited an apparent periodicity of properties. Thus, elements which are similar regarding their chemical properties either have similar atomic weights or have atomic weights that increase in a regular manner. In 1869 Mendeelev published his periodic table of the known elements, leaving several missing spaces to signify several then-unknown elements. In the process he predicted the qualities of what were to be called germanium, gallium and scandium, eventually identified by scientists several decades later. See Michael Gordin, *A Well-Ordered Thing* (Basic Books, New York; 2004).

[64] Bernard Hoekman and Petros Mavroidis note that "[t]he use of WTO dispute settlement procedures is highly skewed towards large and richer players . . . Most WTO members are bystanders. . . . many developing countries do not engage." Bernard Hoekman & Petros Mavroidis, "Preventing the Bad from Getting Worse: The End of the World (Trade Organization) As We Know It?" 32:3 *E.J.I.L.* 743 at 750 (2021).

[65] Simon Evenett and Richard Baldwin profile how the WTO's monitoring function, in particular, has not achieved what it could because of the:

> few resources being devoted to the independent collection of information on trade policy changes by the WTO Secretariat, non-cooperation by some G20 governments, and pressure by other G20 governments on the WTO Secretariat not to report certain policy developments. The fact that the

What then is the probable future of WTO law when seen through the prism of a communitarian theory? Generally speaking, it is possible to detect a broad movement under the treaty from the regular observance of obligations to the more robust assertion of rights in line with the relationship of transition or oscillation mentioned earlier. In short, the nature of WTO arrangements appears to be evolving from a unified egalitarian system based on the idea of a club good toward a more diffuse fairness-based regime based on the idea of individual trade relationships as private goods.

In law this trajectory appears to be taking the form of greater reliance on rights-based flexibilities and regional and other arrangements under the protective guise of GATT Art. XXIV. The theory predicts that with such a movement there will be more emphasis on compacts that are "contractual," retrospective and proof-based. A number of provisions of the USMCA Agreement of 2019, the successor to NAFTA, appear consistent with this characterization.[66] The same is visible in the "Phase 1" Agreement between the United States and China concluded in 2019.[67]

> WTO Secretariat reports have stopped reporting detailed information on "general economic support" measures by G20 governments is telling.
>
> (Evenett & Baldwin, *Revitalising Multilateralism* 26)

Evenett and Baldwin also note that "[i]ntelligent deliberation is difficult in an organisation where many members practice obstruction." Ibid. at 26. Henry Gao has noted how the crisis over the Appellate Body has soured the membership and led in some instances to corrosive behavior. Henry Gao, "Finding a Rule-Based Solution to the Appellate Body Crisis: Looking beyond the Multiparty Interim Appeal Arbitration Arrangement" 24 *J.I.E.L.* 534 at 548 (2021); Robert Howse, "The Limits of the WTO" *A.J.I.L. Unbound* 41 at 42–43 (doi: 10.1017/aju.2022.5) (describing a current environment in the WTO as one where "one must acknowledge that, generally, trust is low").

66 Perhaps the most visible aspect of the new treaty in this regard is that whereas under NAFTA automobile trade was quota-free, quotas totaling 2.6 million Canadian and Mexican vehicles were agreed to as part of treaty-related "side letters." Similarly, quotas of $32.4 billion on Canadian auto parts imports and $108 billion on Mexican auto parts imports were imposed. The USMCA also increased the total North American content requirement for vehicles and for the first time established an auto part context requirement divided into core, principal and complementary parts. Two additional requirements not included in NAFTA but now part of the USMCA are that 70 percent of steel and aluminum content must originate in North America, and 40–45 percent of a vehicle must be produced by workers paid an hourly wage of USD $16 or more.

67 Economic and Trade Agreement between the Government of the United States of America and the Government of the People's Republic of China (15 Jan. 2020). As part of the Agreement China committed that over the period 2020–2022 it would import no less than $200 billion of U.S. goods and services on top of the amounts imported in the base year of 2017 in four broad categories. To that extent, the Agreement was backward-looking. See "New data show the failures of Donald Trump's China trade strategy" 438:9232 *The Economist* (10 Feb. 2021).

Another reason for the departure from multilateralism is disappointed expectations. Originally there was in many quarters the hope that the economic liberalization implied by WTO membership would be accompanied by political liberalization among member states. The two tendencies – of economic and political freedom – were contemplated to be mutually reinforcing.

That hope did not fully materialize. Since 1994 a number of countries have shown themselves to be capable of developing economically as members of the WTO without significant political liberalization.[68] This course of development is now held up as another reason not to fully adhere to the unconditional interdependence called for in the WTO Agreement. In this respect the argument often made about economies promoting state-centered capitalism is thus: They're not really like us and aren't prepared to follow fair rules of the game.[69]

Consequently, a search appears to be on among WTO members for deeper integration with like-minded trading partners. In the current environment, there is much talk of reshoring (or near-shoring/"friend-shoring") production as well as the need to "secure" supply chains.[70] A protective ethos is emerging.[71]

With it, the WTO membership seems to be dividing into two camps, one apparently "liberal democratic," the other plausibly "autocratic," although there is criticism of this simplistic division.[72]

One analysis has noted, "[l]ooking back, we probably put too much emphasis on the power of material forces like economics and technology to drive human events and bring us together."[73] Similarly, Bruno Simma has warned:

[68] Jing Linbo, "The Development of the Strategic Trade Policy and Its Application in China" 50:2 *Chinese Econ.* 97 (2017).

[69] This is particularly noted with respect to the operation of state-owned enterprises and certain types of subsidies that significantly distort international trade, neither of which is fully covered by current WTO rules. See European Commission, "WTO Modernization: Introduction to Future EU Proposals" (18 Sept. 2018).

[70] "Xi's Incubator State" 442:9292 *The Economist* 60 (16 Apr. 2022); Brett Fortnam, "Okonjo-Iweala Hopes Reshoring Is Limited to Critical Industries" 40:18 *Inside U.S. Trade* 14 (6 May 2022); Margaret Spiegelman, "Draft TTC Statement: U.S., EU Plan Early Warning System for Chip Shortages" 40:19 *Inside U.S. Trade* 173948 (13 May 2022).

[71] "Since 2016, there is evidence of a rise in the share of global trade that is subject to trade restrictions, even excluding those related to the U.S.-China trade war." "A Changed World" 441:9266 *The Economist* SR, 12 (9 Oct. 2021).

[72] "Chaguan: Why China Says It Is a Democracy" 441:9274 *The Economist* 61 (4 Dec. 2021).

[73] David Brooks, "The Culture Wars Have Gone Global" *The New York Times* Section SR, 4 (10 Apr. 2022).

> the assumption that a society/community could be held together by means of legal norms alone overestimates the capacity of law and, conversely, underestimates the necessity of a societal consensus as a precondition for the formation of, and in particular the respect for, legal rules.[74]

In the midst of the above, there is an acute sense that "globalization is over,"[75] although that sentiment appears to be exaggerated. Interdependence will continue, but it will likely take a more modest and conditional form than in the past.

What then does this presage in a concrete sense for the future of WTO law and the WTO? Two WTO functions merit consideration: negotiation and dispute settlement.

In terms of negotiation, it has long been recognized that the organization's existing multilateral negotiating framework has become unworkable and that the prospects of successful conclusion of a grand negotiating round, as happened at the end of the Uruguay Round in 1994 and was attempted in the Doha negotiations, is unlikely.[76]

In their place the movement identified above toward a more rights-based arrangement implies greater pluralism, and perhaps inevitably, plurilateral arrangements as the only way to move the agenda forward. Such agreements could take a number of forms including true "open" plurilateral agreements as well as more limited "closed" compacts whose membership and benefits would be circumscribed. Further contributions

[74] Bruno Simma, "From Bilateralism to Community Interest in International Law" 250 *Recueil des Cours* 217 at 245 (1994). In a similar vein Christian Meier has commented:

> The life of a city ... depends on more than a water supply and the import of food, more than a market with true weights and a reliable medium of exchange. The life of a city also depends on certain norms: customs and ethics, the existence of some basic shared principles, rules of behavior and a language that facilitates discussion and conflict resolution. There must also be some basis for unity, or solidarity, that serves to stabilize the population in the event of a crisis.
>
> Christian Meier, *Athens: A Portrait of the City in Its Golden Age* 328 (Metropolitan Books, New York; 1998).

[75] David Brooks, "The Culture Wars Have Gone Global" *The New York Times* Section SR, 4 (10 Apr. 2022).

[76] Hannah Monicken, "Former WTO Director-General: Finding Consensus Largely 'Impossible'" 40:20 *Inside U.S. Trade* 20 (20 May 2022) (former WTO Director-General Roberto Azevedo observing that "[m]ultilateralism requires leadership and commitment, and I think, over time, it was missing [in the WTO] ... And you cannot blame one actor... I think it was quite pervasive").

could be supplied by "sub-multilateral agreements, regional and specific purpose multi-party agreements as well as bilateral compacts."[77]

The difficulty with a pluralized regime is several-fold, however. One is a fear that plurilateral agreements will cannibalize the negotiating agenda supposedly reserved for multilateral discussion, potentially disadvantaging countries that choose to remain outside them. This concern is already being expressed over Joint Statement Initiatives (JSIs) that are viewed in some quarters as unduly selective, in effect eroding the uniformity of commitment achieved in areas such as services and S&DT.[78] Another concern is the possibility of discordant results reached by groups of members negotiating against each other such that WTO disciplines become even more fragmented and "*à la carte.*"[79]

Against these views are perspectives that note that few ongoing negotiations in the WTO have borne much fruit. Beyond them, entire swaths of economic activity – notably in the field of e-commerce – remain untouched by WTO rules.[80] Something should be done to allow for a more relaxed form of "variable geometry," with one solution perhaps being a move toward majority or qualified majority voting in the organization.

There is no easy answer to the current dilemma, which neatly traces the divide identified in a communitarian theory between egalitarian and fairness-based idea-complexes. On one side a strident multilateral strand calls for adherence to "one size fits all" solutions in the image of the single undertaking. On the other, a newer and perhaps more pragmatic strand asserts that the single undertaking is a relic of the past and must be conclusively abandoned. In the meantime changes are coming fast. WTO

[77] Alan Wolff, "WTO 2025: Getting Back to the Negotiating Table" 22–27 Peterson Institute for International Economics Briefing Paper 11 (May 2022); Gregory Schaffer, "Governing the Interface of U.S.-China Trade Relations" 115:4 *A.J.I.L.* 622 at 634 ("For the WTO multilateral system to remain resilient, WTO decisionmakers must acknowledge the shift towards a pluralist approach to trade governance.").

[78] Jane Kelsey, "The Illegitimacy of Joint Statement Initiatives and Their Systemic Implications for the WTO" 25:1 *J.I.E.L.* 2 (Mar. 2022).

[79] The phrase "GATT à la carte" was coined to describe the phenomenon of plurilateral codes agreed during the Tokyo Round (1973–1979), which had their own memberships and dispute settlement mechanisms and which led to forum duplication and forum shopping. Ernst-Ulrich Petersmann, "Current Legal Problems in GATT Dispute Settlement: Proceedings in the Field of Antidumping Law" in Daniel Fridemann & Ernst-Joachim Mestmäcker (eds), *Conflict Resolution in International Trade* 167 at 190*ff* (Nomos Verlagsgesellschaft, Baden-Baden; 1993).

[80] Dan Ciuriak, "World Trade Organization 2.0: Reforming Multilateral Trade Rules for the Digital Age" *CIGI Policy Brief* 152 (11 July 2019).

negotiations will have to move on if the organization hopes to remain relevant in global policy-making.

In terms of dispute settlement, at the time of writing the existing system continues to operate with the activation of panels but without true two-tier review.[81] Over time it is to be expected that differential panel outcomes will manifest themselves, leading to a degree of interpretative incoherence. Depending on the degree of divergence, this may or may not be a manageable problem. As a point of comparison, it is useful to note that the regime of international investment arbitration surveyed in Chapter 7 has operated successfully with significant divergence and without necessarily collapsing. The theory suggests that the creative space provided by disputes for efforts at settlement is probably more important and valuable than resort to retaliation.

On the continuing impasse over the Appellate Body commentators sometimes appear to suggest that the crisis has been triggered by one country – a single, isolated constituency – and that plausible solutions could take the form of amendments or modifications to dispute settlement rules.[82] Once implemented, these will somehow magically "reboot" the system.

[81] At the WTO's 12th Ministerial Conference in July 2022, the membership acknowledged "the challenges and concerns with respect to the [WTO] dispute settlement system including those related to the Appellate Body" and committed to conducting "discussions with the view to having a fully and well-functioning dispute settlement system accessible to all Members by 2024." See WTO MC 12 Outcome Document, WT/MIN(22)/24, para. 4 (22 June 2022).

[82] For Bernard Hoekmann and Petros Mavroidis, the problem lies with the standard of review in ADA Art. 17.6, which was interpreted by the Appellate Body as indistinguishable from the regular standard in DSU Art. 11. According to Hoekmann and Mavroidis, "[t]he U.S. delegation's understanding was that article 17.6 served as a green light for zeroing ... [but] ... the AB only paid [this interpretation] lip service, and frankly, this critique is well founded." Bernard Hoekmann & Petros Mavroidis, "Dispute Settlement at the WTO: Now What?" in *Modernizing the WTO* 14 at 16 (Centre for International Governance Innovation, Waterloo; 2020). For Valerie Hughes the WTO dispute settlement system has been working relatively well but with suspension of work by the Appellate Body could benefit from the use of no-appeal agreements, interim appeal arbitration under DSU Art. 25 and resort to dispute settlement mechanisms contained in other free trade agreements. See Valerie Hughes, "Approaches to Modernizing the Dispute Settlement Understanding" in *Modernizing the WTO* 21 (Centre for International Governance Innovation, Waterloo; 2020). For Giorgio Sacerdoti minor changes to the DSU are possible through binding interpretations under WTO Art. IX:2 or through a facilitated procedure set forth in a Ministerial Decision taken as part of the Uruguay Round negotiations in 1993. However, these could result in looser forms of nonbinding review and risk throwing "the baby out with the bathwater." See Giorgio

However, the view taken here is that the current crisis over the Appellate Body is much deeper and more profound than these views infer, being anchored in contemporary misgivings about the 'good' of unconditional interdependence. This deep-seated concern suggests that simple tweaks to WTO rules are unlikely to resolve the issue.

It may be time to recognize that there appears to be less need for binding, authoritative pronouncements supplied by a single authoritative dispute settlement system. Instead, in line with the view expressed earlier, the organization must redefine its purpose, not as a Kantian "trade enforcer" but as a setting within which common positions can be worked out, with some attention paid to law. In this respect more focus could be devoted to panels' power under DSU Art. 19(1) to make suggestions, as was the case in several instances under GATT 1947.[83] Again, it is the space created for transformative results that is probably most important and valuable about the dispute settlement system.

Such a reorientation will inevitably involve members reassuming greater responsibility for outcomes in order to rebalance what has become an institutional arrangement overly reliant on dispute settlement.

In the meantime, much attention is likely to be paid in the next few years to decision-making under the Multiparty Interim Appeal Arbitration Arrangement (MPIA) as an alternative for resolving disputes appealed by members. WTO members can resort to the use of the MPIA under DSU Art. 25 in place of appeals or resort to it to hear matters at first instance. The MPIA embodies WTO appellate review rules and in a dispute between members that agree to it the arrangement will supersede the previous appeal processes and may also apply to future disputes between them. In this way, the MPIA is designed to overcome the impasse over the Appellate Body.

There will be great pressure for the MPIA to look like, but also to depart from, methods and precedents established by the Appellate Body. The pressure for similarity comes from the desire to satisfy settled expectations. Participants will want the best that was embodied in the

Sacerdoti, "The Challenge of Re-establishing a Functioning WTO Dispute Settlement System" in *Modernizing the WTO* 26 at 30–31 (Centre for International Governance Innovation, Waterloo; 2020).

[83] DSU Art. 19.1 provides that "[i]n addition to its recommendations, the panel or Appellate Body *may suggest ways* in which the Member concerned could implement the recommendations." [italics added]. See Hannah Monicken, "U.S. Welcomes WTO Panel Reports as Proof Dispute Settlement Can Work" 40:22 *Inside U.S. Trade* 5 (3 June 2022) (observing the U.S. position that WTO dispute settlement "should facilitate the resolving of disputes but has often failed to do so").

suspended system to be replicated. Conversely, participating members will want to judiciously sidestep the pitfalls and weaknesses of Appellate Body jurisprudence, notably its disregard of the 90-day time limit for rendering appellate decisions and the sensitive issue of precedential status for Appellate Body decisions.[84]

At the same time, there are a number of reasons to believe the MPIA will be a significant departure from garden variety appellate review. First, it will involve arbitration under DSU Art. 25, not procedures under DSU Art. 17, giving disputing parties greater autonomy over the results. Depending on the parties, that autonomy could be used – or possibly misused – to craft results at variance with the interests of the WTO membership as a whole. Second, awards rendered under the MPIA will be reported to the DSB but because they are not formal dispute settlement results they will not be automatically enforceable. In particular, given its current posture, the United States can be expected to object to efforts at enforcement of MPIA results through the DSB.[85] In addition, due to the fact that MPIA procedures can be disclaimed, Olga Starshinova has pointed out that "[m]embers could act in bad faith and refuse to resolve disputes through the MPIA at any time."[86] Third, few WTO members have agreed to MPIA procedures so far, and a number of major WTO countries appear either uninterested in it or fearful of upsetting their relationship with the United States by doing so.

These factors promise significant caveats to the MPIA's operation. Henry Gao has pointed out how the MPIA may generate a line of dubious half-precedent and a sense of "false comfort" among the membership that two-tier review is being preserved.[87] Nevertheless, after the "constitutionalism" of its founding phase, it seems that the organization

[84] In early 2020 the Office of the U.S. Trade Representative made a number of criticisms of Appellate Body jurisprudence, including that Appellate Body members had repeatedly violated DSU Art. 17.5 with respect to the 90-day time limit for rendering appellate decisions, and that the Appellate Body wrongly claimed that its reports are entitled to be treated as binding precedent and must be followed by panels, absent "cogent reasons," See United States Trade Representative, *Report on the Appellate Body of the World Trade Organization* (Feb. 2020).

[85] See Letter from Ambassador Dennis Shea to WTO Director-General, Roberto Azevedo (5 June 2020); Hannah Monicken, "Shea: U.S. Opposes Use of WTO Budget for Interim Appellate Plan" 38:25 *Inside U.S. Trade* 21 (19 June 2020).

[86] Olga Starshinova, "Is the MPIA a Solution to the WTO Appellate Body Crisis?" 55:5 *J. World Trade* 787 at 800 (2021).

[87] Gao, "Finding a Rule-Based Solution to the Appellate Body Crisis" 24 *J.I.E.L.* 534 at 548–550 (2021).

is transitioning toward a more "contractual" structure as the treaty and its underlying idea of 'good' mature. It is undeniable that appeals decided by arbitration under DSU Art. 25, which stress bilateralism and party autonomy, are consistent with this evolution.

All of these points suggest the unity of the WTO Agreement may wax and wane – and possibly wax again. Patience and a long-term perspective on the treaty are required. To hope the WTO Agreement remains a single, coherent arrangement at all times is wishful thinking. Instead, it is the treaty's ability to tolerate stress – if not outright contradiction – that is most remarkable.[88] This was in fact the record of GATT which, during its existence from 1948 to 1994, experienced intervals of latency and activity, stagnation and renewal.[89] Some commentators forecast an eventual reversion to multilateralism, a move consistent with the communitarian theory's identification of oscillatory tendencies between multilateralism and unilateralism over long intervals.[90]

The theory projects that in order to do so the system will require an acknowledged "good." There is a chance that the WTO could be

[88] Patrick Glenn has noted how legal traditions "which are great and large have of course become great and large because they provide an overarching means of reconciling different views. So their dynamic become impossible to shut down. All that can occur is that some major feature of the tradition is taken as apodictic, by some adherents to the tradition, who then undertake to universalize it." H. Patrick Glenn, *Legal Traditions of the World* (5th ed.) 48 (Oxford University Press, Oxford; 2014).

[89] Robert Hudec, *The GATT Legal System and World Trade Diplomacy* 196 (Butterworth Legal Publishers, Salem, NH; 1990).

[90] For predictions of an eventual return to multilateralism, see Meinhard Hilf & Tim René Salomon, "Running in Circles: Regionalism in World Trade and How It Will Lead Back to Multilateralism" in Ulrich Fastenrath et al. (eds), *From Bilateralism to Community Interest: Essays in Honour of Bruno Simma* 257 at 267 (Oxford University Press, Oxford; 2011) ("after being subject to [fragmentation] for some time, States will consequently start to look for a solution in order to somehow limit the variety of dispute settlement systems to its lowest common denominator."); Alan Wolff, "WTO 2025: Getting Back to the Negotiating Table" 22-7 Peterson Institute for International Economics Briefing Paper 10 (May 2022) ("Fragmentation of the trading system is not a sustainable long-term trend. There will be a return to multilateralism."). For broader accounts of this same oscillatory movement between multilateralism and unilateralism detected in international law, see Matthew Craven, "Unity, Diversity and the Fragmentation of International Law" XIV *Finnish Yearbook I.L.* 3 at 12 (2003) (referring to the fact that "progressive systematization [of international law] appears in tension with that of fragmentation . . . A system is a system by reason of its ability to unify a diversity of experience – it must be simultaneously homogenous and heterogenous, unified but multipolar."); Bruno Simma & Dirk Pulkowski, "Of Planets and the Universe: Self-contained Regimes in International Law" 17:3 *E.J.I.L.* 483 at 529 (2006) (referring to "Unity and multiplicity, stability and change mutually condition[ing] each other").

reconstituted around a set of environmental disciplines that would give the membership common cause – a good that they value – but if recent experience is any indicator, that possibility appears remote. The global effects of climate change are uneven. In such situations it is far from certain that countries will respond to this threat in a coordinated way implying recognition of a good. Instead, when conditions deteriorate sufficiently, people and governments may be prompted to take matters into their own hands.

This scenario may seem gloomy and somewhat apocalyptic, but it is worth keeping in mind if we seek something better.

8.6 Conclusion: Biology as Ideology

What I have highlighted in previous chapters is interdependence. Interdependence is the topic that brings the many disparate threads of this book together, whether in the form of interdependent economic activity, an interdependent view of the relationship between distributive and corrective justice, or interdependent obligations underpinning the normative order of the WTO Agreement.

Interdependence has expanded enormously with recent developments. Notwithstanding recent events, it is likely to continue doing so.

In the meantime we struggle to understand all that is unfolding. Current developments appear novel, complex and incomprehensible.

What I have emphasized in this book is that the issue of community and its maintenance is a perennial one. Interdependence is rarely far from our thoughts. Why? Because it stems from our biology and involves our greatest common attribute as a species: the remarkable ability to cooperate. This forces us to constantly confront the issue of what is just.

In this final chapter I have suggested that the issue involves consideration not only of ourselves but of other future generations and the wider world around us. The issue is essentially identical to the one that Aristotle pondered twenty-five centuries ago when he asked what is it that holds people together?

Aristotle thought about this subject in the context of the *polis*. We think about it in a globalizing world. Despite the difference of scale, the central question remains the same.

BIBLIOGRAPHY

Abi-Saab, Georges, "The WTO Dispute Settlement and General International Law" in Yerxa, Rufus and Wilson, Brian (eds), *Key Issues in WTO Dispute Settlement: The First Ten Years* 9 (World Trade Organization, Geneva; 2005)

Acconci, Pia, "Most-Favoured-Nation Treatment" in Muchlinski, Peter, Ortino, Federico and Schreuer, Christoph (eds), *The Oxford Handbook of International Investment Law* 363 (Oxford University Press, Oxford; 2008)

Afilalo, Ari, "Towards a Common Law of International Investment" 17 *Geo. I.E.L. Rev.* 51 (2004)

Ahmed, Salman and Engel, Rozlyn (eds), *Making U.S. Foreign Policy Work Better for the Middle Class* (Carnegie Endowment for International Peace, Washington, DC; 2020)

Ahn, Dukgeun, "Korea in the GATT/WTO Dispute Settlement System" 6:3 *J.I.E.L.* 597 (2003)

Akerlof, George and Schiller, Robert, *Animal Spirits* (Princeton University Press, Princeton, NJ; 2010)

Alejandro, Roberto, "Rawls's Communitariansm" 23:1 *Can. J. Phil.* 75 (1993)

Aliseda, Atocha, *Abductive Reasoning* (Springer, Dordrecht; 2006)

Allen, Trevor, "Review: Dworkin and Dicey: The Rule of Law as Integrity" 8:2 *O.J.L.S.* 266 (1988)

Allott, Philip, *Eunomia* (Oxford University Press, Oxford; 1990)

The Health of Nations (Cambridge University Press, Cambridge; 2002)

Alschner, Wolfgang, "Aligning Loss and Liability: Towards an Integrated Assessment of Damages in Investment Arbitration" in Marion Jansen, Joost Pauwelyn and Theresa Carpenter (eds), *The Use of Economics in International Trade and Investment Disputes* 283 (Cambridge University Press, Cambridge; 2017)

"Amicable Settlements of WTO Disputes: Bilateral Solutions in a Multilateral System" 13:1 *World Trade Rev.* 65 (2013)

Alston, Philip, "Resisting the Merger and Acquisition of Human Rights by Trade Law: A Reply to Petersmann" 13:4 *E.J.I.L.* 815 (2002)

Alter, Karen, "Resolving or Exacerbating Disputes? The WTO's New Dispute Resolution System" 79:4 *Int'l Aff.* 783 (2000)

Alvarez, José, "Book Review of *The Multilateralization of International Investment Law*" 105 *Am. J. Int'l L.* 377 (2011)

International Organizations as Law-Makers (Oxford University Press, Oxford; 2005)

The Public International Law Regime Governing International Investment (Hague Academy of International Law, The Hague; 2011)

Amerasinghe, Chittharanjan, "Presumptions and Inferences in Evidence in International Litigation" 3 *Law & Prac. Int'l Cts. & Tribunals* 395 (2004)

Antoine, Martin and Mercurio, Bryan, "Doha Dead and Buried in Nairobi" 16:1 *J. Int'l Trade & Pol.* 49 (2017)

Aristotle, *Nicomachean Ethics* (2nd ed.) (Terence Irwin, trans., Hackett Publishing, Indianapolis, IN;1999)

Austin, John, *The Province of Jurisprudence Determined* (J. Murray, London; 1832)

Bacchus, James, "Groping toward Grotius: The WTO and the International Rule of Law" 44 *Harv. Int'l L.J.* 533 (2003)

Bagchi, Aditi, "Distributive Injustice and Private Law" 130 *Hastings L.J.* 105 (2008)

Bagwell, Kyle and Staiger, Robert, "An Economic Theory of GATT" 89:1 *Am. Econ. Rev.* 215 (1999)

"The WTO: Theory and Practice," WTO Staff Working Paper ERSD-2009-11 (11 Nov. 2009).

Baldwin, Richard, "The Causes of Regionalism" 20:7 *World Econ.* 865 (2002)

Balkin, Jack, "Nested Oppositions" 99 *Yale L.J.* 1669 (1990)

Barnett, Randy, "A Consent Theory of Contract" 86:2 *Columbia L. Rev.* 269 (1986)

Baumard, Nicolas, *The Origins of Fairness* (Oxford University Press, Oxford; 2016)

Bederman, David, *The Spirit of International Law* (University of Georgia Press, Athens, GA; 2002)

Bedjaoui, Mohammed, *Towards a New International Economic Order* (UNESCO, Paris; 1979)

Bellamy, Richard, *Liberalism and Pluralism: Towards a Politics of Compromise* (Routledge, London; 2000)

Benson, Peter, "The Basis of Corrective Justice and Its Relation to Distributive Justice" 77 *Iowa L. Rev.* 515 (1992)

Bentes, Pablo, "In Search of a 'Genuine and Substantial' Cause: The Analysis of Causation in Serious Prejudice Claims" in Jansen, Marion, Pauwelyn, Joost and Carpenter, Theresa (eds), *The Use of Economics in International Trade and Investment Disputes* 239 (Cambridge University Press, Cambridge; 2017)

Bernasconi-Osterwalder, Nathalie, Magraw, Daniel, Oliva, Maria Julia, Tuerk, Elisabeth and Orellana, Marcos, *Environment and Trade: A Guide to WTO Jurisprudence* 76 (Earthscan, London; 2006)

Bhagwati, Jagdish, "U.S. Trade Policy: The Infatuation with Free Trade Agreements" in Bhagwati, Jagdish and Kreuger, Anne (eds), *The Dangerous Drift to Preferential Trade Agreements* 1 (AEI Press, Washington, DC; 1995)

Bhala, Raj, "Power of the Past: Towards De Jure Stare Decisis in WTO Adjudication (Part Three of a Trilogy)" 33 *Geo. Wash. Int'l L. R.* 873 (2000)

Bird, Otto, *The Idea of Justice* 10 (F. A. Praeger, New York; 1967)

Blackaby, Nigel, Partasides, Constantine, Redfern, Alan and Hunter, Martin, *Redfern and Hunter on International Arbitration* (5th ed.) (Oxford University Press, Oxford; 2009)

Blair, Tony, "What I've Learned" 383:8531 *The Economist* (2 June 2007)

Bodansky, Daniel, Crook, John and Crawford, James, "The ILC's Articles on Responsibility of States for Internationally Wrongful Acts: A Retrospect" 96 *Am. J. Int'l L.* 874 (2002)

Bonnitcha, Jonathan, Poulsen, Lauge Skovgard and Waibel, Michael, *The Political Economy of the Investment Treaty Regime* (Oxford University Press, Oxford; 2015)

Bonzon, Yves, *Public Participation and Legitimacy in the WTO* (Cambridge University Press, Cambridge; 2014)

Bowles, Samuel and Gintis, Herbert, *A Cooperative Species* (Princeton University Press, Princeton, NJ; 2011)

Bown, Chad, *Self-Enforcing Trade: Developing Countries and WTO Dispute Settlement* (Brookings Institution Press, Washington, DC; 2009)

Bown, Chad and Pauwelyn, Joost (eds), *The Law, Economics and Politics of Retaliation in WTO Dispute Settlement* (Cambridge University Press, Cambridge; 2010)

Bown, Chad and Ruta, Michele, "The Economics of Permissible WTO Retaliation," WTO Staff Working Paper ERSD-2008-04 (2008)

Boyle, Alan and Chinkin, Christine, *The Making of International Law* (2nd ed.) (Oxford University Press, Oxford; 2015)

Breen, Claire, "The Necessity of a Role for the ECOSOC in the Maintenance of International Peace and Security" 12:2 *J. Conflict & Security L.* 261 (2007)

Brilmayer, Leah, "International Justice and International Law" 98 *W. Va. L. Rev.* 610 (1996)

Brooks, David, "Globalization Is Over: The Global Culture Wars Have Begun" *The New York Times* (8 Apr. 2022)

Brower, Charles and Blanchard, Sadie "What's in a Meme: The Truth about Investor-State Arbitration" 52.3 *Colum. J. Transnat'l L.* 689 (2014)

Brownlie, Ian, *System of the Law of Nations: State Responsibility (Part 1)* 52 (Clarendon Press, New York; 1983)

Bruckerhoff, Joshua, "Giving Nature Constitutional Protection: A Less Anthropocentric Interpretation of Environmental Rights" 86 *Tex. L. Rev.* 615 (2008)

Brudner, Alan and Nadler, Jennifer, *The Unity of the Common Law* (2nd ed.) (Oxford University Press, Oxford; 2013)

Brunnée, Jutta and Toope, Stephen, "International Law and Constructivism: Elements of an Interactional Theory of International Law" 39 *Colum. J. Transnat'l L.* 19 (2000)

Legitimacy and Legality in International Law 88 (Cambridge University Press, Cambridge; 2010)

Buchanan, Allen, and Golove, David, "Philosophy of International Law" in Coleman, Jules and Shapiro, Scott (eds), *The Oxford Handbook of Jurisprudence and Philosophy of Law* 868 (Oxford University Press, Oxford; 2004)

Bücheler, Gebhard, *Proportionality in Investor-State Arbitration* (Oxford University Press; Oxford; 2015)

Busch, Marc and Reinhardt, Eric, "Bargaining in the Shadow of the Law: Early Settlement in GATT/WTO Disputes" 24 *Fordham Int'l L.J.* 158 (2000)

"Three's a Crowd: Third Parties and WTO Dispute Settlement" 58:3 *World Politics* 446 (Apr. 2006)

Calabresi, Steven, Agudo, Sarah and Leahy, Kat, "State Bills of Rights in 1787 and 1791: What Individual Rights Are Deeply Rooted in American History and Tradition" 85 *S. Cal. L. Rev.* 1451 (2011–2012)

Cameron, James and Gray, Kevin, "Principles of International Law in the WTO Dispute Settlement Body" 50 *I.C.L.Q.* 248 (2001).

Cameron, Peter, "The Aircraft Negotiations 2004 to 2007: 'This Will Never Fly!'" in OECD, *Smart Rules for Fair Trade* 190 (OECD, Paris; 2011)

Campbell, Tom, *Justice* (3rd ed.) (Palgrave Macmillan, Basingstoke; 2010)

Cane, Peter, "The Anatomy of Private Law Theory" 25:2 *O.J.L.S.* 203 (2003)

Carlarne, Cinnamon, "From the U.S.A. with Love" 37 *Enviro. L.* 301 (2007)

Carmody, Chi "International Decisions: Softwood Lumber Dispute (2001–2006)" 100:3 *A.J.I.L.* 664 (2006)

"Third Parties under GATT" 18 *Mich. J. Int'l L.* 615 (1997)

Carmody, Chios, "WTO Obligations as Collective" 17:2 *E.J.I.L.* 419 (2006).

Carmody, Chios and Garcia, Frank and Linarelli John (eds), *Global Justice and International Economic Law* (Cambridge University Press, Cambridge: 2012)

Carroll, Sean, *The Serengeti Rules* (Princeton University Press, Princeton, NJ; 2016)

Cass, Deborah, "The 'Constitutionalization' of International Trade Law" 12 *E.J.I.L.* 39 (2001)

The Constitutionalization of the World Trade Organization (Oxford University Press, Oxford; 2005)

Cedro, Rafael and Vieira, Bruno, "John Rawls' Justice as Fairness and the WTO" 3:2 *Law & Dev. Rev.* 122 (2010)

Chaitin, Gregory, "The Limits of Reason" 294(3) *Scientific American* 74 (2006)

Chayes, Abraham and Handler Chayes, Antonia, *The New Sovereignty* (Harvard University Press, Cambridge, MA; 1995)

Chen, Yusong and Li, Xiaoling, "Constraints of the WTO Compensation Mechanism and Implications from Recent Practice" 49:4 *J. World Trade* 643 (2015)

Chin, Moya, "What Are Global Public Goods?" 58:4 *Finance & Development* 62 (Dec. 2021).

Chinkin, Christine, *Third Parties in International Law* (Oxford University Press, Oxford; 1993)

Cho, Sungjoon, "A Bridge Too Far" 7 *J.I.E.L.* 219 (2004)

"GATT Non-Violation Issues in the WTO Framework" 39 *Harv. Int'l L. J.* 311 (1998)

Choi, Won-Mog, *"Like Products" in International Trade Law* ix (Oxford University Press, Oxford; 2003)

Choudhury, Barnali "The Façade of Neutrality: Uncovering Gender Silences in International Law" 15:1 *Will. & Mary J. Women & L.* 113 (2008)

Christie, Konstantin and Turtoi, Rodica, "Compensation for Expropriation" *Lexology* (27 Apr. 2020)

Chua, Adrian, "Precedent and Principles of WTO Panel Jurisprudence" 16 *Berkeley J. Int'l L.* 171 (1998)

Chutikul, Kobsak, "Options for a Parliamentary Dimension of the WTO" (Discussion Paper presented at the Parliamentary Conference on the WTO) (17–18 Feb. 2003)

Chyzh, Olga, "Dangerous Liaisons: An Endogenous Model of International Trade and Human Rights" 53:3 *J. Peace Research* 409 (2016)

Ciuriak, Dan, "World Trade Organization 2.0: Reforming Multilateral Trade Rules for the Digital Age," CIGI Policy Brief 152 (11 July 2019)

Clark, Ann Marie, Friedman, Elisabeth and Hochstetler, Kathryn, "The Sovereign Limits of Global Civil Society" 51:1 *World Politics* 1 (1998)

Clift, Jeremy, "What Is Nowcasting?" *Finance & Development* 6 (Mar. 2014)

Collins, Angelo and Stewart, James, "The Knowledge Structure of Mendelian Genetics" 51:3 *Am. Biol. Teach.* 143 (1989)

Collins-Williams, Terry and Wolfe, Robert, "Transparency as a Trade Policy Tool: The WTO's Cloudy Windows" 9:4 *World Trade Rev.* 551 (2010)

Copacino, William, *Supply Chain Management* (St. Lucie Press, Boca Raton, FL; 1997)

Cooper, Thomas, *The Institutes of Justinian* (North-Holland, Amsterdam; 1975)

Cottier, Thomas and Foltea, Marina, "Constitutional Functions of the WTO and Regional Trade Agreements" in Bartels, Lorand and Ortino, Federico (eds), *Regional Trade Agreements and the WTO Legal System* 43 (Oxford University Press, Oxford; 2006)

Cottier, Thomas and Hertig, Maya, "The Prospects of 21st Century Constitutionalism" 7:1 *MaxPlanckUNYB* 261 (2004)

Cottier, Thomas, Oesch, Matthias and Fischer, Thomas, *International Trade Regulation* (Staempfli Publishers, Berne; Cameron May, London; 2005)

Cottier, Thomas and Schefer, Krista, "NVNI Complaints in WTO/GATT Dispute Settlement: Past, Present and Future" in Petersmann, Ernst-Ulrich (ed.), *International Trade Law and the WTO/GATT Dispute Settlement System* 145 (Kluwer, The Hague; 1997)

Covington, J. R., Jr., *The Structure of Legal Argument and Proof* (John Marshall, Houston, TX; 1993)

Crawford, James, *The International Law Commission's Articles on State Responsibility: Introduction, Text and Commentaries* (Cambridge University Press, Cambridge; 2002)

"The Problems of Legitimacy-Speak" 98 *Proc. Annu. Meet. (American Society of International Law)* 271 (2004)

Craven, Matthew, "Unity, Diversity and the Fragmentation of International Law" XIV *Finnish Yearbook I.L.* 3 (2003)

Dagan, Hanoch, "The Distributive Foundation of Corrective Justice" 98 *Mich. L. Rev.* 138 (1999)

Davey, William J., "Compliance Problems in WTO Dispute Settlement" 42:1 *Cornell Int'l L.J.* 119 (2009)

Davey, William, *Non-discrimination in the World Trade Organization* 56 (Hague Academy of International Law, The Hague; 2012)

Debaere, Peter "A Theory of GATT/WTO" Darden Case No. UVA-GEM-0153 (2018)

Delanty, Gerard, *Community* (2nd ed.) (Routledge, New York; 2010)

Delaney, Joachim and Magraw, Daniel Barstow, "Procedural Transparency" in Muchlinski, Peter, Ortino, Federico and Schreuer, Christoph (eds), *The Oxford Handbook of International Investment Law* 752 (Oxford University Press, Oxford; 2012)

di Mascio, Nicholas and Pauwelyn, Joost, "Nondiscrimination in Trade and Investment Treaties" 102 *Am. J. Int'l L.* 48 (2008)

Diamond, Jared, *Collapse* (Viking, New York; 2005)

Dirac, Paul, 119 *Nature* 1001–1002 (untitled supplement) (June 1937)

Dolzer, Rudolph and Schreuer, Christoph, *Principles of International Investment Law* (Oxford University Press, Oxford; 2008)

Douglas, Zachary, "Hybrid Foundations of Investment Treaty Arbitration" 74 *B.Y.I.L.* 151 (2003)

"Property, Investment and the Scope of Investment Protection Obligations" in Douglas, Zachary, Pauwelyn, Joost and Viñuales, Jorge (eds), *The Foundations of International Investment Law* 363 (Oxford University Press, Oxford; 2014)

Dowrick, Frank, *Justice According to the English Common Lawyers* (Butterworth, London; 1961)

Drahos, Peter, "The Regulation of Public Goods" 7:2 *J.I.E.L.* 321 (2004)

Dreyer, Iana and Erixon, Frederik, "An EU-China Trade Dialogue," ECIPE Policy Brief No. 03/2008.

Dunoff, Jeffrey, "Constitutional Conceits: The WTO's Constitution and the Discipline of International Law" 17:3 *E.J.I.L.* 647 (2006)

Dworkin, Ronald, *Justice in Robes* (Belknap Press, Cambridge, MA; 2006)

Law's Empire (Belknap Press, Cambridge, MA; 1986)

Edmundson, William, *John Rawls: Reticent Socialist* (Cambridge University Press, Cambridge, MA; 2017)

Ehring, Lothar, "De Facto Discrimination in WTO Law," Jean Monnet Working Paper 12/01 (2001)

Eisenberg, Melvin, *The Nature of the Common Law* 154 (Harvard University Press, Cambridge, MA; 1988)

Eleftheriadis, Pavlos, "Corrective Justice among States" 2 *Jus Cogens* 7 (2020)

Elkins, Zachary, Ginsburg, Tom, Melton, James, Shaffer, Robert, Sequeda, Juan & Miranker, Daniel, "Constitute: The World's Constitutions to Read, Search and Compare" 27 *Web Semant.* 10 (2014). Available online at constituteproject.org.

Elliott, E. Donald, "Law and Biology: The New Synthesis" 41 *St. Louis U. L.J.* 595 (1997)

Endicott, Martin, "Remedies in Investor State Arbitration" in Kahn, Philippe and Wälde, Thomas (eds), *New Aspects of International Investment Law* 531 (Martinus Nijhoff, Leiden; 2007)

Englard, Izhak, *Corrective and Distributive Justice: From Aristotle to Modern Times* (Oxford University Press, Oxford; 2009)

Eskridge, William, "The Relationship between Obligations and Rights of Citizens" 69 *Fordham L. Rev.* 1721 (2001)

Evans, Gail, *Lawmaking under the Trade Constitution* (Kluwer Law International, London; 1999)

Evenett, Simon and Baldwin, Richard, *Revitalising Multilateralism: Pragmatic Ideas for the New WTO Director-General* (Centre for Economic Policy Research, London; 2020)

Ezzell, Carol, "Clocking Cultures" in *A Matter of Time*, 27:2 *Scientific American* 48 (Summer 2018)

Farmelo, Graham, *The Strangest Man* (Faber & Faber, London; 2009)

Farrell, Henry and Newman, Abraham L., "Weaponized Interdependence: How Global Economic Networks Shape State Coercion" 44:1 *Int'l Security* 42 (2019)

Farrell, Henry, Newman, Abraham L. and Drezner, Daniel (eds), *The Uses and Abuses of Weaponized Interdependence* (Brookings Institution Press, Washington, DC; 2021)

Faulkner, Robert, "Regulating Biotech Trade" 76:2 *International Affairs* (2000)

Federico, Giovanni and Tena-Junguito, Antonio, "A Tale of Two Globalizations: Gains from Trade and Openness 1800–2010," London, Centre for Economic Policy Research (CEPR WP.11128) (2016)

Fefer, Rachel, Schwarzenberg, Andres and Wong, Liana, "Global Value Chains: Overview and Issues for Congress," Congressional Research Service Report R46641 (16 Dec. 2020)

Fehr, Ernest and Gächter, Simon, "Fairness and Retaliation: The Economics of Reciprocity" 14:3 *J. Econ. Perspect.* 159 (Summer 2000)

Feitchner, Isabel, *The Law and Politics of WTO Waivers* (Cambridge University Press, Cambridge; 2012).

Finger, J. Michael and Winters, Alan L., "Reciprocity in the WTO" in Hoekman, Bernard M., Mattoo, Aaditya and English, Philip (eds), *Development, Trade, and the WTO: A Handbook*, Vol. 1, 50 (World Bank, Washington, DC; 2002)

Finnis, John, *Natural Law and Natural Rights* (Oxford University Press, New York; 1980)

Fitzmaurice, Gerald, "Second Report on the Law of Treaties" U.N. Doc. A/CN.4/SER.A/1957/Add.l, *Yearbook of the International Law Commission* (1957)

"Third Report on the Law of Treaties" U.N. Doc. A/CN.4/115, *Yearbook of the International Law Commission* Vol. II (1958)

Flett, James, "The Client's Perspective" in Jansen, Marion, Paulweyn, Joost and Carpenter, Theresa (eds), *The Use of Economics in International Trade and Investment Disputes* 83 (Cambridge University Press, Cambridge; 2017)

Footer, Mary, *An Institutional and Normative Analysis of the World Trade Organization* (Martinus Nijhoff, Leiden; 2006)

"Some Aspects of Third Party Intervention in GATT/WTO Dispute Settlement Proceedings" in Petersmann, Ernst-Ulrich (ed.), *International Trade Law and the GATT/WTO Dispute Settlement System* 211 (Kluwer Law International, London; 1997)

Foster, Sheila and Bonilla, Daniel, "The Social Function of Property: A Comparative Law Perspective" 80 *Fordham L. Rev.* 101 (2011)

France, Anatole, *The Red Lily* 95 (John Lane, London; 1922)

Franck, Thomas, *The Power of Legitimacy among Nations* (Oxford University Press, Oxford; 1990)

Frankel, Susy, "Interpreting the Overlap of International Investment and Intellectual Property Law" 19(1) *J.I.E.L.* 120 (2016)

Frankenberg, Günter, "The Return of the Contract: Problems and Pitfalls of European Constitutionalism" 6 *Eur. L.J.* 257 (2002)

Fried, Charles, *Contract as Promise* 1 (Oxford University Press, Oxford; 1981).

Friedman, Thomas, *The World Is Flat* (Farrar, Straus and Giroux, New York; 2005)

Frydrych, David, "Rights Correlativity" in Balganesh, Shyamkrishna, Sichelman, Ted and Smith, Henry (eds), *Wesley Hohfeld A Century Later: Edited Work, Select Personal Papers, and Original Commentaries* 112 (Cambridge University Press, Cambridge; 2021)

Gagné, Gilbert, *The Trade and Culture Debate: Evidence from US Trade Agreements* (Lexington Books, Lanham, MD; 2016)

Gao, Henry, "Finding a Rule-Based Solution to the Appellate Body Crisis: Looking beyond the Multiparty Interim Appeal Arbitration Arrangement" 24 *J.I.E.L.* 534 (2021)

Garcia, Frank, *Global Justice and the International Economic Law: Three Takes* (Cambridge University Press, Cambridge; 2013)

Trade, Inequality and Justice (Transnational Publishers, Ardsley, NY; 2003)

Gerhart, Peter, *Contract Law and Social Morality* (Cambridge University Press, Cambridge; 2021)

Property Law and Social Morality (Cambridge University Press, Cambridge; 2014)

"Reflections: Beyond Compliance Theory – TRIPS as a Substantive Issue" 32:3 *Case Western Reserve J. Int'l L.* 357 (2000)

Tort Law and Social Morality (Cambridge University Press, Cambridge; 2010)

"Two Constitutional Visions of the World Trade Organization" 24 *U. Pa. J. Int'l Econ. L.* 1 (2003)

Giorgetti, Chiara, "Who Decides Who Decides in International Investment Arbitration?" 35:2 *U. Pa J. Int'l L.* 431 (2013)

Glenn, H. Patrick, *Legal Traditions of the World* (5th ed.) (Oxford University Press, Oxford; 2014)

The Cosmopolitan State (Oxford University Press, Oxford; 2013)

Goodman, John, "An Economic Theory of the Evolution of the Common Law" 7 *J. Legal Studies* 393 (1978)

Goodwin, Doris Kearns, *Team of Rivals* 207 (Simon & Schuster, New York; 2005)

Gordin, Michael, *A Well-Ordered Thing* (Basic Books, New York; 2004)

Grando, Michelle, *Evidence, Proof and Fact-Finding in WTO Dispute Settlement* (Oxford University Press, Oxford; 2009)

Grant, Adam, *Think Again* (Viking, New York; 2021)

Grene, Marjorie and Depew, David, *The Philosophy of Biology* (Cambridge University Press, Cambridge; 2004)

Grossman, Gene and Mavroidis, Petros, "Dispute Settlement Corner: United States – Section 110(5) of the U.S. Copyright Act, Recourse to Arbitration under Article 25 of the DSU: Would've or Should've? Impaired Benefits due to Copyright Infringement" 2:2 *World Trade Rev.* 233 (2003)

Grotius, Hugo, *On the Law of War and Peace* (Stephen Neff ed., Cambridge University Press, Cambridge; 2012)

Guan, Wenwei, "Consensus Yet Not Consented" 17 *J.I.E.L.* 77 (2014)

Guillaume, Gilbert, "The Use of Precedent by International Judges and Arbitrators" 2:1 *J. Int'l Dispute Settlement* 5 (2011)

Halpin, Andrew, "Correlativity and Its Logic" 32:1 *Can. J. L. & Jurisprudence* 83 (2019)

Harford, Tim, "Big Mistake?" *Financial Times* 18 (29–30 Mar. 2014)

Harris, James, *Property and Justice* (Clarendon Press, Oxford; 1996)

Hart, Herbert L. A., *The Concept of Law* 159 (Oxford University Press, Oxford, 1994)

The Concept of Law (2nd ed.) (Oxford University Press, London; 2006)

Hathaway, Oonagh and Shapiro, Scott, "Outcasting: Enforcement in Domestic and International Law" 121:2 *Yale L.J.* 252 (Nov. 2011)

Helfer, Laurence, "Constitutional Analogies in the International Legal System" 37 *Loy. L.A. L. Rev.* 193 (2003)

Heller, Michael, *The Gridlock Economy* (Basic Books, New York; 2008)

Henckels, Caroline, *Proportionality and Deference in Investor-State Arbitration* (Cambridge University Press, Cambridge; 2015)

Henrich, Joseph et al., "Markets, Religion, Community Size, and the Evolution of Fairness and Punishment" 327 *Science* 1480 (19 Mar. 2010)

Heyman, Steven, "Aristotle on Political Justice" 77 *Iowa L. Rev.* 851 (1992)

Hilf, Meinhard and Salomon, Tim René, "Running in Circles: Regionalism in World Trade and How It Will Lead Back to Multilateralism" in Fastenrath, Ulrich, Geiger, Rudolf and Khan, Daniel-Erasmus (eds), *From Bilateralism to Community Interest: Essays in Honour of Bruno Simma* 257 (Oxford University Press, Oxford; 2011)

Hilf, Meinhardt, "Power, Rules and Principles – Which Orientation for WTO/ GATT Law?" 4 *J.I.E.L.* 111 (2001)

Hillman, Jennifer, "An Emerging International Rule of Law – The WTO Dispute Settlement System's Role in its Evolution" 42 *Ottawa L. Rev.* 269 (2010)

"Three Approaches to Fixing the World Trade Organization's Appellate Body: The Good, the Bad and the Ugly?" (Dec. 2018)

Hinton, Alexander (ed.), *Transitional Justice* (Rutgers University Press, New Brunswick, NJ; 2010)

Hoda, Anwarul, *Tariff Negotiations and Renegotiations under the GATT and WTO* (Cambridge University Press, Cambridge; 2001)

Hodges, Christopher "Settlement and its pitfalls in England and Wales" in Hodges, Christopher & Stadler, Astrid, *Resolving Mass Disputes* 106 (Edward Elgar, Cheltenham; 2013)

Hoekmann, Bernard and Mavroidis, Petros, "Dispute Settlement at the WTO: Now What?" in *Modernizing the WTO* 14 (Centre for International Governance Innovation, Waterloo; 2020)

"Preventing the Bad from Getting Worse: The End of the World (Trade Organization) Ss We Know It?" 32:3 *E.J.I.L.* 743 (2021)

Hoff, Karla, "Fairness in Modern Society" 327 *Science* 1467 (19 Mar. 2010)

Hohfeld, Wesley, *Fundamental Legal Conceptions as Applied in Judicial Reasoning* (1919, rev'd ed., Lawbook Exchange, Clark, NJ; 2010)

Holmes, Peter, "The WTO and the EU" in de Búrca, Grainne and Scott, Joanne (eds), *The EU and the WTO* 59 (Hart, Oxford; 2001)

Honkonen, Tuula, "The Development of the Principle of Common but Differentiated Responsibilities and Its Place in International Environmental Regimes" in Kuokkanen, Tuomas, Couzens, Ed, Honkonen, Tuula and Lewis, Melissa (eds), *International Environmental Law-Making and Diplomacy* 160 (Routledge, Milton Park; 2016)

Horn, Henrick, Maggi, Giovanni and Staiger, Robert, "The GATT/WTO as an Incomplete Contract" [unpublished paper] (2005)

Howse, Robert, "Adjudicative Legitimacy and Treaty Interpretation in International Trade Law" in Weiler, Joseph (ed.), *The EU, the WTO and the NAFTA* 35 (Oxford University Press, Oxford; 2000)

"The Limits of the WTO" *A.J.I.L. Unbound* 41. Available at www.cambridge.org/core/journals/american-journal-of-international-law/ajil-unbound (accessed 7 July 2022) (doi: 10.1017/aju.2022.5)

Howse, Robert and Nicolaidis, Kalypso, "Enhancing WTO Legitimacy?" 16:1 *Governance* 73 (2003).

"Legitimacy and Global Governance" in Porter, Roger B., Sauvé, Pierre, Subramanian, Arvind and Bevigilia Zampetti, Americo (eds), *Efficiency, Equity and Legitimacy* 227 (Brookings Institution Press, Washington, DC; 2001)

Hudec, Robert, *Developing Countries in the GATT Legal System* (Gower, London; 1987)

Enforcing International Trade Law (Butterworth Legal Publishers, Salem, NH; 1993).

The GATT Legal System and World Trade Diplomacy (Butterworth Legal Publishers, Salem, NH; 1990)

"Mirror, Mirror, on the Wall: The Concept of Fairness in United States Trade Policy" in Hudec, Robert, *Essays on the Nature of International Trade Law* 227 (Cameron May, London; 1999)

Hufbauer, Gary Clyde and Jung, Eujin, "The USMCA, Newly Jeopardized, Was Never a Free Trade Agreement" Petersen Institute Trade and Investment Policy Watch (4 June 2019)

Hughes, Valerie, "Approaches to Modernizing the Dispute Settlement Understanding" in *Modernizing the WTO* 21 (Centre for International Governance Innovation, Waterloo; 2020)

Hunter, Dan, "No Wilderness of Single Instances" 48:3 *J. Legal Educ.* 365 (1998)

Hutchinson, Allan, *Evolution and the Common Law* (Cambridge University Press, Cambridge; 2005)

Iacovides, Marios and Jansen, Marion, "Lost in Translation: Communication and Interpretation Challenges Related to Economic Evidence in Trade Disputes" in Jansen, Marion, Paulweyn, Joost and Carpenter, Theresa (eds), *The Use of Economics in International Trade and Investment Disputes* 164 (Cambridge University Press, Cambridge; 2017)

IDE-JETRO, *Trade Patterns and Global Value Chains in East Asia* (World Trade Organization, Geneva; 2010)

Ikenberry, John, *After Victory* (Princeton University Press, Princeton, NJ; 2001)

Isaac, Grant and Kerr, William, "The Biosafety Protocol and the WTO: Concert or Conflict?" in Faulkner, Robert (ed.), *The International Politics of Genetically Modified Food* 195 (Palgrave Macmillan, Basingstoke; 2007)

Jackson, John, "The WTO 'Constitution' and Proposed Reforms" 4 *J.I.E.L.* 67 (2001)

World Trade and the Law of GATT (Bobbs-Merrill, Indianapolis, IN; 1969)
The World Trade Organization (Routledge, New York; 1998)
Jaffey, Peter, "Hohfeld's Power-Liability/Right-Duty Distinction in the Law of Restitution" 17:2 *Can. J. L. & Jurisprudence* 295 (2004)
Jansen, Marion, Paulweyn, Joost and Carpenter, Theresa, "Introduction" in Jansen, Marion, Paulweyn, Joost and Carpenter, Theresa (eds), *The Use of Economics in International Trade and Investment Disputes* 5 (Cambridge University Press, Cambridge; 2017).
The Use of Economics in International Trade and Investment Disputes (Cambridge University Press, Cambridge; 2017)
Jenks, C. Wilfred, *A New World of Law?* 226 (Longmans, Harlow; 1969)
Jennings, Robert and Watts, Arthur (eds), *Oppenheim's International Law* (9th ed.) (Longman, Harlow; 1996)
Johnson, Renée, "The U.S.-EU Beef Hormone Dispute" *CRS Report for Congress* R40449 (6 Dec. 2010)
Jones, David and de Villars, Anne S., *Principles of Administrative Law* (5th ed.) 253 (Carswell, Toronto; 2009)
Jordan, Andrew and O'Riordan, Timothy, "The Precautionary Principle: A Legal and Policy History" in Martuzzi, Marco and Tickner, Joel (eds), *The Precautionary Principle*, ch. 3 (World Health Organization, Copenhagen; 2004).
Joseph, Sarah, *Blame It on the WTO* (Oxford University Press, Oxford; 2011)
Kaplow, Louis and Shavell, Steven, *Fairness versus Welfare* (Harvard University Press, Cambridge, MA; 2002)
Kapstein, Ethan, *Economic Justice in an Unfair World* (Princeton University Press, Princeton, NJ; 2006)
Karst, Kenneth, "Why Equality Matters" 17:2 *Ga. L. Rev.* 245 (1983)
Kaufmann-Kohler, Gabrielle, "Arbitral Precedent: Dream, Necessity or Excuse?" 23:3 *Arbitr. Int.* 357 (2007)
Kazazi, Mojtaba, *Burden of Proof and Related Issues* (Kluwer Law International, The Hague; 1996)
Keck, Alexander and Low, Patrick, "Special and Differential Treatment in the WTO: Why, When and How?," WTO Staff Working Paper ERSD-2004-03 (May 2004)
Kelsen, Hans, *General Theory of Law and State* (Transaction Publishers, New Brunswick, NJ; 2008)
Pure Theory of Law (Max Knight, trans., University of California Press, Berkeley; 1967 [Lawbook Exchange, Clark, NJ; rev'd ed, 2005])
Kelsey, Jane, "The Illegitimacy of Joint Statement Initiatives and Their Systemic Implications for the WTO" 25:1 *J.I.E.L.* 2 (Mar. 2022)
Keohane, Robert, "Reciprocity in International Relations" 40:1 *Int'l Org.* 1 (Winter 1986).

Kidane, Won, *The Culture of International Arbitration* (Oxford University Press, New York; 2017)

Kingsbury, Benedict, "The International Legal Order" in Cane, Peter and Tushnet, Mark (eds), *Oxford Handbook of Legal Studies* 271 (Oxford University Press, Oxford; 2003)

Klabbers, Jan, "The Changing Image of International Organizations" in Coicaud, Jean-Marc and Heiskanen, Veijo (eds), *The Legitimacy of International Organizations* 227 (United Nations University Press, Tokyo; 2001)

An Introduction to International Institutional Law (Cambridge University Press, Cambridge; 2009)

Klabbers, Jan, Peters, Anne and Ulfstein, Geir, *The Constitutionalization of International Law* (Oxford University Press, Oxford; 2009)

Knight, Jack, "Justice and Fairness" 1 *Annu. Rev. Polit. Sci.* 425 (1998)

Koestler, Arthur, *Darkness at Noon* (Macmillan, New York; 1941)

Kolb, Robert, *An Introduction to the Law of the United Nations* (Hart, Oxford; 2010)

Theory of International Law (Hart, Oxford; 2016)

Koskenniemi, Martti, *The Gentle Civilizer of Nations* (Cambridge University Press, Cambridge; 2001)

Kriebaum, Ursula, "Evaluating Social Benefits and Costs of Investment Treaties" 33 *ICSID Rev.* 14 (2018)

Kriebaum, Ursula and Schreuer, Christoph, "The Concept of Property in Human Rights Law and International Investment Law" in Breitenmoser, Stephan, Ehrenzeller, Bernhard, Sassoli, Marco, Stoffel, Walter and Wagner Pfeifer, Beatrice (eds), *Human Rights, Democracy and Rule of Law: liber amicorum Luzius Wildhaber* (Dike, Nomos, Zürich, Baden-Baden; 2007)

Krisch, Nico, *Beyond Constitutionalism* (Oxford University Press, Oxford; 2010)

Krishnamurthy, Pavan S., "To Enforce or Manage: An Analysis of WTO Compliance" 32:3 *Emory Int'l L. Rev.* 377 (2018)

Kuhn, Thomas, *The Structure of Scientific Revolutions* (University of Chicago Press, Chicago; 1962)

Kuijper, Pieter-Jan, "The Law of GATT as a Special Field of International Law – Ignorance, Further Refinement or Self-Contained System of International Law" 25 *Neth. Yearbook Int'l L.* 227 (1994)

Kurtz, Jürgen, *The WTO and International Investment Law* (Cambridge University Press, Cambridge; 2016)

Laird, Sam, "Regional Trade Agreements: Dangerous Liasons?" 22:9 *World Econ.* 1179 (1999)

Lang, Andrew and Scott, Joanne, "The Hidden World of WTO Governance" 20:3 *E.J.I.L.* 575 (2009)

Lang, John, "Community Constitutional Law: Article 5 EEC Treaty" 27 *Comm. Mkt. L. Rev.* 645 (1990)

Langford, Malcolm, Behn, Daniel and Lie, Runar Hilleren, "*The Revolving Door in International Investment Arbitration*" 20:2 *J.I.E.L.* 301 (2017)

Langille, Joanna, "Neither Constitution nor Contract: Understanding the WTO by Examining the Legal Limits on Contracting Out through Regional Trade Agreements" 86 *N.Y.U. L. Rev.* 1482 (2011)

Larson, Jane, "Women Understand So Little, They Call My Good Nature 'Deceit': A Feminist Rethinking of Seduction" 93:2 *Columbia L.R.* 374 (1993)

Lau, Simon and Shropp, Simon, "The Role of Economics in WTO Dispute Settlement and Choosing the Right Litigation Strategy – A Practitioner's View" in Jansen, Marion, Pauwelyn, Joost and Carpenter, Theresa (eds), *The Use of Economics in International Trade and Investment Disputes* 55 (Cambridge University Press, Cambridge; 2017)

Law Commission of Canada, "From Restorative Justice to Transformative Justice: Discussion Paper," Law Commission of Canada Catalogue No. JL2–6/1999 (1999)

Lawrence, Robert Z., *Regionalism, Multilateralism, and Deeper Integration* (Brookings Institution, Washington, DC; 1996)

League of Nations, *Commercial Policy in the Interwar Period: International Proposals and National Policies* (League of Nations, Geneva; 1942)

Lee, Edward, "Measuring TRIPS Compliance and Defiance" 18 *J. Intell. Prop. L.* 401 (2010–2011)

Leite, Bernardo, "Brazil to Apply Unilateral Retaliation in Trade Disputes," Grinberg Cordovil Advogados (18 Jan. 2022)

Lester, Simon, Mercurio, Bryan and Davies, Arwel, *World Trade Law* (2nd ed.) (Hart, Oxford; 2012)

Letwin, Shirley, *On the History of the Idea of Law* (Noel Reynolds, ed.) (Cambridge University Press, Cambridge; 2005)

Lévesque, Céline, "The European Commission Proposal for an Investment Court System: Out with the Old, In with the New?" CIGI Investor-State Arbitration Series Paper No. 10 (Sept. 2016).

Levine, Robert, *A Geography of Time* (Basic Books, New York; 1998)

Liang Qichao: Anthology of Works on Law by Liang Qichao (Fan Zhongxin, ed.) (1989) [Hein – World Constitutions Illustrated].

Linbo, Jing, "The Development of the Strategic Trade Policy and Its Application in China" 50:2 *Chinese Econ.* 97 (2017)

Llewellyn, Jennifer and Howse, Robert, "Restorative Justice – A Conceptual Framework," Paper Prepared for the Law Commission of Canada (1998)

Low, Patrick, "WTO Decision-Making for the Future" WTO ERSD-2011-05 (Economic Research and Statistics Division, World Trade Organization, Geneva; 2011)

Lowenfeld, Andreas, *International Economic Law* (2nd ed.) (Oxford University Press, Oxford; 2008)

Lucas, J. R., "Justice" 47 *Philosophy* 229 (1982)

Macaulay, Stewart, "An Empirical View of Contract" 1985 *Wis. L. Rev.* 465 (1985)

MacCormick, Neil, *Legal Reasoning and Legal Theory* (Clarendon Press, Oxford; 1978)

Mackenzie, Ruth, Romano, Cesare, Shany, Yuval and Sands, Philippe (eds), *Manual on International Courts and Tribunals* (Oxford University Press, Oxford; 2010)

Magnus, John, "Compliance with WTO Dispute Settlement Decisions: Is There a Crisis?" in Yerxa, Rufus and Wilson, Brian (eds), *Key Issues in WTO Dispute Settlement* 242 (Cambridge University Press, Cambridge; 2005)

Mann, Erika, "A Parliamentary Dimension to the WTO: More than Just a Vision?!" 7:3 *J.I.E.L.* 659 (2004)

Marboe, Irmgard, *Calculation of Compensation and Damages in International Investment Law* (2nd ed.) (Oxford University Press, Oxford; 2017)

"Assessing Compensation and Damages in Expropriation versus Nonexpropriation Cases", in Beharry, Christine (ed.), *Contemporary and Emerging Issues on the Law of Damages and Valuation in International Investment Arbitration* 111 (Brill Nijhoff, Leiden; 2018)

Marceau, Gabrielle, "Evolutive Interpretation by the WTO Adjudicator" 12:4 *J.I.E.L.* 791 (2018)

Marceau, Gabrielle and Hurley, Mikella, "Transparency and Public Participation at the WTO" 4 *Trade L. & Dev.* 19 (2012)

Marceau, Gabrielle, "WTO Dispute Settlement and Human Rights" 13:4 *E.J.I.L.* 753 (2002)

"Assessing Compensation and Damages in Expropriation versus Non-expropriation Cases" in Beharry, Christina (ed.), *Contemporary and Emerging Issues on the Law of Damages and Valuation in International Investment Arbitration* 111 (Brill Nijhoff, Leiden; 2018)

Mark Anderson, "Settlement or Roll the Dice?" 28:1 *Litigation* 37 (Fall 2001).

Martin, Roger, *The Opposable Mind* (Harvard Business School Press, Boston; 2007).

Maskus, Keith, "Intellectual Property Rights and Economic Development" 32:3 *Case Western Reserve J. Int'l L.* 471 (2000)

Mavroidis, Petros and Sapir, André, *China and the WTO* (Princeton University Press, Princeton, NJ; 2021)

Mavroidis, Petros, "Free Lunches? WTO as Public Good, and the WTO's View of Public Goods" 23:3 *E.J.I.L.* 731 (2012)

The General Agreement on Tariffs and Trade: A Commentary (Oxford University Press, Oxford; 2005)

"Remedies in the WTO Legal System: Between a Rock and a Hard Place" 11:4 *E.J.I.L.* 763 (2000)

Trade in Goods (1st ed.) (Oxford University Press, Oxford; 2007)

Mayr, Ernest, *The Growth of Biological Thought* (Belknap Press, Cambridge, MA; 1982)

McGinnis, John and Movsesian, Mark, "The World Trade Constitution" 114 *Harv. L. Rev.* 511 (2000)

McGivern, Brendan, "Seeking Compliance with WTO Rulings: Theory, Practice and Alternatives" 36:1 *Int. Lawyer* 141 (2002)

McKinsey Global Institute, *Risk, Resilience and Rebalancing in Global Value Chains: Report* (6 Aug. 2020)

McLeod, Ian, *Legal Theory* (Palgrave Macmillan, Basingstoke; 2005)

McLachlan, Campbell, "The Principle of Systemic Integration and Article 31(3)(c) of the Vienna Convention" 54 *I.C.L.Q.* 279 (Apr. 2005)

McLachlin, Campbell, Shore, Laurence and Matthew Weiniger, *International Investment Arbitration: Substantive Principles* (Oxford University Press, Oxford; 2007)

McLachlin, Campbell, "The Principle of Systemic Integration and Article 31(3)I" 54 *I.C.L.Q.* 279 (Apr. 2005)

McMaster, Karen et al., "The Insolvency Review: United Kingdom – England & Wales" in Bernstein, Donald (ed.), *The Insolvency Review* (9th ed.) (Law Business Research, London; 17 Oct. 2021)

McRae, Donald, "The Contribution of International Trade Law to the Development of International Law" 260 *Recueil des Cours* 103 (1996).

"The WTO in International Law" 3:1 *J.I.E.L.* 27 (2000)

Meadows, Donella, *Thinking in Systems* (Chelsea Green, White River Junction, VT; 2008)

Mégret, Frédéric, "Justice" in d'Aspremont, Jean and Singh, Sahib (eds), *Concepts for International Law* 585 (Edward Elgar, Cheltenham; 2019)

Meier, Christian, *Athens: A Portrait of the City in Its Golden Age* (Metropolitan Books, New York; 1998)

Mercurio, Bryan, "Retaliatory Trade Measures in the WTO Dispute Settlement Understanding: Are There Really Alternatives?" in Beladi, Hamid and Choi, Kwan (eds), *Frontiers of Economics and Globalization (Vol. 6) – Trade Disputes and the Dispute Settlement Understanding of the WTO* 397 (Emerald Group, London; 2009)

Meyer, Timothy, "The Political Economy of WTO Exceptions" 99:4 *Wash. U. L. Rev.* 1299 (2022)

Miller, David, *Principles of Social Justice* (Harvard University Press, Cambridge, MA; 1999)

Mitchell, Andrew, "Good Faith in WTO Dispute Settlement" 7 *Melbourne J. Int'l L.* 339 (2006)

Legal Principles in WTO Disputes 182 (Cambridge University Press, Cambridge; 2008)

Moloo, Rahim and Khachaturian, Alex, "The Compliance with the Law Requirement in International Investment Law" 34 *Fordham Int'l L.J.* 1473 (2011)

Muchlinski, Peter, "Caveat Investor – The Relevance of the Conduct of the Investor under the Fair and Equitable Treatment Standard" 55:3 *Int'l & Comp LQ* 527 (2006)

Mullender, Richard, "Two Nomoi and a Clash of Narratives: The Story of the United Kingdom and the European Union" 3 *Issues Leg. Scholarsh.* 9 (2006)

Murphy, John, "The Heterogeneity of Tort Law" 39 *O.J.L.S.* 455 (2019)

Murphy, Sean D., "Contemporary Practice of the United States – State Responsibility for Injury to Aliens: Ex Gratia Payment for Bombing of Chinese Embassy in Belgrade" 94:1 *A.J.I.L.* 127 (Jan. 2000)

Nanto, Dick, *CRS Report for Congress: Globalized Supply Chains and U.S. Policy* R40167 (27 Jan. 2010)

Narlikar, Amrita, "A Grand Bargain to Revive the WTO" in Fitzgerald, Oonagh (ed.), *Modernizing the World Trade Organization: A CIGI Essay Series* 93 (Centre for International Governance Innovation, Waterloo, Ontario; 2020)

"As Multilateral as Apple Pie: Managing a World of Weaponized Interdependence" *The Security Times* 34 (Feb. 2020)

National Research Council, *America's Climate Choices: Panel on Advancing the Science of Climate Change* (The National Academies Press, Washington, DC; 2010)

Newcombe, Andrew and Paradell, Lluis, *Law and Practice of Investment Treaties* (Kluwer Law International, Alphen aan den Rijn; 2009)

Neyers, Jason, "The Inconsistencies of Aristotle's Theory of Corrective Justice" 11 *Can. J.L. & Juris.* 311 (1998)

Nguyen, Son Tan, "The Applicability of Comity and Abuse of Rights in World Trade Organisation Dispute Settlement" 35 *U. Tas. L. Rev.* 95 (2016)

Nikièma, Suzy, *Compensation for Expropriation Best Practices Series* 10 (The International Institute for Sustainable Development, Winnipeg; Mar. 2013)

Nozick, Robert, *Anarchy, State, and Utopia* (Blackwell, Oxford; 1974)

Nussbaum, Martha, "Patriotism and Cosmopolitanism" in Cohen, Joshua (ed.), *For Love of Country*, 3 (Beacon Press, Boston; 1996)

O'Brien, Robert, Goetz, Anne Marie, Scholte, Jan Aart and Williams, Marc, *Contesting Global Governance* (Cambridge University Press, Cambridge; 2000)

O'Cinneade, Colm, "The Right to Equality" 1 *UCL Human Rights Rev.* 78 (2008)

O'Connor, Bernard and Djordjevic, Margareta, "Practice Aspects of Monetary Compensation: The U.S. – Copyrights Case" 8:1 *J.I.E.L.* 127 (2005)

Office of Development Studies, Bureau of Development Policy, United Nations Development Programme, "Global Public Goods: International Cooperation in the 21st Century" (1999)

Office of the United States Trade Representative, *2018 Trade Policy Agenda and 2017 Annual Report of the President of the United States on the Trade Agreements Program* (Mar. 2018)

Ogunmupe, Bayo, "Nigeria: Meaning of Social Justice Today" *Daily Champion* (18 May 2004)

O'Malley, Nathan, *Rules of Evidence in International Arbitration* (Informa, London; 2019)

O'Neill, Onora, *Bounds of Justice* (Cambridge University Press, Cambridge; 2000)

O'Riordan, Patrick, *Global Ethics and Global Common Goods* (Bloomsbury Academic, London; 2015)

Ormerod, Paul, *Positive Linking* (Faber & Faber, London; 2012)

Ortiz-Ospina, Esteban and Beltekian, Diana, "Trade and Globalization" (first published in 2014; last revised in October 2018).

Osakwe, Chiedu, "Future of the Mutilateral Trading System" 10:1 *Asian J. WTO & Int'l Health Law & Pol.* 2 (2015)

Ossa, Ralph, "A 'New Trade' Theory of GATT/WTO Negotiations" 119:1 *J. Pol. Econ.* 122 (2011)

Owada, Hisashi, "Some Reflections on Justice in a Globalizing World" 97 *Am. Soc. Int'l L. Proc.* 181 (2003)

OXFAM International, *Rigged Rules and Double Standards* (Oxfam, Oxford; 2002)

Pahuja, Sundhya, "Trading Spaces: Locating Sites for Challenge within International Trade Law" 14:1 *Australian Feminist L.J.* 38 (2000)

Pandey, B. N. and Saha, Prabhat Kumar, "Special and Differential Treatment in the WTO: Current Anxieties" 61(4) *J. Indian L. Institute* 463 (2019)

Panizzon, Marion, *Good Faith in the Jurisprudence of the WTO* (Hart, Oxford; 2006)

"Good Faith, Fairness and Due Process in WTO Dispute Settlement Practice" in Chaisse, Julien and Balmelli, Tiziano (eds), *Essays on the Future of the World Trade Organization (Vol. II – The WTO Judicial System: Contributions and Challenges)* 26 (Editions interuniversitaires suisses, Geneva; 2008)

Papaefstratiou, Athina Fouchard and Shiroor, Tejas, "Investors' Obligation to Comply with Domestic Law" *TDM* 4 (2019)

Patterson, Dennis (ed.), *A Companion to Philosophy of Law and Legal Theory* (2nd ed.) (Wiley-Blackwell, Malden, MA; 2010).

"Patience, Fairness and the Human Condition" 385:8549 *The Economist* (Evolution) (6 Oct. 2007).

Paulsson, Jan, "Avoiding Unintended Consequences" in Sauvant, Karl and Chiswick-Patterson, Michael (eds), *Appeals Mechanism in International Investment Disputes* 241 (Oxford University Press, New York; 2008).

Pauwelyn, Joost, "Defenses and the Burden of Proof in International Law" in Bartels, Lorand and Paddeu, Frederica (eds), *Exceptions in International Law* 88 (Oxford University Press, Oxford; 2020)

"The Role of Public International Law in the WTO" 95:3 *Am. J. Int'l L.* 535 (2001)

"A Typology of Multilateral Treaty Obligations" 14:5 *E.J.I.L.* 907 (2003)

Pelc, Krzysztof J., "Twenty Years of Third-Party Participation at the WTO" in Elsig, Manfred, Hoekman, Bernard and Pauwelyn, Joost (eds), *Assessing the World Trade Organization* 203 (Cambridge University Press, Cambridge; 2017).

Perry, Stephen, "On the Relationship between Corrective and Distributive Justice" in Horder, Jeremy (ed.), *Oxford Essays in Jurisprudence: Fourth Series* 237 (Oxford University Press, Oxford; 2000)

Peters, Anne, "Global Constitutionalism Revisited" 11 *Intl. Leg. Theory* 39 (Fall 2005).
"Realizing Utopia as a Scholarly Endeavour" 24:2 *Eur. J. Int'l L.* 533 (2013)
Petersmann, Ernst-Ulrich, "Constitutionalism and International Organizations" 17 *Nw. J. Int'l L. & Bus.* 398 (1997)
Constitutional Functions and Constitutional Problems of International Economic Law (University Press, Fribourg; Westview Press, Boulder; 1991)
"Current Legal Problems in GATT Dispute Settlement: Proceedings in the Field of Antidumping Law" in Fridemann, Daniel and Mestmäcker, Ernst-Joachim (eds), *Conflict Resolution in International Trade* 167 (Nomos Verlagsgesellschaft, Baden-Baden; 1993)
"European and International Constitutional Law" in de Búrca, Grainne and Scott, Joanne (eds), *The EU and the WTO* 81 (Hart, Oxford; 2001)
"How to Promote the International Rule of Law-Contributions by the World Trade Organization Appellate Review System" 1 *J.I.E.L.* 25 (1998)
"International Competition Rules for the GATT/WTO World Trade and Legal System" 27 *J. World Trade* 35 (1993)
"International Economic Theory and International Economic Law: On the Tasks of a Legal Theory of International Economic Order" in Macdonald, Ronald St. John and Johnston, Douglas (eds), *The Structure and Process of International Law* (Martinus Nijhoff, Boston; 1983)
"The WTO Constitution and Human Rights" 3 *J.I.E.L.* 19 (2000)
"The WTO Constitution and the Millennium Round" in Bronckers, Marko and Quick, Reinhard (eds), *New Directions in International Economic Law* 111 (Kluwer Law International, The Hague; 2000)
Piotrowski, Jan, "Special Report on Business and the State: Return to Picking Winners" 442:9279 *The Economist* 4 (15 Jan. 2022)
Pirie, Fernanda and Scheele, Judith (eds), *Justice, Community, and Law* (Oxford University Press, Oxford; 2014)
Pogge, Thomas, "Concluding Reflections" in Brock, Gillian (ed.), *Cosmopolitanism versus Non-Cosmopolitanism* 294 (Oxford University Press, Oxford; 2013)
John Rawls: His Life and Theory of Justice (Oxford University Press, Oxford; 2007)
Polanco Lazo, Rodrigo, "Is There a Life for Latin American Countries after Denouncing the ICSID Convention?" 11:1 *TDM* 1 (2014)
Polyviou, Polyvios, *The Equal Protection of the Laws* (Duckworth, London; 1980)
Porterfield, Matthew C., "An International Common Law of Investor Rights?" 27:1 *U. Pa. J. Int'l Econ. L.* 79 (2006)
Prag, Andrew, "The Climate Challenge and Trade: Would Border Carbon Adjustments Accelerate or Hinder Climate Action?" OECD Round Table on Sustainable Development 4 (25 Feb. 2020).
Priel, Dan, "Analytic Jurisprudence in Time" in Bustamante, Thomas and Lopes Decat, Thiago (eds), *Philosophy of Law as an Integral Part of Philosophy* 213 (Hart, Oxford; 2020)

Priest, George, "The Common Law Process and the Selection of Efficient Rules" 6 *J. Legal Studies* 65 (1977)

Qureshi, Asif, *Interpreting WTO Agreements* (Cambridge University Press, Cambridge; 2006)

Radbruch, Gustav, *Legal Philosophy* (Quelle & Meyer, Leipzig; 1932)

Rafi Communiqué, "Endod: A Case Study of the Use of African Indigenous Knowledge to Address Global Health and Environmental Problems" (Mar. 1993)

Rai, Rajnish Kumar, "Effect of the TRIPS-Mandated Intellectual Property Rights on Foreign Direct Investment in Developing Countries" 11:5–6 *J. World Intell. Prop.* 404 (2008)

Ratner, Steven, "From Enlightened Positivism to Cosmopolitan Justice: Obstacles and Opportunities" in Fastenrath, Ulrich, Geiger, Rudolf, Khan, Daniel-Erasmus, Paulus, Andreas, von Schorlemer, Sabine and Vedder, Christoph (eds), *From Bilateralism to Community Interest* 155 (Oxford University Press, Oxford; 2011)

"Survey Article: Global Investment Rules as a Site for Moral Inquiry" 27:1 *J. Polit. Philos.* 107 (2019)

The Thin Justice of International Law (Oxford University Press, Oxford; 2015)

Rawls, John, *A Theory of Justice* (rev'd ed.) (Belknap, Cambridge, MA; 1999)

The Law of Peoples (Harvard University Press, Cambridge, MA; 1999)

Raz, Joseph, *Between Authority and Interpretation: On the Theory of Law and Practical Reason* (Oxford University Press, Oxford; 2009)

Redgwell, Catherine, "Multilateral Environmental Treaty-Making" in Gowland-Debbas, Vera (ed.), *Multilateral Treaty Making* 91 (Martinus Nijhoff, The Hague; 2000)

Reich, Arie, "From Diplomacy to Law" 17 *Nw. J. Int'l L. & Bus.* 775 (1997)

"The Effectiveness of the WTO Dispute Settlement System: A Statistical Analysis," EUI Working Papers 11/2017 (2017)

Reinisch, August, "Investment Arbitration – The Role of Precedent in ICSID Arbitration" in Klausegger, Christian (ed.), *Austrian Arbitration Yearbook 2008* 495 (Manz'sche Verlags- und Universitätsbuchhandlung, Vienna; 2008)

Riggs, Robert, "Legitimate Expectation and Procedural Fairness in English Law" 36 *Am. J. Comp. L.* 395 (1988)

Ripinsky, Sergey and Williams, Kevin, *Damages in International Investment Law* (British Institute of International and Comparative Law, London; 2008)

Ripstein, Arthur, "The Division of Responsibility and the Law of Tort" 72 *Fordham L. Rev.* 1811 (2004)

Robert Bone, "To Encourage Settlement: Rule 68, Offers of Judgment, and the History of the Federal Rules of Civil Procedure" 102:4 *Nw U. L. Rev.* 1561 (2008).

Roberts, Anthea, "Clash of Paradigms: Actors and Analogies Shaping the Investment Treaty System" 107:1 *Am J. Int'l L.* 45 (2013).

Roessler, Frieder and Gappah, Pettina, "A Reappraisal of Non-Violation Complaints under the WTO Dispute Settlement Procedures" in McCory, Patrick, Appleton, Arthur and Plummer, Michael (eds), *The World Trade Organization: Legal, Economic and Political Analysis* 1371 (Springer, New York; 2005)

Roessler, Frieder, "Why Only a Small Part of WTO Law Is Enforced through the WTO Dispute Settlement Procedures and Whether Something Should Be Done about This" (unpublished paper given at www.sipa.columbia.edu/wto/html/papers.html (2006))

Rolland, Sonia, *Development at the WTO* (Oxford University Press, Oxford; 2012)

Rubin, Paul, "Why Is the Common Law Efficient?" 6 *J. Legal Studies* 51 (1977)

Ruessmann, Lawrence, "The Place of Legitimate Expectations in the General Interpretation of the WTO Agreements," K.U. Leuven Institute for International Law Working Paper No. 36 (Dec. 2002)

Ruse-Khan, Henning Grosse, "The Protection of Intellectual Property and International Investment Law" 19(1) *J.I.E.L.* 87 (2016)

Ruta, Michele and Saito, Mika, "Chained Value" *Finance & Development* 52 (Mar. 2014)

Ruta, Michele, "Preferential Trade Agreements and Global Value Chains: Theory, Evidence, and Open Questions" in The World Bank, *Global Value Chain Development Report 2017* (2017)

Sabahi, Borzu, *Compensation and Restitution in Investor-State Arbitration* (Oxford University Press, Oxford; 2011)

Sacerdoti, Giorgio, "The Challenge of Re-establishing a Functioning WTO Dispute Settlement System" in *Modernizing the WTO* 26 (Centre for International Governance Innovation, Waterloo; 2020)

Samans, Richard, Blanke, Jennifer, Corrigan, Gemma and Drzeniek, Margareta, *The World Economic Forum Inclusive Growth and Development Report* (2015)

Samuel, Geoffrey, "'Le droit subjectif' and English Law" 46 *Cambridge L.J.* 264 (1987)

Sandbu, Martin, *The Economics of Belonging* (Princeton University Press, Princeton, NJ; 2022)

Sauvant, Karl (ed.), *Yearbook on International Investment Law & Policy* 679 (Oxford University Press, New York; 2010–2011)

Sauvant, Karl and Ortino, Federico, *Improving the International Investment Law and Policy Regime* (Ministry for Foreign Affairs of Finland, Helsinki; 2014)

Scelle, Georges, *Précis de Droit des Gens* (Recueil Sirey, Paris; 1932)

Schaffer, Gregory, "Governing the Interface of U.S.-China Trade Relations" 115:4 *A.J.I.L.* 622 (2021).

Schaffer, Gregory, Wolfe, Robert and Le, Vinhcent, "Can Informal Law Discipline Subsidies?" 18 *J.I.E.L.* 711 (2015)

Sharpe, Jeremy, "Drawing Adverse Inferences from the Non-production of Evidence" 22:4 *Arbitration International* 549 (2006)

Schermers, Henry and Blokker, Niels, *International Institutional Law* (6th rev'd ed.) (Brill Nijhoff, Leiden; 2018)

Schiefer, David and van der Noll, Jolanda, "The Essentials of Social Cohesion: A Literature Review" 132 *Soc. Indic. Res.* 579 (2017)

Schill, Stephan, "Fair and Equitable Treatment under Investment Treaties as an Embodiment of the Rule of Law," IILJ Working Paper 2006/6 (2006)

The Multilateralization of International Investment Law (2009)

"The Multilateralization of International Investment Law" 2 *Trade, L. & Dev.* 59 (2010)

Schmidtz, David, *Elements of Justice* (Cambridge University Press, Cambridge; 2006)

Schreuer, Christoph and Weiniger, Matthew, "A Doctrine of Precedent?" in Peter Muchlinski, Ortino, Federico and Schreuer, Christoph (eds), *The Oxford Handbook of International Investment Law* 1189 (Oxford University Press, Oxford; 2008)

Schrijver, Nico and Prislan, Vid, "From Mare Liberum to the Global Commons: Building on the Grotian Heritage" 30:1 *Grotiana* 168 (2009)

Schultz, Thomas, "Against Consistency in Investment Arbitration?" in Taylor, Zachary, Pauwelyn, Joost and Viñuales, Jorge (eds), *The Foundations of International Investment Law* 297 (Oxford University Press, Oxford; 2014)

Seabright, Paul, *The Company of Strangers* (Princeton University Press, Princeton, NJ; 2004)

Sebastian, Thomas, "World Trade Organization Remedies and the Assessment of Proportionality: Equivalence and Appropriateness" 48:2 *Harv. Int'l L.J.* 337 (2007)

Sen, Amartya, *Inequality Reexamined* (Harvard University Press, Cambridge, MA; 1995)

Shore, Laurence and Rothkopf, Robert, "For Better or Worse, Is There a Common Law of Investment Arbitration?" in 7 Arthur W. Rovine (ed.), *Contemporary Issues in International Arbitration and Mediation* 292 (Brill Nijhoff, Leiden; 2013).

Sinclair, Michael, "Evolution in Law" 71 *U. Det. Mercy L. Rev.* 31 (1993)

Simma, Bruno, "From Bilateralism to Community Interest in International Law" 250 *Recueil des Cours* 217 (1994)

Simma, Bruno, *The Charter of the United Nations: A Commentary* (2nd ed.) (Oxford University Press, Oxford; 2002)

Simma, Bruno and Paulus, Andreas, "The 'International Community': Facing the Challenge of Globalization" 9 *E.J.I.L.* 266 (1998)

Simma, Bruno and Pulkowski, Dirk, "Of Planets and the Universe: Self-contained Regimes in International Law" 17:3 *E.J.I.L.* 483 (2006)

Simma, Bruno, "Self-Contained Regimes" 16 *Neth. Yearbook Int'l L.* 111 (1985)

Skidelsky, Robert, *John Maynard Keynes* (Macmillan, London; 1992)

Smialek, Jeanna and Swanson, Ana, "The Era of Cheap and Plenty May Be Ending" *The New York Times* (3 May 2022)

Smith, Stephen, *Contract Theory* (Oxford University Press, Oxford; 2004)

"A Duty to Make Restitution" 26 *Can. J. L. & Jurisprudence* 157 (2013)

Smith, Wendy, "Extreme Measures for Dire Poverty, Book Review of *The Aid Trap* by Hubbard, R. Glenn and Duggan, William" 47:1 *Finance & Development* 55 (Mar. 2010)

Solzhenitsyn, Alexander, *One Day in the Life of Ivan Denisovitch* (Dramatic Publishing Company, Chicago; 1963)

Soper, Philip, *A Theory of Law* 14 (Harvard University Press, Cambridge, MA; 1984)

Sourgens, Frédéric, *A Nascent Common Law* (Brill Nijhoff, Leiden; 2015)

Sourgens, Frédéric, Duggal, Kabir and Laird, Ian, *Evidence in International Investment Arbitration* (Oxford University Press, Oxford; 2018)

Spamann, Holger, "The Myth of 'Rebalancing' Retaliation in WTO Dispute Settlement Practice" 9 *J. Int'l Econ. L.* 31 (2006)

St. Augustine, *The City of God*, Vol. 2 (J. M. Dent & Sons, London; 1931)

Staiger, Robert and Sykes, Alan, "Non-Violation" 16:4 *J.I.E.L.* 741 (2013)

Standen, Jeffrey, "The Fallacy of Full Compensation" 73 *Wash. U. L. Q.* 145 (1995)

Starshinova, Olga, "Is the MPIA a Solution to the WTO Appellate Body Crisis?" 55:5 *J. World Trade* 787 (2021)

Steger, Debra, "Strengthening the WTO Rulemaking Function" in *Modernizing the World Trade Organization: A CIGI Essay Series* 97 (Centre for International Governance Innovation, Waterloo, Ontario; 2019)

Steiner, Eva, *French Law* (Oxford University Press, Oxford; 2018)

Strickland, Ruth, *Restorative Justice* (Peter Lang, New York; 2004)

Stone, Christopher, "Common but Differentiated Responsibilities in International Law" 98 *Am. J. Int'l L.* 276 (2004)

Sturma, Pavel, "The International Law Commission between Codification, Progressive Development, or a Search for a New Role" 13:6 *FIU L. Rev.* 1125 (2019)

Sun, Haochen, "The Road to Doha and Beyond: Some Reflections on the TRIPS Agreement and Public Health" 15 *Eur. J. Int'l L.* 123 (2004)

Sunstein, Cass, *The Partial Constitution* (Harvard University Press, Cambridge, MA; 1993)

Suranovic, Stephen, "A Positive Analysis of Fairness with Applications to International Trade" 23:3 *World Econ.* 283 (2000)

Sutter, Karen, Schwarzenberg, Andres and Sutherland, Michael, "COVID-19: China Medical Supply Chains and Broader Trade Issues," Congressional Research Service Report R46304 (23 Dec. 2020)

Suttle, Oisin, "Poverty and Justice: Competing Lenses on International Economic Law," Book Review of John Linarelli (ed.), *Research Handbook on Global Justice and International Economic Law* (2013) and Krista Nadakavukaren

Schefer (ed.), *Poverty and the International Economic Legal System: Duties to the World's Poor* (2013) in 15 *J. World Invest. Trade* 1071 (2014)

Taekema, Sanne, *The Concept of Ideals in Legal Theory* (Kluwer Law International, The Hague; 2003)

Tams, Christian, "Recognizing Guarantees and Assurances of Non-Repetition: *LaGrand* and the Law of State Responsibility" 27:2 *Yale J. Int'l L.* 441 (2002)

Tasioulas, John, "International Law and the Limits of Fairness" 13 *E.J.I.L.* 993 (2002)

Terrebonne, R. Peter, "A Strictly Evolutionary Model of Common Law" 10 *J. Legal Studies* 397 (1981)

Thirlway, Hugh, *The Sources of International Law* (Oxford University Press, Oxford; 2014)

Thomas, Chantal, "The Death of Doha? Forensics of Democratic Governance, Distributive Justice and Development in the WTO" in Carmody, Chios, Garcia, Frank and Linarelli, John (eds), *Global Justice and International Economic Law* 185 (Cambridge University Press, Cambridge; 2012)

Thomas, Joseph Anthony Charles (trans.), *The Institutes of Justinian* (North-Holland, Amsterdam; 1976)

Tladi, Dire, "Codification, Progressive Development, New Law, Doctrine, and the Work of the International Law Commission on Peremptory Norms of General International Law (Jus Cogens): Personal Reflections of the Special Rapporteur" 13:6 *FIU L. Rev.* 1137 (2019)

Tomasello, Michael, *A Natural History of Human Thinking* (Harvard University Press, Cambridge, MA; 2014)

Trachtman, Joel, "Jurisdiction in WTO Dispute Settlement" in Yerxa, Rufus and Wilson, Brian (eds), *Key Issues in WTO Dispute Settlement* 132 (2005)

"The WTO Cathedral" 43 *Stanford J. Int'l L.* 127 (2007)

Tudor, Ioana, *The Fair and Equitable Treatment Standard in the International Law of Foreign Investment* (Oxford University Press, Oxford; 2008)

United States Trade Representative, "Report on the Appellate Body of the World Trade Organization," p. 2 (Feb. 2020)

Vaitheeswaran, Vijay, "A Slow Unravelling" 432:9151 *The Economist* 3 (13 July 2019)

Valcke, Catherine, "Contractual Interpretation at Common Law and Civil Law" in Neyers, Jason, Bronaugh, Richard and Pitel, Stephen (eds), *Exploring Contract Law* 77 (Hart, Oxford; 2008)

Van Banning, Theo, *The Human Right to Property* (Intersentia, Antwerpen; 2002)

Van Damme, Isabelle, *Treaty Interpretation by the WTO Appellate Body* (Oxford University Press, Oxford; 2009)

Van Harten, Gus, "Five Justifications for Investment Treaties" 2 *Trade, L. & Dev.* 19 (2010)

Investment Treaty Arbitration and Public Law (Oxford University Press, Oxford; 2007)

The Trouble with Foreign Investor Protection (Oxford University Press, Oxford; 2020)

Vattel, Emmerich de, *The Law of Nations* (Carnegie Institute of Washington, Washington, DC; 1916)

Vermulst, Edwin and Ikenson, Daniel, "Zeroing under the WTO Ant-Dumping Agreement: Where Do We Stand?" 2:6 *Glob. Trade Cust. J.* 231 (2007)

Vermulst, Edwin and Komuro, Norio, "Antidumping Disputes in the WTO: Navigating Dire Straits" 31 *J. World Trade* 5 (1997)

Villiger, Mark, *Customary International Law and Treaties* (Kluwer Law International, The Hague; 1997)

Waddams, Stephen, *Dimensions of Private Law* (Cambridge University Press, Cambridge, MA; 2003)

Wade, William and Forsyth, Christopher, *Administrative Law* (10th ed.) (Oxford University Press, Oxford; 2009)

Waincymer, Jeffrey, *Procedure and Evidence in International Arbitration* (Kluwer Law International, Alphen aan den Rijn; 2012)

WTO Litigation (Cameron May, London; 2002)

Wälde, Thomas, "Interpreting Investment Treaties: Experience and Examples" in Binder, Christina, Kriebaum, Ursula, Reinisch, August and Wittich, Stephan (eds), *International Investment Law for the Twenty-first Century* 724 (Oxford University Press, Oxford; 2009)

Wälde, Thomas W. and Sabahi, Borzu, "Compensation, Damages, and Valuation" in Peter Muchlinski, Ortino, Federico and Schreuer, Christoph (eds), *The Oxford Handbook of International Investment Law* 1052 (Oxford University Press, Oxford; Sept. 2012)

Waldron, Jeremy, "Rights in Conflict" 99:3 *Ethics* 503 (1999).

Walker, Neil, "The EU and the WTO: Constitutionalism in a New Key" in de Búrca, Grainne and Scott, Joanne (eds), *The EU and the WTO* 31 (Hart, Oxford; 2001)

Walt, Steven, "Eliminating Corrective Justice" 92:7 *Virginia. L. Rev.* 1311 (2006)

Walton, Douglas, *Abductive Reasoning* (University of Alabama Press, Tuscaloosa; 2004)

Weiler, Joseph, "The Rule of Lawyers and the Ethos of Diplomats" 35 *J.W.T.* 191 (2001)

Weinrib, Ernest, "Corrective Justice in a Nutshell" LII:4 *U.T.L.J.* 349 (2002)

The Idea of Private Law (Harvard University Press, Cambridge, MA; 1995)

Weiss, Freidl, "Trade and Investment" in Muchlinski, Peter, Ortino, Federico and Schreuer, Christoph (eds), *The Oxford Handbook of International Investment Law* 182 (Oxford University Press, Oxford; 2008)

Weiss, Thomas, "ECOSOC and the MDGs: What Can Be Done?" in Wilkinson, Rorden and Hulme, David (eds), *The Millennium Development Goals and Beyond* 117 (Routledge, New York; 2012)

Westen, Peter, "The Empty Idea of Equality" 95 *Harv. L. Rev.* 537 (1982)

Whiteman, Marjorie, *Damages in International Law* (U.S. Government Printing Office, Washington, DC; 1937)

Wigmore, John H., *A Treatise on the Anglo-American System of Evidence*, Vol. 1 (3rd ed.) (Little, Brown, Boston; 1940)

William L. Adams, "Let's Make a Deal: Effective Utilization of Judicial Settlements in State and Federal Courts" 72:2 *Or. L. Rev.* 427 (1993)

Wilson, Bruce, "Compliance by WTO Members with Adverse WTO Dispute Settlement Rulings" 10:2 *J.I.E.L.* 397 (2007)

"The WTO Dispute Settlement System and Its Operation: A Brief Overview of the First 10 Years" in Yerxa, Rufus and Wilson, Brian (eds), *Key Issues in WTO Dispute Settlement: The First Ten Years* 25 (Cambridge University Press, Cambridge; 2005)

Wilson, Edmund, *Letters to a Young Scientist* (Liveright Publishing, New York; 2013)

Wintour, Patrick, "Gulf Plunged into Diplomatic Crisis as Countries Cut Ties with Qatar" *The Guardian* (8 June 2017)

Wolf, Martin, "COVID-19 Will Hit Developing Countries Hard" *Financial Times* 17 (10 June 2020)

Wolff, Alan, "WTO 2025: Getting Back to the Negotiating Table," 22-7 Peterson Institute for International Economics Briefing Paper 10 (May 2022)

World Trade Organization, *GATT Analytical Index*, Vol. II (6th ed.) (World Trade Organization, Geneva; 1995)

"Briefs in a Twist" 357:8200 *The Economist* 85 (9 Dec. 2000)

Trade Impacts of LDC Graduation (World Trade Organization, Geneva; 2020)

Wright, Thomas, "Sifting through Interdependence" 36:4 *The Washington Quarterly* 7 (2013)

Xu, Yu-Chong and Weller, Patrick, *The Governance of World Trade: International Civil Servants and the GATT/WTO* (Edward Elgar, Cheltenham; 2004)

Yearbook of the International Law Commission, 1978, Vol. II, Part Two (United Nations, New York; 1979).

Yearwood, Ronnie R. F., *The Interaction between World Trade Organisation (WTO) Law and External International Law* (Routledge, London; 2012)

Young, Oran, "Political Leadership and Regime Formation: On the Development of Institutions in International Society" 45:3 *Int'l Org.* 281 (Summer 1991)

Young, Oran R. and Osherenko, Gail, *Polar Politics* (Cornell University Press, Ithaca, NY; 1993)

Zampetti, Americo Beviglia, *Fairness in the World Economy* (Edward Elgar, Cheltenham; 2006)

Zane, John Maxcy, *The Story of Law* (2nd ed.) (Liberty Fund, Indianapolis, IN; 1998)

INDEX

CAMBRIDGE STUDIES IN INTERNATIONAL AND COMPARATIVE LAW

Books in the Series

181 *A Communitarian Theory of WTO Law*
Chios Carmody

180 *Drones and International Law: A Techno-Legal Machinery*
Mignot-Mahdavi

179 *The Necessity of Nature: God, Science and Money in Seventeenth Century English Law of Nature*
Mónica García-Salmones

178 *Making the World Safe for Investment: The Protection of Foreign Property 1922–1959*
Andrea Leiter

177 *National Governance and Investment Treaties*
Josef Ostřanský and Facundo Pérez Aznar

176 *Who Owns Outer Space? International Law, Astrophysics, and the Sustainable Development of Space*
Michael Byers and Aaron Boley

175 *Intervening in International Justice: Third States before Courts and Tribunals*
Brian McGarry

174 *Reciprocity in Public International Law*
Arianna Whelan

173 *When Environmental Protection and Human Rights Collide*
Marie-Catherine Petersmann Drones and International Law

172 *The International Law of Sovereign Debt Dispute Settlement*
Kei Nakajima

171 *The Everyday Makers of International Law: From Great Halls to Back Rooms*
Tommaso Soave

170 *Virtue in Global Governance: Judgment and Discretion*
Jan Klabbers

169 *The Effects of Armed Conflict on Investment Treaties*
Tobias Ackermann

168 *Investment Law's Alibis: Colonialism, Imperialism, Debt and Development*
David Schneiderman

167 *Negative Comparative Law: A Strong Programme for Weak Thought*
Pierre Legrand

166 *Detention by Non-State Armed Groups under International Law*
Ezequiel Heffes

165 *Rebellions and Civil Wars: State Responsibility for the Conduct of Insurgents*
Patrick Dumberry

164 *The International Law of Energy*
Jorge Viñuales

163 *The Three Ages of International Commercial Arbitration*
Mikaël Schinazi

162 *Repetition and International Law*
Wouter Werner

161 *State Responsibility and Rebels: The History and Legacy of Protecting Investment Against Revolution*
Kathryn Greenman

160 *Rewriting Histories of the Use of Force: The Narrative of 'Indifference'*
Agatha Verdebout

159 *The League of Nations and the Protection of the Environment*
Omer Aloni

158 *International Investment Law and Legal Theory: Expropriation and the Fragmentation of Sources*
Jörg Kammerhofer

157 *Legal Barbarians: Identity, Modern Comparative Law and the Global South*
Daniel Bonilla Maldonado

156 *International Human Rights Law Beyond State Territorial Control*
Antal Berkes

155 *The Crime of Aggression under the Rome Statute of the International Criminal Court*
Carrie McDougall

154 *Minorities and the Making of Postcolonial States in International Law*
Mohammad Shahabuddin

153 *Preclassical Conflict of Laws*
Nikitas E. Hatzimihail

152 *International Law and History: Modern Interfaces*
Ignacio de la Rasilla

151 *Marketing Global Justice: The Political Economy of International Criminal Law*
Christine Schwöbel-Patel

150 *International Status in the Shadow of Empire*
Cait Storr

149 *Treaties in Motion: The Evolution of Treaties from Formation to Termination*
Edited by Malgosia Fitzmaurice and Panos Merkouris

148 *Humanitarian Disarmament: An Historical Enquiry*
Treasa Dunworth

147 *Complementarity, Catalysts, Compliance: The International Criminal Court in Uganda, Kenya, and the Democratic Republic of Congo*
Christian M. De Vos

146 *Cyber Operations and International Law*
François Delerue

145 *Comparative Reasoning in International Courts and Tribunals*
Daniel Peat

144 *Maritime Delimitation as a Judicial Process*
Massimo Lando

143 *Prosecuting Sexual and Gender-Based Crimes at the International Criminal Court: Practice, Progress and Potential*
Rosemary Grey

142 *Capitalism As Civilisation: A History of International Law*
Ntina Tzouvala

141 *Sovereignty in China: A Genealogy of a Concept Since 1840*
Adele Carrai

140 *Narratives of Hunger in International Law: Feeding the World in Times of Climate Change*
Anne Saab

139 *Victim Reparation under the Ius Post Bellum: An Historical and Normative Perspective*
Shavana Musa

138 *The Analogy between States and International Organizations*
Fernando Lusa Bordin

137 *The Process of International Legal Reproduction: Inequality, Historiography, Resistance*
Rose Parfitt

136 *State Responsibility for Breaches of Investment Contracts*
Jean Ho

135 *Coalitions of the Willing and International Law: The Interplay between Formality and Informality*
Alejandro Rodiles

134 *Self-Determination in Disputed Colonial Territories*
Jamie Trinidad

133 *International Law as a Belief System*
Jean d'Aspremont

132 *Legal Consequences of Peremptory Norms in International Law*
Daniel Costelloe

131 *Third-Party Countermeasures in International Law*
Martin Dawidowicz

130 *Justification and Excuse in International Law: Concept and Theory of General Defences*
Federica Paddeu

129 *Exclusion from Public Space: A Comparative Constitutional Analysis*
Daniel Moeckli

128 *Provisional Measures before International Courts and Tribunals*
Cameron A. Miles

127 *Humanity at Sea: Maritime Migration and the Foundations of International Law*
Itamar Mann

126 *Beyond Human Rights: The Legal Status of the Individual in International Law*
Anne Peters

125 *The Doctrine of Odious Debt in International Law: A Restatement*
Jeff King

124 *Static and Evolutive Treaty Interpretation: A Functional Reconstruction*
Christian Djeffal

123 *Civil Liability in Europe for Terrorism-Related Risk*
Lucas Bergkamp, Michael Faure, Monika Hinteregger and Niels Philipsen

122 *Proportionality and Deference in Investor-State Arbitration: Balancing Investment Protection and Regulatory Autonomy*
Caroline Henckels

121 *International Law and Governance of Natural Resources in Conflict and Post-Conflict Situations*
Daniëlla Dam-de Jong

120 *Proof of Causation in Tort Law*
Sandy Steel

119 *The Formation and Identification of Rules of Customary International Law in International Investment Law*
Patrick Dumberry

118 *Religious Hatred and International Law: The Prohibition of Incitement to Violence or Discrimination*
Jeroen Temperman

117 *Taking Economic, Social and Cultural Rights Seriously in International Criminal Law*
Evelyne Schmid

116 *Climate Change Litigation: Regulatory Pathways to Cleaner Energy*
Jacqueline Peel and Hari M. Osofsky

115 *Mestizo International Law: A Global Intellectual History 1842–1933*
Arnulf Becker Lorca

114 *Sugar and the Making of International Trade Law*
Michael Fakhri

113 *Strategically Created Treaty Conflicts and the Politics of International Law*
Surabhi Ranganathan

112 *Investment Treaty Arbitration As Public International Law: Procedural Aspects and Implications*
Eric De Brabandere

111 *The New Entrants Problem in International Fisheries Law*
Andrew Serdy

110 *Substantive Protection under Investment Treaties: A Legal and Economic Analysis*
Jonathan Bonnitcha

109 *Popular Governance of Post-Conflict Reconstruction: The Role of International Law*
Matthew Saul

108 *Evolution of International Environmental Regimes: The Case of Climate Change*
Simone Schiele

107 *Judges, Law and War: The Judicial Development of International Humanitarian Law*
Shane Darcy

106 *Religious Offence and Human Rights: The Implications of Defamation of Religions*
Lorenz Langer

105 *Forum Shopping in International Adjudication: The Role of Preliminary Objections*
Luiz Eduardo Salles

104 *Domestic Politics and International Human Rights Tribunals: The Problem of Compliance*
Courtney Hillebrecht

103 *International Law and the Arctic*
Michael Byers

102 *Cooperation in the Law of Transboundary Water Resources*
Christina Leb

101 *Underwater Cultural Heritage and International Law*
Sarah Dromgoole

100 *State Responsibility: The General Part*
James Crawford

99 *The Origins of International Investment Law: Empire, Environment and the Safeguarding of Capital*
Kate Miles

98 *The Crime of Aggression under the Rome Statute of the International Criminal Court*
Carrie McDougall

97 *'Crimes against Peace' and International Law*
Kirsten Sellars

96 *Non-Legality in International Law: Unruly Law*
Fleur Johns

95 *Armed Conflict and Displacement: The Protection of Refugees and Displaced Persons under International Humanitarian Law*
Mélanie Jacques

94 *Foreign Investment and the Environment in International Law*
Jorge E. Viñuales

93 *The Human Rights Treaty Obligations of Peacekeepers*
Kjetil Mujezinović Larsen

92 *Cyber Warfare and the Laws of War*
Heather Harrison Dinniss

91 *The Right to Reparation in International Law for Victims of Armed Conflict*
Christine Evans

90 *Global Public Interest in International Investment Law*
Andreas Kulick

89 *State Immunity in International Law*
Xiaodong Yang

88 *Reparations and Victim Support in the International Criminal Court*
Conor McCarthy

87 *Reducing Genocide to Law: Definition, Meaning, and the Ultimate Crime*
Payam Akhavan

86 *Decolonising International Law: Development, Economic Growth and the Politics of Universality*
Sundhya Pahuja

85 *Complicity and the Law of State Responsibility*
Helmut Philipp Aust

84 *State Control over Private Military and Security Companies in Armed Conflict*
Hannah Tonkin

83 *'Fair and Equitable Treatment' in International Investment Law*
Roland Kläger

82 *The UN and Human Rights: Who Guards the Guardians?*
Guglielmo Verdirame

81 *Sovereign Defaults before International Courts and Tribunals*
Michael Waibel

80 *Making the Law of the Sea: A Study in the Development of International Law*
James Harrison

79 *Science and the Precautionary Principle in International Courts and Tribunals: Expert Evidence, Burden of Proof and Finality*
Caroline E. Foster

78 *Transition from Illegal Regimes under International Law*
Yaël Ronen

77 *Access to Asylum: International Refugee Law and the Globalisation of Migration Control*
Thomas Gammeltoft-Hansen

76 *Trading Fish, Saving Fish: The Interaction between Regimes in International Law*
Margaret A. Young

75 *The Individual in the International Legal System: Continuity and Change in International Law*
Kate Parlett

74 *'Armed Attack' and Article 51 of the UN Charter: Evolutions in Customary Law and Practice*
Tom Ruys

73 *Theatre of the Rule of Law: Transnational Legal Intervention in Theory and Practice*
Stephen Humphreys

72 *Science and Risk Regulation in International Law*
Jacqueline Peel

71 *The Participation of States in International Organisations: The Role of Human Rights and Democracy*
Alison Duxbury

70 *Legal Personality in International Law*
Roland Portmann

69 *Vicarious Liability in Tort: A Comparative Perspective*
Paula Giliker

68 *The Public International Law Theory of Hans Kelsen: Believing in Universal Law*
Jochen von Bernstorff

67 *Legitimacy and Legality in International Law: An Interactional Account*
Jutta Brunnée and Stephen J. Toope

66 *The Concept of Non-International Armed Conflict in International Humanitarian Law*
Anthony Cullen

65 *The Principle of Legality in International and Comparative Criminal Law*
Kenneth S. Gallant

64 *The Challenge of Child Labour in International Law*
Franziska Humbert

63 *Shipping Interdiction and the Law of the Sea*
Douglas Guilfoyle

62 *International Courts and Environmental Protection*
Tim Stephens

61 *Legal Principles in WTO Disputes*
Andrew D. Mitchell

60 *War Crimes in Internal Armed Conflicts*
Eve La Haye

59 *Humanitarian Occupation*
Gregory H. Fox

58 *The International Law of Environmental Impact Assessment: Process, Substance and Integration*
Neil Craik

57 *The Law and Practice of International Territorial Administration: Versailles to Iraq and Beyond*
Carsten Stahn

56 *United Nations Sanctions and the Rule of Law*
Jeremy Matam Farrall

55 *National Law in WTO Law: Effectiveness and Good Governance in the World Trading System*
Sharif Bhuiyan

54 *Cultural Products and the World Trade Organization*
Tania Voon

53 *The Threat of Force in International Law*
Nikolas Stürchler

52 *Indigenous Rights and United Nations Standards: Self-Determination, Culture and Land*
Alexandra Xanthaki

51 *International Refugee Law and Socio-Economic Rights: Refuge from Deprivation*
Michelle Foster

50 *The Protection of Cultural Property in Armed Conflict*
Roger O'Keefe

49 *Interpretation and Revision of International Boundary Decisions*
Kaiyan Homi Kaikobad

48 *Multinationals and Corporate Social Responsibility: Limitations and Opportunities in International Law*
Jennifer A. Zerk

47 *Judiciaries within Europe: A Comparative Review*
John Bell

46 *Law in Times of Crisis: Emergency Powers in Theory and Practice*
Oren Gross and Fionnuala Ní Aoláin

45 *Vessel-Source Marine Pollution: The Law and Politics of International Regulation*
Alan Khee-Jin Tan

44 *Enforcing Obligations Erga Omnes in International Law*
Christian J. Tams

43 *Non-Governmental Organisations in International Law*
Anna-Karin Lindblom

42 *Democracy, Minorities and International Law*
Steven Wheatley

41 *Prosecuting International Crimes: Selectivity and the International Criminal Law Regime*
Robert Cryer

40 *Compensation for Personal Injury in English, German and Italian Law: A Comparative Outline*
Basil Markesinis, Michael Coester, Guido Alpa and Augustus Ullstein

39 *Dispute Settlement in the UN Convention on the Law of the Sea*
Natalie Klein

38 *The International Protection of Internally Displaced Persons*
Catherine Phuong

37 *Imperialism, Sovereignty and the Making of International Law*
Antony Anghie

36 *Principles of the Institutional Law of International Organizations*
C. F. Amerasinghe

35 *Necessity, Proportionality and the Use of Force by States*
Judith Gardam

34 *International Legal Argument in the Permanent Court of International Justice: The Rise of the International Judiciary*
Ole Spiermann

33 –

32 *Great Powers and Outlaw States: Unequal Sovereigns in the International Legal Order*
Gerry Simpson

31 *Local Remedies in International Law* (second edition)
Chittharanjan Felix Amerasinghe

30 *Reading Humanitarian Intervention: Human Rights and the Use of Force in International Law*
Anne Orford

29 *Conflict of Norms in Public International Law: How WTO Law Relates to Other Rules of International Law*
Joost Pauwelyn

28 –

27 *Transboundary Damage in International Law*
Hanqin Xue

26 –

25 *European Criminal Procedures*
Edited by Mireille Delmas-Marty and J. R. Spencer

24 *Accountability of Armed Opposition Groups in International Law*
Liesbeth Zegveld

23 *Sharing Transboundary Resources: International Law and Optimal Resource Use*
Eyal Benvenisti

22 *International Human Rights and Humanitarian Law*
René Provost

21 *Remedies against International Organisations*
Karel Wellens

20 *Diversity and Self-Determination in International Law*
Karen Knop

19 *The Law of Internal Armed Conflict*
Lindsay Moir

18 *International Commercial Arbitration and African States: Practice, Participation and Institutional Development*
Amazu A. Asouzu

17 *The Enforceability of Promises in European Contract Law*
James Gordley

16 *International Law in Antiquity*
David J. Bederman

15 *Money Laundering: A New International Law Enforcement Model*
Guy Stessens

14 *Good Faith in European Contract Law*
Reinhard Zimmermann and Simon Whittaker

13 *On Civil Procedure*
J. A. Jolowicz

12 *Trusts: A Comparative Study*
Maurizio Lupoi and Simon Dix

11 *The Right to Property in Commonwealth Constitutions*
Tom Allen

10 *International Organizations before National Courts*
August Reinisch

9 *The Changing International Law of High Seas Fisheries*
Francisco Orrego Vicuña

8 *Trade and the Environment: A Comparative Study of EC and US Law*
Damien Geradin

7 *Unjust Enrichment: A Study of Private Law and Public Values*
Hanoch Dagan

6 *Religious Liberty and International Law in Europe*
Malcolm D. Evans

5 *Ethics and Authority in International Law*
Alfred P. Rubin

4 *Sovereignty over Natural Resources: Balancing Rights and Duties*
Nico Schrijver

3 *The Polar Regions and the Development of International Law*
Donald R. Rothwell

2 *Fragmentation and the International Relations of Micro-States: Self-Determination and Statehood*
Jorri C. Duursma

1 *Principles of the Institutional Law of International Organizations*
C. F. Amerasinghe

For EU product safety concerns, contact us at Calle de José Abascal, 56–1°, 28003 Madrid, Spain or eugpsr@cambridge.org.

www.ingramcontent.com/pod-product-compliance
Lightning Source LLC
LaVergne TN
LVHW010340220926
848484LV00004BB/946

* 9 7 8 0 5 2 1 8 7 9 0 0 2 *